STRATEGIC JUSTICE

OXFORD MORAL THEORY

Series Editor
David Copp, University of California, Davis

Drawing Morals
Essays in Ethical Theory
Thomas Hurka

Commonsense Consequentialism
Wherein Morality Meets Rationality
Douglas W. Portmore

Against Absolute Goodness
Richard Kraut

The Lewd, the Rude and the Nasty
Pekka Väyrynen

In Praise of Desire
Nomy Arpaly and Timothy Schroeder

Confusion of Tongues
A Theory of Normative Language
Stephen Finlay

The Virtues of Happiness
A Theory of the Good Life
Paul Bloomfield

Inner Virtue
Nicolas Bommarito

Strategic Justice
Convention and Problems of Balancing Divergent Interests
Peter Vanderschraaf

STRATEGIC JUSTICE

Convention and Problems of Balancing Divergent Interests

Peter Vanderschraaf

OXFORD
UNIVERSITY PRESS

OXFORD
UNIVERSITY PRESS

Oxford University Press is a department of the University of Oxford. It furthers the University's objective of excellence in research, scholarship, and education by publishing worldwide. Oxford is a registered trade mark of Oxford University Press in the UK and certain other countries.

Published in the United States of America by Oxford University Press
198 Madison Avenue, New York, NY 10016, United States of America.

CIP data is on file at the Library of Congress
ISBN 978-0-19-983219-4

For James Hanink and Brian Skyrms

CONTENTS

PREFACE

This book has had an unusually long incubation period. The thesis I set myself to defend is certainly not entirely new. Indeed, versions of this thesis were proposed by some of Plato's Sophist predecessors. I have studied, considered, and reconsidered this thesis with both fascination and a touch of skepticism ever since my first days in graduate school. As I studied parts of the related classic and contemporary literature and began publishing some contributions of my own to this literature, I found myself having to rethink. And rethink. And then rethink some more. I am already looking forward to a great deal more rethinking as readers respond to the ideas I discuss in the pages to follow.

Put simply, and quite roughly, here is the thesis: *Justice is convention.* I believe that this justice-as-convention thesis, properly developed, provides the most cogent characterization of the general theory of justice as conceived of as a system of rules for mutual benefit, or *justice as mutual advantage*, to use the recent terminology Brian Barry has given moral and political philosophers. In this book I have made my own attempt at such a proper development. While justice-as-mutual-advantage and in particular justice-as-convention have ancient roots, I believe justice-as-mutual-advantage has always been a minority view among philosophers. Plato set a template for all future philosophers by raising two interrelated questions: (1) What precisely is justice? (2) Why should one be just? One simple pair of answers to these questions had some currency even in Plato's Athens: (i) Justice is a system of requirements that are conventions, that is, mutually advantageous arrangements, of one's society, and (ii) Given their conventional nature, one has good reason to obey these requirements simply because obedience serves one's own ends given others' expected obedience. Plato thought that justice-as-convention was a position to be taken seriously. As I interpret them, Hugo Grotius, Thomas Hobbes, John Locke, Samuel Pufendorf, and especially David Hume all had enough respect for justice-as-convention that they developed parts of their modern natural law theories in conventionalist terms. Indeed, I think that convention is the backbone of Hobbes' and Hume's quite different moral and political theories.

But historically, I think, not many have been eager to embrace any version of justice-as-mutual-advantage, including justice-as-convention. And while Hobbes and Hume are rightly recognized as two of the greatest justice-as-mutual-advantage theorists, I also think that until recently they have been thought of mainly as outliers among the giants of moral and political philosophy. The conventionalist responses to the content question (1) and the motivational question (2) are indeed simple. As Plato and other perceptive critics have always believed, these responses are too simple. Surely justice could not be *mere* convention. Conventions guide the members of a community to coordinate their actions. The members of a society all follow conventional practices such as using the same form of currency or tying the direction of driving to the same side of a road in order to live together more easily. Could one seriously regard justice as on a par with conventions of money or road traffic? A convention in practice is one of many alternative systems of practices. Could just *any* set of incumbent conventional practices constitute a system of justice?

In light of these pointed questions, justice-as-convention seems plainly wrongheaded. I certainly thought so in the beginning. But like a number of proposals in philosophy that appear similarly outlandish, justice-as-convention never fully disappears. If anything, I think most philosophers regard justice-as-mutual-advantage proposals as something of a permanent irritant. Plato took justice-as-convention to be the main opposing theory to his own, presumably superior, theory of justice. In our own time leading political philosophers such as Brian Barry and Allen Buchanan have felt the need to present fresh and stinging criticisms of the view Barry himself dubbed justice as mutual advantage. And it is no surprise that so many of us have been and remain irritated. It appears that according to justice-as-mutual-advantage and in particular justice-as-convention, practically any set of mutually beneficial arrangements in a given society is officially just, no matter how unevenly the benefits are shared out or how the society's most vulnerable members end up neglected or mistreated.

The reasons justice-as-convention has staying power are also plain. This position offers perhaps the most straightforward answer to the motivational question (2). As for the content question (1), justice-as-convention explains much. Even many opponents of justice-as-convention are ready to grant that it is at least a prerequisite for a satisfactory system of justice that this system be stable and mutually beneficial. The justice-conventionalists simply take this alleged prerequisite as fundamental. According to them, the complex systems of rules of justice actually in force are at bottom parts of much larger families of rules that humans have developed for interacting more effectively and which endure on account of mutual compliance. They accept this position at the risk of making justice somewhat less exalted than some think it should be. I have always respected the main criticisms raised against justice as mutual advantage. But over the years I have reflected on Plato's two questions, I have also come to an ever-deepening appreciation of the power of the justice-conventionalists' answers to these questions.

Over these years I came to the view that a satisfactory formulation of justice-as-convention is possible *if* one has a sufficiently precise and general understanding of convention itself. In this book I present a theory of convention that I believe is sufficiently precise and general, and I use this theory to develop elements of an account of justice in terms of convention. In both wings of this project I make considerable use of game theory, the mathematical theory of interactive decisions. This book falls in an emerging tradition of moral and political philosophy that uses game theory as an analytic platform, a tradition spearheaded by the landmark works of Michael Taylor, Robert Sugden, David Gauthier, Brian Skyrms, Ken Binmore, and Kaushik Basu. These and other existing works in this tradition develop parts of specific moral and political theories that incorporate conventionalist elements, although not all their authors draw an explicit connection between justice and convention. I have set myself to answer a broad question: Is a satisfactory general justice-as-convention theory possible? My own proposed affirmative answer to this question builds upon the general analysis of convention I give here. I define a convention as a system of strategies that characterize an *equilibrium* solution to a problem of coordination that has a plurality of such equilibrium solutions. Conventions of justice are special cases where the corresponding equilibria solve problems of *conflictual coordination*, in which the interests of the agents involved both coincide to some extent and diverge to some extent. Justice understood this way is *strategic* justice.

Like any typical author, I have written this book with the hope that readers will find it most fruitful to read the text from beginning to end. However, given that the book is long and that its audience will not have a uniform background, here I will make some suggestions for what some readers may wish to focus on immediately on a first reading. Chapter 1 is introductory, and readers already having a background in applications of game theory in moral and political philosophy may want to proceed immediately to the later chapters and refer back to Chapter 1 only as needed. Chapter 2 presents the core of my own game-theoretic theory of convention. Readers familiar with previous related game-theoretic accounts of convention by other authors may find that the main new material they will need for the later chapters is concentrated in §2.2–§2.4, where I discuss alternative senses of how a convention can be arbitrary and how to define convention in proper generality so as to encompass all conventions of conflictual coordination. Chapters 3–8 develop some of the fundamental components of a general account of justice in terms of the account of convention developed in Chapter 2. I think they will read most naturally in the order given, but readers who understand the basics of the account of convention given in Chapter 2 should be able to turn first without serious difficulty to any of these later chapters that they find of most interest. For example, readers who are especially interested in the problem of reconciling justice with self-interest may turn to Chapter 7 before studying Chapters 3–6. The concluding chapter, Chapter 8, gives a general characterization of justice in terms of convention and builds upon ideas developed in Chapters 3–7.

Whenever I have discussed or quoted from classic texts in philosophy, I have used editions or translations of these texts that I believe in all cases are both accessible to a general audience and respected by specialists of the relevant era. I give identifying information on these editions in the References. I refer to a classic work originally composed in a language other than English using the title by which I believe the work is most commonly known among English-speaking users. For examples, I use *De Cive* and not *On the Citizen*, and I use *The Rights of War and Peace* and not *De Iure Belli ac Pacis* to refer to these two works, written respectively by Hobbes and by Grotius. When I repeatedly discuss, cite, or quote from a classic text that has a lengthy name, I state the full name of this text the first time I discuss it in the main text and thereafter use an abbreviated name. The three most important specific cases of this are Hume's *A Treatise of Human Nature*, which I usually refer to as *Treatise*; Hume's *An Enquiry Concerning the Principles of Morals*, which I usually refer to as *Enquiry*; and Locke's *Second Treatise of Government*, which I usually refer to as *Second Treatise*. Using the abbreviated titles *Treatise* and *Second Treatise* to refer, respectively, to Hume's and Locke's great works should cause no difficulty since I discuss no other classic works with the word "treatise" in the original title or, in the case of translated works, in the English equivalent of the original title. The abbreviated name *Enquiry* should cause no difficulty, as I refer to Hume's *An Enquiry Concerning Human Understanding* directly only once in the main text. In all cases where a classic text has an associated referencing system that has become most common among scholars of this text, I use this referencing system. In particular, in rough decreasing order of frequency of citations and quotations: (1) For Hume's enquiries, I give section and paragraph number, and for *A Treatise of Human Nature* I give book, part, section, and paragraph number. For instance, *Enquiry* 3.1:20 refers to the 20th paragraph of Section 3.1 of *An Enquiry Concerning Principles of Morals*, and *Treatise* 3.2.2:22 refers to the 22nd paragraph of Book 3, Part 2, Section 2 of *A Treatise of Human Nature*. (2) For Hobbes' *Elements of Law: Part I, Human Nature, De Cive*, and *Leviathan*, I give the chapter and paragraph number. For instance, *Leviathan* 13:8 refers to the 8th paragraph of Chapter 13 of *Leviathan*. (3) For Locke's *Second Treatise of Government*, I give the section number. (4) For Plato's works, I give corresponding Stephanus numbers. (5) For Aristotle's works, I give corresponding Bekker numbers. (6) For Thucydides' *The History of the Peloponnesian War*, I give book and chapter number. (7) For Sidgwick's *The Methods of Ethics*, I give the page number of the seventh and final edition. (8) For Pufendorf's *On the Law of Nature and of Nations*, I give book, chapter, and paragraph number. (9) And for Aquinas' *Summa Theologiae*, I give volume, question, and article number. For the remaining classic works, each of which is cited only once, I give the citation according to the associated reference system in more detail.

Conventions of pronoun use in the English language remain somewhat in flux in the twenty-first century. In this book I have adopted a rule of using traditionally feminine pronouns such as "she" or "her" when referring to a generic individual person. When I discuss a 2-agent game where the agents are referred to with the generic names "Agent 1" and "Agent 2" or "Party 1" and "Party 2," my default rule is to use traditionally feminine pronouns to refer to Agent 1 or Party 1 and traditionally masculine pronouns to refer to Agent 2 or Party 2. I believe this latter rule makes it easier for readers to distinguish between the two agents engaged in the game. Regarding the first rule, I appreciate that views on generic pronoun use are currently somewhat polarized, and that some authors have expressed concern that readers may find frequent use of feminine pronouns distracting, as this practice might be taken as calling repeated attention to continuing gender inequalities to no real avail. On this question I regard adopting a traditionally female pronoun rule at the present time as an appropriate step, albeit a tiny one, in the direction of greater gender equality. After many decades of the predominant use of traditionally male pronouns to refer to generic persons, if some adopt a traditionally female pronoun rule for at least a few decades, perhaps whatever consciousness the use of this rule raises may in the long run contribute in a small way toward greater gender equality. Like many other authors, I find the use of "they" as a singular pronoun jarring, and I further believe this practice, which presumably sidesteps the relevant gender issue, tends to make English-language texts slightly harder to read. All this said, here I will express my respect for those who disagree with the policies I have just described and have employed in this book.

ACKNOWLEDGMENTS

Several institutions and many individuals contributed significantly to the completion of this work. I am privileged to recognize some of them here.

My research was generously supported by the Institute for Advanced Study, where I was a member of the School of Social Sciences for the 2011–12 academic year, and by the Center for the Humanities at the University of California, Merced, which awarded me a faculty fellowship for the spring 2014 semester. My colleagues in cognitive science and philosophy at the University of California, Merced, have created an intellectually exciting and supportive environment for research and writing. My visiting appointments in the philosophy departments at the University of North Carolina at Chapel Hill in the 2006–7 academic year and at Boston University in the 2007–8 academic year were exceptionally fruitful, due largely to my interactions with the extraordinary professorial and graduate student colleagues of both these departments.

Many colleagues influenced the final text directly by their responses to earlier versions of written sections. I particularly thank Julia Annas, Jacob Barrett, Jenna Bednar, Ken Binmore, Andrea Christelle, David Copp, Diana Richards Doyle, Russell Golman, Keith Hankins, Govert den Hartogh, Hartmut Kliemt, Brian Kogelmann, Bernd Lahno, Peter Lewis, Nate Olson, Scott Page, C. D. C. Reeve, Susanne Sreedhar, Stephen G. W. Stich, Robert Sugden, Michael Taylor, Amie Thomasson, Kevin Vallier, Chad Van Schoelandt, and, posthumously, Edward McClennen. Other colleagues influenced the text more indirectly, via the conversations and correspondence I enjoyed with them on some of its major themes. For this I particularly thank Brad Armendt, Cristina Bicchieri, Andreas Blume, James Doyle, John Duffy, Emily Evans, Dean Foster, Drew Fudenberg, Vijay Krishna, Steven Kuhn, Sharon Lloyd, Eric Maskin, Gerald Postema, Gerasimos Santas, Giacomo Sillari, John Thrasher, Michael Walzer, and Paul Weithman. Gerald Gaus and Christopher Morris merit special mention, not only because I have learned so much from both of them via their published writings and their informal conversation but also because of their unflagging good counsel and encouragement during the final years in which I was completing the book. I'm especially grateful to Jerry Gaus for studying earlier versions of this book in entirety in manuscript form and for his splendid recommendations, which are reflected in the final text. The late Gregory Kavka also merits special mention, both because I had the great fortune to participate in several of his graduate courses before we lost him and because I continue to learn from his remarkable body of published and unpublished writings. James Hanink was my principal philosophy professor during my undergraduate career at Loyola Marymount University. Brian Skyrms directed my doctoral thesis in graduate school at the University of California, Irvine. Jim and Brian have remained my esteemed colleagues and good friends since I completed my formal philosophical training. As Jim and Brian are the two individuals who had the greatest influence on my formation as a philosopher, I believe it fitting to dedicate the book to the two of them.

With the permissions of the original publishers, I have incorporated material from a number of previously published journal articles and book chapters. In most cases the material taken from these earlier pieces is seriously revamped, as my thinking on the issues I discussed in them has evolved and, I hope, matured. These earlier pieces include "Joint Beliefs in Conflictual Coordination Games" (with Diana Richards), *Theory and Decision* 42 (1997); "Knowledge, Equilibrium and Convention," *Erkenntnis* 49 (1998); "Instituting the Hobbesian Commonwealth," *Pacific Philosophical Quarterly* 82 (2001); "Justice-Conventionalism, Justice-Platonism and the Social Contract," in *The Social Institutions of Capitalism: Evolution and Design of Social Contracts*, ed. Pursey Heugens, Hans van Oosterhout, and Jack Vromen (Cheltenham, UK: Edward Elgar, 2003); "The Circumstances of Justice," *Politics, Philosophy and Economics* 5 (2006); "War or Peace? A Dynamical Analysis of Anarchy," *Economics and Philosophy* 22 (2006); "Covenants and Reputations," *Synthese* 157 (2007); "The Invisible Foole," *Philosophical Studies* 147 (2010); "Justice as Mutual Advantage and the Vulnerable," *Politics, Philosophy and Economics* 10 (2011); "A Governing Convention?," *Rationality, Markets and Morals* 4 (2013); "Game Theoretic Interpretations of Hobbes," in *The Bloomsbury Companion to Hobbes*, ed. Sharon A. Lloyd (London: Bloomsbury Academic, 2013); "In a Weakly Dominated Strategy Is Strength: Evolution of Optimality in Stag Hunt Augmented with a Punishment Option," *Philosophy of Science* 83 (2016); and "Learning Bargaining Conventions," *Social Philosophy & Policy* 35 (forthcoming).

Adam Gjesdal contributed substantially to the preparation of the index of this book. A team led by Sue Warga and Sudha Ramprasath skillfully copy-edited the entire text. Production manager Shalini Balakrishnan guided the process of bringing the text to its final published form. Isla Ng at Oxford University Press assisted greatly with the final production of the book. Peter Ohlin, my editor at Oxford University Press, merits special mention for his remarkable support at every stage of this project's development.

Helen Zheng Altenbach, Yue Deng, Laura Hackstein, Claudia Vanderschraaf, and Ted Vautrinot all granted me permission to use their first names in many of the game-theoretic examples that appear in this book. A number of these examples involve stories of musicians and are in part inspired by the music I have enjoyed in performances in ensembles including Helen, now cellist with the Los Angeles Opera and the Hollywood Bowl Orchestra; Yue, now artist in residence at the University of Alberta; Laura and Claudia, founding members of the Santa Barbara String Quartet; and Ted, now with the Ted & Lucy Project and One Less Monkey.

My late mother, Cornelia, my father, John, my brothers Frits and Robert, and their families have given me the inestimable support of a loving extended family throughout my academic career and especially as I worked on this project. Simply by their company, my nieces Maggie, Gracie, and Libbie and my nephew Nathan have helped me to remain more focused and more determined to work through many of the hard questions discussed in the pages that follow, even though they are too young to understand the specifics of a professional philosopher's work. My spouse, Claudia Vanderschraaf, was unflaggingly patient and supportive throughout the latter stages of this project, especially in those moments when I was less than ideal company. Claudia's unexpected arrival in my life only a few short years ago was one of a number of personal and professional turning points for me that roughly coincided, and certainly it was the most fortunate.

STRATEGIC JUSTICE

1 DILEMMAS OF INTERACTION

Crusoe is given certain physical data (wants and commodities) and his task is to combine and apply them in such a fashion as to obtain a maximum resulting satisfaction. There can be no doubt the he controls exclusively all the variables upon which this result depends—say the allotting of resources, the determination of the uses of the same commodity for different wants, etc.

Thus Crusoe faces an ordinary maximum problem, the difficulties of which are of a purely technical—and not conceptual—nature, as pointed out.

Consider now a participant in a social exchange economy. His problem has, of course, many elements in common with a maximum problem. But it also contains some, very essential, elements of an entirely different nature. He too tries to obtain an optimum result. But in order to achieve this, he must enter into relations of exchange with others. If two or more persons exchange goods with each other, then the result for each one will depend in general not merely on his own actions but on those of others as well. Thus each participant attempts to maximize a function (the above-mentioned "result") of which he does not control all variables. This is certainly no maximum problem, but a peculiar and disconcerting mixture of several conflicting maximum problems.

—JOHN VON NEUMANN AND OSKAR MORGENSTERN,
Theory of Games and Economic Behavior

Introduction

For nearly two centuries economists and philosophers have used Defoe's tale of Robinson Crusoe as a foil for their discussions of economic and political concepts. Defoe's story motivates the *Crusoe economy* concept, where a single agent acts as both producer and consumer, so trade, monetary currency, and prices are absent. A Crusoe economy characterizes a decision-theoretic problem where an agent seeks to identify a best choice given the inanimate constraints of "Nature," such as amounts of available resources. As critics of the Crusoe economy concept have always stressed and advocates have always acknowledged, few if any economic agents are ever in a situation like Robinson Crusoe in his solitary state, where only inanimate constraints are relevant to his decisions. Exchange drives actual economies. And exchange rests upon the interrelated decisions of multiple agents. Taking this to be a fundamental economic truth, John von Neumann and Oskar Morgenstern in the 1940s developed the foundations of *game theory*, a theory where decisions interact.[1] Von Neumann and Morgenstern viewed game theory as no less than a formal theory of all economic exchanges. As game theory continues to develop in the twenty-first century, its applications continue to expand far beyond the scope of traditional economics. One can characterize game theory as the formal theory of all social interactions.

Von Neumann and Morgenstern use the Robinson Crusoe story to help motivate their own position that economic decisions are typically interdependent. A variation of this story also helps to shed light upon the relational character of justice. In rather different ways, Aristotle and David Hume argue that justice presupposes a community of distinct and interdependent individuals.[2] As Defoe tells the story, during Crusoe's long stay as the lone inhabitant of the island off the Venezuelan coast, he has only the Bible for reading material. But suppose instead that Crusoe's island library is larger and includes Thomas Hobbes' *De Cive*, John Locke's *Second Treatise of Government*, and Jean-Jacques Rousseau's *Discourse on the Origin and Foundations of Inequality Among Men*. With more than ample time on his hands, Crusoe studies *De Cive* carefully and realizes he appears to be in the State of Nature as Hobbes describes it. But when he later studies Locke's *Second Treatise* and Rousseau's *Second Discourse*, Crusoe learns that Locke and Rousseau have accounts of the State of Nature that differ in interesting ways both from Hobbes' account and from each other. Crusoe wonders, "Whose, if any, account of the State of Nature is the right account?" But he also concludes that at least while he remains alone, for practical purposes he need not reject any of the three accounts he has so carefully studied. For by virtue of being solitary, Crusoe is in the peculiar case where the practical outcomes of being in Hobbes's, or Locke's, or Rousseau's State of Nature are bound to coincide. Once Man Friday joins Crusoe, how both understand the particulars of what it means to be in the State of Nature may become a good deal more important to Crusoe, and to Friday as well. Given that Crusoe and Friday live *together*, they can adopt a system of justice that regulates how they share the burdens and the benefits this togetherness might generate.[3] And how they understand the State of Nature may significantly shape this system.

---

1. Von Neumann and Morgenstern presented their theory in *Theory of Games and Economic Behavior* (Princeton, NJ: Princeton University Press, 1944). I will discuss some of the history and impact of their treatise in §1.2.

2. *Nicomachean Ethics*, Book V, especially Chapters 9 and 11, and *An Enquiry Concerning the Principles of Morals* 3.1:20.

3. Given the account of justice I develop in later chapters, this arguably does not happen in Defoe's story, where Friday and Crusoe fall into a relationship resembling that of a slave and his master.

This twist on the Crusoe story suggests another moral, namely, that game theory provides a vehicle for philosophers to analyze justice more precisely and rigorously than in times past. Problems of justice are characteristically problems of interaction. Why not use game theory to study and evaluate the formal structures of such problems? Richard Braithwaite, the first professional philosopher to use game theory to model a problem of moral philosophy, conjectured in 1954 that game theory might ultimately transform various branches of political and moral philosophy, much as probability and statistics had transformed the social sciences.[4] Such a transformation has yet to occur—Braithwaite himself suggested this process might take centuries—but game theory is now already an important tool for moral and political philosophers.

In this introductory chapter I will give some initial applications of game-theoretic reasoning to problems of justice together with a short review of some of the main concepts from game theory I use in the chapters to follow. In §1.1 I introduce five specific problems of justice. Some of these problems appear in classics of philosophy, some in classics of the social sciences, and some from works of history and even fiction. Each of these problems is important in its own right and helps to motivate important parts of the discussions in subsequent chapters. In §1.2 I discuss some of the basics of noncooperative game theory that are important for analyzing problems of justice and more generally for developing an analysis of convention sufficiently general to characterize such problems. In §1.3 I return to the §1.1 problems and reformulate them as game-theoretic problems. Along the way I discuss some additional game-theoretic concepts germane to some of these specific problems and that I will also use in subsequent chapters. The game-theoretic reformulation of each problem reveals precisely why the agents involved would have difficulty arriving at a mutually satisfactory resolution of this problem, and why a "solution" of this problem calls for some principle or principles of justice to guide their conduct.

§1.1. Five Motivating Problems

Problem 1.1. The Farmer's Dilemma

One is obligated to keep one's promises. In *A Treatise of Human Nature*, David Hume argues that the obligations of promises are in a certain sense not natural. Hume maintains that this seemingly outrageous claim in fact follows straightforwardly once one recognizes that promises are intelligible only as a matter of human conventions and that the obligations of promises cannot add anything to

4. Richard Braithwaite, *Theory of Games as a Tool for the Moral Philosopher* (1955; Bristol: Thoemmes Press, 1994).

morality, properly understood. To set up his analysis of promises, Hume gives a striking example that casts doubt upon the rationality of exchange. Two neighboring farmers each expect a bumper crop of corn. Each farmer realizes that when her corn ripens she will require her neighbor's help in the harvest, or else a substantial portion of this corn will rot in the field. Since their corn will ripen on different days, the two farmers can ensure themselves full harvests by helping each other when their crops ripen. Yet Hume claims that prudential reasoning leads the farmers to work alone, even knowing they could have enjoyed a substantial mutual benefit had they worked together.

> Your corn is ripe today; mine will be so tomorrow. 'Tis profitable for us both, that I shou'd labour with you to-day, and that you shou'd aid me to-morrow. I have no kindness for you, and know you have as little for me. I will not, therefore, take any pains on your account; and should I labour with you upon my own account, in expectation of a return, I know I shou'd be disappointed, and that I shou'd in vain depend upon your gratitude. Here then I leave you to labour alone: You treat me in the same manner. The seasons change; and both of us lose our harvests for want of mutual confidence and security.[5]

What leads to this disastrous, and easily avoidable, result? Hume assumes that each farmer analyzes this problem from a purely selfish perspective, desiring only to possess in the end the greatest possible amount of corn in her barn, regardless of what happens to the other farmer. But does the farmers' complete lack of altruistic concern for each other explain their failure to work together? After all, each farmer stands to gain a substantial net economic benefit if they help each other, and both know it. The outcome where the farmers work together is *Pareto optimal* or simply *optimal*, that is, neither can do better in this exchange situation without worsening the other's situation. Yet the two farmers fail to reap this net economic benefit. As a result of their apparently "rational" analyses of their situation, they end up in the suboptimal outcome where each loses a large part of her harvest. Some of Hume's readers have dubbed this problem Hume's *Farmer's Dilemma*.[6]

---

5. *A Treatise of Human Nature* 3.2.5:8.

6. See especially Jordan Howard Sobel, *Taking Chances: Essays on Rational Choice* (Cambridge: Cambridge University Press, 1994), ch. 13, and Peter Vanderschraaf, "The Informal Game Theory in Hume's Account of Convention," *Economics and Philosophy* 14 (1998), pp. 215–247 (henceforth Vanderschraaf 1998a), and "Knowledge, Equilibrium and Convention," *Erkenntnis* 49 (1998), pp. 337–369 (henceforth Vanderschraaf 1998b).

Each of Hume's farmers in this interaction has the preferences of an individual who regards her good as consisting solely of material goods and services, and who acts so as to maximize personal expected payoff, defined solely in terms of the material goods and services she expects to acquire. Such an individual views any act for the benefit of another solely as a positive cost to oneself, and considers incurring such a cost only as a means toward securing a higher expected payoff for oneself. This sort of individual is sometimes referred to as *homo economicus*, a label that emerged partly in response to a definition of economic man, attributed to John Stuart Mill, as an individual concerned solely with seeking wealth who acts so as to achieve the greatest amount of personal wealth at the least personal cost.[7] Many scholars, from Wilfredo Pareto early in the twentieth century to Ken Binmore and Gerald Gaus in our own time, rightly argue that such a conception of *homo economicus* is really a straw man conception, at least if one wishes to use the term "*homo economicus*" to refer to an agent who reasons according to canonical principles of economics.[8] In fact, both serious interests in ends other than material gain and passionate concern for the welfare of others are fully compatible with the notion of *homo economicus*, properly understood. I take it to be a commonsense belief that very few if any actual persons who have lived on our planet are either as selfish or as materialistic as this caricature of *homo economicus* attributed to Mill. And the empirical evidence supporting this belief is considerable. Many if not most people act at least some of the time with the aim of fulfilling ends other than material gain. And many if not most people act with the aim of benefitting others, even at significant personal cost, at least some of the time.[9] Insofar as Hume's analysis of his Farmer's Dilemma depends upon an evidently defective moral psychology, one might be inclined to dismiss this analysis.

---

7. John Stuart Mill, "On the Definition of Political Economy: And on the Method of Investigation Proper to It," in *Essays on Some Unsettled Questions of Political Economy* (1836; London: London School of Economics and Political Science, 1948), pp. 137–138, 144.

8. See Vilfredo Pareto, *Manual of Political Economy*, trans. Ann S. Schwier, ed. Ann S. Schwier and Alfred N. Page (1927; New York: Augustus M. Kelley, 1971), ch. 1, sec. 24; Ken Binmore, *Playing Fair* (Cambridge, MA: MIT Press, 1994), pp. 18–24; and Gerald Gaus, *On Philosophy, Politics, and Economics* (Belmont, CA: Thomson Wadsworth, 2008), pp. 15–30.

9. Of course, the fact that people sometimes make personal sacrifices that advance others' interests does not on the face of it imply that psychological egoism is untrue. Defenders of psychological egoism can maintain that such purportedly "altruistic" acts are acts of higher-order self-interest, as when one helps another at some first-order (personal) cost in order to advance the second-order good of self-satisfaction. Hume himself is aware of this. Hume's own view is that the dispute over psychological egoism is both probably irresolvable and of little practical importance, since whether or not services to others are at some deep level expressions of self-love, it remains the case that others benefit from such services and that consequently we believe they should be encouraged (*Enquiry*, Appendix II).

In fact, Hume himself rejects this cartoonish conception of the person. When he discusses the natural temper of typical people, Hume writes:

> So far from thinking, that men have no affection for any thing beyond themselves, I am of the opinion, that tho' it be rare to meet with one, who loves any single person better than himself; yet 'tis as rare to meet with one, in whom all the kind affections, taken together, do not over-balance all the selfish.[10]

Hume takes the material sacrifices that family members often make for one another as convincing evidence that actual people are not so as selfish as the *homo economicus* caricature described above. Hume also explicitly maintains both in *Treatise* and in *An Enquiry Concerning the Principles of Morals* that individuals desire certain goods that cannot be received or taken away directly via a voluntary or involuntary exchange, including in particular peace of mind.[11] When it comes to economic goods, Hume takes the plausible view that most individuals are only moderately selfish, and that typically their benevolence extends primarily toward those with whom they have developed personal relationships, particularly family and friends.[12] Hume takes it to be a mundane empirical fact that people will often act for the benefit of those with whom they have developed relationships, and especially with people they love, even if they expect to receive no advantage as a result.[13] In cases such as these, the preference structure of the Farmer's Dilemma does not apply.

Nevertheless, the straw man conception is useful for framing a discussion of Hume's Farmer's Dilemma. Hume directs the Farmer's Dilemma argument specifically at individuals engaged in self-interested commerce. Hume believes such commerce typically occurs between individuals who lack the developed personal ties that would motivate any of them to act with a primary or even partial aim of promoting the other's interests in an exchange.[14] Hume poses the Farmer's Dilemma argument as a general problem for agents contemplating some extended property exchange or transfer in which they could derive mutual benefit from economic exchange but where any of the agents must wait upon any of the others to provide a good or service not immediately present. Such transactions typically take place between individuals who are either strangers to each another, or who

10. *Treatise* 3.2.2:5.

11. *Treatise* 3.2.2:7, 3.3.6:6; *Enquiry* 9.2:23.

12. *Treatise* 3.2.2:8, 3.2.5:8, 3.2.7:1.

13. *Treatise* 3.2.5:8.

14. *Treatise* 3.2.5:8.

at best regard each other as mere acquaintances, not friends. The selfish, materialistic *homo economicus* caricature of the previous paragraph may be a woefully inadequate model of actual persons in general, but the preferences of individuals in the context of economic exchanges will very often resemble the preferences of such an individual. So evidently Hume cannot resolve his Farmer's Dilemma by appealing to the farmers' "better natures."

Hume introduces the Farmer's Dilemma in the context of his analysis of promises, and so one might naturally suppose that promises will figure prominently in any solution to this problem that Hume might offer. And indeed, Hume does believe that promises are crucially important for supporting economic exchange. But Hume does not believe that the mere fact that one promises creates a reason that one ought to keep the promise. The Farmer's Dilemma apparently shows not only that it is irrational for either farmer to help the other farmer but also that it would be irrational for either to trust the other's promise to help. When Hume first presents the Farmer's Dilemma, he does not say that the farmers make any explicit agreement to help each other before the corn in either of their fields ripens. But an exchange of promises apparently would do nothing to change the logic of their predicament. If the farmers make a prior agreement to help each other harvest their corn, then should the farmer whose corn ripens later keep her promise, then the farmer whose corn ripened earlier and who has benefitted from her help appears to fare better by breaking his promise when her corn eventually ripens. The farmer whose corn ripens later should anticipate this betrayal and break her promise to prevent the other farmer from exploiting her. The end result is the same as if they had not exchanged promises in the first place.

Farmer's Dilemma reasoning evidently shows that rational, self-interested individuals will not engage in such commonplace exchanges as the sale of houses and the trade of commodities, since these kinds of transactions require a trust that such agents would know better than to give.[15] Hume concludes that little or no economic exchange could take place at all in a society of individuals who take the Farmer's Dilemma to its logical conclusion. Among a population of agents who reason like Hume's farmers, the requisite trust would tend not to arise; hence Hume's gloomy preliminary conclusion that no such exchanges would take place in such a population.

Problem 1.2. Claim or Concede?

In 1954, Richard Braithwaite gave his inaugural lecture as Knightbridge Professor of Moral Philosophy at Cambridge University. In his Cambridge lecture, entitled

15. *Treatise* 3.2.5:8.

Theory of Games as a Tool for the Moral Philosopher, Braithwaite considered the problem of dividing a fixed quantity of a resource between two individuals, each of whom would like to receive all of the available resource.[16] Braithwaite presented a story to motivate this problem, which I paraphrase: Two musicians, Matthew and Luke, live in adjacent apartments. Luke plays the piano and Matthew plays the trumpet. Both have schedules that permit them only the same particular hour each day for playing their instruments. Unfortunately for Luke and Matthew, the walls in their apartments are thin. Each can hear the other's playing almost as well as he can hear his own playing. Each admittedly finds the other's playing somewhat pleasant, but each most wants to be able to play his instrument undisturbed. So the best outcome from the perspective of each is to play his instrument while the other keeps quiet. Luke and Matthew must decide how they will try to use a limited resource, in this case time for playing their instruments, over which they have conflicting interests.[17] Braithwaite asks: "Can any plausible principle be devised stating how they should divide the proportion of days on which both of them play, Luke alone plays, Matthew alone plays, neither play, so as to obtain maximum production of satisfaction compatible with fair distribution?"[18]

Braithwaite's musician problem is closely related to several other problems analyzed in contemporary classics of social science and biology. R. Duncan Luce and Howard Raiffa present such a problem in one of these classics, their 1957 book *Games and Decisions*. Luce and Raiffa note that this particular problem has various possible interpretations. They offer the following interpretation, perhaps hoping to amuse their readers:

> A man, player 1, and a woman, player 2, each have two choices for an evening's entertainment. Each can either go to a prize fight (α_1 and β_1) or to a ballet (α_2 and β_2). Following the usual cultural stereotype, the man much prefers the fight and the woman the ballet; however, to both it is more important that they go out together than that each see the preferred entertainment.[19]

Some may find the stereotypes Luce and Raiffa use in their interpretation annoying, but their analysis of this problem in *Games and Decisions* was pioneering

16. Braithwaite (1994).

17. Like Braithwaite, I assume that Luke and Matthew are unable to take measures like soundproofing their rooms or moving elsewhere that would effectively eliminate their resource division problem.

18. Braithwaite (1994), p. 9.

19. R. Duncan Luce and Howard Raiffa, *Games and Decisions: Introduction and Critical Survey* (New York: John Wiley and Sons, 1957), p. 91.

in 1957. Partly in honor of their fine work, an entire class of coordination problems having a mixture of conflict and coordination like Luce and Raiffa's ballet/prize-fight problem have become known as *Battle of the Sexes* problems.[20] Like Braithwaite's Neighboring Musicians problem, in a 2-agent Battle of the Sexes problem apparently one of the agents involved must "give in" to the wishes of the other in order for them to coordinate successfully. One obvious way Luce and Raiffa's Battle of the Sexes problem differs from Braithwaite's problem is that in the former the woman and the man coordinate exactly when they choose the same alternative, while in the latter Luke and Matthew coordinate exactly when each chooses the alternative that is the opposite of his neighbor's choice.

In his great 1960 book *The Strategy of Conflict*, Thomas Schelling considers the predicament of two individuals who unexpectedly parachute into a certain area, presumably because they could no longer safely remain in the aircraft in which they were flying, and who need to meet quickly in order to be rescued.[21] Neither parachutist knows where in the area the other has landed. Worse, they have no way of communicating with each other. But both know that each has a map of the area. Do the parachutists have good prospects of finding each other in time to be rescued? Each parachutist knows that the other could be searching for her in any position within a sizeable radius, even if she believes the other is searching for her only within the area charted on his map and that the other believes she limits her search to this area as well. There are infinitely many different places within the mapped area they might find each other, that is, infinitely many different ways for them to coordinate. But there are also infinitely many different ways for them to miscoordinate by looking for each other in the wrong places until it is too late. Their problem is exacerbated if both dislike walking. For while both want to meet, in general any location where they might meet will be less satisfactory from the perspective of one and more satisfactory from the perspective of the other than some of the many available alternatives depending upon how much walking each of these alternatives requires. One way to view the structure of this *Parachutists* problem is as an extension of the Neighboring Musicians problem where the two agents involved have a great many more options available to them and where one might "win" and the other "lose" to *a certain degree*, depending upon how far each must walk in order to achieve the mutually desired outcome of meeting.

Finally, in his 1982 book *Evolution and the Theory of Games*, John Maynard Smith explores how certain stable patterns of conduct might evolve when the

---

20. This is the name Luce and Raiffa give their interpretation of this problem (1957, p. 90).

21. Thomas Schelling, *The Strategy of Conflict* (Cambridge, MA: Harvard University Press, 1960), pp. 54–55, 58–59. Schelling evidently assumes they cannot be rescued separately.

members of a population interact. Early in this book Maynard Smith considers a problem of conflict over a resource:

> Imagine that two animals are contesting a resource of value V. By 'value', I mean that the Darwinian fitness of an individual obtaining the resource would be increased by V. Note that the individual which does not obtain the resource need not have zero fitness. Imagine, for example, that the 'resource' is a territory in a favorable habitat, and that there is adequate space in a less favorable habitat in which losers can breed. Suppose, also, that animals with a territory in a favorable habitat produce, on average, 5 offspring, and that hose breeding in the less favorable habitat produce 3 offspring. Then V would equal $5-3=2$ offspring. Thus V is the *gain* in fitness to the winner, and losers do not have zero fitness.[22]

As Maynard Smith frames the simplest version of this *Hawk-Dove* problem, each individual in such a contest either *escalates* until injured or until the other retreats or *displays only* at first and then retreats at once if the other escalates. Maynard Smith refers to escalators as *hawks* and to those who display only as *doves*. Like Luce and Raiffa's Battle of the Sexes problem and Schelling's Parachutists problem, Maynard Smith's Hawk-Dove problem resembles Braithwaite's Neighboring Musicians problem in that each side "wins" exactly when this side tries to insist upon claiming the good at stake, in this case by escalating, and the other side acquiesces, in this case by displaying only. But in the Neighboring Musicians, Battle of the Sexes, and Parachutists problems, each of the alternative outcomes where the two agents miscoordinate might be equally bad for them both, while in Hawk-Dove, one of the miscoordination outcomes is worse for both sides than the other. For when both sides are doves, they share the use of the resource, but when both are hawks, both run the risk of injury in an escalating conflict.

Problem 1.3. The Stag Hunt

In the *Second Discourse*, Jean-Jacques Rousseau gives an example meant to illustrate the origins of cooperation among self-interested individuals so as to achieve mutual benefit:

> If a deer was to be caught, everyone clearly sensed that this required him faithfully to keep his post; but if a hare happened to pass within reach

---

22. John Maynard Smith, *Evolution and the Theory of Games* (Cambridge: Cambridge University Press, 1982), pp. 11–12.

> of one of them, he will, without a doubt, have chased after it without a scruple and, after catching his prey, have cared very little about having caused his Companions to have missed theirs.[23]

As Rousseau frames this problem of commitment, each hunter wants as much meat as she can get from the hunt. Enough hare live in the woods to ensure that each hunter can guarantee herself the meat of a hare if she hunts alone for hare. But enough deer also live in the woods to ensure that if all hunt together for deer, then together they will catch a deer. A captured deer that they will divide amongst themselves will yield each hunter much more meat than she would get from a captured hare. But in order to catch a deer, the hunters must all work together, or else any deer any of them hunt will escape. If any hunter believes that any of the other hunters will fail to hunt for deer, then she had better hunt for hare, since otherwise she will catch nothing and gain no meat at all from the hunt.

Rousseau's *Stag Hunt* story has captured the imagination of many philosophers and social scientists interested in the problem of explaining cooperation for mutual benefit. In fact, Rousseau was not the first to propose a Stag Hunt problem. To illustrate his account of convention in *Treatise*, Hume presents an example of two rowers who must row in unison in order to move their boat forward. Hume notes that the rowers are able to synchronize their rowing, even though they do not explicitly promise one another to row in a certain way, so long as each expects the other to row as she rows. In this rowboat problem, each rower gets what she most wants, which is to move the boat forward, precisely by choosing the same pattern of rowing as the other rower, in which case the other rower gets what she most wants as well. But if for some reason either rower thinks that the other rower will not pull his oar in the same way as she would pull her own oar, then she will not pull her oar after all. Each rower "plays it safe" by not pulling her oar, since then she at least saves herself the energy she would have expended by rowing.[24]

Thomas Hobbes presents some even earlier Stag Hunt problems in his writings. In *Elements of Law, De Cive*, and *Leviathan* Hobbes presents a system of general moral precepts he refers to as *laws of nature*. Hobbes' system is one of the most important modern contributions to the long natural law tradition in moral philosophy. Like the natural law theorists of the scholastic tradition, Hobbes includes in his system prohibitions against stealing and against aggressing against

---

23. *Discourse on the Origin or Foundations of Inequality Among Men,* Part II, para. 9.

24. Brian Skyrms and Jordan Howard Sobel also note that Hume's rowboat example is structurally similar to Rousseau's Stag Hunt. See Brian Skyrms, *The Stag Hunt and the Evolution of Social Structure* (Cambridge: Cambridge University Press, 2004), p. 2; Jordan Howard Sobel, *Walls and Vaults: A Natural Science of Morals (Virtue Ethics According to David Hume)* (Hoboken, NJ: John Wiley and Sons, 2009), pp. 283–284.

others. But interestingly, Hobbes gives his prohibitions against stealing and aggression in conditional form. In his *Leviathan* statement of the first law of nature, Hobbes declares:

> *That every man ought to endeavor Peace, as far as he has hope of obtaining it; and when he cannot obtain it, that he may seek, and use, all helps and advantages of Warre.* The first branch of which Rule, containeth the first, and Fundamentall Law of Nature; which is, *to seek peace, and follow it*. The Second, the summe of the Right of Nature; which is, *By all means we can, to defend our selves.*[25]

From this first fundamental law it follows that one must refrain from injuring or killing others, but only on condition that one believes one need not injure or kill others in order to protect one's own life. Hobbes claims that a second law of nature follows immediately from the first which, among other things, requires that one must refrain from seizing another's goods without permission, but again only on condition that one expects others to refrain from seizing one's own goods without permission.[26] For Hobbes, one is released from the general prohibitions against aggression and stealing in certain special circumstances, namely, when one cannot count on those with whom one interacts to obey these prohibitions with respect to oneself. Using helpful terminology from Gregory Kavka's work, according to Hobbes one may permissibly violate the prohibitions of the first and second laws of nature *defensively* with respect to another when the other disregards these prohibitions with respect to herself or she has good reason to expect the other to disregard these prohibitions with respect to herself. But Hobbes' natural law forbids violating the prohibitions against aggression and stealing *offensively*, by aggressing against or stealing from another when one *does* expect the other to obey these prohibitions with respect to oneself or when the other *does* obey these prohibitions with respect to oneself.[27] One can interpret reasoning and conduct with respect to certain of Hobbes' moral requirements,

---

25. *Leviathan* 14:4. Hobbes gives a parallel statement of this law of nature in *De Cive* 2.2. In *Elements of Law: Part I, Human Nature* 14:14 Hobbes also declares that reason requires one to seek peace when one can hope to attain peace before officially introducing natural law precepts in 15:1.

26. *Leviathan* 14:5. Hobbes gives parallel texts in *De Cive* 2.3 and *Elements of Law I* 15.2 summarizing the positive requirements of the *Leviathan* second law and proceeds immediately in those respective works to discuss how one can relinquish or transfer rights to goods. This conditional form of this law is articulated most clearly in *Leviathan*.

27. Gregory Kavka, *Hobbesian Moral and Political Theory* (Princeton, NJ: Princeton University Press, 1986), 139, and "The Rationality of Rule-Following: Hobbes's Dispute with the Foole," *Law and Philosophy* 14 (1995), p. 8.

such as the first and second laws of nature, as Stag Hunt reasoning and conduct. One presumably fares better in a peaceful condition where one and the others with whom one interacts all obey the positive requirements of these laws against offensive violation than one fares in a warlike state liable to ensue if all fail to obey these positive requirements. But if one obeys these positive requirements with respect to others who do not reciprocate, then one suffers exploitation that one could avoid by violating these requirements defensively. Like hunting hare in Rousseau's coordination problem, one plays it safe when one does not obey the positive requirements of Hobbes' first two laws of nature. But by playing it safe, one undermines everyone's chances of achieving the peaceful outcome all realize they can achieve if all follow the positive requirements, same as hunting hare undermines everyone's chances of sharing a captured deer in Rousseau's problem.

Problem 1.4. Contribute or Free-Ride?

In *Treatise*, Hume uses a pair of examples of groups that could benefit by draining a meadow they possess to illustrate some of the problems that can arise in joint projects.

> Two neighbors may agree to drain a meadow, which they possess in common; because 'tis easy for them to know each others mind; and each must perceive, that the immediate consequence of his failing in his part, is, the abandoning the whole project. But 'tis very difficult, and indeed impossible, that a thousand persons shou'd agree in any such action; it being difficult for them to concert so complicated a design, and still more difficult for them to execute it; while each seeks a pretext to free himself of the trouble and expense, and would lay the whole burden on others.[28]

If two can succeed, why are a thousand prone to fail? One serious problem facing the thousand is deciding just how they should all proceed. Should they dig wells? Or should they dig trenches that allow the surface water to drain into a nearby pond? Or should they lay pipes and draining tile beneath the surface? And the thousand would have to settle several issues allied with each method they might consider. If some were to propose digging wells, others might well ask questions of the following sort: "How many wells would we have to dig, and how deep would each well have to be?," "Where in the meadow would we dig the wells?," and "Would not laying pipe and draining tile be less tiring than digging wells?" On top of all this, the thousand would have to decide how to divide the labor and

---

28. *Treatise* 3.2.7:8.

expenses needed to complete the task. If they dig wells, then some will have to dig, some will have to move the dug earth, some will have to build scaffolding with which others can lift and lower diggers, and so on. Some if not all will also have to contribute toward providing the necessary tools and raw materials plus the food, drink, first aid, and anything else they expect those laboring in the meadow will need in order to finish the job. Disputes among the thousand would likely erupt over how to assign the various tasks and contribution amounts needed to execute any proposed method of meadow draining, adding more confusion to an already confused situation.

The thousand people in Hume's meadow draining example would most likely fail in their joint venture partly because each individual would be in the dark as to just how she should contribute. Hume gives an additional reason why they are prone to fail. Hume observes that each of the thousand would really rather drop out and leave the others to complete the project than to contribute herself. If one contributes to the project and in the end the group fails, then one apparently will have incurred a personal cost for nothing. And one might expect one's personal contribution to make little difference. Given a thousand potential contributors, would withholding one's own contribution appreciably affect the likelihood that they will successfully drain the meadow? If one does contribute, are the chances the thousand will ultimately succeed really significantly greater? Moreover, individuals among the thousand might reason that since there are so many potential contributors, quite possibly no one will even take note of whether or not a particular individual among the thousand contributes. If the thousand possess their meadow in common, same as the pair in Hume's first meadow draining example possess their meadow in common, then presumably should the thousand somehow complete their project, each of them will then be able to enjoy the benefits of the drained meadow whether or not she contributed herself. In short, each of the thousand people in Hume's meadow draining example might conclude that she may as well withhold her own contribution, given that both the likelihood that the meadow will be drained and her own access to the meadow should it be drained are for all practical purposes independent of her own activity.

A drained meadow possessed in common is an example of a *public good.* A public good for a given community is *nonexcludable,* that is, a good that once available is available to every community member, whether or not this member contributes to its provision. Most public goods that can be generated by the efforts of community members must be *jointly supplied,* that is, only the joint contributions of a significant percentage of community members produce an appreciable amount of the public good. Examples of jointly supplied public goods include the relative security from foreign attack that stems from an effective national defense and an environment with relatively low levels of pollution. A drained meadow possessed in common is another example, since the draining requires the joint effort of a number of the common possessors. Hume argues that, paradoxically, as the number of potential contributors to this public good grows, the prospects for the provision of this good actually diminish. Two can succeed, whereas a thousand will most likely fail.

In a similar vein, in his classic 1965 work *The Logic of Collective Action*, Mancur Olson argued that the level of public good provision declines as the population of potential providers increases.[29] Olson's arguments stress the increasing insignificance of personal contribution as group size grows, while Hume gives more emphasis to the complexities of organizing individuals to work together for a common good. Yet they arrive at the same conclusion. Put in the terminology that emerged after Olson's work, typically when individuals would all benefit if all of them were to contribute toward providing a public good, each individual is tempted to "free-ride," withholding her own contribution. A free-rider enjoys the benefits of the public good at no personal cost so long as not too many others also free-ride. As the group size grows, so does the temptation to free-ride, and so does the likelihood that no amount of the public good is provided at all. Olson himself claimed that unless the group size is quite small, in the absence of outside incentives rational, self-interested group members will not contribute to achieving their group's interests.[30] This claim has become known as Olson's *zero contribution thesis*. *The Logic of Collective Action* was a key early work in *public choice theory*, which analyzes traditional problems of politics using the formal tools of contemporary economics. Much of contemporary public choice theory is driven by the study of problems, such as public goods problems, where unrestricted pursuit of individual interest can lead to outcomes at odds with group interest. Hume's meadow draining example illustrates a central problem of public choice: In a society with a sizeable population, some goods, such as security from foreign aggression and breathable air, can exist only as jointly supplied public goods. Given the free-rider problem, how can such public goods exist?

Problem 1.5. Acquiesce or Resist?

The plot of Giacomo Puccini's opera *Gianni Schicchi* includes a striking problem of decision and commitment. Here is a summary of the relevant part of the plot: Buoso Donati, a wealthy resident of Florence, has died. Before Buoso's

---

29. Mancur Olson, *The Logic of Collective Action* (Cambridge, MA: Harvard University Press, 1965), p. 35.

30. Olson (1965), p. 2.

death is announced publicly, his relatives study his will and learn to their rage that Buoso has bequeathed his fortune to a monastery rather than to them. The relatives then seek the advice of Gianni Schicchi, a newcomer to Florence. Sizing up the situation, Schicchi suggests to the relatives that he impersonate Buoso and draw up a new and false will, which will name the relatives as Buoso's principal heirs. The relatives agree to Schicchi's proposal. Schicchi indeed successfully impersonates Buoso, and in the relatives' presence he dictates a new will to a notary. But to their astonishment and renewed rage, Schicchi dictates to the notary that the principal part of Buoso's fortune is to be left not to them but to Gianni Schicchi! For a moment the relatives consider exposing Schicchi's treachery to the authorities. However, the punishment for falsifying a will in Florence is severe. Anyone implicated in falsifying a will in Florence first suffers the loss of a hand by amputation and afterward is banished from the city. If the relatives were to expose Schicchi, they would still lose Buoso's fortune to the monastery in the end and would also expose themselves. So they reluctantly accept the situation.

In his *History of the Peloponnesian War*, Thucydides presents a dialog attributed to representatives of Athens and the island of Melos who met in 416 B.C.E. outside the Melian city soon after the arrival of a large military contingent of Athenians and their allies. According to Thucydides, the Athenian representatives gave the Melians a choice: join the Delian League peaceably, or face destruction.[31] The Melians wished to continue their policy of neutrality. Joining the Delian League would effectively require Melos to side with Athens and its empire in their ongoing conflict with the Peloponnesian League, led by Sparta. Both sides were well aware that the Athenians had arrived in overwhelming force, and that the Athenians were negotiating at all only to save themselves the costs of a siege they expected would surely succeed. Quite early in their exchange, the Athenian ambassadors came to what they thought was the real point of their meeting, and the Melians responded with a warning:

> *Athenians*: let's work out what we can do on the basis of what both sides truly accept: we both know that decisions about justice are made in human discussions only when both sides are under equal compulsion; but when one side is stronger, it gets as much as it can, and the weak must accept that.
>
> *Melians*: Well then, since you put your interest in place of justice, our view must be that it is in your interest not to subvert this rule that is good for all: that a plea for justice and fairness should do some good for a man who has fallen into danger, if he can win over his judges, even if he is not perfectly

31. *The History of the Peloponnesian War* V:91–93.

> persuasive. And this rule concerns you no less than us: if you ever stumble, you might receive a terrible punishment and be an example to others.[32]

The Athenians dismissed this warning and argued that if their positions were reversed, the Melians would be the ones demanding that the Athenians acquiesce or face certain destruction.[33] The Melian representatives ultimately concluded that they could not surrender without a fight and keep their honor. They also insisted that they had to trust in the gods and in the hope that the Spartans might come to their aid, despite their own past refusal to side with Sparta in the war. The Athenians ended the negotiations, but not before accusing the Melians of wishful thinking and warning them a last time that their defiance would lead to their total destruction. The Athenian force then besieged the Melian city and ultimately defeated the Melians. Thucydides reports that following the Melians' surrender, the victorious Athenians killed all the surviving Melian men of military age and sold the surviving Melian women and children into slavery.[34]

Thucydides' account of the tragic end of the Melians recorded in his *History of the Peloponnesian War* may seem very far removed from Puccini's amusing conclusion to his opera *Gianni Schicchi*. Yet these two stories have important elements in common. Each is a story of one side placing the other side in an apparently helpless position. Each is also a story of the side in the stronger position trying to exploit the other side's knowledge of its relative weakness. Gianni Schicchi betrays the relatives he has promised to help, because Schicchi knows what the relatives know, namely, that the relatives cannot expose Schicchi without also exposing themselves. Schicchi rightly predicts that the relatives would rather allow Schicchi to keep the fortune they have so coveted and to at least continue residing in Florence with their bodies intact than suffer the same severe punishment he would suffer if they were to expose his betrayal. The Athenians offered the Melians an apparently easy choice: become vassals of the Athenian empire or suffer utter destruction. The Athenian ambassadors were right when they warned the Melians that neither the gods nor any earthly allies would save the Melians from defeat. Of course, the stories of the Athenians and the Melians and of Gianni Schicchi and Buoso's relatives differ in one important way: the victims in Thucydides' story ultimately resisted as best they could, while the victims in Puccini's opera simply acquiesced. The Melians chose the course they knew could lead to their own destruction, while Buoso's relatives chose what they recognized was the safer option.

---

32. *The History of the Peloponnesian War* V:89–90.

33. *The History of the Peloponnesian War* V:105.

34. *The History of the Peloponnesian War* V:112–116.

These two examples raise important questions regarding interactions between individuals and groups who differ so much with respect to relative advantage in the interaction that one side is effectively at the mercy of another. Does prudence require that the relatively helpless simply accept whatever the relatively more advantaged parties may do to them, including betraying, mistreating, or even killing them? Schicchi anticipates that Buoso's relatives will conclude they should acquiesce if he takes advantage of their gullibility and places them in a relatively helpless position. And the relatives acquiesce, just as they "should." But the Melian representatives refused to give in to what they considered an unjust ultimatum, even though the Athenian ambassadors rightly warned them that resistance would be futile. Must any appeal to justice be framed in terms of prudential interests? Or is justice simply irrelevant in the interactions between parties so disparate in power that one side cannot effectively resist the other? The Melian representatives tried to persuade the Athenian ambassadors that violating justice by attacking the Melians would not in the end serve Athenian interests. They believed, probably rightly, that they could persuade the Athenians to treat them with restraint only by convincing the Athenian ambassadors that the Athenians would be prudent to exercise such restraint. And the Athenian ambassadors simply asserted that in a situation like theirs, where one side is overwhelmingly stronger than the other, the weaker side must simply accept whatever terms the strong offer. The Athenian ambassadors endorsed the position that justice is indeed irrelevant when one relatively powerful side interacts with another relatively helpless side. But many would deny this claim. And if given the opportunity to query these ambassadors, many would ask them: "What is justice for, if not to ensure that the interests of the powerless are protected?"

§1.2. Noncooperative Game Theory

In 1944, von Neumann and Morgenstern established game theory as an important new branch of social science by publishing their treatise *Theory of Games and Economic Behavior*. Von Neumann and Morgenstern viewed their work as laying the foundations of a precise and rigorous theory of economic and sociological problems in general. In the early 1950s, John Nash published a series of essays that made tremendous strides in the research program von Neumann and Morgenstern started.[35] One can rightly regard von Neumann, Morgenstern, and Nash as the primary creators of the *classical game theory* that explores how ideally rational and knowledgeable agents interact.

The more fundamental part of von Neumann, Morgenstern, and Nash's game theory is the theory of *noncooperative games*, where agents interact with

35. Nash's essays on game theory are reprinted as they originally appeared in the journals where they were first published in a single volume, together with an introductory essay by Ken Binmore, in *Essays on Game Theory* (Cheltenham, UK: Edward Elgar, 1996).

		Agent 2 (Ted)		
		R	P	S
	R	(0, 0)	(– 1, 1)	(1, – 1)
Agent 1 (Yue)	P	(1, – 1)	(0, 0)	(– 1, 1)
	S	(– 1, 1)	(1, – 1)	(0, 0)

R = rock, S = scissors, P = paper

FIGURE 1.1 Rock-Paper-Scissors

no preexisting binding agreements that restrict their actions.[36] According to the account of convention I develop and use in this book, a convention can emerge in a community without any prior explicit agreements or commitments. The noncooperative theory is the primary branch of game theory for analyzing conventions. A noncooperative game is characterized by a set of *agents*, their sets of *pure strategies*, and the *payoffs* each receives at each possible strategy combination. The *Rock-Paper-Scissors* game summarized in Figure 1.1 is such a noncooperative game in *strategic form*.[37] Yue is the row agent, or Agent 1 by convention, and Ted is the column agent, Agent 2.[38] Each must choose exactly one of the three pure strategies rock (R), scissors (S), or paper (P). Each chooses independently and privately. The joint outcome of their choices is one of the game's pure strategy combinations or profiles. Each pure strategy profile (s_1, s_2) has an associated payoff vector $(u_1(s_1, s_2), u_2(s_1, s_2))$ where Agent i's payoff $u_i(s_1, s_2)$ is the ith component.[39] Strategic form games model interactions where each agent chooses her own strategy without being able to causally influence or even observe the other agents' strategy choices in advance. In a strategic form game, agents choose independently and as if they were choosing simultaneously. The payoffs are von Neumann–Morgenstern utilities, reflecting the relative intensities of each

36. Von Neumann and Morgenstern also developed the foundations of *cooperative game theory*, where interacting agents can have such preexisting binding agreements. In one of his essays, Nash argued that a cooperative game should be viewed as part of a larger noncooperative game in which the agents might in the initial moves establish binding agreements. See John Nash, "Two-Person Cooperative Games," *Econometrica* 21 (1953), pp. 128–140, reprinted in Nash (1996), pp. 34–46.

37. Von Neumann and Morgenstern referred to such games as *normal form* games. Some game theorists continue to use von Neumann and Morgenstern's original terminology.

38. In this book I refer to generic individuals engaged in a game as *agents* or *parties* in order to emphasize that most of the games I discuss summarize problems of justice.

39. Here and throughout this book, "$u_i(s)$" denotes Agent i's payoff in an n-agent game at the pure strategy profile $\boldsymbol{s} = (s_1, \ldots, s_n)$.

agent's preferences over the various possible outcomes. In *Theory of Games and Economic Behavior*, von Neumann and Morgenstern proved a representation theorem that showed how one can derive cardinal utilities for an agent who has preferences over the outcomes that can depend upon her acts that satisfy certain consistency axioms. Such von Neumann–Morgenstern utilities are unique up to a choice of scale.[40] Von Neumann and Morgenstern's representation theorem secured the respectability of cardinal utility theory in economic theory.[41] And von Neumann–Morgenstern utilities make possible a rigorous analysis of noncooperative games.

Given the interdependence of the agents' decisions and the potential for conflicting preferences over outcomes, how can a noncooperative game be "solved"? In *Theory of Games and Economic Behavior*, von Neumann and Morgenstern argued that a solution of such a game must result from some strategy selection procedure such that each agent would willingly follow this procedure knowing that the other agent knows this and also selects a strategy according to this procedure.

> Let us now imagine that there exists a complete theory of the zero-sum two-person game which tells a player what to do, and which is absolutely convincing. If the players knew such a theory then each player would have to assume that his strategy has been "found out" by his opponent. The opponent knows the theory, and he knows that a player would be unwise not to follow it. Thus the hypothesis of the existence of a satisfactory theory legitimizes our investigation of the situation when a player's strategy is "found out" by his opponent. And a satisfactory theory can exist only if we are able to harmonize the two extremes Γ_1 and Γ_2,—strategies of player 1 "found out" or of player 2 "found out."[42]

In *The Dynamics of Rational Deliberation*, Brian Skyrms observes that von Neumann and Morgenstern's argument evidently presupposes more than that the agents use some general algorithmic procedure for selecting strategies and

40. Von Neumann and Morgenstern (1944), appendix.

41. In fact, Von Neumann and Morgenstern rediscovered some of the results of Frank Ramsey's 1926 essay "Truth and Probability." Ramsey showed that if an agent has a sufficiently rich preference ordering over lotteries and follows certain axioms of coherent decision-making, this agent can derive both a cardinal utility function and a subjective probability measure over the various outcomes of her decisions. See Frank Ramsey, "Truth and Probability," in *Philosophical Papers*, ed. D. H. Mellor (1926; Cambridge: Cambridge University Press, 1990), pp. 52–94.

42. Von Neumann and Morgenstern (1944), p. 148.

know that they use this procedure.[43] In a noncooperative game each agent has certain beliefs reflecting the likelihood that the other agents follow certain strategy profiles. These beliefs can be summarized with precision as a probability distribution the agent assigns over the strategy profiles the others can follow. This probability distribution is the agent's *conjecture* over the other agents' strategy profiles. A *best response* given one's conjecture is a strategy that maximizes one's expected payoff according to the probabilities of this conjecture. Suppose that in the Figure 1.1 Rock-Paper-Scissors game Yue and Ted both know they follow exactly one and the same rule: Follow a best response given my conjecture. This is simply a special case of the principle of *Bayesian rationality*, according to which one's rational choice from among a set of available options is an option that maximizes one's expected utility given one's beliefs. Then Yue and Ted both follow the same theory for strategy selection and both know this, but they can still arrive at an outcome neither finds satisfactory. If Yue's conjecture assigns probability 1 to Ted's choosing P and Ted's conjecture assigns probability 1 to Yue's choosing R, then by following their best responses the outcome will be the profile (S,S). Plainly each would prefer to deviate from (S,S) if she were to discover that her counterpart will follow S given his conjecture. So this single rule of expected utility maximization is not by itself a satisfactory theory of strategy selection according to von Neumann and Morgenstern's standards. The "complete theory" of strategy selection von Neumann and Morgenstern speak of actually presupposes that each agent can reconstruct all of the reasoning a counterpart employs in selecting a strategy. Such a theory would have to include not only a common rule or algorithm the agents use but also all of the *inputs* to this rule or algorithm. And such a theory would have to characterize an *equilibrium* of the game, that is, no agent would have reason to deviate unilaterally from her part of the *strategy system* this theory prescribes.

Nash defined an equilibrium concept rooted in Bayesian rationality and established existence conditions for this concept for a general class of noncooperative games.[44] Nash's equilibrium concept incorporates *mixed strategies*, where each agent randomizes over her pure strategies in a manner probabilistically independent of the other agents' randomizations.[45] Pure strategies become special

---

43. Brian Skyrms, *The Dynamics of Rational Deliberation* (Cambridge, MA: Harvard University Press, 1990), pp. 13–16.

44. John Nash, "Equilibrium Points in *n*-Person Games," *Proceedings of the National Academy of Sciences of the United States* 36 (1950), pp. 48–49, reprinted in Nash (1996), p. 9, and "Non-Cooperative Games," *Annals of Mathematics* 54 (1951), pp. 286–295, reprinted in Nash (1996), pp. 22–31.

45. In a game, agents' strategies are probabilistically independent if the joint probability distribution over the pure strategy combinations defined by their strategies is a product measure

cases of mixed strategies where a pure strategy is chosen with probability 1. Von Neumann had employed mixed strategies in his analysis of *zero-sum games*, where one agent gains exactly when the other agents lose. Rock-Paper-Scissors is such a zero-sum game. A zero-sum game can fail to have any equilibria in pure strategies, but von Neumann showed that in any 2-agent zero-sum game, the agents follow an equilibrium in mixed strategies by following security strategies that satisfy the *maximin* rule: Identify the minimum expected utility possible given each strategy, then choose the strategy yielding the maximum of these minimums.[46] In the Figure 1.1 game, Yue and Ted have the same maximin strategy, the mixed strategy $\sigma = \frac{1}{3}R \oplus \frac{1}{3}S \oplus \frac{1}{3}P$, where one follows R, P, and S with probability $\frac{1}{3}$ each. Neither Agent i can improve her *maximin payoff*, the expected payoff $E_i(u_i(\sigma,\sigma)) = 0$ she achieves by following σ, by following any other strategy. So (σ,σ) is an equilibrium.[47] Von Neumann's application of maximin reasoning in solving 2-agent zero-sum games cannot be extended to even the simplest of non-zero-sum games. But Nash realized that if the agents can follow mixed strategies, a wide class of games have equilibria rooted in the Bayesian rationality principle. Nash defined an equilibrium as a mixed strategy profile such that no agent can improve upon her expected payoff by deviating from this profile when the other agents follow their respective ends of this profile. Nash proved that every noncooperative game with finitely pure strategy profiles, determined by a finite set of agents each of whom has finitely many pure strategies, has such a *Nash equilibrium*. Since by definition every agent in the game follows the Bayesian principle of utility maximization at a Nash equilibrium, another way of phrasing Nash's result is that for every game with finitely many possible outcomes in pure

---

of each agent's individual strategy. So if σ_i is Agent i's mixed strategy and if $\boldsymbol{\sigma}$ is the joint probability distribution over the pure strategy combinations defined by all the agents' mixed strategies, then $\boldsymbol{\sigma} = \sigma_1 \cdots \sigma_n$.

46. John von Neumann, "Zur Theorie der Gesellshaftsspiele," *Mathematische Annalen* 100 (1928), pp. 295–320, and von Neumann and Morgenstern (1944), §17. Von Neumann's result is known as the *minimax theorem*, which gets its name because in a zero-sum game an Agent i's maximin payoff coincides with the minimax payoff, which is the lowest expected payoff that Agent i's counterparts can force her to accept without knowing in advance which strategy Agent i follows.

47. Here and throughout this book, (i) "$\oplus$" denotes a probabilistic or *convex combination* operator for strategies or strategy profiles, so that $\lambda_1 s_1 \oplus \cdots \oplus \lambda_n s_n$ with $\lambda_i \geq 0$ for $i \in \{1,\ldots,n\}$ and $\lambda_1 + \cdots + \lambda_n = 1$ is the convex combination where strategy or strategy profile s_i is followed with probability λ_i, and (ii) "$E_i(\cdot)$" denotes Agent i's expectation operator, so that $E_i(u_i(\boldsymbol{f}))$ is Agent i's expected payoff at the (possibly probabilistic) system of strategy profiles $\boldsymbol{f}$. Special cases of such systems include pure strategy and mixed strategy profiles where agents' strategies are probabilistically independent. In Chapter 2, I will discuss *correlated* strategy systems.

strategies, there is an outcome in mixed strategies where individual Bayesian rationality coincides with joint Bayesian rationality. Nash's fundamental theorem led to the Nash equilibrium becoming the central solution concept for noncooperative games. In more recent years, alternative interpretations of mixed strategies have led to important generalizations of the Nash equilibrium concept, which I will discuss in Chapter 2.

Nash's equilibrium existence theorem did not establish a general method for solving games, since a game need not have a unique Nash equilibrium. The strategic form game of Figure 1.2 provides a dramatic example of this phenomenon. In this *unanimity game*, each agent has the pure strategies $A_1,\ldots,A_n$, and each achieves her best outcome exactly when both follow the same pure strategy. One can interpret this *Encounter Problem* game as a situation where Yue and Ted search for each other in a shopping mall with n different stores. A_i is the strategy of visiting Store i, and Ted and Yue find each other exactly when they both visit the same Store i. The Encounter Problem has n different Nash equilibria in pure strategies, namely, (A_1,A_1), (A_2,A_2), . . ., and (A_n,A_n). Each of these pure strategy equilibria is *strict*, that is, an agent who deviates unilaterally from any of these pure strategy equilibria strictly lowers her payoff. Each of these pure strategy equilibria is also (Pareto) optimal, that is, there is no other outcome of the game at which both agents fare at least as well and at least one of them fares better in terms of expected payoff.[48] In fact, on the face of it Yue and Ted seem to have no good reason to prefer any one of these strict equilibria over any of the others. Moreover, these pure strategy equilibria are not the only Nash equilibria available to the agents. For $n = 2$, the Encounter Problem has a third Nash equilibrium in mixed strategies, where Yue and Ted independently follow $\sigma^* = \frac{1}{2}A_1 \oplus \frac{1}{2}A_2$. For $n = 5$, the Encounter Problem has in addition to the five strict pure strategy Nash equilibria another twenty-six mixed strategy Nash equilibria. For $n = 10$, the Encounter Problem has 1,023 Nash equilibria in total! At most of these Nash equilibria the two agents do not achieve their best outcomes, although by definition they follow strategies that maximize their expected utilities. For instance, in the $n = 2$ case, at the mixed strategy Nash equilibrium (σ^*,σ^*) Ted and Yue both achieve an expected payoff of only $\frac{1}{2}$, less than what both achieve if they follow either (A_1,A_1) or (A_2,A_2). The (σ^*,σ^*) equilibrium is *Pareto inferior* to

48. An outcome $s=(s_1,\ldots,s_n)$ of an n-agent game is (Pareto) optimal or *(Pareto) efficient* if for every outcome $s'=(s'_1,\ldots,s'_n)$, if $u_1(s')\geq u_1(s)$, $u_2(s')\geq u_2(s)$ . . . , and $u_n(s')\geq u_n(s)$ then $s'=s$. That is, no other outcome s' yields any Agent i a higher expected payoff than Agent i receives at s and none a lower expected payoff than any receives at s.

Agent 2 (Ted)

		A_1	A_2		A_m
	A_1	$(1,1)$	$(0,0)$	$\cdots$	$(0,0)$
Agent 1 (Yue)	A_2	$(0,0)$	$(1,1)$	$\cdots$	$(0,0)$
	$\vdots$	$\vdots$	$\vdots$	$\ddots$	$\vdots$
	A_m	$(0,0)$	$(0,0)$	$\cdots$	$(1,1)$

FIGURE 1.2 Encounter Problem

both (A_1, A_1) and (A_2, A_2), and, conversely, (A_1, A_1) and (A_2, A_2) are both *Pareto superior* to or *Pareto improvements* over the maximin equilibrium.[49]

The Encounter Problem illustrates what is perhaps the most interesting and challenging problem of game theory, namely, the problem of *equilibrium selection.* By following any Nash equilibrium of this game, the agents all satisfy the Bayesian rationality principle given their mutual expectations. If each agent expects the other agents to follow their parts of a certain equilibrium, then she maximizes her expected utility by following her own part of this equilibrium. Even for $n = 2$, the simplest nontrivial case, it is by no means obvious *which* equilibrium Ted and Yue should follow. The suboptimal mixed Nash equilibrium (σ, σ) exhibits a certain symmetry, in that at this equilibrium Yue and Ted both follow the mixed strategies that give equal weight to each of their pure strategy options. But why should this property lead them to follow this Nash equilibrium? After all, Yue and Ted achieve an outcome best for them both by following one of the pure strategy Nash equilibria. But there is the rub. The two pure strategy Nash equilibria (A_1, A_1) and (A_2, A_2) are equally good from the perspective of each agent. How should they choose? And the equilibrium selection problem for the Figure 1.2 game only grows exponentially more complex as n increases. In cases like the Encounter problem, where there are multiple equilibria, how would agents pick one equilibrium over all the others? For that matter, why would one expect that agents engaged in a game like this would settle upon any equilibrium at all?

One can think of the payoff structures of Rock-Paper-Scissors and the Encounter Problem as illustrating two extreme cases of interactions between two individuals, the first being one wheretheir interests are diametrically opposed, and the second where their interests coincide perfectly. Thomas Schelling developed this idea in

49. More generally, an outcome s' of an n-agent game is *Pareto inferior* (*superior*) to an outcome s is if $u_i(s') \leq u_i(s)$ $(u_i(s') \geq u_i(s))$ for each Agent i with strict inequality for at least one Agent i. If s' is Pareto superior to s then s' is said to *Pareto dominate* s or to *Pareto improve upon* s.

The Strategy of Conflict. Schelling argued that one can use game theory to model a host of interaction problems, of which *pure conflict* problems and *pure coordination* problems represent extreme cases. Schelling also argued that pure conflict and pure coordination games represent extreme cases of what agents want their counterparts to know, or not to know, regarding the pure strategies they select. In a pure coordination game such as the Encounter Problem, each agent will want the other agents to know which pure strategy she will follow. Conversely, in a pure conflict game such as Rock-Paper-Scissors, each agent will want to keep secret which pure strategy she will follow. And one way to keep the pure strategy one will follow in the end a secret even from oneself is to employ a completely mixed strategy.

Schelling proposed a reorientation of game theory in which all noncooperative games should be regarded as falling along a continuum of which the games of pure conflict and pure coordination are the endpoints. The payoff structure of a game-theoretic model of an interaction should reflect the extent to which the agents' interests agree and, correspondingly, the extent to which each agent will want her counterparts to be able to guess her chosen pure strategy. The more the agents' interests disagree, the closer the corresponding game's payoffs will be to zero-sum game payoffs, while the more their interests agree, the closer the game's payoffs will be to pure coordination game payoffs. In *Theory of Games and Economic Behavior*, von Neumann and Morgenstern emphasized the theory of zero-sum games, the games of pure conflict. Perhaps more than any other single work, *The Strategy of Conflict* helped to expand the application of noncooperative game theory beyond problems of pure conflict resolution to problems of social interaction in general. Much of the analysis to follow in this book will concentrate on interactions that fall somewhere in between the extremes of Schelling's continuum, in that they contain elements of both conflict and coordination.

§1.3. Revisiting the Motivating Problems

Problem 1.1. The Farmer's Dilemma

One can summarize the structure of the interaction between the two farmers in the Farmer's Dilemma Hume presents in *Treatise* with the tree diagram given in Figure 1.3.[50] In many situations, agents might want to take into account any sequential structure their interaction may have if they are able to do so. The Figure 1.3 game characterizes a game in *extensive form* that explicitly incorporates the temporal

50. Brian Skyrms, Jordan Howard Sobel, and I use this game to model Hume's Farmer's Dilemma. See Brian Skyrms, "The Shadow of the Future," in *Rational Commitment and Social Justice: Essays for Gregory Kavka*, ed. Jules Coleman and Christopher Morris (Cambridge: Cambridge University Press, 1998), pp. 12–22; Vanderschraaf (1998a); Sobel (2009), pp. 270–271.

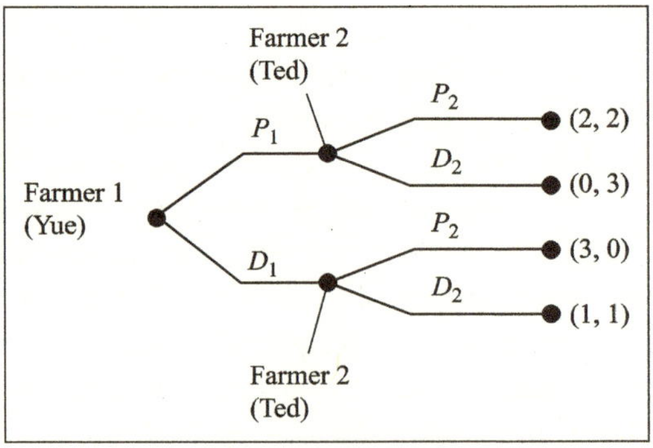

P_i = Farmer i performs, D_i = Farmer i defects, $i \in \{1,2\}$

FIGURE 1.3 Farmer's Dilemma

ordering of the agents' moves. Each possible outcome of an extensive form game has an associated payoff vector such that Agent *i*'s payoff is the *i*th component of the vector, and this outcome corresponds to a terminal node of the associated game tree. In this game, each farmer when she is to act can either perform (P_i) by helping the other farmer or defect (D_i) by not helping. Yue, the first farmer, moves either P_1 or D_1 first. This is a game of *perfect information* since the second farmer, Ted, moves next after observing Yue's initial move. Ted can move either P_2 or D_2 if Yue first moves P_1, and either P_2 or D_2 if Yue first moves D_1. Using the Figure 1.3 game, one can paraphrase Hume's argument that neither farmer will help the other as follows: Yue reasons that if she were to choose P_1, then Ted's best response would be to choose D_2. So Yue rules out the P_1, P_2-outcome, and then must decide whether to choose P_1 and arrive at the P_1, D_2-outcome or to choose D_1. Since the P_1, D_2-outcome is Yue's worst outcome, to avoid this outcome Yue will choose D_1. Ted will then choose D_2, his best response to Yue's choice of D_1. According to this *backward induction* analysis, the two farmers will follow the outcome where each follows D_i at the time she is to choose her action.[51] In a game of perfect information, one identifies a backward induction solution by starting at the terminal nodes of the game and then stepwise deleting branches of the tree that are not best responses for the agent who is to move at the preceding node given the remaining branches. The branch of the Figure 1.3 Farmer's Dilemma remaining at the end of this stepwise procedure is the branch of the D_1, D_2-outcome.

The backward induction analysis of the Farmer's Dilemma plainly rests upon specific assumptions regarding what the two agents in the game know about each other and upon Yue's reasoning regarding a subjunctive conditional, since Yue draws a crucial conclusion in her reasoning regarding what would occur if she

51. Skyrms (1998) and Vanderschraaf (1998a) credit Hume with an informal backward induction analysis of his Farmer's Dilemma example.

were to choose a strategy she does not choose in the end. Specifically, this backward induction analysis presupposes (i) the two farmers understand the interaction structure, that is, they know the game, (ii) they follow strategies that are best responses in terms of expected payoff, that is, they are Bayesian rational, and (iii) Yue knows that Ted is Bayesian rational and knows the game.[52] The Farmer's Dilemma has a single Nash equilibrium in pure strategies, and this equilibrium is entirely characterized by the two agents' best responses at each possible stage in the interaction.[53] This equilibrium is especially easy to identify in the strategic form representation of the Farmer's Dilemma game, which is given in Figure 1.4. In the Figure 1.4 game, $(D_1; D_2\text{-if-}P_1, D_2\text{-if-}D_1)$ is the Nash equilibrium in pure strategies.

One might wonder whether or not the two farmers would be more likely to help each other harvest their corn if they could each choose either to perform or to defect without either knowing ahead of time what the other has done. Some of Hume's own texts suggest that Hume believes the real barrier to cooperation in the Farmer's Dilemma is that the two farmers cannot exchange their labor simultaneously.[54] Figure 1.5 depicts an extensive form game tree closely related to the Figure 1.3 game tree. In the Figure 1.5 game, Yue again moves either P_1 or D_1 first, but now Ted does not observe Yue's move before moving himself. Yue's move at the first stage places Ted at an *information set*, indicated by the bubble connecting the P_1- and D_1-nodes in the Figure 1.5 tree. An agent's information set at a given stage when she moves reflects her uncertainty regarding the prior moves in the game. When each agent in an extensive form game has no uncertainty regarding the previous moves, as was the case in the Figure 1.3 Farmer's Dilemma game,

---

52. Exploring the specific knowledge conditions needed to support backward induction solutions for certain classes of extensive form games has become an important part of the research on epistemic foundations of game-theoretic solution concepts. Some important works in this specific area include Philip Reny, "Rationality in Extensive Form Games," *Journal of Economic Perspectives* 6 (1992), pp. 103–118; Cristina Bicchieri, *Rationality and Coordination* (Cambridge: Cambridge University Press, 1993); and Robert Aumann, "Backward Induction and Common Knowledge of Rationality," *Games and Economic Behavior* 8 (1995), pp. 16–19.

53. The Figure 1.3 game also has some partially mixed Nash equilibria where Yue follows D_1 and Ted follows a mixed strategy of the form

$$\sigma_2^* = (1-y)\cdot(P_2\text{-if-}P_1, D_2\text{-if-}D_1) \oplus y\cdot(D_2\text{-if-}P_1, D_2\text{-if-}D_2)$$

where $y \geq \frac{1}{2}$. But at any of these equilibria Yue and Ted are to follow the same path as the pure strategy equilibrium path.

54. See especially Hume's preliminary discussion of exchange in *Treatise* 3.2.5:8 immediately prior to his presentation of the Farmer's Dilemma example and Hume's discussion of the difficulties of physically delivering certain goods in property transference in *Treatise* 3.2.4:2.

		Farmer 2 (Ted)			
		P_2-if-P_1 P_2-if-D_1	P_2-if-P_1 D_2-if-D_1	D_2-if-P_1 P_2-if-D_1	D_2-if-P_1 D_2-if-D_1
Farmer 1 (Yue)	P_1	(2, 0)	(2, 0)	(0, 3)	(0, 3)
	D_2	(3, 0)	(1, 1)	(3, 0)	(1, 1)

P_i = Farmer i performs, D_i = Farmer i defects, $i \in \{1, 2\}$

FIGURE 1.4 Farmer's Dilemma in Strategic Form

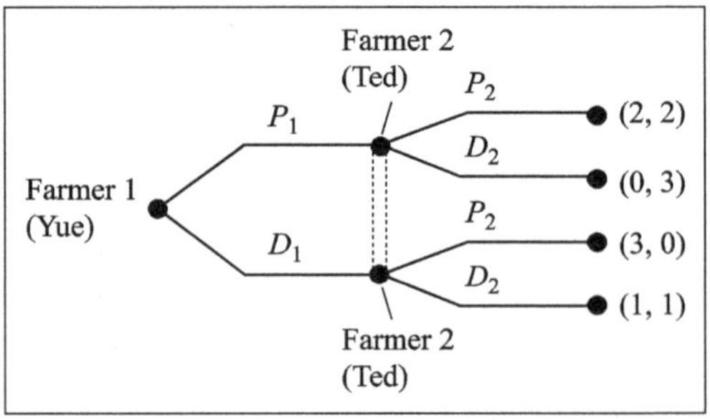

P_i = Farmer i performs, D_i = Farmer i defects, $i \in \{1, 2\}$

FIGURE 1.5 Prisoner's Dilemma in Extensive Form

the game is a game of perfect information where the information sets in this game all reduce to the decision nodes corresponding to the agents' actual moves. But in the Figure 1.5 game, at the information set connecting the P_1- and D_1-nodes, Ted has some nontrivial uncertainty regarding Yue's initial move. At this information set, Ted must choose his move knowing he might be at either the P_1- or the D_1-node. Games like the Figure 1.5 game, with information sets consisting of more than a single node, are games of *imperfect information*.

Interpreted through the lens of game theory, Hume's argument that the two farmers are bound to fail to help each other makes free use of the perfect information structure of the Figure 1.3 extensive form game. By taking away this perfect information, does one alter the interaction so as to make P_i a best response for either or both of the farmers? In fact, in the Figure 1.5 game P_i can never be a best response for either farmer. Figure 1.6 gives the strategic form representation of the Figure 1.5 game. The Figure 1.6 payoff matrix characterizes a *Prisoner's Dilemma*, the most famous and the most studied of all noncooperative games. According to the payoff structure of the Figure 1.6 matrix, D_i strictly dominates P_i for both farmers, that is, choosing D_i yields each farmer a greater payoff than choosing P_i no matter what strategy the other

		Farmer 2 (Ted) P_2	Farmer 2 (Ted) D_2
Farmer 1 (Yue)	P_1	$(2,2)$	$(0,3)$
Farmer 1 (Yue)	D_1	$(3,0)$	$(1,1)$

P_i = Farmer i performs, D_i = Farmer i defects, $i \in \{1,2\}$

FIGURE 1.6 Prisoner's Dilemma in Strategic Form

farmer chooses.[55] One consequence of this strict dominance is that even if either farmer expects that for some reason her counterpart will not follow his own best response, D_i remains her unique best response. Consequently, if each chooses her own best option, they settle into the (D_1, D_2) outcome, where neither helps the other, even though each would receive a higher payoff at the (P_1, P_2) outcome, where both perform. (D_1, D_2) is the unique Nash equilibrium of this Prisoner's Dilemma game, and in order to predict in advance that the two farmers will follow this equilibrium, one need assume only that each farmer knows her own payoffs in the game and is Bayesian rational.

The Prisoner's Dilemma has many interpretations in the literature and has generated a wealth of research in disciplines ranging from economics to psychology to philosophy. As Russell Hardin has pointed out, the Prisoner's Dilemma models cases of bilateral exchange so naturally that it might better have been called the *Exchange* game.[56] For example, here I interpret the Prisoner's Dilemma as a variant of Hume's story of a possible exchange of labor between two farmers, where each farmer chooses either to help or to not help as if the two were choosing simultaneously. The Farmer's Dilemma game summarizes an exchange where one side can observe the other's choice before choosing. Some

---

55. In an n-agent game, Agent i's strategy s_{ij} *weakly dominates* Agent i's strategy s_{ik} if

$$u_i(s_{ij}, \mathbf{s}_{-i}) \geq u_i(s_{ik}, \mathbf{s}_{-i}) \tag{1}$$

for every strategy profile $\mathbf{s}_{-i}$ the other agents can follow and with strict inequality for at least one strategy profile the other agents can follow. If inequality (1) is strict for every strategy profile $\mathbf{s}_{-i}$ available to the agents other than Agent i, then s_{ij} *strictly dominates* s_{ik}.

56. Russell Hardin, "Exchange Theory on Strategic Bases," *Social Science Information* 2 (1982), pp. 251–272, *Morality Within the Limits of Reason* (Chicago: University of Chicago Press, 1988), pp. 41–42, and *Indeterminacy and Society* (Princeton, NJ: Princeton University Press, 2003), pp. 20–21.

refer to this game as *Sequential Prisoner's Dilemma*. It is worth noting that while the preferences of the two farmers in the Figure 1.4 and Figure 1.5 games are assumed to be entirely selfish, this is not a necessary condition for an interaction to be a Prisoner's Dilemma. Indeed, Edna Ullmann-Margalit and Derek Parfit give examples of 2-agent Prisoner's Dilemmas where each agent has completely altruistic preferences.[57]

Problem 1.2. Claim or Concede?

Braithwaite's Neighboring Musicians example and Schelling's Parachutists example can be summarized as games of *impure coordination*, where the two agents have multiple equilibria available to them and they disagree over which equilibrium each regards as most desirable. Figure 1.7 summarizes a simple 2-agent impure coordination game where each agent has two pure strategies. Both agents would like to coordinate their choices, but each prefers the outcome of one of the two coordinated act pairs over the other. Hence the agents' payoffs do not coincide exactly at the outcomes where they do coordinate. One can interpret this game as a simple version of Braithwaite's Neighboring Musicians, where pure strategy G is the strategy of playing one's instrument all of the available time and pure strategy M is the strategy of keeping quiet all of the available time. One can also interpret this game as a much simplified version of Schelling's Parachutists problem, where the two parachutists know both their locations and where G is the strategy of remaining stationary and M is the strategy of walking all the way to the other parachutist. The Figure 1.7 game has three Nash equilibria, namely, the two pure strategy equilibria (G,M) and (M,G) and the mixed equilibrium $\sigma^* = (\sigma^*, \sigma^*)$, where $\sigma^* = \frac{4}{9}M \oplus \frac{5}{9}G$. At the mixed equilibrium σ^*, the agents will coordinate only $\frac{40}{81}$ of the time, and each agent's expected payoff is $\frac{20}{9}$, less than her payoff if they follow the strict equilibrium where she "gives in" and follows M while the other follows G.[58] The strict equilibria (M,G) and (G,M) are

57. Edna Ullmann-Margalit, *The Emergence of Norms* (Oxford: Oxford University Press, 1977), p. 48, n. 7, and Derek Parfit, "Is Common-Sense Morality Self-Defeating?," *Journal of Philosophy* 76 (1979), pp. 533–545.

58. If the two agents follow σ^*, then they will follow the (M,G) and the (G,M) outcomes with probability $\frac{4}{9}\cdot\frac{5}{9} = \frac{20}{81}$ each, so they will coordinate with probability $\frac{20}{81} + \frac{20}{81} = \frac{40}{81}$ and miscoordinate at either (M,M) or (G,G) with probability $\frac{41}{81}$. At σ^* each Agent i's expected payoff is $E_i(u_i(\sigma^*)) = 0\cdot\left(\frac{4}{9}\right)^2 + 4\cdot\frac{4}{9}\cdot\frac{5}{9} + 5\cdot\frac{5}{9}\cdot\frac{4}{9} + 0\cdot\left(\frac{5}{9}\right)^2 = \frac{20}{9}$.

		Agent 2 M	Agent 2 G
Agent 1	M	(0, 0)	(4, 5)
	G	(5, 4)	(0, 0)

FIGURE 1.7 Parachutists/Symmetric Neighboring Musicians

such that neither gains in terms of payoff if either unilaterally deviates. Because of this kind of coincidence of interests, the Figure 1.7 game and similar games with this kind of coincidence of interests are known as coordination games, and their strict equilibria are known as *coordination equilibria*.[59] But because the interests of the two agents also fail to coincide completely over the alternative outcomes, the Figure 1.7 game is also known as a game of impure coordination. In this game, even though the two agents want to coordinate their strategies, each of them might be tempted to threaten the other agent by insisting that she will play her end of the equilibrium that is best for her no matter what. But if both make and carry out such threats, they will miscoordinate on (G,G). On the other hand, if each believes the other's threat and consequently both give in, they will miscoordinate on (M,M). To be certain of coordinating at one of the two pure strategy Nash equilibria, exactly one agent will have to give in, and obviously neither wants to be the "patsy" who gives in.

Figure 1.8 summarizes a game equivalent to the game Luce and Raiffa give in their presentation of Battle of the Sexes.[60] Like the Figure 1.7 Parachutists game, this Battle of the Sexes game has two coordination Nash equilibria, (A, A), (B, B), and a mixed Nash equilibrium where Agent 1 follows $\sigma_1^* = \frac{3}{5}A \oplus \frac{2}{5}B$ and Agent 2 follows $\sigma_2^* = \frac{2}{5}A \oplus \frac{3}{5}B$. At the mixed Nash equilibrium each agent's expected payoff is $\frac{1}{5}$, so each agent fares strictly worse at this equilibrium than at either of the coordination Nash equilibria, same as in the Figure 1.7 game.[61] The equilibrium selection problem for the two agents here is much like that of the Figure 1.7 game, except that they coordinate by choosing the same pure strategy options. So one might think of Battle of the Sexes as a Parachutists problem "in reverse." Conversely, one

59. See Schelling (1960), pp. 83–99, and David Lewis, *Convention: A Philosophical Study* (Cambridge, MA: Harvard University Press, 1969), p. 14. I discuss Lewis' work further in Chapter 2.

60. See Luce and Raiffa (1957), p. 90.

61. The expected payoffs at this and the other mixed Nash equilibria of 2-agent games discussed below in this chapter are obtained by computations similar to those of note 58.

might think of Parachutists as "reverse Battle of the Sexes." But in each of these problems, in order for the two agents involved to be sure they will coordinate successfully, exactly one must give in to the preferences of the other. Who shall give in?

An additional complication in an impure coordination problem emerges if the agents have asymmetric payoffs. Braithwaite points this out in his own analysis of the Neighboring Musicians problem. Suppose that Luke's and Matthew's payoffs in this problem are those given in Figure 1.9. The Figure 1.9 payoffs are equivalent to the payoffs Braithwaite gives in the example of his Cambridge lecture. (M,G) and (G,M) are again the pure strategy equilibria of this revised Neighboring Musicians game, while $\sigma^* = (\sigma_1^*, \sigma_2^*)$ is the mixed equilibrium where $\sigma_1^* = \frac{1}{10}M \oplus \frac{9}{10}G$ and $\sigma_2^* = \frac{3}{8}M \oplus \frac{5}{8}G$. At σ^*, Luke's expected payoff is $\frac{9}{4}$ and Matthew's expected payoff is $\frac{4}{5}$, so Luke and Matthew would both achieve higher expected payoffs at either of the pure strategy equilibria where one gives in completely to the other, same as in the Figure 1.7 and Figure 1.8 games. In this game, Matthew's payoffs reflect his preference for the cacophony of (G,G) over the complete quiet of (M,M), while Luke's payoffs reflect the opposite preference. Hence, Matthew is more willing than Luke to suffer the consequences if they both carry out threats to play no matter what. Put another way, Matthew has a *threat advantage* in this impure coordination game. Still, if Matthew is certain that Luke will play his piano, then he had better back down and follow the (G,M) equilibrium. So even if the asymmetry in payoff structure appears to make the game more favorable to Matthew, this is no guarantee that they will settle

		Agent 2: A	Agent 2: B
Agent 1	A	$(2, 1)$	$(-1, -1)$
	B	$(-1, -1)$	$(1, 2)$

FIGURE 1.8 Battle of the Sexes

		Agent 2 (Matthew): M	Agent 2 (Matthew): G
Agent 1 (Luke)	M	$(1, -1)$	$(3, 8)$
	G	$(6, 1)$	$(0, 0)$

FIGURE 1.9 Braithwaite Game

upon Matthew's preferred equilibrium. How do the agents take the asymmetries in payoffs into account, so that they settle upon an equilibrium?

Figure 1.10 summarizes the *Hawk-Dove* game Maynard Smith analyzes in his work on the evolution of stable behaviors. In Hawk-Dove, each agent can choose to adopt either a conciliatory *"dove"* strategy (D) or a more aggressive *"hawk"* strategy (H). V is the value of the resource and C is the expected cost of injury an agent might suffer in the conflict that occurs at the (H,H) outcome. When $C > V$, Hawk-Dove has two strict equilibria, (D,H) and (H,D), and a mixed Nash equilibrium where each follows $\sigma^* = \frac{C-V}{C} \cdot D \oplus \frac{V}{C} \cdot H$. The agents' preferences over the alternative Nash equilibria conflict, same as in the Battle of the Sexes and Braithwaite games. Each agent's best outcome occurs when she follows "hawk" and the other follows "dove." But this Hawk-Dove game is not an impure coordination game. In pure coordination games such as the Figure 1.2 Encounter Problem and impure coordination games such as the Figure 1.8 Battle of the Sexes and the Figure 1.9 Braithwaite games, if one agent deviates unilaterally from a strict Nash equilibrium, then neither agent fares better in terms of payoff in the game. In the Hawk-Dove game, if either agent were to deviate by herself from her best equilibrium, where she chooses H and the other chooses D, then she would raise the other's payoff while lowering her own. Hawk-Dove is one of a class of *conflictual coordination games* where agents have strictly differing preferences over a plurality of strict equilibria.[62] The class of conflictual coordination games contains the impure coordination games as special cases.

A variety of interesting interpretations of games with Hawk-Dove structure appear in the game theory literature. One interpretation, inspired by part of the plot of the film *Rebel Without a Cause*, has each agent driving straight towards the other in her car on a narrow road. According to this interpretation, one agent wins this *"Chicken"* game if she follows H by driving straight on this narrow road till the end while the other follows D by swerving off the road, and they crash their cars into each other if both follow H. Steven Brams uses a Hawk-Dove game to model the Cuban missile crisis of 1962, suggesting a more general interpretation where in a given crisis situation between two roughly equal powers each side is tempted to adopt an aggressive policy, corresponding to H, in hopes that the other side will back down, corresponding to D, and a mutually

62. My thanks to Diana Richards Doyle for suggesting the term "conflictual coordination game." See Peter Vanderschraaf and Diana Richards, "Joint Beliefs in Conflictual Coordination Games," *Theory and Decision* 42 (1997), pp. 287–310. The class of conflictual coordination games discussed in this book is more general than that discussed in Vanderschraaf and Richards (1997).

		Agent 2	
		D	H
Agent 1	D	$(\frac{V}{2}, \frac{V}{2})$	$(0, V)$
	H	$(V, 0)$	$(\frac{V-C}{2}, \frac{V-C}{2})$

$C > V > 0$

FIGURE 1.10 Hawk-Dove

destructive war erupts if both adopt the aggressive policy.[63] A number of authors, including Robert Sugden, Brian Skyrms, and myself, use Hawk-Dove in a manner similar to Maynard Smith's use in our discussions of the origins of property.[64] Sugden and I draw inspiration from some of Hume's examples of the establishment of first property rights.[65] Suppose two agents each would like to acquire some good. Each can either offer to share the use of this good with the other (corresponding to D) or claim ownership of the good (corresponding to H). If both choose D, then they indeed share the use of this good. If exactly one of them chooses H, then the H-chooser becomes owner of the good and the D-chooser leaves the encounter empty-handed. But if both choose H, then a mutually damaging fight breaks out.

Problem 1.3. The Stag Hunt

In Rousseau's description of the Stag Hunt, defecting from the hunting party by hunting hare is a security strategy for each hunter. However, if they all perform by hunting deer, all will end up with a better overall payoff. Figure 1.11 summarizes this problem for a hunting party of two with the payoff matrix of a game known as 2-agent *Assurance* or *Stag Hunt*.[66]

---

63. Steven Brams, *Game Theory and Politics* (New York: Free Press, 1975), pp. 40–42. Brams gives a second and more complex model of the Cuban missile crisis on pp. 42–44, involving rules for selecting a strategy conditional on the strategy choice of the counterpart agent.

64. Robert Sugden, *The Economics of Rights, Co-operation and Welfare*, 2nd ed. (Houndmills, UK: Palgrave Macmillan), pp. 58–65; Brian Skyrms, *Evolution of the Social Contract*, 2nd ed. (Cambridge: Cambridge University Press, 2014), pp. 66–67; Vanderschraaf (1998a, 1998b). Sugden also uses a repeated Hawk-Dove game to model Hobbes' State of Nature. I will propose a different game-theoretic model of the Hobbesian State of Nature in Chapter 5.

65. See especially *Treatise* 3.2.3 for such examples.

66. Many authors have discussed games with a payoff structure that is isomorphic or nearly isomorphic to that of the Figure 1.13 game. Some refer to games with this general structure as Stag Hunt games, while others refer to such games as Assurance games. Amartya Sen was perhaps the first to analyze the Stag Hunt game. Sen considers an n-agent version of Stag Hunt in "Isolation, Assurance and the Social Rate of Discount," *Quarterly Journal of Economics* 81 (1967), pp. 112–124.

		Agent 2: P	Agent 2: D
Agent 1	P	$(3,3)$	$(0,2)$
	D	$(2,0)$	$(2,2)$

P = perform (hunt deer), D = defect (hunt hare)

FIGURE 1.11 Assurance/Stag Hunt

The pure strategies for each agent in this game are *perform* (P) and *defect* (D), which are directly analogous to the pure strategies in the Prisoner's Dilemma and Farmer's Dilemma games discussed above. This 2-agent Stag Hunt has the pure strategy Nash equilibria (P,P), where both perform and catch a deer, and (D,D), where both defect by hunting hare. There is also a mixed equilibrium at which each hunter follows $\sigma^* = \frac{2}{3}P \oplus \frac{1}{3}D$ and has an expected payoff of 2. (P,P) is the Pareto optimal Nash equilibrium. However, the hunters will not reach this equilibrium unless each has a sufficiently high expectation that the other will perform. If Agent 1 has little or no confidence that Agent 2 will perform, then Agent 1 must defect in order to avoid her worst payoff. If the hunters mistrust each other and each decides to play it safe and defect, then they will settle upon the Pareto inferior equilibrium (D,D). Even though the (P,P) equilibrium is the best outcome of this game for both hunters, they cannot reach (P,P) without a high degree of mutual trust. In Stag Hunt, the equilibrium selection problem becomes one of explaining how and to what extent agents come to trust or mistrust each other.

Many interesting problems involving mutual trust can be modeled as Stag Hunt games. As indicated in §1.1, one can interpret Hobbes' formulation of his first two *Leviathan* laws of nature as giving recommendations for conduct in social situations having a Stag Hunt structure. The Figure 1.11 game summarizes a very simple case where just two individuals must each decide whether or not to obey the positive requirements of these two laws of nature with respect to each other when they interact. Given this interpretation of the game, P is the strategy of obeying the positive requirement of one of these Hobbesian laws, and D is the strategy of not obeying this positive requirement. For example, if both individuals engaged in the game lay down their rights with respect to each other's goods, as the positive part of the second law of nature stated in *Leviathan* requires, then they follow the optimal (P,P) equilibrium. But if either individual has reason to believe the other will not follow P, then this individual may violate the positive requirement of the second law defensively by following D. Stag Hunt analyses of natural law precepts such as those found in Hobbes' system have sparked a growing contemporary philosophical literature.[67]

Problem 1.4. Contribute or Free-Ride?

Mancur Olson's *The Logic of Collective Action* helped to cement an understanding of public goods as nonexcludable goods that typically must be supplied jointly if they are to be supplied at all. In a later pioneering work, *Governing the Commons*, Elinor Ostrom adopted a more refined classification of collective action problems and their associated goods. In Ostrom's taxonomy, both public goods and *common pool resources* are goods that are jointly supplied and nonexcludable to a high degree. But common pool resources have the additional property of being *subtractable* to a high degree, that is, an agent's use of the available good can diminish the amount of this good available for others.[68] The problems of public good and common pool resource provision are frequently *threshold problems*. Each individual has the option of either performing by contributing toward the provision of the good or defecting by free-riding. The good may be a "lumpy" or *step good*, that is, no amount of the good is provided unless a certain threshold number of the population performs. Suppose, for example, that in order to keep the water in a regional lake safe for use, a minimum number of manufacturers must perform by implementing costly pollution control measures. If a minimal number do not perform, then there is a loss of joint gains. However, if sufficiently many manufacturers do perform, then any single manufacturer would be tempted to free-ride so long as its free-riding does not cause the amount of pollution in the lake to exceed safe levels. Negotiating an agreement to limit pollution into the lake is a coordination problem with conflictual elements, since each manufacturer would prefer to fall in a group that free-rides while enjoying the benefits of water safe for use paid for by the performing manufacturers. Other environmental problems that share this theoretical structure include those of regulating fishing and whaling and the use of ecosystems such as tropical rain forests. Given that every potential contributor to maintaining a common pool resource might be tempted to free-ride, these provision problems are often referred to as *commons dilemmas*.[69]

---

67. See especially Jean Hampton, *Hobbes and the Social Contract Tradition* (Cambridge: Cambridge University Press, 1986), §3.3–§3.4; Kavka (1986), ch. 9, (1995); Skyrms (2004); Peter Vanderschraaf and Andrea Christelle, "Convention and Natural Law" (unpublished manuscript, 2012).

68. Elinor Ostrom, *Governing the Commons: The Evolution of Institutions for Collective Action* (Cambridge: Cambridge University Press, 1990), ch. 2. Ostrom (1990, 32) credits Michael Taylor with recognizing the difference between public goods and common pool resources in Taylor's *The Possibility of Cooperation* (Cambridge: Cambridge University Press, 1987), p. 3.

69. Garrett Hardin introduced the phrase "tragedy of the commons" into the vocabulary of science with his 1968 essay "The Tragedy of the Commons," *Science* 162 (1968), pp. 1243–1248.

P

	P	D
P	$(3,3,3)$	$(3,5,3)$
D	$(5,3,3)$	$(2,2,0)$

D

	P	D
P	$(3,3,5)$	$(0,2,2)$
D	$(2,0,2)$	$(2,2,2)$

P = perform, D = defect

FIGURE 1.12 Three-in-a-Boat

One can model these sorts of threshold problems with games having more than two agents. Figure 1.12 summarizes a 3-agent game where Agent 1 chooses the row, Agent 2 chooses the column, and Agent 3 chooses the matrix. This game is called *Three-in-a-Boat* because according to one of its better-known interpretations, the three agents are individuals in a boat where only two need row in order to move the boat forward. According to this interpretation, the best outcome for any one of these three is to defect (D) by relaxing while the other two perform (P) by rowing.[70] One can also interpret this game as a 3-agent version of Rousseau's Stag Hunt problem where each of three hunters again performs by hunting for deer with the others and defects by hunting for hare by herself, but only two need to perform in order for them capture a deer. This game has four Nash equilibria in pure strategies, namely, the three optimal equilibria (D,P,P), (P,D,P), and (P,P,D), where exactly one agent defects, and the suboptimal equilibrium (D,D,D), where all three defect. This game also has a variety of suboptimal Nash equilibria involving mixed strategies.[71] Although (D,P,P), (P,D,P), and (P,P,D) are optimal, it is not a foregone conclusion that the agents in this game are likely to follow any of these equilibria. Three-in-a-Boat is similar to the Neighboring Musicians, Parachutists, and Hawk-Dove games of Figures 1.7 and 1.10 in that each agent might be tempted to adopt an aggressive posture in hopes of driving the other agents to perform. If the others believe that Agent i will defect *alone*, then they will settle into the equilibrium most favorable to Agent i. There seems no clear way to prioritize among the three optimal Nash equilibria. Why should they follow the Nash equilibrium most favorable to any one of them, rather than one of the other two optimal Nash equilibria? The (D,D,D) outcome is the worst pure strategy Nash equilibrium for all, but D is each agent's security

70. See Michael Taylor and Hugh Ward, "Chickens, Whales and Lumpy Goods: Alternative Models of Public-Goods Provision," *Political Studies* 30 (1982), pp. 350–370. Taylor discusses this game further in Taylor 1987, ch. 2. Hampton (1986), p. 177–180, uses this game to model Hume's meadow draining problem.

71. At some of these Nash equilibria, one of the three agents follows the pure strategy D and the other two agents each follow the mixed strategy $\sigma^* = \frac{2}{3}P \oplus \frac{1}{3}D$, and at these partially mixed Nash equilibria each agent's expected payoff is 2.

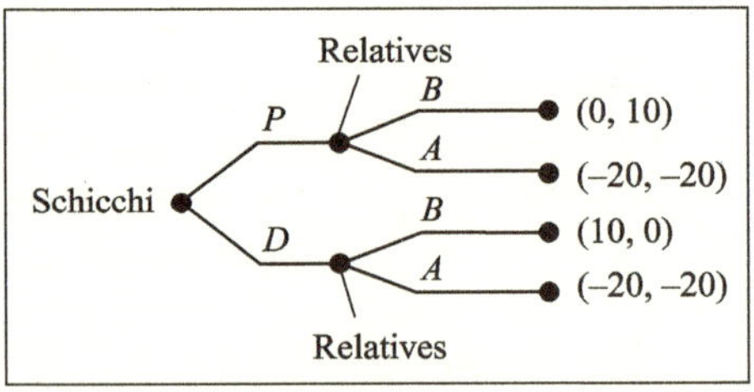

P = perform (honor agreement with relatives), D = defect (double-cross relatives)

B = back down (accept situation), A = accuse (expose both Schicchi and themselves)

FIGURE 1.13 *Gianni Schicchi*

strategy and (D,D,D) is a strict Nash equilibrium. Moreover, (D,D,D) is the only pure strategy Nash equilibrium that is symmetric in terms of the agents' payoffs. So one might suspect that three agents engaged in this threshold game are likely to settle into the suboptimal equilibrium. And if this is indeed the case, this would seem to be bad news for those who seek to explain how groups can adequately provide public goods and maintain common pool resources adequately via voluntary contributions. If even as few as three are unlikely to produce a threshold good in a problem as simple as Three-in-a-Boat, what chance do larger groups have of generating adequate levels of public goods and common pool resources in more complex settings?

Problem 1.5. Acquiesce or Resist?

Figure 1.13 summarizes an extensive form representation of a *Gianni Schicchi* game reflecting the key decisions the agents, Schicchi and Buoso's relatives, must make in the plot of Puccini's opera.[72] Schicchi, who moves first, can either *keep his promise* (P) and name the relatives as Buoso's principal heirs in the new false will or *double-cross* (D) by naming himself Buoso's principal heir. After they observe Schicchi's move, the relatives can either *back down* (B), thereby accepting the terms of the false will, or *accuse* (A), thereby exposing both Schicchi and themselves. One can more easily identify the Nash equilibria of the *Gianni Schicchi* game by examining its strategic form representation, given in Figure 1.14.

---

72. William Harper models the interaction between Gianni Schicchi and Buoso's relatives with a different *Chain Store* game. See William Harper, "Causal Decision Theory and Game Theory: A Classic Argument for Equilibrium Solutions, a Defense of Weak Equilibria, and a New Problem for the Normal Form Representation," in *Causation in Decision, Belief Change, and Statistics II*, ed. W. Harper and B. Skyrms (Dordrecht: Kluwer, 1988), 25–48, and "Ratifiability and Refinements (in Two-Person Noncooperative Games)," in *Foundations of Decision Theory*, ed. M. Bacharach and S. Hurley (Oxford: Blackwell, 1991), 263–293. In Harper's Chain Store model, the relatives act only if Schicchi defects. I prefer the Figure 1.15 game because this game allows the relatives to act whether Schicchi defects or performs.

		Relatives			
		B-if-P B-if-D	B-if-P A-if-D	A-if-P B-if-D	A-if-P A-if-D
Schicchi	P	(0, 10)	(0, 10)	(– 20, – 20)	(– 20, – 20)
	D	(10, 0)	(– 20, – 20)	(10, 0)	(– 20, – 20)

P = perform, D = defect, B = back down, A = accuse

FIGURE 1.14 *Gianni Schicchi* in Strategic Form

$(P; B\text{-if-}P, A\text{-if-}D)$, $(D; B\text{-if-}P, B\text{-if-}D)$, and $(D; A\text{-if-}P, B\text{-if-}D)$ are all pure strategy Nash equilibria. There are additional partially mixed Nash equilibria where Schicchi follows P and the relatives follow a mixed strategy $\sigma_2^* = y \cdot B\text{-if-}C, A\text{-if-}D \oplus (1-y) \cdot B\text{-if-}C, B\text{-if-}D$ with probability $y \geq \frac{1}{3}$. If $y > \frac{1}{3}$, then P is Schicchi's unique best response, which appears to show that the relatives could ensure that Schicchi will keep his promise by informing Schicchi that they will follow σ_2^* with $y > \frac{1}{3}$. However, one must remember that Schicchi, by double-crossing, places the relatives in a hopeless position. The relatives would be irrational to carry out a threat to follow A-if-D, and for that matter they would be irrational to carry out a threat to follow A-if-P. Assuming Schicchi knows that the relatives know their payoffs at the alternative outcomes and choose according to Bayesian rationality, Schicchi can rule out the A-if-D and the A-if-C branches of the tree. Of the remaining two branches, Schicchi fares better at the D, B-branch, so Schicchi's unique rational move given his own rationality and what he knows about the relatives is to follow D at the onset. Given that both agents have mutual knowledge that both are rational and know the structure of the game, the *Gianni Schicchi* game has only one credible solution, the Nash equilibrium $(D; B\text{-if-}P, B\text{-if-}D)$. But since there are other Nash equilibria, including Nash equilibria where Schicchi follows P, this suggests the need for some formal criterion that distinguishes between these equilibria and rules out all but the $(D; B\text{-if-}P, B\text{-if-}D)$ equilibrium.

In 1965, Reinhard Selten proposed just such a criterion.[73] Selten observed that a strategy profile might be an equilibrium of an extensive form game and yet not be an equilibrium of all its *subgames*. Each information set that is a single nonterminal node of a game in extensive form determines a proper subgame, since if this information set is reached, then the strategy options and payoffs still available to the agents constitute a smaller extensive form game starting at this node. Selten argued that any credible solution of an extensive form game

73. Reinhard Selten, "Spieltheoretische Behandlung eines Oligipolmodells mit Nachfragtragheit," *Zeitschrift für die gesamte Staatswissenschaft* 121 (1965), pp. 301–334, 667–689.

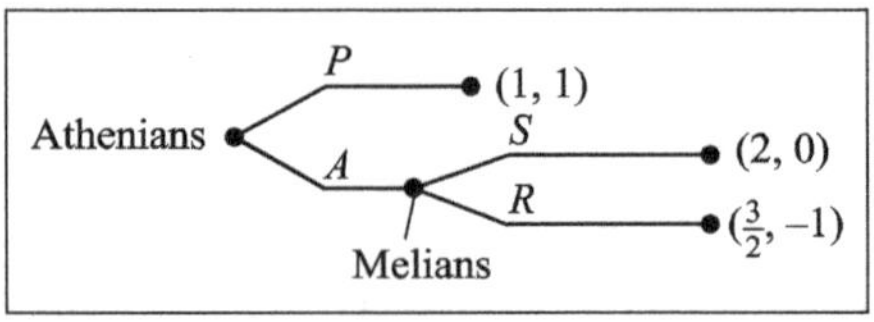

P = offer peace, A = attack
S = surrender, R = resist

FIGURE 1.15 Melian Invasion I Game

must define an equilibrium of each of its subgames. An equilibrium with this property is called *subgame perfect*. The intuition behind Selten's argument is that if an agent selects a strategy for the overall game, she should be willing to stick with this strategy at any point in the game in which she might find herself. For instance, in the *Gianni Schicchi* game, the $(P; B\text{-if-}P, A\text{-if-}D)$ equilibrium is not subgame perfect, since following A in the subgame starting at the D-node of the game tree is not an equilibrium strategy for the relatives. $(D; B\text{-if-}P, B\text{-if-}D)$ is the only subgame perfect equilibrium of the *Gianni Schicchi* game, so in this case Selten's subgame perfection criterion selects the uniquely credible solution of the game. $(D; B\text{-if-}P, B\text{-if-}D)$ is also the backward induction solution of the *Gianni Schicchi* game, and in general in finite games of perfect information the subgame perfect equilibria coincide with the outcomes that survive backward induction. Subgame perfection is one of many *refinements* of the Nash equilibrium concept game theorists have proposed for selecting Nash equilibria in noncooperative games.[74] For the special case of games of perfect information, I believe that subgame perfection is often an important "lower bar" a credible solution to the game should meet.

On the surface, the strategic structure of the interaction between the Athenians and the Melians may seem simpler than that between the agents in the *Gianni Schicchi* game. Figure 1.15 summarizes a *Melian Invasion I* game in extensive form. The Athenians, who move first, can either *offer peace* (P) or *attack* (A). The Melians move only if the Athenians attack, in which case the Melians either *surrender* (S) or *resist* (R). The payoffs reflect the Athenians' correct belief that if they attack and the Melians resist, they will destroy the Melians at relatively low cost. In this game, the backward induction solution is the A,S-outcome. If this game does in fact adequately summarize their interaction, then if the Melians are Bayesian rational and know the payoff structure, and if the Athenians know

74. For fine overviews of the best-known Nash equilibrium refinements, see Bicchieri (1993) and Eric van Damme, *Stability and Perfection of Nash Equilibria*, 2nd ed. (Berlin: Springer, 2002).

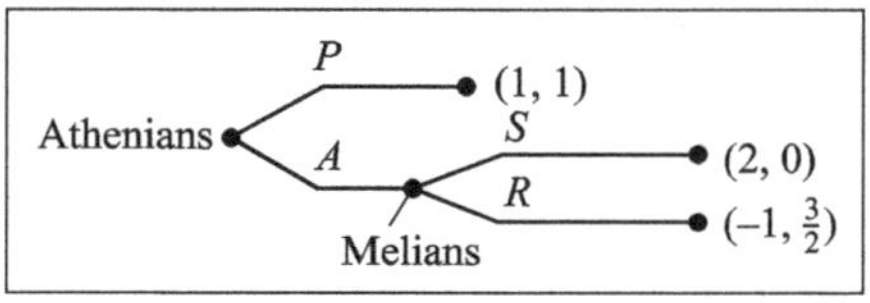

P = offer peace, A = attack
S = surrender, R = resist

FIGURE 1.16 Melian Invasion II Game

this about the Melians and also are rational and know the payoff structure, then the A,S-outcome is the only credible solution. But according to Thucydides, in their negotiations the Melians tried to convince the Athenians that attacking might not serve their own interests well. As part of their argument, the Melians claimed that they might yet prevail, especially if the Spartans sent aid. Figure 1.16 summarizes a *Melian Invasion II* game where the Melians are victorious if the Athenians attack and they resist. Suppose the Melians and the Athenians recognized that their interaction would have a Melian Invasion II game structure if the Spartans did send aid to the Melians. In the Figure 1.16 game, the backward induction solution is the outcome where the Athenians follow P, and $(P, R\text{-if-}A)$ is the unique Nash equilibrium in pure strategies.

The classical game theory of von Neumann, Morgenstern, and Nash presupposes that all the agents are Bayesian rational and all know the entire payoff structure of the game. The classical theory also presupposes that all agents know their counterparts are like themselves, in that their counterparts also are Bayesian rational and know the payoff structure of the game. These assumptions are the beginnings of possible *common knowledge* in game theory, a topic to be discussed further in subsequent chapters. But these assumptions are often violated to at least some extent in real-world situations, and such violations may make profound differences in how the agents in the game might analyze their situation and choose strategies. And in cases where these assumptions are violated, one must consider not only the individual agents' uncertainties regarding the game but also their uncertainties about other agents' uncertainties and so on, to arbitrarily high levels. In 1967–68 John Harsanyi published a series of essays that inaugurated a theory of such *games of incomplete information*.[75] Harsanyi proposed modeling various kinds

75. John Harsanyi, "Games with Incomplete Information Played by 'Bayesian' Players, I–III: Part I. The Basic Model," *Management Science* 14 (1967), pp. 159–182, "Games with Incomplete Information Played by 'Bayesian' Players, I–III: Part II, Bayesian Equilibrium Points," *Management Science* 14 (1968), pp. 320–334 (henceforth Harsanyi 1968a), and "Games with Incomplete Information Played by 'Bayesian' Players, I–III: Part III. The Basic

of structural uncertainty with *types* that define the different possible characteristics of the agents, such as their payoffs and beliefs over counterparts, that might not be common knowledge at the onset. Probabilities over types are *consistent* given a *common prior probability* over a set of states that define the types such that each agent's probabilities over other agents' types are just her probabilities conditional on her own type. Harsanyi showed that given consistent probabilities, a game of incomplete information can be recast as an extensive form game where Nature makes the initial move of choosing the state defining the agents' actual types.

Since the Melian representatives did tell the Athenian representatives that they would trust that the gods and human allies would help the Melians prevail in their just cause, the Athenians, had they known some game theory, could have analyzed the strategic situation as a game of incomplete information where the Melians were either of *inferior* type (θ_1), in which case the relevant game is the Figure 1.15 game, or of *superior* type (θ_2), in which case the relevant game is the Figure 1.16 game. After applying the *Harsanyi transformation* to these two games, the Athenians and the Melians have for their analysis the extensive form game summarized by Figure 1.17, in which the Figure 1.15 and Figure 1.16 games are embedded. The Melians know whether or not Spartan aid is on the way and hence know their own type. The Athenians' uncertainty over the Melians' type is reflected by the information set connecting their choice nodes in the game following Nature's initial move. In the Figure 1.17 game, P can be part of a Nash equilibrium if the probability that the Melians are of superior type is sufficiently high. More specifically, $(P; S\text{-if-}\theta_1, R\text{-if-}\theta_2)$ is a Nash equilibrium if the Athenians' and the Melians' common prior probability for the true state being θ_2 is $\frac{1}{3}$ or greater.[76] Otherwise the only Nash equilibrium is the outcome where the Athenians follow A and the Melians follow S at each state. In fact, the Athenians thought the chance that the Melians could prevail was negligible, and events proved the Athenians right. Had they used the Figure 1.17 game to analyze their situation, the Athenians might have concluded that, given that the prior probability that the true state was θ_2 was exceedingly low, their unique best strategy was to pursue A. Of course, this analysis raises an unsettling question: Is conquering and then exploiting those who have done nothing to provoke attack always rational just so long as one is sufficiently confident that these innocents are too powerless to resist effectively?

Probability Distribution of the Game," *Management Science* 14 (1968), pp. 486–502 (henceforth Harsanyi 1968b).

76. To see why, first note that the Melians, who know their type, have the unique equilibrium strategy $s_2^* = S\text{-if-}\theta_1, R\text{-if-}\theta_2$. If the common prior probability that the Melians are of the inferior θ_1-type is $x = \mu(\theta = \theta_1)$, then the Athenians' pure strategy expected payoffs are $E_1(u_1(P, s_2^*)) = 1$ and $E_1(u_1(A, s_2^*)) = 2 \cdot \mu(\theta = \theta_1) - 1 \cdot \mu(\theta = \theta_2) = 2 \cdot x - 1 \cdot (1 - x) = 3x - 1$ so $E_1(u_1(P, s_2^*)) \geq E_1(u_1(A, s_2^*))$ when $x \leq \frac{2}{3}$, or, equivalently, $\mu(\theta = \theta_2) \geq \frac{1}{3}$.

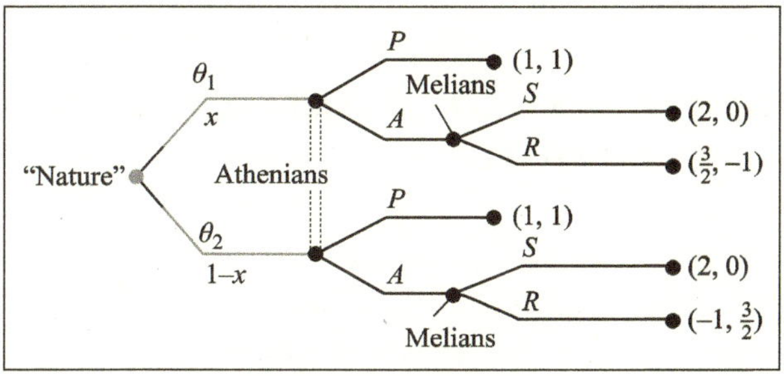

P = offer peace, A = attack

S = surrender, R = resist

θ_1 = Melians are inferior, θ_2 = Melians are superior,

FIGURE 1.17 Combined Melian Invasion Game

Conclusion

The five motivating problems I have discussed in this chapter illustrate what is really a mundane point: Problems of justice have strategic aspects. This point is easy to miss if one thinks of strategic reasoning as applicable to zero-sum interactions only. Before the 1980s, many economists who were misled by von Neumann and Morgenstern's emphasis on zero-sum games drew the analogous conclusion that game theory is not relevant to most economic transactions. The strategies employed in poker games, team sport contests, and military battles have no clear applications to problems involving justice. If strategic reasoning were always zero-sum game reasoning, then one might conclude that such reasoning has no place in justice. But this way of thinking of strategies and strategic reasoning is surely too narrow. If strategic reasoning really were limited to zero-sum interactions, it would consist primarily of thinking about how to outwit opponents. As Schelling, and Hume before him, clearly recognized, strategic reasoning in most cases involves agents' attempts to coordinate their thinking with that of their counterparts in such a way that each one has correct beliefs regarding the intentions of the others and knows the others have mirroring correct beliefs regarding one's own intentions. One wants *only* one's own beliefs about the others' intentions to be correct in a zero-sum situation. Understood in its proper generality, strategic reasoning is important in social interactions with corresponding games running the gamut of Schelling's continuum, from games of pure conflict to games of pure coordination. The five problems of this chapter are representative problems of justice in that they have elements of coordination as well as conflict, and as such have equilibria that the agents involved follow on condition that they have the right coordinated expectations regarding one another.

2 COORDINATION, CONFLICT, AND CONVENTION

> Every member of society is sensible of this interest: Every one expresses this sense to his fellows, along with the resolution he has taken of squaring his actions by it, on condition that others will do the same. No more is requisite to induce any one of them to perform an act of justice, who has the first opportunity. This becomes an example to others. And thus justice establishes itself by a kind of convention or agreement; that is; by a sense of interest, suppos'd to be common to all, and where every single act is perform'd in expectation that others are to perform the like. Without such a convention, no one wou'd ever have dream'd, that there was such a virtue as justice, or have been induc'd to conform his actions to it.
>
> —DAVID HUME, *A Treatise of Human Nature*

Introduction

Conventions pervade social life to such a great degree that we can easily overlook their importance and fail to reflect upon their nature and origins. We employ conventions when we carry out the most mundane tasks of day-to-day life. We rely upon the conventions of a language in order to communicate, upon conventions of monetary currency in order to purchase services and goods, and so on. So cogent analyses of the nature and the origins of conventions would be valuable contributions to social philosophy. Such analyses are chiefly the product of the early modern and contemporary philosophical eras. Prior to the seventeenth century, philosophers would occasionally highlight certain properties of specific conventions without trying to define conventions in general. Several of the great figures of early modern moral philosophy incorporated important conventionalist insights into their accounts of natural law. David Hume, building upon many such insights of his own, gave an explicit analysis of conventions and their origins. Hume's watershed analysis has helped motivate a developing contemporary body of research in philosophy and the social sciences on conventions.

Many who allow that purely coordinative practices are conventions would balk at the idea that norms of social morality or of justice could also be conventions. Some might be tempted to conclude that claims that we have justice by convention are at bottom only challenges to justice, much as John Rawls alleges that egoism is really a challenge to alternative conceptions of right rather than a genuine conception of right.[1] My goal in this chapter is to present an account of convention rich enough and precise enough to provide the foundation for a satisfactory conventionalist analysis of justice. In §2.1 I set the stage by reviewing elements of several past philosophical discussions of convention. Plato and Aristotle give representative premodern discussions of conventions where they view conventions as arbitrary and changeable practices not directly connected with justice. David Hume gives perhaps the first true philosophical analysis of conventions, which is motivated in part by the idea that justice can and should be understood in terms of convention. Hume takes the monumental step of analyzing convention as a system of coordinated reciprocal expectations, foreshadowing David K. Lewis' contemporary and now classic theory of conventions that incorporates game theory and Lewis' analysis of *common knowledge*. Hume's and Lewis' analyses have inspired much of the recent work on convention, including the analysis I offer here. In §2.2 I discuss how conventions are arbitrary. I argue that there are in fact two different senses of arbitrariness associated with conventions, an *indifference-sense* arbitrariness, where each of a set of conventions is equally good from the perspective of all the agents hoping to coordinate, and a *discretionary-sense* arbitrariness, where such agents always have a variety of options for coordinating by following one of a plurality of available conventions. I argue that conflictual coordination problems have associated conventions that are always discretionary-sense arbitrary with respect to each other, and yet can also be more or less equitable. I conclude that one can in principle define norms of justice as conventions while simultaneously maintaining that conventions are arbitrary. In §2.3 I discuss how a subjectivist interpretation of the Nash equilibrium concept motivates a more general *correlated equilibrium* concept. I then show that conventions are naturally characterized by strict correlated equilibria of games having a plurality of such equilibria. Finally, in §2.4 I argue that an adequate analysis of convention should allow for the possibility that agents predicate their current choices on the history of past interactions and that such an analysis should be applicable to whole families of related social interactions. Here I present a new definition of convention in terms of correlated equilibrium and common knowledge over a family of repeated games. This is the definition of convention I shall use in the remainder of this book.

---

1. John Rawls, *A Theory of Justice* (Cambridge, MA: Harvard University Press, 1971), p. 136. Rawls claims here that rational parties would regard egoism not as a viable candidate conception of right in his original position, but rather as what they would fall into in the event they cannot agree upon a conception of right.

§2.1. A Sampling of Earlier Discussions of Convention

Examples and Proto-Analysis in Plato and Aristotle

Plato and Aristotle present particularly good representative premodern discussions of convention in some of their works, particularly the *Cratylus* and *Nicomachean Ethics*, that are of special interest here because in the relevant parts of these works Plato and Aristotle treat convention as largely orthogonal to justice, a view very different from those of some of the early moderns, especially Grotius, Hobbes, and Hume.[2]

In the *Cratylus*, Plato considers the possibility that names are purely conventional, and in the *Gorgias* and the *Republic* he considers the possibility that justice is merely a system of conventions that regulate a given society. Convention plays a particularly prominent role in the *Cratylus*. Near the beginning of the dialog, Hermogenes states his own conventionalist view of names:

> no one is able to persuade me that the correctness of names is determined by anything besides convention and agreement. I believe that any name you give a thing is its correct name. If you change its name and give it another, the new one is as correct as the old. For example, when we give names to our domestic slaves, the new ones are as correct as the old. . . . No name belongs to a particular thing by nature, but only because of the rules and usage of those who establish the usage and call it by that name.[3]

Hermogenes pits his own view against the view, which he attributes to Cratylus, that each thing has a naturally correct name.[4] The dialog progresses into a careful evaluation of Hermogenes' conventionalism and Cratylus' naturalism, and culminates in a discussion of the Heracliteian doctrine of flux and the Platonic doctrine of forms and the import of these doctrines for knowledge of language.[5] In the *Cratylus* an analysis of the nature of linguistic expressions leads to a serious examination of ontological commitments. So one can read

---

2. To be sure, I am not claiming that the passages from the *Cratylus* and the *Nicomachean Ethics* I discuss below summarize everything interesting that Plato and Aristotle have to say regarding convention, only that they represent one way to view the relationship between justice and convention.

3. *Cratylus* 384d1–8.

4. *Cratylus* 383a3–4.

5. A naturalism that is rather more refined than that Hermoneges attributes to Cratylus at the beginning. See *Cratylus* 392b–394e.

the *Cratylus* as foreshadowing the more contemporary philosophy of language tradition of Frege, Russell, Quine, and Kripke. The *Cratylus* also suggests certain ways of understanding the nature of convention. Hermogenes' initial statement suggests that conventions are closely related to certain sorts of rules and agreements. Much deeper into the dialog, Socrates and Cratylus agree that convention is the same as usage or habit.[6] In several places Socrates and Cratylus indicate that a conventionalist believes that things are assigned their names purely by chance.[7] And at one point Socrates claims that Cratylus may have unwittingly committed himself to having entered into a convention with only himself, a position both appear to regard as odd at the least if not definitely unacceptable.[8] These scattered remarks are not a sufficient basis for a full-fledged analysis of convention, and I do not claim Plato tried to analyze convention fully in the *Cratylus* or elsewhere in his corpus. But these remarks do highlight two related ideas that I believe Plato accepted and which are important in premodern philosophers' understandings of convention. The first of these ideas is that a convention is an arbitrary practice, in that this practice is adopted and followed with no presumption that it is a uniquely correct practice. Put another way, a given conventional practice that has come into force and is then followed because of custom or habit could be replaced by some other practice that would serve just as well. This convention might have been established by some deliberate means, say by some agreement, but the end result is the same as if the convention had been established by chance. The second idea is that a convention is a practice relative to a certain community, and presumably a community of more than one. Given the arbitrary nature of conventions, the conventions the members of a given community follow need not be the practices of other communities.

In *Nicomachean Ethics*, Aristotle considers the convention of money: "by social convention money has come to serve as a representative of demand. And this is why money is called *nomisma*, because it exists not by nature but by convention (*nomos*), and it is within our power to change its value and to render it worthless."[9] Assuming Aristotle regards monetary currency a generic example

---

6. *Cratylus* 434e1–5. Francesco Ademollo translates the Greek "διά γε τὸ ἐ'θος" into English as "habit" in *The* Cratylus *of Plato: A Commentary* (Cambridge: Cambridge University Press, 2011), p. 395, while C. D. C. Reeve translates this as "usage" (Aristotle, *Politics*, trans. Reeve [Indianapolis: Hackett, 1998], pp. 86–87). In private correspondence, Reeve informed me that he regards "habitual use" as an alternate acceptable translation.

7. *Cratylus* 397a4–b1, 402b1–3, 434a1.

8. *Cratylus* 435a5–10.

9. *Nicomachean Ethics* 1133a29–32.

of a convention, this passage suggests that Aristotle understands a convention as a useful social practice that the members of society can change and even render useless. This understanding implies that a convention is purely artificial, which would explain why Aristotle maintains that money exists by law and not by nature. Interestingly, the Greek *nomos* can be translated as "convention" as well as "law."[10] This general view regarding convention that I attribute to Aristotle is of course quite similar to the corresponding views I attribute to Plato. Aristotle does not make it clear whether he believes that the convention of money is to be understood as a general practice that has many different instantiations in different societies, including various forms of coinage and paper currency, or as the particular monetary practice of a given society. I think this ambiguity poses no serious difficulty. Aristotle can maintain that he uses the term "convention" both in a general sense, referring to an entire class of similar social practices that can all serve a given useful end, and in a particular sense, referring to the actual practice of a particular society. Aristotle also does not bother to explain how the members of society can change the convention of monetary currency or make it useless. On the surface the explanation is obvious. The members of a society change a convention of money when they stop accepting payment in their exchanges in units of the forms of currency they have been using and start accepting payment in units of some other form of currency. If, for example, the members of a certain society abandon the exclusive use of certain Louis D'or coins in favor of the exclusive use of certain paper assignat certificates, then the old coinage becomes useless for purchases and other transactions requiring money. In another society whose members exchange all goods and services via bartering, the convention of money in its general sense is useless, for an alternative convention of bartering prevails. But a deeper explanation is needed. Why would a Louis D'or convention dissolve in favor of an assignat convention? Why would a society use any monetary convention in trade rather than just barter? David Hume would ultimately provide an explicit answer to such questions.

Note that according to this interpretation, for Aristotle particular conventions are at least somewhat arbitrary. I will argue below in §2.2 that in a certain sense Hume, Lewis, and their contemporary successors, including myself, would all agree with Plato and Aristotle that conventions are arbitrary practices. But if arbitrariness really is characteristic of conventions, then one might naturally doubt the relevance of conventions in serious discussions of justice. Both Plato and Aristotle in the end reject the proposal that justice is a system of conventions, and many if not most of their successors agree that this proposal should be

10. My thanks to Govert den Hartogh for alerting me to this.

rejected.[11] On the face of it, this widespread rejection of the justice-conventionalist proposal is no more surprising than the relative lack of analysis of convention in premodern philosophy. Philosophers may be infamous for their disagreements, but in the main they do agree that justice is anything but arbitrary. But as I noted in the Preface, justice-conventionalism is an ancient idea that recurs over the centuries in different forms. Plato and Aristotle took justice-conventionalism seriously even though they firmly opposed the idea. The idea comes up again with considerable new force in the early modern period of philosophy, together with a new analysis of convention.

Hume's Watershed Analysis

David Hume was perhaps the first philosopher to propose a general analysis of convention. Hume credits Hugo Grotius with a similar understanding of convention in Grotius' discussion of the origins of property.[12] Thomas Hobbes, Samuel Pufendorf, and John Locke also present analyses of specific social practices that foreshadow Hume's discussion of convention.[13] Yet Hume's treatment of convention is pioneering, as he gives conditions that characterize conventions in general and a novel explanation of their origins. Hume's analysis of convention is somewhat scattered in Book III, Part II of *Treatise* and Appendix III of *Enquiry*.[14] No single passage captures all of the nuances of Hume's analysis. Yet one rich passage in *Treatise*, which I quote below in two parts, summarizes its core. In the first part of this passage, a snippet of which I quoted earlier in §1.1, Hume gives a conventionalist analysis of the stability of property rights that one can extrapolate into a definition of convention:

> It is only a general sense of common interest; which sense all the members of the society express to one another, and which induces them to regulate

11. See, for example, *Republic* 612b1–3, *Nicomachean Ethics* 1134b18–30, *Politics* 1280b10. Representative texts where Plato and Aristotle state some of their own views regarding justice that oppose justice-conventionalism include *Gorgias* 527b3–15, *Republic* 443b3–444a2, and *Nicomachean Ethics* 1135a8–13.

12. *Enquiry* Appendix III:8 n. 1. In this footnote Hume quotes most of Articles 4 and 5 of Book II, Chapter II of Grotius' *The Law of War and Peace*, where Grotius discusses the origins of property.

13. *Leviathan* 14:4–5, *On the Law of Nature and of Nations* II.3:13, *Second Treatise* §20, §46.

14. In addition to the passage from *Treatise* 3.2.2:10 quoted below, some of the most important passages in Hume's work concerning convention appear in *Treatise* 3.2.2:22, 3.2.3:4–11, and 3.2.5:11 and in *Enquiry* Appendix III:7–8. The relevant part of *Treatise* 3.2.2:22 is quoted as the epigraph of this chapter.

> their conduct by certain rules. I observe, that it will be for my interest to leave in another the possession of his goods, *provided* he will act in the same manner with regard to me. He is sensible of a like interest in the regulation of his conduct. When this common sense of interest is mutually express'd, and is known to both, it produces a suitable resolution and behavior. And this may properly enough be call'd a convention or agreement betwixt us, tho' without the interposition of a promise; since the actions of each have a reference to those of the other, and are perform'd on the supposition, that something is to be performed on the other part. Two men, who pull the oars of a boat, do it by agreement or convention, tho' they have never given promises to each other.[15]

Here Hume characterizes a convention in terms of a rule or practice people follow for mutual benefit. Hume's examples in this part of the passage are respect of property rights and the rowboat example discussed in Chapter 1. General conformity with the practice is mutually beneficial in that each individual involved fares better if all involved follow this practice than if all fail to follow the practice. In the vocabulary of modern economics, general conformity with a Humean convention is Pareto superior over general nonconformity. But Hume requires more than that the practice be mutually beneficial. He also requires that given the choice between conforming or not conforming, a given involved individual serves her interests better if she conforms on condition that the others involved conform as well. Hume indicates later in his discussion of the Farmer's Dilemma, exchange, and promises that he does not insist that all involved conform with a convention all of the time.[16] General conformity suffices, meaning roughly that most individuals involved conform at least most of the time. So for Hume a convention is a stable practice, in the sense that if the individuals involved generally conform with the practice in question, each individual serves her own interests by continuing to conform. Yet Hume clearly recognizes that the fact that a certain practice is both stable and mutually beneficial if the individuals involved do follow this practice is not sufficient reason for such individuals to actually follow this practice. Hume argues that mutual expectations of conformity are

---

15. *Treatise* 3.2.2:10.

16. *Treatise* 3.2.5:9–10. Here Hume refers to a convention where others withdraw their trust in case one breaks a promise, which obviously indicates that a convention of promise keeping remains in force even if some occasionally violate this convention. In his discussion of the Sensible Knave in *Enquiry* 9.2:22, Hume explicitly acknowledges it may be possible to occasionally violate a requirement of justice without destroying the mutually beneficial system of justice conventions. I discuss conventions of promises and the challenge of the Sensible Knave more extensively in Chapter 7.

what underwrite actual conformity with the practice. Each involved individual conforms because she expects the others involved to conform. Indeed, Hume concludes that the mutual expression of the "general sense of common interest" is what really produces a convention. That is, what characterizes a convention is each individual expressing that she knows the practice is mutually beneficial and stable and that she intends to conform. The mutual expression of this general sense of common interest generates the mutual expectations of conformity that produce actual conformity.

Just how do the individuals involved in following a conventional practice mutually express the "general sense of common interest" that produces conformity? One might naturally think that people generate the necessary mutual expectations via covenants, that is, by exchanging promises to conform. However, Hume denies that conventions are generally established by exchanging promises. Indeed, Hume maintains that promises themselves are practices arising from certain conventions, so for Hume this purported explanation of the origins of conventions is circular.[17] In the second part of the core passage, Hume offers a different explanation for the origins of conventions:

> Nor is the rule concerning the stability of possession the less deriv'd from human conventions, that it arises gradually, and acquires force by a slow progression, and by our repeated experience of the inconveniences of transgressing it. On the contrary, this experience assures us still more, that the sense of interest has become common to all our fellows, and gives us a confidence of the future regularity of their conduct. And 'tis only on the expectation of this, that our moderation and abstinence are founded. In like manner are languages gradually establish'd by human conventions without any promise. In like manner do gold and silver become the common measures of exchange, and are esteem'd sufficient payment for what is of a hundred times their value.[18]

According to Hume, the members of a population learn to follow various conventions through experience. Here Hume argues that people who interact repeatedly can learn to follow a convention via some trial and error process, by which their expectations regarding each other gradually converge and characterize the convention that produces their mutually beneficial conduct. Elsewhere, Hume gives more detailed explanations of how certain conventions first emerge. For example, Hume argues that people frequently start to acquire certain sorts

17. *Treatise* 3.2.2:10, 3.2.5:1.

18. *Treatise* 3.2.2:10.

of property through *accession*, that is, by associating some connection between a good one possesses and another good that is connected to the former and in some sense inferior to the former. According to Hume, accession explains how one becomes the owner of goods such as the produce of one's garden even before one takes possession of this produce.[19] The important point to note here is that Hume maintains that the members of society learn to follow conventions via *inductive inferences*. This is quite remarkable, since Hume famously maintains that while people make inductive inferences as a matter of routine, at a deep level there is no rational justification of inductive inference.[20] Hume in fact remarks that conventions of justice are analogous to superstitions.[21] Moreover, Hume argues that the members of a society continually reinforce the mutual expectations that characterize a convention by following the stable and mutually beneficial practice of this convention. Put another way, the members of society mutually express the common sense of interest associated with a certain convention by actually following the practice of this convention in their interactions. Each member of society then expects the others to conform, because they have conformed in the past. And they can mutually express their common sense of interest in this manner, and thereby reinforce the mutual expectations of the convention, even if they no longer know who first tried to act for mutual benefit in this manner or when in their history sufficiently many members of their society gave up different alternatives in favor of conforming to this particular practice so that they established *this* practice as *their* convention.

Summarizing, one can paraphrase the two main ideas of Hume's analysis of convention as follows:

(H1) A convention for a given society is a general sense of common interest its members know and mutually express. That is, each member of society knows that a certain rule or practice is mutually beneficial and stable and expresses her knowledge of this fact and her intention to conform with this practice, so that all expect each other to conform.

(H2) The members of a given society learn to follow a convention by inductive inferences. In particular, they mutually express the general sense of common interest by conforming with the practice, in effect teaching each other to continue conforming given that they have conformed in the past.

---

19. *Treatise* 3.2.3:10.

20. Perhaps Hume's best-known statements of these claims are in *Enquiry Concerning Human Understanding* 4.2:3 and 4.2:21.

21. *Enquiry* 3.2:37.

Hume's analysis bears a family resemblance to the proto-analyses I attribute to Plato and Aristotle above. I believe Plato, Aristotle, and Hume all agree that conventions are artificial, that is, human communities create conventional practices and can change these practices. However, Hume's, Plato's, and Aristotle's treatments of convention also differ fundamentally in several obvious ways. With respect to the claims I gave at the start of this section, this is the most important difference: While Aristotle and Plato maintain that justice cannot be understood in terms of convention, Hume clearly regards justice as a special class of conventions.

Lewis' Contemporary Analysis

David Lewis launched a contemporary philosophical literature on conventions with his 1969 monograph *Convention: A Philosophical Study*. Lewis acknowledges that he presents a theory of convention similar to Hume's theory.[22] Nevertheless, Lewis' theory introduces two key innovations. First, Lewis uses game theory as scaffolding for his own analysis of coordination problems, drawing inspiration from Schelling's study of coordination games. For Lewis, a convention is a special kind of equilibrium of a coordination game. This corresponds to Hume's requirement that a conventional practice be a stable practice. Lewis also argues that the equilibrium requirement is a necessary, but not sufficient, condition for his account of convention. This leads to Lewis' second major innovation. Lewis requires that the individuals who follow a convention have common knowledge that they follow a given equilibrium of a game and that were their beliefs about each other's conduct appropriately different, they would follow some other equilibrium. Lewis presents an explicit analysis of common knowledge,[23] an analysis later refined by various other authors.[24] Informally, Lewis–common knowledge for a group that a proposition *A* obtains implies that each group member has reason to believe that *A* obtains, each group member has reason to believe that each group member has reason to believe that *A* obtains, and so on. The analysis of common knowledge and its various applications has become an important area of research in its own right. Sparked in large part by Lewis' work, common knowledge has become an integral part of contemporary analyses of conventions.

22. Lewis (1969), pp. 3–4.

23. Lewis (1969), pp. 52–60.

24. Vanderschraaf (1998b); Robin Cubitt and Robert Sugden, "Common Knowledge, Salience and Convention: A Reconstruction of David Lewis' Game Theory," *Economics and Philosophy* 19 (2003), pp. 175–210, and Giacomo Sillari, "A Logical Framework for Convention," *Synthese* 147 (2005), pp. 379–400.

In *Convention*, Lewis sets himself to defend the following platitude: There are conventions of language.[25] Lewis particularly wishes to respond to a special challenge raised against this platitude. Bertrand Russell, and Willard Quine and William Alston after him, argued that there are no linguistic conventions, except perhaps some set up by formal agreement, because they thought that agents would need language in order to establish a "convention" of language.[26] As Russell put it:

> The community that speaks a language has learnt it, and modified it by processes almost all of which are not deliberate, but the results of causes operating according to more or less ascertainable laws. If we trace any Indo-European language back far enough, we arrive hypothetically (at any rate according to some authorities) at the stage when language consisted only of the roots out of which subsequent words have grown. How these roots acquired their meanings is not known, but a conventional origin is clearly just as mythical as the social contract by which Hobbes and Rousseau supposed civil government to have been established. We can hardly suppose a parliament of hitherto speechless elders meeting together and agreeing to call a cow a cow and a wolf a wolf.[27]

Russell's doubts that the meanings of the original roots of the words of a language could be conventional echo the skeptical doubts regarding language conventionalism Plato raises in the exchanges of the *Cratylus*. Lewis believes the key to answering this Russellian challenge is an analysis of convention that can account for the origins of at least some conventions without referring to any preexisting linguistic conventions. Lewis provides just such an analysis, and then applies his analysis in an argument that a convention of meaning is established when agents have common knowledge that they follow a *signaling system equilibrium* of an appropriate *signaling game*. And since on Lewis' analysis of convention agents do not necessarily require preliminary discussion or "cheap talk" to pick an equilibrium, the circularity that worried Russell, Quine, and Alston

---

25. This is exactly how Lewis states this platitude near the end of *Convention*, on p. 203. In the introduction, Lewis states the platitude in a different way: "Language is ruled by convention" (p. 1).

26. Bertrand Russell, *The Analysis of Mind* (London: George Allen and Unwin, 1921), p. 190; Willard Quine, "Truth by Convention," in *Philosophy of Mathematics: Selected Readings*, 2nd ed., ed. Paul Benacerraf and Hilary Putnam (1936; Cambridge: Cambridge University Press, 1983), pp. 329–354; William Alston, *Philosophy of Language* (Englewood Cliffs, NJ: Prentice Hall, 1964), p. 57.

27. Russell (1921), p. 190.

is avoided.[28] Pure coordination games are the games Lewis needs to develop his overall argument, and while Lewis does not limit his analysis of convention to pure coordination games only, most of his specific examples of convention are pure coordination examples.[29]

Lewis defines a convention as a *coordination equilibrium* of a game that agents follow on account of their common knowledge that they all follow *this* equilibrium and no other. Lewis defines a coordination equilibrium of a noncooperative game as a strategy profile such that no agent is better off if any agent unilaterally deviates from this profile.[30] As with Nash equilibria in general, a coordination equilibrium is strict if any agent who deviates unilaterally from this equilibrium is strictly worse off. A social situation where agents can follow a Lewis-convention is summarized by a noncooperative game with multiple strict coordination equilibria. Agents who follow a Lewis-convention in this situation must follow one of the game's strict coordination equilibria. However, for Lewis to follow such an equilibrium is not a sufficient condition for agents to be following a convention. For suppose that the agents engaged in one of these social situations characterized by a game with multiple strict coordination equilibria fail to analyze their situation properly at all, but happen to follow a strict coordination equilibrium R by sheer luck. Lewis does not count accidental coordination of this sort as a convention.

Suppose next that each of these agents maximizes her expected payoff given what she knows regarding this situation, and that part of what each agent knows is the payoff structure of this game. If each agent expects the others to follow their ends of R, her own end of R is her unique best response. So all follow R. Are they now following a convention? Not necessarily, contends Lewis in a subtle argument.[31] Each follows her best response in the game because she expects the others to follow their ends of R. But each agent might believe that the others all follow their ends of R mindlessly out of habit. In this case each agent of course best responds by following her end of R. They coordinate, but in this case partly because each falsely believes that others act in this situation like automata. Lewis thinks that a proper account of convention should exclude cases where agents happen to coordinate on the basis of false beliefs they have regarding their reasoning, or lack thereof, with respect to the coordination problem at hand. In

---

28. Lewis presents his account of signaling systems in Chapter IV of *Convention*.

29. An interesting and important exception is Lewis' discussion of Rousseau's Stag Hunt (1969, pp. 7, 47).

30. Lewis (1969), p. 14. Coordination equilibria were discussed in §1.3.

31. Lewis (1969), p. 59.

particular, like Hume before him, Lewis requires that the agents who follow a convention must have mutual expectations that each acts with the aim of coordinating with the others. In Lewis' account of convention, the necessary mutual expectations obtain if each of these agents knows that:

A_1: All are (Bayesian) rational.
A_2: All know the payoff structure of the game.
A_3: All intend to follow their respective ends of the coordination equilibrium R.
A_4: There is at least one other coordination equilibrium R' in the game different from R.

Suppose the agents' beliefs are appropriately augmented, so that each agent does know that A_1, A_2, A_3, and A_4 are the case. Again they coordinate on R. Are they *now* following a convention? Still not necessarily, says Lewis. For what if it turns out that some Agent i believes that some of the others believe that all other than themselves follow their ends of R mindlessly out of habit? Then Agent i has a false belief regarding the others' reasoning with respect to this coordination problem. Lewis is incorporating the following key point in his account of convention, although he does not state this point explicitly in this argument: Any agent who follows a convention must not believe that she has an ability to reason through propositions relevant to her decision in the coordination problem that the others involved lack. If Agent i concludes correctly that she should follow her end of R because she knows that A_1, A_2, A_3, and A_4 are the case, then she should expect that counterpart Agent j can also correctly conclude that he should follow his end of R because he knows that A_1, A_2, A_3, and A_4 are the case. That is, if first-order mutual knowledge where each Agent i knows that A_1, A_2, A_3, and A_4 are the case supports a convention, then evidently second-order mutual knowledge of A_1, A_2, A_3, and A_4 where each Agent i knows that each Agent j knows that A_1, A_2, A_3, and A_4 are the case must obtain. But can *third-order* mutual knowledge that A_1, A_2, A_3, and A_4 are the case then fail? No, argues Lewis. For if Agent i thought that Agent j did not know that Agent i knew that A_1, A_2, A_3, and A_4 were the case, then Agent i would have a false belief about Agent j. The key point kicks in again: If each Agent i can draw the conclusion involving second-order knowledge that each Agent j can conclude that he should follow his end of R because he knows that A_1, A_2, A_3, and A_4 obtain, then she should conclude that each Agent j can draw a parallel second-order knowledge conclusion. To conclude otherwise, Agent i would have to assume that she has some reasoning ability enabling her to draw conclusions regarding A_1, A_2, A_3, and A_4 that some counterpart Agent j lacks. So if second-order mutual knowledge that A_1, A_2, A_3, and A_4 are the case supports a convention, then the agents must have third-order mutual knowledge that A_1, A_2, A_3, and A_4 are the case. And the argument can be continued for higher levels of mutual knowledge.

Lewis concludes that a necessary condition for agents to be following a convention is that their preferences to follow the corresponding coordination equilibrium be common knowledge. Lewis' conclusion extends Hume's recognition that conventions are rooted in reciprocal expectations and Schelling's insight that individuals can coordinate successfully if they have arbitrarily high levels of mutual expectations that they will choose a given coordination point.[32] In the 1960s and 1970s a number of philosophers and social scientists independently proposed different analyses of common knowledge.[33] Common knowledge and related multi-agent epistemic concepts have become important research areas in philosophy, social science, and computer science. Lewis gave one of the earliest explicit definitions of common knowledge, and he was the first to incorporate common knowledge in an analysis of convention. Lewis adopts a key assumption in his analysis: In order to have common knowledge of some proposition E, the agents involved must have reason to believe that they are *symmetric reasoners* with respect to some *basis state* of affairs A^* that gives each reason to believe that E obtains, that is, that they share the same "rationality, inductive standards and background information" with respect to some state of affairs A^* that *indicates* to each that E is the case.[34] A^* indicates to Agent i that E is the case when she has reason to believe E is the case exactly when she has reason to believe that A^* is the case.[35] Lewis effectively assumes that each Agent i has reason to believe that all can infer any conclusion from A^* that she can infer. E is Lewis–common knowledge for the agents of a group N when (i) each Agent i in N has reason to believe that A^* obtains, (ii) A^* indicates to each Agent i in N that all in N have reason to believe that A^* obtains, (iii) all in N have reason to believe that they are symmetric reasoners with respect to A^*, and (iv) A^* indicates to each Agent i in N that E is the case.[36] Given sufficient epistemic powers, the agents of N who have Lewis–common knowledge of E can all infer that each Agent i in N knows that E is the case, each Agent i in N knows that each Agent j in N knows that E is the case, and so on, ad infinitum.[37]

---

32. Schelling (1960), p. 54.

33. Giacomo Sillari and I give an overview of the early history of common knowledge in "Common Knowledge," *The Stanford Encyclopedia of Philosophy*, Spring 2014 ed., ed. Edward N. Zalta, http://plato.stanford.edu/archives/spr2014/entries/common-knowledge.

34. Lewis (1969), p. 53.

35. Lewis (1969), pp. 52–53.

36. Lewis (1969), p. 56.

37. This is proved formally in Vanderschraaf (1998b).

So on Lewis' account, a convention for a set of agents is a strict coordination equilibrium that the agents follow on account of their common knowledge of their rationality, of the payoff structure of the relevant game, and that each agent follows her part of the equilibrium. Lewis' final definition of convention reflects his awareness that a regularity in behavior could be a convention to a certain degree:

> A regularity R in the behavior of members of a population P when they are agents in a recurrent situation S is a *convention* if and only if it is true that, and it is common knowledge in P that, in almost any instance of S among members of P,
>
> (1) almost everyone conforms to R;
> (2) almost everyone expects almost everyone else to conform to R;
> (3) almost everyone has approximately the same preferences regarding all possible combinations of actions;
> (4) almost everyone prefers that any one more conform to R, on condition that almost everyone conform to R;
> (5) almost everyone would prefer that any one more conform to R', on condition that almost everyone conform to R',
>
> where R' is some possible regularity in the behavior of members of P in S, such that almost no one in almost any instance of S among members of P could conform both to R' and to R.[38]

For Lewis, R could be the convention members of some population P follow in a recurrent situation S even if a few of the members of P fail to follow R, a few of the members of P do not expect others to follow R, and so on. Lewis frankly acknowledges that he cannot identify a way to measure the degree of conventionality as a single number that does not seem to him quite artificial.[39] Lewis does not directly address a related question that will motivate some of the discussion below in §2.4: How much deviance can an incumbent convention R for a population P withstand before R ceases to be a convention of P?

What accounts for agents following a particular coordination equilibrium, when they might have followed a different coordination equilibrium or even miscoordinated altogether? Lewis maintains that agents select and maintain a *salient* equilibrium characterizing *their* convention, that is, an equilibrium that is somehow prominent or conspicuous to them all.[40] Lewis argues that salience can

---

38. Lewis (1969), p. 78.

39. Lewis (1969), pp. 79–80.

40. Lewis (1969), p. 35.

arise from a variety of different factors, including explicit agreement, precedent, environmental clues, and in general any background knowledge the agents have in common. As Lewis acknowledges, the notion of salience is present in Schelling's *The Strategy of Conflict*,[41] and in fact David Hume presents even earlier insights into coordination by salience in *Treatise* and *Enquiry*.[42] Salience plays a key role in Lewis' response to Russell's, Quine's, and Alston's skeptical doubts regarding conventions of language. For while a verbal agreement can make a certain equilibrium salient, such agreements are not the only source of salience. For Lewis, the generation of salience from factors such as precedent and environmental clues implies that a convention can emerge in a population without antecedent communication. So Lewis has the tools to build his response to those skeptical of the idea that there are genuine conventions of language.

§2.2. The Arbitrariness of Conventions

Plato in the *Cratylus* and Aristotle in *Nicomachean Ethics* speak of conventions as if they are characteristically arbitrary practices. David Lewis declares that it is redundant to speak of an arbitrary convention.[43] But if conventions are arbitrary, how are they arbitrary? There are at least two different ways to understand the arbitrariness of conventions, and I believe one is likely to undervalue the role conventions may play in moral and political philosophy if one does not take care to avoid conflating them.[44] A pair of examples illustrates the distinction. The first example is a slight variation of one of Lewis' examples in *Convention*.[45] Suppose a cellist, Claudia, and a violinist, Laura, regularly perform together in public. They frequently need to discuss their plans for obtaining the necessary

---

41. Schelling develops his views on coordination and focal points primarily in Schelling (1960), chs. 2 and 3.

42. See especially *Treatise* 3:1.1–3 and *Enquiry* 3.2.

43. Lewis (1969), p. 70.

44. In several of their works on convention, Margaret Gilbert and Andrei Marmor draw a distinction much like the distinction I draw in this section between indifference-sense arbitrariness and discretionary-sense arbitrariness. See Margaret Gilbert, *On Social Facts* (Princeton, NJ: Princeton University Press, 1989), §4.2, §8.5, and "Social Convention Revisited," *Topoi* 27 (2008), pp. 5–16, and Andrei Marmor, "On Convention," *Synthese* 107 (1996), pp. 349–371, and *Social Conventions: From Language to Law* (Princeton, NJ: Princeton University Press, 2009), ch. 1. Gilbert and Marmor use the distinction they identify to develop their own alternative accounts of convention that do not employ game-theoretic concepts. Here I argue that indifference-sense arbitrariness and discretionary-sense arbitrariness are both captured by an equilibrium analysis of convention.

45. Lewis (1969), pp. 5, 43–44.

		Laura	
		C	R
Claudia	C	$(0,0)$	$(1,1)$
	R	$(1,1)$	$(0,0)$

C = call, R = receive

FIGURE 2.1 Cell Phone

sheet music, for rehearsal, and for other arrangements for their performances. When they converse on their cell phones, occasionally the transmission is interrupted. To resume a conversation on their cell phones after such an interruption, exactly one of them must call the other. For each musician the cost of conversing on her cell phone is the same whether she receives or calls, so neither has a strict preference over either receiving or calling. Laura and Claudia care only that they coordinate. They are indifferent over the alternative ways they might coordinate. Figure 2.1 summarizes a *Cell Phone* pure coordination game that characterizes their problem.

The two strict Nash coordination equilibria (C,R) and (R,C) are equally good from the musicians' individual perspectives. Likewise, each regards the miscoordination outcomes (C,C) and (R,R) as equally bad. One way for Claudia and Laura to solve their coordination problem is to always follow the (C,R) equilibrium, that is, Claudia always calls and Laura always receives after an interruption. Another is to follow the (R,C) equilibrium always. Or they can adopt a *contingency strategy* by tying their actions to some piece of background information. One such contingency strategy is

S': C if my colleague initiated the call, R if I initiated the call.

If Laura and Claudia both adopt this contingency strategy, then either would fare strictly worse if she were to deviate unilaterally from S'. In this case they follow a strict *correlated equilibrium* at which they consistently coordinate, so called because they correlate their acts with their background information. Robert Aumann gave the first formal analyses of correlated equilibrium in a pair of now classic essays.[46] Correlated equilibrium will play a very prominent role in the discussion

46. Robert Aumann, "Subjectivity and Correlation in Randomized Strategies," *Journal of Mathematical Economics* 1 (1974), pp. 67–96, and "Correlated Equilibrium as an Expression of Bayesian Rationality," *Econometrica* 55 (1987), pp. 1–18.

of convention to follow. Of course, Claudia and Laura can achieve a variety of solutions of their coordination problem both regard as equally good as the (C,R), (R,C), or (S',S') solutions via any number of other contingency strategies. In fact, there are infinitely many distinct correlated equilibria of this game that yield the two musicians payoffs equivalent to those of the two strict Nash equilibria (C,R) and (R,C). To see why, suppose that following an interruption Laura and Claudia can both observe the outcome ω of a random experiment with two possible outcomes ω_1 and ω_2 where ω_1 occurs with probability λ and ω_2 occurs with probability $1-\lambda$. If they conform with the strategy system

$$f_\lambda(\omega) = \begin{cases} (C,R) \text{ if } \omega = \omega_1 \\ (R,C) \text{ if } \omega = \omega_2 \end{cases}$$

then Claudia and Laura are at a correlated equilibrium since if either unilaterally deviates from this system, her payoff will drop from 1 to 0, so each strictly prefers to conform so long as her colleague conforms. At this correlated equilibrium each achieves her best payoff in the entire coordination game each time the experiment is run. This correlated equilibrium is also a coordination equilibrium according to Lewis' definition because if either deviates alone from the equilibrium, both the deviator and the one who conforms end up with lower payoffs. Since f_λ satisfies these properties for any $\lambda \in [0,1]$, the Figure 2.1 game has infinitely many different strict coordination equilibria. Any one of these equilibria could characterize a convention for Claudia and Laura as Lewis defines convention. In their Cell Phone problem, Claudia and Laura follow a Lewis-convention if they have common knowledge that they follow contingency strategy S'. But Laura and Claudia both regard all of the different strict correlated equilibria of the Figure 2.1 game as equally good. So if they follow the (S',S') convention, they do so knowing that neither would fare better were they to change to some other Lewis-convention that would resolve this Cell Phone problem. The (S',S') convention is arbitrary in the sense that the individuals involved have no reasons to choose to follow (S',S') rather than some other coordination equilibrium other than reasons no one could infer from studying the structure of their interaction problem. The reasons they settle into following (S',S') could appear frivolous to an outsider and possibly to Claudia and Laura themselves, given that they are indifferent over the alternative conventions available to them. I will call the sort of arbitrariness of conventions illustrated in this example arbitrariness in the *indifference sense*.

The second example is Luce and Raiffa's impure coordination game Battle of the Sexes, introduced in §1.1 and summarized in Figure 1.8. Here is an interpretation somewhat different from Luce and Raiffa's interpretation: After performing together, Claudia (Agent 1) and Laura (Agent 2) wish to dine together at either Arigato Sushi (A), Claudia's favorite restaurant, or Café Buenos Aires (B), Laura's favorite restaurant. As in the Cell Phone game, in this Battle of the Sexes game Claudia and Laura can coordinate at either of two strict Nash coordination equilibria. However, their preferences over these strict Nash equilibria fail to coincide. (A,A) is Claudia's favorite Nash equilibrium and (B,B) is Laura's favorite Nash equilibrium. Consequently, they are prone to miscoordinate if each tries to follow her most preferred equilibrium. Either (A,A) or (B,B) can be a Lewis-convention for Laura and Claudia given appropriate common knowledge. Laura and Claudia also have more coordination equilibria available to them in Battle of the Sexes if they can follow contingency strategies. If for any given $\lambda \in [0,1]$ Claudia and Laura follow the contingency strategy system

$$f_\lambda(\omega) = \begin{cases} (A,A) \text{ if } \omega = \omega_1 \\ (B,B) \text{ if } \omega = \omega_2 \end{cases}$$

for the random experiment outcomes ω_1 and ω_2 described in the preceding paragraph, then they follow a strict coordination correlated equilibrium in this Battle of the Sexes game.[47] Any one of these correlated equilibria characterizes a Lewis-convention available to Laura and Claudia. However, in this situation Claudia and Laura care very much which convention they do follow. If they conform with their respective ends of a given Lewis-convention of their Battle of the Sexes problem defined by f_{λ^*} for some $\lambda^* \in [0,1]$, they do so knowing that at some of the other strict equilibria that might have settled into, one of them would have fared better and the other worse than they fare at f_{λ^*}.[48] If in fact they follow this f_{λ^*} convention, at least one of them would prefer that they switch to some other Lewis-convention. None of the possible f_λ equilibrium Lewis-conventions in this Battle of the Sexes problem is indifference-sense arbitrary with respect to any of the others.

47. This follows from an argument much like that of previous paragraph. If Claudia and Laura can observe the results of the random experiment described above and they follow the contingency strategy system defined by f_λ, then if either unilaterally deviates from f_λ both their payoffs will strictly drop. Hence f_λ defines a strict correlated coordination equilibrium, and if Claudia and Laura have common knowledge that they follow this equilibrium, then they follow a Lewis-convention.

48. If they follow f_λ for $\lambda = \lambda^*$, then Claudia's expected payoff is

$$2 \cdot \lambda^* + 1 \cdot (1 - \lambda^*) = \lambda^* + 1$$

One can argue that an impure coordination problem like Battle of the Sexes always has conventions that are indifference-sense arbitrary with respect to each other on the grounds that different underlying randomization schemes can produce correlated equilibria having the same alternation probabilities and the same expected payoff vector. For instance, in Battle of the Sexes a $f_{\frac{10}{19}}$ convention where Laura and Claudia follow (A, A) with probability $\frac{10}{19}$ and (B, B) with probability $\frac{9}{19}$ can be characterized in a number of different ways. Claudia and Laura might observe the toss of a biased coin that lands heads up with probability $\frac{10}{19}$ and then follow (A, A) if this coin lands heads up and (B, B) if this coin lands tails up. Or they might observe the spin of a fair American roulette wheel and follow (B, B) if the ball lands in one of the black slots and follow (A, A) otherwise.[49] And so on. These conventions are all arbitrary in the indifference sense with respect to each other, but the corresponding correlated equilibria all define the same joint probability distribution over the alternative strategy profiles of the Battle of the Sexes game. I will call a set of conventions that are arbitrary in the indifference sense with respect to each other *nontrivial* if the conventions of this set all share the same expected payoff vector and include correlated equilibria where the agents in the corresponding game follow alternative strategy profiles according to different probabilities. The conventions of the Cell Phone problem that can be characterized by the contingency strategy systems of the form f_λ for $\lambda \in [0,1]$ form a nontrivial indifference-sense arbitrary set. But in Battle of the Sexes, the sets of conventions that are indifference-sense arbitrary with respect to each other are all trivial.

Nevertheless, if Claudia and Laura do end up following one of the f_λ conventions of Battle of the Sexes, their convention is still arbitrary in another

---

and Laura's expected payoff is

$$1 \cdot \lambda^* + 2 \cdot (1 - \lambda^*) = 2 - \lambda^*.$$

If they switch to some other contingency strategy system

$$f_{\lambda'}(\omega) = \begin{cases} (A, A) \text{ if } \omega = \omega_1 \\ (B, B) \text{ if } \omega = \omega_2 \end{cases}$$

where $\lambda' \neq \lambda^*$, then Claudia's and Laura's respective expected payoffs are $\lambda' + 1 > \lambda^* + 1$ and $2 - \lambda' < 2 - \lambda^*$ if $\lambda' > \lambda^*$ and $\lambda' + 1 < \lambda^* + 1$ and $2 - \lambda' > 2 - \lambda^*$ if $\lambda' < \lambda^*$.

49. This follows because eighteen of the thirty-eight slots on an American roulette wheel are black.

		Laura A	Laura B
Claudia	A	(1, 1)	(− 1, 0)
	B	(0, − 1)	(1, 1)

FIGURE 2.2 Coordination Game A

sense. They follow this f_λ convention knowing that there are other strict equilibria available to them, each of which could have defined their followed convention given a different set of mutual expectations. The Battle of the Sexes and Cell Phone problems illustrate a general feature of Lewis' analysis of convention that I, too, maintain is characteristic of conventions: For any convention that guides conduct in a given situation, there is an alternative that could also serve as a convention in this same situation. The individuals involved always have a variety of options, each of which can be "their" convention if they adopt this alternative rather than any of the others. While they might adopt a given convention for reasons other than deliberate choice, in principle they can always choose to follow a convention different from one they do in fact follow. In this sense, which I shall call the *discretionary sense*, Lewis can rightly say that it is redundant to speak of an arbitrary convention.[50]

Many pure coordination games have at least one set of equilibria corresponding to conventions that are a nontrivially indifference-sense arbitrary set. Nevertheless, for an interaction to have available conventions with nontrivially indifference-sense arbitrariness it is neither necessary nor sufficient that the underlying game be a game of pure coordination. The coordination *Game A* of Figure 2.2 is not a pure coordination game since Claudia's worst outcome occurs at (A,B) while Laura's worst outcome occurs at (B,A). But the strict Nash equilibria (A,A) and (B,B) and the correlated equilibria where they alternate between (A,A) and (B,B) according to appropriate contingency strategies are all equally good from both Laura's and Claudia's perspectives. All the conventions of this game are arbitrary in the indifference sense with respect to each other, although plainly the joint probability distributions over the four pure strategy profiles that define these conventions vary.

On the other hand, the coordination *Game B* of Figure 2.3 is a pure coordination game, but any two alternative conventions Laura and Claudia might

50. As I interpret Marmor, discretionary-sense arbitrariness is the leading idea behind his own definition of arbitrariness. See Marmor (1996), pp. 351–352, and (2009), ch. 1.

		Laura: A	Laura: B
Claudia	A	$(2,2)$	$(0,0)$
	B	$(0,0)$	$(1,1)$

FIGURE 2.3 Coordination Game B

follow where they alternate between (A,A) and (B,B) according to different probabilities have different expected payoff vectors, and consequently are not arbitrary in the indifference sense with respect to each other.[51] The Nash equilibrium (A,A) is uniquely optimal, so the corresponding convention would be the best convention Claudia and Laura could follow in terms of expected payoff. However, this by no means guarantees that Laura and Claudia will actually follow the (A,A) convention. Suppose that before they interact in the situation with the Figure 2.3 structure for the first time, Claudia and Laura together observe another pair of musicians, Helen and Yue, in an interaction Laura and Claudia believe also has a Figure 2.3 game structure, and that they observe Yue and Helen follow the outcome corresponding to (B,B). Then in their own interactions having the Figure 2.3 game structure, Claudia and Laura might in the end follow the (B,B) Nash equilibrium convention because the actions they observed in the interaction between Helen and Yue have made (B,B) salient to them both, even though (B,B) is strictly suboptimal. I note that it is not necessarily the case that Helen and Yue were following the (B,B) convention themselves. Perhaps they were following some correlated equilibrium convention of alternation between (A,A) and (B,B), and Laura and Claudia happened to see Yue and Helen interact precisely at some time when the contingency strategy system of their convention required Helen and Yue to both follow B. In any event, this example shows that agents like Claudia and Laura could possibly end up following a convention that yields each of them the worst payoff of any of the available conventions on account of their observations of others interacting in a like situation.

51. One can infer this by inspection of the Figure 2.3 game, but also analytically as follows: For $\lambda \in [0,1]$ let f_λ denote the strategy system defined above for Battle of the Sexes. Then if Claudia and Laura follow either of the conventions characterized by f_{λ_1} or f_{λ_2}, then for $i \in \{1,2\}$ the respective expected payoffs for them both are $2\cdot\lambda_i + 1\cdot(1-\lambda_i) = 1+\lambda_i$. So if their respective expected payoffs at f_{λ_1} and f_{λ_2} are equal, then $\lambda_1 = \lambda_2$.

On the other hand, impure coordination games always will have some conventions having no indifference-sense arbitrariness with respect to each other. This follows at once from the definition of an impure coordination game as a game where the agents have conflicting preferences over the pure strategy Nash equilibria. Still, in some impure coordination games some conventions can be nontrivially arbitrary in the indifference sense with respect to each other. Figure 2.4 summarizes an *Extended Battle of the Sexes* game illustrating this phenomenon. One can interpret this game as an extension of Laura's and Claudia's restaurant problem, where they now have a third option, Cajun Kitchen (C), that both regard as a second-best choice for dining after performing. As with the Figure 1.8 game, this game has an associated continuum of correlated equilibria corresponding to conventions Laura and Claudia might follow yielding at least one of them an expected payoff lower than her payoff at her favorite equilibrium. This extended game also has a new coordination Nash equilibrium, namely (C,C). The (C,C) Lewis-convention is plainly not arbitrary in the indifference sense with respect to all of the other available conventions, since Claudia would prefer the (A,A) convention over the (C,C) convention and Laura would prefer the (B,B) convention over the (C,C) convention. But the (C,C) convention is indifference-sense arbitrary with respect to the correlated equilibrium convention where Claudia and Laura follow (A,A) and (B,B) with probability $\frac{1}{2}$ each. This example highlights an important point only hinted at above: Discretionary-sense arbitrariness is a property common to all the conventions of a given coordination problem, but indifference-sense arbitrariness is a property that is characterized only with reference to some subset of the available conventions. Put another way, discretionary-sense arbitrariness and indifference-sense arbitrariness are both relational properties, but while any convention is discretionary-sense arbitrary with respect to all other conventions of the given coordination problem, a convention is indifference-sense arbitrary only

		Laura		
		A	B	C
	A	$(2, 1)$	$(-1, -1)$	$(-1, -1)$
Claudia	B	$(-1, -1)$	$(1, 2)$	$(-1, -1)$
	C	$(-1, -1)$	$(-1, -1)$	$(\frac{3}{2}, \frac{3}{2})$

FIGURE 2.4 Extended Battle of the Sexes

with respect to a specific subset of the available conventions of this coordination problem, namely, the subset of conventions that are expected payoff equivalent to the given convention.

Here I have argued that the common and old view that conventions are essentially arbitrary practices is in a certain sense correct. All conventions of a given coordination problem are arbitrary in the discretionary sense with respect to each other. In this sense Lewis is right to claim that it is redundant to speak of arbitrary conventions. But it does not follow from this point that those involved in a coordination problem never care which of the available conventions they follow in the end. More particularly, it does not follow that convention is a notion orthogonal to justice. In even the simplest cases of impure coordination problems, there are alternative conventions over which the agents' preferences directly conflict. And at least some of these conventions may strike some as unfair. In their Battle of the Sexes problem, (A, A) and (B, B) are coordination equilibria characterizing two of the Lewis-conventions available to Claudia and Laura, but Laura might well complain that the (A, A) convention is definitely unfair to her and Claudia might similarly complain that the (B, B) convention is definitely unfair to her. But if justice and convention are related in any interesting way, what is the nature of this relationship? I believe an answer to this question will depend in part upon a more general analysis of convention than those considered this far. I turn to this more general analysis in the next two sections.

§2.3. Convention and Correlated Equilibrium

I discussed some specific examples of correlated equilibrium conventions of the Cell Phone and Battle of the Sexes problems in §2.2. To show more generally how conventions can be characterized as correlated equilibria, I will use the Hawk-Dove game with payoff structure summarized by Figure 2.5.

		Agent 2	
		M	G
Agent 1	M	$(6, 6)$	$(2, 7)$
	G	$(7, 2)$	$(0, 0)$

$M =$ "dove," $G =$ "hawk"

FIGURE 2.5 Hawk-Dove

(M,G) and (G,M) are the strict Nash equilibria of this game. By definition, at either of these equilibria each agent has a decisive reason to conform with her end of the equilibrium given that she expects the other agent to conform. These equilibria also depend upon the agents' reciprocal expectations in the following way: When each agent can infer that she should follow her end of one of these equilibria given that she expects her counterpart to follow his end of this equilibrium, she can also infer that she should follow some different strategy given certain different expectations regarding her counterpart's strategy choice. For instance, if the two agents have common knowledge that they are rational, that they know the structure of the Hawk-Dove game, and that each expects the other to follow the other's part of (G,M), then each has sufficient reason to follow her own part of (G,M). Nevertheless, from their common knowledge of the payoff structure of Hawk-Dove, they know that had Agent 1 believed with sufficiently high probability that Agent 2 would choose G, then Agent 1 would have chosen M. Similarly, they know that had Agent 2's beliefs about Agent 1 been in a certain manner different, Agent 2 would have deviated from (G,M).

Suppose that the Hawk-Dove game summarizes a problem of initial ownership. Each agent when she finds some good she believes might not already be owned must decide whether to follow G and claim the good as her own or follow M and concede to the other the right to use this good. Given this interpretation, a strict Nash equilibrium supported by the stated common knowledge conditions would seem to be a prime example of a convention as Hume would describe one. And in fact, according to the account of convention I will propose, both (G,M) and (M,G) together with the appropriate common knowledge conditions are conventions of Hawk-Dove. But neither of these strict Nash equilibria can be an equilibrium of a Lewis-convention. For at either of these equilibria, the agent who chooses M would prefer that the other agent deviate and also choose M. Given that each at first thinks the other will follow her end of a strict Nash equilibrium, if the M-chooser could convince the G-chooser that, contrary to fact, she will be aggressive, the G-chooser would have good reason to deviate from the strict equilibrium. To be sure, were such a deception successful, the agents could no longer be said to be following a convention, since mutual "chickening out" is an unstable outcome of Hawk-Dove. This example illustrates the following general point I attribute in an informal manner to Hume and adopt myself: At the equilibrium of a convention the interests of the agents need be aligned only to the extent that each has a decisive reason to follow her end of this equilibrium given that she expects the others to follow their ends of this equilibrium. So the equilibrium of a convention need not be a coordination equilibrium. Interestingly, the specific requirements Lewis gives regarding agents' reciprocal expectations in a convention are virtually identical to those I adopt and attribute to Hume. Lewis argues that a necessary property of a convention is that agents have common knowledge of a *mutual expectations criterion*:

> Each agent has a decisive reason to conform to her part of the convention given that she expects the other agents conform to their parts.[52]

This mutual expectations criterion is satisfied for any Humean-style convention where there is potential for agents' interests to be in enough conflict that the defining equilibrium is not a coordination equilibrium. Lewis-conventions actually satisfy a much stronger property, namely, common knowledge of a *public intentions criterion*:[53]

> Each agent desires that her choice of action is common knowledge among all agents engaged in the game.

This is clearly the case since, by definition, if agents follow a coordination equilibrium, then no agent's payoff could improve if any agent were to deviate.

I have used the Hawk-Dove game to show that an analysis of conventions need not be limited, as Lewis supposed, to social situations having "solutions" corresponding to coordination equilibria. Conventions can, in fact, regulate situations where none of the corresponding strict Nash equilibria are coordination equilibria. I will next use the Hawk-Dove game to illustrate the more fundamental claim stated at the beginning of this section, namely, that convention is analyzed most naturally in terms of correlated equilibrium. The primary solution concept in noncooperative game theory has been the Nash equilibrium concept. According to a traditional interpretation rooted in the work of von Neumann, Morgenstern, and Nash, agents are at a Nash equilibrium if each agent employs a mixed strategy that maximizes her expected utility given the other agents' mixed strategies. By definition, an agent's mixed strategy is a function with a domain that is the set of outcomes of some private random experiment mapped into the counterdomain of the agent's pure strategies. *Ex post*, the pure strategy the agent follows is defined by the outcomes of her random experiment *ex ante*. Since each agent pegs her pure strategies on the outcomes of her own private experiment, the agents' mixed strategies in a game are probabilistically independent. But just why would agents engaged in a game follow mixed strategies? After all, many individuals who have never studied game theory, and many who have, frequently interact with no direct

52. Lewis (1969), pp. 25–27.

53. I argued for this point in Vanderschraaf (1998b).

reference to private random experiments. Indeed, cases where the individuals who interact do follow mixed strategies are quite exceptional. Does this imply that the Nash equilibrium concept, so important in the mathematical theory of games, is of little relevance for explaining the outcomes of most actual interactions?

In *Games and Decisions*, Luce and Raiffa point out that a primary argument in favor of supposing that agents would ever mix their strategies is that mixing can keep one's opposing counterparts in a game uncertain as to which pure strategy one will ultimately play.[54] This might be a compelling rationale for mixed strategies in games of pure conflict where each agent wants the others to fail to guess which pure strategy she will follow. But in a great many games, each agent will want the others to coordinate their pure strategies with her own to at least some extent. This kind of coordination may be quite unlikely if the agents all follow explicitly mixed strategies, which by definition are probabilistically independent. For example, suppose that n agents are engaged in a pure coordination game where each has the two pure strategies L and R, and each receives a positive payoff of 1 if they all follow L or they all follow R and a payoff of 0 at any other outcome. For $n = 2$, this game is equivalent to the Encounter Problem of Figure 1.2 with two pure strategies. One can think of this as a *Highway* game, where each agent's pure strategy corresponds to driving either on their *right side* (R) or on their *left side* (L) of a road, and a suboptimal halt of traffic is bound to ensue unless the agents all drive on their same side of the road. The Highway game has 2^n pure strategy profiles. Only two of these pure strategy profiles, $(L,\ldots,L)$ and $(R,\ldots,R)$, are Nash equilibria. The agents' prospects for coordinating by all driving on the same side in the Highway game can be quite poor if all follow completely mixed strategies, even if all follow the same mixed strategy and this mixed strategy places high probability on the same pure strategy. For $n = 10$, if the agents all adopt the same mixed strategy $\sigma = \frac{9}{10} \cdot L \oplus \frac{1}{10} R$, they coordinate in their Highway game with probability approximately 0.3487. For $n = 20$, if the agents all follow σ they coordinate with probability approximately 0.1216, and for $n = 50$, if the agents all follow σ they coordinate with probability only approximately 0.0052.[55]

54. Luce and Raiffa (1957), 75. Luce and Raiffa add that many do not believe this is a fully satisfactory defense of mixed strategies and they do not claim themselves that this is a fully satisfactory defense.

55. In order to achieve coordination, the n agents must either all follow L or all follow R. If each agent follows $\sigma = \frac{9}{10} L \oplus \frac{1}{10} R$, then this coordination event occurs with probability $\left(\frac{9}{10}\right)^n + \left(\frac{1}{10}\right)^n$, and $\left(\frac{9}{10}\right)^{10} + \left(\frac{1}{10}\right)^{10} \approx 0.3487$, $\left(\frac{9}{10}\right)^{20} + \left(\frac{1}{10}\right)^{20} \approx 0.1216$, and $\left(\frac{9}{10}\right)^{50} + \left(\frac{1}{10}\right)^{50} \approx 0.0052$.

I believe the explicitly mixed strategies of classical game theory are of limited value either descriptively or normatively. Individuals seldom mix their strategies in actual interactions, and in many games that are not games of pure conflict, the agents are likely to arrive at suboptimal nonequilibrium outcomes if they all follow completely mixed strategies. Nevertheless, it does not follow that the Nash equilibrium concept is suspect. For there is another way to interpret probabilities over pure strategies in game theory. As noted above, one argument proposed in favor of mixed strategies is that mixing can make one's counterparts uncertain as to which pure strategy one will actually follow. However, it is not necessary for an agent to mix her own strategies in order to generate uncertainty in the minds of the other agents. An alternative way to interpret the probabilities of mixed strategies is as the probabilities in the minds of the other agents regarding what one will do. Suppose that in a noncooperative game the agents do not announce their intended strategies, either pure or mixed. Each agent still has a probability distribution over the others' strategies, reflecting her uncertainty regarding the others' actions. This probability distribution is the agent's conjecture that describes precisely her beliefs over the alternative strategy profiles the others might follow. Suppose that each agent's conjecture is *consistent* with the other agents' conjectures, that is, the probability she assigns agrees with the probabilities the others assign to a given counterpart's pure strategy. And suppose the conjectures satisfy probabilistic independence, so that each conjecture over the joint strategy profiles of an agent's counterparts is equivalent to the product of the agent's marginal conjectures over each individual counterpart's pure strategies. Then if the agents have common knowledge of the payoff structure of the game, their Bayesian rationality, and their conjectures, the probabilities of their conjectures over pure strategies are equivalent to the probabilities of a Nash equilibrium in explicitly mixed strategies.[56] So one can reinterpret Nash equilibrium as *equilibrium-in-conjectures*. If agents are at equilibrium-in-conjectures regarding what their counterparts will do, then each may choose a pure strategy that is her end of a corresponding equilibrium strategy combination. Hence the equilibrium-in-conjectures reinterpretation of Nash equilibrium avoids the objections one might raise against explicitly mixed strategies. Moreover, replacing randomized strategies in game theory with conjectures appears to reflect

56. This is proved in Adam Brandenburger and Eddie Dekel, "Rationalizability and Correlated Equilibrium," *Econometrica* 55 (1987), pp. 1391–1402, Brandenburger and Dekel, "The Role of Common Knowledge Assumptions in Game Theory," in *The Economics of Missing Markets, Information and Games*, ed. Frank Hahn (Oxford: Clarendon Press, 1988), pp. 46–61, and Peter Vanderschraaf, *Learning and Coordination* (New York: Routledge, 2001) (henceforth Vanderschraaf 2001b), Chapter 2.

the actual predicament of the agents. Each agent wants to maximize her expected utility, which she can always do by choosing a pure strategy given what she believes her opponents will do, and her beliefs may be quantified by a subjective probability distribution over the opponents' act combinations. For these reasons, I will adopt the equilibrium-in-conjectures approach in the remainder of this book.[57]

The strategies of a Nash equilibrium must be probabilistically independent. Aumann recognized that the agents engaged in a game could have conjectures that characterize a system of strategies that are not probabilistically independent yet are still in equilibrium. To illustrate Aumann's great insight, I return to the Hawk-Dove game, again using the initial ownership interpretation. When an agent finds a certain good, she might ascertain whether or not she is also the first to find that this good is not already claimed by someone else. For example, if the agents indicate their claims to goods by marking them, an agent can conclude she is such a *first finder* if upon finding the good by herself she can see that no one else has marked this good appropriately. Of course, an agent might not be able to ascertain that she is the first finder of an unowned good, particularly if she sees her counterpart agent nearby when she finds this good before she can inspect the good for markings. In short, there are three possible worlds:

ω_1: Agent 1 ascertains that she is first finder.
ω_2: Agent 2 ascertains that he is first finder.
ω_0: Neither agent ascertains that she is first finder.

Each agent can tell whether or not she really is first finder. But if she concludes she is not first finder, then she does not know whether or not the other agent is first finder. In this case she knows that the other agent might either ascertain that he is first finder or be as unsure about whether or not she is first finder as she is regarding him. Now suppose that heading into their encounter each agent knows her partner is similarly situated, in that the partner has the same inferential abilities as herself and has the same ability to ascertain whether or not he is first finder. So as they head into their encounter they have common knowledge that Agent 1 knows either that $\{\omega_1\}$ or $\{\omega_0, \omega_2\}$ is the case and that Agent 2

57. Some of the other authors who adopt the subjectivist interpretation of equilibrium in noncooperative games include Aumann (1974), (1987), pp. 1–18; Skyrms (1990), chs. 2 and 7; Ken Binmore and Adam Brandenburger, "Common Knowledge and Game Theory," in Ken Binmore, *Essays on the Foundations of Game Theory* (Oxford: Basil Blackwell, 1990), pp. 105–150, and Bicchieri (1993), ch. 2.

knows either that $\{\omega_2\}$ or $\{\omega_0, \omega_1\}$ is the case. Each agent can then follow the contingency strategy:

f_i: G if I (Agent i) ascertain I am first finder, M otherwise.

The contingency strategy system $f = (f_1, f_2)$ defines a function over the set of possible worlds $\Omega = \{\omega_0, \omega_1, \omega_2\}$ with values defined by

$$f(\omega) = \begin{cases} (G, M) \text{ if } \omega = \omega_1 \\ (M, G) \text{ if } \omega = \omega_2 \\ (M, M) \text{ if } \omega = \omega_0 \end{cases}.$$

Figure 2.6.a summarizes the pattern of strategy profiles the agents follow according to f.

Now suppose that when heading into their encounter, each agent believes, based upon past experiences, the three possible worlds are equally likely. That is, they have a common prior probability distribution that assigns equal probabilities to the elements of Ω. Figure 2.6.b summarizes the joint probability distribution f defines over the strategy profiles of the Hawk-Dove game. If the agents both follow their ends of f, then each achieves an expected payoff of

$$E_i(u_i(f)) = 7 \cdot \frac{1}{3} + 2 \cdot \frac{1}{3} + 6 \cdot \frac{1}{3} = 5.$$

If either Agent i deviates unilaterally from f by following some other function $g_i \neq f_i$ from Ω to her pure strategies, Agent i does not improve her expected payoff.

(a)

		Agent 2	
		M	G
Agent 1	M	$(6,6)^{\omega_0}$	$(2,7)^{\omega_2}$
	G	$(7,2)^{\omega_1}$	$(0,0)$

M = "dove," G = "hawk"

(b)

		Agent 2	
		M	G
Agent 1	M	$\frac{1}{3}$	$\frac{1}{3}$
	G	$\frac{1}{3}$	0

M = "dove," G = "hawk"

Shaded cells are visited with positive probability.

FIGURE 2.6 a. Strategy System f Applied to Hawk-Dove b. Partially Correlated Equilibrium Distribution of Hawk-Dove

If, for instance, $g_1(\omega) = G$ for $\omega \in \{\omega_0, \omega_1, \omega_2\}$, that is, Agent 1 follows G no matter what, her expected payoff is then

$$E_1\left(u_1\left(g_1, f_2\right)\right) = 7 \cdot \frac{1}{3} + 0 \cdot \frac{1}{3} + 7 \cdot \frac{1}{3} = \frac{14}{3} < 5.$$

f is a *partially correlated equilibrium*, so-called because the agents' individual strategies are imperfectly correlated according to their different information partitions. Agent 1's and Agent 2's respective information partitions are $\mathcal{H}_1 = \{\{\omega_1\}, \{\omega_0, \omega_2\}\}$ and $\mathcal{H}_2 = \{\{\omega_2\}, \{\omega_0, \omega_1\}\}$.[58] In this example, the equilibrium depends upon the agents having differential and imperfect information over the possible worlds, reflected by their different partitions. If, say, Agent 1 were to discover at ω_0 that ω_0 is the actual world, then f would no longer be an equilibrium since in this eventuality Agent 1 would prefer to deviate from f. Similarly, if the prior probability distribution were sufficiently different from the Figure 2.6.b distribution then f would cease to be an equilibrium. If for some reason both agents were to believe that ω_0 occurs with probability 1, then both would prefer to deviate from f. So correlated equilibrium is clearly a concept rooted in the agents' conjectures given their private information. Aumann formulates his correlated equilibrium concept under the assumptions that the agents engaged in the game have common knowledge of the game, their rationality, their information partitions of the possible worlds, and a common prior probability distribution over these worlds. Given this much common knowledge, the agents' conjectures define a correlated equilibrium of the game.[59]

Aumann presented his correlated equilibrium concept in an abstract manner, because he was mainly concerned with establishing conceptual connections between common knowledge, Bayesian rationality, and equilibrium in subjective conjectures. Aumann did not explore alternative explanations of the origins of agents' knowledge partitions or their probabilities over the relevant possible worlds. I believe that examining alternative interpretations of games with an eye to explaining how the agents might come to partition their information and how they might form their probabilities sheds light upon a complementary relationship between correlated equilibrium and convention. The correlated equilibrium

58. A partition of a set Ω is a collection of sets $\mathcal{H} = \{H_1, H_2, \ldots\}$ such that $H_i \cap H_j = \varnothing$ for $i \neq j$ and $\bigcup_i H_i = \Omega$.

More formally, f is a correlated equilibrium because neither Agent i cannot improve her expected payoff by deviating unilaterally to some function g_i that is *measurable* with respect to her information partition $\mathcal{H}_i$, that is, a function g_i that is constant on each cell of Agent i's partition $\mathcal{H}_i$.

59. Aumann proves this as the main theorem of his 1987 essay (p. 7).

f described in the previous paragraph illustrates this point. This correlated equilibrium corresponds to the common convention, reviewed by Hobbes in *Leviathan* and Hume in *Treatise*, where ownership of a previously unowned good is conceded to the individual who finds and claims the good first.[60] One might think of the two agents as perhaps foraging for firewood or prospecting for gold. They follow a first finder convention that characterizes a version of the familiar "finders keepers" rule if they think each has an equal chance of ascertaining she is first finder of an unclaimed quantity of the good first: each claims the good for herself if she knows she is first finder and they share the use of the good if neither knows who is first finder.

Of course, property rights can be established in many other ways. In *Leviathan*, Hobbes gives in his thirteenth law of nature recommendations that goods that cannot be used in common be used in turn or assigned according to lot.[61] In his fourteenth *Leviathan* law, Hobbes recommends first seizure and primogeniture as forms of natural lotteries for assigning goods.[62] Suppose that when the two contest over a good, ω_i denotes the possible world where Agent i has the prior claim according to primogeniture and both know who has this prior claim. Then in the Figure 2.5 Hawk-Dove game, for any common prior over the possible worlds $\boldsymbol{\Omega} = \{\omega_1, \omega_2\}$ the function $\boldsymbol{h}$ from $\boldsymbol{\Omega}$ into the outcomes defined by

$$\boldsymbol{h}(\omega) = \begin{cases} (G,M) \text{ if } \omega = \omega_1 \\ (M,G) \text{ if } \omega = \omega_2 \end{cases}$$

is a correlated equilibrium characterizing the establishment of ownership according to primogeniture. But another correlated equilibrium, namely, function $\boldsymbol{h}'$ from $\boldsymbol{\Omega}$ into the outcomes defined by

$$\boldsymbol{h}'(\omega) = \begin{cases} (M,G) \text{ if } \omega = \omega_1 \\ (G,M) \text{ if } \omega = \omega_2 \end{cases}$$

assigns ownership according to which of the two agents has the *lower* priority according to primogeniture. $\boldsymbol{h}$ and $\boldsymbol{h}'$ respectively characterize primogeniture and

60. *Leviathan* 15:27, 28, *Treatise* 3.2.3:6–7.

61. *Leviathan* 15:26.

62. *Leviathan* 15:27. My thanks to Amie Thomasson, who first alerted me to the possibility of viewing primogeniture as a convention that can regulate conduct in a situation of partial conflict.

"reverse primogeniture" conventions. Here the agents' information partitions are $\mathcal{G}_1 = \mathcal{G}_2 = \{\{\omega_1\},\{\omega_2\}\}$, and ω_i is a *public state of affairs* or *public fact*. $\boldsymbol{h}$ and $\boldsymbol{h}'$ are *perfectly correlated equilibria* for any common prior distribution over the possible worlds because the two agents' strategies are perfectly correlated with public facts.[63] Interestingly, if heading into the encounter the two possible worlds are equally, then for each Agent i the expected payoffs of following $\boldsymbol{h}$ and $\boldsymbol{h}'$ are $E_i\left(u_i\left(\boldsymbol{h}\right)\right) = E_i\left(u_i\left(\boldsymbol{h}'\right)\right) = \frac{9}{2} < 5$. At these particular perfectly correlated equilibria, both fare less well than they fare at the partially correlated equilibrium f given above. So agents can sometimes follow an equilibrium predicated upon their having less than perfect information regarding the possible worlds that is better for all than some of the equilibria where they all have the same perfect knowledge of which of the possible worlds is actual.[64] And as these examples indicate, the possible conventions for conveying property ownership are perhaps limited only by our imaginations, much as Hume suggested long ago in his discussions of conventions and property rights.

The examples I have examined in these past two sections suggest that one can define conventions in general in terms of correlated equilibria. And in fact some authors have proposed correlated equilibrium definitions of convention.[65] In these earlier definitions, a convention is characterized by a strict correlated equilibrium of a game having multiple strict correlated equilibria together with the agents' having common knowledge that they follow this strict equilibrium and no other. This definition is well suited for analyzing certain conventions, such as the conventions of Hawk-Dove, where the underlying game is a conflictual coordination game. In a conflictual coordination game the agents are prone to miscoordinate at a nonequilibrium outcome if each tries to follow her most preferred strict equilibrium. Conflictual coordination games include impure coordination games such as Battle of the Sexes as a special case, but also include games such as Hawk-Dove where the set of strict equilibria need not be coordination equilibria. So these earlier correlated equilibrium definitions generalize Lewis' definitions of convention to many situations of partial conflict lying outside the scope of Lewis' analysis. However, I believe these earlier definitions are still insufficiently general.

---

63. One can show that neither player can profit from a unilateral deviation from either $\boldsymbol{h}$ or $\boldsymbol{h}'$ by arguments similar to that given above to show that f is a correlated equilibrium.

64. Aumann (1974) was the first to show this.

65. Vanderschraaf (1998b) and (2001), ch. 4; Herbert Gintis, *The Bounds of Reason: Game Theory and the Unification of the Behavioral Sciences* (Princeton, NJ: Princeton University Press, 2009), ch. 7; and Samuel Bowles and Herbert Gintis, *A Cooperative Species: Human Reciprocity and Its Evolution* (Princeton, NJ: Princeton University Press, 2011), §5.5.

Conflictual coordination games such as Hawk-Dove have conventions that the agents involved can follow with reference only to a given current interaction. But what if agents consider tying their acts in a current interaction to the history of past interactions? And what if agents might follow rules for interacting in whole families of similar situations rather than for just one kind of situation summarized by a single game? These possibilities open the door to exploring an even more general class of conventions than the conflictual coordination conventions I have considered thus far. I turn to conventions of this more general class in the next section.

§2.4. Defining Convention

In Chapter 1, I claimed that one can view Hume's Farmer's Dilemma as a challenge against the rationality of keeping promises to honor one's end of an exchange. In §1.3 I used the Prisoner's Dilemma to summarize a variation of Hume's Farmer's Dilemma where the exchange has no sequential structure. Figure 2.7 summarizes a Prisoner's Dilemma similar to the Figure 1.6 game where each agent either *performs* (P) by keeping her promise to complete her part of an exchange or *defects* (D) by breaking her promise. Using the terminology introduced in Chapter 1, one violates a covenant offensively by defecting when one expects one's counterpart to perform or knows one's counterpart has already performed.[66] As discussed before, in an exchange having a structure like that of a Farmer's Dilemma or a Prisoner's Dilemma, each party exposes herself to exploitation if she performs and achieves her most preferred outcome by defecting when her counterpart performs. So why not defect and take advantage of others' performance if one can?

Nevertheless, soon after he introduces his Farmer's Dilemma example, Hume warns against offensively violating covenants. I will discuss Hume's warning at

		Agent j	
		P	D
Agent i	P	$(1, 1)$	$(-2, 1)$
	D	$(2, -1)$	$(-1, -1)$

P = perform, D = defect

FIGURE 2.7 Prisoner's Dilemma

66. See Problem 1.1 of §1.1.

some length in Chapter 7, but the main underlying idea is captured in a single sentence:

> When a man says *he promises any thing*, he in effect expresses a resolution of performing it; and along with that, by making use of this form of words, subjects himself to the penalty of never being trusted again in case of failure.[67]

Here Hume maintains that an offensive violator should expect to lose opportunities for future exchange. If the expected benefits of future exchange outweigh the immediate gains of an offensive violation, then one has good prudential reason to keep one's promises. A rough summary of Hume's argument for a community of just two agents employs a *repeated* Prisoner's Dilemma played out over indefinitely many periods of interaction. Suppose that each of these agents adopts the following *history-dependent strategy*:

Tr: Follow P each period of interaction until and including the first period the other follows D, then afterward follow D.

The Tr strategy, known in the game theory literature as *trigger* or *grim*, specifies for each agent a well-defined course of action for each Prisoner's Dilemma at each period of interaction that might be reached given what they have done in the Prisoner's Dilemmas of earlier periods. Specifically, Tr requires one to perform at each period on condition that the other has never offensively violated and to defect otherwise. If the two agents have sufficiently high probabilities of continued interaction, then the strategy profile (Tr, Tr) is an equilibrium of this *indefinitely repeated game* with an *equilibrium path* where they follow (P, P) at each period. To see why, let δ_i and δ_j denote Agent i's and Agent j's respective probabilities that the sequence of Prisoner's Dilemma games continues at a given period, so that δ_i^t and δ_j^t are Agent i's and Agent j's respective probabilities that the sequence continues at the tth future period.[68] The agents' *discount factors* are δ_i and δ_j. If both follow Tr, then Agent i's expected payoff is

$$E_i\left(u_i\left(Tr, Tr\right)\right) = \sum_{t=1}^{\infty} 1 \cdot \delta_i^t = \frac{\delta_i}{1-\delta_i}$$

67. *Treatise* 3.2.5:10.

68. This follows because for Agent i the events of the sequence (A_t) of events where

$$A_t = \left[\text{the sequence of Prisoner's Dilemmas continues at period } t\right]$$

are probabilistically independent.

because both follow P at each period t. Now suppose that g_{i1} is some strategy for engaging in the repeated Prisoner's Dilemma that requires Agent i to offensively violate at period $t = 1$. If Agent i follows g_{i1} while Agent j continues to follow Tr, then

$$E_i\left(u_i\left(g_{i1}, Tr\right)\right) \leq 2\delta_i + \sum_{t=2}^{\infty}(-1)\cdot\delta_i^t = 2\delta_i - \frac{\delta_i^2}{1-\delta_i}$$

because after gaining the 2 payoff of the (D,P) outcome if they engage at period $t = 1$, at any period $t > 1$ where they engage Agent i can achieve a payoff no better than the -1 payoff of (D,D) because Agent j will follow D. Hence $E_i\left(u_i\left(Tr,Tr\right)\right) \geq E_i\left(u_i\left(g_{i1},Tr\right)\right)$ when $\frac{\delta_i}{1-\delta_i} \geq 2\delta_i - \frac{\delta_i^2}{1-\delta_i}$ or $\delta_i \geq \frac{1}{3}$. By a similar argument, if g_{iT} is some other strategy that requires Agent i to offensively violate for the first time at some period $T > 1$, $E_i\left(u_i\left(Tr,Tr\right)\right) \geq E_i\left(u_i\left(g_{iT},Tr\right)\right)$ when $\delta_i \geq \frac{1}{3}$. So if $\delta_i \geq \frac{1}{3}$ then Tr is a best response for Agent i when Agent j follows Tr.[69] By a parallel argument, if $\delta_j \geq \frac{1}{3}$, Tr is a best response for Agent j when Agent i follows Tr. So if $\delta_i \geq \frac{1}{3}$ and $\delta_j \geq \frac{1}{3}$ then (Tr,Tr) is an equilibrium of this indefinitely repeated Prisoner's Dilemma. Moreover, if $\delta_i > \frac{1}{3}$ and $\delta_j > \frac{1}{3}$, then (Tr,Tr) is *path-observance strict*, that is, any strategy that requires either agent to deviate unilaterally from the equilibrium path defined by (Tr,Tr) yields this agent a strictly lower expected payoff. The indefinitely repeated Prisoners' Dilemma game has many other equilibria that are also path-observance strict, including the strategy profile where both agents defect at each interaction period, and the agents might follow any of these equilibria given appropriate mutual expectations.[70] So a path-observance strict equilibrium (Tr,Tr) is effectively discretionary-sense arbitrary with respect to all the other path-observance strict equilibria. Hence I will maintain that a path-observance strict (Tr,Tr) equilibrium characterizes a convention, defined in terms of history-dependent strategies, for this indefinitely repeated interaction.

69. If some strategy $g_i^* \neq Tr$ never requires Agent i to offensively violate, then should Agent 1 deviate unilaterally from (Tr,Tr) and follow g_i^*, her expected payoff will again be $\frac{\delta_i}{1-\delta_i}$ because both will still follow (P,P) at each period.

70. This result in an example of a *folk theorem* of repeated games. I discuss folk theorems further in Chapter 7.

Of course, there are many other history-dependent strategies to consider even for the simple case of dyadic exchanges. Here I will give just one more example to indicate some of the rich possibilities. Suppose the agents in a community of $n \geq 2$ agents who, like Hume's farmers, seek to directly promote only their own economic interests in exchanges of labor or goods can either perform or defect in a covenant they enter into, and also have the option of declining to enter into such a covenant in the first place. Each member of the community when paired with another member can either first consent to enter into an exchange or *shun* (S), that is, decline to covenant so that no exchange takes place with this counterpart. If both consent, then this member can *perform* (P) her end of their covenant, keeping her promise, or *defect* (D), breaking her promise. The relevant interaction between a pair of agents in this community is summarized by the *Covenant* game of Figure 2.8.

This game embeds the Figure 2.8 Prisoner's Dilemma into a larger game where either side can initially avoid an exchange with the other by shunning. An agent presumably consents only when she expects her partner to perform if he also consents. If the members of this community are matched with partners who might change over time in individual Covenant games played repeatedly over an indefinite time horizon, then they can follow equilibria where all perform in exchanges if all follow their required paths. For example, suppose ω_1 denotes the state where no community member has followed D over the previous two periods and ω_2 is the state where over the previous two periods at least one has offensively violated a covenant by following D. Then if all in the community follow the contingency strategy

$$h^*: P \text{ if the current state is } \omega_1, S \text{ if the current state is } \omega_2.$$

then they are at a path-observance strict equilibrium of the indefinitely repeated game on condition that each has a discount factor $\delta_i > \frac{\sqrt{5}-1}{2} \approx 0.618$.[71] This is a correlated equilibrium where the agents tie their acts in individual encounters to the possible worlds of the set $\Omega = \{\omega_1, \omega_2\}$ that are public events. The underlying idea of this all-follow-h^* equilibrium is that if anyone offensively violates in a given period, then no one is willing to enter into a covenant with anyone for the following two periods, but following this *punishment cycle*, all resume entering into and performing their parts of covenants until the next offensive violation. Any offensive violator suffers in terms of a lower overall payoff for deviating from the path defined by the equilibrium. The all-follow-h^* equilibrium is a *community enforcement convention* since the community members can follow a variety of

71. This follows from Proposition A3.3 of Appendix 3.

		Agent j		
		P	D	S
	P	$(1,1)$	$(-2,2)$	$(0,0)$
Agent i	D	$(2,-2)$	$(-1,-1)$	$(0,0)$
	S	$(0,0)$	$(0,0)$	$(0,0)$

P = perform, D = defect, S = shun

FIGURE 2.8 Covenant Game

other equilibria of the indefinitely repeated Covenant Game. I will discuss some of these alternatives further in Chapter 7.

In light of the motivating examples of this section, §2.2, and §2.3, I am now ready to state a general definition of convention. This definition is rooted in the idea that a convention is characterized by the reciprocal expectations that underwrite a discretionary-sense arbitrary equilibrium, and it accounts for conventions involving history-dependent strategies as well as simpler cases of pure and conflictual coordination. Here I state the definition in terms of the main necessary game-theoretic concepts somewhat informally. A more formal and technically detailed analysis is given in Appendix 1.

Definition. Given a community N of agents who can be matched in each period in a game Γ_t from the sequence of games or *supergame* (Γ_t), f is a *convention* if, and only if,

(C1) f defines a path-observance strict equilibrium of (Γ_t).
(C2) There is some strategy profile $f' \neq f$ such that f' also defines a path-observance strict equilibrium of (Γ_t).
(C3) (C1) and (C2) are common knowledge among the members of N.

If, in addition,

(C4) Each Agent $i \in N$ in fact expects the other agents in N to follow their parts of f.
(C5) (C4) is common knowledge among the members of N.

then f is the *incumbent convention* for the members of N.

(C1) is the requirement that f be a correlated equilibrium of the sequence of base games such that any Agent i expects to fare strictly worse by deviating unilaterally from the path of f. (C2) is the requirement that f be discretionary-sense arbitrary, that is, there is some alternative f' to f such that conforming to f' is also each agent's unique best response given that the other conform to f'. If (C4) obtains, then in fact each agent expects the others to follow *this* equilibrium of the supergame, rather than any of the alternative equilibria that are different available conventions. The common knowledge requirements (C4) and (C5) are to be understood in terms of an analysis of common knowledge similar to Lewis' analysis, where the hierarchy of epistemic claims that characterizes common knowledge forms a chain of implications rather than the actual steps in anyone's reasoning.[72] This specifics of this analysis of common knowledge are also summarized in Appendix 1.

As the repeated Prisoner's Dilemma and repeated Covenant game examples show, according to this definition it is possible for a convention to be characterized by equilibria of indefinitely repeated games even where the profile of actions this convention prescribes in a given interaction period is not an equilibrium of the base game. The conventions of these examples depend upon the *ex ante* history of acts the various members have followed. Certain refinements of this definition characterize previous and less general accounts of convention. A convention is *simple* if its equilibrium is a correlated equilibrium of the base game Γ_t for each t, regardless of what agents may have done in the past. In the Highway game of §2.3, the equilibria $(L,\dots,L)$ and $(R,\dots,R)$ of each base game where n_t motorists drive at each period t characterize simple conventions. A simple convention is *basic* when the agents involved always engage in exactly the same base game Γ at every period t. The various correlated equilibrium conventions of Hawk-Dove discussed above in §2.3 are examples of basic conventions. A simple convention f is a *Lewis-convention* if for each pair of agents $i, j \in N$, Agent j's expected payoff does not improve if Agent i deviates unilaterally from f, that is, f is a coordination equilibrium. The $(L,\dots,L)$ and $(R,\dots,R)$ conventions of the Highway game and the conventions of the Cell Phone and Battle of the Sexes games discussed in §2.2 are all examples of Lewis-conventions.

Two further important refinements summarize certain ways a convention can withstand at least some noncompliance. In an actual community, individual members might occasionally deviate from what an incumbent convention requires, possibly by mistake or to test the resolve of their fellow community members. Such "fallibility" of community members can be summarized as follows: For a strategy profile $f = (f_1,\dots,f_n)$, at each period t suppose each

72. Lewis (1969), p. 53, made it clear that this is how one is to interpret the hierarchy of epistemic claims in his analysis of common knowledge.

Agent i follows her part f_i with probability $1-\varepsilon_i$ and deviates from the path specified by f_i with probability ε_i. The *aberration probabilities* ε_i, $i \in N$, define mixed strategies for the agents in each base game. If $\varepsilon_i > 0$, then at any given period there is some positive chance that Agent i "slips" and deviates from what f requires her to do at this period. A convention $f = (f_1, \ldots, f_n)$ is *aberration stable* if for some $\varepsilon > 0$, following the mixed strategy in each base game defined by f and $\varepsilon_i = \varepsilon$ yields each Agent i a greater expected payoff than any strategy $g_i \neq f_i$ that has Agent i deviate from the path f_i specifies. A convention f is *self-correcting* if following a deviation from the path f requires at some period t by some Agent i, the agents will return to a sequence equivalent to that specified by f at period $t = 1$ provided there are no further deviations until the agents make this return. The property of being self-correcting is stronger than that of aberration stability, since a self-correcting convention actually "resets" itself to a path equivalent to that where no deviation took place. Simple conventions are always self-correcting because these conventions characterize strict equilibria of the base games. The h^* community enforcement convention of the indefinitely repeated Covenant Game is self-correcting, because if any agent deviates from the path where all follow P by following D at a given period, then all in the community, including the deviator, fare best by following S in each Covenant Game over the next two periods and then "starting over" by following P again as h^* requires on condition that each expects everyone to continue to follow h^* after the deviation.[73] The (Tr, Tr) convention of indefinitely repeated Prisoner's Dilemma is aberration stable but not self-correcting. For if one of the two agents deviates from the path $(P,P),(P,P),\ldots$ and follows D at some period T_0, then both agents will prefer to follow D for every period $t > T_0$ as Tr requires. But of course they can never resume the optimal path $(P,P),(P,P),\ldots$ because of the completely unforgiving character of Tr.

Conclusion

A satisfactory conventionalist analysis of justice requires a satisfactory analysis of convention. I have argued that many reject conventionalist justice proposals like the proposals Plato summarizes in the *Gorgias* and the *Republic* on the basis of an old and mistaken view that all conventions are indifference-sense arbitrary with respect to each other. It is true that in many social situations all of the possible associated conventions are indifference-sense arbitrary with respect to each other. I grant that these sorts of conventions have little to do with

73. As with the discount conditions for this equilibrium (see note 71), this follows from Proposition A3.3 of Appendix 3.

justice, since by definition the agents who desire to coordinate their behavior in such situations do not care which alternative convention they actually follow. Many of these conventions are the conventions of situations having a pure coordination game structure falling at one of the endpoints of Schelling's proposed game-theoretic continuum. But in a great many situations, the agents who hope to coordinate are not indifferent over which alternative convention they follow, and in many such situations the preferences the individual agents have over these alternatives come into conflict. Many conventions are the conventions of conflictual coordination game situations, so the notion of convention applies to a much larger part of Schelling's continuum than the pure coordination game endpoint. Agents will follow certain equilibria of such conflictual coordination games only given the right reciprocal expectations regarding their chosen strategies. So the corresponding conventions of these conflictual coordination problems have discretionary-sense arbitrariness, even if the agents involved care very much which alternative convention they follow.

The game-theoretic definition of convention given in this chapter is designed to capture all of the possible conflictual coordination conventions. The conventions available to the members of a community are differentiated by equilibria that are discretionary-sense arbitrary with respect to each other, but this in no way implies that all conventions of a given interaction need be equally good from the respective perspectives of the individual community members. In some settings, some of the available conventions might be equitable and others much to the advantage of some at the expense of others. Like the work of Lewis, and that of Hume before him, my analysis allows for conventions to be created deliberately, possibly by an edict or an explicit pact, but also allows for convention to emerge "spontaneously," so to speak, according to other sources of salience such as precedent or environmental clues. So one can explain the origins of conventions without falling into a vicious regress of the sort that Russell, Quine, and Alston feared. Indeed, the fact that agents can coordinate according to a wide variety of common background information is precisely what motivates the *correlated* equilibrium analysis of convention proposed here. As I have shown above, cases of conflictual coordination conventions range from basic conventions that can regulate how goods are distributed among claimants, as in the primogeniture and first finder conventions of Hawk-Dove, to the history-dependent conventions where individual agents might be tempted to exploit the good conduct of others in individual instances, such as the examples of path-observance strict equilibrium conventions of repeated Prisoner's Dilemma and Covenant games discussed above. In short, this definition is designed for analyzing the conventions of justice.

3 THE CIRCUMSTANCES OF JUSTICE

Reverse, in any considerable circumstance, the condition of men: Produce extreme abundance or extreme necessity: Implant in the human breast perfect moderation and humanity, or perfect rapaciousness and malice: By rendering justice totally *useless*, you thereby totally destroy its essence, and suspend its obligation upon mankind.

The common situation of society is a medium amidst all these extremes. We are naturally partial to ourselves, and to our friends; but are capable of learning the advantage resulting from a more equitable conduct. Few enjoyments are given us from the open and liberal hand of nature; but by art, labour, and industry, we can extract them in great abundance. Hence the ideas of property become necessary in civil society: Hence justice derives its usefulness to the public: And hence alone arises its merit and moral obligation.

—DAVID HUME, *An Enquiry Concerning the Principles of Morals*

Introduction

Justice, whatever it may be, presupposes a certain background context. David Hume, and Plato and Aristotle before him, recognized that unless parties are constrained by certain limiting conditions, one might doubt that justice can exist between these parties. These *Circumstances of Justice* are the set of conditions that give rise to the problems that are simultaneously problems of coordination and of conflict. In *A Theory of Justice*, John Rawls describes the Circumstances of Justice as "the normal conditions under which under which human cooperation is both possible and necessary."[1] In *Theories of Justice*, Brian Barry suggests that one might define justice as the terms of this cooperation given these circumstances.[2]

A *State of Nature* in Hobbes' political philosophy is a state of complete anarchy. According to Hobbes' classic analysis, the individuals in a State of Nature as he describes it inevitably fall into a war of all

1. Rawls (1971), p. 126.

2. Brian Barry, *Theories of Justice* (Berkeley: University of California Press, 1989), p. 148.

against all. Consequently, says Hobbes, there is no justice in a State of Nature: "To this warre of every man against every man, this also is consequent; that nothing can be Unjust. The notions of Right and Wrong, Justice and Injustice have there no place."[3] Plainly, Hobbes is another giant of political philosophy who explicitly argues that justice presupposes a certain context. For Hobbes, at least part of this context is to be in what he takes to be the only viable alternative to life in a State of Nature, which is life under the rule of a sovereign that wields virtually unlimited power over its subjects.[4]

The Circumstances of Justice and the Hobbesian State of Nature are two of the canonical building blocks of political philosophy. But a close look at these two building blocks leads to an unsettling surprise. The generally accepted account of the Circumstances of Justice given by authors such as H. L. A. Hart in *The Concept of Law* and John Rawls in *A Theory of Justice* closely resembles key parts of Hobbes' analysis of human nature and the background conditions of human interaction in general. In fact, careful study of Hobbes' analysis reveals that the people in a Hobbesian State of Nature are also in the Circumstances of Justice as described in this accepted account. How could people be in conditions in which justice is "both possible and necessary" if they are also doomed to a war of all against all that precludes justice?

This apparent anomaly motivates much of the analysis of this chapter. In §3.1, I review an account of the Circumstances of Justice that is attributed to Hume and that I maintain is the received account in the contemporary philosophical literature. Here I conclude that this *Standard Account* of the Circumstances of Justice is so widely accepted because its conditions typically do obtain between parties that restrain their own conduct according to "ordinary" norms of justice. But I also argue that this account raises serious questions that I address in subsequent sections. In §3.2, I argue that Hobbes' State of Nature is a situation where the circumstances of the Standard Account obtain and yet justice inevitably fails to exist. This shows that the Standard Account circumstances are not sufficient conditions for justice. In §3.3, I compare the Standard Account circumstances more closely with Hume's own presentation of the Circumstances of Justice and show that the Standard Account diverges significantly from Hume's account. I argue further in this section that the Standard Account circumstances are also not necessary conditions for justice. Having rejected the specifics of the Standard Account, in §3.4 I take another look at some specific examples of conflictual coordination games and threshold public goods games with an eye toward motivating another account of the Circumstances of Justice. Here I show that the essentials

3. *Leviathan* 13:13.

4. Hobbes gives one of his best statements of this conclusion in *Leviathan* 17:13.

of the Circumstances of Justice properly understood are captured by interactions as simple in structure as Braithwaite's Neighboring Musicians and Rousseau's Stag Hunt. In §3.5, I generalize from the examples of §3.4 and present an alternative set of conditions I call the *Generic Circumstances of Justice*. I argue that the Generic Circumstances are the necessary conditions for norms of justice to exist between parties. But I also conclude that the Generic Circumstances are in a certain sense not sufficient conditions for justice. The Generic Circumstances do not by themselves specify *which* norms serve as the norms of justice for a given community. Rather, they are a preamble, though a crucially important preamble, to any cogent answer to the question "What is justice?"

§3.1. The Standard Account

Philosophers long before Hume recognized that certain limiting conditions at least appear to be necessary conditions for justice. In Book II of *Republic*, Plato considers a condition similar to what below will be called rough equality when he has Glaucon present the fable of the Lydian shepherd who acquires the power of invisibility.[5] In *Politics*, just before he characterizes justice as the organization of a political community,[6] Aristotle also describes a condition similar to rough equality: "Anyone who cannot form a community with others, or who does not need to because he is self-sufficient, is no part of a city-state—he is either a beast or a god."[7] In *Leviathan*, Hobbes acknowledges a similar condition when he argues that men are by nature equal.[8]

However, more contemporary philosophers who discuss the Circumstances of Justice widely agree that David Hume presents the clearest and most complete analysis of these circumstances. They also agree in the main upon the specific set of conditions that constitutes the Circumstances of Justice that presumably emerge from Hume's analysis. For the remainder of this chapter, I will refer to these conditions as the Standard Account of the Circumstances of Justice.[9] Contemporary expositions of the Standard Account are based primarily upon Hume's discussion in Section 3.1 of *Enquiry*, which is more detailed and, on the surface, more systematic than the corresponding discussion

---

5. *Republic* 358e2–360d6. I discuss the fable of the Lydian shepherd at greater length in Chapter 7.

6. *Politics* 1253a37–38.

7. *Politics* 1253a28–30.

8. *Leviathan* 13:1, 3.

9. Similar expositions of the Standard Account are given by H. L. A. Hart, *The Concept of Law*, 3rd ed. (Oxford: Clarendon Press, 2012), ch. IX.2; Rawls (1971), §22; David Gauthier,

in *Treatise*.[10] According to the Standard Account, individuals or *parties* are in the Circumstances of Justice with respect to each other when the following conditions obtain:

(S1) *Moderate variable scarcity*. The goods that justice ordinarily regulates are neither so abundant that all parties can have as much as will satisfy all their wants and needs nor so easy to obtain that any party can acquire more without cooperating with others at some private cost. But the parties can produce more if they do cooperate. The goods are neither so scarce nor so hard to produce that more cannot be made available by joint effort. Co-opting a term David Gauthier coins in his analysis of bargaining, the parties are capable of producing a *cooperative surplus*.[11]

(S2) *Moderate selfishness*. Parties tend to prefer that their own needs and wants be satisfied, and they act so as to satisfy their needs and wants. They also tend to be unwilling to sacrifice the satisfaction of their own interests for the sake of satisfying the interests of others with whom they have no strong personal ties. However, parties do not generally care nothing for their fellows. Using Hart's terminology, the individuals capable of following a system of justice are neither perfectly mercenary *devils* nor perfectly altruistic *angels*.[12] In fact, they are intermediate between these two extremes and, in particular, are partial to having their own wants and needs satisfied.

(S3) *Rough equality*. All parties have limited and roughly equal powers, so that the plans of each can be thwarted by the others. Individuals may differ somewhat in their powers, which might include intellectual capacity, physical strength, and various possessions.[13] Yet no party can enforce its will on all using its own powers alone. Every party is vulnerable to attack or otherwise having its own attempts to carry out its plans blocked by the united efforts of some of the others. This condition implies that others can by combining their efforts deprive any individual of a share of the goods at stake.

Morals by Agreement (Oxford: Clarendon Press, 1986), ch. V, sec. 1.1; Barry (1989), §18; and D. Clayton Hubin, "The Scope of Justice," *Philosophy and Public Affairs* 9 (1979), pp. 3–24, especially pp. 6–7.

10. The most important passages in *Treatise* where Hume discusses the Circumstances of Justice appear in 3.3.2:15–18.

11. Gauthier (1986), p. 130.

12. Hart (1994), p. 196.

13. The Standard Account tacitly adopts a Hobbesian account of natural and instrumental power, which I discuss a bit further in §4.1.

Some authors add additional conditions to the list. Hume himself adds requirements that individuals are neither self-sufficient nor isolated from each other.[14] Rawls extends the list with certain facts regarding the diversity of individuals. Rawls notes that people have diverging conceptions of the good and plans for realizing these conceptions, and also a plurality of philosophical, religious, social, and political commitments. Rawls counts these facts as *subjective* Circumstances of Justice.[15] However, while these and the other extra conditions some have included on their lists help to clarify the Standard Account, they add nothing essential to it. For instance, Hume's interdependence requirement is implicit given moderate variable scarcity. Rough equality implies that parties can interact, for an isolated individual's activities cannot be thwarted by any others. Rawls' subjective Circumstances of Justice go far in explaining why the interests of individuals conflict to some extent. But that these interests do conflict is already implied by moderate variable scarcity and moderate selfishness.[16] In short, conditions (S1)–(S3) adequately summarize the Standard Account.

One point needs to be addressed in order to clarify the subsequent discussion. (S1)–(S3) are purportedly the background conditions of justice, but they are background conditions only. The Standard Account provides no direct answer to the all-important question "What is justice?" Still, one can infer that the Standard Account presupposes the following interrelated ideas: (1) Justice regulates the distribution of goods among a group of parties that need or want these goods, keeping in mind that the "goods" at stake can include some relief from burdens such as taxation or military service, and (2) justice requires individual parties to make contributions or sacrifices that enable other parties to receive greater shares of these goods. These assumptions seem unproblematic, and I think indeed philosophers generally regard the substance of (1) and (2) as uncontroversial. I will adopt these assumptions myself in my discussion of the Standard Account. However, in §3.5 I will argue that (1) and (2) are not sufficiently general to serve as background assumptions regarding the structure of interactions that can be regulated by norms of justice, and there I will propose an alternative that includes these assumptions as a special case.

The Standard Account might appear to be such a fine account of the background conditions for justice that this account requires little if any further

---

14. *Enquiry* 3.1:20.

15. See Rawls (1971), p. 127, and Lecture II, Section I of "Kantian Constructivism in Moral Theory," *Journal of Philosophy* 9 (1980), pp. 515–572, reprinted in *Collected Papers*, ed. Samuel Freeman (Cambridge, MA: Harvard University Press, 1999), pp. 303–358.

16. In fact, Rawls says that his summary of the Circumstances of Justice adds nothing essential to Hume's account, even though Hume does not explicitly mention Rawls' subjective circumstances. See Rawls (1971), pp. 127–128.

analysis. And in fact, I believe that with only a few notable exceptions over the past century, professional philosophers have in the main accepted the Standard Account as clearly correct.[17] I suspect the Standard Account has become the received account of the Circumstances of Justice because this account captures a large part of our actual experience of justice. The Standard Account describes conditions that typically obtain and that go far in accounting for why people usually comply with the ordinary requirements of justice, such as keeping promises and respecting property rights. If we imagine, as Hume invites us to, a world where any of the conditions of the Standard Account fail, we question the relevance of justice in this world. If we examine situations, such as famines or wars, where the conditions of the Standard Account come near to failing, we find that the parties in these situations tend to ignore the ordinary requirements of justice in their dealings with each other.

Nevertheless, upon closer examination the wide acceptance of the Standard Account is surprising on several counts. Hume uses the thought experiments and the case studies of Section 3.1 of *Enquiry* specifically to defend his claim that justice has value only when it serves the public interest. But the philosophers who adopt the Standard Account that is allegedly based upon Hume's *Enquiry* Section 3.1 discussion are not necessarily interested in proving or disproving Hume's claim that justice has no intrinsic value. Rather, they adopt this account as the set of conditions that presumably make justice both possible and necessary. In fact, I believe that it is by no means so clear in what sense the Standard Account describes Circumstances of Justice. Are (S1)–(S3) really necessary or sufficient conditions for justice to exist between parties? Or are they both or neither? Hume bases his own theory of justice in large part upon his account of convention with an eye to explaining property rights. I have claimed that the Standard Account attributed to Hume is the received account of the Circumstances of Justice. Yet Hume's theory of justice is plainly not the received theory of justice. Does the Standard Account fit neatly into *any* theory of justice? Moreover, Section 3.1 of *Enquiry* gives clear textual evidence that Hume would not accept all of the particulars of the Standard Account. Yet contemporary expositors claim to be merely following Hume's analysis in their summaries of the Standard Account. Should one accept the Standard Account if this account is not even faithful to the supposedly classic statement of the Circumstances of Justice?

These are serious questions. Below I will try to answer these questions and to show that the answers contain good reasons for rejecting some of the specifics

17. Some of these exceptions include C. D. Broad, *Five Types of Ethical Theory* (Oxford: Clarendon Press, 1930), ch. IV; Hubin (1979); and Jonathan Harrison, *Hume's Theory of Justice* (Oxford: Clarendon Press, 1981), especially "Epilogue: Justice in the *Enquiry* Section III." I will discuss their objections to the Standard Account in §3.3.

of the Standard Account and insights useful for constructing a more satisfactory alternative set of Circumstances of Justice. However, first I will examine the problem raised at the start of this chapter. The Standard Account attributed to Hume purportedly describes the conditions where justice is in some sense "possible and necessary." Yet Hobbes' classic analysis of life in a State of Nature bears striking similarities to the Standard Account, and according to this analysis, in a State of Nature justice is not possible!

§3.2. The Standard Account Meets *Leviathan*

In various works, but most famously in *Leviathan*, Thomas Hobbes concludes that individuals in their *natural condition* or State of Nature will fall into war with each other,[18] even though he also insists that reason requires individuals to seek peace whenever they can hope to achieve peace.[19] Hobbes' conclusion might seem even more surprising on the surface given that he characterizes a State of Nature simply as a state where individuals are at liberty to treat each other as they please, being free both from a common power that can effectively restrict their conduct and from antecedent obligations with respect to each other.[20] Hobbes also concludes as a corollary that there can be no justice between people who remain in a Hobbesian State of Nature.[21] I will employ elements of Hobbes' celebrated argument for the inevitability of war between people who find themselves in their natural condition in my own analysis of interaction in anarchy in Chapter 4. For the present discussion it is important to note that Hobbes bases this argument upon certain characteristics he attributes to people in general as parts of his account of human nature. Gregory Kavka summarizes six of these characteristics in his fine analysis of Hobbes' argument. I repeat Kavka's summary together with supporting citations from *Leviathan*:[22]

1. *Egoism*. Individuals are primarily concerned with their own well-being, and act accordingly. (*Leviathan* 11:1, 14:8)

---

18. *Elements of Law I* 14:12, *De Cive* 1:12, *Leviathan* 13:8.

19. *Elements of Law I* 14:14, *De Cive* 2:2, *Leviathan* 14:3.

20. *De Cive* 8.1, *Leviathan* 13:8, 17:1, 31:1.

21. *Leviathan* 13:13, 15:3.

22. Kavka (1986), pp. 33–34. Most of these supporting citations are Kavka's. Kavka also gives a similar list of human characteristics in an earlier critical study of Hobbes' argument for the inevitability of war between people in a State of Nature. See Gregory Kavka, "Hobbes's War of All Against All," *Ethics* 93 (1983): 292–293.

2. *Death aversion*. Individuals are strongly averse to their own death, and act accordingly. (*Leviathan* 11:4, 13:9, 14)
3. *Concern for Reputation*. Individuals care about their reputations, about what others think about them, and they act accordingly. (*Leviathan* 13:7)
4. *Forward lookingness*. Individuals care about their future (as well as present) well-being, and act accordingly. (*Leviathan* 11:2)
5. *Conflicting Desires*. Satisfaction of one person's desires often interferes with, or precludes, satisfaction of another person's. This may result from material scarcity, opposed claims to the same particular objects, incompatible ideals or values, competing aspirations for domination or preeminence, and so on. (*Leviathan* 13:3)
6. *Rough Equality*. People are fairly equal in their intellectual and bodily powers. They are equal enough, in any case, that each is vulnerable to death at the hands of others. (*Leviathan* 13:1–2)

These six characteristics are fully compatible with the conditions of the Standard Account of the Circumstances of Justice. Indeed, the conflicting desires, egoism, and rough equality conditions of this list closely resemble the conditions (S1)–(S3) that summarize the Standard Account. Moreover, nothing in the Standard Account precludes the parties being in a Hobbesian State of Nature with respect to each other. Evidently, Hobbes' classic analysis of life for people in their natural condition exposes a deficiency in the Standard Account. People could be in the circumstances of the Standard Account with respect to each other, but if they are also in a Hobbesian State of Nature with respect to each other, then according to Hobbes they are doomed to a war of all against all that blocks the possibility that justice exists between them.

Hobbes makes it clear that the State of Nature is a state of extreme scarcity because people caught in this state cannot hope to work productively either separately or together, not because natural resources are in short supply.[23] In other words, people in the Hobbesian State of Nature are in conditions of moderate variable scarcity. A number of "proof texts" in *The Elements of Law, De Cive*, and *Leviathan* appear to confirm the old stereotype that Hobbes is a psychological egoist.[24] But several major contemporary studies of Hobbes' *Leviathan* project, including especially studies by Bernard Gert, Francis McNeilly, Jean Hampton, and Gregory Kavka, cast doubt upon the stereotype.[25] The authors

23. *Leviathan* 13:3, 9.

24. For examples, see *Elements of Law I* 9:10, 12:6, *De Cive* 1:1, 10, 13, 6:4, and *Leviathan* 14:8, 15:16, 27:8.

25. Bernard Gert, "Hobbes and Psychological Egoism," *Journal of the History of Ideas* 27 (1967), pp. 503–520; Francis S. McNeilly, *The Anatomy of* Leviathan (London: Macmillan,

of these studies argue that the occasional passages in which Hobbes appears to endorse psychological egoism in *Leviathan* do not agree with other, more representative texts in which Hobbes suggests that he really espouses a less egoistic view of human nature. More to the point, they argue persuasively that even if Hobbes is occasionally paying lip service to the doctrine of psychological egoism, he does not use this doctrine as a premise in his main arguments.[26] I concur with Hampton and Kavka that in his main arguments Hobbes can and in fact does rely upon a view of humans as largely but not exclusively self-regarding.[27] One can summarize the psychological premises that Hobbes actually employs in his main arguments with a doctrine Kavka calls *predominant egoism*. According to predominant egoism, the self-interested motives of most people usually take precedence over their non-self-interested motives, especially when these motives conflict.[28] Predominant egoism is compatible with what seems manifestly the case, namely, that most people act selflessly some of the time and some saintly people act selflessly a great deal of the time. Hobbes' overall argument does not require an assumption that people are perfectly selfish devils. In fact, the doctrine of predominant egoism would make a good alternative statement of the moderate selfishness condition of the Standard Account.

So the conditions of the Standard Account obtain between people in their natural condition. What are the implications for the Standard Account? Hobbes would say that his analysis of the State of Nature shows that the Standard Account is obviously incomplete. Hobbes could even characterize the central project of *The Elements of Law, De Cive*, and *Leviathan* as his demonstration that a crucial circumstance of justice, one that Hume fails to acknowledge in his analysis in Section 3.1 of *Enquiry*, is that the parties live in a civil society under the rule of an

---

1968), §5.9; Hampton (1986), §1.3; Kavka (1986), §2.3. Gert, McNeilly, and Hampton argue that Hobbes is not a psychological egoist, at least not in *Leviathan*, surface appearances to the contrary. Kavka concludes that Hobbes' commitment to psychological egoism is at best ambiguous.

26. Moreover, it is not certain that Hobbes is paying such lip service to psychological egoism. A number of commentators argue that since Hobbes' definition of a person's good is simply what that person desires, maybe nothing in principle in Hobbes' theory blocks the possibility that sometimes a person's good is to procure some benefit for someone else. See *Leviathan* 6:7.

27. Hampton (1986), p. 24; Kavka (1986), pp. 33–34, 50. Kavka (1986), pp. 44–51, concludes that there is textual evidence on both sides of the claim that Hobbes really believed in psychological egoism, even though Kavka agrees with Gert and McNeilly that Hobbes does not really make use of psychological egoism in his main arguments against anarchy.

28. Kavka (1986), p. 50, argues that Hobbes relies upon predominant egoism to develop his main argument against anarchy, despite Hobbes' ambiguous commitment to psychological egoism.

absolute sovereign rather than in their natural condition. Hobbes' conclusion that a State of Nature must result in a war of all against all has become a cornerstone of modern political philosophy. Any philosopher who would defend a form of social order other than a state must confront Hobbes' analysis of the State of Nature. Hobbes' defense of his bleak conclusion has been reconstructed and analyzed many times over. Many accept some reconstructed version of Hobbes' argument as clearly sound. Many others who reject Hobbes' argument admit that Hobbes was right in his conclusion. In Chapter 4 I will argue that Hobbes' argument is inconclusive, but that an alternate argument based upon Hobbes' assumptions summarized above vindicates his conclusion. Like Kavka, who defends a reconstruction of Hobbes' argument, I find Hobbes' analysis all the more remarkable because, with the exception of egoism, Hobbes' assumptions regarding human nature in this argument are so mundane.[29] Moreover, we have already seen that the predominant egoism Hobbes actually uses in his argument amounts to the moderate selfishness of the Standard Account. Those who accept the Standard Account can rightly say that characteristics such as concern for reputation and forward-lookingness are not part of this account, at least not explicitly. But again, Hobbes' assumptions are ordinary, undeniable facts of human life. Even if they go beyond the assumptions of the Standard Account, this presents no difficulty for anyone who mounts a Hobbesian criticism of the Standard Account.

§3.3. The Standard Account Meets Hume's Account

The §3.2 analysis shows that the Standard Account definitely does not give sufficient conditions for justice to exist between rational parties. Are conditions (S1)–(S3) at least necessary conditions of justice? I believe (S1)–(S3) might serve as necessary conditions for justice if one accepts Hume's rather unusual account of justice as coextensive with a system of rules that regulate property rights. But (S1)–(S3) do not serve so well for other accounts of justice. As some others have noticed, the conditions of the Standard Account can fail in some settings where justice seems especially necessary. One might conclude that Hume tailors his presentation of the Circumstances of Justice to fit his own theory of justice, and consequently want to reject or at least seriously amend Hume's presentation. However, I would like to suggest another possibility more charitable to Hume, if not to some of Hume's recent interpreters. Here I will argue that the Standard Account departs from Hume's own presentation in important ways. I believe that Hume's presentation fits our intuitions regarding justice better than does the Standard Account. Putting the point another way, one can read Hume as giving

29. See Kavka (1986), p. 33.

an account of the Circumstances of Justice meant for use in developing any cogent theory of justice. On this reading, some of the contemporary discussions of the circumstances may be projecting Hume's own theory of justice into the Standard Account.

Hume maintains that the survivors of a shipwreck are perfectly reasonable to forget about who owned the ship's cargo before the wreck and to use this cargo to sustain themselves for as long as they can. Hume argues that in a besieged town, people cannot be blamed for breaking into granaries and sharing out the grain among themselves long before they are starving, no matter who owned the grain before the siege began. Hume uses these examples to support his claim that justice serves no purpose under conditions of severe scarcity.[30] But some object, arguing that justice can certainly play an important role when the goods at stake are extremely scarce. If the survivors of a shipwreck have only a single biscuit left for food, they might very well divide the biscuit equally or draw lots for it. C. D. Broad rightly observes that we would applaud equal division or a fair lottery as being just and disapprove of a mad scramble for the biscuit.[31] Hume himself suggests that in a famine, people should share what little bread they have *equally*. Hume's *Enquiry* analysis establishes only that the ordinary rules of property are suspended when people suffer a catastrophe and must ration what little they still have. When Hume says that justice is useless in such unhappy circumstances, he is referring to his own account of justice as the ordinary rules of property. But *moderate* scarcity is not a prerequisite for justice more generally conceived.

Moderate selfishness is also not a prerequisite for justice. If the parties who must interact are perfectly selfish devils, then they surely need justice, not only to ensure that they get shares of the goods they want, but also to avoid the costly struggle they can expect in the absence of justice.[32] Hume uses his own Farmer's Dilemma example in *Treatise* to illustrate how economic exchange requires parties to keep their promises, and Hume explicitly says that the corn farmers in this example have no kind motives for each other. On the other hand, completely unselfish parties can also have a need for justice. A simple variant of Broad's example illustrates the point: If the survivors of a shipwreck are all perfectly selfless angels, then each will be tempted to leave all of what little food they have for the others. But if each angel yields to temptation completely, all will starve, even though each angel is acting so as to prevent the others from starving. Knowing this, the angels

30. *Enquiry* 3:1–8.

31. See Broad (1930), pp. 95–98. In their analyses of the Standard Account, Hubin (1979), pp. 9–10, and Harrison (1981), pp. 265–266, make similar points.

32. Hubin (1981), p. 10, raises a similar point in his discussion of *Enquiry* 3.1:9. Unlike me, Hubin interprets Hume's "society of ruffians" as referring to a society of perfectly selfish people.

need to divide the food so that all get shares, even though this requires each of them to yield somewhat to the wishes of the others. What is necessary for justice is not moderate selfishness but a moderate conflict of interests. These interests can be completely selfish, utterly selfless, or somewhere in between.

Interestingly, Hume's texts suggest that he does not think that moderate selfishness is what is needed for justice to serve a purpose. When he argues that people who all care as much for the welfare of others as each cares for her own welfare have no use for justice, Hume is not speaking of perfectly selfless people.[33] Rather, Hume is arguing justice is useless for people who are perfect *utilitarians* and, consequently, have no biased interests favoring any particular people. Such perfect utilitarians might need some rules for coordinating their practices so that they maximize happiness, but they would not need justice because their interests never conflict.[34] No one would mind giving up any share for the sake of another if by doing so she would increase aggregate happiness. In game-theoretic parlance, such people do not need justice because they are in a pure coordination game. In *Treatise*, Hume argues that if people "persu'd their own interest, without any precaution, they would run headlong into every kind of injustice and violence."[35] According to Hume's *Treatise* analysis, *unrestrained* selfishness is an impediment to justice, not selfishness itself. When Hume argues that justice becomes useless if one falls "into the society of ruffians," he has in mind individuals who are perfectly malicious, not perfectly selfish.[36] Justice cannot exist between perfectly malicious people because their interests are in complete conflict. These people are caught in a zero-sum game in which anyone's gains are the others' losses.

What of the rough equality condition of the Standard Account? At first blush, this condition seems both especially plausible and somewhat appealing, in that it seems to repudiate the view, embraced by Plato and Aristotle, that some classes of people are naturally inferior to others. However, as several authors argue forcefully, upon closer scrutiny this rough equality condition leads to conclusions that actually run opposite to our intuitions regarding justice.[37] We normally think that justice is especially necessary in cases where some are tempted to take

---

33. *Enquiry* 3.1:6.

34. Harrison's discussion of moderate selfishness is somewhat similar to mine. Harrison argues that a society of perfectly benevolent people would still need rules for coordinating their benevolence. Unlike me, Harrison thinks that such coordinating rules would be rules of justice. See Harrison (1981), pp. 266–267.

35. *Treatise* 3.3.2:21.

36. *Enquiry* 3.1:9.

37. See especially Barry (1989), pp. 162–163; Barry, *Justice as Impartiality* (Oxford: Oxford University Press 1995), pp. 41–43; and Allen Buchanan, "Justice as Reciprocity Versus

advantage of others who cannot effectively resist. What is justice for, if not to protect the helpless from exploitation? We tend to believe that people are owed the benefits of justice because they are rational beings, who have their own plans of life that no one should obstruct arbitrarily. Indeed, many argue that to be a person is to be such a rational being. To be sure, if a being is simply incapable of exercising powers of rationality, this being is liable to also be incapable of resisting the aggressions of other beings who *can* exercise powers of rationality. But we tend to regard this helplessness as a *by-product* of lacking rationality. Perhaps only rational beings are owed justice, but we tend to believe it is their rationality itself and not the relative power rationality gives them that is why they are owed justice. How any account of justice addresses the powerless members of society says a great deal regarding the plausibility of this account, and this issue will be central in the discussion in Chapter 8. For now, I reemphasize that the rough equality of the Standard Account simply does not mesh with our everyday beliefs regarding the purpose of justice.

There is a further problem with the rough equality condition of the Standard Account: It is not Hume's rough equality condition. In one of his thought experiments in Section 3.1 of *Enquiry*, Hume argues that if humans lived together with a race of rational creatures who were so comparatively weak, both in body and in mind, that they could never effectively resist humans, then no justice would exist between the humans and the members of this other race.[38] The plot of a Rod Serling story originally presented on the television anthology series *The Twilight Zone* illustrates Hume's thought experiment: Two Earth astronauts, Fletcher and Craig, land their disabled spacecraft on a planet inhabited by people the size of Earth ants. Fletcher works hard at repairing their ship. Meanwhile, Craig starts ordering the natives to provide him with water, food, and entertainment, and terrorizes them into obeying by killing some of them by simply stepping on them. When Fletcher discovers Craig's conduct, he tries to protect the natives. But when he has finished repairing the craft, Fletcher is unable to persuade Craig to leave the planet with him. Unwilling either to harm Craig or to remain marooned, Fletcher reluctantly leaves. Craig then proclaims himself the god of this planet, and the native people have no choice but to worship him and live as his slaves, or else more will die under his boot. This part of Serling's story "The Little People" shows that the rough equality condition of the Standard Account does not accurately reflect Hume's discussion in *Enquiry*. According to Hume's thought experiment, as soon as Craig and Fletcher arrived on the

---

Subject-Centered Justice," *Philosophy and Public Affairs* 19 (1990), pp. 227–253. I discuss Barry's and Buchanan's views regarding exploitation of the vulnerable further in Chapter 8.

38. *Enquiry* 3.1:18.

scene no justice could exist between them and the now helpless native people. However, on the Standard Account, the two astronauts and the natives remained in the Circumstances of Justice *until Fletcher left*. True, the natives were utterly at the astronauts' mercy. But Fletcher together with the natives could restrain Craig's conduct, even though the natives could not add any relatively appreciable amount of force to Fletcher's efforts against Craig.[39]

Interestingly, Hume's discussion of rough equality looks on the surface like something of an afterthought. Hume gives no explicit discussion of rough equality when he discusses the Circumstances of Justice in *Treatise*. And in Section 3.1 of *Enquiry*, in the particularly fine pair of summary paragraphs quoted above in the epigraph to this chapter, Hume reviews his argument and reiterates his main conclusion before he has mentioned anything like rough equality.[40] When Hume does eventually discuss significant asymmetries in relative power, he is simply giving an alternative argument for a point he believes he has already established: Justice exists only because the restraints on conduct that justice requires serve the interests of all parties involved. Still, Hume was right to recognize both that something like rough equality is a circumstance distinct from the circumstances he discusses regarding scarcity and human motivation and that people tend to disregard justice when dealing with beings they regard as their inferiors.

In fact, Hume's analysis in *Enquiry* makes much better intuitive sense than the rough equality condition of the Standard Account. If one accepts rough equality as stated in the Standard Account, then this condition places no clear limits on what creatures can be counted as parties in the Circumstances of Justice. Suppose that on the planet featured in "The Little People," the native people coexisted with "little squirrels" and "little frogs," two species whose members also lived under conditions of moderate scarcity and showed at most limited altruism toward their fellow species members. Then these "little squirrels" and "little frogs" were technically parties along with the native people according to the Standard Account so long as each Earth astronaut remained to restrain the other, even if they were so relatively tiny that the Earth astronauts remained unaware of their existence. Philosophers have traditionally accepted both Aristotle's view that human beings are the only creatures capable of perceiving justice and Epicurus' related view that there can be no justice between humans and nonhuman creatures.[41] A recent body of philosophical work challenges the latter traditional

39. Serling's story ends with the natives freed after a pair of even larger aliens visit the planet and crush Craig to death by accident!

40. *Enquiry* 3.1:12–13.

41. See *Politics* 1253a15–18 and *Principal Doctrines* XXXII.

position in interesting ways.[42] I will consider the possibility that the scope of justice extends beyond humans and human institutions at more length in Chapter 8. But while I do not wish merely to assume the traditional position here, I will agree with Hume that at least some nonhuman species fall outside the scope of justice.[43] This assumption does not commit me to supposing that any sort of maltreatment of creatures such as squirrels or frogs is a matter of moral indifference. Similarly, Hume does not think that if humans were to coexist with a race of relatively weak beings like the tiny beings in "The Little People" then the humans should think they have license to maltreat these weaker beings, since he expressly maintains that "we should be bound, by the laws of humanity, to give gentle usage to these creatures."[44] Still, the point remains that the Standard Account gives no clear guidelines for establishing the proper scope of the applicability of justice.

The actual idea that Hume's thought experiment conveys is that for justice to exist between parties, every proper subset of the parties can, when they unite, have some restraining effect on any individual party in the complement subset. This implies that each party can by her own actions hinder to *some* extent any other party's attempts to claim all the goods that that party desires. Such parties are necessarily rational, as Hume explicitly requires. Furthermore, even if some groups are relatively powerless against other groups, they can remain in the Circumstances of Justice as Hume describes them, because each individual in a weaker group can restrain any individual in a stronger group at least somewhat. This explains how Hume can consistently maintain that the invading "civilized EUROPEANS" were wrong to think themselves outside the Circumstances of Justice with respect to the "barbarous INDIANS" native to North America.[45] In Hume's time, Native North Americans may have been powerless against the united might of the better-armed invading Europeans, but an individual Native North American could appreciably restrain any one of these invading Europeans, just as an individual invading European could appreciably restrain any Native North American.

---

42. See especially Martha Nussbaum's *Frontiers of Justice* (Cambridge, MA: Harvard University Press, 2007).

43. *Enquiry* 3:1:19.

44. *Enquiry* 3.1:18.

45. *Enquiry* 3.1:19. Here Hume says that Europeans in general, including himself, were on account of their "great superiority" over Native Americans *tempted* to regard themselves outside the Circumstances of Justice with respect to the Native Americans. This admittedly falls short of a point-blank declaration that the Europeans were mistaken, and in fact Barry claims Hume is here trying to shy away from the full implications of his own account of the Circumstances of Justice (1989, p. 162). But I think reading Hume here as hinting the Europeans really were mistaken makes sense given the interpretation of Hume's account of rough equality proposed here.

Pure strategy Nash equilibrium cells darkly shaded, mutual modesty outcome lightly shaded.

		Party 2	
		M	G
Party 1	M	(η_1, η_2)	(β_1, α_2)
	G	(α_1, β_2)	$(0, 0)$

M = modest (claim none), G = greedy (claim all)

$\alpha_i > \beta_i > 0, \alpha_i > \eta_i, \; i \in \{1, 2\}$

FIGURE 3.1 2×2 Conflictual Coordination Game

§3.4. Playing Instruments and Hunting Stags

Fair Division Problems

In his Cambridge lecture, Richard Braithwaite presented a specific impure coordination problem in order to motivate his original method for resolving problems of fair division. As discussed in §1.1, Braithwaite's coordination problem has two agents, Matthew and Luke, who have a conflict over a limited resource, in this case time for playing one's instrument uninterrupted. Figure 3.1 summarizes a family of 2-agent conflictual coordination games that characterize situations like Matthew and Luke's predicament.

In any game summarized by the Figure 3.1 matrix for specific values of the parameters α_i, β_i, and η_i, $i \in \{1,2\}$, each party can follow either of two extreme options that are the pure strategies: be *greedy* (G) and claim all of the resource at hand, or be *modest* (M) and claim none. Figure 3.1 summarizes the simplest nontrivial class of conflictual coordination games, where there are only two parties, each having only two pure strategies. Nevertheless, the Figure 3.1 matrix characterizes quite a rich variety of conflictual coordination games, some of which will by now be familiar. If $\beta_1 > \eta_1$ and $\beta_2 > \eta_2$, then the game is an impure coordination game. Schelling's Parachutists game of Figure 1.7 and Braithwaite's Neighboring Musicians game of Figure 1.9 are specific instances of such "backward Battle of the Sexes" games, and the Braithwaite game is a backward Battle of the Sexes with nontrivial payoff asymmetries. If $\eta_1 > \beta_1$ and $\eta_2 > \beta_2$, then the corresponding Figure 3.1 game has a Hawk-Dove structure. The Figure 2.5 game is such a Hawk-Dove game with a symmetric payoff structure. Any game having the Figure 3.1 payoff structure has three Nash equilibria, namely, (G, M), which is Party 1's ideal point in the entire game; (M, G), which is Party 2's ideal point in the entire game; and the mixed Nash equilibrium $\left(\sigma_1^*, \sigma_2^*\right)$, where Party 1's and

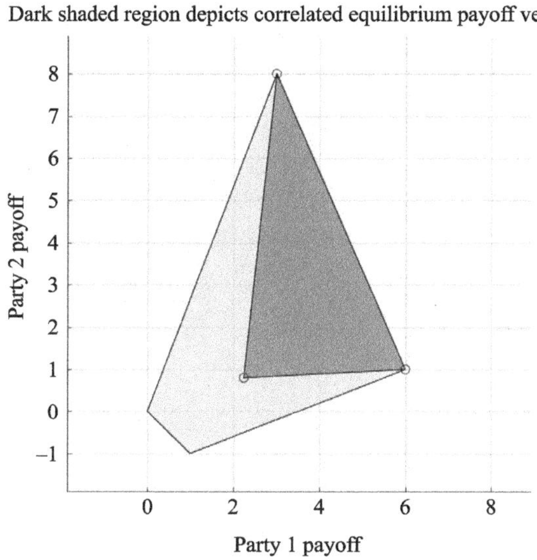

FIGURE 3.2 Correlated Equilibrium Payoff Vectors of Braithwaite Game

Party 2's respective mixed strategies are $\sigma_1^* = \frac{\beta_2}{\alpha_2+\beta_2-\eta_2}\cdot D \oplus \frac{\alpha_2-\eta_2}{\alpha_2+\beta_2-\eta_2}\cdot H$ and $\sigma_2^* = \frac{\beta_1}{\alpha_1+\beta_1-\eta_1}\cdot D \oplus \frac{\alpha_1-\eta_1}{\alpha_1+\beta_1-\eta_1}\cdot H$.[46] Any such game also has a large set of perfectly correlated equilibria that are characterized by various probability distributions over (G,M), (M,G), and (σ_1^*,σ_2^*). Figure 3.2 depicts the set of payoff vectors of the perfectly correlated equilibria of the Figure 1.9 Braithwaite game. And for cases where the payoffs η_1 and η_2 of the mutual modesty outcome (M,M) are sufficiently great relative to the β_1 and β_2 payoffs that are respectively Party 1's and Party 2's worst efficient equilibrium payoffs, then the corresponding Figure 3.1 game also has partially correlated equilibria with payoff vectors that lie outside the set of the perfectly correlated equilibrium payoff vectors. Figure 3.3 depicts the set of payoff vectors of the perfectly correlated equilibria of the Figure 2.5 Hawk-Dove game.

Braithwaite analyzes the asymmetric conflictual coordination game that summarizes his Neighboring Musicians problem with Luke in the Party 1 position and Matthew in the Party 2 position using the theory of bargaining developed by

46. At this mixed Nash equilibrium Party 1's and Party 2's expected payoffs are given by

$$E_i\left(u_i\left(\sigma_1^*,\sigma_2^*\right)\right) = \frac{\alpha_i\beta_i}{\alpha_i+\beta_i-\eta_i},\ i \in \{1,2\}.$$

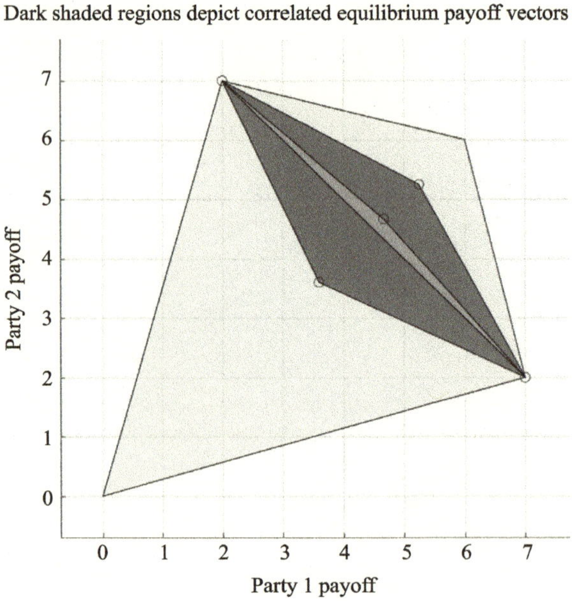

FIGURE 3.3 Correlated Equilibrium Payoff Vectors of Hawk-Dove Game

John Nash.[47] Luke and Matthew can claim fractions of the available playing time. Their claims are *compatible* if, when combined, they do not exceed the available amount of playing time. Each of the musicians gets the share he claims if their claims are compatible, and otherwise both get nothing. Nash argued that one can analyze any bargaining problem either from the perspective of a rational arbiter, who employs certain axioms to determine a fair division of the resource between the parties, or from the perspective of the parties themselves, who try to resolve the problem via some bargaining process.[48] Braithwaite takes the axiomatic approach. He defends a procedure that divides the resource so that, following a special rescaling of their respective payoffs, Luke and Matthew follow an alternation scheme between Luke's ideal outcome (G,M) and Matthew's ideal outcome (M,G) where the two achieve equal relative gains from their respective payoffs at the *nonagreement point* (G,G).[49]

Not everyone agrees with Braithwaite's favored solution to a two-player bargaining problem. In fact, Nash proposed a solution in his original analysis of the

47. John Nash, "The Bargaining Problem," in Nash (1996), pp. 1–8, and "Two-Person Cooperative Games," in Nash (1996), pp. 34–46.

48. Nash (1996), pp. 34–46.

49. I discuss Braithwaite's specific solution further in §5.2.

bargaining problem that yields a result for the Braithwaite game quite different from that of Braithwaite's solution. The bargaining problem will reappear in various places in this book, especially in Chapter 5 and Chapter 8, but the relative merits of axiomatic solutions are not crucial to the analysis of this section. What are crucial are the structure of the underlying game and two properties that any outcome of this game must possess in order to merit serious consideration as a just resolution of the game. I couch this discussion in terms of Braithwaite's game, but the specific properties of this game and its equilibria illustrate more general properties of the conflictual coordination games that summarize fair division problems and their equilibria. Regarding Matthew and Luke, each can affect both his own payoff and the payoff the other receives by changing his strategy. They have this kind of interdependence because their game has multiple strict equilibria. Since their preferences over the strict equilibria conflict, in order to coordinate either Luke must give in completely, Matthew must give in completely, or both must give in to a certain extent. I will assume that for any outcome of their division problem to be considered a just outcome, the following conditions must be satisfied: (1) Each must prefer to follow this outcome if the other follows this outcome, and (2) each must receive a positive share of the good at stake. Condition (1) is the requirement that the resolution of the division problem be an equilibrium outcome. Condition (2) says that each must give in to the other to some extent, and in particular neither is to give in completely to the other.

Can Luke and Matthew settle upon such an outcome? They can, by following a correlated equilibrium equivalent to their alternating between their respective ideal points (G,M) and (M,G) with some positive probability each. A simple contingency strategy system that characterizes such a correlated equilibrium is for Luke and Matthew to observe their landlord each morning toss a coin and then at the hour available for playing follow (G,M) if the coin landed heads up that morning and (M,G) if the coin landed tails up that morning. If the landlord uses a coin that lands heads up with probability $\lambda \in [0,1]$, then Matthew and Luke alternate between (G,M) and (M,G) with respective probabilities λ and $1-\lambda$. For each value of $\lambda \in [0,1]$, this contingency strategy system defines a strict and perfectly correlated equilibrium of the Figure 1.9 game, so condition (1) is satisfied. But to allow $\lambda \in [0,1]$ is to allow too much. If the landlord were to use a trick coin that lands heads up with probability $\lambda = 0$ or $\lambda = 1$, then the resulting contingency strategy system would have Luke and Matthew follow (M,G) all of the time if $\lambda = 0$ and (G,M) all of the time if $\lambda = 1$. Both of these strategy systems are still technically correlated equilibria, but they characterize the two strict Nash equilibria of the Figure 1.9 game where either Luke or Matthew receives none of the resource at stake. However, if the coin-toss probabilities are such that $\lambda \in (0,1)$, then Matthew and Luke each receive positive shares of the resource, and each sacrifices some fraction of the resource he would like to claim, thereby allowing the other to receive a larger share. So for $\lambda \in (0,1)$, both condition (1) and condition (2) are satisfied. Moreover, such a coin-toss equilibrium yields both Matthew and Luke greater payoffs than they receive at the nonagreement point where neither gives in. This example illustrates the following general point regarding fair division problems: In order for the distribution to be just, whatever mechanism is used to assign the agents their shares must characterize a correlated equilibrium of the corresponding conflictual coordination game different from any one of the agents' various ideal points.

I framed the discussion of necessary conditions for a just outcome in the Braithwaite game using some of the terminology of axiomatic bargaining theory. This terminology illuminates certain crucial aspects of the structure of the Braithwaite game, and of course the above discussion dovetails with Braithwaite's own analysis of this game in terms of axiomatic bargaining theory. But the vocabulary of bargaining theory is not necessary for analyzing candidates for just resolutions of conflictual coordination games in general. Moreover, the candidates for such just resolutions need not always be limited to perfectly correlated equilibria consisting of alternation schemes over the agents' alternative favorite Nash equilibria. The Figure 2.5 Hawk-Dove game is a conflictual coordination game of the Figure 3.1 matrix form with $\alpha_i = 7$, $\beta_i = 2$, and $\eta_i = 6$, $i \in \{1,2\}$. In this game, any perfectly correlated equilibrium where the two parties alternate between the strict Nash equilibria (G, M) with probability $\lambda \in (0,1)$ and (M, G) with probability $1-\lambda$ is a candidate just resolution for this conflictual coordination game. But this game also has many partially correlated equilibria that can also be candidate just resolutions. One such partially correlated equilibrium characterizes the first finder convention discussed in §2.3. At this equilibrium the parties alternate between (G, M), (M, G), and (M, M) with probability $\frac{1}{3}$ each. This first finder equilibrium effectively enables each party to follow her most preferred outcome some of the time because her partner yields to her interests to some extent, and as discussed in §2.3, the overall expected payoff vector of this equilibrium Pareto dominates the payoff vector of the perfectly correlated equilibrium where the parties alternate between (G, M) and (M, G) with probability $\frac{1}{2}$ each.

If one expands the set of pure strategies available to the parties, then it is even possible for agents to have candidate just resolution equilibria that are constructed using none of the game's Nash equilibria.[50] Figure 3.4 summarizes

50. My thanks to Brian Kogelmann for alerting me to this possibility and suggesting that a correlated equilibrium of the 3×3 game in Aumann (1974, pp. 72–73) that is summarized in

Pure strategy Nash equilibrium cell darkly shaded, cells contributing to partially correlated equilibrium lightly shaded.

		Party 2		
		M	G	S
	M	$(6,6)^{\omega_0}$	$(2,7)^{\omega_2}$	$(0,3)$
Party 1	G	$(7,2)^{\omega_1}$	$(0,0)$	$(0,3)$
	S	$(3,0)$	$(3,0)$	$(3,3)$

M = modest (claim none), G = greedy (claim all)

S = opt out

FIGURE 3.4 Hawk-Dove with Opt-Out Option

a conflictual coordination game where each party has three pure strategies. This game is somewhat similar to the Covenant game of Figure 2.8 that extends a 2-agent Prisoner's Dilemma with a preliminary "opt-out" option. One can think of the Figure 3.4 game as embedding a Hawk-Dove game in a larger Assurance-like game where each party's "safe" strategy is to opt out (S) and the pure strategies M and G predicated on trying to enter into the Hawk-Dove subgame are both risky and potentially better in terms of expected payoff than the safe strategy. But this game may not seem obviously a conflictual coordination game since neither of the parties' respective ideal points is a Nash equilibrium. This game has one Nash equilibrium in pure strategies, namely, (A, A), and two other Nash equilibria in

---

Figure 3.A illustrates this phenomenon. Aumann showed that the Figure 3.A game has a partially correlated equilibrium where the two agents follow (M,M), (G,M), and (M,G) with probability $\frac{1}{3}$ each, even though these strategy profiles include no Nash equilibria.

		Party 2		
		M	S	G
	M	$(6,6)$	$(0,0)$	$(2,7)$
Party 1	S	$(0,0)$	$(4,4)$	$(3,0)$
	G	$(7,2)$	$(0,3)$	$(0,0)$

FIGURE 3.A Aumann's Extended Hawk-Dove

mixed strategies.[51] The parties also have a variety of strict correlated equilibria available to them where each achieves her favorite outcome with positive probability. Some of these equilibria are of the form

$$f_x(\omega)=\begin{cases}(G,M) \text{ if } \omega=\omega_1\\(M,G) \text{ if } \omega=\omega_2\\(M,M) \text{ if } \omega=\omega_0\end{cases}.$$

where the parties have common knowledge that (i) Party 1's and Party 2's respective information partitions over the possible worlds $\Omega=\{\omega_0,\omega_1,\omega_2\}$ are $\mathcal{H}_1 = \{\{\omega_1\},\{\omega_0,\omega_2\}\}$ and $\mathcal{H}_2 = \{\{\omega_2\},\{\omega_0,\omega_1\}\}$, and (ii) their prior probabilities over the possible worlds of Ω are such that both believe ω_0 occurs with probability $\frac{1}{3}$, ω_1 occurs with probability x, and ω_2 occurs with probability $\frac{2}{3}-x$ where $x\in\left(\frac{1}{6},\frac{1}{2}\right)$. These partially correlated equilibria are of course quite similar to the first finder equilibrium of the ordinary Figure 2.5 Hawk-Dove game discussed in §2.3. At such an f_x equilibrium, the parties achieve an overall expected payoff vector of $\left(\frac{10}{3}+5x,\frac{20}{3}-5x\right)$.[52] And their preferences over these f_x equilibria diverge according to the value of x. In fact, while there are more correlated equilibria of the Figure 3.4 game than the set of f_x equilibria, no strict correlated equilibrium of this game is the most preferred equilibrium for both parties.[53] So this game is indeed a conflictual coordination game, with many distinct candidate just resolution equilibria.

Threshold Public Good Problems

Braithwaite was specifically interested in the problem of assigning shares of a divisible good fairly. Rousseau's Stag Hunt problem motivates a game-theoretic model

---

51. These Nash equilibria are $\boldsymbol{\sigma}_1^*=(\sigma_1^*,\sigma_1^*)$ where $\sigma_1^*=\frac{2}{3}M\oplus\frac{1}{3}G$ and $\boldsymbol{\sigma}_2^*=(\sigma_2^*,\sigma_2^*)$ where $\sigma_2^*=\frac{3}{7}M\oplus\frac{3}{14}G\oplus\frac{5}{14}A$.

52. For $x\in\left(\frac{4}{15},\frac{6}{15}\right)$, this expected payoff vector Pareto dominates the payoff vectors of all three Nash equilibria.

53. The elementary computations that establish these claims are similar to those in §2.3 that establish the first finder strategy system f, defined in that section as a strict partially correlated equilibrium of the Figure 2.5 Hawk-Dove game.

Pure strategy Nash equilibrium cells shaded.

		Party 2	
		P	D
Party 1	P	(V_1, V_2)	$(-c_1, \beta_2)$
	D	$(\beta_1, -c_2)$	$(0, 0)$

P = contribute, D = defect

$V_i = \alpha_i - c_i > \beta_i \geq 0,\ c_i > 0,\ i \in \{1, 2\}$

FIGURE 3.5 2-Party Threshold Public Good Game

of a somewhat different kind of problem that can involve requirements of justice. The Figure 3.5 game generalizes the Stag Hunt model of Rousseau's problem presented in §1.3 for the special case where there are two hunters. The Figure 3.5 game is equivalent to a game where each Party i can guarantee herself a payoff of at least 1 by following D, thereby avoiding a cost $c_i > 0$ of contributing, and if both parties contribute, then each achieves a payoff of $1 + V_i$ where $V_i = \alpha_i - c_i \geq \beta_i \geq 0$ and β_i reflects any additional payoff Party i might achieve by defecting when the other party contributes.[54] The Stag Hunt of Figure 1.11 is equivalent to an instance of the Figure 3.5 game where for each Party i, $V_i = \frac{1}{2}$ and $\beta_i = 0$, so that $c_i = 1$ and $\alpha_i = \frac{3}{2}$. In general, in any game with the Figure 3.5 payoff structure the (P, P) equilibrium is the best outcome for both parties. However, each party runs a risk of arriving at her worst outcome in the game if she contributes. Moreover, each party might by following the safe strategy D secure for herself her own best expected payoff by effectively lowering her counterpart's payoff. If, say, Party 1 defects because her conjecture ascribes low probability that Party 2 will contribute and in fact Party 2 *does* contribute, then Party 1 improves her own expected payoff by effectively worsening her partner's payoff. In this case Party 1 defects in order to gain the guaranteed minimum payoff she nets by avoiding her contribution cost. This is her Bayesian rational choice given her conjecture. But her choice then results in her partner absorbing his contribution cost and gaining nothing in return, his worst outcome in the game. The parties might try to establish reciprocal expectations that together they will generate the public good by exchanging promises to contribute. And if they do exchange such promises and

54. The Figure 3.5 game is obtained from the described game simply by subtracting the constant 1 that is also the minimum guaranteed payoff for each Party i from each outcome of the described game.

one of them defects in the end, the contributor who kept her promise is liable to accuse the defector of having committed an injustice against her.

As I discussed in Chapter 1, David Hume and Mancur Olson after him argued that in the absence of some sort of enforcement mechanism, a public good tends to be less well supplied as the number of potential contributors increases. Correspondingly, to commit an injustice by breaking one's promise to contribute to a multiparty public good problem might appear ever more tempting as the number of parties who make such promises increases, in part because in many cases these parties might be able to achieve the public good even if not all of them keep their promises to contribute. Figures 3.6 and 3.7 summarize two generalized 3-party threshold public good problems. As in the 2-party games with the Figure 3.5 payoff structure, in 3-party games with the Figure 3.6 and Figure 3.7 payoff structures each Party i sustains a contribution cost $c_i > 0$ if she follows P, and they can achieve a public good worth $\alpha_i > \beta_i + c_i$ to Party i apart from her contribution cost if sufficiently many of them follow P. For a game with Figure 3.6 payoff structure, the parties generate the public good only if all three contribute. This is a

Pure strategy Nash equilibrium cells shaded.

P	P	D
P	(V_1, V_2, V_3)	$(-c_1, \beta_2, -c_3)$
D	$(\beta_1, -c_2, -c_3)$	$(\beta_1, \beta_2, -c_2)$

D	P	D
P	$(-c_1, -c_2, \beta_3)$	$(-c_1, \beta_2, \beta_3)$
D	$(\beta_1, -c_2, \beta_3)$	$(0, 0, 0)$

P = contribute, D = defect

$V_i = \alpha_i - c_i > \beta_i \geq 0,\ c_i > 0,\ i \in \{1, 2, 3\}$

FIGURE 3.6 3-Party Public Good Problem, Threshold $T = 3$

Pure strategy Nash equilibrium cells darkly shaded, mutual contribution outcome lightly shaded.

P	P	D
P	(V_1, V_2, V_3)	(V_1, α_2, V_3)
D	(α_1, V_2, V_3)	$(\beta_1, \beta_2, -c_3)$

D	P	D
P	(V_1, V_2, α_3)	$(-c_1, \beta_2, \beta_3)$
D	$(\beta_1, -c_2, \beta_3)$	$(0, 0, 0)$

P = contribute, D = defect

$V_i = \alpha_i - c_i > \beta_i \geq 0,\ c_i > 0,\ i \in \{1, 2, 3\}$

FIGURE 3.7 3-Party Public Good Problem, Threshold $T = 2$

3-party version of Rousseau's Stag Hunt and the *participation threshold* is $T = 3$. If all three exchange promises to contribute, then this might raise their expectations that each will indeed follow P, and if one or more keep their promise and one or more of the others in the end defect, the contributors can accuse the defectors of injustice. As in a 2-party Figure 3.5 game, in such a 3-party game a defector takes advantage of any contributors because the defector guarantees herself a certain minimum payoff by allowing her contributing counterparts to fall into their worst outcomes of the entire game.

In a Figure 3.7 game, only two parties need to cooperate in order to generate the public good, so the participation threshold is $T = 2$. The Three-in-a-Boat game of Figure 1.12 is equivalent to an instance of this threshold public good problem with $\alpha_i = \frac{5}{2}$, $\beta_i = 0$, and $c_i = 1$ for each Party i. If all three in a game having a Figure 3.7 structure promise to contribute, then each Party i might be tempted to break her own promise for two reasons. Breaking her word ensures she gains the guaranteed minimum payoff of defection. And only two of them need to keep their word in order for them to generate the public good. If they do in fact exchange promises to contribute, each knows that she and her partners are all capable of taking advantage of the others' trust by free-riding. Injustice might possibly "pay," in that one might be able to profit from others' good conduct by breaking one's own promise to cooperate. Interestingly, in all of these threshold public good games a party can possibly take advantage of the others by following her maximin strategy. The injustice of breaking one's promise to contribute in such situations amounts to playing it safe.

Given that (P,P,P) is not an equilibrium of the Three-in-a-Boat game, one might think there is little hope that if all three promise each other to contribute in one such game that they would all keep their word, as justice requires. But if the three engage in this game indefinitely often, they can follow some history-dependent strategy that defines an equilibrium of this indefinitely repeated game where all three contribute at each engagement. For example, if each of the three parties follows the strategy

$f^{(k)}$: Follow P at the first period, then follow P unless some party has deviated from the profile (P,P,P) over any of the immediately past k periods, and otherwise follow D,

then for sufficiently high discount factors $f^{[k]} = \left(f^{(k)}, f^{(k)}, f^{(k)}\right)$ is a path-observance strict correlated equilibrium. Since the three parties could also follow another path-observance correlated equilibrium of the indefinitely repeated Three-in-a-Boat game where they alternate between the strict Nash equilibria (D,P,P), (P,D,P), and (P,P,D) over successive periods, $f^{[k]}$ is a convention. One can think of $f^{[k]}$ as a "blinking" equilibrium since if any party deviates from the required sequence of repetitions of (P,P,P) where each keeps her promise to contribute, all three then defect for a punishment cycle of length k periods. Consequently, the system "blinks" to the suboptimal (D,D,D) equilibrium outcome during the punishment cycle outcome no matter who might have taken advantage of the others' contributions by breaking her promise to contribute. Both the "blinking" equilibrium and the "taking turns" equilibrium characterize conventions that require each party to refrain from following her own ideal outcome where she defects and the others contribute all of the time.

§3.5. An Alternative Account

At this point, I am ready to generalize from the above examples and propose a set of conditions that I contend are necessary background conditions for justice. As I did in the definition of conventions given in Chapter 2, here I will use game-theoretic vocabulary to define these Generic Circumstances of Justice. The members of a set $N = \{1,\ldots,n\}$ of parties are in the Generic Circumstances of Justice with respect to each other when their interaction is summarized by a game Γ such that the following obtain:

(G1) *Baseline outcomes.* Γ has a set of outcomes Ψ defined as follows: For each Party i there is at least one strategy profile $\underline{s}_{ij} = \left(s'_{1j},\ldots,s'_{i-1j},\underline{s}_{ij},s'_{i+1j},\ldots,s'_{nj}\right)$ of Γ that Party i ranks higher according to her preferences than the other parties rank $\underline{s}_{ij}$ according to their preferences. Ψ is the set of strategy profiles of the form $\underline{s}_k = \left(\underline{s}_{1j_1},\ldots,\underline{s}_{nj_n}\right)$ where each Party i tries to follow her end of one of these $\underline{s}_{ij}$ profiles.

(G2) *Cooperative surplus outcomes.* Γ has a set of outcomes Ξ such that (i) each outcome $\xi \in \Xi$ is strictly Pareto-superior to the outcomes of Ψ, that is, all of the parties of N strictly prefer ξ over each $\underline{s}_k \in \Psi$, and (ii) the parties of N do not all have the same preferences over all the outcomes of Ξ.

(G3) *Reciprocal expectations.* The parties of N have common knowledge that for some $\Xi_0 \subseteq \Xi$ with more than a single element, for each $\xi \in \Xi_0$, parties when active can follow strategies $f_{\xi i}$, $i \in N$, such that $f_\xi = \left(f_{\xi 1},\ldots,f_{\xi n}\right)$ is a path-observant strict correlated equilibrium with equilibrium path equivalent to ξ.

The Generic Circumstances summarize the structure of any social interaction that could be regulated by a norm, or set of norms, such that one who violates any these norms is liable to be accused of committing an injustice. The underlying game of the Generic Circumstances could be as simple as the Braithwaite game or a 2-party Stag Hunt game, where two parties each begin with only two pure strategies and try to find a rule for selecting an outcome that would work for them even if they engage in this game only once. Or the game could be very much more complicated, with many players who move at different times and whose chosen moves can depend upon the history of past play. What matters is that (i) the game that characterizes the relevant social interactions lies somewhere in between the pure conflict and pure coordination endpoints of Schelling's spectrum outlined in *The Strategy of Conflict* and (ii) one runs some risk of suffering an outcome one especially wants to avoid if one tries to follow a mutually beneficial equilibrium and some of the others let one down by failing to follow their parts of this equilibrium.

Like the Standard Account circumstances, the Generic Circumstances are also obviously defined with reference to some community of parties. Who or what can count as parties? As the language used in Generic Circumstances suggests, paradigmatic parties are individual human persons, who can make choices that affect themselves and others. However, I do not want to foreclose the possibility that parties could be other sorts of entities. For example, these circumstances might be applicable in principle to nations, in a manner analogous to the manner in which Hobbes claims heads of state are in a State of Nature with respect to one another.[55] To be sure, if certain corporate or nonhuman entities can be counted as parties in the Generic Circumstances, then one needs to supply some account of what it means for these entities to have relevant preferences and common knowledge.[56] I do not pursue these issues in depth here. But I reiterate that in principle, the parties in the Generic Circumstances could be corporate or nonhuman entities as well as individual human persons.

(G1) and (G2) together make precise how the parties in the Generic Circumstances have interests in common, but only imperfectly in common. The conflict of interests implied by these conditions is a conflict over preferences only. This conflict is compatible with the parties being perfectly selfish, moderately selfish, and completely unselfish. (G2) reflects the idea that the parties can by coordinating their efforts produce a cooperative surplus, although parties might not all

---

55. *Leviathan* 13:12.

56. For corporate entities one would obviously need to rephrase the Generic Circumstances without the gendered language I have used for convenience. Also, according to certain proposed analyses of personhood, some members of some nonhuman species might count as persons. I discuss nonhuman species somewhat further in Chapter 8.

agree which possible cooperative surplus is most desirable. (G1) reflects the idea that it is also possible for each party to achieve some outcome from which she derives some relative benefit for herself at the expense of others. The 2-party and 3-party threshold public good games of §3.4 illustrate (G1) and (G2), since the parties can generate a cooperative surplus if all contribute, but each might gain at the others' expense by defecting when the others contribute. If there is only one such pure strategy profile for each Party i where Party i can achieve a relative benefit at the expense of others, then the baseline or "free-for-all" strategy profile that results if each party tries to gain at the expense of the others corresponds roughly to the nonagreement point of a bargaining problem like that of Braithwaite's neighboring musician game or to Hobbes' State of Nature war. In the 2-party and 3-party threshold public good games of §3.4, the free-for-all strategy profiles are those where every party defects. (G3) reflects the idea that the parties are at least in principle capable of following one of a number of correlated equilibria that are better for all than falling into some state like the Hobbesian war where no one restrains her own conduct for mutual benefit. Given how I have defined conventions in Chapter 2, (G3) says that the parties have available to them a set of conventions that are not all indifference-sense arbitrary with respect to each other, and each of which is better for all than a free-for-all outcome. Not all such conventions need be strictly optimal. In the indefinitely repeated Three-in-a-Boat game, the blinking equilibrium is not strictly optimal. Three parties who follow the blinking equilibrium could still generate their public good at a different equilibrium that is strictly optimal such as the taking-turns equilibrium, which releases one of them from contributing at each period.

In many cases of special interest, some of the outcomes over which the parties' preferences conflict are also the most preferred outcomes of particular individual parties. These are cases of fair division, where one expects a just resolution to share out the benefits of interaction so that all parties receive more than each would receive by giving in completely to the preferences of others. I summarize these *Generic Circumstances with Division* as follows:

(D1) *Ideal and baseline outcomes.* For each Party i of N, an *i-ideal outcome* is a strategy profile $\left(M_{1j},\ldots,M_{i-1j},G_{ij},M_{i+1j},\ldots,M_{nj}\right)$ of Γ that Party i ranks highest according to her preferences. Ψ is the set of strategy profiles of the form $\boldsymbol{G}_k^* = (G_{1j_1},\ldots,G_{nj_n})$ where each Party i tries to follow an i-ideal outcome.
(D2) *Cooperative surplus outcomes.* Γ has a set of outcomes Ξ with more than a single element such that (i) each outcome $\xi \in \Xi$ is strictly Pareto superior to the outcomes of Ψ, and (ii) no outcome of Ξ is an i-ideal outcome for any Party i of N.
(D3) *Reciprocal expectations.* The parties of N have common knowledge that each active party can follow at least one strategy f_i that is her end of a strict

correlated equilibrium $f = (f_1, \ldots, f_n)$ of Γ that is equivalent to a cooperative surplus outcome $\xi \in \Xi$.

Conditions (D1), (D2), and (D3) are special cases of (G1), (G2), and (G3), respectively, and reflect the idea that parties in the Generic Circumstances with Division are engaged in a conflictual coordination game. The equilibria of (D3) characterize simple conventions of the underlying conflictual coordination game. The Braithwaite game illustrates (D1), (D2), and (D3) where Luke's and Matthew's respective ideal outcomes are (G,M) and (M,G), (G,G) is their baseline outcome, and candidate norms of justice include perfectly correlated equilibria of the form $\lambda \cdot (M,G) \oplus (1-\lambda) \cdot (G,M)$, $\lambda \in (0,1)$. The extended Hawk-Dove game of Figure 3.4 also illustrates (D1), (D2), and (D3) where (G,G) is the baseline outcome, (G,M) and (M,G) are Party 1's and Party 2's respective ideal outcomes, and some of the candidate norms of justice are partially correlated equilibria where the parties follow all three of (M,M), (G,M), and (M,G) with positive probability.

The Generic Circumstances with Division refine the conditions of the Standard Account. (D1), (D2), and (D3) reflect the "innocent" assumptions of the Standard Account mentioned in §3.1, namely, that justice regulates the distribution of some set of goods and minimally requires all parties to yield to some extent to the wishes of the others in order to achieve mutual overall benefit. The Generic Circumstances (G1), (G2), and (G3) reflect these assumptions of the Standard Account as well, but they also allow for cases where all parties can achieve their best outcomes by together following certain requirements of justice. The strictly optimal (P,P) conventions of 2-agent Figure 3.5 Stag Hunt games illustrate this phenomenon, since in any of these games any equilibrium of the form $\lambda \cdot (P,P) \oplus (1-\lambda) \cdot (D,D)$ for $0 < \lambda \le 1$ characterizes a convention better for each side than the free-for-all outcome (D,D), but the (P,P) convention requires the parties to follow the ideal point for them both.[57] This example also illustrates how the Generic Circumstances (G1), (G2), and (G3) summarize the background conditions for ordinary norms of justice such as norms of promise keeping as well as norms of fair division. For this reason, the Generic Circumstances (G1), (G2), and (G3) can fit neatly into a variety of different theories of justice. For instance, the Generic Circumstances could underwrite theories in the impartial spectator tradition of Adam Smith, such as John Harsanyi's utilitarian theory or

57. For each Party i,

$$E_i\left(u_i\left(\lambda \cdot (P,P) \oplus (1-\lambda) \cdot (D,D)\right)\right) = V_i \cdot \lambda > 0 = E_i\left(u_i(D,D)\right).$$

This is why such a 2-agent Stag Hunt game can satisfy (G3).

John Rawls' more egalitarian theory, or theories in the Hobbesian contractarian tradition, such as David Gauthier's and Gregory Kavka's theories, or of course Hume's theory and theories inspired by Hume, such as Robert Sugden's and Brian Skyrms' evolutionary theories and Ken Binmore's theory that combines elements of evolution and rational choice.

The Generic Circumstances refer in several places to *active* parties, suggesting that some of the parties might in some sense be inactive at least some of the time. I make this qualification in order that the Generic Circumstances will cohere with widely held views regarding justice in an important way that the Standard Account does not. I have already noted that the Generic Circumstances with Division include a certain "self-sacrificing" condition, stated explicitly as part (ii) of the mutual expectations condition (D2). The (G1) condition of the more general Generic Circumstances also implies a pair of conditions of reciprocal restraint:

(G1A) *Interdependence I.* Each Party *i* can, when Party *i* is to act, follow a strategy that prevents some other parties who are to receive payoffs from receiving their highest possible payoffs.
(G1B) *Interdependence II.* For each Party *i*, there is at least one other active Party *j* that can follow a strategy such that when Party *j* is to act, Party *j* prevents Party *i* from receiving Party *i*'s highest possible payoff.

Interdependence I and II replace the rough equality condition of the Standard Account. These two conditions allow for the possibility that some parties are active at different times and some receive their payoffs at different times. As noted in §3.3, rough equality in the Standard Account evidently implies that people who are especially vulnerable fall outside the scope of justice. In particular, the very young, the very aged, the severely ill, and the severely disabled all seem to fall outside justice given the Standard Account. The interdependence conditions (G1A) and (G1B) open the door to the inclusion of vulnerable persons within the scope of justice. Interdependence I requires only that each party can have some influence over the prospects of some of the others during the times that she can exercise her powers of rationality. So long as anyone, even a severely disabled person, can refuse to cooperate with others sometime during his life, she inconveniences them and thus affects their prospects. This of course implies that the class of parties counted as active parties is very wide indeed, since I have included no predetermined minimum amount of time a party must be able to restrain others to any extent in order to be counted active. Interdependence II implies that no party is ever immune from some restraint by any other parties. This implies that a party might be prevented from exploiting other parties currently unable to protect themselves by *third parties* who are capable of exercising some restraining force.

So, unlike the circumstances of the Standard Account, the generic account circumstances do not necessarily limit justice to parties capable of forcing others to promote their own interests via their own might. The reciprocal restraining conditions outlined in the previous paragraph allow for a wider scope of justice that can include parties who might be unable to enforce others' compliance with requirements of justice themselves. One can even construct conflictual coordination games that explicitly model the times when parties are completely helpless using *overlapping generations models*. In these games, equilibria can exist that require the active parties to give positive shares of the goods at stake to the parties who are helpless. I will discuss such overlapping generations models further in an examination of the complex issue of how justice applies to vulnerable parties in Chapter 8. However, here I reiterate that the relative restraining power that parties have and that are described by the Interdependence I and Interdependence II conditions is a by-product of their being able to exercise their powers of rationality during some parts of their lives. The Generic Circumstances do not assume that relative power is the ultimate reason parties are owed justice. The Generic Circumstances do assume that parties can under ordinary circumstances lay claim to shares of the goods at stake, as can any person seeking justice. When a party exercises the restraining power of the interdependence condition, this party claims a share, and receives the claim to the degree that others concede. The others can refuse to concede at all, but the party can still prevent them from receiving everything they would have received in the absence of this party's claim.[58]

Conclusion

In this chapter I have examined the necessary background conditions for justice in a given society. I have agreed with the prevailing view among contemporary philosophers that David Hume presented an especially clear and cogent analysis of these Circumstances of Justice. But I have taken issue with large parts of the Standard Account of these circumstances so widely accepted and so commonly attributed to Hume. The alternative Generic Circumstances of Justice I have proposed are inspired partly by Hume's analysis and partly by an examination of Hobbes' account of the State of Nature, a situation where the conditions of the

58. As Peter Lewis pointed out to me, without the implicit assumption that parties deliberately claim shares when they restrain others according to the Interdependence I and Interdependence II conditions, one might think that nonhuman creatures such as insects and even inanimate entities such as hurricanes would fall within the scope of the Generic Circumstances simply because these entities can interfere with the lives of people. I will discuss the question of justice toward nonhuman creatures further in Chapter 8.

Standard Account obtain and yet the parties involved can expect no justice. The idea I have tried to capture in outlining the Generic Circumstances of Justice is that parties have the right background conditions for justice when (i) they have available to them a variety of conventions over which their preferences differ to some extent, (ii) they can by working together generate a cooperative surplus characterized by some of these conventions, but (iii) each is also vulnerable to being taken advantage of by others who aim for outcomes better for themselves that result in their fellow parties suffering relative losses. As a very important special case, I proposed Generic Circumstances with Division to capture the background conditions of distributive justice. Parties are in these more specialized circumstances when they have available to them multiple simple conventions that are better for all than a free-for-all outcome, where each tries to follow her part of an outcome ideal for herself and none of these conventions is an ideal outcome for any party. The Generic Circumstances with Division reflect the idea that distributive justice typically requires parties to restrain their own claims somewhat in order that other parties can enjoy greater benefits.

I have claimed here that the Generic Circumstances are necessary conditions for justice. Are they sufficient conditions? Plainly, they are not. The Generic Circumstances are background conditions that effectively set certain formal constraints upon norms of justice. Such norms must characterize equilibria of the underlying games, so that parties have good reason to follow them given the right expectations. Specifically, these norms must be conventions. These conventions must lead all to an outcome better for all than a free-for-all outcome, and they must not allow any individual parties to benefit too much at the expense of others, since otherwise they could not plausibly be considered the conventions of justice. But the fact that parties in the Generic Circumstances have such mutually beneficial conventions available to them by no means implies that they actually follow any such conventions. Such parties might be in the Generic Circumstances and not have the requisite reciprocal expectations that would render a candidate norm for justice the norm that characterizes their incumbent convention. Indeed, such parties might end up in a free-for-all outcome of no restraint, even though they have common knowledge that they have available to them alternatives better for them all.

Moreover, not just any equilibrium satisfying the formal constraints implied by the Generic Circumstances need be a *just* equilibrium. An incumbent convention might satisfy these formal constraints and yet still be quite unfavorable for some parties, so much so that more favored parties open themselves to mockery when they claim the status quo is just. As the Generic Circumstances themselves suggest, a satisfactory theory of justice requires some account of equilibrium refinement or selection that will pick out specific sets of norms as satisfactory the norms of justice. I will apply one approach to equilibrium selection, an *inductive learning* approach, to explore the origins of equilibria regarded as fair conventions of certain bargaining problems in Chapter 5. But in my opinion there is still no fully satisfactory theory for picking out the just equilibria for all bargaining problems. And a bargaining problem as Nash defines it is but one of a very large family of interactions where the parties involved are in the Circumstances of Justice as defined here, and a relatively simple such problem in its structure at that. To be sure, I certainly do not think that giving a proper definition of the class of equilibria that are a society's norms of justice is a hopeless task. As I will argue in Chapter 8, the key to giving such a definition will be providing equilibrium refinement or selection criteria that do not import ad hoc a preexisting theory of justice. But specifying the Circumstances of Justice is really just the first move beyond defining conventions toward analyzing justice in conventionalist terms.

4 THE DYNAMICS OF ANARCHY

You have the same propension, that I have, in favor of what is contiguous above what is remote. You are, therefore, naturally carry'd to commit acts of injustice as well as I. Your example both pushes me forward in this way by imitation, and also affords me a new reason for any breach of equity, by showing me, that I shou'd be the cully of my integrity, if I alone shou'd impose on myself a severe restraint amidst the licentiousness of others.

—DAVID HUME, *A Treatise of Human Nature*

Introduction

In Chapter 3, I used Thomas Hobbes' analysis of life in the natural condition of mankind or State of Nature to criticize one account of the circumstances of justice. There I claimed that a State of Nature as Hobbes describes it is a state where the circumstances of justice obtain according to what I have called the Standard Account, and yet in this state there can be no justice. But this claim of course presupposes that Hobbes is correct to conclude that justice is necessarily absent in a State of Nature. And not everyone believes that Hobbes is correct. John Locke, for one, argues that people in a State of Nature are obliged to obey a law of nature requiring them to treat one another with some restraint. So evidently Locke thinks that some form of justice can obtain in a State of Nature. Whose position is the correct position?

The State of Nature has become one of the cornerstone concepts of political philosophy, even though some of the great figures who introduced this concept, including Locke and Hobbes, differed somewhat over exactly what a State of Nature might be. What political philosophers, including Hobbes and Locke, do generally grant is that a community of individuals living in anarchy are in a State of Nature.[1] In this chapter I will take a closer look at anarchy, understood as a condition where individuals lack an effective government that in particular can, by using its own resources, including possibly coercive

1. The descriptive discussion of anarchy in this chapter should be clearly distinguished from certain forms of political anarchism whose adherents believe that some form of government might be morally acceptable on condition that such a government avoids the use of coercive force.

force, restrain their conduct. My analysis here will be descriptive in character. I will be trying to answer this question: What is the likely outcome of life in anarchy? The right answer to this question will, of course, be of crucial importance to those who would raise normative challenges against the rule of states. As Christopher Morris argues forcefully in his fine work *An Essay on the Modern State*, the fact that practically all of the Earth's population currently lives under the rule of some state should not lull political philosophers into concluding that acceptable social life necessarily presupposes life under the rule of a state.[2] In *A Cooperative Species*, Samuel Bowles and Herbert Gintis point out that for at least 95% of the time biologically modern humans have lived on earth, they have lived without governments of the sort Hobbes thought were necessary for any sort of viable social order.[3] If people in modern times could live peaceably in anarchy, then governments capable of wielding coercive force might be an unnecessary evil. My own interest in analyzing anarchy is closely related to those concerned with justifying or challenging the rule of states. I wish to determine whether or not individuals in anarchy are in the Generic Circumstances of Justice as I have defined these circumstances in Chapter 3. Put another way, my analysis here is motivated by this question: Does strategic justice presuppose some enduring social institutions, such as states, that restrict the freedoms of individuals, possibly via coercive force?

Descriptive analyses of anarchy have become a staple of political philosophy since Hobbes' and Locke's great works on the State of Nature. Authors inspired by Hobbes' and Locke's works have followed their lead and given primarily a priori analyses of anarchy. These authors have tried to demonstrate that some social outcome such as a war or a peace is bound to occur in anarchy as the result of the decisions the individuals in anarchy are sure to make once they surmise their situation. I regard the arguments in this tradition as static in character, because they assume that the individuals in anarchy decide once and for all how they respond given that they are in anarchy. I believe that while some of these a priori analyses have much to teach us, a different and more dynamically oriented analysis of anarchy is needed. In §4.3 I present such a dynamical analysis of anarchy using a game-theoretic *Variable Anticipation Threshold* model.[4] Previous game-theoretic models of anarchy are static in the sense I have just described. Models

2. Christopher Morris, *An Essay on the Modern State* (Cambridge: Cambridge University Press, 1998).

3. Bowles and Gintis (2011), p. 110.

4. I first presented the Variable Anticipation Threshold model of State of Nature interaction in "War or Peace? A Dynamical Analysis of Anarchy," *Economics and Philosophy* 22 (2006), pp. 243–279 (henceforth Vanderschraaf 2006b).

of this sort produce a deterministic prediction of anarchy's outcome via a priori analysis. In §4.1 I review Hobbes' and Locke's alternative analyses of anarchy and the static Prisoner's Dilemma and Stag Hunt models of State of Nature interaction previous authors have introduced that are based upon Hobbes' and Locke's divergent conclusions. In §4.2 I set the stage for the §4.3 analysis by discussing two such static models that allow for the possibility that different behavioral types of individuals are present in anarchy. I argue that once one incorporates such behavioral diversity into the analysis, any conclusions one might draw from the use of such static models will rest upon unrealistic assumptions regarding the agents' common knowledge of their situation. However, a model of anarchy that incorporates alternative types of agents can be developed as a dynamical model, one that assumes no common knowledge in anarchy. In the Variable Anticipation Threshold model of §4.3, individuals modify their behavior dynamically as they learn from repeated interactions. I present specific instances of this model in which the dynamical systems that characterize the beliefs of the individuals in anarchy converge to different equilibria corresponding to either peace or war, depending on the initial conditions. One striking finding presented here is that individuals are liable to converge to Hobbes' war of all against all even if only a small percentage of them actually prefer to exploit others' cooperation. The presence of only a few "nasty" individuals gradually drives all, including those inclined to be "nicer," to imitate the "nasty" conduct of these few. This dynamical analysis suggests that the Hobbesian war in anarchy is indeed inevitable in most realistic circumstances. In short, I vindicate Hobbes' conclusion with a quite un-Hobbesian analysis.

§4.1. Two Accounts of Anarchy

Given the central role that a State of Nature plays in both Hobbes' and Locke's political theories, it is somewhat surprising how little attention either Hobbes or Locke gives to explicitly defining a State of Nature. This is especially surprising in the case of Hobbes, who states detailed definitions of so many situations and activities, ranging from definitions of war and peace to definitions of laughter and weeping.[5]

In the Preface to *De Cive*, Hobbes says that one may call the condition of men outside civil society the State of Nature.[6] At first blush, this looks like an official definition, so that for Hobbes, "State of Nature" is simply another name

5. See *Elements of Law I* 14:11, 9:13–14 and *Leviathan* 13:8, 6:42–44.

6. *De Cive*, Preface 14. Hobbes uses the term "state of nature" in *De Cive*. In *Elements of Law*, Hobbes sometimes refers to the State of Nature as the "estate of nature." In *Leviathan*,

for absence of government. But other short texts scattered in his political writings suggest Hobbes has a somewhat deeper analysis in mind. In *Elements of Law*, Hobbes describes the State of Nature as "the estate of liberty and right of all to all."[7] In *Leviathan*, Hobbes declares that people are in a State of Nature when they "live without a common Power to keep them all in awe."[8] As Kavka rightly observes, this *Leviathan* text indicates that for Hobbes, a State of Nature is to be understood in terms of relations.[9] More specifically, if a set of parties are in a Hobbesian State of Nature with respect to each other, then no common third party exists that exerts authority over them, such that they obey and expect each other to obey this third party. Hobbes later states that such authority is typically backed up by coercive force, including punishment for disobedience.[10] But elsewhere in *De Cive*, Hobbes also characterizes a State of Nature as a state where people have formed no agreements with each other and where everyone has a right to all things.[11] In *Leviathan*, Hobbes declares that the one way people can have civil society, the alternative to the State of Nature, is for all of them to obey, and expect each other to obey, a sovereign, and these expectations are of the sort people would have if they had made a covenant with each other to obey this sovereign.[12] Hobbes also likens heads of states as being with respect to each other in positions analogous to those of gladiators in an arena.[13] This suggests that the parties in a State of Nature could be collective entities such as nations as well as individual people. In the continued absence of an effective world government, nation-states might be in circumstances approximating a Hobbesian State of Nature to the degree that they lack reciprocal obligations created by treaties or that they disregard these obligations. All this suggests that Hobbes would approve of the following definition: Parties are in a State of Nature with respect to each other when these parties are completely free both from the authority of some common third party and from antecedent obligations with respect to each

---

Hobbes uses the terms "condition of mere nature" and "naturall condition" to refer to the State of Nature.

7. *Elements of Law I* 14:12.

8. *Leviathan* 13:8.

9. Kavka (1986), pp. 88–89.

10. *Leviathan* 15:3, 17:1.

11. *De Cive* 1:10. Hobbes also says in *Elements of Law I* 14:10 and *Leviathan* 14:4 that in a State of Nature one has a right to all things.

12. *Leviathan* 17:13.

13. *Leviathan* 13:12.

other.[14] In short, one quick description of a Hobbesian State of Nature is *anarchy without morality*. And Hobbes confirms this by stating that the existence of justice between parties in their interactions is contingent on the parties not being in a State of Nature:

> Where there is no common Power, there is no Law: where no Law, no Injustice. Force, and Fraud, are in warre the two Cardinall vertues. Justice, and Injustice are none of the Faculties neither of the Body, nor Mind. If they were, they might be in a man that were alone in the world, as well as his Senses, and Passions. They are Qualities, that relate to men in Society, not in Solitude. It is consequent also to the same condition, that there be no Propriety, no Dominion, no Mine and Thine distinct; but onely that to be every mans, that he can get; and for so long, as he can keep it.[15]

Hobbes famously claims that in a State of Nature as he describes it, "there is no way for any man to secure himselfe, so reasonable, as Anticipation."[16] What exactly is Anticipation? Hobbes gives an official definition: For one to Anticipate is "by force or wiles to master the persons of all men he can."[17] But this account of Anticipation is too restrictive if taken to its literal extreme. Hobbes makes explicit claims that adult people have roughly equal mental and physical powers.[18] So an individual in a Hobbesian State of Nature with respect to others and equipped with only her own force and wiles will seldom, if ever, be able to completely master any of these others for more than a brief time unless she severely injures or kills him, in which case there would seem to be little if anything left to master. Moreover, given rough equality, such an individual can expect only rare opportunities to kill or to seriously wound a State of Nature counterpart without running serious risk of death or serious injury herself. It is conceivable that a cunning, charismatic individual might be able to persuade some to obey her every

---

14. This definition is inspired in part by Kavka's analysis of a Hobbesian State of Nature (1986, p. 88), although Kavka refers only to a common power in his definition and does not mention of obligations created by covenant. As Kavka observes, the concept of a State of Nature might have elements of vagueness, both because possibly more than one specific set of power relations might be sufficient for parties to be out of a State of Nature and because coercive power can be a matter of degree (1986, pp. 88–89). Kavka's discussion suggests that a more refined definition of State of Nature is possible.

15. *Leviathan* 13:14.

16. *Leviathan* 13:4.

17. This is Hobbes' only description of Anticipation in *Leviathan*. The term "anticipate" appears in only one other passage in *Leviathan* (11:9).

18. *Elements of Law I* 14:1–2, *De Cive* 1:3, *Leviathan* 13:4.

command without question.[19] Yet such complete mastery by wiles alone would also be fleeting while parties remain in a State of Nature. In order to maintain her cadre of fanatical disciples, who are roughly her equals in their own mental powers, such an individual must be capable of regulating all communication among these disciples and all information from the outside. Control over information flow of this sort is characteristic of many institutions that function within a society ruled by an effective government, including possibly the government itself. But such control would not exist in a Hobbesian State of Nature. For as Hobbes himself suggests, one of the disadvantages of anarchy is that it is difficult if not impossible to generate mutual or common knowledge or otherwise regulate the flow of information among a group of people.[20]

Hobbes needs a more general definition of Anticipation, one that captures the idea that any individual in the State of Nature is capable of Anticipating against other individuals in the State of Nature. And, in fact, he suggests a more general definition in *De Cive*, where he says that to Anticipate is to attack another preemptively in an attempt to get the better of the other.[21] This idea can be fleshed out in terms of Hobbes' analysis of power. In *Leviathan* Hobbes famously maintains that people restlessly seek power in order to live well.[22] Hobbes defines power formally as means by which one can obtain some future goods. Along with one's *natural* powers of body and of mind, such as physical strength and eloquence, one may acquire *instrumental* powers, such as wealth, reputation, and friends, by fortune or by using one's natural powers.[23] Hobbes devotes more attention to instrumental powers than to natural powers, which is not surprising since Hobbes thinks that a typical person's endowment of natural powers is relatively fixed and roughly the same as that of any other typical person, while in principle there is no limit to the endowment of instrumental powers one might acquire. Importantly, one can acquire more of some instrumental powers, such as external goods and reputation, via encounters with others.[24] In the Hobbesian State of Nature, the instrumental powers others possess are a primary source of

19. Sharon Lloyd suggested this possibility to me in conversation, pointing out that an especially charismatic person in a Hobbesian State of Nature might be able to persuade some of her State of Nature companions to follow her bidding without question, perhaps for religious reasons.

20. *Leviathan* 13:9.

21. *De Cive*, Preface 12.

22. *Leviathan* 11:2.

23. *Leviathan* 10:1–2.

24. An important exception for Hobbes is good luck, which Hobbes in *Leviathan* 10:2 identifies with the secret working of God.

the additional power each individual seeks. One can increase one's total power endowment by appropriating some of the goods others possess. Moreover, one can increase one's *relative* power by diminishing the power endowments of others. In the State of Nature, any individual might find it difficult if not impossible to gain total mastery of others, at least most of the time. But such an individual might find it fairly easy to increase her own relative power in the State of Nature. Hobbes can define Anticipation against others as the permanent or even temporary seizure of *some* of their power. Under this definition, one can Anticipate against another by killing or seriously wounding her, thereby achieving complete mastery but gaining only in that one removes a rival permanently or at least for a very long time. Or one can take an easier and less dangerous path and aim for merely partial mastery over another. One can Anticipate against another simply by seizing some of the goods she possesses. One can also Anticipate by humiliating another in public, which enhances one's reputation for toughness while correspondingly diminishing the victim's reputation. One can even Anticipate against another by occupying some of her physical and mental powers in a conflict. Interestingly, if an Anticipator gains only partial mastery over another, she does not completely eliminate this other as a rival, but on the other hand she might be able to make better use of some of this other's services than she could have if she had killed or wounded this other. For the remainder of this chapter, I will employ this more general definition of Anticipation.

As is well known, Hobbes concludes that individuals in the State of Nature do *not* make themselves more secure when they all do what is allegedly "so reasonable." For when individuals Anticipate against each other, they fall into a conflict that includes costly defensive posturing and occasional violent fighting. Such individuals are in a state of war, a war that profits no one. And this war is a consequence of each individual following the course of action Hobbes claims to be the most reasonable. Hence Hobbes' notorious description of life in the State of Nature:

> In such condition, there is no place for Industry; because the fruit thereof is uncertain: and consequently no Culture of the Earth; no Navigation, nor use of the commodities that may be imported by Sea; no commodious Building; no Instruments of moving, and removing such things as require much force; no Knowledge of the face of the Earth; no account of Time; no Arts; no Letters; no Society; and which is worst of all, continuall feare, and brutal danger of violent death; And the life of man, solitary, poore, nasty, brutish, and short.[25]

---

25. *Leviathan* 13:8, 9.

In *The Second Treatise of Government*, John Locke claims that people in the State of Nature he analyzes might arrive at a rather different outcome:

> And here we have the plain *difference between the State of Nature, and the State of War*, which however some Men have confounded, are as far distant, as a State of Peace, Good Will, Mutual Assistance, and Preservation, and a State of Enmity, Malice, Violence and Mutual Destruction are one from another. Men living together according to reason, without a common Superior of Earth, with Authority to judge between them, is properly the State of Nature. But force, or a declared design of force upon the Person of another, where there is no common superior on Earth to appeal to for relief, is the *State of War*.[26]

Locke maintains that philosophers such as Hobbes are wrong to identify the State of Nature with the state of war. In fact, in the quoted passage from §19 of *Second Treatise*, Locke suggests that when people act according to reason, the State of Nature is a state of peace. Locke also expressly denies that people in a State of Nature should think themselves free to treat each other any way they please, and maintains there is morality in this state:

> Though this be a *State of Liberty*, yet it is *not a State of Licence*, though Man in that State have an uncontroleable Liberty, to dispose of his Person or Possessions, yet he has not Liberty to destroy himself, or so much as any Creature in his Possession, but where some nobler use, than its bare Preservation calls for it. The *State of Nature* has a Law of Nature to govern it, which obliges every one: And Reason, which is that Law, teaches all Mankind, who will but consult it, that being all equal and independent, no one ought to harm another in his Life, Liberty, or Possessions.[27]

Nevertheless, in §21 of *Second Treatise*, Locke speaks of the State of Nature as a state of war after all. Some of Locke's readers accuse Locke of blatantly contradicting himself.[28] On a more charitable reading, Locke is simply arguing that people in a State of Nature might end up *either* at peace or at war, or even

---

26. *Second Treatise* §19.

27. *Second Treatise* §6.

28. See Crawford B. Macpherson, *The Political Theory of Possessive Individualism: Hobbes to Locke* (Oxford: Oxford University Press, 1962), ch. V, sec. 4, and John J. Jenkins, "Locke and Natural Rights," *Philosophy* 42 (1967), pp. 149–154.

in some intermediate state between peace and war. A. John Simmons reads Locke this way, contending that the outcome of the Lockean State of Nature is indeterminate.[29]

What accounts for Hobbes' and Locke's divergent conclusions? Locke and Hobbes propose differing accounts of the State of Nature, but this is no real answer to the question because their accounts overlap considerably. Hobbes and Locke agree that people in anarchy are in a State of Nature. In *Elements of Law*, *De Cive*, and *Leviathan*, Hobbes defines his State of Nature as a state of anarchy with no preexisting obligations. In *Second Treatise* §14 and §15, Locke maintains that people are in a State of Nature with respect to each other when they are not ruled by a government they have consented to obey. So for Locke, anarchy is a sufficient but not a necessary condition for a State of Nature to exist between parties.[30] True, Locke's description of a State of Nature includes a law of nature, but Hobbes would agree with Locke on this point:

> The Lawes of Nature oblige *in foro interno*, that is to say, they bind to a desire they should take place: but *in foro externo*; that is, to the putting them in act, not alwayes. For he that should be modest, and tractable, and performe all he promises, in such time, and place, where no man els should do so, should but make himselfe a prey to others, and procure his own certain ruine, contrary to the ground of all Lawes of Nature, which tend to Natures preservation.[31]

Hobbes believes that people can ascertain what the basic requirements of the natural law are even when they live in their natural condition of political freedom. Indeed, in each of his presentations of the law of nature in *Elements of Law*, *De Cive*, and *Leviathan*, Hobbes describes what laws of nature are and summarizes many of the most important of these laws in the context of his corresponding discussion in these works of the State of Nature. But unlike Locke, who seems to think that people in anarchy might follow certain moral requirements, Hobbes believes that people who find themselves in anarchy will certainly not follow these requirements. Since Hobbes and Locke agree that anarchy characterizes a State of Nature, perhaps they disagree over what rational people in anarchy do

29. See A. John Simmons, "Locke's State of Nature," *Political Theory* 3 (1989), pp. 449–470, and *On the Edge of Anarchy: Locke, Consent and the Limits of Society* (Princeton, NJ: Princeton University Press, 1993), ch. 1.

30. For fine critical studies of Hobbes' and Locke's accounts of the State of Nature, see Kavka (1983), (1986), ch. 3, and Simmons (1989), (1993), ch. 1.

31. *Leviathan* 15:36. Hobbes gives parallel texts in *Elements of Law I* 17:10 and *De Cive* 3:27.

because they disagree over what these people are like. This is a common interpretation of this dispute between Hobbes and Locke and is well summarized by a pair of game-theoretic models of interaction in anarchy proposed as summaries of Hobbes' and Locke's arguments.

A number of philosophers maintain that Hobbes is arguing that people in a State of Nature are trapped in a Prisoner's Dilemma.[32] According to a Prisoner's Dilemma reading of Hobbes, each individual in a Hobbesian State of Nature has two available pure strategies, namely, either *cooperate* with (P) or *Anticipate* against (D) those she encounters. To cooperate with another is to treat this other as an ally. Cooperation includes endeavoring for peace with the other and laying down one's original State of Nature rights to what the other possesses. This is what the first two *Leviathan* laws of nature in Hobbes' system require of an individual, on condition that others reciprocate.[33] Again, one Anticipates against another by seizing at least some of this other's power. To Anticipate against another is to treat the other as an enemy. What happens when parties in a State of Nature meet? According to the Prisoner's Dilemma reading, when both parties cooperate, they are at *peace* with each other. When both Anticipate, they are at *war*. This corresponds to Hobbes' accounts of war as a state in which all know that all are predisposed to fight, and peace as a state where all trust each other not to fight.[34] When one cooperates and the other Anticipates, the Anticipator gains power at the expense of the cooperator. One can assume an Anticipator exploits a cooperator by seizing some of the cooperator's power without serious resistance. One might alternatively assume that a cooperator will resist Anticipation as best she can but will fare worse against an Anticipator than would another who Anticipates, because Anticipators prepare themselves better for conflict than do cooperators. Figure 4.1 summarizes the outcome of a pairwise encounter in the Hobbesian State of Nature.

The key reason so many attribute Prisoner's Dilemma reasoning to Hobbes is that Hobbes explicitly asserts that Anticipation is everyone's most reasonable option in the State of Nature, even though the peace that results if all cooperate is better for all than the war that results if all Anticipate. Hobbes' assertion leads

32. See especially Brian Barry, *Political Argument: A Reissue with a New Introduction* (1965; Berkeley: University of California Press, 1990), pp. 253–254; Rawls (1971), p. 238; David Gauthier, "Thomas Hobbes: Moral Theorist," in *Moral Dealing: Contract, Ethics and Reason* (Ithaca, NY: Cornell University Press, 1990), pp. 11–23; Kavka (1986), pp. 109–113; Michael Taylor, *The Possibility of Cooperation* (Cambridge: Cambridge University Press, 1987), ch. 6; and Edwin Curley, "Introduction to Hobbes' *Leviathan*," in Hobbes, *Leviathan*, ed. Edwin Curley (Indianapolis: Hackett, 1994), pp. xxiv–xxv.

33. See *Elements of Law I* 15:2, *De Cive* 2:2–3, and *Leviathan* 14:4–5.

34. *Leviathan* 13:8.

		Party 2	
		P	D
Party 1	P	Peace between Party 1 and Party 2	Party 2 gains more power, Party 1 is exploited
	D	Party 1 gains more power, Party 2 is exploited	War between Party 1 and Party 2

$P =$ cooperate, $D =$ Anticipate

FIGURE 4.1 Two Parties in a Hobbesian State of Nature

Pure strategy Nash equilibrium cell shaded.

		Party 2	
		P	D
Party 1	P	(β_1, β_2)	$(0, \alpha_2)$
	D	$(\alpha_1, 0)$	(η_1, η_2)

$P =$ cooperate, $D =$ Anticipate

$\alpha_i > \beta_i > \eta_i > 0,\ i \in \{1, 2\}$

FIGURE 4.2 State of Nature as Prisoner's Dilemma

some of his readers to surmise that Hobbes is presenting an informal dominance argument. In a pairwise State of Nature encounter, D strictly dominates P if one assumes the following four claims: (i) One's best outcome occurs if one Anticipates and the other cooperates, since then one enhances her security by gaining power at the expense of the other. (ii) One's second-best outcome occurs if both cooperate, since then they are at peace and she loses none of her original resources. (iii) One's third-best outcome occurs if both Anticipate, for then they are at war and one consequently loses some of her original resources. And (iv) One's worst outcome occurs if one cooperates and the other Anticipates. If one cooperates with an Anticipator, then one loses an even greater share of her original resources than she loses if she Anticipates and they are at war. Given these claims, the parties' preferences characterize a Prisoner's Dilemma, summarized in Figure 4.2.

According to the logic of the Prisoner's Dilemma, by following their strictly dominant strategies the two parties settle into the unique Nash equilibrium (D, D), the outcome of war. One can extend this logic to a larger population of parties in anarchy. Assuming the gains of Anticipation, the losses of exploitation, and the costs of conflict increase monotonically with the number of parties one encounters, rational parties will all Anticipate. From these premises, sometimes attributed to Hobbes, we have arrived at the war of all against all.

As noted above, on a sympathetic reading Locke is arguing that the outcome of anarchy is indeterminate. In several passages, Locke states that one should leave another in peace and in possession of her goods unless she first acts, or overtly threatens to act, aggressively without provocation.[35] But if another party strikes first, Locke allows that one may justly punish this aggressor until one has reason to believe that the aggressor will change and treat others peaceably in the future:

> in the State of Nature, for want of positive Laws, and Judges with Authority to appeal to, *the State of War once begun, continues*, with a right to the innocent Party, to destroy the other whenever he can, until the aggressor offers Peace, and desires reconciliation on such Terms, as may repair any wrongs he has already done, and secure the innocent for the future.[36]

Locke would say that one should Anticipate against another only if one expects the other to Anticipate, and one should expect this only if the other overtly threatens to Anticipate or has Anticipated before. When parties Anticipate against each other, they are at war, but Locke claims that even in anarchy warring parties can make peace. Locke's discussion also suggests that a rational individual *prefers* to Anticipate against another only when she expects the other to Anticipate. According to this interpretation of Locke, if two parties in the State of Nature have the preferences of rational individuals, then their encounter has the structure of a Stag Hunt game, summarized in Figure 4.3.[37] In Stag Hunt, no strategy is strictly dominant. To cooperate is the better strategy, provided that one expects the other to cooperate. To Anticipate is to forgo the chance of realizing the outcome that is best for both, in exchange for being certain not to suffer one's own worst outcome. The (D,D) outcome of war remains an equilibrium in this Stag Hunt game. But now the (P,P) outcome of peace is also an equilibrium, and (P,P) is optimal. If anarchy really has a Stag Hunt structure,

35. *Second Treatise* §16, §19.

36. *Second Treatise* §20.

37. In this Stag Hunt, if one party plays it safe by Anticipating, this party's prospects are actually improved somewhat over the outcome where both Anticipate if the other cooperates. This makes intuitive sense since if one Anticipates against a cooperator, then one is spared the costs of conflict that ensue if one's counterpart also Anticipates.

Pure strategy Nash equilibrium cells shaded.

		Party 2	
		P	D
Party 1	P	(α_1, α_2)	$(0, \beta_2)$
	D	$(\beta_1, 0)$	(η_1, η_2)

$P =$ cooperate, $D =$ Anticipate

$\alpha_i > \beta_i > \eta_i > 0,\ i \in \{1, 2\}$

FIGURE 4.3 State of Nature as Stag Hunt

then war is not inevitable after all. Indeed, as the (P, P) equilibrium is optimal, some authors suggest that this is the equilibrium rational individuals will select.[38] By extending the logic of the Stag Hunt game over all of the parties in anarchy, the outcome where all cooperate is an optimal equilibrium that all will follow if each party expects the others to reciprocate cooperation. We have arrived at peace from Lockean premises.

Philosophers use the Prisoner's Dilemma or the Stag Hunt in their attempts to complete the Hobbesian project of predicting the outcome of anarchy as the result of agents' rational decisions. To be sure, neither of these games fully summarizes the predicament of individuals in anarchy. Few actual encounters between people who coexist for any length of time can be described completely by the payoff matrix of a single strategic form game. Indeed, as I shall argue below, the analysis of interaction in anarchy changes dramatically when one explicitly considers how parties might interact repeatedly over time with neighbors. In §4.3 these factors will be modeled explicitly with iterated games embedded in a spatial structure. But first I will consider a crucial part of Hobbes' own treatment of the preferences of individuals in anarchy that cannot be adequately captured by either the Stag Hunt or the Prisoner's Dilemma game.

Gregory Kavka also suggests that Locke's State of Nature can be modeled as a Stag Hunt game in "Political Contractarianism" (unpublished manuscript, 1989). In this essay Kavka also proposes Stag Hunt as a model of a Hobbesian State of Nature in which all parties are *moderates*, who only prefer to Anticipate in self-defense. In §4.2 I give a more detailed discussion of moderates in anarchy.

38. Jean Hampton argues that the optimality of the (P, P) equilibrium implies that rational agents will follow this equilibrium in a 2-agent Stag Hunt. See Hampton (1986), pp. 67–68. More generally in his analysis of coordination David Gauthier argues that if a strategy profile in a game is uniquely both optimal and an equilibrium, then agents having common knowledge of rationality and the game's payoffs should follow this equilibrium See David Gauthier, "Coordination," reprinted in Gauthier (1990), pp. 274–297.

§4.2. Hybrid A Priori Models of Anarchy

The Prisoner's Dilemma and the Stag Hunt models of anarchy reviewed in §4.1 yield different results because they are developed from different sets of assumed preferences. If these two games accurately summarize the key elements of Hobbes' and Locke's analyses of anarchy, then the dispute between Hobbesians and Lockeans is a dispute over psychology. However, I suspect that neither of the game-theoretic models of anarchy considered in §4.1 accurately reflects human psychology. For the Prisoner's Dilemma and Stag Hunt models of interaction in anarchy presuppose that parties have identical preferences over the alternative outcomes. It is admittedly possible that all parties in a Hobbesian State of Nature share the same set of preferences. So the Hobbesian State of Nature could have a Prisoner's Dilemma or a Stag Hunt structure. But these are endpoint cases. It is also possible that the preferences of parties in a Hobbesian State of Nature *vary* to some extent. The likelihood that such variance is present in a State of Nature grows as the number of parties in this State of Nature grows. In this section I will examine two hybrid models of anarchy that incorporate heterogeneous preferences across parties.

Gregory Kavka developed a contemporary Hobbesian analysis of anarchy that incorporates different *types* of parties.[39] As noted in §4.1, the Hobbes scholars who attribute an informal Prisoner's Dilemma analysis of anarchy to Hobbes rely upon Hobbes' claim that Anticipation is one's most reasonable option. However, for Anticipation to be each individual's unique best option, it is not necessary that Anticipation be each individual's strictly dominant option. In fact, Hobbes may have understood this informally. Consider what Hobbes says in *Leviathan* immediately after recommending Anticipation as the most reasonable course of action in the Hobbesian State of Nature:

> And this is no more than his own preservation requireth, and is generally allowed. Also, because there be some, that taking pleasure in contemplating their own power in acts of conquest, which they pursue farther than their security requires; if others, that otherwise would be glad to be at ease within modest bounds, should not by invasion increase their power, they would not be able, long time, by standing only on their defence, to subsist. And by consequence, such augmentation of dominion over men, being necessary to a man's conservation, it ought to be allowed him.[40]

39. Kavka (1986), §3.4, (1989). As I discuss below in note 42, Michael Taylor briefly considered a type-based model of Hobbesian State of Nature interaction before Kavka, but Taylor did not pursue this idea in depth.

40. *Leviathan* 13:4. A similar text appears in *Leviathan* 11:2.

Pure strategy Nash equilibrium cell shaded.

		Party 2	
		P	D
Party 1	P	(α_1, β_2)	$(0, \alpha_2)$
	D	$(\beta_1, 0)$	(η_1, η_2)

$P =$ cooperate, $D =$ Anticipate

$\alpha_i > \beta_i > \eta_i > 0,\ i \in \{1, 2\}$

FIGURE 4.4 State of Nature as Assurance Dilemma

Hobbes identifies two types of parties in the State of Nature. Parties of only one of these two types prefer to Anticipate against cooperators. I will follow Kavka's terminology and refer to parties of this aggressive type as *dominators*. The more "modest" parties are *moderates*.[41] Both types most fear exploitation and prefer peace over war. However, a moderate most prefers mutual cooperation, while a dominator most prefers to exploit cooperators. Kavka argues that when a moderate meets a dominator in the State of Nature their encounter has the structure of a game Kavka dubs the *Assurance Dilemma*.[42] Figure 4.4 summarizes an Assurance Dilemma where Party 1 is a moderate and Party 2 is a dominator.

The moderate has Stag Hunt preferences, while the dominator has Prisoner's Dilemma preferences, so the Assurance Dilemma is a hybrid of these two games. An Assurance Dilemma has a determinate outcome if both know their preferences and at least the moderate knows that they are engaged in an Assurance Dilemma and that they are both rational. For D is Party 2's strictly dominant choice, and Party 1, knowing this and knowing Party 2 is rational, concludes that her own choices are effectively between (P, D) and (D, D). Since Party 1 prefers (D, D) over (P, D), she chooses D. Hence (D, D) is the unique *rationalizable* strategy profile of the Assurance Dilemma; that is, (D, D) is the only strategy profile compatible with the parties having common knowledge of their rationality and the

41. Kavka (1986), p. 97. In his later 1989 essay, Kavka calls the dominators *glory seekers*.

42. Kavka (1989). In Taylor (1987), pp. 140–141, and its predecessor volume *Anarchy and Cooperation* (London: John Wiley and Sons, 1976), pp. 109–110, Michael Taylor considered briefly an Assurance Dilemma game as a model of Hobbesian State of Nature interaction without naming the game. However, Taylor preferred a Prisoner's Dilemma interpretation of the Hobbesian State of Nature because he believed that Hobbes' texts supported the view that Hobbes thought Anticipation is *every* party's strictly dominant strategy in the State of Nature (1976, pp. 110–111, 1987, pp. 129–141). Kavka developed his Assurance Dilemma analysis of Hobbesian State of Nature interaction independently of Taylor's earlier work.

payoff structure of their game.[43] Kavka calls this game the Assurance *Dilemma* because (D,D) is the unique Nash equilibrium of this game even though only one of the parties prefers to deviate from the optimal (P,P) outcome. Kavka maintains that the Assurance Dilemma is

> the best simple representation of Hobbes's analysis of the problem of anarchy. Since it relies on less cynical assumptions about human nature than the standard prisoner's dilemma view, we may call this the *Kinder-Gentler* Interpretation of Hobbes's state of nature.[44]

The Assurance Dilemma model incorporates preferences that are "kinder and gentler" than Prisoner's Dilemma preferences. Still, if encounters in the Hobbesian State of Nature have an Assurance Dilemma preference structure, one can predict that rational parties with sufficient mutual knowledge of their situation will go to war. Hobbes' own texts indicate that he attributes "kinder, gentler" preferences to people than do many of his followers. If only all in the State of Nature were moderates, then peace would be an equilibrium. Alas, this is not likely to be the case. Dominators are likely to be present in the State of Nature, and these dominators will start a spiral of expected Anticipation that leads all to go to war.[45] The Assurance Dilemma illustrates a simple case of how this spiral unfolds.

Kavka's Assurance Dilemma model is an important step forward in the analysis of the Hobbesian State of Nature, but it has its shortcomings. The Assurance Dilemma model summarizes a compelling argument for why mutual Anticipation is inevitable when a rational moderate and a rational dominator meet and the moderate recognizes the dominator as such. But how often does this happen? When dominators meet, their encounter is a Prisoner's Dilemma.

---

43. Doug Bernheim and David Pearce introduced the rationalizability concept in B. D. Bernheim, "Rationalizable Strategic Behavior," *Econometrica* 52 (1984), pp. 1007–1028, and David Pearce, "Rationalizable Strategic Behavior and the Problem of Perfection," *Econometrica* 52 (1984), pp. 1029–1050. If a game has a unique rationalizable strategy profile, as do the Prisoner's Dilemma and the Assurance Dilemma, then this profile is the unique Nash equilibrium of this game.

Kavka (1989, pp. 9–10) gives a similar argument that (A,A) is the determinate solution of the Assurance Dilemma. In his argument, Kavka does not state the necessary assumptions regarding the parties' knowledge of their situation. Also, Kavka was evidently unaware that his argument is an informal rationalizability argument.

44. Kavka (1989), p. 10. I have followed the exact punctuation, capitalization, and emphases in Kavka's unpublished manuscript.

45. Kavka (1986), §3.4–6, (1989).

When moderates meet, their encounter is a Stag Hunt. If moderates can identify the dominators in their midst, then of course they should be able to identify the other moderates. Such moderates might adopt the contingency strategy of cooperating with moderates and Anticipating against dominators. The premises necessary to enable one to predict that parties in an Assurance Dilemma will surely follow (D, D) on account of their rationality also imply that when moderates are present in a Hobbesian State of Nature, the outcome need not be Hobbes' war of all against all. Indeed, if the moderates in anarchy consistently cooperate with the other moderates and Anticipate against the dominators, the outcome is the intermediate state between peace and war that Simmons argues Locke predicted![46]

Kavka may not have fully recognized this problem for his Assurance Dilemma model. But he was evidently aware that not all encounters in anarchy will be Assurance Dilemmas. Kavka argues that the moderate parties in a Hobbesian State of Nature will reason *as if* they were in an Assurance Dilemma because these parties in fact *cannot* distinguish the dominators from the moderates. Given that the moderates are uncertain as to whether or not the other parties they meet are dominators, Kavka argues that their best choice is to play it safe and Anticipate. Consequently, these cautious moderates together with the dominators generate more expected Anticipation in an ever-increasing spiral.[47] Again, Hobbes himself gives a similar argument:

> we cannot tell the good and the bad apart, hence even if there were fewer evil men then good men, good, decent people would still be saddled with the constant need to watch, distrust, anticipate and get the better of others, and to protect themselves by all possible means.[48]

Hobbes, and Kavka after him, maintains that the moderates' uncertainty as to whether or not other parties they encounter are dominators ultimately leads the moderates to avoid ever running the risk of being exploited. Following their reasoning, a moderate will treat any other party she encounters as if she were certain that this other party is a dominator. Hence, from the perspective of a moderate, anarchy does have an Assurance Dilemma structure in which one's only rational alternative is to Anticipate.

Hobbes, and later Kavka, concludes that the parties' uncertainty regarding party types they meet is a key reason the Hobbesian State of Nature converges to

46. Simmons (1989), (1993), ch. 1.

47. Kavka (1986), pp. 104–107, (1989).

48. *De Cive* Preface 12.

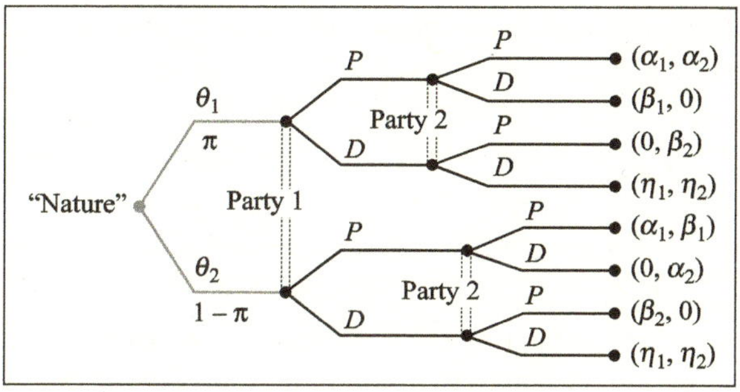

P = cooperate, D = Anticipate

θ_1 = Party 2 is a moderate, θ_2 = Party 2 is a dominator

FIGURE 4.5 State of Nature as π-Assurance

war. However, this uncertainty suggests an alternative, and more general and flexible, hybrid game-theoretic model of the Hobbesian State of Nature. As noted above, when a moderate encounters another party, the *actual* structure of this encounter is either Stag Hunt or Assurance Dilemma, depending upon the other's type. Suppose moderate Party 1, who is uncertain as to counterpart Party 2's type, considers the possibilities as if the type of party she meets is selected for her by "Nature." If Party 2 is a θ_1-type, he is a moderate and the game is Stag Hunt. If Party 2 is a θ_2-type, he is a dominator and the game is Assurance Dilemma. The Figure 4.5 game summarizes the extensive form game corresponding to this game of incomplete information that results from applying the Harsanyi transformation. I will call this game *π-Assurance*, where π is Party 1's probability that Party 2 is a θ_1-type.

π-Assurance is a probabilistic hybrid of the Stag Hunt and the Assurance Dilemma games. What should moderate Party 1 do in this game? The answer to this question is indeterminate. For either cooperation or Anticipation could be Party 1's better option, depending upon the specific payoffs Party 1's preferences generate and the probabilities Party 1 ascribes over Party 2's possible types.[49] Kavka's Assurance Dilemma is a special case of π-Assurance where $\pi = 0$. Indeed, this is my main reason for rejecting the Assurance Dilemma as a hybrid game-theoretic model of anarchy. The Assurance Dilemma model presupposes that a moderate's uncertainty over party types should lead her to act as if she is certain

49. A dominator is also faced with a game of incomplete information. However, the analysis of this game is trivial. If the dominator's counterpart is a moderate, then they are in an Assurance Dilemma, while if the dominator's counterpart is also a dominator, then they are in a Prisoner's Dilemma. So D is the dominator's strictly dominant strategy in this game of incomplete information since D is the dominator's unique best strategy given any probability distribution he has over his counterpart's types.

to meet only θ_2-type parties in her encounters. But why should moderate parties be so pessimistic? Even if Party 1 cannot distinguish the dominators from the other moderates, she might believe that she will seldom encounter a dominator. Consequently, her value for π will be relatively high. If π is sufficiently high, then cooperation can be Party 1's best response given what she expects Party 2 to choose if Party 2 is a θ_1-type.[50] The π-Assurance model accommodates this possibility, and indeed accommodates any possible beliefs a moderate party might have regarding her counterpart's payoff types and alternative strategies.

The π-Assurance game can have equilibria where both parties cooperate as well as the equilibrium where both Anticipate. This game also exposes certain difficulties that arise when one tries to predict war or peace in anarchy via a static a priori analysis alone. In order to identify the equilibria of the π-Assurance game, one needs to know the payoffs for both parties at each possible outcome and the moderate Party 1's probability distribution over Party 2's payoff types. Even if one has this much information, this does not imply that one can now identify some outcome of the game as *the* solution the parties will follow. One cannot predict which equilibrium of the game the parties will follow, or even that they follow an equilibrium at all, unless one assumes that they have common knowledge of their rationality, the complete payoff structure of the Harsanyi transformation game, and their conjectures over each other's strategies in this game. Common knowledge of the Harsanyi transformation game includes common knowledge of the probability distribution over payoff types. Where would all this common knowledge come from? Beyond all this, the Figure 4.5 game of incomplete information characterizes a pairwise encounter between a *particular* pair of parties in anarchy. Whatever one might ultimately conclude by analyzing this game of incomplete information need not characterize the behavior of *all* of the parties in anarchy. For there are no good reasons to suppose that either the moderates or the dominators in anarchy share a single payoff function over alternative outcomes because they share a preference set over these outcomes. And there are no good reasons to suppose that the parties in anarchy share a unique probability distribution over the types and strategies of their counterparts.[51]

---

50. If Party 1 follows P, then Party 2's unique best response is $s_2^* = P\text{-if-}\theta_1, D\text{-if-}\theta_2$. We have $E_1(u_1(P,s_2^*)) \geq E_1(u_1(D,s_2^*))$ or $\alpha_1\pi + \eta_1 \cdot (1-\pi)$ when $\pi \geq \dfrac{\eta_1}{\alpha_1 - \beta_1 + \eta_1}$.

51. In other words, I deny that the parties in anarchy would have a common prior probability distribution over the possible states that characterize their situation. A common prior is assumed in some of the literature on the foundations of game theory, but I concur with many game theorists that it is doubtful that the common prior assumption always obtains for actual individuals engaged in a game.

In short, I believe a more flexible game-theoretic model is necessary, one in which payoffs and probabilities vary across the individuals in anarchy over *ranges*, rather than across discrete types only. I believe that one can develop such a model by relaxing some of the assumptions of the π-Assurance model and by considering repeated interactions in the Hobbesian State of Nature. This opens the door to a dynamical analysis of anarchy based upon how parties learn over time. I propose such a model in the following section.

§4.3. A Dynamical Model of Anarchy

This section introduces a Variable Anticipation Threshold model of interaction in anarchy. This model simulates interactions among individual agents who coexist and interact in conditions reflecting a Hobbesian State of Nature. The Variable Anticipation Threshold model contributes to the recent and growing body of research on *agent-based modeling*. Agent-based models simulate, often with computer experiments, the actions of the members of a population who can have a variety of differing individual characteristics and who can meet and interact in a spatial structure. Here I use the agent-based approach with the aim of giving a more satisfactory analysis of what is likely to happen in a community in their natural condition as Hobbes describes this condition. In this section I describe the Variable Anticipation Threshold model and the results of computer experiments using this model informally. This model and computer experiments based upon this model are described in full detail in Appendix 2.

In the Variable Anticipation Threshold model, members of a population of N individual parties interact repeatedly over discrete time periods. At each interaction period, each Party i in N can meet one or more *partner* parties. When parties meet, each either cooperates with (P) or Anticipates against (D) her partners. The possible outcomes of an interaction between partners are defined by the 2-party payoff matrix of Figure 4.6. The Figure 4.6 matrix characterizes a family of 2 × 2 games whose payoffs vary according to the parameters $x_i > 1$, $\alpha_i \geq 0$ for $i \in N$. Most of the game-theoretic

		Party j	
		P	D
Party i	P	(x_i, x_j)	$(0, 1+\alpha_j)$
	D	$(1+\alpha_i, 0)$	$(1, 1)$

P = cooperate, D = Anticipate

$x_k > 1,\ \alpha_k \geq 0,\ k = i, j$

FIGURE 4.6 Hobbesian State of Nature Interaction

literature on interactions between members of a large population assumes all share a single set of payoffs, so the games of all engagements are identical. As discussed in §4.2, this assumption is unlikely to be compatible with the preferences of all in an actual group of people in anarchy. The hybrid models of §4.2 employ two different payoff types, but these models are still insufficiently general because they do not reflect the relative intensity of preferences that different individuals might have over alternative outcomes. In the Variable Anticipation Threshold model, the variable parameters reflect differing intensities of preferences via the variable payoffs. In an interaction defined by the Figure 4.6 matrix, x_i is a "cooperation parameter," as $x_i - 1$ reflects how much Party i prefers peace over war, and α_i is Party i's "temptation parameter," as α_i determines how much Party i desires the gains of exploiting another party. If $x_i > 1 + \alpha_i$, Party i is a *moderate*. If $x_i = 1 + \alpha_i$, Party i is a *weak dominator*. And if $1 + \alpha_i > x_i$, Party i is a *strict dominator*.[52] If two partners are both strict dominators, their game is a Prisoner's Dilemma. If both are moderates, their game is a Stag Hunt. If one is a moderate and the other a strict dominator, their game is an Assurance Dilemma. So for a moderate, the payoffs of an encounter with a given partner in anarchy are like those of a π-Assurance game where the moderate is uncertain as to whether or not her partner is also a moderate. However, as we shall see, the Variable Anticipation Threshold model does not assume the common knowledge needed for an a priori analysis of the strategies parties follow in the π-Assurance model.

In the Variable Anticipation Threshold model, there can be as many distinct payoff functions as there are distinct parties in N. At each time period, each Party i of N ordinarily chooses a strategy that maximizes expected payoff given her current conjectures, although the model allows for the possibility that a party occasionally deviates from following her best response in a given interaction by mistake or as an experiment. At each period t, Party i's conjecture is characterized by $\lambda_i(t)$, her current probability that a given partner Anticipates. Each Party i has an *anticipation threshold* λ_i^*, a value such that Party i maximizes expected utility by following D when $\lambda_i(t) > \lambda_i^*$. Otherwise Party i maximizes expected utility by following P.[53] That is, Party i plays it safe and Anticipates when her current probability $\lambda_i(t)$ exceeds this threshold.

52. If $x_i = 1 + \alpha_i$, then Anticipation is Party i's weakly dominant strategy since Party i always does at least as well by following D rather than P and does strictly better if Party j follows A. If $x_i > 1 + \alpha_i$, then Anticipation is Party i's weakly dominant strategy. These properties motivate the names "weak dominator" and "strict dominator."

53. When $\lambda_i(t) < \lambda_i^*$, then P is Party i's unique best response. When $\lambda_i(t) = \lambda_i^*$, then any mixed strategy $xP \oplus (1-x)D$ for $x \in [0,1]$, including P itself, is a best response for Party i.

The epistemic assumptions of the Variable Anticipation Threshold model are quite weak compared to the mutual knowledge assumptions implicit in Kavka's Assurance Dilemma model and the common knowledge assumptions of the π-Assurance model. Each party in the Variable Anticipation Threshold model is an expected payoff maximizer and knows her own payoffs. But this model does not assume a party knows the payoffs of any of her partners or even that her partners are necessarily also expected payoff maximizers. If the payoff functions and the rationality of the parties were common knowledge, then moderates could adopt contingency strategies in which they cooperate only with other moderates. Similarly, if the identities of parties who Anticipate against cooperators were common knowledge, then parties could adopt history-dependent strategies similar to the "grim" strategy or the untargeted punishment cycle strategy I discussed in §2.4, which agents can follow as their parts of an equilibrium of an indefinitely repeated Prisoner's Dilemma or Covenant Game. However, there are no mechanisms in the Variable Anticipation Threshold model for generating any mutual or common knowledge among the parties. Indeed, creating such mechanisms would be just the sort of cooperative endeavor Hobbes expressly denies is possible while people remain in anarchy. The Variable Anticipation Threshold model does not assume that parties can identify which of their partners are dominators or have a history of exploiting others. This is in line with Hobbes' belief that the parties in anarchy are unable to distinguish between the types of partner parties they encounter.

The strategies the parties in the Variable Anticipation Threshold model follow depend crucially upon how they form their conjectures. Intuitively, one would expect a party's probability that a current partner will Anticipate to increase monotonically according to the number of past partners who Anticipated. The Variable Anticipation Threshold model reflects this intuition by incorporating a rule for forming conjectures known among game theorists as *weighted fictitious play*. The weighted fictitious play process is a variation on Rudolf Carnap's system of inductive logic where an agent forms her subjective conjecture over the likelihoods of events in a given event set as a probability distribution that is a mixture of a prior probability distribution over these events and the observed frequencies of each of these events over time.[54] In game theory the interpretation of a fictitious play process is that in a game repeated over time periods, at each period each agent engaged in the game updates her conjecture over her counterparts' strategy profiles according to the frequency of past observed profiles and then

54. Carnap's final system of inductive logic was published posthumously as "A Basic System of Inductive Logic, Part 2," in *Studies in Inductive Logic and Probability*, ed. Richard Jeffrey (Berkeley: University of California Press, 1980), II, pp. 7–155.

follows a best response given her updated conjecture. In order to update her conjecture according to such a process, an agent only needs to know her own payoffs and the strategies her counterparts have followed in the past. These are epistemic assumptions applicable to the parties of the Variable Anticipation Threshold model. And while weighted fictitious play is surely an oversimplified model of inductive learning, this model fits the findings of laboratory experiments on simple coordination games fairly well.[55] The specific cases of the Variable Anticipation Threshold model presented below use distributions of the discount factors that are compatible with these experimental results. The mathematical definition of this model is summarized in Appendix 2.

The probabilities $\lambda_i(t)$ for the parties of N in the Variable Anticipation Threshold model form a dynamical system that evolves as a function of the discount factors, the priors, and the strategies followed by each party's partners across time periods. To complete the Variable Anticipation Threshold model, an account of how parties meet their partners is needed. Most of the game-theoretic literature assumes either that each agent in a game interacts exclusively with a fixed set of counterpart agents or that at each time period agents are matched with new counterparts selected completely at random from a large population. Neither of these extremes is a good approximation of how individuals in anarchy are likely to interact. The Variable Anticipation Threshold model defines each party's partners as those parties that are sufficiently near her, and allows parties to migrate over time and encounter new partners that previously were a relatively short distance away. More specifically, in the Variable Anticipation Threshold model parties occupy cells in a two-dimensional lattice. At time period t, Party i's partners are the parties in the cells immediately adjacent to Party i's cell in the lattice. At period $t+1$, Party i may if possible move to a new cell in the lattice, particularly in order to move away from partners who Anticipated at period t.

To illustrate how one can use the Variable Anticipation Threshold model to analyze the emergence of war or peace in anarchy, I will summarize the results of several computer experiments. Figure 4.7 summarizes the initial state of a computer simulation of the interactions among a population N of 1,256 parties in a two-dimensional lattice. In this simulation, the parties' payoff function parameters were distributed so that $x_i > 1 + \alpha_i$ for each Party i of N,

55. See Yin-Wong Cheung and Daniel Friedman, "Individual Learning in Normal Form Games: Some Laboratory Results," *Games and Economic Behavior* 19 (1997), pp. 46–76. Colin Camerer summarizes the results of these and related experimental studies in *Behavioral Game Theory: Experiments in Strategic Interaction* (Princeton, NJ: Princeton University Press, 2003), pp. 283–295.

White cells represent moderates who follow P. Dark grey cells represent moderates who follow D. Light gray cells are unoccupied.

FIGURE 4.7 Initial State of a Population of All Moderates in the Variable Anticipation Threshold Model

so that every party was a moderate. The prior probabilities $\lambda_i(0)$ for $i \in N$ were distributed so that initially Anticipation was the unique best response for approximately half the parties. At period $t+1$, if any of Party i's neighbors Anticipated at period t, Party i would migrate to a neighboring unoccupied cell if possible. Otherwise, Party i would migrate if possible with probability 0.25 to a neighboring unoccupied cell. These migration rules reflect the idea that parties would definitely flee from Anticipators if they could, and otherwise would move if they could at random. The system was allowed to evolve for 1,000 periods or *generations*. Within 50 generations, the system converged to a state where all parties follow P, even though slightly more than half of them began by following D. This system converged to the equilibrium of peace because every party was a moderate. Each Party i's Anticipation threshold satisfied $\lambda_i^* > 0$, so cooperation was her unique best response if enough partners cooperated. Consequently, the initially high dispersion of Anticipators was rapidly overwhelmed by the spread of the P strategy as the parties learned through their experience with their partners.

A second experiment tests the stability of the all-P equilibrium in a population of all moderates. In this simulation, 1,257 parties occupied sites in a two-dimensional lattice, and their payoffs again were distributed so that all were moderates. Once more the priors were distributed so that initially approximately half Anticipated, and the migration rules had each party move if possible when a neighbor Anticipated, and otherwise had each party move if possible with probability 0.25. However, in this simulation parties had some tendency to occasionally deviate from their best responses. In each generation 2% of the parties followed either P or D at random instead of following their best responses to their beliefs formed by weighted fictitious play. One can interpret these random *mutations* as mistakes or experiments. This system was allowed to evolve for 10,000 generations. Even though the system was continually bombarded by a relatively high 2% rate of mutation, the parties rapidly gravitated toward the all-P equilibrium and remained near this equilibrium throughout the duration of the simulation. This and the previous example illustrate a general phenomenon: *When all in the population are moderates, universal cooperation is an attracting equilibrium of the dynamical system.* A population of rational individuals in anarchy can converge to a state of peace, provided that all of them are moderates whose best outcome is the outcome of reciprocal cooperation.

What happens when dominators are present in the population? Figure 4.8 summarizes the initial state of a population N of 1,256 parties in a two-dimensional lattice. This time, the priors were all set at $\lambda_i(0) = 0$. That is, each party initially had a zero probability for the event that any partner Anticipates. Once again, at each successive time period, a party moved if possible if a neighbor Anticipated in the previous time period and otherwise moved if possible with probability 0.25. However, in this population the payoff functions were such that approximately 0.88% of the parties were strict dominators. Initially, each moderate followed P given her prior beliefs, while each dominator followed D, his strictly dominant

White cells represent moderates who initially follow *P*. Black cells represent dominators. Light gray cells are unoccupied.

FIGURE 4.8 Initial State of a Mixed Population in the Variable Anticipation Threshold Model

strategy. This system was allowed to evolve for 1,000 generations. Even though nearly all of the parties began by cooperating, the D-strategy gradually spread through and overtook the population. Figure 4.9 shows the state of this population at various generations.

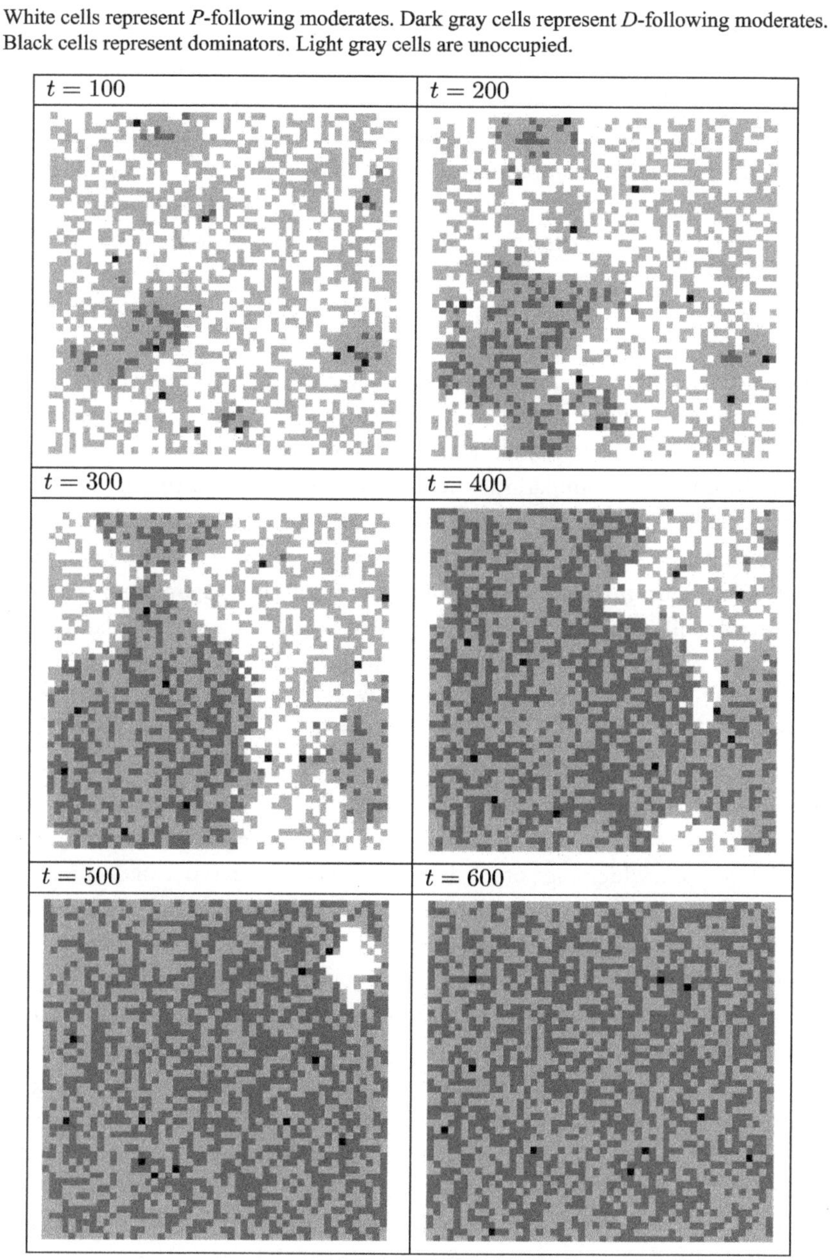

FIGURE 4.9 States of a Mixed Population Who Update Beliefs According to the Variable Anticipation Threshold Model

In fewer than 600 generations, the entire system had converged to the all-A equilibrium even though fewer than 1% of the parties were dominators.

In a fourth simulation, 1,268 parties in a two-dimensional lattice again began with priors all set at $\lambda_i(0) = 0$. These parties followed the same migration rules as in the previous experiments. Approximately 0.71% of the parties in this population were strict dominators. In this population at every generation parties mutated at the rate of 2%. This system was allowed to evolve for 10,000 generations. In fewer than 500 generations the system gravitated to the all-A equilibrium of war and remained near this equilibrium for the remaining generations despite the high rate of mutation. These latter two examples illustrate another general phenomenon: *When some in the population are strict dominators, universal Anticipation is an attracting equilibrium of the dynamical system, while universal cooperation is never an equilibrium.*

A variety of additional computer experiments, the results of which are summarized in Appendix 2, test the sensitivity of the Variable Anticipation Threshold model to variations in the parameters. The properties of the Variable Anticipation Threshold model proved surprisingly robust to changes in the parameters that govern population size, density, movement, mutation, and partnership. In every simulation where all the moderates in the population initially followed P, when the payoffs were distributed so that a small percentage of the population were strict dominators, the system converged fairly rapidly to the all-D equilibrium even if the dominators received no help from moderates who occasionally mutated to D. When parties could mutate, populations with dominators present would always remain near the all-D equilibrium even if the system was bombarded steadily by mutation rates as high as $\varepsilon = 0.02$. On the other hand, in each simulation where the payoffs were distributed so that the parties' Anticipation thresholds were all positive and bounded away from 0, so that all were moderates, when all began by following P the system would always remain near the all-P equilibrium even with the relatively high mutation rate of $\varepsilon = 0.02$. So for a wide range of model parameters, the presence of dominators is both a sufficient and a necessary condition to destabilize the all-P state and drive the system to the all-D equilibrium of war.

In general, in the populations where all are moderates, cooperation can spread throughout the system even if a large percentage of the population begin by Anticipating and parties mutate at a high rate. All-P is an attracting equilibrium of such systems because Anticipation is no party's best strategy in the long run. Every party eventually learns to follow P except possibly for occasional generations in which she mutates, because even if D is initially her best response given a sufficiently pessimistic conjecture, she encounters sufficiently many cooperators over time to convert her to follow P as her best response. If a party Anticipates initially or Anticipates because of a mutation, her neighbors will try to move away from her, but they will not persist in doing so because this party will not persist in Anticipating. When all parties are moderates, all can learn to cooperate.

On the other hand, in the populations containing some strict dominators, the moderates gradually convert to Anticipation because of the activity of these strict dominators. While strict dominators might form only a tiny part of the population in such systems, they always Anticipate except possibly for occasional and rare periods when they mutate, because for them Anticipation is strictly dominant. Neighboring parties might try to move away from these dominators, but they cannot avoid them in the long run, so the parties near the strict dominators suffer *persistent* Anticipation. Since parties cannot distinguish persistent Anticipators from others in the system, they cannot adopt contingency strategies that treat persistent Anticipators differently than the others. The moderate parties that begin by cooperating convert to Anticipation when sufficiently many of their neighbors persistently Anticipate. At first, moderates convert to Anticipation only when they are in the proximity of strict dominators whom they cannot flee. Gradually the consistent Anticipation of the strict dominators creates "clusters" of neighboring parties who have converted to Anticipation because their updated $\lambda_i(t)$ probabilities now exceed their Anticipation thresholds. These clusters of Anticipators in effect form a critical mass of converts to Anticipation, since they grow and produce a "contagion" of Anticipation that overtakes the entire population. In populations containing any strict dominators, the all-P state of peace cannot be an equilibrium of the corresponding dynamical system. Indeed, given the distribution of Anticipation thresholds in this population, the only equilibrium of this system is the all-D equilibrium of war. A population of rational individuals in anarchy might converge to Hobbes' war of all against all even if only a few of them are strict dominators and all of the moderates cooperate at first. In effect, a few "bad apples" can spoil the entire "barrel"![56]

Conclusion

One tradition in political philosophy tries to deduce what sort of society emerges as the result of rational choices in particular circumstances. Hobbes is a giant of this tradition. At the beginning of his rational choice account of the social contract, Hobbes took the extraordinary step of taking the natural condition of humankind to be a condition of complete freedom, and then argued that the rational choices of the individuals in such a State of Nature inevitably lead to war. But as we have seen, given a variation in social preferences across people that Hobbes explicitly acknowledges, the war of all against all in anarchy need not inevitably follow from the individuals' a priori rational decisions. Locke may have

56. My thanks to Brian Skyrms for suggesting this metaphor.

recognized this when he challenged the Hobbesian claim that the outcome of a State of Nature is bound to be war.

A second tradition in political philosophy analyzes how society might evolve as its members modify their behavior in light of experience. Hume is a giant of this tradition. Hume argued that injustice breeds more injustice, as people tend to follow the lead of those they encounter who commit acts of injustice. In this chapter I have presented a dynamical analysis of anarchy inspired by Hume's argument. I have used a specific model, the Variable Anticipation Threshold model, to explore how the interactions of a population in anarchy might evolve. Special cases of this model show that when individuals in a population learn from experience and modify their behavior accordingly, they can converge either to a social equilibrium of war or to a social equilibrium of peace depending upon the composition of the population. When all in the population have social preferences corresponding to the preferences of a moderate, they can settle into a state of peace. On the other hand, the presence of but a few dominators in the population can lead others to imitate their example, as Hume predicted, so that they all ultimately end up at war, as Hobbes predicted.

The key elements of the Variable Anticipation Threshold model are the variable payoffs that determine differential Anticipation thresholds across the population, the spatial structure and rules that determine the movement of individuals, and the learning rules that underwrite the dynamical system of the individuals' expectations. This agent-based dynamical model is designed to reflect some of the background conditions likely to obtain in any sizable State of Nature population. As I indicated in §4.3, this type of dynamical model has a number of advantages over the static a priori models of anarchy, such as those discussed in §4.1 and §4.2, which are more common in the literature on Hobbes' and Locke's accounts of anarchy. The variable payoffs evidently reflect actual human psychology, since in real human societies some, but not all, similarly situated individuals exploit others. A variable-payoffs model is faithful to the texts of classical political philosophers such as Hobbes and Locke, who allow for the possibility that some in anarchy will act like moderates and some like dominators. The existing static models of anarchy either incorporate unrealistically pessimistic assumptions regarding human nature, as does the Assurance Dilemma model, or rest upon unrealistically strong epistemic assumptions, as does the π-Assurance model. An agent-based dynamical model can account for how Anticipation spreads in anarchy as individuals learn from their interactions. In the Variable Anticipation Threshold model, when dominators are present the population converges to the equilibrium of the Hobbesian war simply because the individual parties migrate across a spatial structure and update their beliefs according to a simple inductive rule. Of course, as is generally the case with models of social processes, the Variable Anticipation

Threshold model is somewhat stylized, and one might wish to explore models that are even more complex and accordingly more realistic. For instance, one might consider extensions of the Variable Anticipation Threshold model where parties migrate according to more complex movement rules and update their beliefs according to more sophisticated learning rules. Yet the simpler Variable Anticipation Threshold model of anarchy suggests that the route to vindicating Hobbes' claim that anarchy inevitably leads to war is not Hobbes' own static a priori approach but the dynamical approach Hume proposed informally.

The Variable Anticipation Threshold model also suggests a promising route to resolving the dispute between the Hobbesians and the Lockeans. The presence in every civil society of some individuals who repeatedly commit robberies, homicides, and other violent crimes is strong evidence that some dominators will be present in any sizable population. Hobbes explicitly acknowledges that one must expect that some individuals in a society are dominators, although he allows that the dominators might be in the minority. And nothing Locke says suggests that he would deny this. Again, I maintain that Locke and Hobbes are not really at odds over their accounts of human psychology. I believe the real crux of the dispute between the Lockeans and Hobbesians is the set of assumptions one makes regarding mutual and common knowledge in anarchy, not the set of assumption regarding human psychology. If all are moderates and this is common knowledge, then all can infer that universal cooperation characterizes an equilibrium for their society, so it is also common knowledge that they can sustain the peace of universal cooperation. Similarly, if moderates and dominators are present in the population and the identities of the moderates and the dominators are common knowledge, then the parties would have the information they need to sustain an equilibrium where each moderate follows the contingency strategy of cooperating exactly with the other moderates. If one assumes this much common knowledge, then the Lockeans are right. But the Hobbesians would deny that people in anarchy can acquire all this common knowledge, or even that individuals in anarchy can have first-order mutual knowledge of everyone's type. If individuals do not know enough about others to enable them to distinguish between moderates and dominators, then they cannot follow contingency strategies that depend on party type. Such individuals must rely upon what they learn over time from direct experience interacting with others. The Variable Anticipation Threshold model shows that war can be inevitable when individuals in anarchy base their strategies upon inductive learning and even a few dominators are present. When individuals cannot identify the types of parties they encounter, a small number of dominators can spark the war of all against all that Hobbes predicted. Of course, common knowledge of the party types of all and complete lack of knowledge of any party types other than one's own type are endpoint cases. Mutual and even common knowledge may be attainable for some communities in certain realistic circumstances, including possibly civil society, and I will discuss contingency strategies based upon such mutual or common knowledge further in Chapter 7. Common and mutual knowledge may be unattainable in many other realistic circumstances, including especially complete anarchy. The analysis here suggests that mechanisms that facilitate the transmission of information across the members of society are a prerequisite for social cooperation, in part to enable them to follow appropriate contingency strategies that support such cooperation.

5 PLAYING FAIR

Norms do not as a rule come into existence at a definite point in time, nor are they the result of a manageable number of identifiable acts. They are, rather, the resultant of complex patterns of behavior of a large number of people over a protracted period of time.

—EDNA ULLMANN-MARGALIT, *The Emergence of Norms*

Introduction

I open this chapter with a look at two apparent anomalies observed in strategic interactions. The first of these apparent anomalies is an observed reluctance of individuals in certain situations to accept offers of free money. In 1982, Werner Güth, Rolf Schmittberger, and Bernd Schwarze reported their findings in an experimental study of an *Ultimatum* game where a *Proposer* subject offered a share of a monetary stake to another *Recipient* subject, who then either accepted this share, leaving the Proposer with the rest, or rejected the offer, leaving both with nothing.[1] Güth, Schmittberger, and Schwarze had twenty-one pairs of subjects engage in this Ultimatum game in a first round, and a week later rematched these subjects into new pairs who engaged in this Ultimatum game again. In both rounds the stakes were between 4 and 10 German marks. Overall, the average Proposer's offer was 37% in the first-week round and 33% in the second-week round, and in the first-week round 50% was the modal offer. In these forty-two Ultimatum games, eight Recipients rejected proposals. In seven of these cases the Proposer offered one-fourth or less of the stake, but in all save one of these cases acceptance would have netted the Recipient at least 1 mark. In the years since Güth, Schmittberger, and Schwarze's study, many social scientists and philosophers have constructed laboratory experiments on a host of different Ultimatum games that vary the background conditions of the original Güth, Schmittberger, and Schwarze study. The experimental findings remain empirically consistent. In general, Proposers offer an average of about 40% of the

---

1. Werner Güth, Rolf Schmittberger, and Bernd Schwarze, "An Experimental Study of Ultimatum Bargaining," *Journal of Economic Behavior and Organization* 3 (1982), pp. 367–388.

available monetary stake, and Recipients reject low offers of around 20% about half the time.[2]

Any positive offer in an Ultimatum game is apparently one of the proverbial offers one cannot refuse. Indeed, one can view the Ultimatum game as a generalization of the *Gianni Schicchi* game introduced in Chapter 1 where the Proposer's choice, like Schicchi's choice in the Figure 1.13 game, places her counterpart in a subgame where the counterpart's only Bayesian rational choice is to acquiesce. Why don't most Proposers try to exploit their position in the game and make the lowest possible positive offer? Why don't Recipients always accept any positive offer?[3] One answer to these questions is likely to occur to many who are not committed to the cartoonish view of *homo economicus* as a perfectly selfish individual whose utility function increases according to personal material gain and nothing else: Money isn't everything. Or at least, one's own monetary fortune is not everything for everyone. A standard backward induction analysis of the Ultimatum game that has the Recipient accepting all positive offers and the Proposer offering the lowest possible positive share presupposes agents much like Hume's two corn farmers, each seeking only to maximize her own monetary gain regardless of what the other might gain.[4] Yet nothing blocks the possibility that one's payoff in an Ultimatum game might depend in part on factors other than the amount of material good one receives from the interaction, including especially the amount one's partner receives. Indeed, some of the impure coordination games discussed in earlier chapters reflect this idea, since the agents in these games get some satisfaction from the shares their partners receive as well as their own shares. If each agent's payoffs in an Ultimatum game can depend in part upon how the money is distributed, the observed outcomes in Ultimatum game experiments are no longer so mysterious. A Recipient might reject offers he considers too low out of envy at what the Proposer would gain were he to accept. And a Proposer might offer a larger share than she "should" partly out of benevolence toward the Recipient. Perhaps more interestingly, a Proposer who like one of Hume's corn farmers has no kindness for her partner might

---

2. Camerer (2003), §2.1, summarizes some of the best known results of Ultimatum game experiments.

3. If the Proposer offers nothing, then in terms of monetary payoff acceptance would still be a Recipient's best response but not a unique best response, since in this case the Recipient receives a zero monetary payoff either by rejecting or accepting.

4. Assuming these preferences and that money can be divided into only finitely many increments, the Ultimatum game has two subgame perfect equilibria, one where the Recipient accepts all offers and the Proposer offers nothing and the other where the Recipient accepts all positive offers and the Proposer offers the lowest possible positive amount. To guarantee herself a positive net gain, the Proposer will offer this smallest positive amount.

still offer more than the lowest possible positive share because she anticipates that her partner might care how the wealth is shared out and might punish her for offering too little and claiming too much for herself. More generally, the claimants in a division problem might try to avoid reaching outcomes that are too far from outcomes they consider fair, either because they are predisposed to try to be fair themselves, or because they know some they encounter are so disposed and might sanction what they perceive to be unfair conduct, or both. This hypothesis has been tested and confirmed in a variety of experimental settings.[5] As Cristina Bicchieri puts it in *The Grammar of Society*, certain people in certain contexts exhibit a *taste for fairness*.[6]

The role a taste for fairness can play in the Ultimatum game is disarmingly simple. Figure 5.1 summarizes an Ultimatum game where the stake is 10, shares are in increments of 1, and the payoffs of Proposer and Recipient are identical with their own monetary gains. The usual backward induction solution of the Figure 5.1 game has the Proposer offering 1 and the Recipient accepting all offers. What happens if the payoffs can reflect some preference for fairness? Bicchieri proposed a payoff function that can depend upon both one's monetary gain and some commitment to a fairness norm relevant to the context of interaction.[7] Suppose the Proposer has no serious commitment to fairness in this Ultimatum game herself, but the Recipient believes that fairness in this game requires equal division of the stake and he is sufficiently committed to this norm that he prefers to reject offers that stray too far from at least half the stake. Figure 5.2 summarizes an Ultimatum game with the same monetary payoffs as the Figure 5.1 game, but where payoffs are now defined by the Bicchieri norm-dependent function.[8] This game can also be solved by backward induction, but now the backward induction solution has the Proposer offering 40% of the stake. In many realistic situations, agents in the Proposer and Recipient roles might be uncertain just

5. Alvin Roth, "Bargaining Experiments," in *Handbook of Experimental Economics*, ed. John H. Kagel and Alvin E. Roth (Princeton, NJ: Princeton University Press, 1995), pp. 253–348, and Camerer (2003), ch. 2, summarize the most important experimental results.

6. Cristina Bicchieri, *The Grammar of Society: The Nature and Dynamics of Social Norms* (Cambridge: Cambridge University Press, 2006), ch. 3.

7. Bicchieri (2006), pp. 112–117.

8. Bicchieri's payoff function for a Recipient who receives the offer x is

$$u_2(x) = x - k_2 \cdot \max(N_2 - x, 0),$$

where N_2 is the amount the Recipient believes he should receive according to a fairness norm and $k_2 > 0$ reflects how averse the Recipient is to receiving an amount lower than N_2 (2006, p. 116). In the Figure 5.2 game, the Recipient's payoffs are defined as $u_2(x)$ where $N_2 = 5$ and $k_2 = 1$.

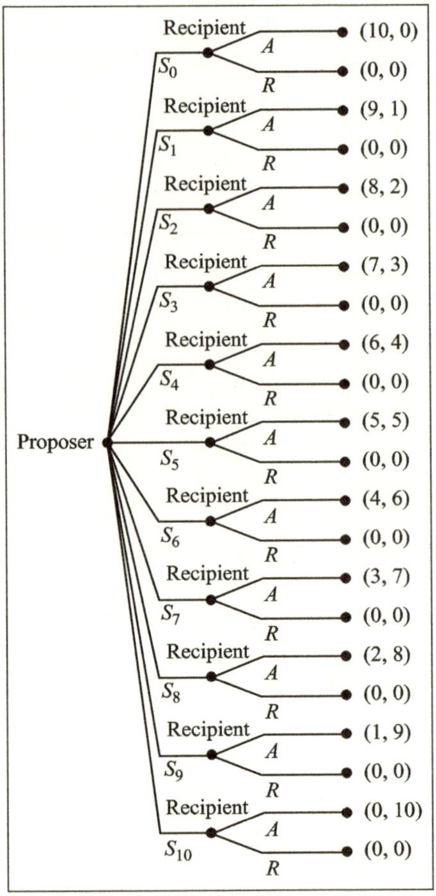

S_i = offer i, $i \in \{1, \ldots, 10\}$, A = accept, R = reject

FIGURE 5.1 Ultimatum Game

how committed their partners are to a relevant fairness norm. In such situations the Ultimatum game becomes a game of incomplete information where types of agents vary according to strength of commitment to a fairness norm. But so long as the chances of being matched with a partner strongly committed to a fairness norm are at or above a certain threshold, even the most narrowly egoistic agents' best strategies result in an outcome at or near the outcome specified by this norm.

The study of the theoretical underpinnings of this tendency for individuals to follow outcomes they perceive to be fair or at least nearly fair is today yet another lively and rapidly expanding area of research influenced by and influencing game theory. A now vast body of empirical evidence confirms that a *social preference* to follow outcomes that all involved regard as fair exists, is widespread, and affects

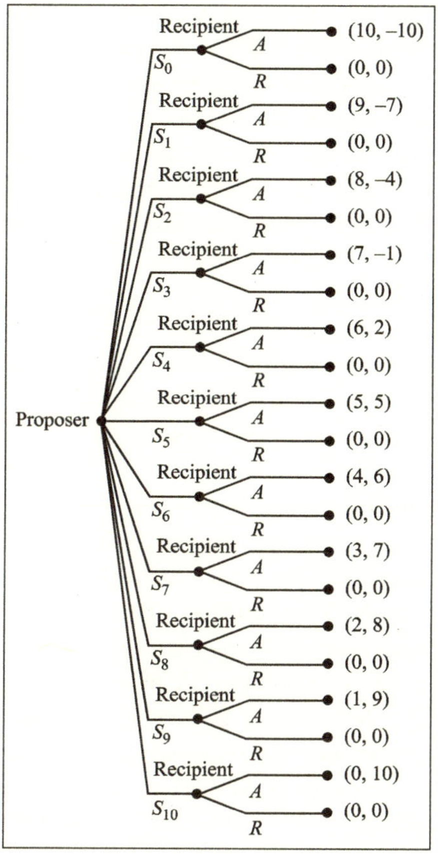

S_i = offer i, $i \in \{1, ..., 10\}$, A = accept, R = reject

FIGURE 5.2 Revised Ultimatum Game

the outcomes of interactions in a variety of contexts. But just where do these social preferences come from? If one appeals to commitments to norms to explain otherwise "anomalous" conduct in situations like the Ultimatum game, then the obvious next question to ask is: Where do the fairness norms come from? In the preceding paragraph, I appealed to a norm of equal division. But why should there be any presumption that goods in a certain division problem be shared out equally, or in any other particular way?

The second apparent anomaly is an observed tendency for some individuals to punish those they perceive to be taking advantage of others' good conduct even when they must absorb a material cost in order to carry out such punishments. In 2000, Ernst Fehr and Simon Gächter published an experimental study of a game that tested subjects' ability to generate a common pool resource by their own voluntary contributions.[9] Groups of four were matched from a pool of twenty-four to engage in a game where each could contribute a share of an initial endowment to add to a common payoff pool that would be divided equally among the four group members in proportion to the sum of contributions. Group members could achieve an optimal outcome in terms of final monetary fortune if each contributed her full endowment, but each would maximize her own expected fortune by contributing nothing whatever the others contributed. Social scientists had run a great many similar public good and common pool resource experiments before Fehr and Gächter's study, including many that had a similar apparent multiagent Prisoner's Dilemma structure. What made this study special was that Fehr and Gächter incorporated treatments that allowed group members to fine each other immediately after their contribution game, both with stable groups whose members engaged repeatedly over twenty periods and random groups where at each of twenty periods the subjects were all randomly reassigned to new groups of four and then engaged with their newly assigned partners. In both the stable group and the random group treatments, over the first ten periods group members engaged in the contribution game with no fining, and over the remaining ten periods they engaged in the contribution game with fining. Not surprisingly, over the no-fining periods the contribution rates converged to near zero levels. But in the stable group treatment, when fining was allowed a contribution rate of nearly 95% of the endowment was maintained. And in the random group treatment, when fining was allowed a contribution rate of over 50% of the endowment was maintained. This last result was all the more remarkable because Fehr and Gächter specifically designed their random group treatment so that group members could not fine strategically, at least not on their own behalf, in expectation of profiting over future periods for having a known tendency to fine. The reason for the groups' successes in the Fehr and Gächter experiments is plain. Their subjects had the option of meting out *targeted punishment*, which many used to punish partners who contributed less than the group average.[10] But at least some of those who did fine were evidently *altruistic punishers*, since fining did help to sustain relatively high group contribution rates but by

9. Ernst Fehr and Simon Gächter, "Cooperation and Punishment in Public Goods Experiments," *American Economic Review* 90 (2000), pp. 980–994.

10. In an earlier seminal study, Elinor Ostrom, James Walker, and Roy Gardner incorporated targeted punishment in a similar manner by having subjects play a public goods game and then allowing subjects to fine their partners at some personal cost. This earlier study differed from the Fehr and Gächter study in that in all of their treatments, the subjects in the Ostrom, Walker, and Gardner study played their game repeatedly with the same partners, so that those who could fine could fine strategically. See Elinor Ostrom, James Walker, and Roy Gardner, "Covenants With and Without a Sword: Self-Governance Is Possible," *American Political Science Review* 86 (1992), pp. 404–417.

experimental design cost punishers some share of their own endowment with no expectation of direct future monetary reward. Why would individuals punish at such personal material costs?

Empirical tests of the presence of altruistic punishers in certain interactions form an integral part of a vibrant contemporary body of research on *strong reciprocity*. Many surprising social phenomena can be explained as a consequence of the presence in human communities of strong reciprocators who are predisposed to act for the benefit of their group and to punish free-riders. In particular, a large body of analytical models, experiments, and field studies support the hypothesis that groups of moderate size can sustain high levels of public good or common pool resource provision and consequently thrive if some of their members are strong reciprocators.[11] The potential explanatory power of strong reciprocity is easy to illustrate with the 3-agent Three-in-a-Boat threshold public good game of Figure 1.12. In this game, each of the outcomes (D,P,P), (P,D,P), and (P,P,D), where exactly one defects and the public good is provided, is an optimal Nash equilibrium, and the nonprovision outcome (D,D,D), where all defect, is a suboptimal Nash equilibrium, though D is always each agent's "safe" strategy. Three-in-a-Boat is one of the simplest nontrivial games where free-riding is possible, since each agent's best outcome occurs when she defects while her two partner agents perform. As I discussed in Chapter 1, the agents' prospects for generating the public good might appear quite poor, precisely because free-riding is possible. Indeed, models of inductive learning applied to this game indicate that absent any preexisting commonly accepted contingency strategies, agents will be unlikely via trial-and-error learning to coordinate on an equilibrium where they provide the public good. For example, when a weighted fictitious play learning model similar to the model used in §4.3 is applied to the Figure 1.12 game, approximately 37.67% of the possible initial conjectures converge to those of one of the provision equilibria, (D,P,P), (P,D,P), or (P,P,D), while approximately 62.33% of these initial possible conjectures converge to those of the nonprovision equilibrium (D,D,D).[12] Figure 5.3 illustrates different orbits of weighted fictitious play for an

11. Some fine collections of research on issues connected to strong reciprocity include Herbert Gintis, Samuel Bowles, Robert Boyd, and Ernst Fehr, eds., *Moral Sentiments and Material Interests: The Foundations of Cooperation in Everyday Life* (Cambridge, MA: MIT Press, 2005) and Jean Ensminger and Joseph Henrich, eds., *Experimenting with Social Norms: Fairness and Punishment in Cross-Cultural Perspective* (New York: Russell Sage Foundation, 2014).

12. These and the other estimated frequencies of convergence were determined by computer simulations that are summarized in Appendix 2.

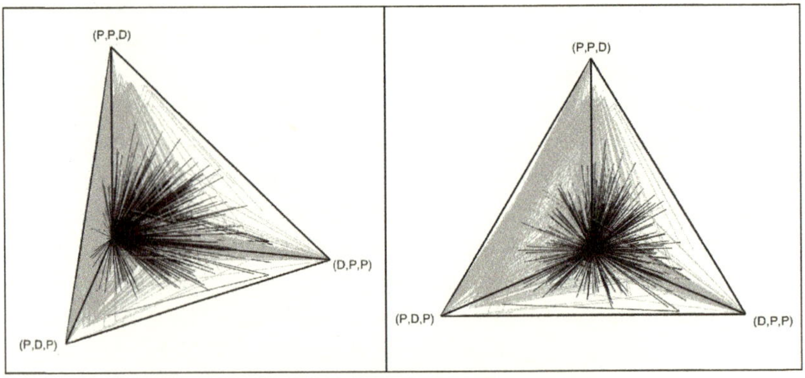

Side and overhead views of the simplex tetrahedron
Orbits for optimal Nash equilibria are gray Orbits for the suboptimal Nash equilibrium are black.

FIGURE 5.3 1,000 Weighted Fictitious Play Orbits of Agent in a Three-in-a-Boat Game

agent in this Three-in-a-Boat game where this agent's initial conjectures are chosen at random.[13] The nonprovision equilibrium is by far the most likely outcome of this inductive learning process.

The agents' prospects for achieving an optimal equilibrium increase dramatically if targeted punishment is possible. Suppose some of the agents in a population who engage in the Three-in-a-Boat game are strong reciprocators who punish free-riders. A strong reciprocator incurs a personal cost $r > 0$ in order to inflict a cost $p \geq r$ against the free-rider. If a fraction x of this population are reciprocators while the remaining $1-x$ are the more "ordinary" *egoists* who simply try to maximize their expected payoffs according to the Figure 1.12 Three-in-a-Boat payoffs, and the probabilities of being matched with a particular type of agent are independent, then in the resulting public goods game free-riding can be a much less attractive option. Suppose for example that $\frac{1}{10}$ of the population are reciprocators who punish at personal cost $r = 1$, inflicting the punishment

13. An *orbit* of weighted fictitious play is the sequence of updated conjectures this learning process generates from an initial conjecture. For this $3 \times 2 \times 2$ game, the conjecture for any of the three agents is characterized by the point in a tetrahedron where each vertex corresponds to one of the counterparts' four available pure strategy profiles. For this game, each vertex of this tetrahedron that characterizes Agent 1's possible conjectures characterizes one of the four pure strategy Nash equilibria. For example, the point $(0,0,0,0)$ that defines the conjecture $\mu_1(D,D) = 1$ where Agent 1 believes with probability 1 that Agent 2 and Agent 3 both follow D characterizes the equilibrium (D,D,D), since at this conjecture Agent 1's best response is also D.

P

	P	*D*
P	(3.000, 3.000, 3.000)	(2.910, 4.260, 2.910)
D	(4.260, 2.910, 2.910)	(1.983, 1.983, 0.714)

D

	P	*D*
P	(2.910, 2.910, 4.260)	(0.714, 1.983, 1.983)
D	(1.983, 0.714, 1.983)	(1.974, 1.974, 1.974)

P = perform, *D* = defect

FIGURE 5.4 Strategic Form of Threshold Public Good Game with Reciprocators, $\mu\left[\text{Agent is a reciprocator}\right]=\frac{1}{10}$, $r=1$, $p=3$

cost $p=3$, while the remaining $\frac{9}{10}$ of the population are egoists.[14] Figure 5.4 summarizes this new public good game.[15] In the Figure 5.4 game, the provision and nonprovision Nash equilibria are the same as in the original Figure 1.12 Three-in-a-Boat game. But now the relative expected gain from unilateral defection is considerably less, given that an egoist who free-rides receives punishment if one or both counterparts turn out to be reciprocators. When weighted fictitious play is applied to the Figure 5.4 game, now approximately 64.13% of the possible initial conjectures converge to those of one of the provision equilibria, while only 35.87% of these initial possible conjectures converge to those of the nonprovision equilibrium. Figure 5.5 illustrates different orbits of weighted fictitious play for an agent in this new public good game where the initial conjectures are chosen at random in this agent's part of the simplex. The presence of only a small proportion of such strong reciprocators turns the original Three-in-a-Boat game into a game where now a provision equilibrium is the more likely outcome of this inductive learning process.

14. These parameters are in fact somewhat on the conservative side of what is common in the strong reciprocity literature. Fehr, Fischbacher, and Gächter report that in a variety of experiments at least 40% of subjects exhibit strong reciprocity while the conduct of the remainder suggests they are purely selfish. See Ernst Fehr, Urs Fischbacher, and Simon Gächter, "Strong Reciprocity, Human Cooperation and the Enforcement of Social Norms," *Human Nature* 13 (2002), pp. 1–25. In many human subject and computer simulation experiments on strong reciprocity, a punishee's cost p of at least three times the punisher's cost r is commonly applied. For example, in their group selection model of the evolution of altruistic punishment, Robert Boyd, Herbert Gintis, Samuel Bowles, and Peter Richerson assign to a punishee a cost $p=4r$. See "The Evolution of Altruistic Punishment," *Proceedings of the National Academy of Sciences* 100 (2003), pp. 3531–3535, reprinted in Gintis et al. (2005), pp. 215–227.

15. See Appendix 2 for details on the construction of this game.

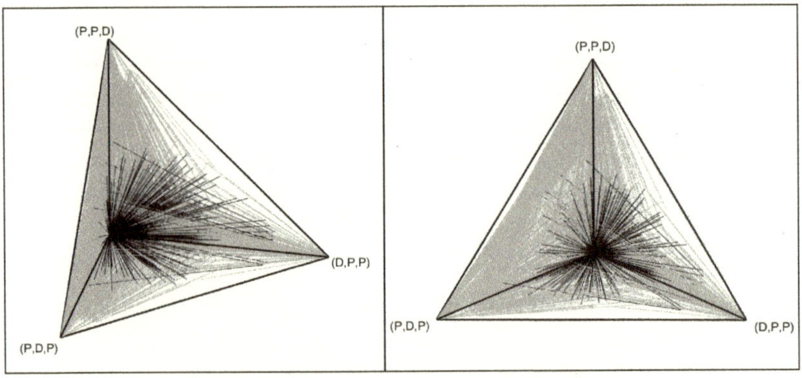

Side and overhead views of the simplex tetrahedron
Orbits for optimal Nash equilibria are gray. Orbits for the suboptimal Nash equilibrium are black.

FIGURE 5.5 1,000 Weighted Fictitious Play Orbits of Agent in Figure 5.4 Game

Situations such as the Ultimatum game and the threshold public good games discussed above support the general claim that fairness norms and strong reciprocity are important in social life, and that in particular they can help explain otherwise "anomalous" prosocial conduct. In fact, this general claim dovetails with Hobbes' claims that some members of society are more willing to exploit their fellow members than are others and that certain norms of fair division and of punishment are laws of nature. Indeed, I think the emergence of cooperation out of the State of Nature depends upon the presence of at least some individuals who tend to act more for the benefit of others and to follow norms of restraint than do Hobbesian dominators. For as I have analyzed the State of Nature in Chapter 4, if *everyone* in society were a dominator, then the State of Nature really would have the structure of a huge Prisoner's Dilemma and no way of life other than the war of all against all would be possible. But this leaves us with questions of origins and persistence. How do fairness norms emerge in a community? Where do strong reciprocators come from, and how can they coexist with others who would willingly exploit their prosocial conduct?

I believe a tendency for individuals to "play fair" in certain interactions can evolve in populations, with the end result that such populations converge to *fairness equilibria*. This idea is not new.[16] However, the specific interactions I use in this chapter to illustrate this idea yield novel insights into the nature of "playing

16. Some of the landmark works that have developed this idea include Robert Axelrod, *The Evolution of Cooperation*, rev. ed. (New York: Basic Books, 2006); Robert Boyd and Peter J. Richerson, *Culture and the Evolutionary Process* (Chicago: University of Chicago Press, 1985); Sugden (2004); and Skyrms (2014).

fair." These specific interactions are the bargaining problem and a variation on the Stag Hunt. The remainder of this chapter is structured as follows: In §5.1 I discuss alternative approaches to solving the 2-agent bargaining problem. I conclude that the standard a priori analyses of the bargaining problem are not fully satisfactory and that since the bargaining problem is a coordination problem, one should analyze this problem in terms of salience and dynamic learning concepts. I show by example that communities of agents who engage in various bargaining problems and who form their conjectures according to a form of inductive learning reach a variety of equilibria, and the distribution of these equilibria tends toward a particular *egalitarian solution* of the bargaining problem. This is one example of how a fairness norm might evolve. In §5.2 I revisit the Stag Hunt. Many studies of the Stag Hunt support the general conclusion that the suboptimal equilibrium where neither side performs is likely to emerge unless the optimal payoffs of mutual performance are significantly greater than those of the safe suboptimal equilibrium. I consider an extension of the Stag Hunt where an agent who performs alone can punish her defecting partner at some cost to herself. I show that when a population of agents who learn inductively engage in this *Augmented Stag Hunt*, their prospects for converging to an optimal equilibrium where each side performs are greatly enhanced. The punishing strategy can form part of an optimal equilibrium of an evolved population even though this altruistically punishing strategy is weakly dominated. Those who follow this "irrational" strategy are in effect altruistic punishers. So Augmented Stag Hunt illustrates how a form of strong reciprocity might evolve.

§5.1. Fair Division

Aristotle claims everyone agrees upon a *proportionality principle* of distributive justice, according to which the ratios of the values of shares received and of the recipients' worth are equal. According to this principle, equals according to the criteria of worth are to receive equally valuable shares.

> All men think justice to be a sort of equality; . . . For they say that what is just is just for someone and that it should be equal for equals. But there still remains a question: equality or inequality of what? Here is a difficulty which calls for philosophical speculation.[17]

In fact, the formal proportionality principle Aristotle thinks is universally accepted is itself a matter for philosophical speculation. This principle is not a consequence of the orthodox logic of rational choice, according to which a rational

17. *Politics* 1282b18–22. See also *Politics* 1280a8–30 and *Nicomachean Ethics* 1131a–1131b22.

		Laura M	Laura G
Claudia	M	$(0,0)$	$(0,1)$
Claudia	G	$(1,0)$	$(0,0)$

M = modest (claim none), G = greedy (claim all)

FIGURE 5.6 Chocolate Cake Basis Game

agent consistently chooses options that are best in the sense of maximizing expected utility or payoff. One of the simplest of resource division problems is the *Chocolate Cake* problem, where hungry claimants each claim a share of a cake, and then each receives the share she has claimed if their claims are *compatible*, so that there is enough cake to supply each her own claim, and otherwise receives nothing because the cake spoils while they spat over having made incompatible claims. When the claimants are assigned payoffs reflecting their preferences for cake, their problem becomes a *demand game*. When there are two claimants and the payoff each receives is exactly equal to the fraction defining her received share of cake, the 2×2 Figure 5.6 game is a basis for defining the payoff structure of this demand game. In this basis game, the claimants Claudia and Laura each can be *modest* and claim no cake at all (M) or *greedy* and claim the entire cake (G). G is each claimant's weakly dominant strategy. If Laura and Claudia are limited to choosing either M or G, then apparently if they both choose rationally they end up at (G,G) and both get nothing. But they can do better if their strategy set is enriched so that each can claim any desired fractional share of cake. Indeed, if Claudia claims $x_1 \in (0,1)$ and Laura claims $1-x_1$, then they follow a convention equilibrium of this demand game. If Laura were to deviate unilaterally from the claim pair $(x_1,1-x_1)$ by claiming less, she would get less than her original claim $1-x_1$, and if she were to deviate by claiming more, than she would get nothing. Similarly, Claudia would get less than her original claim x_1 were she to unilaterally deviate. So $(x_1,1-x_1)$ is a strict equilibrium and characterizes a convention because this claim pair is one of many distinct strict equilibria of this game. The perfect symmetry of the payoff structure of this game reflects an important background assumption, namely, that neither Claudia nor Laura is more deserving than the other of this chocolate cake. In this situation they are equals with respect to the relevant criteria of worth. If Aristotle is right, then all would agree that Laura and Claudia should receive equal shares of chocolate cake. But Claudia and Laura might not accept this conclusion so blithely. A rational agent placed in a division problem like the Chocolate Cake demand game might make one of any number of different claims, depending on how cautious or aggressive she might be and how cautious or aggressive she expects her counterpart claimant to be. The convention of the $\left(\frac{1}{2},\frac{1}{2}\right)$ equilibrium where each claims half is only one of a whole continuum of conventions available to Claudia and Laura. Even if both do follow strategies according to orthodox standards of rational choice, equal division of the cake does not follow from this fact or even from their having common knowledge of this fact.

Because the above Chocolate Cake problem has a perfectly symmetric payoff structure reflecting the claimants' equal worth with respect to shares of the cake, it is at least clear that according to the Aristotelian principle in this problem each claimant's fair share should be half of the cake. For a division problem with payoff asymmetries, what counts as a fair share might not be at all obvious. Figure 5.7 gives a 2-agent game equivalent to the Matthew-Luke game Braithwaite presented in his Cambridge lecture. The Figure 5.7 game is a rescaled Figure 1.9 game where Luke's and Matthew's payoffs are now normalized so that the worst possible payoff for each is 0 and the best possible payoff for each is 1. Matthew and Luke have available to them a family of correlated equilibrium conventions where for each $x \in [0,1]$ they follow (G, M) for x of the time and (M, G) the remaining $1-x$ of the time. The rescaling makes certain differences between the two neighboring musicians even more clear. While Matthew and Luke each most desires to play his instrument undisturbed, Matthew's own dislike for listening to Luke play solo compared to his own playing solo is greater than Luke's dislike for listening to Matthew play solo compared to his own playing solo. Neither Luke nor Matthew prefers the resulting silence if both are modest over listening to the other to play solo, but Matthew dislikes silence even more than Luke. Conversely, Luke, but not Matthew, regards the cacophony that ensues if both are greedy as the worst possible outcome, so Matthew has the threat advantage. Matthew and Luke might agree with Braithwaite that the solution they ultimately follow should be fair. But given the asymmetries in this game, Luke and Matthew might have

		Laura	
		M	G
Claudia	M	$(\frac{1}{6}, 0)$	$(\frac{1}{2}, 1)$
	G	$(1, \frac{2}{9})$	$(0, \frac{1}{9})$

M = modest (claim none), G = greedy (claim all)

FIGURE 5.7 Braithwaite Basis Game

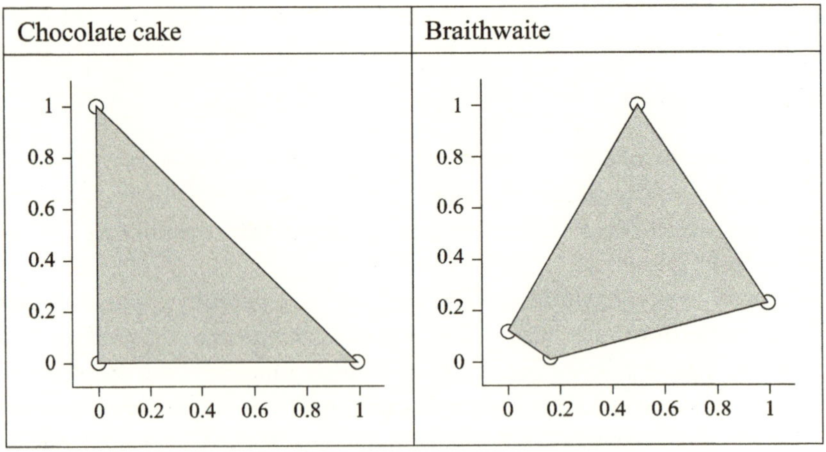

FIGURE 5.8 Feasible Sets of Chocolate Cake and Braithwaite Demand Games

some difficulty agreeing upon proper formal criteria of fairness that would serve even to narrow down the set of outcomes to be considered candidate solutions, let alone pick a uniquely fair solution.

The simple symmetric and asymmetric demand games presented here have the basic structure of a bargaining problem as formulated by John Nash. Nash characterized a given bargaining problem as a *feasible set* that is the set of all the payoff vectors the agents involved might achieve by taking some agreed-upon joint action together with a baseline or *nonagreement point* that is the payoff vector corresponding to the outcome that ensues in case they fail to agree. In many cases where the bargaining problem is also a problem of dividing some fixed quantity of a good, the feasible set is defined simply as the set of payoff vectors determined by compatible claims. In a division problem any set of compatible claims of the good at stake corresponds to a unique point in this set.[18] I will use this definition of the feasible set in all of the fair division bargaining problems discussed here. Figure 5.8 depicts the feasible sets of the Chocolate Cake and the Braithwaite demand games according to this definition.

In his own discussion of fair division problems, Nash proceeded from the premises that each agent's payoff is nondecreasing in the amount of good she receives and that the nonagreement point is the outcome where each claimant claims all of the good at stake, so that no agent receives any. In the Chocolate Cake and Braithwaite games, this second premise implies that (G,G) defines

18. In some presentations of axiomatic bargaining theory, the feasible set is defined as a *comprehensive set*. The comprehensive set extension of the compatible payoff vector set reflects an additional assumption that each agent is free to destroy without cost any of the good she might receive from a division defined by compatible claims.

the nonagreement point. The feasible set payoffs of the Chocolate Cake and Braithwaite games reflect the first premise, since each agent in fact fares better than she fares at the nonagreement point if she receives a positive share of the good at stake. In each of the Figure 5.8 sets, the part of the boundary joining the ideal points for each of the two agents is the *Pareto frontier*.[19] A bargaining problem is *nontrivial* if its Pareto frontier consists of more than a single point.[20] In both the Chocolate Cake and the Braithwaite games, the Pareto frontier is the set of payoff vectors defined by the alternation schemes $x\cdot(G,M)\oplus(1-x)\cdot(M,G)$, $x\in[0,1]$, where the agents follow a strict correlated equilibrium.

Nash argued that in principle one can analyze any bargaining problem either *axiomatically* by considering which allocations satisfy certain formal desiderata, or from the perspective of agents who settle upon an allocation via some *strategic bargaining process*.[21] Nash regarded these two approaches as complementary.[22] According to Nash's own proposed axiomatic solution, if at a set $\boldsymbol{x}=(x_1,\ldots,x_n)$ of claims that can but need not be compatible each Agent i's payoff is $u_i(\boldsymbol{x})$ and $(u_{01},\ldots,u_{0n})$ is the payoff vector of the nonagreement point so that Agent i receives u_{0i} at this point, then the good is divided so as to maximize the *Nash product*, $(u_1(\boldsymbol{x})-u_{01})\cdots(u_n(\boldsymbol{x})-u_{0n})$. In the Chocolate Cake demand game, the Nash product is $x\cdot(1-x)$, which is maximized at $x=\frac{1}{2}$, so that at the Nash solution Claudia and Laura follow (G,M) for half the time and (M,G) the remaining half of the time. In the Braithwaite game, at the Nash solution Luke and Matthew follow the (G,M) outcome $\frac{1}{14}$ of the time and the (M,G) outcome $\frac{13}{14}$ of the time.[23]

---

19. In an n-agent division problem, if each Agent i claims $x_i\in[0,1]$ and $x_1+\cdots+x_n=1$, then this set of compatible claims defines a point along the Pareto frontier.

20. A simple example of a trivial bargaining problem is a 2-agent division problem where each Agent i can claim some fraction x_i of a good at stake and $x_i=1$ corresponds to G and $x_i=0$ corresponds to M, same as in the Chocolate Cake and Braithwaite problems, but where $u_i(x_1,x_2)=0$ for any set of claims, compatible or incompatible. This example summarizes a situation where neither agent happens to derive any positive payoff from receiving any amount of the good at stake.

21. Nash, "Two-Person Cooperative Games," in Nash (1996), pp. 34–46. See Alvin Roth, *Axiomatic Models of Bargaining* (Berlin: Springer, 1979) and William Thomson and Terje Lensberg, *Axiomatic Theory of Bargaining with a Variable Number of Agents* (Cambridge: Cambridge University Press, 1989) for fine surveys of axiomatic solution concepts for bargaining problems.

22. Nash (1996), p. 35.

23. The Nash product of the Braithwaite Demand Game is $x\cdot\left(\frac{5}{3}-\frac{14x}{9}\right)$, which is maximized at $x=\frac{15}{28}$, which in turn defines the Pareto frontier point $\left(\frac{15}{28},\frac{17}{18}\right)\approx(0.536,0.944)$.

Two other axiomatic solution concepts, both first introduced by Howard Raiffa, rival Nash's solution in importance.[24] Raiffa, and Braithwaite after him, concurred with Nash that the outcome where each agent claims all of the good at stake defines the nonagreement point. According to one of Raiffa's solutions, one first scales payoffs so that each Agent *i*'s most desired and least desired outcomes have respective payoffs 1 and 0, and then picks the point on the Pareto frontier yielding the agents equal gains from their individual nonagreement point payoffs according to this payoff scale. In the Braithwaite Demand Game, this *egalitarian solution* has Claudia and Laura follow (G, M) for $\frac{7}{23}$ of the time and (M, G) for $\frac{16}{23}$ of the time. Braithwaite, who took inspiration from Nash's analysis of bargaining but who also thought Nash's solution of Braithwaite's demand game problem is plainly too lopsided in Laura's favor, defended a variation of Raiffa's egalitarian solution as the basis for a fair division in this problem.[25] Another of Raiffa's solutions selects a point on the Pareto frontier at which the ratio of each Agent *i*'s received payoff less her nonagreement point payoff to her ideal payoff where she gets all the resource less her nonagreement point payoff is the same for all the agents. Some years after Raiffa's work, Ehud Kalai and Meir Smorodinsky axiomatized this solution.[26] In the Braithwaite demand game, at this *Kalai-Smorodinsky solution* the two agents follow (G, M) for $\frac{4}{11}$ of the time and (M, G) for $\frac{7}{11}$ of the time. In *Morals by Agreement* David Gauthier defended a *minimax relative concession solution* for the *n*-agent bargaining problem that is

Solving $z \cdot \left(\frac{1}{2}, 1\right) + (1 - z) \cdot \left(1, \frac{2}{9}\right) = \left(\frac{15}{28}, \frac{17}{18}\right)$ yields $z = \frac{1}{14}$, so at the Nash solution Luke claims $\frac{1}{14}$ and Matthew claims $\frac{13}{14}$.

24. Howard Raiffa, "Arbitration Schemes for Generalized Two-Person Games," in *Contributions to the Theory of Games*, ed. H. Kuhn and A. W. Tucker (Princeton, NJ: Princeton University Press, 1953), 2, pp. 361–387.

25. Braithwaite's solution differs from Raiffa's egalitarian solution in that Braithwaite adopts a different scaling of the payoffs. Consequently, at Braithwaite's egalitarian solution the agents follow (G, M) for $\frac{16}{43}$ of the time and (M, G) for $\frac{27}{43}$ of the time.

26. Ehud Kalai and Meir Smorodinsky, "Other Solutions to Nash's Bargaining Problem," *Econometrica* 16 (1975), pp. 29–56.

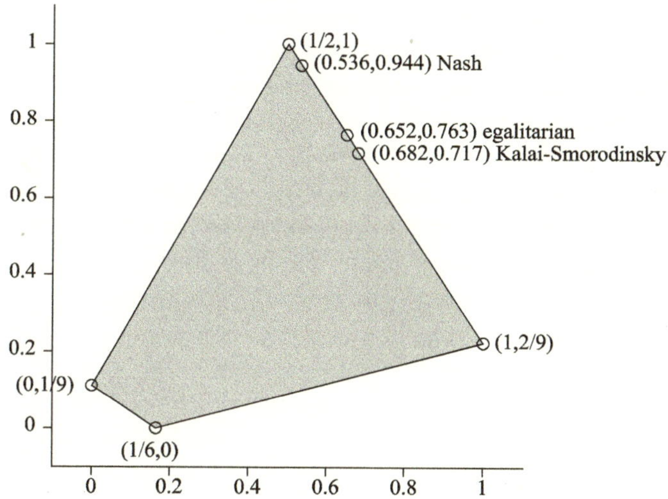

FIGURE 5.9 Axiomatic Solutions of the Braithwaite Demand Game

the Kalai-Smorodinsky solution in the 2-agent case.[27] While Raiffa, Kalai, and Smorodinsky refrained from declaring that the Kalai-Smorodinsky solution is generally superior to others, when Gauthier published *Morals by Agreement* he maintained that minimax relative concession solves the bargaining problem.[28] The Nash, egalitarian, and Kalai-Smorodinsky solutions of the Braithwaite Demand Game are depicted in Figure 5.9.

Braithwaite and Gauthier may have thought that the axiomatic approach can produce *the* fair solution to any given division problem, even if they defended different solutions. But is any axiomatic solution fully satisfactory? Each of the various axiomatic solution concepts game theorists have proposed fails to satisfy some property central to motivating some competing solution concepts. For example, the shares of the egalitarian solution can vary according to one's choice of payoff scales, and Nash and Kalai and Smorodinsky require their solution concepts to satisfy scale invariance.[29] On the other hand, if the feasible set is expanded with new payoff vectors that increase the possible gain of exactly one

27. Gauthier (1986). Chapter V. Gauthier presented an earlier defense of minimax relative concession in "Rational Cooperation," *Nous* 8 (1974), pp. 53–65.

28. In more recent work, Gauthier endorses a closely related principle of *maximin proportionate gain* that he discussed in Gauthier (1986), pp. 14–15, 154–155, but now defends using arguments inspired by Ariel Rubinstein's analysis of strategic bargaining discussed in the next paragraph. See Gauthier, "Twenty-Five On," *Ethics* 124 (2012), pp. 601–624.

29. Raiffa's and Braithwaite's alternative egalitarian solutions of the Braithwaite demand game illustrate how this solution concept can fail to satisfy scale invariance.

Agent i, then it is possible that the Nash solution of the expanded bargaining problem actually leaves Agent i worse off than at the Nash solution of the original problem. The Kalai-Smorodinsky and egalitarian solutions satisfy monotonicity properties that guarantee that an Agent i does not lose as the result of the feasible set being enlarged with payoff vectors more favorable to Agent i herself. And the Kalai-Smorodinsky solution is not stable when it is reapplied across subgroups. If the Kalai-Smorodinsky solution is applied first to all of the good and all the claimants are assigned their shares accordingly, and then if this concept is reapplied to the fraction of the good originally assigned to some proper subset of the claimants, the reapplication could leave some in this subset worse off than they were according to the original application. The Nash and egalitarian solutions satisfy reapplication stability properties that forestall this defect of the Kalai-Smorodinsky solution. Plainly, the Nash, Kalai-Smorodinsky, and egalitarian solutions all have drawbacks that accompany their virtues. In fact, any solution concept that requires a Pareto optimal division and equal division when the feasible set is perfectly symmetric is unstable with respect to either expansion of the feasible set in any agent's favor, reapplication across subgroups, or rescaling of payoffs.[30]

Game theorists have made some important steps toward completing the *Nash program* of relating the axiomatic and strategic bargaining approaches Nash proposed, but the strategic bargaining approach in its present state is of limited value for predicting the outcomes ideally rational and knowledgeable agents would follow in bargaining problems. Some of the central results of the *alternating offers* models of bargaining first proposed in the 1970s and 1980s by Ingolf Stähl and Ariel Rubinstein show that a pair of rational agents who are to exchange successive proposals for allocation of an infinitely divisible good will converge to a unique solution given common knowledge of their rationality, their payoffs, the bargaining procedure, and how much each discounts her payoff for the share she ultimately receives over the time periods during which they can submit new proposals.[31] As the length of these time periods approaches zero this solution for the Rubinstein model maximizes the *weighted Nash product* $(u_1(x)-u_{01})^{\alpha_1} \cdot (u_2(x)-u_{02})^{\alpha_2}$ for $\alpha_1, \alpha_2 \geq 0$. In this product α_i reflects Agent i's bargaining power and is defined as an increasing function of Agent i's discount factor, so a more patient agent has greater bargaining power. And for the special

30. John Thrasher gives a fine critique of the role of the symmetry axiom in bargaining theory in "Uniqueness and Symmetry in Bargaining Theories of Justice," *Philosophical Studies* 167 (2014), pp. 683–699.

31. Ingolf Stähl, *Bargaining Theory* (Stockholm: Economic Research Institute, 1972) and Ariel Rubinstein, "Perfect Equilibrium in a Bargaining Model," *Econometrica* 50 (1982), pp. 97–109.

case where $\alpha_1 = \alpha_2 = 1$, this product is the ordinary Nash product. This result is conceptually remarkable, since it shows how the outcome of an axiomatic solution could emerge from agents' individual strategic moves in certain special circumstances. But even assuming the underlying common knowledge of payoffs and discount factors that seldom, if ever, exists among agents in actual bargaining situations, alternating offers models such as the Rubinstein model give determinate solutions only for the 2-agent case where the good is infinitely divisible. In a bargaining problem with three or more agents, given sufficiently large discount factors the corresponding alternating offers models can converge to such a large set of distinct equilibria that these models do not even serve to narrow down the set of equilibrium outcomes the bargaining agents might reach in any interesting way.[32] And even in the 2-agent case, if the good is divisible only up to finitely many increments, like a sum of money, then two agents who otherwise satisfy the assumptions of the Rubinstein model might settle into practically any outcome better for both than the nonagreement point.[33]

In sum, each of the two rational choice approaches Nash proposed for analyzing the bargaining problem yields a negative moral along with its positive conclusions. The axiomatic approach shows that every bargaining problem has a unique solution satisfying several of a set of intuitively appealing properties, but no axiomatic solution concept satisfies all these properties. One who follows Braithwaite and Gauthier's lead and defends a certain axiomatic solution as the fair solution of division problems will have to "pick her poison" and decide which sort of solution instability to accept. The strategic bargaining approach shows that a highly stylized model of the process of bargaining between rational agents will for a 2-agent bargaining problem where the good is infinitely divisible reach a solution that coincides with an axiomatic solution. But for bargaining problems outside this narrow class, this approach yields no determinate results.

So far I have argued that neither of the two rational choice approaches Nash proposed for analyzing the bargaining problem is fully successful, at least not given the results both positive and negative discovered over the decades since Nash's original work. A quite different approach emphasizes learning and focal points. This approach exploits the fact that in a nontrivial bargaining problem, the Pareto frontier allocations all characterize correlated equilibrium conventions.

---

32. Martin J. Osborne and Ariel Rubinstein show by example that a 3-agent extension of the 2-agent Rubinstein model can converge to any outcome of the Pareto frontier in *Bargaining and Markets* (San Diego: Academic Press, 1990), pp. 63–65. Osborne and Rubinstein credit the example and the 3-agent extension of the Rubinstein model to Avner Shaked.

33. Eric Van Damme, Reinhard Selten, and Eyal Winter showed this in "Alternating Bid Bargaining with a Smallest Money Unit," *Games and Economic Behavior* 2 (1990), pp. 188–201.

Lewis argued that a convention can emerge and persist in a community if the defining equilibrium is salient for these community members, that is, this equilibrium "stands out" to them all. Schelling had much the same idea when he argued that agents can coordinate successfully by their all recognizing a certain outcome as a focal point of *their* interaction.[34] Hume gave much earlier salience–focal point explanations of the origins on conventions. In particular, Schelling and Hume argued that focal points can be crucial for the agents involved in a resource division problem.[35] Focal point explanations of efficient allocations in bargaining problems are illustrated in many examples in ordinary life and in the laboratory. In unstructured bargaining experiments, where the details of the bargaining process are left to the subjects themselves, subjects try to follow certain divisions they regard as focal.[36]

What makes a focal point focal? Schelling and Lewis, and Hume before them, frankly acknowledge that the agents tend to employ different sets of contextual clues in different situations where they hope to coordinate, and that consequently the answer to this question is indeterminate.[37] The bargaining problem as Nash formulates it might seem especially open-ended with respect to focal points given the huge number of strategy profiles, and accompanying payoff vectors, defined by various claim combinations available to the agents in any nontrivial bargaining problem. In principle, any outcome of a bargaining problem could be focal simply because the bargaining agents can distinguish this outcome from all of the others. But, as already noted, empirical evidence confirms that in many bargaining problems the agents involved do use focal points to coordinate on efficient divisions. What could explain the origins of the focal point effect? This effect can stem from learning. Game theorists have traditionally treated the learning and the focal point approaches to equilibrium selection separately. In fact, these two approaches are better viewed as interdependent. Any focal point effect in a coordination situation depends crucially upon what the agents trying to concert their actions know about each other. Trial-and-error learning can serve as one source of this knowledge. In bargaining problems, agents can learn to follow certain types of equilibria more often than others even when they have no

34. Schelling (1960), p. 57.

35. Schelling (1960), ch. I, and *Treatise* 3.2.3, especially p. 10, n. 5, where Hume argues that a natural allocation of several bottles of wine among three claimants follows from an application of a rule of accession.

36. See Roth, "Bargaining Experiments," in Kagel and Roth (1995), pp. 253–348, and Camerer (2003), ch. 4.

37. See especially Schelling (1960), pp. 54–58; Lewis (1969), pp. 35–38; and *Treatise* 3.2.3:4, n. 1, 3.2.4:1–2 and *Enquiry* 3.2:35–37.

contextual information other than their own individual payoffs, and the results of the learning process can lead them to regard certain solutions as focal.

In the remainder of this section I will explore how a focal point effect could emerge from learning by applying a weighted fictitious play model of inductive learning to some specific 2-agent bargaining problems. This model is similar to the weighted fictitious play model of learning in the State of Nature applied in §4.3. The interpretation of the weighted fictitious play process applied here is summarized as follows: A fixed pair of Bayesian rational agents engage in a specific demand game repeated over time periods. At each period each agent updates her conjecture over her counterpart's strategies according to the frequency of past observed profiles, and then follows a best response given her updated conjecture. To update according to this process, each agent need only know her own payoffs in the demand game and the strategies the counterpart has followed in the past. The mathematical details of this weighted fictitious play process are summarized in Appendix 2.

I begin with the Chocolate Cake problem. For this problem and for the asymmetric bargaining problems discussed below, I will apply weighted fictitious play to a corresponding demand game with *claim precision* $\delta = \frac{1}{100}$, that is, each agent may claim any fraction $\frac{m}{100}$ of the good where $m \in \{0,1,\ldots,100\}$. Each convention equilibrium $\left(\frac{m}{100}, \frac{100-m}{100}\right)$ where $m \in \{1,\ldots,99\}$ of this Chocolate Cake demand game is an attractor of the weighted fictitious play dynamic. But the different convention equilibria do not all have the same attracting power. The *basin of attraction* for weighted fictitious play of a strict Nash equilibrium is the set of possible initial conjectures according to this learning process, and the *size* of this basin is the fraction of the simplex of all possible conjectures defined by the conjectures of this basin.[38] Figure 5.10 summarizes the relative sizes of the basins of attraction of the weighted fictitious play dynamic applied to this Chocolate Cake demand game.

As one would expect, the limits of the orbits starting from initial points chosen at random in the belief simplex are distributed across the set of convention equilibria. But the $\left(\frac{1}{2}, \frac{1}{2}\right)$ equilibrium has the largest basin of attraction, and the distribution of orbit limits is centered around this equilibrium. This indicates that

38. The attraction frequencies of the weighted fictitious play process applied to the threshold public goods games described in §5.1 are actually sizes of basins of attraction. For example, for the Figure 1.12 Three-in-a-Boat game the basin of attraction of the (D, D, D) equilibrium for this weighted fictitious play process has size 0.6269.

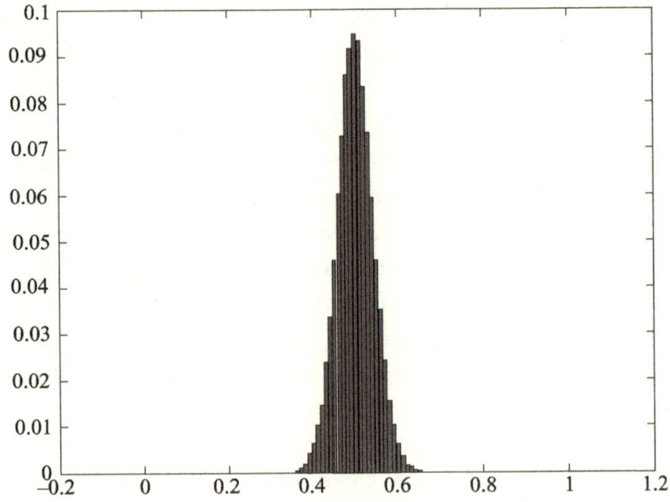

FIGURE 5.10 Relative Sizes of Basins of Attraction of Chocolate Cake Demand Game with Claim Precision $\delta = \frac{1}{100}$

inductive learners who engage repeatedly in a structurally symmetric bargaining problem like the Chocolate Cake problem might settle into a variety of division conventions, *and* that they will have some tendency to converge to the equal division convention. This dovetails with everyday experience, where parties in a completely symmetric division problem might regard equal division as salient and follow the equal division equilibrium most of the time, but perhaps not always.

In the Chocolate Cake bargaining problem, the Nash, Kalai-Smorodinsky, and egalitarian solutions all coincide at the $\left(\frac{1}{2}, \frac{1}{2}\right)$ point of equal division. Do inductive learners tend to converge to equilibria at or near any of these axiomatic solutions in an asymmetric bargaining problem? I consider next three such asymmetric problems. In *Morals by Agreement*, David Gauthier presents a simple example to illustrate how the Nash and Kalai-Smorodinsky solutions can differ.[39] Figure 5.11 summarizes the underlying *Gauthier basis game* and the feasible set that characterizes the corresponding demand game. In the Gauthier demand game, Laura's payoffs are the same as in the Chocolate Cake game, but Claudia's payoff at (M,G), where she concedes all of the good to Laura, is $\frac{1}{2}$ and Claudia receives an addition of $\frac{1}{2}x$ to her (M,G) payoff for any

39. Gauthier (1986), pp. 147–148.

(a)

		Laura: M	Laura: G
Claudia	M	$(0,0)$	$(\frac{1}{2},1)$
	G	$(1,0)$	$(0,0)$

M = modest (claim none), G = greedy (claim all)

(b)

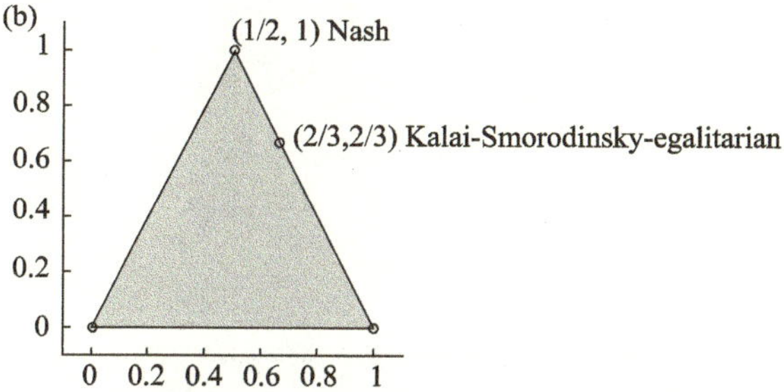

FIGURE 5.11 a. Gauthier Basis Game b. Feasible Set of Gauthier Demand Game

positive share x of the good she receives. In the Gauthier basis game, G is Laura's weakly dominant strategy, whereas either M or G can be Claudia's best response given her conjecture regarding Laura, so it appears that Laura has the upper hand. The Kalai-Smorodinsky and egalitarian solutions of the Gauthier demand game coincide at $\left(\frac{2}{3},\frac{2}{3}\right)$, and at this point Claudia's share is $\frac{1}{3}$ and Laura's share is $\frac{2}{3}$.[40] The Nash solution is $\left(\frac{1}{2},1\right)$, and the corresponding Nash equilibrium is (M,G), where Laura receives all of the good while Claudia receives none. The asymmetry in their preferences over the other's ideal point gives Laura a perfect threat advantage according to Nash's theory, even though (G,G) is the worst possible outcome for both. The Nash solution might strike one as plainly unfair, and it certainly seems to strike Gauthier this way. The Kalai-Smorodinsky-egalitarian solution may appear more equitable since this solution awards Claudia a positive share yet still respects Laura's apparent advantage to some extent. Figure 5.12 summarizes the relative sizes of the basins of attraction of weighted fictitious play applied to the Gauthier demand game with $\delta = \frac{1}{100}$ claim precision.

40. Gauthier uses this game partly to illustrate how the Nash and Kalai-Smorodinsky solutions can differ, without mentioning the egalitarian solution.

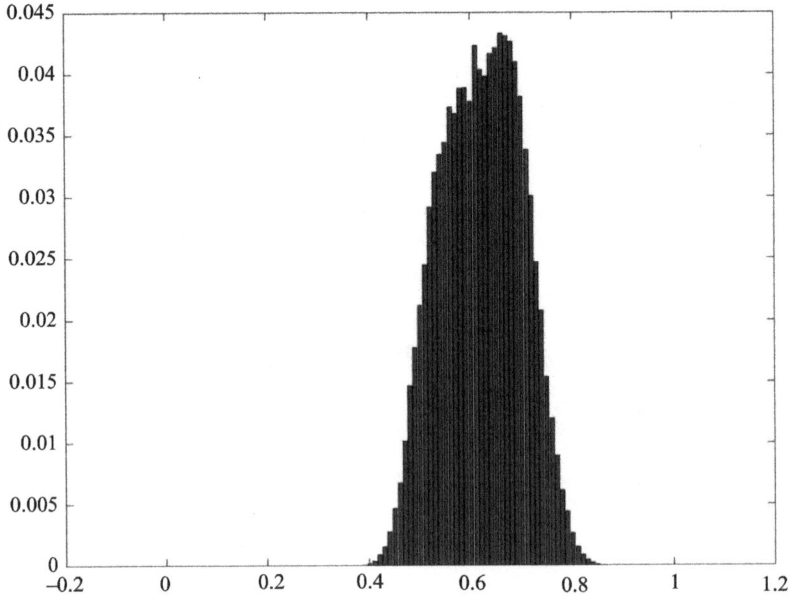

FIGURE 5.12 Relative Sizes of Basins of Attraction of Gauthier Demand Game with Claim Precision $\delta = \frac{1}{100}$

As was the case with the Chocolate Cake game, in the Gauthier game the weighted fictitious play process converges to a whole distribution of convention equilibria. But in this game, the orbits tend to converge to equilibria near the Kalai-Smorodinsky and egalitarian solution, and the modal attractors are particularly close to this solution. The Nash solution has a negligible basin of attraction. The Kalai-Smorodinsky- egalitarian solution looks like the "winner" over the Nash solution for the Gauthier demand game.

The next example is based upon an asymmetric impure coordination basis game. Figure 5.13 depicts the payoff structure of a 2×2 *False Mirror* basis game together with the feasible set of the corresponding demand game.[41] False Mirror gets its name because the geometric symmetries of the feasible set might give one the immediate impression that the solution of this bargaining problem should be $\left(\frac{13}{16}, \frac{13}{16}\right)$, where each receives half of the good. But the False Mirror basis game is asymmetric in its nonequilibrium outcomes, and the corresponding demand game is asymmetric with respect to threat advantage.

41. Luce and Raiffa (1957), p. 139, introduced this game as part of their critical discussion of alternate procedures for analyzing bargaining problems. The name "False Mirror" is my own.

(a)

Claudia \ Laura	M	G
M	$(\frac{3}{8}, 0)$	$(\frac{5}{8}, 1)$
G	$(1, \frac{5}{8})$	$(0, \frac{3}{8})$

M = modest (claim none), G = greedy (claim all)

(b)

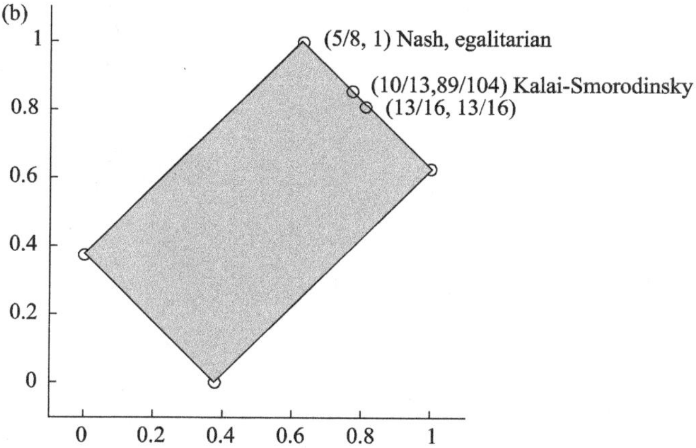

FIGURE 5.13 a. False Mirror Basis Game b. Feasible Set of False Mirror Demand Game

Laura has a greater tolerance than Claudia for suffering the consequences of arriving at the nonagreement point (G,G) and consequently has the threat advantage. In this bargaining problem the Kalai-Smorodinsky solution is $\left(\frac{10}{13},\frac{89}{104}\right)$, at which Claudia receives $\frac{5}{13}$ and Laura receives $\frac{8}{13}$ of the good. The Nash and the egalitarian solutions coincide at $\left(\frac{5}{8},1\right)$, where the agents follow the (M,G) equilibrium. Figure 5.14 summarizes the relative sizes of the basins of attraction of weighted fictitious play applied to the False Mirror demand game with $\delta = \frac{1}{100}$ claim precision. The Nash-egalitarian solution is the modal attracting equilibrium, and the entire distribution of orbit limits is skewed toward this solution.

The final example I will examine is Braithwaite's bargaining problem. In this bargaining problem the Nash, Kalai-Smorodinsky, and egalitarian solutions are mutually distinct. Figure 5.15 summarizes the relative sizes of the basins of

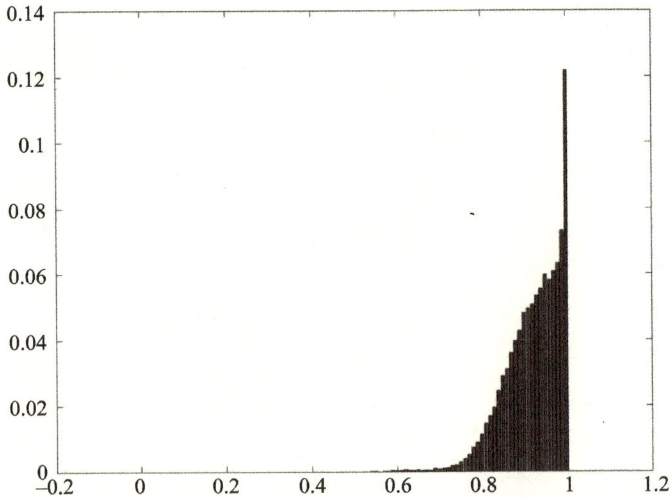

FIGURE 5.14 Relative Sizes of Basins of Attraction of False Mirror Demand Game with Claim Precision $\delta = \frac{1}{100}$

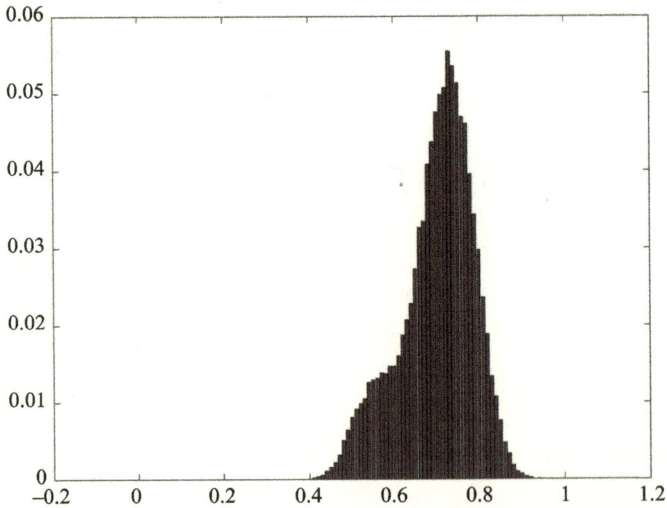

FIGURE 5.15 Relative Sizes of Basins of Attraction of Braithwaite Demand Game with Claim Precision $\delta = \frac{1}{100}$

attraction of weighted fictitious play applied to the Braithwaite demand game with claim precision $\delta = \frac{1}{100}$. Once more the egalitarian solution has a certain attracting power for this form of inductive learning. For this game the distribution of the orbits of the weighted fictitious play process is centered quite near the equilibrium of the egalitarian solution. The equilibrium nearest the Nash solution has a negligible basin of attraction. The equilibria closest to the Kalai-Smorodinsky and egalitarian solutions have non-negligible basins of attraction, but the basins of the latter equilibria are larger than those of the former, reflecting the stronger attracting power of the egalitarian solution. Interestingly, here the distribution of basin sizes shows a slight bimodality, with the smaller peak skewed toward the equilibrium of equal division that disregards Luke's and Matthew's payoffs. This indicates that the equal division has some small independent attracting power of its own, though far less than that of the egalitarian solution.

What do these numerical examples reveal? I conjecture that they illustrate how two general rules for dividing a good, namely, one rule that assigns claimants equal shares and another that aims to assign claimants equal relative benefits, could come into force in many contexts and how the equilibria they define even come to be regarded as focal points of division problems. In the bargaining theory Nash established, these rules are made precise as the egalitarian solution, with the equal relative benefits rule taking priority over the equal shares rule when the outcomes of these two rules do not coincide perfectly. In each of these examples populations of inductive learners converge to a variety of equilibria whose distribution is concentrated at or near the equilibrium of the egalitarian solution. The payoff scalings of these examples reflect the assumption that in the context of the particular bargaining problem, each agent would receive the same relative benefit at her ideal point, where she receives all of the good at stake, that the other would receive at his ideal point. I believe this assumption in turn reflects the predicament of claimants in many actual 2-agent division problems. I conjecture that for such problems, while many different bargaining conventions can emerge from trial-and-error learning, egalitarian solution equilibria may become psychologically prominent because these equilibria tend to be attracting points of such learning.

§5.2. Costly Punishment and Joint Cooperation

I have claimed that Hobbes, Locke, Hume, and Rousseau all discuss interactions having a Stag Hunt structure. They all use their various Stag Hunt interactions to illustrate the possibility of mutual cooperation for mutual benefit, and they all acknowledge that a suboptimal outcome is likely if the interacting parties lack sufficient faith in one another. Can the agents in a Stag Hunt learn to cooperate, as Rousseau seems to have believed? Figure 5.16 summarizes a 2-agent Stag Hunt game where each Agent i can either perform (P) or defect (D) and where the parameter α reflects how much the agents prefer the optimal (P,P) equilibrium over the (D,D) equilibrium.

		Agent 2	
		P	D
Agent 1	P	$(1+\alpha, 1+\alpha)$	$(0,1)$
	D	$(1,0)$	$(1,1)$

P = perform, D = defect

FIGURE 5.16 Stag Hunt

Along with the two strict Nash equilibria (P,P) and (D,D), the Figure 5.16 Stag Hunt has a third Nash equilibrium in mixed strategies (σ^*,σ^*) where each agent follows the mixed strategy $\sigma^* = \frac{1}{1+\alpha}P \oplus \frac{\alpha}{1+\alpha}D$ and has an expected payoff of 1. As discussed in 1.3, the Stag Hunt presents agents with a problem where risk and optimality are in tension. Defecting is the safe strategy, and each agent will be unwilling to perform if she lacks sufficient confidence that the other also will perform. Agents who engage in a Stag Hunt game can learn to follow (P,P) from repeated experience, same as they might learn to follow any other basic convention equilibrium of any game having multiple strict equilibria. But the suboptimal (D,D) equilibrium also characterizes a basic convention equilibrium that agents can learn to follow from repeated experience. Not surprisingly, for a variety of dynamical learning models the likelihood of agents settling into either strict equilibrium depends on the magnitude of α. To illustrate the point, I will apply another weighted fictitious process to some specific instances of the Figure 5.16 game. The interpretation of this *representative weighted fictitious play* process is that members of a community enter into a given game at different times and update their conjectures regarding their current interaction partners according to their private initial beliefs and what each of them has observed from the history of interactions.[42] When $\alpha = 1$, for representative weighted fictitious play the set of conjectures defining the (P,P) equilibrium has a basin of attraction $\Delta_{(P,P)}$ of size $m(\Delta_{(P,P)}) \approx 0.750$, and the set of conjectures defining the (D,D) equilibrium has a basin of attraction $\Delta_{(D,D)}$ of size $m(\Delta_{(D,D)}) \approx 0.250$. No other set of conjectures, including the set defining the mixed equilibrium (σ^*,σ^*), is an attracting point of representative weighted fictitious play.[43] For this Stag Hunt, the members of a

42. See Appendix 2 for a detailed description of this representative weighted fictitious play process.

43. In the examples discussed in this section, the sizes of basins of attraction for the representative weighted fictitious play process are estimated numerically by computer simulations that are summarized in Appendix 2.

community are more likely to learn to follow the optimal convention equilibrium because this equilibrium yields each a payoff so much greater than the guaranteed payoff of defecting. But the likelihood of settling into the suboptimal (D,D) equilibrium grows as the value of α decreases. For $\alpha = \frac{1}{2}$, where the Figure 5.16 game is equivalent to the Figure 1.11 Stag Hunt, the basins of attraction $\Delta_{(P,P)}$ and $\Delta_{(D,D)}$ of the (P,P) conjectures and the (D,D) conjectures for representative weighted fictitious play have sizes $m(\Delta_{(P,P)}) \approx 0.395$ and $m(\Delta_{(D,D)}) \approx 0.605$. For $\alpha = \frac{1}{4}$, these basins of attraction of representative weighted fictitious play have sizes $m(\Delta_{(P,P)}) \approx 0.020$ and $m(\Delta_{(D,D)}) \approx 0.980$. Agents who learn inductively according to this processes can learn to follow the optimal (P,P) for any value of $\alpha > 0$, but the likelihood of their settling into the safe (D,D) equilibrium increases markedly as the extra benefit of the optimal equilibrium reflected in the value of α decreases.

A simple extension of the Figure 5.16 game can dramatically change the agents' prospects for learning to perform together in a Stag Hunt for any $\alpha > 0$. If one agent in a 2-agent Stag Hunt game performs and her partner defects, the performer will presumably be disappointed in her partner, since she trusted her partner enough to perform herself. This performer ran the risk of arriving at her worst possible outcome of the game, and her defecting partner indeed placed her at this outcome. I will label an agent who defects in a 2-agent Stag Hunt when her partner performs a *provocative defector* precisely because she has let her performing partner down.[44] As the name suggests, a provocative defector might incite a punitive response from her now angry partner. Suppose that the Stag Hunt interaction is expanded as follows: If either agent performs alone, once she realizes her partner has defected provocatively because she received the payoff corresponding to leaving a hunt empty-handed, she can then immediately punish her partner. Figure 5.17 summarizes a corresponding *Augmented Stag Hunt* game in strategic form. The pure strategies P and D in Augmented Stag Hunt in effect simply replicate performing and defecting, respectively, in the ordinary Figure 5.16 Stag Hunt. The substantively new addition is the vengeful strategy R, which has an agent first perform and then punish if her partner has defected, incurring a *punisher's cost* $r > 0$ and inflicting a *punishee's cost* $p \geq r$ on her defecting partner. Embellishing Rousseau's original story, one can think of a punisher picking a

44. The term "provocative defector" is obviously similar to and influenced by Gregory Kavka's term "offensive violator," which I have used elsewhere in this book. However, a provocative defector in this context need not be an offensive violator since I do not assume any of the agents in this Stag Hunt have an antecedent obligation to perform.

		Agent 2		
		P	D	R
	P	$(1+\alpha, 1+\alpha)$	$(0,1)$	$(1+\alpha, 1+\alpha)$
Agent 1	D	$(1,0)$	$(1,1)$	$(1-p, -r)$
	R	$(1+\alpha, 1+\alpha)$	$(-r, 1-p)$	$(1+\alpha, 1+\alpha)$

$P = C_1, B_2\text{-if-}D_1,\ D = D_1, R = C_1, R_2\text{-if-}D_1,\ \alpha > 0,\ r \geq 0,\ p \geq 0$

FIGURE 5.17 Augmented Stag Hunt

fight with the provocative defector and possibly even destroying the defector's hare in the process, but knowing the conflict will prove costly for them both. This 3×3 symmetric game has five Nash equilibria in pure strategies, namely, the four equilibria (P,P), (P,R), (R,P), and (R,R) where each agent's payoff is $1+\alpha$ and the equilibrium (D,D) where each agent's payoff is 1. This game also has a large set of Nash equilibria involving mixed strategies. The strategy profile (σ^*, σ^*) where $\sigma^* = \frac{1}{1+\alpha}\cdot P \oplus \frac{\alpha}{1+\alpha}\cdot D$ is a Nash equilibrium with payoff vector $(1,1)$, and any strategy profile (σ_1', σ_2') where $\sigma_1' = x_1 P \oplus (1-x_1) R$ and $\sigma_2' = x_2 P \oplus (1-x_2) R$ for $x_1, x_2 \in [0,1]$ is a Nash equilibrium with the optimal payoff vector $(1+\alpha, 1+\alpha)$. However, the suboptimal (D,D) is the only strict Nash equilibrium of this game. In a context where agents learn as representatives of larger populations, one can interpret a mixed strategy as a *polymorphism* where the mixing probabilities are the proportions in the populations that follow given pure strategies. Given this interpretation, Augmented Stag Hunt has many optimal polymorphic equilibria where everyone in the community follows either P or R.

By introducing the new R strategy, Augmented Stag Hunt greatly increases the set of optimal Nash equilibria available to the two agents over the single optimal (P,P) equilibrium of ordinary Stag Hunt. However, it is by no means clear that a rational agent would ever follow the R strategy. Since $r > 0$, the acquiescing P weakly dominates the punishing R. One might regard following R as a rudimentary form altruistic punishment. I say "rudimentary" because successful altruistic punishers benefit their own groups at some costs to themselves, while it is not immediately clear that Augmented Stag Hunt punishers will tend to benefit anyone as a result of their costly punishments. Indeed, I do not assume punishers in Augmented Stag Hunt belong to any well-defined subgroups in the population that engage in this game, and the models of this section are selection models at the individual level. The requirement that $p \geq r$ reflects the intuition that an agent would be unwilling to punish if the punisher's cost were

		Agent 2		
		P	D	R
	P	$(\frac{5}{4}, \frac{5}{4})$	$(0, 1)$	$(\frac{5}{4}, \frac{5}{4})$
Agent 1	D	$(1, 0)$	$(1, 1)$	$(1, 0)$
	R	$(\frac{5}{4}, \frac{5}{4})$	$(0, 1)$	$(\frac{5}{4}, \frac{5}{4})$

$R = P$

FIGURE 5.18 Extended Stag Hunt with Duplicate P-Strategies, $\alpha = \frac{1}{4}$

greater than the punishee's cost, and is in line with much of the experimental literature on punishment where the punishee's cost is equal to or greater than the punisher's cost.[45]

How likely are particular strategies of the Augmented Stag Hunt to evolve over time? To address this question, I will apply dynamical models of learning to the Augmented Stag Hunt. First, I will apply representative weighted fictitious play to some representative examples. To establish a baseline of comparison, I first apply this dynamic to the 3×3 game characterized by Figure 5.18. The Figure 5.18 game is effectively a degenerate Augmented Stag Hunt game with $r = p = 0$, so that there is no punisher's cost or punishee's cost associated with R. In this 3×3 game, if either strategy R or P is deleted, the resulting 2×2 game is equivalent to the Figure 5.16 Stag Hunt with $\alpha = \frac{1}{4}$, so that R and P are effectively copies or "clones" of the same strategy of simply performing, while D remains the strategy of defecting. For the representative weighted fictitious play process the basin of attraction $\Delta_{(D,D)}$ of the (D, D) equilibrium conjectures has size $m\left(\Delta_{(D,D)}\right) \approx 0.928$. The basins of attraction for the optimal equilibria in this game together constitute only a share 0.059 of the distribution simplex. For this game, the suboptimal (D, D) equilibrium is by far the most powerful attractor of representative weighted fictitious play.

Nevertheless, the attracting power of the set of optimal equilibria increases dramatically when there are positive punisher and punishee costs in Augmented Stag Hunt. I will illustrate this phenomenon with the Augmented Stag Hunts of Figures 5.19 and 5.20. For the Figure 5.19 game, the punisher's cost $r = \frac{1}{4}$ is equivalent to the difference α between the optimal value of half a deer and the

45. See note 13.

		Agent 2		
		P	D	R
	P	$(\frac{5}{4}, \frac{5}{4})$	$(0, 1)$	$(\frac{5}{4}, \frac{5}{4})$
Agent 1	D	$(1, 1)$	$(1, 1)$	$(-\frac{1}{4}, -\frac{1}{4})$
	R	$(\frac{5}{4}, \frac{5}{4})$	$(-\frac{1}{4}, -\frac{1}{4})$	$(\frac{5}{4}, \frac{5}{4})$

FIGURE 5.19 Augmented Stag Hunt, $\alpha = \frac{1}{4}$, $r = \frac{1}{4}$, $p = 1 + r = \frac{5}{4}$

	Agent 2		
	P	D	R
P	$(\frac{5}{4}, \frac{5}{4})$	$(0, 1)$	$(\frac{5}{4}, \frac{5}{4})$
D	$(1, 0)$	$(1, 1)$	$(-1, -1)$
R	$(\frac{5}{4}, \frac{5}{4})$	$(-1, -1)$	$(\frac{5}{4}, \frac{5}{4})$

FIGURE 5.20 Augmented Stag Hunt, $\alpha = \frac{1}{4}$, $r = 1$, $p = 1 + r = 2$

value of a hare and the punishee's cost $p = r + 1 = \frac{5}{4}$ is the value of half a deer. In this game the basin of attraction of the (D, D) equilibrium for representative weighted fictitious play has size $m(\Delta_{(D,D)}) \approx 0.400$, and the basins of attraction of the optimal equilibria take up the share 0.600 of the distribution simplex, with the basin of attraction of the (P, P) equilibrium having size $m(\Delta_{(P,P)}) \approx 0.596$. For the Figure 5.20 game, where the punisher's cost $r = 1$ is the value of a hare and the punishee's cost $p = r + 1 = 2$ is the value of two hares, the basin of attraction for (D, D) has size $m(\Delta_{(D,D)}) \approx 0.280$ and the basins of attraction of the optimal equilibria take up 0.720 of the distribution simplex with $m(\Delta_{(P,P)}) \approx 0.718$. The key to these improvements in the agents' prospects for achieving an optimal equilibrium is the magnitude of the punishee's cost. The basins of attraction of optimal equilibria take up a larger share of the distribution simplex than that of the suboptimal equilibrium because $p = r + 1 > 1$, that is, the punishee's cost is greater than the gain of provocative defection and consequently the punishee suffers a non-negligible net loss. Strikingly, for this inductive learning dynamic, equilibria that include the punishing strategy R have very small positive basins of attraction of their own. This is because P weakly dominates R so that in the limit, most of the agents who followed the punishing strategy R in the beginning as their parts of an optimal polymorphic equilibrium gradually convert to P. The mere presence of the R strategy that punishes provocative defectors transforms the original Stag Hunt into a new game where mutual performance is more likely to emerge than mutual defection. Perhaps even more strikingly, optimal equilibria become more likely to emerge as the magnitude of the punishment increases. The Figure 5.19 and Figure 5.20 games illustrate this phenomenon. Punishing might appear to be even more "irrational" in the Figure 5.20 game than in the Figure 5.19 game because the punishment cost in the former game is greater, but allowing for the presence of R-followers in the Augmented Stag Hunt with the greater punishment cost leads to even better prospects for the emergence of optimal equilibria.

It is instructive to examine the outcomes when other dynamics are applied to Augmented Stag Hunt games such as the specific games discussed above. Here I will consider a variation of *weighted best response*, a continuous time dynamic that complements the discrete time representative weighted fictitious play processes. Like representative weighted fictitious play, weighted best response models the process of inductive learning in a community. But while representative weighted fictitious play learners update conjectures at successive time periods, weighted best response learners update conjectures over continuous time intervals, so this learning process can have easily identifiable geometric properties for various games.[46] To reflect the possibility that some population members might make mistakes or experiment, one can introduce *mutation* into the learning process, so that at any given time $\delta > 0$ of the population updaters follow a strategy chosen at random while the remaining $1 - \delta$ update according to their best responses. This results in a *perturbed* weighted best response dynamic with mutation rate δ. For any $\delta > 0$, if an orbit of the perturbed weighted best response dynamic approaches a limit, this limit is a Nash equilibrium. In the following examples I will apply perturbed weighted best response with mutation rate $\delta = 0.01$. Again for purposes of comparison with nontrivial Augmented Stag Hunts, I first examine the Figure 5.18 game that extends ordinary Stag Hunt with duplicate P strategies. Figure 5.21 depicts a phase diagram of orbits of the perturbed weighted best response dynamic applied to the triangular simplex of possible conjectures of the Figure 5.19 game.[47]

46. See Appendix 2 for a more detailed description of the weighted best response dynamic.

47. The simplex of possible conjectures for a 3×3 symmetric game can be represented as a triangle where each point corresponds to a mixed strategy conjecture and in particular each vertex

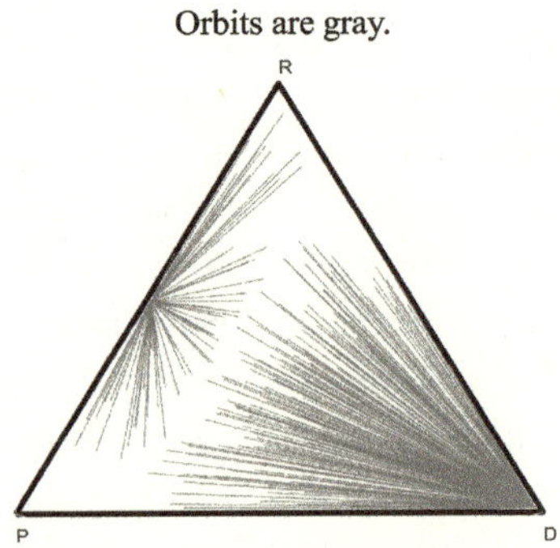

FIGURE 5.21 Perturbed Weighted Best Response Dynamic Applied to Figure 5.18 Game

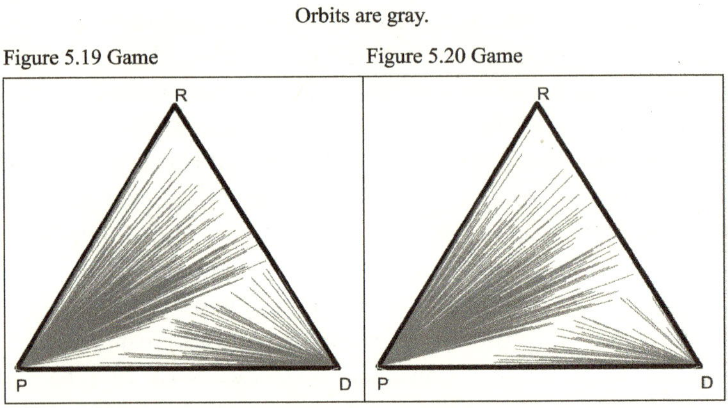

FIGURE 5.22 Perturbed Weighted Best Response Dynamic Applied to Figure 5.19 and Figure 5.20 Games

For this game, the points that define the conjectures that all in the population follow D and the polymorphism $\sigma' = \frac{1}{2}P \oplus \frac{1}{2}R$ are both attractors of the dynamic. The basin of attraction of the strategy σ' that defines an optimal polymorphic equilibrium (σ', σ') is much smaller than the basin of attraction of the strategy D that defines the suboptimal but uniquely strict equilibrium (D, D).

As was the case for the discrete representative weighted fictitious play process, the attracting power for weighted best response dynamics of strategies that define optimal equilibria is dramatically greater for true Augmented Stag Hunt games

---

corresponds to one of the pure strategies. The phase diagrams of this section were created in MatLab by plotting 300 orbits of the perturbed weighted best response dynamic with initial point chosen at random in the possible conjecture simplex.

where the punitive strategy R results in positive costs for both punisher and provocative defector. Figure 5.22 depicts phase diagrams of perturbed weighted best response dynamics applied to the Figure 5.19 and Figure 5.20 games. For these games, there are again two basins of attraction and the D-point is still an attractor, but with a basin that is now by far the smaller basin of attraction. In both these games, the point that defines P is now the other attractor, and this point has by far the larger basin of attraction. Moreover, the basin of attraction of the P-point is even larger for the Figure 5.20 game than for the Figure 5.19 game, even though the weakly dominated R-strategy of the former game is apparently even more "irrational" than the weakly dominated than that of the latter game. Again, this is because the net loss a punishee suffers for provocative defection is even greater in the Figure 5.20 game than in the Figure 5.19 game. Interestingly, the attracting point of the larger basin in these games is that of the acquiescing pure strategy P rather than some polymorphism when some follow P and the rest follow R. This result is similar to that of discrete representative weighted fictitious play applied to these games where a large majority of orbits converged to conjectures of optimal equilibria and nearly almost of these converged to the conjectures of the (P,P) equilibrium. Again, the mere presence of the punitive but weakly dominated R strategy greatly increases the likelihood of the population converging to the optimal equilibrium where all follow P. However, the system is continually "bombarded" by random mutant strategies, so some few are always following D and R even when the system is close to the P-point. Indeed, as Figure 5.22 illustrates, the orbits approach the attracting D-, σ-, and P-points quite closely without ever quite reaching them. So even though a population might seldom need to "use" R-following punishers in the limit to approach the equilibrium where all follow P, the continuing presence of some few R-followers may serve to maintain the stability of the P-point equilibrium.

In this section I have shown by example that a population prone to converge to the defecting equilibrium of the ordinary Stag Hunt has much better prospects for settling into an equilibrium where each side performs when their strategy set is expanded to include the weakly dominated punishing strategy. In the numerical examples of Augmented Stag Hunts with positive punisher costs discussed here, optimal equilibria of mutual performance are far more likely to emerge than the equilibrium of defection, even though in the corresponding ordinary 2×2 Stag Hunt the reverse is the case and the (D,D) equilibrium is far more likely to emerge than the (P,P) equilibrium. This phenomenon generalizes across a wide class of Augmented Stag Hunts for a variety of dynamical updating processes. When $p - r \geq 1$, that is, the punishee's net loss is at least as great as the punisher's net loss, then for weighted best response and other related dynamics the basin of attraction of strategies involving P and R only is larger than the basin

Agent 2

	D	R
D	$(1,1)$	$(1-p,\ -r)$
R	$(-r, 1-p)$	$(1+\alpha, 1+\alpha)$

FIGURE 5.23 Reduced Figure 5.17 Game

of attraction of strategy D for *any* value of $\alpha > 0$, even though the size of the basin of attraction of P in the ordinary Stag Hunt approaches zero as α approaches zero.[48] Informally, the reason the punishing R strategy promotes performance so dramatically is that R introduces a secondary element of coordination into the Stag Hunt. Figure 5.23 highlights this by summarizing the 2×2 game that results when the acquiescing P is deleted. This is a coordination game where following D no longer guarantees one the minimum payoff of the (D, D) equilibrium. When $p - r \geq 1$, in the Figure 5.23 game the punishing R has much greater attracting power than P has in the corresponding ordinary 2×2 Stag Hunt. For many dynamical processes such as the learning dynamics discussed here, each of the polymorphisms of the form $\sigma' = xP \oplus (1-x)R$ for $x > 0$ has a contribution from R that gives all strategies that include P some additional "pull." Individually, each σ' might have relatively weak attracting power, especially compared against the attracting power of D, but collectively these polymorphic strategies can win out a substantial majority of the time. In a sense, then, the weakly dominated strategy of punishment gives the performers in a population greater strength.

Conclusion

In this chapter I have explored how the members of a community can learn to "play fair" in certain interactions, so that they tend to follow certain fairness equilibria of these interactions. The analysis here contributes to the ongoing research program of recent years that explores how tendencies to treat others fairly and to punish those who fail to do likewise can evolve in a population. The above analyses of the 2-agent bargaining problem and the Augmented Stag Hunt complement other studies that show how fairness norms and strong reciprocity

48. This result is proved for the *replicator dynamics* that are frequently used to model the evolution of strategies in both human and nonhuman populations in Peter Vanderschraaf, "In a Weakly Dominated Strategy Is Strength: Evolution of Optimality in Stag Hunt Augmented with a Punishment Option," *Philosophy of Science* 83 (2016), pp. 29–59. The proof of this result for weighted best response dynamics is similar to the proof in Vanderschraaf (2016).

norms can emerge. The analyses of these two specific problems also yield some more general philosophical morals.

The analysis of the Augmented Stag Hunt of §5.2 shows how a strategy that is effectively an altruistic punishment strategy can evolve and support a polymorphic equilibrium of mutual performance. The learning models used in this analysis are representative models that can be interpreted this way: At successive points in time, individual members of a population who engage in a game update their conjectures regarding the strategies counterparts will follow according to the strategies they have observed fellow members follow, then meet partners and engage in the game with these partners, following their best responses given their current conjectures. These representative models do not assume the population members always engage with the same partners, or with partners from certain proper subgroups, or even that they can distinguish between proper subgroups and then adopt subgroup-dependent contingency strategies. Most of the existing models of the evolution of strong reciprocity phenomena like altruistic punishment are *group selection* models. These models are used to support arguments of this very rough general form: If a group includes a certain portion of strong reciprocators, then this group will exhibit greater fitness than similarly structured groups that lack strong reciprocators. Such greater group fitness can be explicated in terms of a group's tendency to grow in numbers or to be stable with respect to invasions of noncooperative behaviors. While the emerging strong reciprocity tradition has done much to revive interest in group selection, the idea remains somewhat controversial in evolutionary theory. For my own part, I regard group selection models as a valuable part of a larger explanation of social cooperation, but I would not want to rely solely upon them. Group selection models obviously presuppose *groups*, and presumably the process of group formation requires at least some forms of cooperative conduct. In particular, well-defined groups might not exist among the parties in a Hobbesian State of Nature where by definition these parties have no obligations toward one another. Strong reciprocity has great explanatory power. Given its importance, one might wonder if an alternative explanation of the evolution of strong reciprocity that does not appeal to group selection might be available. The §5.2 analysis of the Augmented Stag Hunt is an *individual selection* analysis that illustrates how a form of strong reciprocity that benefits one's whole population can evolve.

In the 2-agent bargaining problems examined in §5.1, the simple process that mimics inductive learning results in a distribution of equilibria concentrated at or near the egalitarian solution. Braithwaite gave an a priori argument that the fair solution to a 2-agent bargaining problem is the egalitarian solution.[49] In

---

49. Again, Braithwaite's use of a payoff scale different from the Raiffa scale used in the Figure 5.7 game produces a solution different from the egalitarian solution based on the Figure 5.7 game. See note 25.

Chapter 8 I will argue that the egalitarian solution, but not the Nash solution or the Kalai-Smorodinsky solution, belongs to a family of solutions that characterize the just bargaining conventions. So one can view the §5.1 results as lending some empirical support in the form of computer experimental results to Braithwaite's and my own conclusions. Another and surely more controversial conclusion one can draw from the §5.1 analysis is that it lends support for admitting interpersonal utility comparisons into the analysis of fair division problems. As Raiffa recognized when he first introduced the egalitarian solution, this solution concept presupposes that the utilities of the agents can be measured against each other according to some common scale, so that it makes sense to refer to points where all benefit equally with respect to the nonagreement point. For this axiomatic solution, the "poison" one must pick is to incorporate interpersonal utility comparisons. Many follow Nash in doubting that one can compare utilities across individuals in a meaningful way. Others, such as John Harsanyi, argue that interpersonal utility comparisons are unavoidable in any reasonable theories of morality and justice, and that rather than evade the issue philosophers and social scientists must strive to develop rigorous logical foundations for interpersonal utility comparisons.[50] Skeptics continue to ask, "But how?," although I believe significant progress has been achieved in recent years.[51] Luce and Raiffa took a more mitigated stance in the 1950s, and I think their position continues to have merit. Luce and Raiffa acknowledge that interpersonal utility comparisons have yet to be put on a scientific footing, but they also point out that in many actual bargaining situations the bargainers themselves make informal references to interpersonal utility comparisons, and that mathematical abstractions of such situations should reflect such comparisons.[52] When he introduced the egalitarian solution, Raiffa did this by converting the payoffs of each agent to a 0–1 scale. The §5.1 examples use this specific conversion. These examples show that when

50. John Harsanyi, "Cardinal Welfare, Individualistic Ethics, and Interpersonal Comparisons of Utility," *Journal of Political Economy* 63 (1955), pp. 309–332, and *Rational Behavior and Bargaining Equilibrium in Games and Social Situations* (Cambridge: Cambridge University Press, 1977), ch. 4. However, it is important to note that Harsanyi (1977), §9.11, states that while he believes interpersonal utility comparisons are crucial in making moral value judgments, he is much more doubtful that they should play a direct role in the solution of a bargaining problem. Unlike Raiffa and Braithwaite, Harsanyi does not consider the bargaining problem a proper tool for analyzing principles of fair division.

51. Ken Binmore has produced a particularly sophisticated theory of interpersonal utility comparisons based upon *empathetic preferences*. Binmore develops elements of his theory in various writings, but gives his most comprehensive presentation in Binmore (1994), ch. 4, and *Game Theory and the Social Contract*, vol. II, *Just Playing* (Cambridge, MA: MIT Press, 1998), ch. 2.

52. Luce and Raiffa (1957), pp. 131–132.

the agents' payoffs are scaled this way, the egalitarian solution has a certain pull in the learning process.

If one grants that interpersonal utility comparisons make sense in some contexts, then one can establish an equivalence between Aristotle's proportionality principle and the egalitarian solution of the bargaining problem. So the analysis of bargaining problems in §5.1 in fact suggests a focal point explanation for the wide acceptance of Aristotle's principle. To apply the proportionality principle, claimants need to agree upon how to ascertain the value of a quantity of the good at stake and upon the relevant criteria of worth.[53] If they can agree, then the claimants have a common standard for measuring their gains relative to their worth, but as Aristotle observes more than once, claimants tend to disagree over the criteria of worth.[54] Suppose that Laura and Claudia have resolved these problems and agree how to measure both the value of a share of the good at stake and their relative worth. If Claudia and Laura conform their respective claims x_1 and x_2 to Aristotle's principle, then these claims must satisfy

$$\frac{w_1 + V(x_1)}{w_2 + V(x_2)} = \frac{w_1}{w_2}$$

or equivalently

$$w_1^{-1}V(x_1) = w_2^{-1}V(x_2)$$

where $V(x_i)$ is the value of a share x_i of the good and $w_1 > 0$ and $w_2 > 0$ are the respective measures of Claudia's and Laura's relative worth with respect to this good.[55] If Claudia's and Laura's payoffs are calibrated to equal their weighted gains so that $u_1(x_1) - u_{01} = w_1^{-1}V(x_1)$ and $u_2(x_2) - u_{02} = w_2^{-1}V(x_2)$, then the egalitarian solution of the corresponding demand game is the value of $x \in [0,1]$ that solves

53. *Politics* 1280a11–19, *Nicomachean Ethics* 1131a20–24. In his fine reconstruction of Aristotle's account of distributive justice, David Keyt interprets Aristotle as maintaining that people tend to agree upon how to value shares of the good at stake, and tend to disagree mainly over which criteria are relevant criteria of worth. See David Keyt, "Aristotle's Theory of Distributive Justice," in *A Companion to Aristotle's* Politics, ed. David Keyt and Fred D. Miller Jr. (Oxford: Basil Blackwell, 1991), p. 242.

54. *Nicomachean Ethics* 1131a25–28, *Politics* 1280a18–19.

55. For the first version of Aristotle's formula given here, which reconstructs Aristotle's final formulation in *Nicomachean Ethics* 1131b4–10, I draw upon Keyt (1991), pp. 241–242.

$$w_1^{-1}V(x) = w_2^{-1}V(1-x)$$

which is the Aristotelian proportionate solution of their division problem.[56] For example, in the Chocolate Cake problem where Claudia and Laura are assumed to be equally worthy with respect to shares of the cake, the Aristotelian solution becomes the solution to $u_1(x_1) = x_1 = u_2(x_2) = x_2$, namely, $x_1 = x_2 = \frac{1}{2}$. If asked just why everyone accepts the formal proportionality principle for dividing a good justly, Aristotle can take a helping hand from Hume, Schelling, and Lewis and respond that this principle defines a focal convention of the equivalent bargaining problem.

I began this chapter by examining a pair of apparently anomalous phenomena observed and tested rigorously in the laboratory. Rejecting positive offers perceived as too lopsided in Ultimatum games and punishing defectors at a personal cost in public good games are explainable as products of an evolved tendency in our species to treat others fairly and to punish those who fail to do likewise. This tendency to "play fair" influences conduct and how we think about our conduct far beyond laboratory settings. A general requirement to "play fair" is deeply rooted in the natural law tradition from antiquity. A number of the great figures in both the classical and the modern natural law traditions maintain that requirements of the natural law follow from some version of the Golden Rule.[57] These natural law requirements correspond to the principle "Do unto others as you would have them do unto you," since they require one to act for the benefit of others, possibly at some personal cost. One way, though admittedly not the most common way, to understand such natural moral law precepts is as distinguished conventions. Hume articulates this idea explicitly, maintaining both that the requirements of justice are conventions and that one can rightly refer to these requirements as laws of nature.[58] Hobbes' first two *Leviathan* laws of nature that include positive requirements to abstain from aggression against another and from seizing another's possessions without permission illustrate the conventionalist viewpoint. Given the Stag Hunt summaries of these two laws of nature discussed in §1.3, the strategy these two laws summarize is to perform unless one cannot expect others to reciprocate, and this strategy characterizes

56. Binmore (1998), pp. 397–399, gives a similar argument for the equivalence of the Aristotelian proportionality rule in division problems and the egalitarian solution of the bargaining problem.

57. See especially Aquinas, *Summa Theologiæ* I–II Q 94 A 4, Q 99 A 1–3; Hobbes, *Elements of Law I* 17:9, *De Cive* 3:27, and *Leviathan* 14:5, 15:35; and Pufendorf, *On the Law of Nature and of Nations* II.3.

58. *Treatise* 3.2.1:19, 3.2.2:9–10.

optimal Stag Hunt conventions. These two Hobbesian laws of nature forbid offensive violations of the prohibitions against aggression and stealing but permit defensive violations of these prohibitions, and reflect a modified version of the Golden Rule of the Gospel: "Do unto others as you would have them do unto you to the extent you can expect others to reciprocate."[59] Our evolved tendency to "play fair" helps to explain the origins of natural law requirements understood as special conventions.

In Chapter 4 I argued that Hobbes was right to conclude that war is inevitable in a State of Nature. There I argued that a key underlying circumstance that drives State of Nature parties to war is their inability to generate common knowledge, so that they cannot adopt contingency strategies for treating the more aggressive differently from the more modest. One can think of the Chapter 4 analysis as applying to a large undifferentiated population who find themselves bereft of the protection a government ordinarily provides and the expectations of mutual aid created by personal ties. One can understand this chapter as giving at least part of a story of how parties might escape the Hobbesian State of Nature, and the analysis here as applying to smaller groups who are able to learn what to expect from one another and to generate common knowledge of their mutual expectations. I think Hobbes and Hume would agree with the spirit of the analysis here. Hume in *Treatise* is clear that small communities whose members have learned to follow the fundamental natural laws concerning stability of possession, transferring possession, and promise keeping are antecedent to government and that government is in fact founded upon these natural laws.[60] And I think it is no mistake that in all three of his major treatises on politics and morals Hobbes presents his account of natural law before he discusses the origins of civil society. But what about cooperation on a grand scale, so that a large society becomes capable of industry, importing and exporting goods, arts, letters, public goods including public safety, and all of the other benefits of social life that Hobbes argues State of Nature parties would be without? Hobbes and Hume argue that as a leaderless community grows in size, it becomes more unstable as its members grow confused over how they should work together and are increasingly tempted to free-ride.[61] I am hardly unorthodox in agreeing with Hobbes and Hume that at some point, a community needs government in order to coordinate their actions in some of their most important collective action problems. Government is the topic of the following chapter.

---

59. Kavka attributes a similar *copper rule* to Hobbes: "Do unto others as they do unto you" (1986, p. 347). In a graduate seminar he led after he published *Hobbesian Moral and Political Theory*, Kavka in oral conversation gave a more refined version: "Do unto others as you expect them to do unto you."

60. *Treatise* 3.2.8:3.

61. *Leviathan* 17:3–4 and *Treatise* 3.2.8:8. The *Treatise* discussion includes Hume's example of draining the meadow discussed in Chapter 1.

6 A LIMITED LEVIATHAN

[A]lthough social activity is required prior to the creation of an agency agreement with the ruler, this activity, when properly understood, is both prepolitical and possible for Hobbesian people to perform. . . . [H]er institution is accomplished when the subjects, by various means, perform (what are perceived as) individually rational actions creating a *convention* among themselves that she will rule over them. Only insofar as this convention exists does the sovereign have the power base enabling her to rule. So the people who establish and maintain this convention are the sovereign's employer. Or, to put it another way, the sovereign is hired by the sum of the individuals whose actions maintain this convention, and the sovereign is fired when these individuals no longer find it rational to act so as to maintain this convention.

—JEAN HAMPTON, *Hobbes and the Social Contract Tradition*

Introduction

The social contract is an ancient idea, with a long and multifaceted tradition. According to one common recounting of the history of pre-twentieth-century political philosophy, discussions of the social contract first emerge in the Sophist tradition, reappear from time to time in the Roman and Scholastic traditions, reach full flower in the early modern tradition of Hobbes, Pufendorf, Locke, and Rousseau, and then suffer abrupt and apparently decisive refutation at the hands of David Hume. Starting in the mid-twentieth century, contractarianism has enjoyed a tremendous revival. But exactly what is the social contract? In fact, contractarianism encompasses a large family of both political and moral theories.[1] In its most generic sense, a social contract for a given society corresponds to a body of norms for regulating the interactions of its members. When Glaucon discusses justice in *Republic* and Gerald Gaus discusses social morality in his recent *The Order of Public Reason*, they discuss the social contract in this generic

1. In the inaugural issue of *Journal of Applied Ethics and Philosophy* Michael Davis published an essay titled "Fourteen Kinds of Social Contract." See *Journal of Applied Ethics and Philosophy* 1 (2009), pp. 8–19.

sense.[2] There is also a more restricted sense of the social contract corresponding specifically to the state that regulates civil society. Locke in *The Second Treatise of Government* and Rousseau in *The Social Contract* concentrate on this segment of contractarianism. I will adopt Jean Hampton's helpful terminology and refer to theories with the more generic scope as *moral contractarian* theories and those focusing on the state as *state contractarian* theories.[3] There are also normative and explanatory sides of the contractarian tradition. The normative side tries to answer the question "Why should we obey certain institutions?" and the explanatory side tries to answer the question "How did we fall under the sway of certain institutions?" The normative and the explanatory sides correspond roughly to the views that a social contract is the product of rational choice or of cultural evolution, respectively. John Rawls in *A Theory of Justice* and David Gauthier in *Morals by Agreement* present important contemporary normative moral contractarian theories rooted in rational choice. Robert Sugden presents important explanatory moral contractarian works rooted in evolution in *The Economics of Rights, Co-operation and Welfare*, and Brian Skyrms does so in *Evolution of the Social Contract*.

Until fairly recently, David Hume was viewed primarily as the archetypical anti-contractarian because of his severe criticisms of actual consent theories of government. Plainly, Hume will have no truck with actual consent state contractarianism. But since the end of the 1970s philosophers can no longer so complacently label Hume an opponent of contractarianism. For in 1979 David Gauthier and in 1986 Robert Sugden in independent works presented compelling arguments that Hume is in fact a moral contractarian who explains the requirements of justice in terms of his own watershed analysis of convention.[4] I think Hume can also be regarded a state contractarian of a different stripe. More specifically, I believe Hume's discussions of government help point to a way of understanding the relationship between rulers and the ruled in a civil society as a kind of implicit state contract where the members of a society can via conventions establish and maintain a mutually satisfactory relationship between those who govern and those who are governed where each side restrains its conduct with respect to the other.

2. Gerald Gaus, *The Order of Public Reason: A Theory of Freedom and Morality in a Diverse and Bounded World* (Cambridge: Cambridge University Press, 2011).

3. Jean Hampton, "Two Faces of Contractarian Thought," in *Contractarianism and Rational Choice: Essays on David Gauthier's* Morals by Agreement, ed. Peter Vallentyne (New York: Cambridge University Press, 1991), p. 32.

4. Gauthier, "David Hume: Contractarian," in Gauthier (1990), pp. 45–76; Sugden (2004).

In the sections to follow, I present the outlines of a *coordination regime* or *governing convention* analysis of the state.[5] In such a coordination regime, the governed support their governors by obeying them and in return the governors support the governed by providing them with services they find adequate and refraining from exploiting them. So the members of such a society can have an effective yet limited state, even though the governed and their governors have no actual contract according to the usual understanding of contracts. I draw inspiration from Hume's and Hobbes' works, which may seem doubly surprising since Hume is not usually thought of as a state contractarian of any sort and Hobbes, who can justly be credited for developing a prototype modern state social contract theory, is not usually associated with arguments for a government that acts within limits. And I draw inspiration from Russell Hardin's and Jean Hampton's more recent works, as they explored the possibility of a conventionalist account of government.[6] Hardin's and Hampton's analysis of the relationship between the ruled and their rulers in a state is primarily conceptual. My analysis here is somewhat more formal, in that I focus on the structure of the governing convention and present game-theoretic models meant to make explicit the conditions under which such a state social contract can exist.

In §6.1 I review a pair of problems, namely, the problem of *trust* in an asynchronic exchange and the problem of *leadership selection*. The Trust problem is structurally similar to the problem of establishing and then maintaining a governing convention, assuming the sovereign of the state has been chosen, while the Leadership Selection problem is structurally similar to the problem of selecting the sovereign. I use these problems to motivate the models of the remaining sections. In §6.2 I discuss aspects of Hobbes' accounts of the creation of commonwealth and the relationship between the sovereign and the subjects in a commonwealth. I argue that Hobbes anticipates much of contemporary contractarianism by using the system of agreements in his commonwealth by institution process,

---

5. "Coordination regime" is Russell Hardin's term, while "governing convention" is Jean Hampton's term. See especially Russell Hardin, *Liberalism, Constitutionalism and Democracy* (Oxford: Oxford University Press, 1999), p. 15, and Jean Hampton, *Political Philosophy* (Boulder, CO: Westview Press, 1997), p. 78. Hardin frequently uses the simpler phrase "a coordination" to refer to a coordination regime. In her earlier 1990 essay "The Contractarian Explanation of the State," *Midwest Studies in Philosophy* 15 (1990), pp. 344–371, Hampton uses the term "leadership convention." Hampton uses these terms in a somewhat wider sense than I will use the term "governing convention." For Hampton, the governing convention defines government offices and officeholders as well as the authority of the governors. In this chapter, the governing convention refers specifically to the convention that characterizes this authority.

6. Hardin (1999), ch. 3; Hampton (1986), chs. 8, 9, (1990), (1997), ch. 3.

agreements I interpret as hypothetical, to develop an *isomorphism argument* for justifying actual commonwealths. I argue that Hobbes' device of commonwealth by institution fails to do the justificatory work Hobbes intended, but that his isomorphism argument strategy is a valuable approach to justifying certain commonwealths. In §6.3 I introduce a repeated *Humean Sovereignty* stage game model of the relationship between rulers and the ruled. Here I argue that this repeated game model shows that a governing convention is indeed conceptually possible. I also argue that Hume's account of the origins and the maintenance of government incorporates the idea of a governing convention in an informal manner. In §6.4 I argue that one can keep the basic idea, inspired by Hobbes, that to select a sovereign is to select one of the many equilibria of a complex conflictual coordination game. But while I argue in §6.2 that State of Nature parties would not be able to choose their sovereign by following some electoral process in a hypothetical truce, as Hobbes supposes, here I argue these parties could settle upon a democratic commonwealth due to the natural salience of the equilibrium that characterizes democracy.

§6.1. Two Problems

Problem 6.1. Trust in Exchange

In the Figure 1.13 game I used in Chapter 1 to summarize Puccini's version of the *Gianni Schicchi* story, Schicchi moves first after Buoso's relatives have already hired him, and he defects, acquiring Buoso's fortune when the relatives back down, their only rational response. In a different version of the story, the relatives show greater foresight, but still fail to gain Buoso's fortune. In this version, the relatives have at the start a relatively small sum worth 1 utile to them, and Buoso's fortune is worth 9 utiles to them. The relatives *perform* (P_1) at the cost 1 by hiring Schicchi and paying him their initial small sum to draw up a new will that shares Buoso's fortune between Schicchi and themselves, with two-thirds of the fortune going to the relatives and the remaining third to Schicchi. They *defect* (D_1) by not hiring Schicchi. Schicchi, who has the same cardinal utilities for money as the relatives, *performs* (P_2) by willing two-thirds of Buoso's fortune to the relatives and one-third to himself, as he has promised, and he *double-crosses* (D_2) by willing all of the fortune to himself. Figure 6.1 summarizes this *Reverse Gianni Schicchi* game.[7]

7. In this version of the story, I assume the terms of whatever new will Schicchi draws up are binding. One could also suppose that since the Relatives know that if they hire Schicchi their only rational response is to acquiesce to whatever Schicchi does, they foresee that this interaction has effectively just the three possible outcomes of the Figure 7.1 game.

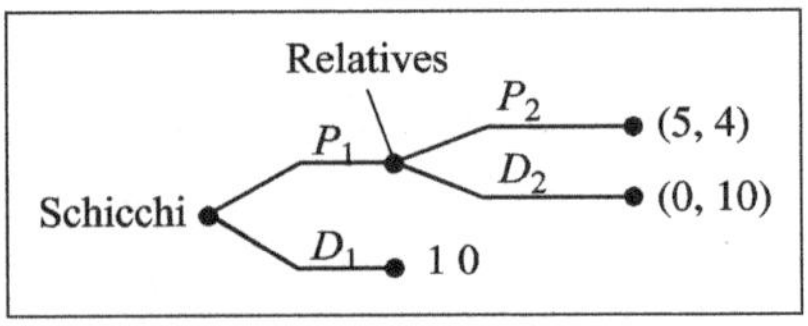

P_i = perform, D_i = defect, $i \in \{1, 2\}$

FIGURE 6.1 Reverse *Gianni Schicchi*/Trust Game

In this game, $(D_1; D_2\text{-if-}P_1)$ is the unique subgame perfect equilibrium. By following their end of this equilibrium and defecting, the Relatives gain none of the fortune, but at least they keep their hiring fee. But both sides would fare better if both were to perform. The Figure 6.1 game is also known as a *Trust* game, since the agent that moves first could expect to net a substantial gain *if* this side could only trust the other side to share the spoils of some venture given the chance. And yet rationality apparently dictates that the agent that moves first not give the other side that chance. Trust games summarize a variety of possible exchanges between two parties who, like Hume's corn farmers, seek only to maximize personal gain of services or goods from the exchange and where one party generates all of the cooperative surplus if the other party chooses to invest initially. So a *one-sided Farmer's Dilemma* would also be an apt name for this game.[8]

What could remove the temptation to defect in an exchange? The two parties could exchange promises to perform, creating a contract. But why would they keep their promises? To break a promise is to violate justice, but this is no real reply if one has no account of why such parties would do what justice requires. If the parties are in a Hobbesian State of Nature, making a contract to complete their exchange would evidently be pointless. As Hobbes himself puts it, "covenants without the sword are but words, and of no strength to secure a man at all."[9] A penalty for failing to perform as promised in a contract is one "sword" that might make such a promise more than cheap talk. If an exchange originally having the Figure 6.1 Trust game structure is augmented so that each Party i suffers such a penalty of expected magnitude p_i for breaking her promise to perform, then the Figure 6.2 game summarizes the parties' revised situation.[10]

8. The Trust game is sometimes referred to as *one-sided Prisoner's Dilemma*, but I prefer *one-sided Farmer's Dilemma* since the Trust game has an explicit sequential structure.

9. *Leviathan* 17:2. See also *Leviathan* 14:18.

10. I say *expected* magnitude since Party i might suffer the penalty only with a certain probability.

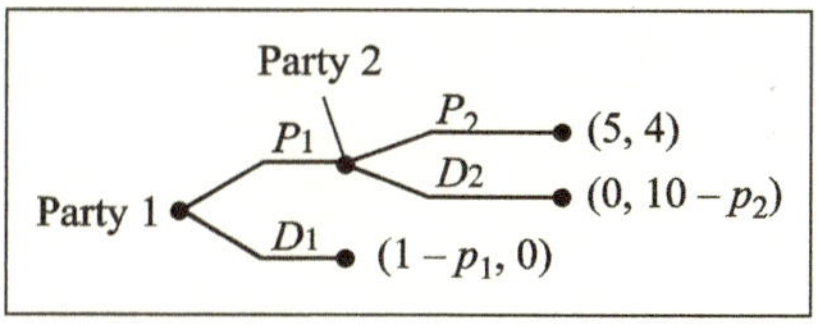

P_i = perform, D_i = defect, $i \in \{1,2\}$

FIGURE 6.2 Trust Game Augmented with Penalties

For sufficiently large values of p_i, P_i becomes each party's strictly dominant strategy and (P_1,P_2) is then the unique equilibrium.[11] The Figure 6.2 game summarizes in rough manner the strategic structure of the interaction between two parties who have formed a contract enforceable by some third party capable of meting out punishment in case of failure to perform. If such a third party exists and is willing to administer appropriate punishments against defectors, then the parties have sufficient reason to honor the contract they have formed.

Problem 6.2. Leadership Selection

The specter of war should lead people to prefer life in a civil society with effective government over life in their natural condition of complete freedom. So argue Thomas Hobbes and David Hume.[12] Hobbes, in particular, is emphatic that only *civil society* or *commonwealth* can save people from warring with each other and that a civil society must be ruled by a sovereign that can direct the actions of these people according to its own will.

> Since therefore a *combination* of several wills in the same end is not adequate to the preservation of peace and stable defense, it is required that there be a *single will* among all of them in matters essential to peace and defense. This can only happen if each man subjects his *will* to the *will* of a *single* other, to the *will*, that is, of one *Man* or of one *Assembly*, in such a way that whatever one wills on matters essential to the common peace may be taken as the will of all and each.[13]

---

11. For the Figure 6.2 game, P_1 is strictly dominant when $p_1 > 1$ and P_2 is strictly dominant when $p_2 > 6$.

12. *Elements of Law I* 19, *De Cive* 5, *Leviathan* 17, and *Treatise* 3.2.6.

13. *De Cive* 5:6. See also *Elements of Law I* 19:6 and *Leviathan* 17:13.

A_1

	A_1	P_2	A_3	V	D
P_1	(6, 4, 4)	(3, –1, 2)	(3, –1, 2)	(3, –1, 2)	(3/2, 1/3, 4/3)
A_2	(0, 0, 0)	(2, 3, –1)	(0, 0, 0)	(0, 0, 0)	(0, 1, 0)
A_3	(0, 0, 0)	(0, 0, 0)	(0, 0, 0)	(0, 0, 0)	(0, 1, 0)
V	(0, 0, 0)	(0, 0, 0)	(0, 0, 0)	(0, 0, 0)	(0, 1, 0)
D	(1, 0, 0)	(1, 0, 0)	(1, 0, 0)	(1, 0, 0)	(1, 1, 0)

A_2

	A_1	P_2	A_3	V	D
P_1	(3, 2, –1)	(–1, 3, 2)	(0, 0, 0)	(0, 0, 0)	(0, 1, 0)
A_2	(0, 0, 0)	(4, 6, 4)	(0, 0, 0)	(0, 0, 0)	(0, 1, 0)
A_3	(0, 0, 0)	(–1, 3, 2)	(0, 0, 0)	(0, 0, 0)	(0, 1, 0)
V	(0, 0, 0)	(–1, 3, 2)	(0, 0, 0)	(0, 0, 0)	(0, 1, 0)
D	(1, 0, 0)	(1/3, 3/2, 4/3)	(1, 0, 0)	(1, 0, 0)	(1, 1, 0)

P_3

	A_1	P_2	A_3	V	D
P_1	(3, 2, –1)	(0, 0, 0)	(–1, 2, 3)	(0, 0, 0)	(0, 1, 0)
A_2	(0, 0, 0)	(2, 3, –1)	(–1, 2, 3)	(0, 0, 0)	(0, 1, 0)
A_3	(2, –1, 3)	(2, –1, 3)	(4, 4, 6)	(2, –1, 3)	(4/3, 1/3, 3/2)
V	(0, 0, 0)	(0, 0, 0)	(–1, 2, 3)	(0, 0, 0)	(0, 1, 0)
D	(1, 0, 0)	(1/3, 4/3, 3/2)	(1, 0, 0)	(1, 0, 0)	(1, 1, 0)

V

	A_1	P_2	A_3	V	D
P_1	(3, 2, –1)	(0, 0, 0)	(0, 0, 0)	(0, 0, 0)	(0, 1, 0)
A_2	(0, 0, 0)	(2, 3, –1)	(0, 0, 0)	(0, 0, 0)	(0, 1, 0)
A_3	(0, 0, 0)	(0, 0, 0)	(0, 0, 0)	(0, 0, 0)	(0, 1, 0)
V	(0, 0, 0)	(0, 0, 0)	(0, 0, 0)	(5, 5, 5)	(0, 1, 0)
D	(1, 0, 0)	(1, 0, 0)	(1, 0, 0)	(1, 0, 0)	(1, 1, 0)

D

	A_1	P_2	A_3	V	D
P_1	(3/2, 4/3, 1/3)	(0, 0, 1)	(0, 0, 1)	(0, 0, 1)	(0, 1, 1)
A_2	(0, 0, 1)	(4/3, 3/2, 1/3)	(0, 0, 1)	(0, 0, 1)	(0, 1, 1)
A_3	(0, 0, 1)	(0, 0, 1)	(0, 0, 1)	(0, 0, 1)	(0, 1, 1)
V	(0, 0, 1)	(0, 0, 1)	(0, 0, 1)	(0, 0, 1)	(0, 1, 1)
D	(1, 0, 1)	(1, 0, 1)	(1, 0, 1)	(1, 0, 1)	(1, 1, 1)

P_i = proclaim oneself leader, A_i = authorize Party i as leader

V = submit to majority rule, D = Anticipate

Party 1 chooses row, Party 2 chooses column, Party 3 chooses matrix.

Equilibrium outcomes are shaded.

FIGURE 6.3 3-Party Leadership Selection

But Hobbes insists just as emphatically that civil society is an artificial institution, created by the people its sovereign rules.[14] How could a people create a civil society "from scratch"? One central reason the creation of government de novo poses such a challenging problem from both the normative and the explanatory perspectives is that the people who are to create their government must do so knowing that whoever runs this government will be running *them*. How are they to decide who should have the right to govern them?

Such a Leadership Selection problem can prove quite formidable even for groups who have only a few options to choose from. The Figure 6.3 game summarizes a problem where three parties must choose how they are to be led in order for them to work together productively. In this 3-party impure coordination game, Party 1 chooses the row, Party 2 chooses the column, and Party 3 chooses the matrix. Each Party i has five pure strategies: *proclaim* itself leader

14. *Leviathan*, introduction.

(P_i), *authorize* the other Party j as leader (A_j) or the other Party k as leader (A_k), submit to *majority rule* (V), or give up and *Anticipate* (D), treating the others as enemies. As the pure strategy descriptions suggest, a natural interpretation of this game is as three parties in a State of Nature trying to establish a commonwealth, where they can establish a single-party sovereign if one of them proclaims and the others authorize this one, or establish a democratic sovereign if all submit to majority rule, or go to war if all Anticipate.[15]

This game has five pure strategy Nash equilibria, namely, (P_1, A_1, A_1), (A_2, P_2, A_2), (A_3, A_3, P_3), (V, V, V), and (D, D, D). From the perspective of each Party i, the best outcome is the equilibrium where this party follows P_i and the others follow A_i, so that Party i is established as leader; second-best is the equilibrium where all follow V, forming a democracy; and the two tied for third-best are the equilibria where exactly one other Party j follows P_j and Party i and the remaining Party k both follow A_j, so both end up as Party j's subordinates. The (D, D, D) equilibrium is worse for all than any of the equilibria where they have some form of leadership, but for each of them D is the "safe" maximin strategy. There are 120 possible nonequilibrium outcomes, and some of these miscoordination outcomes are worse than others from the perspective of each. For instance, Party 2's worst outcomes occur if Party 1 proclaims itself leader, Party 3 authorizes Party 1, and Party 2 tries to follow one of the optimal equilibria other than the (P_1, A_1, A_1) equilibrium where Party 1 is established as leader, since Party 2 now faces an opposing coalition formed by Party 1 and Party 3. All the parties prefer any of the four equilibria where either one of them is established as leader or they have a democracy over any of the many alternatives. But one might doubt that these three parties will succeed in reaching any of these four optimal equilibria, given not only their conflicting preferences over these equilibria but also the extreme instability of all of the miscoordination outcomes where at least one party tries to follow one of the optimal equilibria and the other two do not also aim for this equilibrium, since she thereby leaves herself even more vulnerable to the other two than she would be by Anticipating. These parties might therefore have some tendency to gravitate toward the suboptimal (D, D, D) equilibrium. One might have difficulty imagining just how much more complicated the corresponding impure coordination problem would be for a whole multitude of individuals trying to choose how to be led.

15. Hampton (1986, pp. 150–151) uses a similar but simpler 3-agent game to model the problem of selecting the Hobbesian sovereign. Hampton's game is much like a reduced Figure 6.3 game where each Party i is limited to the three pure strategies P_i, A_j, and A_k, so that majority rule and mutual Anticipation are no longer possible outcomes.

§6.2. Hobbes' Attempt to Justify Commonwealth

Hobbes identifies two ways to create a commonwealth. A commonwealth established by the people who submit themselves to some person or assembly of persons as their ruler out of fear of this person or assembly is a commonwealth created *naturally* or by *acquisition*.[16] In many if not most cases, a commonwealth by acquisition is imposed upon people by force, possibly by conquest or by coup. A commonwealth established by the mutual agreement of individuals in their "naturall condition" of political freedom is a commonwealth by *design* or by *institution*.[17] Commonwealth by institution is a possibility logically distinct from commonwealth by acquisition, but as a matter of historical record, there are no clear-cut examples of actual commonwealths that were not commonwealths created by acquisition. I believe that Hobbes uses commonwealth by institution to justify commonwealths, not to explain them.[18] Hobbes leaves it to his readers to piece together how this justification is supposed to work. In the following schematized *sovereign by institution argument*, I reconstruct the justification Hobbes never clearly gave, trying to be both fully faithful to Hobbes's own thought and as favorable to Hobbes' overall project as possible:

P1. If every rational person wants to live in a society of the form *X*, then a society of the form *X* is justified.
P2. Every rational person wants to live in a society of the form *X* if the following conditional is true: If any group of rational persons in the State of Nature could create the kind of society in which they are to live, they would institute a society of the form *X*.
P3. If any group of rational persons in the State of Nature could create the kind of society in which they are to live, they would institute a commonwealth ruled by an absolute sovereign.

---

16. *Elements of Law I* 19:11, *De Cive* 5:12, 8:1, *Leviathan* 17:15, 20:1.

17. *Elements of Law I* 19:11, *De Cive* 5:12, 8:1, *Leviathan* 17:15, 18:1. My use of the terminology of contracts and agreements throughout this chapter is consistent with that of Hobbes. Hobbes defines a *contract* as a reciprocal transfer of rights between two or more parties (*De Cive* 2.9, *Leviathan* 14:9). Each party of a contract performs her part by delivering that which she has transferred her right over to the other parties of the contract. In case at least one of the parties does not perform immediately upon transferring her rights, so that the others must trust her to perform at some future time, Hobbes calls the contract an *agreement* or *covenant* (*De Cive* 2.9, *Leviathan* 14:11). An express sign of contract indicating future performance is a promise (*Leviathan* 14:13), and performance after the creation of the covenant is keeping one's promise or *keeping faith* (*Leviathan* 14:11).

18. Several of Hobbes' interpreters have drawn similar conclusions, although they do not clearly spell out what sort of justification Hobbes has in mind. See, for instance, McNeilly (1968), p. 222; Kavka (1986), p. 181; and Hampton (1986), pp. 172–173.

P4. Every rational person wants to live in a commonwealth ruled by an absolute sovereign.
C. A commonwealth ruled by an absolute sovereign is justified.

In this argument, P1 is the standard of justification I attribute to Hobbes. P2 says that one knows that P1 is satisfied when one determines that a substitution instance of "society of the form *X*" in

If any group of rational persons in the State of Nature could create the kind of society in which they are to live, they would institute a society of the form *X*.

makes this counterfactual true. If we grant Hobbes the exceptionally strong premises of this argument, particularly P3, then commonwealth by institution justifies absolute sovereignty, even though parties perhaps never institute a commonwealth in fact.

I have stated the sovereign by institution argument in this much detail in order to make it fully clear just how I believe Hobbes is trying to justify commonwealths. A choice or agreement made in certain hypothetical circumstances is the basis of much of contemporary political contractarianism, led by the works of John Harsanyi, John Rawls, and David Gauthier.[19] The idea of a hypothetical social contract is present in Kant's essay known as "Theory and Practice,"[20] and it is foreshadowed in Adam Smith's works and indeed in Hume's works.[21] But I believe Hobbes employed this idea even earlier in his account of commonwealth

19. Rawls' and Gauthier's best-known presentations of their hypothetical contractarian theories are in *A Theory of Justice* and *Morals by Agreement*, respectively. Harsanyi first presented his hypothetical contractarian theory in the essays "Cardinal Utility in Welfare Economics and the Theory of Risk Taking," *Journal of Political Economy* 61 (1953), pp. 343–345, and Harsanyi (1955).

20. Immanuel Kant, "On the Common Saying: That May Be Correct in Theory, but It Is of No Use in Practice," in *Practical Philosophy*, trans. and ed. Mary J. Gregor (1793; Cambridge: Cambridge University Press, 1996), pp. 274–309.

21. Smith's use of the device of an impartial spectator in *Theory of Moral Sentiments* foreshadows Harsanyi's and Rawls' theories where a principle or principles of justice are chosen from behind a veil of ignorance. In *Treatise*, Hume speaks of a "judicious spectator" who evaluates moral characteristics from an impartial standpoint (*Treatise* 3.3.1:14). On p. 27 of "Of the Independency of Parliament," in *Political Essays*, ed. Knud Haakonssen (Cambridge: Cambridge University Press, 1994), pp. 24–27, Hume speaks of an "impartial examiner" who evaluates political arrangements. In *Treatise* Hume also discusses briefly how he believes that people who perceive the need for government "wou'd naturally assemble together, wou'd chuse magistrates, determine their power, and *promise* them obedience" (*Treatise* 3.2.8:3). Gauthier was perhaps the first to attribute hypothetical contractarian reasoning to Hume in "David Hume: Contractarian," in Gauthier (1990), pp. 45–76. Harsanyi (1977, pp. 48–49) acknowledges that rational choice

by institution, which is why I claim that Hobbes' theory is a prototype modern contractarian theory.[22] For Hobbes argues in Part I of *Leviathan* that people in the State of Nature are generally unable to covenant with each other. Further, Hobbes argues that the State of Nature need not be an actual event in human history in order for his theory to be applicable to his readers. For even if one sets aside Hobbes' argument for the inevitability of war in the State of Nature from his eminently modest and plausible assumptions regarding human nature, Hobbes notes that one can infer just how miserable life would be in a State of Nature by extrapolating from the conditions of civil war and how guarded people are even in civil society.[23] And when he introduces his *Leviathan* account of generating commonwealth at the start of Part II, Hobbes says the people form the covenants to authorize some person or assembly of persons as their sovereign *as if* they exchanged the relevant promises, and I take him to imply that the contract system of commonwealth by institution is hypothetical.[24] If I am granted this interpretation of Hobbes, then the important questions are: (1) How does this hypothetical contract system work?, and (2) What does this hypothetical contract system prove?[25]

To create a Hobbesian commonwealth "from scratch," those who would exit the State of Nature must accomplish two tasks.[26] First, they must select the individual or assembly of individuals that is to serve as their sovereign. Then once

---

contract theories such as his own are part of Smith's impartial spectator tradition. But Rawls in *A Theory of Justice* pp. 184–189 draws a sharp distinction between his justice as fairness and impartial spectator theories, claiming that the latter depend upon sympathy and that his theory avoids this dependence.

22. In saying this I am going against the grain of John Rawls' view of his own project in *A Theory of Justice*. There Rawls states that his is a theory that generalizes and abstracts from the contractarian theories of Locke, Rousseau, and Kant (1971, p. 11), but specifically distances his own theory from Hobbes' theory (1971, p. 11 n. 4). However, in lectures on Hobbes' political theory he presented in 1983, Rawls observes that one can plausibly interpret Hobbes' theory as a hypothetical contractarian theory without committing himself to this interpretation. See John Rawls, *Lectures on the History of Political Philosophy*, ed. Samuel Freeman (Cambridge, MA: Harvard University Press, 2007), pp. 33–34.

23. *De Cive*, Preface 9, *Leviathan* 13:10, 11.

24. *Leviathan* 17:13.

25. Kavka (1986), §1.3, §5.1, and §10.3, also maintains that Hobbes is essentially a hypothetical contract theorist, although Kavka does not point to any specific supporting textual evidence. And as remarked in note 22, above, Rawls also considers a hypothetical contractarian interpretation of Hobbes plausible.

26. Hampton (1986), ch. 6, and Kavka (1986), ch. 5, give somewhat similar though less detailed multistage reconstructions of Hobbesian commonwealth by institution. Neither Hampton nor Kavka argue, as I argue here, that the Leadership Selection problem is unsolvable if the parties try to choose their sovereign according to some electoral process, as Hobbes suggests.

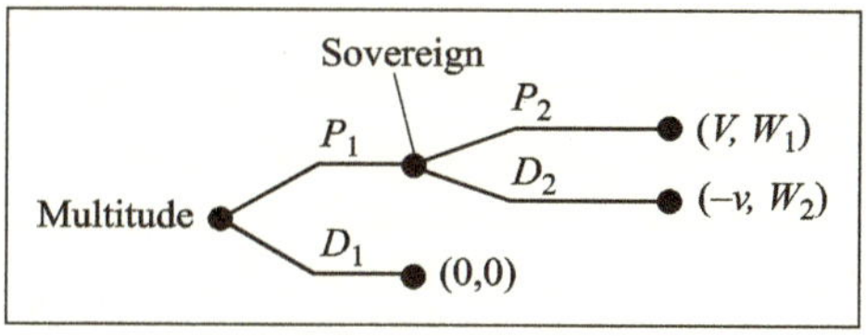

P_1 = authorize, D_1 = abstain

P_2 = perform, D_2 = defect

$V > 0, v > 0, W_1 > 0, W_2 > 0$

FIGURE 6.4 Hobbesian Sovereignty

they have chosen some candidate individual or assembly, they must all then *authorize* the actions of this candidate as if these actions were their own, thereby surrendering their rights of self-government to this candidate.[27] Each then expects all to generally obey this sovereign's commands, and consequently has good reasons to obey this sovereign herself. I believe that the initial candidate selection problem is by far the more challenging task facing the parties, but for the moment I will suppose that the parties trying to create their commonwealth have already solved this problem. The parties all know the identity of the sovereign candidate. This candidate becomes sovereign once they authorize it, and afterward is capable of ruling effectively and providing the parties who are now its subjects with the benefits for which they created their sovereign.

I use the Figure 6.4 game to summarize this final stage of establishing the Hobbesian sovereign. In this *Hobbesian Sovereignty* game, the Multitude moves first and either *authorizes* (P_1) or *abstains* (D_1). If the Multitude abstains its

---

27. Hobbes uses the term "authorize" only in *Leviathan* 17:13 and 18:1, when he discusses commonwealth by institution. In the corresponding texts of *Elements of Law* and *De Cive*, Hobbes speaks of all the people surrendering their rights to the sovereign (*Elements of Law I* 19:7, 10, *De Cive* 5:7). Hobbes' introduction of the new term "authorize" in *Leviathan* has sparked an interesting discussion as to whether or not authorization is a substantive addition to Hobbes' political theory in *Leviathan*. David Gauthier launched a literature on this question in ch. 4 of *The Logic of Leviathan: The Moral and Political Theory of Thomas Hobbes* (Oxford: Clarendon Press, 1969), arguing that Hobbes introduces authorization in *Leviathan* as an important new part of establishing the sovereignty that Hobbes introduces in *Leviathan*. Sharon Lloyd and Susanne Sreedhar defend positions similar to Gauthier's. See Sharon Lloyd, *Ideals as Interests in Hobbes's* Leviathan: *The Power of Mind over Matter* (Cambridge: Cambridge University Press, 1992), ch. 6, and Susanne Sreedhar, *Hobbes on Resistance: Defying the Leviathan* (Cambridge: Cambridge University Press, 2010), ch.3. Gregory Kavka and Luciano Venezia defend a *redundancy interpretation* of authorization in this context, arguing that Hobbes' use of the authorization vocabulary in his discussion of commonwealth by institution adds nothing substantive beyond transferring self-government rights. See Kavka (1986), §10.1, and Luciano Venezia, *Hobbes on Legal Authority and Political Obligation* (Houndmills, UK: Palgrave Macmillan, 2015), §5.1. I favor the redundancy interpretation myself, but the discussion here does not depend upon the specifics of either view of authorization.

constituent individuals and the unauthorized candidate in the role of Sovereign all remain the State of Nature. If the Multitude authorizes, the Sovereign then either *performs* (P_2) by providing good government or *defects* (D_2) by ignoring the Multitude's needs and possibly even exploiting the Multitude. If the Sovereign performs, the Multitude receives a payoff of $V > 0$ as the value of good government and the Sovereign's payoff is $W_1 > 0$. If the Sovereign defects, its payoff is then $W_2 > 0$ and the Multitude's payoff is $-v < 0$, so they are even worse off than they were in the State of Nature. If $W_2 > W_1$, then the Figure 6.4 game has the same preference structure as the Figure 6.1 Trust game, and the subgame perfect equilibrium is $(D_1, D_2\text{-if-}P_1)$. In this case, the Multitude would do better to stay in the State of Nature. But if $W_1 > W_2$, and Hobbes' discussion indicates this is in fact the case, then $(P_1, P_2\text{-if-}P_1)$ is the subgame perfect equilibrium.

Choosing a candidate to authorize as the sovereign is a complex coordination problem. The Leadership Selection game of §6.1 is a special case of this problem where only three parties must choose. I now note that the $5\times5\times5$ Figure 6.3 game interpreted as three State of Nature parties are trying to establish their civil society abstracts from all the logical possibilities, since in addition to single party rule and democracy there are several coalitions of two, each of which in theory could be a sovereign assembly. Including all these possibilities would generate an $8\times8\times8$ game, even though only three parties are trying to establish commonwealth. In general, if there are n parties in the State of Nature, there are $2^n - 1$ logically possible candidates for sovereign. The 3-party Leadership Selection game together with the Hobbesian Sovereignty game illustrate the basic properties of the problem of instituting Hobbesian commonwealth in the n-party case. Given n State of Nature parties, each strategy profile of the corresponding Leadership Selection game in which Party i proclaims itself sovereign and each of the others authorizes Party i is a strict Nash equilibrium, and Party i strictly prefers this equilibrium over all other equilibria of the game. So the leadership selection problem is plainly a conflictual coordination problem. One of all the many equilibria where a civil society is established becomes salient when a single candidate has sufficient support from the others. An election can indicate such support. If, for instance, some candidate Party i wins an election for sovereign, then salience is achieved if the coalition of Party i's supporters is strong enough and stable enough to intimidate all of the parties into complying with the corresponding equilibrium where Party i is sovereign. This last stage is summarized by the first move of the Figure 6.4 Hobbesian Sovereignty game, where all of the other $n-1$ parties together authorize Party i. In this manner, the commonwealth by institution process is completed.

Hobbes gives us no good argument for why the parties in the State of Nature would be able to suspend their war long enough to form agreements to authorize a sovereign and then actually honor the terms of these agreements. Given the interpretation of commonwealth by institution as a hypothetical contract, perhaps this should surprise no one. Hobbes can simply *stipulate* that any circumstance obtains throughout the commonwealth by institution process, so long as (i) this circumstance by itself does not affect the likelihood that any particular candidate is instituted as sovereign and (ii) no party is compelled to authorize any candidate. Hobbes can use this *truce rule* to create hypothetical conditions that allow parties to complete commonwealth by institution.[28] Beyond simply being at truce, to elect a sovereign the parties would have to be able to communicate and make any of their negotiations common knowledge, and choose individuals who would administer the selection mechanism and announce the results truthfully. This cannot be done in an actual Hobbesian State of Nature, where there is "no Knowledge of the face of the Earth; no account of Time; no Arts; no Letters; [and] no Society," but the truce rule permits these preconditions for completing the commonwealth by institution process to obtain.[29]

The agreements of the commonwealth by institution process are agreements between State of Nature parties to follow certain procedures for choosing the sovereign candidate and to authorize the sovereign candidate selected according to these procedures. The sovereign candidate is not a party to any of the agreements of this process. Using the Hobbesian Sovereignty game again as a foil, since both the Multitude and the Sovereign fare better if both perform than they fare in the State of Nature, one might think the Multitude would want to form a covenant with the sovereign before its move and promise to authorize in exchange for the sovereign's promise to perform. However, Hobbes insists that there can be no covenant between State of Nature parties and a sovereign candidate or later between a sovereign and the sovereign's subjects.[30] Hobbes concludes this in large part because he concludes that it would be impossible to resolve any claim of breach of such an alleged "covenant."[31] One way to illustrate Hobbes' point is that if there were such a "covenant" between the sovereign and its subjects, then the true structure of their

---

28. I introduced this version of the truce rule in "Instituting the Hobbesian Commonwealth," *Pacific Philosophical Quarterly* 82 (2001), pp. 383–405 (henceforth Vanderschraaf 2001a). My own truce rule is motivated by Kavka's suggestion (1986, p. 237) that one stipulate that Hobbesian parties are at truce while they negotiate their social contract.

29. *Leviathan* 13:9.

30. *Leviathan* 18:4.

31. This is Hobbes' most important argument against the claim that a sovereign could form a covenant with its subjects, but not his only argument. In *Leviathan*, Hobbes also argues that prior to its authorization a sovereign could not form a covenant with the whole multitude in the State of Nature as the other party, since they are not yet united, and any covenants it might form with each of the individuals in the multitude would be void upon its authorization "because what act soever can be pretended by any one of them for breach thereof is the act both of

relationship would be like that of the augmented Trust game of Figure 6.2, where a third party enforces performance, which for Hobbes would be absurd. For if some third party could act as judge between sovereign and subjects in such a dispute, then this third party would be the "real" sovereign, and then the question of who could adjudicate between this "real" sovereign and the "real" subjects would arise all over again. Similarly, Hobbes maintains it makes no sense to claim the sovereign is bound by laws of the commonwealth that bind its subjects.

> For to be subject to Lawes, is to be subject to the Common-wealth, that is, to the Soveraign Representative, that is, to himself; which is not subjection, but freedome from the Lawes. Which errour, because it setteth the Lawes above the Soveraign, setteth also a Judge above him, and a Power to punish him, which is to make a new Soveraign; and again for the same reason a third, to punish the second; and so continually without end, to the Confusion and Dissolution of the Common-wealth.[32]

Hobbes concludes from this regress argument that the sovereign itself must be the final arbiter in all disputes between members of its commonwealth,[33] and that it would be futile to claim that the sovereign ever breaks faith with its subjects.[34]

Hobbes clearly acknowledges that citizens might be oppressed in any commonwealth.[35] The Hobbesian Sovereignty game captures the idea that once the State of Nature parties have authorized their chosen sovereign candidate, they are effectively at their sovereign's mercy. After they authorize, the Subjects would appear to be in much the same position as the native inhabitants of the world of Rod Serling's "The Little People," discussed in Chapter 3, once astronaut Craig has proclaimed himself their god. Indeed, Hobbes declares that the creation of commonwealth is "the Generation of that great LEVIATHAN, or rather (to speak more reverently) of that *Mortall God*, to which wee owe under the *Immortal God*, our peace and defence."[36] The Subjects in the Hobbesian Sovereignty game can of course forestall all this by abstaining, but then they would remain in the State

---

himself, and all the rest" (18:4). I doubt the soundness of this argument myself, but this argument of Hobbes is not crucial for the analysis of this section.

32. *Leviathan* 29:9.

33. *Leviathan* 18:11.

34. *Leviathan* 18:4. See also *De Cive* 6:18. Hampton gives splendid reconstructions and analyses of Hobbes' regress argument in Hampton (1986), ch. 4, and "Democracy and the Rule of Law," in *The Rule of Law*, ed. Ian Shapiro (New York: New York University Press, 1994), pp. 13–44.

35. *De Cive* 10:2.

36. *Leviathan* 17:13.

of Nature. Hobbes acknowledges that people in civil societies frequently express dissatisfaction with their governments, at least in private, but insists that the worst calamities that might befall a people in civil society at the hands of their sovereign pale in comparison when compared with what they might expect in the State of Nature.[37] Hobbes maintains that the interests of the Sovereign go hand in hand with the interests of its Subjects. The Sovereign's power increases just as the subjects' level of well-being increases.[38] And if the Subjects do generally suffer disadvantages because their regime "malfunctions," the Sovereign suffers disadvantages as well.[39] The Figure 6.4 Hobbesian Sovereignty game reflects Hobbes' reasoning given that the Sovereign's payoffs satisfy $W_1 > W_2$, in which case the Multitude and the Sovereign follow their respective ends of the subgame perfect equilibrium $(P_1, P_2\text{-if-}P_1)$ by authorizing and performing. If Hobbes is right about the alignment of the Sovereign's and the Subjects' interests, then at the last stage of the commonwealth by institution process the State of Nature parties apparently have good reason to authorize the chosen sovereign candidate without trying in vain to first form a contract with the sovereign candidate.

Yet even if one agrees with Hobbes that the parties have good reason to authorize at the end of the commonwealth by institution process, real problems would emerge earlier in this process. Nothing can compel the parties to comply with the results of the selection stage. Since different parties strictly prefer different candidates, would not parties unhappy with the results of the selection phase try to scuttle the agreement by holding out for another candidate? Hobbes' own solution to the holdout problem is to simply leave them behind in the State of Nature.[40] I propose an analogous solution by stipulating that the truce is over immediately following the selection stage and that this is common knowledge throughout the commonwealth by institution process. This ensures that at the end of the selection stage, each party must choose between either authorizing the chosen candidate as sovereign or resuming the State of Nature war, which now is war with the other holdouts and possibly with those who have authorized. Any intransigent holdouts now are likely to be in an even more dangerous situation than they were in the original State of Nature, since they may now be at war with a commonwealth, or at least with a large coalition trying to establish a commonwealth by acquisition over the holdouts. *If* this coalition is both

37. *Leviathan* 18:20.

38. *Leviathan* 19:4. Here Hobbes in fact claims that in the case of monarchy, the interests of the sovereign are *identical* with those of its subjects.

39. *De Cive* 10:2.

40. *De Cive* 6:2, *Leviathan* 18:3.

sufficiently numerous and stable to form a commonwealth in its own right, then any remaining opposing parties will be too relatively weak to pose a serious threat to this coalition and the holdout problem is solved. Yet this might easily fail to be the case after the election, particularly if the winner is backed by only a minority of the parties. At this stage, one might want to buttress Hobbes' argument by stipulating that the election be such that the winner is backed by a coalition of parties large enough to form a viable commonwealth at the authorization stage, at least with respect to any possible holdouts. But can the parties successfully elect a candidate under such a constraint? We have arrived at the most serious problem of all for Hobbes' commonwealth by institution.

So far, this reconstruction of Hobbes' commonwealth by institution presents a plausible case for why parties would carry out an *authorization stage* after the *selection stage*. Unfortunately, a crucial difficulty is likely to emerge at the *preliminary stage*. If the candidate that wins the election does not win by a sufficiently overwhelming majority, then even those who have voted for this winner might be reluctant to authorize in the end, since the winner lacks the "mandate" that would make it salient. If the parties foresee that no candidate is likely to win with the necessary mandate in the end, they will not have a good reason to choose their sovereign in this manner. Moreover, it is well established that given at least three alternative candidates, the candidate an electorate ultimately recognizes as the winner can vary according to the rules governing the election. Hobbes does not explain in detail either in *Leviathan* or in his other writings how parties trying to institute a commonwealth are to elect their sovereign. This omission is not necessarily a lapse on Hobbes' part. The results of contemporary social choice theory were of course unknown to Hobbes, and they indicate that the preliminary stage would be vastly more complicated than Hobbes could have imagined. If there are even as few as three candidates for the post of sovereign, then there is no way to guarantee that certain parties cannot try to rig the voting mechanism so as to produce an outcome more favorable to them in particular. The impossibility result of Gibbard and Satterwaithe shows that in general, nothing can prevent this kind of trickery.[41] When a group has to select one of three or more options, if they use a determinate method such as voting that depends upon the preferences of more than one group member, and if the method does not depend upon keeping an option that is everyone's least preferred option under consideration, then the

41. Allan Gibbard and Mark Satterwaithe proved this result independently in the 1970s, and today their impossibility theorem bears both their names. See Allan Gibbard, "Manipulation of Voting Schemes: A General Result," *Econometrica* 41 (1973), pp. 587–601, and Mark Satterwaithe, "Strategy-Proofness and Arrow's Conditions: Existence and Correspondence Theorems for Voting Procedures and Social Welfare Functions," *Journal of Economic Theory* 10 (1975), pp. 187–216.

method is *manipulable*. That is, some subgroup, by misrepresenting their true preferences, can change the outcome that would emerge when all vote according to their true preferences to an outcome more favorable to those in the subgroup.

Commonwealth by institution, as Hobbes constructs it, will fail, because the State of Nature parties will find themselves deadlocked at the preliminary stage. We can plausibly assume there would be three or more candidates for sovereign among the parties, none of whom is the favorite of an overwhelming majority. There is no determinate method for choosing the sovereign available to the parties that is not open to manipulation by some faction or factions of parties who misrepresent their preferences. Nothing prevents any party from misrepresenting preferences during the commonwealth by institution process. And there is no reason to suppose that the State of Nature parties are not savvy enough to realize all this. Beyond these considerations, the parties know that they have only one chance to execute the selection and authorization stages. Since Hobbes argues that sovereign's powers are irrevocable once conferred[42] and that the current sovereign has the exclusive right to choose its own successor,[43] the parties will have to live with the commonwealth they establish indefinitely, or at least until such time as the sovereign of this commonwealth loses its ability to protect its subjects.[44] Each party already has good reason to mistrust any proposal for a voting scheme. Given how fateful their ultimate choice is, when any party suggests a particular voting scheme, the other parties have a powerful incentive to reject the suggestion. One cannot solve this problem by fiat, the way I have been solving other problems with repeated applications of the truce rule. Stipulating the use of a particular voting method such as a Borda count or approval voting violates clause (i) of the truce rule. This aside, to impose some selection mechanism such as a particular voting rule on State of Nature parties is to restrict their political freedom. If some power can compel the parties to follow a particular selection mechanism, then the parties are apparently no longer in a State of Nature.

Having argued that parties cannot complete Hobbes' commonwealth by institution process, I now contend that commonwealth by institution does not do quite the justificatory work Hobbes would want it to do in support of his overall theory. Hobbes believes that commonwealth by institution yields essentially the same result as commonwealth by acquisition. In particular, the type of dominion,

---

42. *Leviathan* 18:1–6.

43. *Leviathan* 19:14–15.

44. As I will discuss in §6.3, the subjects can depose their sovereign by withdrawing their obedience. But as I will discuss below in the conclusion, the subjects may find it difficult both to coordinate their disobedience in order to depose an unsatisfactory sovereign and to find a suitable replacement.

including the sovereign's specific rights with respect to the commonwealth and the subjects' obligations to obey their sovereign, is the same in both types of commonwealth.[45] I believe Hobbes avows this equivalence between commonwealth by acquisition and institution as part of his attempt to show that subjects are morally obliged to obey the sovereign. This may not seem apparent at first, since Hobbes gives an account of political obligation specific to commonwealth by acquisition, arguing that the vanquished who surrender to a conqueror promise either expressly or tacitly their permanent obedience to this conqueror as sovereign,[46] that those who live openly under this sovereign's protection consent tacitly to obey this sovereign,[47] and that the descendants of those who have consented to obey this sovereign in these ways are obliged to obey this sovereign or its current successor via their obligations to obey their parents.[48] Many commentators have argued that these are dubious grounds for political obligation. Hume gives the right rebuttals to these arguments in "Of the Original Contract,"[49] arguing that consent cannot create a binding obligation to obey one's government if not *freely* given, which in general it is not when a conqueror or usurper gains power,[50] and that even if one's ancestors did consent to the rule of a government, no one thinks that the obligations may have created really are transitive across generations.[51] But granting, as I grant, that Hobbes' specific commonwealth by acquisition arguments are part of one more failed actual consent account of political obligation, Hobbes still has commonwealth by institution. I believe Hobbes uses commonwealth by institution as part of an *isomorphism argument* characteristic of more modern contractarian theories. Commonwealth by institution justifies a certain kind of social structure, namely, commonwealth ruled by an absolute sovereign. If Hobbes can show that the results of commonwealth by acquisition are in the right respects isomorphic to those of commonwealth by institution, might then subjects have an obligation to obey their sovereign without having consented to obey in fact?

---

45. *Leviathan* 20:2, 3, 14. See also *De Cive* 8:6.

46. *Leviathan* 20:10–11. See also *De Cive* 8:1.

47. *Leviathan*, "A Review and Conclusion," 6.

48. *Leviathan* 20:5–8.

49. David Hume, "Of the Original Contract," in Hume (1994), pp. 186–201. Though of course I do not claim that Hume meant to criticize Hobbes specifically in this essay.

50. Hume (1994), 192–193. Here Hume says specifically that people in general are unable to freely give their tacit consent and that fear alone, not consent, is the reason people obey a conqueror or usurper.

51. Hume (1994), p. 189. Unlike Hobbes, Hume evidently does not believe that a coerced promise made to a usurper or conqueror is binding.

I answer, "No. But Hobbes still gave us a valuable tool for evaluating social institutions." The results of commonwealth by institution do not give sufficient conditions for political obligation because hypothetical choices or agreements in general do not oblige. Robert Nozick is reputed to have said, "A hypothetical contract is not worth the paper it's not written on." In *An Essay on the Modern State*, Christopher Morris states the relevant problem with hypothetical agreements far more clearly: "Hypothetical agreement requires no act or engagement of the will and so does not commit one in the way that consent, express or tacit, does."[52] Of course, to be fair to Hobbes, who tried so hard to prove that subjects are morally obligated to obey their sovereign, one might add that perhaps *nothing* can establish this kind of political obligation. Morris notes that among contemporary political philosophers, the consensus is that there are no such obligations, at least not of the sweeping sort in Hobbes' account of sovereignty.[53] And in fact, more contemporary hypothetical contractarians such as Harsanyi and Rawls make no claims that their theories establish any political obligations. But this does not mean either that people can have no good moral reasons for obeying their states or that hypothetical contractarianism is worthless. Much like a lens can help the viewer see an object in ways not possible with the naked eye, a hypothetical choice or contract can help agents examine institutions in ways they cannot given the conflicts and confusions of everyday life. The real value of a hypothetical choice or contract is as a heuristic device for determining how well, or how poorly, some institution would serve a community even when this institution does not happen to be in force. If an incumbent institution, such as an incumbent Hobbesian sovereign, would have been chosen in certain counterfactual circumstances, this might signify that this institution is morally acceptable and thus give individuals at least one moral reason to respect and perhaps even obey this institution. If, on the other hand, this institution would not have been chosen in these counterfactual circumstances, then this might be grounds for considering the reform of, or, in extreme circumstances, even the abolition of this institution.[54] Viewed this way, commonwealth by institution serves as a device for determining a necessary, if perhaps not sufficient, normative condition for whether or not one should either support or work to reform one's government.

52. Morris (1998), p. 7 n. 6. See also pp. 125–126.

53. Morris (1998), p. 216. I think the view Morris expressed in 1998 view remains largely true today. Richard Dagger gives a fine overview of recent philosophical approaches to arguing for political obligation as well as criticisms of these approaches in "Political Obligation," in *The Stanford Encyclopedia of Philosophy*, Summer 2010 ed., ed. Edward N. Zalta, http://plato.stanford.edu/archives/sum2010/entries/political-obligation.

54. Gerald Gaus presents a similar view of the value of hypothetical contractarianism for evaluating principles of social morality in Gaus (2011), §14.2.

§6.3. A Governing Convention

Life might not work out so pleasantly for both sovereign and subjects as Hobbes supposes. Hume, whose own views regarding human weaknesses are close to those of Hobbes, claims such weaknesses may easily pervert government and turn the governors into tyrants.[55] And as Locke puts it in a famous acerbic response to defenders of Hobbesian-style absolutism:

> As if when men, quitting the State of Nature, entered into Society, they agreed that all of them but one should be under the restraint of Laws; but that he should still retain all the Liberty of the State of Nature, increased with Power, and made licentious by Impunity. This is to think that Men are so foolish that they take care to avoid what Mischiefs may be done them by *Pole-cats* or *Foxes*, but are content, nay, think it Safety, to be devoured by *Lions*.[56]

Locke and Hume rightly doubt that the subjects of a Hobbesian commonwealth could trust their sovereign to treat them as well as Hobbes seems to think a sovereign who understands his political theory should. Indeed, it is by no means clear that the sovereign would not serve its own interests best by exploiting its subjects, perhaps even to the point where they are worse off than they would be in the State of Nature. Then the relationship between subjects and sovereign reflected in the Hobbesian Sovereignty game would have a Trust game structure after all where the Sovereign's payoffs satisfy $W_2 > W_1$, so defecting is the Sovereign's best option.

On the other hand, the subjects might not be so helpless in civil society as the Hobbesian Sovereignty game model suggests. The Hobbesian Sovereignty game model abstracts away from the interactions between an instituted Sovereign and the Multitude over time. What if these interactions over time are modeled explicitly? Figure 6.5 depicts a *Humean Sovereignty* stage game. The Figure 6.5 extensive form game summarizes one of a sequence of interactions between agents in the roles of Sovereign and Subject who engage in this game repeatedly over an indefinite time horizon. The repeated Humean Sovereignty game is therefore somewhat similar to other indefinitely repeated games such as the repeated

---

55. *Treatise* 3.2.10:4.

56. *Second Treatise of Civil Government* §93. See also §136. Interestingly, while some read Locke's §93 as a direct response to Hobbes, Peter Laslett argues that it is likely that here Locke's direct target is Filmer. See note 32 in the Laslett-edited edition of Locke's *Two Treatises of Government.*

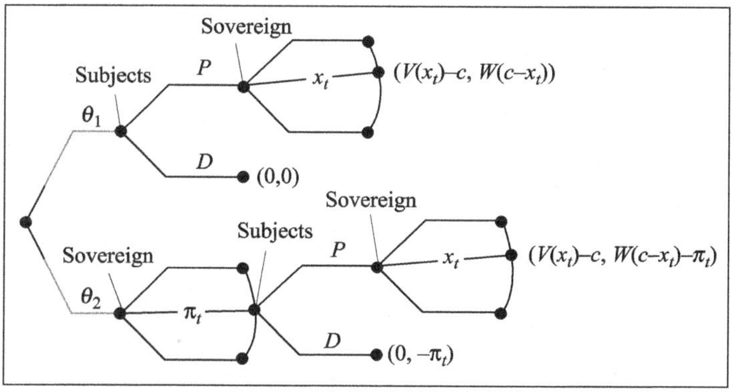

P = obey, D = disobey, θ_0 = State of Nature, θ_1 = commonwealth

$V(c) > c,\ c > V(0),\ c > 0,\ W(c) > W(0) > 0$

FIGURE 6.5 Humean Sovereignty Stage Game

Prisoner's Dilemma and the repeated Covenant Game discussed in §2.4. In this repeated stage game one agent is fixed in every period in the role of the Subjects, while agents in the other role of the Sovereign might vary over time. One can think of the agent in the role of the Subjects as roughly the same multitude of people in each period that can establish or maintain civil society, while the agent in the role of the Sovereign in a given period might at a later period be replaced by a new agent that assumes this role according to the moves the two agents in the game might follow. At the start of each period, either the Subjects and the Sovereign are in an established commonwealth (θ_1) or they are back in the State of Nature (θ_0). If they are in state θ_1, the Subjects can *obey* their Sovereign (P) at a cost $c > 0$. If the Subjects obey, then they keep their current Sovereign in power, and both will be in state θ_1 in the next period. The Subjects can also neutralize the activity of the incumbent Sovereign by *disobeying* (D) and saving themselves the cost of obedience. Disobedience puts both the Subjects and the Sovereign back in the State of Nature, and both will be in state θ_0 in the next period. If they are in state θ_1 and the Subjects obey, then the Sovereign has resources of value c and responds by choosing $x_t \in [0,c]$, which for $x_t = x$ is *performing to the degree* x. If they are in state θ_0, then the Sovereign first chooses $\pi_t \geq 0$ at a cost π_t and places them in a subgame that proceeds as if the initial game were at state θ_1. At either state, if the Subjects obey, then their payoff is $V(x_t)-c$, and the Sovereign's payoff is $W(c-x_t)$ if the state is θ_1 and $W(c-x_t)-\pi_t$ if the state is θ_0. And at either state, if the Subjects disobey, then their payoff is 0, and the Sovereign's payoff is 0 if the state is θ_1 and $-\pi_t$ if the state is θ_0. The functions $V(\cdot)$ and $W(\cdot)$ are such that as x_t increases, $V(\cdot)$ increases and $W(\cdot)$ decreases, so that as the Sovereign increases its degree of performance, the Subjects fare better and the Sovereign fares worse.[57] $W(0) > 0$ and $V(c) > c > V(0)$, so the Sovereign receives some positive payoff even if it performs to the highest degree $x_t = c$, and the Subjects receive a negative payoff if $x_t = 0$ and their highest positive payoff if $x_t = c$. If at either state the Subjects disobey, then the agent in the role of Sovereign is replaced by a fresh agent in the following period.

In the Humean Sovereignty stage game, if the Subjects obey, then the Sovereign maximizes its immediate payoff by choosing $x_t = 0$, effectively spending everything on itself and nothing on its Subjects, and the Subjects are then left with a lower payoff than their State of Nature payoff. This reflects the idea that a sovereign could gain its own best payoff by exploiting its subjects, thereby leaving them even worse off than they would be in the State of Nature. But if the Sovereign exploits its Subjects' obedience in a given period, the Subjects might retaliate by disobeying at a future period. When the state is θ_1, so the Subjects and the Sovereign are in an established commonwealth, disobedience has the effect of a successful rebellion. When the state is θ_0, the agent in the Sovereign role is a new sovereign candidate that actually becomes sovereign only if the Subjects obey. And from the Subjects' point of view some candidates for the post of Sovereign are better than others. In the θ_0 state, the Sovereign agent's choice of π_t is a signal indicating to the Subjects the degree of performance the Sovereign "offers" if they now obey. When the Subjects contemplate obeying for the first time a candidate for Sovereign, π_t is their indicator of how well they can expect this candidate to serve them if they in effect authorize this candidate. Assuming a given signal π_t reflects, perhaps imperfectly, a candidate's ability to perform, the Subjects in the State of Nature might choose to wait until they receive a sufficiently high signal indicating that the current candidate is "good enough." In a candidate can expect the Subjects to obey given a sufficiently "good" signal, the candidate has incentive to increase its signal if it can, at a higher signaling cost.

If the agents engage in the stage game only once, then given the usual assumption that they have common knowledge of the game and their Bayesian rationality, the Subjects' best choice is to disobey at either state and the Sovereign's best choices are $\pi_t = 0$ at state θ_0 and $x_t = 0$ if the Subjects obey at either state. But equilibria for both are available in the indefinitely repeated game. The Subjects can adopt the following contingency strategy:

f_1: At θ_0, P if $\pi_t \geq \pi^*$ and D otherwise, and at θ_1, P if $x_{t-1} \geq x^*$ and D otherwise,

57. Equivalently, $V(\cdot)$ and $W(\cdot)$ are both strictly increasing functions.

where $\pi^* > 0$ is their *signaling threshold* and $x^* > 0$ is their *performance threshold*. Informally, in the State of Nature the Subjects will at period t obey and effectively establish a new regime ruled by the current sovereign-candidate if this candidate's signal π_t is "good enough," and in an established commonwealth the Subjects will at period t obey if the incumbent sovereign performed "well enough" at period $t-1$. But if in the State of Nature a candidate's signal does not meet the Subjects' threshold requirement, then the Subjects opt to wait one more period in the State of Nature in hopes that a better candidate will come along. And if in a commonwealth an incumbent sovereign's performance does not meet the Subjects' threshold requirement in a given period, then at the next period the Subjects depose this sovereign and return to the State of Nature. So the Subjects can have some leverage over their Sovereign given that they are in effect able to punish the Sovereign for poor performance. Now suppose the Sovereign's contingency strategy is

f_2: At θ_0, $\pi_t = \pi^*$ if $\pi_t' \geq \pi^*$ and $\pi_t = 0$ otherwise, and $x_t = \overline{x} \geq x^*$ if the Subjects follow P and $\pi_t' \geq \pi^*$ and $x_t = 0$ otherwise, and at θ_1, $x_t = \overline{x} \geq x^*$ if the Subjects follow P and $\pi_{t_0} \geq \pi^*$ at the last period t_0 in state θ_0, and $x_t = 0$ otherwise,

where $\pi_t' > 0$ is a value reflecting how well the Sovereign can signal at period t, and the Sovereign is capable of performing at any level $x_t \in [0, c]$ if $\pi_t' \geq \pi^*$ but might be incapable of performing at level x^* if $\pi_t' < \pi^*$. Informally, the Sovereign's strategy is to signal at $\pi_t = \pi^*$ if it can and at $\pi_t = 0$ otherwise; then, if definitely capable, to adopt a policy of always performing at least at the Subjects' threshold level if the Subjects obey, but to spend all on itself if not definitely capable and the Subjects obey. The Sovereign has some leverage even when the Subjects set their performance threshold x^* sufficiently high so that $V(x^*) > c$, so that obedience is worth their while if the Sovereign in turn performs at or above their performance threshold. The Sovereign then has incentive to try to perform over time at a level the Subjects find satisfactory. From their side, the Subjects can depose an incumbent Sovereign if the Sovereign fails to meet their acceptability threshold. But the higher their standard x^*, the longer they can expect to languish in the State of Nature waiting for a satisfactory replacement Sovereign if they depose the incumbent.

Under fairly general conditions the Subjects and the Sovereign can be at an equilibrium of an indefinitely repeated Humean Sovereignty stage game where at each period the Subjects obey and the Sovereign performs at an acceptable level. This result follows from the economic theory of *search*, which explores some of the reasons certain resources in an economy might go unused for some time.[58]

---

58. I give a sketch of the proof of this result in Appendix 4. The proof is a variation of the proof of the existence of a reservation wage equilibrium in a model of search unemployment that

In the repeated Humean Sovereignty game, Sovereign and Subjects occupy roles analogous to those in search theory of a prospective employer and a worker seeking employment, and acceptable performance threshold for the Subjects defined by x^* is analogous to a *reservation wage* the prospective employer must offer in order to successfully hire the worker. So a stable and mutually beneficial relationship can obtain between Subjects and Sovereign where the Subjects obey and the Sovereign provides the Subjects benefits they find more satisfactory than the "benefits" of remaining in the State of Nature. The state where at each period the Subjects disobey and the Sovereign would defect if installed by the Subjects' obedience is also an equilibrium—the suboptimal equilibrium where both Sovereign and Subjects remain in the State of Nature. The Subjects and the Sovereign have available to them alternative equilibria they might settle into, according to their conjectures over each other's chosen strategies. So the (f_1, f_2) equilibrium of the indefinitely repeated Humean Sovereignty game characterizes a convention, a governing convention between a ruled people and their ruler or rulers.

I think Hume recognized that the relationship between governors and the governed is ordinarily a conventional relationship, and that this governing convention is more stable the more nearly the interests of the governed balance with those of their governors. This is why I call the Figure 6.5 game the *Humean* Sovereignty stage game. Put another way, for Hume, government is maintained via a self-enforcing "contract."[59] This claim may seem surprising given Hume's repeated denials that our obligations to our governments stem from our explicit or tacit consent.[60] For Hume, mutual recognition that government is a human invention that serves the public interest is the real root of political obligation.[61] He also points out that the governments of recorded history have their origins in usurpation or conquest.[62] But Hume is only an anti-state contractarian according

---

Nancy L. Stokey and Robert E. Lucas give in §10.7 of *Recursive Methods in Economic Dynamics* (Cambridge, MA: Harvard University Press, 1989). Stokey and Lucas base their analysis on the model presented in John J. McCall, "Economics of Information and Job Search," *Quarterly Journal of Economics* 84 (1970), pp. 113–126.

59. Hobbes indicates in his response to the Foole in *Leviathan* 15 that some covenants made in the State of Nature might be self-enforcing, despite his belief that any purported covenant between sovereign and subjects or a sovereign candidate and State of Nature parties necessarily involves third-party judgment and enforcement. I think Hobbes maintains this because in *Leviathan* 17:14 he notes the tendency of the individuals in a large group to disagree with each other, rendering them unable to proceed effectively against their sovereign or even agree whether or not their sovereign has honored its covenant with them. I discuss the ability of subjects to unite further in the concluding section of this chapter. I discuss Hobbes' Foole further in Chapter 7.

60. *Treatise* 3.2.8–9; "Of the Original Contract," pp. 186–201.

61. *Treatise* 3.2.10:4.

62. *Treatise* 3.2.10:4; "Of the Original Contract," pp. 189–190.

to the more limited understanding of a contract as a system of promises enforceable by some third party. Hume suggests the governed themselves can keep the conduct of their governors at least somewhat in check by the threat of revolt. Indeed, he observes that even the most tyrannical regimes are incapable of depriving the people under their rule the right of resistance.[63] Hume argues that people turn to and respect governors in the first place because they perceive that it is in the direct interests of the governors that certain projects such as the generation of public goods are executed for the benefit of all.[64]

Moreover, Hume argues that a government can be examined from the perspective of an "impartial examiner" in order to ascertain how well it serves the public interest.[65] So Hume's discussion of governments contains a normative element that complements its explanatory elements. Hume admits that it may be difficult if not impossible to give precise particular conditions either for an optimally designed government or for when armed insurrection is justified.[66] But he maintains that all would accept the general principle that political obligation ceases should the government cease to provide mutual advantage and security.[67] Game theory facilitates a more precise contemporary reformulation of these ideas. The Humean Sovereignty game model summarizes how a people might depose their repressive regime if their plight becomes "bad enough." Hume's insights regarding a "judicious spectator" or "impartial examiner" foreshadow the impartial spectator central to Adam Smith's moral theory and the contemporary moral contractarian theories in the impartial spectator tradition such as John Harsanyi's and John Rawls' veil of ignorance theories.[68] These insights also illuminate how one can understand the relationship between rulers and ruled as a coordination regime. The ruled will continue to obey so long as their ruler provides sufficient benefits, and what counts as sufficient benefits can be ascertained from the perspective of an impartial spectator.

---

63. *Treatise* 3.2.10:16.

64. *Treatise* 3.2.7:6, 8.

65. "Of the Independency of Parliament," p. 26. In *Treatise* 3.3.1:14 Hume also speaks of evaluating moral qualities from the perspective of a "judicious spectator."

66. *Treatise* 3.2.10:16; "Of the Independency of Parliament," p. 26.

67. *Treatise* 3.2.10:4, 16.

68. See Rawls (1971) and *Justice as Fairness: A Restatement*, 2nd ed., ed. Erin Kelly (Cambridge, MA: Harvard University Press), and Harsanyi (1977), ch. 4, for summaries of their moral contractarian theories. Rawls (1971), pp. 186–188, draws a sharp distinction between his justice as fairness theory and impartial spectator theory, claiming the latter depends upon sympathy and that his theory avoids this dependence. Obviously, I prefer to regard Rawls' theory as an impartial spectator theory, and I do so because of Rawls' use of a veil of ignorance.

§6.4. Democracy via Salience

How can Hobbes' commonwealth by institution be changed so that the parties can complete the process? In a State of Nature with three or more candidates for sovereign, there is no method of *voting* in a sovereign that cannot be manipulated by parties who misrepresent their preferences, but there is a method for selecting a candidate that is not open to such manipulation, namely, choosing the sovereign *at random*. The parties could complete the commonwealth by institution process if they could agree to follow the outcome where some candidate for sovereign is chosen by lot. To forestall worries that the lottery might be rigged in favor of any candidate, one can invoke the truce rule once more and stipulate that the lottery gives each candidate an equal chance of becoming sovereign. For example, in the 3-party case summarized by the Figure 6.3 game, the parties can follow a *die-is-cast* equilibrium where Party i proclaims and the others authorize Party i exactly when Party i wins a fair game determined by the throwing of a single die. Such a die-is-cast equilibrium is a correlated equilibrium where prior to the die throw each Party i's expected payoff is equal to that of her counterpart, and the result of the die throw picks a strict Nash equilibrium that is exactly one party's most preferred equilibrium where this party is sovereign. Given the earlier assumption that the truce is over after the selection stage, if n parties can agree upon such a lottery as their selection mechanism at the preliminary stage and the lottery is executed at the selection stage,[69] then the winning candidate is evidently the salient candidate at the authorization stage.[70]

Choosing a lottery as selection mechanism at the preliminary stage enables the parties to avoid deadlock at this stage. The lottery method has another interesting advantage: the results of this method coincide rather well with commonwealth by acquisition. Suppose parties in a State of Nature wage war until some party emerges as the winner of the conflict. Then the parties all drift into the equilibrium where the victor is the sovereign. If we think of the fortunes of war as somewhat random, then commonwealth by acquisition is much like commonwealth by institution where the sovereign is chosen by lot.[71] One might argue

---

69. I allow for the possibility that both individual parties and groups of parties might be candidates for sovereign included in the lottery at the preliminary stage. Nothing precludes a given Party i from having some chance of winning the lottery by herself as an individual party, in which case she would become monarch, and having some chance of winning as part of various groups, each of which would become a sovereign assembly.

70. Hampton rightly argues that no random equilibrium selection mechanism can make an equilibrium of a coordination game salient if the selected equilibrium is not renegotiation-proof (1986, p. 160). Ending the truce immediately after the selection stage is my way of addressing Hampton's worry.

71. And this is in line with Hobbes' assumption that in the State of Nature, individuals are roughly equal in their natural powers (*Leviathan* 13:1, 2).

that the sovereign one actually lives under could have been chosen by some natural lottery or chance device one's society would have used had they all suddenly been thrust into their "naturall condition" and given the task of instituting a commonwealth. Hence the results of commonwealth by institution and commonwealth by acquisition are isomorphic. By adding in a few ancillary premises,[72] the earlier sovereign by institution argument can be modified, so that P3 can be replaced with

P3′. If any group of rational persons in the State of Nature could create the kind of society in which they are to live, they would institute a commonwealth ruled by an absolute sovereign *chosen by a (possibly natural) lottery.*

This modified sovereign by institution argument would yield

C′. A commonwealth ruled by an absolute sovereign chosen by a (possibly natural) lottery is justified.

and from this extension it follows that the sovereign that emerges from the natural lottery of war is justified.

This modification of the commonwealth by institution process would produce the isomorphism Hobbes would want, but the modified premise (P3′) is dubious, to say the least. Some institutions that assign benefits or burdens to individuals by lot may be justified. Drafting individuals by lot into military service in wartime may be a case in point. However, I will take it for granted that most people would protest that they have no good reason to surrender their political rights to some person or group of persons merely because a chance event makes this person or this group conspicuous to them all. A commonwealth ruled by a sovereign chosen at random is unlikely to pass even the standard of justification I attribute to Hobbes in the original sovereign by institution argument, namely,

---

72. For instance, P3′ could be obtained as follows:

P3′.1. If any group of rational persons in the State of Nature could institute the kind of society in which they are to live, they would institute a commonwealth ruled by an absolute sovereign chosen according to a procedure that is nonmanipulable.

P3′.2. A (possibly natural) lottery is the only mechanism for choosing an absolute sovereign that is nonmanipulable.

P3′. If any group of rational persons in the State of Nature could create the kind of society in which they are to live, they would institute a commonwealth ruled by an absolute sovereign chosen by a (possibly natural) lottery.

P3′.2. might in fact be dubious unless one understands the relevant mechanism to be one deliberately created for the purpose of selecting a candidate. As I argue below, the parties might select a certain form of sovereignty because of its natural salience.

that every rational person finds life in this kind of commonwealth preferable to life in any alternative type of society. If one must be a subject, then one would want to be ruled by a sovereign that governs well. If the sovereign is chosen at random, then the parties run a considerable risk of falling under the rule of an incompetent sovereign, or even a sovereign that persecutes some or all of them for no good reason. Even if subjects are able to depose an unsatisfactory sovereign, as discussed in §6.3, this modification of the commonwealth by institution process simply fails as a justificatory tool. Still, the lottery method of selection suggests another possible modification of the commonwealth by institution process that I will discuss shortly.

Evidently, what the parties really want is the *best-qualified* candidate to be their monarch. Perhaps the parties could select this candidate without falling into deadlock at the preliminary stage if they were constrained for part of the commonwealth by institution process by a veil of ignorance similar to the veils Harsanyi and Rawls use in their hypothetical choice theories. Suppose the parties at the preliminary stage are temporarily deprived of knowledge of certain characteristics by which they ordinarily distinguish themselves and each other. In particular, each party is temporarily ignorant of her own particular abilities and social status.[73] Then the parties could agree to select the best-qualified candidate as their sovereign, assuming that they can identify this individual if their veil of ignorance is lifted at the selection stage. Stipulating a veil of ignorance at the preliminary stage in this manner violates the truce rule, but perhaps in a way the parties could accept, since the selection mechanism would now be biased toward the candidate all expect to be the best sovereign. Yet even if the parties would want to select their sovereign in this manner, the results would now diverge with very high probability from those of commonwealth by acquisition. Their use of the veil of ignorance might prevent deadlock at the preliminary stage, but this modification of commonwealth by institution fails to produce the desired isomorphism between commonwealth by institution and commonwealth by acquisition.

In any event, there is a perhaps more natural resolution to the equilibrium selection problem in commonwealth by institution. In the 3-party Leadership Selection game of Figure 6.3, each Party i's payoff at the democracy equilibrium (V,V,V) is greater than Party i's payoff at the equilibria where Party i is the subject of one of the other two parties. In this game I have assumed that each party would rather form part of a democracy than live as a subject under an absolute monarch. I now explicitly assume that in the general n-party case, each party would prefer to sharing sovereignty with the others in a democracy over

73. In his revisionist Hobbesian contractarian theory, Kavka employs a veil of ignorance less stringent than Rawls' veil. Kavka's parties know their own personal characteristics but not their social positions (1986, pp. 193–194).

living as an absolute monarch's subject. This perhaps marks a departure from one of Hobbes' own positions, namely, that monarchy is generally the best form of commonwealth.[74] If Hobbes is right, then perhaps every party should prefer life in some absolute monarchy, whether she is the monarch or this monarch's subject, over life in every other possible civil society. But this is quite implausible. As argued above, one might reasonably suppose that any party's best possible outcome is to be an absolute monarch, since in this case this party has absolute power over the others while being above the laws of the commonwealth herself. However, individual parties would likely prefer being part of some sovereign assembly over being an absolute monarch's subject so as not to be subject to the monarch's arbitrary whims. Even so, if my stated assumption departs from Hobbes, this departure does little violence to Hobbes' assumptions regarding human nature. Individuals who want above all to avoid the bleak consequences of a State of Nature war will want to avoid any possibility of suffering punishment at the arbitrary order of a monarch. And it is doubtful that the alleged strict preferability of monarchy over other forms of commonwealth really follows from Hobbes' assumptions. Hobbes' arguments for monarchy and against democracy have been criticized many times over in the literature. Without delving into the specifics of these criticisms, I will simply propose that if the parties regard democracy as a viable form of commonwealth each would prefer over being someone else's subject, then to authorize all as democratic sovereign might be the naturally salient outcome of the three-stage process.

Again, in the Figure 6.3 game the payoffs of the (V, V, V) equilibrium reflect each party's strict preference to form part of a democracy over becoming another party's subject. This equilibrium has a certain natural salience, since it is the only strict Nash equilibrium at which each party is sure to escape the dangers of *both* being in the State of Nature and being a subject. So perhaps these properties would lead the parties to agree to settle upon this equilibrium at the preliminary stage, and there would be little incentive to hold out at the authorization stage since to do so would be to run the risk of ending up either a subject or even back in war. As noted in §6.2, extending the Figure 6.3 game so as to include all possible assemblies as candidates for sovereign produces a $8 \times 8 \times 8$ game, which I do not reproduce here. But in the $8 \times 8 \times 8$ game, (V, V, V) is still the only strict Nash equilibrium where each party avoids both the State of Nature war and the pitfalls of being a subject, and this conclusion extends to the corresponding all-V equilibrium of the n-party case. One might argue that an additional advantage of democracy, and one that lends more support to the salience of an all-V equilibrium, is that focusing on this equilibrium does not require the parties to go through

74. *De Cive* Preface 22, 10:3, 6–8, 17–19, *Leviathan* 19:4.

any cumbersome deliberations over which proper subsets of themselves to consider as viable candidates for an aristocracy. Monarchy and aristocracy remain as possibilities, along with the problem of subgroups possibly rigging the outcome by misrepresenting preferences. Yet if the parties all regard democracy as a better alternative than winding up a subject, then perhaps they will be able to settle upon democracy as a compromise that is uniquely second-best from each individual party's perspective, and consequently the best achievable outcome from a social perspective. The selection "mechanism" in this new modification of the commonwealth by institution process is natural salience.

If one accepts this line of reasoning, then one can use this modified version of Hobbesian commonwealth by institution to justify civil society ruled democratically. In the sovereign by institution argument schema, one can replace "absolute sovereign" by "democratic sovereign" in P3, P4, and C. Of course, doing so raises an interesting new question: Should we be suspicious of P2? If the parties would institute a democratic commonwealth when each would rather be an absolute monarch, then is democracy what rational people really prefer over any other type of society? In fact, P2 stands because it employs commonwealth by institution to justify a form of commonwealth, not any particular instance of this form. The isomorphism between commonwealth by institution and commonwealth by acquisition becomes an isomorphism of the government's form, not the specifics of particular governments such as who serves in what office, which would be simply impossible to achieve. And this isomorphism makes good intuitive sense. One can certainly argue that any rational person would rather receive her usual paycheck from her employer than a state lottery ticket, even if she would strictly prefer winning the state lottery over receiving her paycheck. Similarly, one can argue that even individuals with Hobbesian preferences can prefer democracy over monarchy, given that in a monarchy one is almost certain to end up a subject. So commonwealth by institution can produce the quite un-Hobbesian conclusion that democracy, not monarchy, has the strongest Hobbesian justification.

One can obtain a similar result by analyzing the commonwealth by institution process as a multiagent bargaining problem. I argued in Chapter 5 that perhaps no axiomatic solution to the general n-agent bargaining problem is fully satisfactory. Still, in the special case where a bargaining problem is completely symmetric in structure across the agents, the main proposed axiomatic solution concepts all assign the agents equal shares of the good at stake.[75] In this special

---

75. See, for example, Thomson and Lensberg (1989). These solution concepts incorporate a *symmetry axiom*, which is a formal statement that the agents have no differences in natural bargaining ability. I discuss symmetry in bargaining problems further in Chapter 8, especially note 75.

case the equal share solution also has a certain salience, being the unique Pareto optimal solution with no asymmetries in the distribution of shares. In this special case the equal shares solution is also the egalitarian solution that, as I argued in Chapter 5, the members of a community might come to regard as salient from what they learn in 2-agent bargaining problems. This is directly relevant for the discussion here given a continuing background assumption of equally situated parties. In Hobbes' State of Nature, the parties are roughly equal. If in fact the parties are *exactly* equal with respect to their relative powers and their relative preferences for alternative positions in civil society,[76] then the corresponding impure coordination game is entirely symmetric and the solution of the resulting bargaining problem gives each party an equal share of sovereignty. This solution can correspond to the correlated equilibrium where each of the n parties rules as sovereign for $\frac{1}{n}$ of the time if this equilibrium happens to be Pareto optimal. But this solution can also correspond to the equilibrium of democracy if this equilibrium is Pareto optimal, which will be the case if the payoff for each party at the democracy equilibrium exceeds the average payoff of the other equilibria where some party or parties is sovereign and the rest are subjects. Since I argued above that parties will all regard democracy as the second-best of all possible outcomes, I think it very likely that each party's democracy payoff really is greater than her average payoff at the equilibria of the other possible forms of sovereignty. So a bargaining problem analysis supports a second general argument for the salience of democracy.

Conclusion

Hobbes, and Hume after him, rejected the idea that a contract of the sort that obligates parties legally or is more generally subject to third-party arbitration could underwrite the relationship between a sovereign and its subjects. But Hume recognized in an informal manner that rulers and the ruled can establish and maintain a state contract by convention. And Hobbes and Hume both recognized how a state might be judged from the perspective of agents in special hypothetical circumstances, as evidenced by Hobbes' device of commonwealth by institution and Hume's device of an impartial examiner. Here I have used game theory to defend two main claims inspired by Hobbes' and Hume's insights: (1) a governing convention can indeed regulate the interactions between the ruled and their rulers, and (2) democratic government can be justified

76. Exact equality in relative powers is reflected by the symmetry axiom.

using an isomorphism argument, in that parties finding themselves in the State of Nature would choose this form of government.

The indefinitely repeated Humean Sovereignty game summarizes how a balance of power can exist between Sovereign and Subjects that ensures that the Sovereign serves its Subjects adequately in return for the Subjects' obedience. In this setting, there can be a contract between Subjects and their Sovereign that they enforce without appealing to an outside arbitrating power. The equilibrium of the indefinitely repeated Figure 6.5 game where over time the Subjects obey and the Sovereign performs at an acceptable level is a simple example where a governed people and their governor or governors can police a mutually beneficial agreement themselves. Moreover, while they could form this self-enforcing agreement explicitly, this is not a necessary feature of such an agreement. The agents in the positions of Subjects and Sovereign could before the start of play first form a covenant as Hobbes defines it by exchanging promises to follow their ends of an equilibrium based upon the appropriate performance threshold x^*. In this manner they might settle into the equilibrium where at each period the Subjects follow P and obey and the Sovereign follows $\bar{x} \geq x^*$ quite rapidly, perhaps even immediately. Such an explicit covenant could have an effect similar to that Russell Hardin argues a written constitution has on focusing the expectations of the governed very rapidly on a set of governing policies, which in a well-designed constitution characterize a complex but stable social equilibrium that includes a governing convention.[77] But as Hume would remind us, the ruled and their rulers seldom if ever draw up such an explicit contract that regulates their relationship. And the ruled and their rulers might not need any such explicit contract in order to establish and maintain an appropriate balance of power. For the agents involved may be able to learn to follow the equilibrium of a governing convention as Subjects depose initially unsatisfactory Sovereign agents and search for various sovereign candidates until they find a candidate that performs at equilibrium level. In short, as is the case with conventions in general, a governing convention can emerge via some process other than formal agreement.

I have argued that one can model the problem of choosing a sovereign as an n-agent impure coordination game whose strict equilibria correspond to the alternative conventions of sovereign-candidates becoming sovereign. The Leadership Selection game of §6.1 is a simple special case of such a game where three parties try to establish a commonwealth. I have also used the Leadership Selection game to develop a conventionalist justification of democracy. As I have interpreted him, Hobbes clearly recognized that most if not all commonwealths are created by acquisition, but he argued that actual commonwealths are in the

77. Hardin (1999), ch. 3.

end justified because the results of commonwealth by acquisition coincide with those of commonwealth by institution. Hobbes' own isomorphism argument fails, but his isomorphism argument strategy is compelling. I contend that democracy is an acceptable form of government because this would be the object of State of Nature parties' choice. This choice can be, but need not be, the result of a hypothetical covenant. Assuming that the parties in a hypothetical State of Nature truce find the equilibrium of democracy sufficiently salient, they could all exchange promises to follow this equilibrium. This would be enough to establish the desired isomorphism between State of Nature choice and actual democratic commonwealths. But the salience itself can be enough to lead the parties to follow the equilibrium corresponding to a convention of democratic government. Either way, convention is plainly an integral part of this isomorphism argument. I should add that the isomorphism argument does not necessarily show that democracy is the *only* acceptable form of government. Another way to gauge the acceptability of a government is to use Hume's idea of examining a governing convention from the perspective of an impartial examiner. I have not explored this alternative in depth in this chapter, but it may be that many nondemocratic states are acceptable according to this alternate conventionalist standard.

Almost needless to say, the arguments of this chapter leave important questions unanswered, and the accompanying the game-theoretic models oversimplify in several ways the relationships one would expect to find between the rulers and the ruled in actual civil societies. The Leadership Selection games abstract away many of the important specific policies and structures any sovereign must establish just for routine functioning. Even an absolute monarch will need to create subordinate offices with substantial powers that can be wielded directly against segments of the subject population and possibly against the monarchy itself. The isomorphism argument of §6.4 might justify democracy, but how exactly is a democracy to function in practice? What sorts of legislators and what sort of legal system will a democratic commonwealth establish? These are questions I am admittedly not prepared to address in detail here, except to observe that quite a variety of actual democratic states might be justified according to the isomorphism argument, and plainly it need not be the case that all such states are equally good in an absolute sense. What some may find more troublesome is that the isomorphism argument itself sets no official limits upon the democratic sovereign. This argument does not rule out a tyranny of the majority in principle. I concede that this may be a serious objection if one uses the isomorphism argument alone in evaluating the governing structures of a state. But the isomorphism argument is not the only tool at hand for evaluating these structures. One can apply both the isomorphism argument and an impartial examiner analysis of the governing convention that regulates a given state to assess this state's governing structures. A governing convention will generally set limits upon a democratic leviathan's activities. What these limits are and whether or not they are satisfactory from the perspective of an impartial examiner will depend upon the specifics of the particular governing convention.

A leading idea of the indefinitely repeated Humean Sovereignty game model is that subjects can choose either to maintain their incumbent sovereign or to depose this incumbent and initiate a search for a new sovereign they hope will serve them better. The model presupposes somewhat unrealistically that the Subjects always interact with exactly one counterpart in the position of the Sovereign. Either the Subjects maintain an incumbent Sovereign with their continued obedience or, in case they are currently in the State of Nature, they interact with a single Sovereign candidate. Put another way, the §6.3 model oversimplifies by presupposing that at each period, the Leadership Selection problem is already effectively solved. In fact, the process of identifying a suitable replacement for a deposed sovereign would likely be more complex, involving multiple competing candidates that might not all be equally salient from the Subjects' perspective. Indeed, this process might somewhat resemble the process of instituting Hobbesian commonwealth "from scratch." I have treated the problems of selecting a sovereign and creating and maintaining a governing convention somewhat separately, as though State of Nature parties first select an equilibrium of their n-agent Leadership Selection game corresponding to their chosen sovereign candidate and then authorize this candidate with first obedience, as in the Humean Sovereignty game. But new insights into the acceptability of governments may be discovered in a more general model that integrates these processes.

Another way the Humean Sovereignty game model oversimplifies is in treating the Subjects as a single unified coalition that can act at will either to support or to depose the Sovereign.[78] If subjects of a commonwealth cannot easily disobey *together*, or if many of them are unwilling to disobey in protest against how their sovereign treats others, then the sort of tyranny Hume feared might well result. In fact, the dynamics of revolution are exceedingly complicated, and revolutions are quite hard to predict beforehand in large part because those under the rule of any regime might have trouble organizing simultaneous disobedience.[79] Moreover,

78. Of course, the Hobbesian Sovereignty game model of §6.2 also oversimplifies in just this manner.

79. In "Game Theory Meets Threshold Analysis: Reappraising the Paradoxes of Anarchy and Revolution," *British Journal for the Philosophy of Science* 59 (2008), pp. 579–617, I argue that the process of revolution is best modeled by integrating the game-theoretic approach with the threshold analysis approach to analyzing social change first proposed by Thomas Schelling and Mark Granovetter. See Thomas Schelling, *Micromotives and Macrobehavior* (New York: W. W. Norton, 1978), ch. 7, and Mark Granovetter, "Threshold Models of Collective Behavior," *American Journal of Sociology* 83 (1978), pp. 1420–1443.

one might complain that if the Subjects could coordinate their obedience and disobedience so smoothly as they evidently can in the Figure 6.4 and Figure 6.5 games, then they would not need a Sovereign in the first place. One response to this complaint is that a widespread withdrawal of obedience might be easier for a populace to achieve than the widespread coordination of activities an effective government can generate, simply because it takes little specific instruction to know how to stop obeying some authority. The problem of the sovereign oppressing groups that are too weak to launch a successful revolt by themselves might be offset to some extent by both the sympathy and the fear of those in stronger groups. Those belonging to stronger groups might be willing to rebel in part because they want their sovereign to treat all its subjects well, and in part because they fear that the sovereign's oppression of the weak signals that the sovereign is prepared to oppress *them*. Whether these last claims are entirely true or not, the facts remain that successful revolutions occasionally occur even in societies of millions and that generally the parties involved, including revolutionaries themselves, have at best a vague grasp of the circumstances that will trigger a successful revolution. Conversely, the rulers of an incumbent regime might not know exactly how well the ruled regard the status quo, but they might well realize that they should not push the ruled too far or else widespread mutiny might erupt.

One can view the discussion in §6.34 of the indefinitely repeated Humean Sovereignty stage game as presenting an informal existence theorem. Given appropriate constraints on their payoff functions and discount factors, the Subjects and the Sovereign in this indefinitely repeated game have available to them an equilibrium that characterizes a governing convention. But under what conditions are governing conventions likely to emerge and persist in the real world? As I have indicated in the immediately preceding paragraphs, I think this is an open question. In this chapter I have discussed in admittedly rough outline some of the conditions that make a governing convention possible and some of the variations of these conditions that may affect the chances that a governing convention rather than a tyranny or anarchy prevails for a given society. Much more work needs to be done if we are to better understand the nature of governing conventions. Still, I hope I have adequately defended this core idea: State social contractarianism makes sense when one interprets the underlying "contract" as a self-enforcing and not necessarily explicit body of rules, that is, as a convention.

7 THE FOOLE, THE SHEPHERD, AND THE KNAVE

> [A]lthough the performance of duties towards others and the exercise of social virtue seem to be *generally* the best means to the attainment of the individual's happiness . . . it appears improbable that this coincidence is complete and universal. We may conceive the coincidence becoming perfect in a Utopia where men were as much in accord on moral as they are now on mathematical questions, where Law was in perfect harmony with Moral Opinion, and all offences were discovered and duly punished: or we may conceive the same result attained by intensifying the moral sentiments of all members of the community, without any external changes (which indeed would then be unnecessary). But just in proportion as existing societies and existing men fall short of this ideal, rules of conduct based on the principles of Egoistic Hedonism seem liable to diverge from those which most men are accustomed to recognise as prescribed by Duty and Virtue.
>
> —HENRY SIDGWICK, *The Methods of Ethics*

Introduction

"That *honesty is the best policy*, may be a good general rule; but is liable to many exceptions: And he, it may, perhaps be thought, conducts himself with most wisdom, who observes the general rule, and takes advantage of all the exceptions."[1] The Sensible Knave that David Hume introduces at the end of the main text of *Enquiry* presents this claim as part of a challenge against justice. Taken by itself, the second part of the Knave's remark seems rather innocuous. The Knave appears to be recommending simply that one obey a general rule when obedience serves this rule's good purpose, and to break this rule in the exceptional cases where obedience fails to serve this purpose. But when he applies his general recommendation to the rule he states in the first part of his remark, the Knave's conclusion is anything but harmless. Hume himself defends the common view that justice is necessarily inflexible. Hume argues that members of society must honor the requirements of justice even when particular circumstances tempt

1. *Enquiry* 9.2:22.

them to deviate from these requirements, or else confusion and chaos will follow.[2] If the Knave is right, then those who accept this piece of common wisdom and who do try to follow the rules of justice without exception are simply mistaken.

The Foole of Thomas Hobbes' *Leviathan* has his own skeptical challenge against justice. The Knave asserts that sometimes one foresees that one can profit substantially from a particular breach of justice without seriously disturbing the fabric of society.[3] The Knave thinks that one should take advantage of such "golden opportunities" and commit the occasional act of injustice accordingly. The Foole agrees with the Knave in outline, but unlike the Knave, the Foole does not concern himself with how his own transgressions might undermine the system of justice that regulates his society, at least not directly. The Foole simply claims that he should disregard justice when by violating the requirements of justice he best serves his own interests, and that injustice in fact best serves his own interests when he need not fear the punishments or the disapproval of other people.

What could eliminate one's need for the esteem of others and the fear of others' punishments? In Book II of *Republic*, Glaucon claims that one can achieve this sort of independence from the approval and power of others by acquiring godlike power. To illustrate his point, Glaucon recounts the tale of a Lydian commoner who rises to the throne of his country. In Glaucon's version of this story, this commoner is a shepherd who is an unnamed ancestor of the later Lydian king Gyges.[4] This shepherd finds a ring and quickly discovers that with this ring, he can make himself invisible to others at will. The shepherd enters the palace of the Lydian king, and then uses his power of invisibility to seduce the king's wife, kill the king with her aid, and finally seize the rule of the kingdom for himself.[5] Glaucon thinks that the moral of this fable is clear.

> Let's suppose, then, that there were two such rings, one worn by the just person, the other by the unjust. Now no one, it seems, would be so incorruptible that he would stay on the path of justice, or bring himself to keep away from other people's possessions and not touch them, when he could

---

2. *Treatise* 3.2.6:9. See also *Treatise* 3.2.2:22 and *Enquiry* Appendix 3:3–6, 10.

3. *Enquiry* 9.2:22.

4. There are other versions of this story. According to Herodotus, the commoner who seized the Lydian throne was Gyges himself, a palace guard who under pressure from the Lydian queen killed King Kandaules and became king in Kandaules' place. See Herodotus, *The Landmark Herodotus: The Histories*, trans. Andrea L. Purvis, ed. Robert B. Strassler (New York: Anchor Books, 2007), Book I.8–13.

5. *Republic* 359d–360b.

> take whatever he wanted from the marketplace with impunity, go into people's houses and have sex with anyone he wished, kill or release from prison anyone he wished, and do all the other things that would make him like a god among humans. And in so behaving, he would do no differently than the unjust person, but both would pursue the same course.
>
> This, some would say, is strong evidence that no one is just willingly, but only when compelled.[6]

Glaucon claims that anyone who acquires power of sort the ring of Gyges would furnish would have no reason to be just.[7] For no one could constrain such an individual either by threatened force or the actual use of force so that she would refrain from injustice.

The Sensible Knave, the Foole, and Gyges' ancestor the Lydian Shepherd are three fictitious characters who throw the rationality of justice into doubt. The challenges of these three are certainly not the only challenges great figures in the history of moral and political thought have raised against justice over the centuries. Carneades, Machiavelli, Montaigne, and Nietzsche are but a few who pose skeptical questions against justice different from those Hume, Hobbes, and Plato consider in their respective discussions of the Knave, the Foole, and the Shepherd. Yet the challenges of these three have captured the imaginations of philosophers in a special way, and each of these three challenges has generated a large and important literature. One might suppose that the Knave, the Foole, and the Shepherd are so prominent among philosophers because their challenges are presented by three of the greatest defenders of justice. But there is a deeper reason for their prominence. While Hume, Hobbes, and Plato give quite different answers to the question "What is justice?," they agree that justice requires one to act with restraint toward others. And they recognize that if one could commit some injustices with impunity, then one would be tempted to conclude that rigorously restraining one's own conduct, as justice requires, runs against one's self-interest. Hume, Hobbes, and Plato take this worry very seriously. The challenges of the Knave, the Foole, and the Shepherd are perhaps the strongest challenges against the prudential rationality of justice ever raised. Indeed, some have concluded that Hume, Hobbes, and Plato were fooled in the end by their own fictitious creations!

In this chapter I will explore to what extent justice can be vindicated in light of these three challenges. Not surprisingly, the game-theoretic analysis of

---

6. *Republic* 360b–c.

7. The Lydian Shepherd is referred to as an ancestor of Gyges in *Republic* Book II, but in Book X (612b) the invisibility ring is referred to as the ring of Gyges.

convention I have proposed earlier will figure prominently in the analysis below. One important overall conclusion I draw is that certain general responses to the three challenges are significantly more effective when they are combined. This may seem quite a trivial point to make. But in practice philosophers have tended to address the challenges of the Knave, the Foole, and the Shepherd separately and to develop responses to one of these challenges, often building upon Hume's or Hobbes' or Plato's original response to this challenge, largely without reference to the other two. The end result is three fairly distinct philosophical literatures on the Knave, the Foole, and the Lydian Shepherd.[8] One great exception to what I have just claimed is David Gauthier's 1982 essay "Three Against Justice: The Foole, the Sensible Knave and the Lydian Shepherd."[9] Gauthier was the first to consider all three challenges in the same work, and perhaps also the first to argue that philosophers can draw different morals from each of the three challenges. Plainly I draw some inspiration from Gauthier's essay. However, my own goals and conclusions are quite different from Gauthier's, so much so that I seldom refer to the specifics of Gauthier's essay in the main sections of this chapter. Gauthier does not try to show to what extent the three challenges are refutable.[10] Gauthier is mainly concerned with trying to show how the three challenges illuminate the nature of justice as a virtue that restrains the conduct of interdependent individuals and how they imply a dependence relationship between justice and human sociability. I am more concerned with the task Gauthier largely leaves aside, that is, determining to what extent one can refute the three challenges. Consequently, I am also more directly concerned with trying to understand why each of these

8. Here are short lists of recent contributions to these literatures I think are especially valuable. For the Foole: Kavka (1995); Kinch Hoekstra, "Hobbes and the Foole," *Political Theory* 25 (1997), pp. 620–654; Sharon Lloyd, "Hobbes's Reply to the Foole: A Deflationary Definitional Interpretation," *Hobbes Studies* 18 (2005), pp. 50–73. For the Knave: Gerald J. Postema, "Hume's Reply to the Sensible Knave," *History of Philosophy Quarterly* 5 (1988), pp. 23–40; David Gauthier, "Artificial Virtues and the Sensible Knave," *Hume Studies* 28 (1992), pp. 401–428; and Jason Baldwin, "Hume's Knave and the Interests of Justice," *Journal of the History of Philosophy* 42 (2004), pp. 277–296. For the Lydian Shepherd: David Copp, "The Ring of Gyges: Overridingness and the Unity of Reason," *Social Philosophy and Policy* 14 (1997), pp. 86–106.

9. David Gauthier, "Three Against Justice: The Foole, the Sensible Knave and the Lydian Shepherd," *Midwest Studies in Philosophy* 7 (1982), pp. 11–29, reprinted in Gauthier (1990), pp. 129–149.

10. Gauthier maintains that in response to Hobbes' and Hume's original replies to their challenges, the Foole and the Knave would point out that the most these replies show is that one needs to *appear* to be just, but Gauthier does not consider this objection or how Hobbes and Hume might answer it further (1990, p. 145). Gauthier argues that Plato's response to the objection of the Shepherd, which is to develop an account of justice such that justice is intrinsically valuable, is really unnecessary since Glaucon has by hypothesis set the Shepherd outside the circumstances of justice (1990, p. 148).

challenges against justice has such great force and what resources one must marshal if one hopes to refute these challenges.

In §7.1 I discuss the general problem of reconciling just conduct with rational prudence, and Hobbes' special challenge for those who would try to solve this problem that he states through the words of the Foole. I claim that the direct rebuttal Hobbes mounts against the Foole and Hume's related *Treatise* argument against breaking promises are *social-sanctions* arguments, one of two general types of arguments philosophers present to defend the prudential rationality of justice. In §7.2 I discuss the specifics of the challenge Glaucon and Adeimantus raise against justice in *Republic* using the story of the Lydian Shepherd. Here I argue Glaucon and Adeimantus design their challenge to compel Socrates to defend the prudential rationality of justice solely in terms of goods that are inextricably tied to justice. I argue that such an *inseparable-goods* argument is the other general type of argument employed in defense of the prudential rationality of justice. In §7.3 I present and evaluate a *folk theorem interpretation* of Hobbes' response to the Foole. According to this interpretation, Hobbes refutes the Foole by arguing that the Foole interacts with partners who follow a convention of conditional cooperation such that they punish those known to follow the Foole's advice and offensively violate rules of justice. I consider a number of objections against this folk theorem argument and conclude this argument is compelling given the right background conditions but in the end is inconclusive. In §7.4 I consider what happens if the Foole obtains the concealment power of the Lydian Shepherd's invisibility ring. I present new folk theorem arguments to show that the now *Invisible Foole* can have good prudential reasons to avoid offensively violating rules of justice, despite his having acquired the ring's concealment power. I argue that, like Hobbes' folk theorem response to the ordinary Foole, these conventionalist responses to the Invisible Foole have some force but are not decisive. In §7.5 I examine how the social-sanctions and the inseparable-goods approaches to vindicating the prudential rationality of justice are related. I argue that one can develop more effective arguments for the prudential rationality of justice by integrating these two approaches.

§7.1. The Reconciliation Project and the Foole's Challenge

One of the oldest and most difficult problems of moral philosophy is what Gregory Kavka dubs the *Reconciliation Project*, the attempt to show that duty coincides with self-interest or, to be more precise, that moral conduct is required by or at least compatible with rational prudence.[11] Plato's arguments

11. Gregory Kavka, "The Reconciliation Project," in *Morality, Reason and Truth*, ed. David Copp and David Zimmerman (Totowa, NJ: Rowan and Allanheld, 1984), p. 297.

in *Gorgias* and *Republic* that justice is profitable and injustice unprofitable for the actor herself are early contributions to this project. Henry Sidgwick, who discusses the relationship between self-interest and duty extensively in *The Methods of Ethics*, gives near the end of his work a striking description of what he takes to be the consequences of failing to complete the project of reconciling the two:

> practical reason would still impel us decisively to the performance of duty in the more ordinary cases in which what is recognized as duty is in harmony with self-interest properly understood. But in the rarer cases of a recognized conflict between self-interest and duty, practical reason, being divided against itself, would cease to be a motive on either side; the conflict would have to be decided by the comparative preponderance of one or other of two groups on non-rational impulses.[12]

For moral theorists working in any nonegoistic tradition such as Thomism, Kantianism, or utilitarianism, reconciling the moral requirements of their systems with rational prudence is a real challenge. Once the various moral requirements within one of these systems are established according to the standards of its tradition, the relationship between compliance with these requirements and self-interest must be worked out "on the back end," so to speak. And cases where morality requires significant effort and perhaps significant self-sacrifice are "hard" cases precisely because in these cases one cannot easily demonstrate the compatibility of duty and self-interest using the same resources of the moral tradition that produced the moral requirements. Indeed, Kavka believes that most modern philosophers regard the Reconciliation Project as hopeless.[13] Kant himself might have regarded the project as hopeless and perhaps even pointless. Even Sidgwick, the greatest of the classical utilitarians, himself concluded in the end that the duties utilitarianism prescribes cannot be fully reconciled with self-interest without resorting to a belief in divine sanctions or some similar belief.[14]

But on a natural reading of Hobbes' account of the natural moral law, Hobbes has an elegant and perhaps startling proposal for completing the Reconciliation Project. In *Elements of Law* and *De Cive* Hobbes complains that prior to his own work no one had produced a universally accepted account of natural law.[15]

---

12. *Methods of Ethics*, p. 507.

13. Kavka (1984), p. 297.

14. *Methods of Ethics*, pp. 496–509.

15. *Elements of Law I* 15:1, *De Cive* 2:1.

In *De Cive* and *Leviathan*, Hobbes gives what he takes to be the right definition of natural law. Hobbes' *Leviathan* definition is particularly succinct:

> A LAW OF NATURE, (*Lex Naturalis*,) is a Precept, or generall Rule, found out by Reason, by which a man is forbidden to do, that, which is destructive of his life, or taketh away the means of preserving the same, and to omit, that, by which he thinketh it may be best preserved.[16]

Of course, earlier accounts of natural law such as Aquinas's account included precepts requiring one to preserve one's own life. Many of these older accounts have substantially richer foundations than the Hobbesian account, incorporating a variety of contentious theological and philosophical doctrines that Hobbes eschews. Moreover, in earlier systems of natural law the requirement to preserve one's *own* life is derived from fundamental premises, whereas Hobbes makes this requirement itself fundamental.[17] Taken at face value, this characterization of a natural law precept makes the requirements of Hobbes' moral theory compatible with rational prudence *by definition*.[18] This is a move analogous to Galileo's postulating that the natural state of matter is to be in motion and Cantor's defining an infinite set to be a set that can be mapped one-to-one with one of its proper subsets. That is, one takes the phenomenon that is hard to explain according to previous theories, in this case the compatibility of moral requirements with self-interest, as fundamental and then proceeds to build a new theory that aspires to

16. *Leviathan* 14:3. See also *De Cive* 2:1.

17. For example, Aquinas takes as one of his fundamental natural law precepts a requirement to preserve human life without specifying that this requirement refers to any particular humans (*Summa Theologiæ* I.II Q. 94 A.2), and then later derives a prohibition against suicide as a theorem of his system (*Summa Theologiæ* II.II Q.64 A.5).

18. This way of reading Hobbes' natural law project is consistent with several fine twentieth-century works on Hobbes, including John W. N. Watkins, *Hobbes's System of Ideas: A Study in the Political Significance of Philosophical Theories* (London: Hutchinson, 1965); Gauthier (1969), (1986), (1990); Hampton (1986); and Kavka (1986).

To be sure, there are other ways to interpret Hobbes' project. For example, in her fine recent book *Morality in the Philosophy of Thomas Hobbes* (Cambridge: Cambridge University Press, 2009), Sharon Lloyd argues that the real basis of Hobbes' natural law is a reciprocity principle characterized by a negative version of the Golden Rule. Howard Warrender presented an earlier influential portrayal of Hobbes' natural law as a divine command theory in *The Political Philosophy of Hobbes: His Theory of Obligation* (Oxford: Oxford University Press, 1957). These two examples alone illustrate the range of interpretive possibilities.

This much said, I will continue as I have started, taking Hobbes' *De Cive* and *Leviathan* definitions of a natural law precept as his point of origin for building his moral theory. For the project I attribute to Hobbes is of great intrinsic philosophical interest whether or not one agrees with my interpretation of Hobbes.

be more satisfactory overall. Hobbes certainly thought he was presenting the first moral and political philosophy worthy of the name.[19] I suspect he would have viewed himself as having established a modern moral philosophy to complement the modern physics and contemporary set theory initiated respectively by Galileo and Cantor.

Can Hobbes develop requirements from his definition of natural law precepts that look anything like *moral* requirements? The Foole in effect challenges Hobbes to give a good answer to this question. One specific law of nature Hobbes presents in each of his systematic presentations of natural moral law is a law requiring one to honor the promises one makes in covenants.[20] A requirement to keep one's promises is certainly a standard moral requirement. Hobbes regards this particular law of nature as so important that in *Leviathan* 15 he actually states that failure to perform one's end of a covenant is the definition of injustice.[21] But in *Leviathan* 15 Hobbes also recognizes that one might doubt that this requirement really should be part of the natural law given the way Hobbes has defined natural law precepts. Hobbes gives grounds for this doubt with the Foole's challenge. The Foole claims that in certain circumstances, he acts against rational prudence if he honors his promise:

> the question is not of promises mutuall, where there is no security of performance on either side; as when there is no Civill Power erected over the parties promising; for such parties are no Covenants: But either where one of the parties has performed already, or where there is a Power to make him performe; there is the question whether it be against reason, that is, against the benefit of the other to performe, or not.[22]

As stated in Chapter 1, one violates a requirement of justice offensively if one disobeys this requirement with respect to certain others when these others do

---

19. Hobbes gives a famous self-assessment of his political philosophy in the Epistle Dedicatory of *Elements of Philosophy*, in *The English Works of Thomas Hobbes of Malmesbury*, ed. Sir William Molesworth (1839; London: John Bohn, 1962), vol. I, p. ix: "Natural Philosophy is therefore but young; but Civil Philosophy yet much younger, as being no older . . . then my own book *De Cive*." Hobbes gives other choice expressions of his low opinion of moral and political philosophers before him in the Epistle Dedicatory to *De Cive, Leviathan* 31:41, and *Leviathan* 46.

20. *Elements of Law I* 16:1, *De Cive* 3:1, *Leviathan* 15:2.

21. *Leviathan* 15:2. See also *Leviathan* 15:7. In *Leviathan* 14:7, Hobbes gives a more general definition of justice as fulfilling all of one's obligations, a special case of which are the obligations created by covenants.

22. *Leviathan* 15:5.

obey with respect to oneself or one can count on these others to so obey. The conditions under which the Foole thinks he should break his promise look very much like the conditions that define offensive violation of a covenant. In particular, the Foole is aware that if he enters into a covenant with another who honors her promise and performs first, then he has already received whatever benefits were promised him by the terms of the covenant. In this instance, the Foole claims it would be irrational for him to honor his commitment, for if he did so he would incur a cost to himself with no expectation of any further benefit.

Of course, if the Foole is right, then why would anyone who enters into a covenant ever perform first? Hume raises this very point when he presents the Farmer's Dilemma. Figure 7.1 summarizes another Farmer's Dilemma game where each Agent i can either *perform* (P_i) or *defect* (D_i). In the Figure 7.1 game, for each Agent i, the payoff of mutual performance is 1, $g_i > 0$ is her extra gain if she defects and her counterpart performs, $-l_i$ where $l_i > c_i > 0$ is her loss if she performs and her counterpart defects, and $-c_i$ is her loss if both defect. The Figure 1.3 Farmer's Dilemma is equivalent to an instance of the Figure 7.1 game with $g_i = l_i = c_i = 1$ for each Agent i. Suppose the two agents exchange promises to perform, thereby forming a covenant. Then if Agent 1 performs, Agent 2 has an opportunity of the sort the Foole describes, and if Agent 2 follows the Foole's advice he will defect. From the node following P_1, D_2 constitutes an offensive violation. Following Hume's analysis of the Farmer's Dilemma discussed in Chapter 1, Agent 1 will defect at the outset to forestall arriving at her worst possible outcome. Agent 1 is trying to avoid exploitation, so her following D_1 is a defensive violation of the covenant. Of course Agent 2 will then respond by defecting, and in this case from the node following D_1, D_2 is a defensive violation of the covenant for Agent 2.

Both Hobbes and Hume maintain that self-interested agents can have good reason to perform in covenants. They think that agents like the Foole, and likewise the farmers, err by analyzing the benefits of a covenant and the costs of performing in this covenant as if this covenant were the only covenant relevant

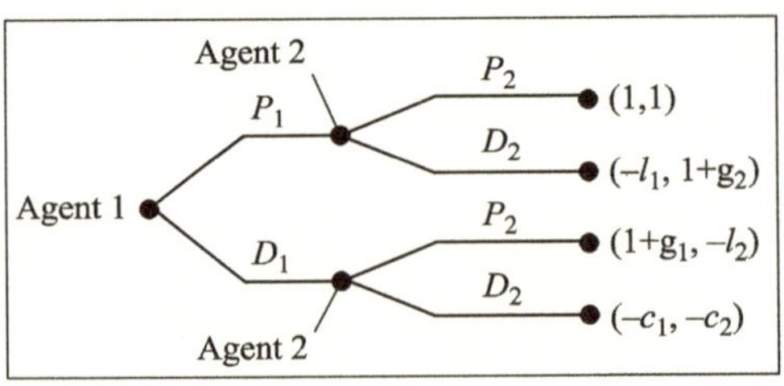

$g_i > 0, l_i > c_i > 0,\ g_i - l_i < 1,\ i \in \{1, 2\}$

FIGURE 7.1 Farmer's Dilemma

to their interests. Under ordinary circumstances, a single interaction like the commitment problem Hume's farmers face is embedded in a complex sequence of social interactions that occur over time. If one reasons that she can expect many opportunities for mutually beneficial cooperation with others in her community, then if one honors her promise made in a covenant and performs on a given occasion, she indicates to others that she will perform on other occasions, so they will be willing to make and perform in covenants with her in the future. As Hume puts it:

> I learn to do a service to another, without bearing him any real kindness; because I forsee, that he will return my service, in expectation of another of the same kind, and in order to maintain the same correspondence of good offices with me or with others. And accordingly, after I have serv'd him, and he is in possession of the advantage arising from my action, he is induc'd to perform his part, as foreseeing the consequences of his refusal.[23]

What about the Foole's claim that he should not reciprocate, but instead should fail to perform when the time comes? Such failure constitutes an offensive violation of a covenant. The Foole certainly could not claim that he does not expect the other agent not to perform when it is his time to perform. The other agent's performance is a fait accompli. Hobbes and Hume give similar warnings against offensive violation. Here is the key part of Hobbes' warning when he addresses the Foole:

> He therefore that breaketh his covenant, and consequently declareth that he thinks he may with reason do so, cannot be received into any society, that unite themselves for Peace and Defense, but by the errour of them that receive him; nor when he is received, be retayned in it, without seeing the danger of their errour; which errours a man cannot reasonably reckon upon as the means of his security: and therefore if he be left, or cast out of Society, he perisheth; and if he live in Society, it is by the errours of other men.[24]

According to Hobbes and Hume, one who follows the Foole's advice and offensively violates a covenant might enjoy an immediate gain by taking advantage of others' compliance. However, they also maintain that prudentially rational and

---

23. *Treatise* 3.2.5:9.

24. *Leviathan* 15:5. A corresponding part of Hume's warning in *Treatise* 3.2.5:10 is quoted in §2.4.

well-informed agents will refuse to enter into covenants with one who has offensively violated a covenant in the past. To lose all such opportunities for future benefits of cooperation far outweighs any immediate gain from a single offensive violation, think Hobbes and Hume.

This kind of rebuttal to the Foole is a social-sanctions rebuttal. One time-honored approach toward defending the prudential rationality of keeping promises, and more generally acting morally, is to argue that one is liable on the one hand to enjoy positive social sanctions as a reward for being just and on the other hand to suffer undesirable social sanctions as punishment for being unjust. Such positive social sanctions will typically include others' reciprocal good conduct toward oneself, while negative social sanctions might range from mild but perceptible disapproval from others to severe punishments, including capital punishment. According to Hobbes, the Foole is liable to suffer the punishment of being ostracized by those who know of his injustice. The social-sanctions tradition, which I will also call the *justice-reciprocalist* tradition, is the tradition of Hugo Grotius, David Hume, and Thomas Hobbes. Philosophers in this tradition argue further that one must be just in order to help generate and maintain a system of reciprocal expectations that the members of society will follow mutually beneficial practices such as respecting property rights. Indeed, some of the philosophers in this tradition might also be called *justice-conventionalists* since they argue that the particular norms of justice in a society are precisely those rules its members follow because they expect to enjoy reciprocal benefits by following them.[25] For these philosophers a conventional structure becomes part of their analysis of norms of justice.

§7.2. Glaucon and Adeimantus' Challenge

In *Republic*, Plato considers several alternative accounts of justice, including a proto-contractarian account Glaucon proposes early in Book II.

> People say, you see, that to do justice is naturally good and to suffer injustice bad. But the badness of suffering it far exceeds the goodness of doing it. Hence, those who have done and suffered injustice and who have tasted both—the ones who lack the power to do it and avoid suffering it—decide that it is profitable to come to an agreement with each other

25. In earlier essays I used "justice-conventionalism" to refer to what I here call "justice-reciprocalism." See "Justice-Conventionalism, Justice-Platonism and the Social Contract," in *The Social Institutions of Capitalism: Evolution and Design of Social Contracts*, ed. Pursey Heugens, Hans van Oosterhout, and Jack Vromen (Cheltenham, UK: Elgar, 2003), pp. 141–163, and "The Invisible Foole," *Philosophical Studies* 147 (2010), pp. 37–57.

		Others: V	Others: J	Others: U
Agent i	V	–	–	4th
	J	–	2nd	–
	U	1st	–	3rd

V = victim, J = just, U = unjust

FIGURE 7.2 Justice as a Mean Between Extremes

> neither to do injustice nor to suffer it. As a result, they begin to make laws and covenants; and what the law commands, they call lawful and just. That, they say, is the origin and very being of justice. It is in between the best and the worst. The best is to do injustice without paying the penalty; the worst is to suffer it without being able to take revenge. Justice is in the middle between these two extremes.[26]

According to Glaucon's discussion, any individual evidently achieves her best outcome in encounters when she commits injustices against others who cannot punish her injustices, her worst outcome when she is herself the helpless victim of injustices, and an intermediate outcome when all act justly. Suppose that one can adopt one of three strategies in a given encounter: Be *unjust* (U) and try to exploit others, be *just* (J) and act cooperatively with others who are not unjust and retaliate against those who are unjust, and be a *victim* (V) and render oneself helpless, say by disarming completely. Then Glaucon would say an individual agent arrives at her best outcome when she follows U and the others follow V, at her worst outcome when she follows V and the others follow U, and at an intermediate outcome when all follow J. Glaucon states that people generally find it profitable to follow the state where all abstain from injustice, so I will assume that all strictly prefer the all-J outcome over the all-U outcome. The Figure 7.2 matrix summarizes the preference structure Glaucon attributes to typical people over the possible outcomes he discusses explicitly.

To summarize the essentials of Glaucon's proposal, it is only necessary to suppose that (i) as already indicated, J-followers matched against each other fare better than U-followers matched against each other, (ii) J-followers matched against V-followers fare at least as well as J-followers matched against each

26. *Republic* 358e–359b.

		Agent 2		
		V	J	U
	V	(4, 4)	(4, 4)	(−3, 9)
Agent 1	J	(4, 4)	(5, 5)	(−1, 3)
	U	(9, −3)	(3, −1)	(0, 0)

V = victim, J = just, U = unjust

FIGURE 7.3 2-Agent Proto-Contractarian Game

other, and (iii) U-followers matched against J-followers also fare less well than J-followers matched against each other. The additional assumptions (ii) and (iii) are plausible since J-followers presumably never exploit V-followers, of course are never exploited by V-followers, and retaliate against U-followers. The stated assumptions together also render the all-J outcome, which Glaucon regards as the intermediate outcome, an equilibrium of the underlying game. According to this game-theoretic translation of Glaucon's argument, Glaucon is giving an informal argument that justice emerges and remains stable because the all-J outcome is the one equilibrium better for all than the all-U outcome, which resembles the Hobbesian war of all against all.

One plausible game-theoretic summary of Glaucon's proposal in the 2-agent case is the game summarized by the Figure 7.3 matrix. The payoffs of this game reflect the idea that a just person strictly prefers that others are just over others being victims, and both just and unjust persons prefer that others are victims over others being unjust. That is, I suppose a just person would rather enjoy the benefits of the active cooperation of other just persons over that of victims, who, being unable to defend themselves, might also be far less able to contribute effectively to joint tasks and projects than other just persons. And I suppose that both just and unjust persons rank the outcome of conflict with unjust persons lower than the outcomes of meeting victims. The Figure 7.2 game is a blend of Stag Hunt and Prisoner's Dilemma, which is easily seen if one examines the reduced 2×2 games that result when one removes the profiles where either agent follows V and when one removes the profiles where either agent follows J. Both (U,U) and (J,J) are strict Nash equilibria, but (J,J), where both are just, is better for both than (U,U).

Glaucon does not merely assume that people regard being unjust against helpless victims as the best outcome, being a helpless victim of injustice as the worst, and all being just as somewhere in between. He defends his claim using what has become one of philosophy's most celebrated thought experiments, asking Socrates to consider what would happen if an ordinarily just person and an ordinarily unjust person were both given the power of the ring of Gyges. Glaucon claims that the conduct of both would be the same, that is, both would commit injustices with impunity. Glaucon thinks the moral of the Lydian Shepherd fable is clear: Anyone who possesses the power to act as if he were a god among humans has no reason to be just. By acting as a god among humans, Glaucon evidently means that one can commit any injustices against others with impunity, for they will be powerless to resist. For example, if anyone in the role of Agent 1 in the Figure 7.3 game were to come into possession of the invisibility ring, then this would be tantamount to eliminating the strategy profiles in this game where Agent 2 follows J or U, since Agent 2 now is apparently completely helpless with respect to Agent 1.

Socrates does not challenge the conclusion Glaucon initially draws from his thought experiment, though he might have done so. For the power of the invisibility ring did not make the Lydian Shepherd like a god among humans in all respects. The ring may have given the Shepherd the power of invisibility, but not the power of invulnerability. Indeed, a blind assassin with exceptional senses of hearing and smell might have been able to dispatch the Shepherd even while the Shepherd was using the ring. In any event, Glaucon proceeds to argue that the real good of justice is the good reputation one typically gains from being just. Glaucon suggests that the outcome best for oneself is to do the greatest injustice while maintaining the greatest reputation for justice.[27] Glaucon's discussion of the importance of reputation suggests an alternative moral of the fable of the Lydian Shepherd: One has no reason to be just if one has the power to perfectly conceal one's identity when committing injustices. For then one cannot damage one's reputation when one commits injustices. Presumably the Shepherd had a reputation for being just before he found the ring. The Shepherd might have used his ring differently. Rather than setting himself up as the tyrant over all the other Lydians, he might have committed injustices against various Lydian people, exploiting them with impunity while invisible, but never revealing that it was he who possessed the ring. Then the other Lydians apparently would have been helpless victims, but not because the Shepherd was acting like a god among humans. The Lydians would simply not have known whom to punish when the Shepherd exploited some of them while invisible.

Glaucon, and later Adeimantus, challenges Socrates to show that someone who is bound to have a perfect reputation for injustice still has a good reason to

27. *Republic* 362a–362b.

be just and that someone who is bound to have a perfect reputation for justice still should refrain from being unjust. And Adeimantus anticipates the sort of argument he thinks Socrates will have to give:

> "Socrates, you amazing man," we said, "of all of you who claim to praise justice, beginning from the earliest heroes of old whose accounts survive up to the men of the present day, not one has ever blamed injustice or praised justice except by mentioning the reputations, honors and rewards that are their consequences. No one has ever adequately described what each does itself, through its own power, by its presence in the soul of the person who possesses it, even if it remains hidden from gods and humans. No one, whether in poetry or in private conversations, has adequately argued that injustice is the greatest evil a soul can have in it, and justice the greatest good. If all of you had spoken in this way and had tried to persuade us from our earliest youth, we would not now be guarding against one another's injustices, but each would be his own best guardian, afraid that by doing injustice he would be living on intimate terms with the worst thing possible."[28]

Adeimantus maintains that in order to meet the challenge he and Glaucon have laid out, Socrates must show what Adeimantus thinks no one has ever shown. Socrates presumably must show that there is some good intrinsic to justice that is so valuable that one is better off being just even if one has a perfect reputation for injustice and suffers the consequences of having such a reputation. Such an inseparable-goods defense of the prudential rationality of justice is based upon the following premise: Justice provides or preserves for its practitioner a good or goods she can obtain through no other means. This good or goods are unlike goods such as money, material goods, or labor, which one might be able to obtain by means other than being just. The inseparable-goods tradition is the tradition of Aristotle, Aquinas, and of course Plato. Since Plato gives some of the earliest inseparable-goods arguments in favor of the prudential rationality of justice, I will also call this tradition the *justice-Platonist* tradition.[29] However, as will become evident immediately below, a justice-Platonist need not adopt Plato's own account of the goods that are inseparable from justice.

---

28. *Republic* 366d–367a.

29. In Vanderschraaf (2003) and Vanderschraaf (2010), I used only the terms "justice-Platonist" and "justice-Platonism" to refer to the tradition that uses what I call here inseparable-goods arguments.

Socrates' key problem, thinks Adeimantus, is that if he accepts the challenge, then he must give some sort of inseparable-goods argument in favor of justice, since he may not appeal to any of the goods that come with others' good offices, as do Hobbes and Hume. Adeimantus even foresees which particular good Socrates will argue is both the greatest human good and the good intrinsic to justice, namely, a soul free from the corruption that injustice causes. To be sure, this is not the only good one might claim one can obtain or preserve only by being just. For example, Aquinas gives a quite different sort of inseparable-goods argument for the prudential rationality of respecting property rights when he argues that theft is a mortal sin.[30] For Aquinas, this kind of injustice brings with it the possibility that one will be excluded from enjoying heaven in the next life. Needless to say, this argument is predicated upon God's knowing the details of one's conduct history and rewarding justice or punishing injustice in certain ways. In the concluding chapter of *The Methods of Ethics*, Sidgwick observes that if one can assume the existence of a divine being who will certainly reward those who perform their duties and punish those who violate their duties, in a next life if not in this life, then duty and self-interest are reconciled immediately.[31] Sidgwick does not help himself to this assumption, and in the end finds himself unable to complete the Reconciliation Project fully. Adeimantus will not allow Socrates such a quick out, since Adeimantus assumes that the perfectly unjust person he describes can conceal his injustices even from the gods. But divine-sanctions arguments are certainly a common form of the inseparable-goods argument, and of course they illustrate how a good that allegedly one can obtain or keep only by being just can be defined in terms of certain special sorts of sanctions.

Adeimantus seems to think that Socrates has little prospect of mounting a successful inseparable-goods argument. Of course, Socrates does accept the challenge and gives exactly the sort of inseparable-goods argument Adeimantus expects. One of the core positions Plato defends in *Gorgias* and *Republic* is the following: If one commits an injustice and thus becomes unjust, this causes one's soul to become corrupt, and to have such a corrupt soul is the worst misfortune one could suffer. Socrates insists that rational prudence requires one to be just in order to maintain one's greatest good, namely, a healthy soul. I will not consider the merits of Socrates' arguments here. Instead, I will consider what, if any, moral Hobbes and like-minded philosophers in the social-sanctions tradition should draw from the fable of the Lydian Shepherd.

30. *Summa Theologiæ* II.II Q. 66 A. 6.

31. *Methods of Ethics* Book IV, Concluding Chapter.

§7.3. Hobbes' Response to the Foole Interpreted as a Folk Theorem Response

Hobbes maintains that the Foole's reasoning is flawed, and that the Foole should not offensively violate covenants even when he thinks offensive violation will be profitable. One quite natural interpretation of Hobbes' response is also quite easy to state and to analyze using the account of convention proposed in Chapter 2. According to this *folk theorem interpretation*, a requirement to abstain from offensively violating covenants can be part of an incumbent convention for a community. In game theory, the folk theorems are a body of results that establish existence conditions for sets of equilibria of indefinitely repeated games.[32] One example of a folk theorem is the argument given in §2.4 that (Tr,Tr), where Tr is the history-dependent strategy of performing exactly when one's partner has never defected, is for sufficiently high discount factors an equilibrium of indefinitely repeated Prisoner's Dilemma with a fixed pair of agents.[33] The rough underlying idea of the folk theorem interpretation can be expressed as a playground saying: "No one wants to play with a cheater." I believe Hobbes' response to the Foole builds upon this idea using informal proto-game-theoretic arguments.[34] Both his response and its effectiveness can be analyzed more clearly using the game theory developed in our own time.

In his warning to the Foole against offensively violating a covenant, Hobbes attributes to the individuals the Foole can expect to encounter the following policy: Perform in covenants with partners who have never offensively violated any of their past covenants, and shun those who *have* offensively violated any of their past covenants. Hume in his discussion of promises assumes that people typically follow just this policy. Suppose a pair of individuals meet, where each must decide whether or not to enter into a covenant and then, if they have formed a covenant, whether or not to honor her part without knowing in advance what

32. Folk theorems get their name because early game theorists knew of and discussed some of these results informally for years before the proofs of any of these results were first published.

33. John Nash discovered the first folk theorem in the 1950s when he proved this result. Nash never published his folk theorem. In an early experimental game theory study, Merrill Flood quotes from a private communication he received from Nash where Nash shared his discovery of this result. See note 11 in Merrill M. Flood, "Some Experimental Games," *Management Science* 5 (1958), pp. 5–26.

34. Robert Sudgen and Brian Skyrms were perhaps the first to draw an explicit connection between folk theorems in game theory and Hobbes' response to the Foole, but neither proposed an explicit community enforcement model as I do here. See Sugden (2004) and Brian Skyrms, "The Shadow of the Future," in *Rational Commitment and Social Justice: Essays for Gregory Kavka*, ed. Jules L. Coleman and Christopher W. Morris (Cambridge: Cambridge University Press, 1998), pp. 12–21.

		Agent 2		
		P_2	D_2	S_2
	P_1	$(1,1)$	$(-l_1, 1+g_2)$	$(0,0)$
Agent 1	D_1	$(1+g_1, -l_2)$	$(-c_1, -c_2)$	$(0,0)$
	S_1	$(0,0)$	$(0,0)$	$(0,0)$

P_i = perform, D_i = defect, S_i = shun, $i \in \{1,2\}$

$g_i > 0,\ l_i > c_i > 0,\ g_i - l_i < 1,\ i \in \{1,2\}$

FIGURE 7.4 Covenant Game

the other does. The Figure 7.4 Covenant game summarizes the structure of such interactions. As with the Covenant game discussed in §2.4, in this Covenant game each Agent i has three pure strategies: *shun* (S_i), which is to decline to enter into a covenant, *perform* (P_i), which is to keep the promise that is her part of the covenant they have entered into, and *defect* (D_i), which is to break this promise. They enter into a covenant exactly when neither shuns. The Figure 2.8 Covenant game is a special case of the Figure 7.4 game with $g_i = c_i = 1$ and $l_i = 2$ for each Agent i. For the Covenant game, the general policy Hobbes and Hume discuss in their warnings against offensive violation is characterized by the contingency strategy

h^*: P_i if partner Agent j is *innocent*, S_i if Agent j is *guilty*,

where one's partner is either innocent or guilty and becomes and remains guilty if she offensively violates a covenant.[35] I will call any strategy of the form h^* together with specified conditions for innocence and guilt that render an offensive violator guilty a *Hobbesian-Humean strategy*.[36]

35. This is a sufficient, but possibly not necessary, condition for guilt. A Hobbesian-Humean strategy as just summarized is unambiguous if one assumes that any h^*-follower executes this strategy perfectly and in particular always shuns guilty counterparts. If one allows that h^*-followers can make mistakes, including failing to shun correctly, then one needs to clarify the conditions for innocence and guilt in case one deviates from h^* by failing to shun a guilty agent. For example, one can define an agent as guilty in case she has offensively violated *or* has failed to shun a guilty counterpart within the specified past. Hobbes and Hume do not consider such possibilities. However, the discussion in this section does not depend upon the specific innocence-guilt conditions involving such mistakes in shunning.

36. In the game theory literature, such strategies are also known as *standing strategies*. Robert Sugden and Robert Boyd launched a literature on standing strategies with various innocence

If two parties are to engage in a single Covenant game only once and they have common knowledge that they are Bayesian rational and know the payoff structure of this game, then mutual shunning would seem to be the predictable result.[37] For each Agent i, D_i weakly dominates P_i, so each apparently should disregard the strategy profiles where either performs. And in the profiles that remain, each simultaneously maximizes expected payoff and avoids her worst possible outcome (D_1, D_2) by following S_i.[38] Another way to reach this conclusion is to note that both can infer that were they to form a covenant, they would then have placed themselves in a Prisoner's Dilemma where each would surely defect, so each is better off avoiding the covenant at the outset.[39] But as discussed in §2.4, if parties are to engage in a sequence of Covenant games of indefinite length, then they have available to them a great many new history-dependent strategies, and many of these strategies can characterize equilibria where the parties fare better than they fare at the equilibrium of mutual shunning. One such example of such an equilibrium is based upon the strategy profile where each agent in a community follows h^*, in which any Agent i is guilty exactly in case she has followed D_i at any time period in the past. To defect is now always an offensive violation. This Hobbesian-Humean strategy h^* is of course quite similar to the grim strategy Tr, discussed in §2.4 and above, for engaging in an indefinitely repeated Prisoner's Dilemma with a fixed partner. If the parties are all sufficiently patient, that is, their discount factors are sufficiently high, then the profile where all follow h^* is an equilibrium of their indefinitely repeated Covenant game. This follows from a derivation similar to that given in §2.4 for (Tr, Tr) applied to indefinitely repeated Prisoner's Dilemma. The all-h^* profile is an equilibrium of this indefinitely repeated Covenant game when the discount factors satisfy $\delta_i \geq \frac{g_i}{1+g_i}$ for each Agent i. And if this inequality is strict, then offensively violating a

---

and guilt conditions that can support patterns of cooperation in communities. See Sugden (2004), §6.3–4, and Robert Boyd, "Mistakes Allow Evolutionary Stability in the Repeated Prisoner's Dilemma," *Journal of Theoretical Biology* 136 (1989), pp. 47–56.

37. The two brief arguments that follow in fact incorporate only some lower-order mutual knowledge of Bayesian rationality and payoff structure. So the common-knowledge assumptions stated here are sufficient but not necessary.

38. In the Covenant game, there are other Nash equilibria, including (D_1, S_2), (S_1, D_2), and two other equilibria where one agent follows S_i and the other follows a partially mixed strategy. At (S_1, S_2) and at all of these other Nash equilibria, no covenant is formed because at least one agent shuns. But unlike (S_1, S_2), at these other equilibria S_i can cease to be Agent i's best response in case the other deviates unilaterally by mistake.

39. In extensive form representations of the Figure 7.4 Covenant game, in the subgame perfect equilibria each Agent i follows S_i at her first move in the game.

covenant strictly lowers Agent i's overall payoff, so the all-h^* equilibrium is path-observance strict.[40]

In the indefinitely repeated Covenant game, if the parties choose between following the Hobbesian-Humean strategy just described and following the Foole's recommendation to defect offensively when one expects thereby to achieve the gain of exploiting one's partner, then their possible interactions are summarized by the Figure 7.5 matrix. In the Figure 7.5 game, each community member follows either the pure strategy F^*, the Foole's strategy, or h^*, where any Agent i in the community is guilty exactly when she has offensively violated a covenant in a past period t with her partner Agent $i(t)$. When the parties choose between F^* and h^* and are all sufficiently patient, their indefinitely repeated Covenant game is transformed into a Stag Hunt. The Stag Hunt structure of the Figure 7.5 game is more obvious for specific numerical values of the free parameters. The Figure 7.6 game is a special case of the Figure 7.5 game where $g_i = c_i = 1$, $l_i = 2$, and $\delta_i = \frac{3}{4}$ for $i \in \{1,2\}$.

Using the Figure 7.5 matrix, one can summarize the folk theorem interpretation of Hobbes' response to the Foole this way: At the initial interaction, if the

		Agent $i(t)$: h^*	Agent $i(t)$: F^*
Agent i	h^*	$\left(\frac{1}{1-\delta_i}, \frac{1}{1-\delta_{i(t)}}\right)$	$\left(-l_i, 1+g_{i(t)}\right)$
	F^*	$\left(1+g_i, -l_{i(t)}\right)$	$\left(-c_i, -c_{i(t)}\right)$

h^* = Hobbesian-Humean strategy, F^* = Foole's strategy

FIGURE 7.5 Repeated Covenant Game Turned into Stag Hunt

		Agent $i(t)$: h^*	Agent $i(t)$: F^*
Agent i	h^*	$(4, 4)$	$(-2, 2)$
	F^*	$(2, -2)$	$(-1, -1)$

$g_i = c_i = 1,\ l_i = 2,\ \delta_i = \frac{3}{4},\ i \in \{1,2\}$

FIGURE 7.6 Numerical Example of Repeated Covenant Game Turned into Stag Hunt

40. I gave the definition of a path-observance strict equilibrium in §2.4.

Foole follows F^* and the counterpart Agent $i(1)$ follows h^*, then at the initial interaction the Foole defects while his partner Agent $i(1)$ performs, so the Foole violates offensively and gains the exploitation payoff $1+g_i$, which includes the extra gain g_i of exploiting Agent $i(1)$, who follows P. But afterward the Foole receives no positive payoff because the other partners he meets shun him, given that they also follow h^*. Since all in the community expect that $\delta_j > \frac{g_j}{1-g_j}$ or $\frac{1}{1-\delta_j} > 1+g_j$ for each Agent j in the community, the Foole should expect to do worse if he offensively violates in the beginning than he would if he follows P_i, which he would follow if he were to adopt h^* like his fellow community members. So the Foole should not offensively violate at the initial round of play. And if the state where everyone in the community follows h^* is an equilibrium of the indefinitely repeated game, then by an exactly similar argument one can show the Foole that he should expect to fare strictly worse if he offensively violates at any round of play than if he obeys Hobbes' natural law and consistently performs with his Humean counterparts. This is a folk theorem argument where compliance with a norm requiring one to perform with innocent partners is maintained via *community enforcement*.[41]

Did Hobbes refute the Foole, as Hobbes seems to have thought? Given the folk theorem interpretation, the answer to this question is plainly: "It depends." The discussion in the preceding paragraph shows by example that if a Hobbesian-Humean strategy for appropriate innocence and guilt conditions characterizes an equilibrium for a community whose members regularly must choose whether or not to perform their respective ends of covenants, and if the Foole expects his fellow community members to all follow this Hobbesian-Humean strategy, then the Foole's best response is to consistently perform.[42] But these are big ifs.

---

41. Community enforcement of social norms has become an important area of analytical and empirical research. In game theory the community enforcement literature was launched in large part by two seminal essays by Michihiro Kandori and Glenn Ellison. See Michihiro Kandori, "Social Norms and Community Enforcement," *Review of Economic Studies* 59 (1992), pp. 63–80, and Glenn Ellison, "Learning, Local Interaction and Cooperation," *Econometrica* 61 (1993), pp. 1047–1071. One of the finest empirical studies on community enforcement published so far is Natalie Henrich and Joseph Henrich's *Why Humans Cooperate* (Oxford: Oxford University Press, 2007), where they analyze the community enforcement of social norms in the Chaldean community of metropolitan Detroit.

42. The Covenant game is one of the simplest nontrivial games that summarizes the actions associated with a covenant. But one can prove the relevant folk theorems for more complex games involving covenants, such as a larger extensive form game where if parties exchange promises, they might then enter into either a Prisoner's Dilemma or a Farmer's Dilemma as one of the proper subgames.

The Foole can raise a number of serious objections to the claim that following a Hobbesian-Humean strategy really is his own best course of action. For one thing, the Foole might challenge the claim that h^* really does characterize an equilibrium of the repeated game. What if some of the members' discount factors are not sufficiently high, as might be the case if they expect their community to break up in the near future? Hobbes will have to hedge his reply and assert that the Foole should expect to live in a stable community whose members expect to interact with each other for some time, so their discount factors should be sufficiently high to make the all-h^* profile an equilibrium. Perhaps this is a plausible assumption under ordinary circumstances, but already one can see that the persuasive force of Hobbes' response to the Foole depends upon context. If the Foole interacts with others in a sufficiently unstable community, then offensive violation might be the Foole's best response to others' performance after all, given that the Foole thinks it sufficiently unlikely that the sequence of covenants in this community will continue much longer.

The Foole can raise other serious objections against Hobbes' response to his challenge. Gregory Kavka supplied the Foole with one such objection, an objection Brian Skyrms subsequently refined.[43] Here is a paraphrase of Kavka's argument:[44] Suppose it is common knowledge in the community that for some value u, say $u = 1{,}000{,}000$, no one lives to see her uth opportunity to enjoy the benefits of others' reciprocal cooperation in covenants. If any agents in the community were somehow to reach the $u-1$st round of interactions involving covenants, they should analyze this interaction as a single game in isolation, there being no later such interaction. Thus parties familiar with the reasoning of Hobbes' Foole and Hume's farmers would not perform at the $u-1$st interaction. But if this is the case, then should any reach the $u-2$nd round, they can disregard the future and treat the interaction of the $u-2$nd round as a single game in isolation, and so they would not perform at the $u-2$nd interaction. And the same reasoning applies to the $u-k$th potential round for each $k > 2$. By this backward induction argument, or an appropriately strengthened version of it, the Foole can conclude that rational agents never perform, in which case the Foole would act against reason were he to obey Hobbes' law of nature requiring promise keeping after all. Skyrms

43. Kavka (1983), Kavka (1986), pp. 130–133, Skyrms (1998). John Nash, and later R. Duncan Luce and Howard Raiffa, pointed out that if a fixed pair of agents are to play a Prisoner's Dilemma only finitely many times, then by applying backward induction reasoning these agents can conclude that each should defect at each round of play. See Flood (1958), note 11, and Luce and Raiffa (1957), pp. 98–99. Kavka's argument and Skyrms' refinements are inspired by Luce and Raiffa's analysis.

44. My paraphrase generalizes Kavka's original argument slightly, since Kavka speaks specifically of an iterated Prisoner's Dilemma while I allow a more general class of games to form the interaction sequence. See note 42.

observes that the force of Hobbes' response to the Foole depends crucially upon common knowledge conditions that Hobbes does not consider. If the community members are rational and know the structure of the indefinitely repeated game but lack common knowledge of a specific upper bound to the number of possible interaction periods, then they will be unable to anchor Kavka's backward induction argument. Consequently, they might then be able to follow an equilibrium characterized by some Hobbesian-Humean strategy. But, perhaps paradoxically, if the community members have common knowledge of the game, their rationality, and a specific upper bound to the number of possible interactions, then the Foole can conclude that it is *never* rational to perform.[45]

Kavka's argument shows that the members of a community of rational agents are liable never to perform in covenants if they have too much common knowledge. The Foole can also argue that the same result is likely if the members of such a community have too little common knowledge. If community members cannot reliably distinguish innocent from guilty partners, then they simply cannot follow a Hobbesian-Humean strategy correctly. Whether or not the members of a community can successfully employ a Hobbesian-Humean strategy will depend upon how information is transmitted among its members. And some centralization of this information transmission may be needed. If the Foole's community transmits information regarding who is guilty and who is innocent solely via decentralized and private communication, then this community may be unable to sustain an equilibrium of a Hobbesian-Humean strategy for the simple reason that the very same members who are prone to follow the Foole's advice, for personal gain, are also prone to spread false reports, for personal gain, about who is innocent and who is guilty. Then if the Foole not only offensively violates at least some of his covenants but also lies and spreads reports that his victims offensively violated against *him*, he may well be able to successfully exploit fellow community members on a continuing basis.[46]

---

45. Skyrms (1998), pp. 16–19.

46. I defend this conclusion in Peter Vanderschraaf, "Covenants and Reputations," *Synthese* 157 (2007), pp. 167–195. In the 1990s, Richard Gaylord and Louis D'Andria presented a computer model of agents who meet in a Covenant game in *Simulating Society: A* Mathematica *Toolkit for Modeling Socioeconomic Behavior* (New York: Springer, 1998), ch. 3. In the Gaylord-D'Andria model all information is transmitted via exchanges of private "blacklists" of offensive violators. In their system, agents who follow the h^* strategy I attribute to Hobbes and Hume, where blacklisted agents are shunned, fare better over time than agents who offensively violate. But in the Gaylord-D'Andria model each blacklist includes only the identities of agents who actually are offensive violators. In Vanderschraaf (1997) I use computer simulations to show that if agents can effectively lie, with the result that the identities of innocent agents appear on these blacklists, then offensive violators who add the identities of their innocent victims to blacklists fare better than h^* followers. For once h^*-followers meet these lying offensive violators, they start applying h^* incorrectly, shunning innocent victims and failing to shun offensive violators.

Finally, suppose conditions are such that the members of the Foole's community are able to follow the equilibrium of a Hobbesian-Humean strategy, so the Foole should set aside the above objections to Hobbes' response. Even then, the Foole can argue that Hobbes' response to his challenge is not decisive.[47] For the Foole can observe that he can adapt the same folk theorem argument that shows that a Hobbesian-Humean strategy is a path-observance strict equilibrium of the relevant supergame of interactions involving covenants to show that this is only one of many convention equilibria of this supergame. In his reply to the Foole, Hobbes assumes that the Foole interacts with the members of a community who all follow h^* with his stated guilt and innocence conditions. Hume assumes much the same in his *Treatise* discussion of promises. In fact, if one sets no arbitrary limits on the strategies they consider, in the relevant system of indefinitely repeated games each community member has uncountably many different history-dependent strategies to choose from, so the real supergame is a great deal more complex than a Stag Hunt. Indeed, if the parties can choose from a sufficiently rich set of history-dependent strategies, then a whole continuum of different path-observance strict equilibria of the relevant supergame becomes possible. To illustrate, Figure 7.7 depicts the set of payoff vectors corresponding to path-observance strict equilibria of the indefinitely repeated Figure 2.8 Covenant game.

Equilibrium payoff vectors lie in the dark shaded region of the convex set of payoff vectors bounder by the larger parallelogram.

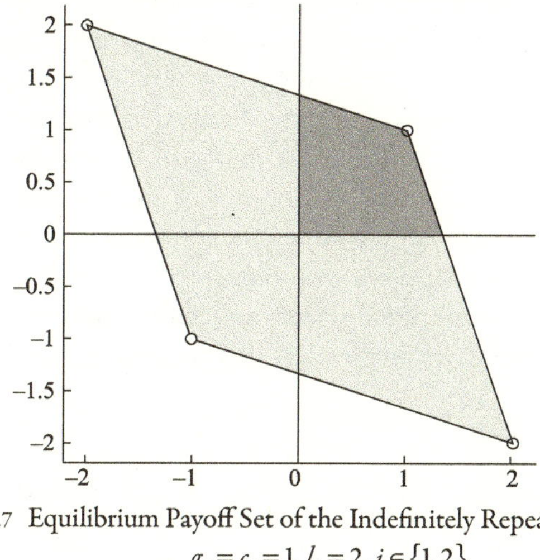

FIGURE 7.7 Equilibrium Payoff Set of the Indefinitely Repeated Covenant Game, $g_i = c_i = 1, l_i = 2, i \in \{1,2\}$

47. Skyrms (1998), p. 16, recognizes the gist of the objection given here.

As Figure 7.7 shows graphically, a supergame of covenant interactions can indeed have infinitely many distinct convention equilibria. The Foole can ask Hobbes, "If my partners are able to follow an equilibrium of your h^* strategy, then why should they not be able to follow different equilibria of other history-dependent strategies that you never consider? Which, if any, of all these convention equilibria should I expect my partners to follow?"

Hobbes can admit that the objections available to the Foole are serious, but he can also counter that in most ordinary circumstances the Foole will find that he is in a community following a convention characterized by a Hobbesian-Humean strategy and should therefore follow the Hobbesian law of nature requiring promise keeping. As noted already, Hobbes can argue that ordinarily the Foole should expect to interact within a relatively stable community, so its members should have discount factors that can render an all-h^* profile, where h^* is a Hobbesian-Humean strategy, an equilibrium. Hobbes can rightly claim that Kavka's backward induction argument against the rationality of performing in covenants relies upon certain common knowledge unlikely to obtain in actual communities. In particular, one might doubt that the members of any actual community have the common knowledge of a least upper bound on the number of possible relevant interactions that would allow them to anchor Kavka's induction argument.[48]

Hobbes can also acknowledge that community members may be unable to follow a Hobbesian-Humean strategy correctly if they must rely upon privately transmitted information, but he can point out that this is one of the primary reasons communities create and maintain certain institutions that facilitate the common knowledge that can underwrite Hobbesian-Humean strategies. Indeed, Hobbes would argue that one of the most important benefits of life in civil society is the security the sovereign provides, which facilitates the generation of common knowledge. The sovereign itself might be a source of common knowledge of who in civil society are to be regarded as innocent or guilty. Private institutions can and frequently do serve much the same function for the communities they serve. To give only one example, in our own time merchants and consumers successfully exchange services and goods involving credit because it is common knowledge in the community of credit users that possessing certain credentials

48. In private conversation, Kavka informed me that he thought his backward induction argument does not require common knowledge of a *least* upper bound. I disagreed with Kavka then and continue to do so now, because I believe a rational agent is committed to adopting particular strategies in a single base game only if she can expect to engage in this game with some probability, albeit possibly a very low probability. Consequently I believe that the parties at the $u-1$ st round of Kakva's argument paraphrased above conclude they will not perform at this round only if they know this round could possibly be reached.

such as an activated credit card indicates that the possessor is in good credit standing. Credit grantors and merchants follow a Hobbesian-Humean strategy of extending credit or accepting credit payments exactly with those they identify as being in good credit standing. The common knowledge that certain screening programs reliably indicate good credit standing is possible in part due to the existence of credit bureaus that record the reports of credit grantors regarding their customers.[49] Obviously, the effectiveness of any institutionalist argument Hobbes might present to the Foole to argue that communities can follow Hobbesian-Humean strategies correctly will depend upon how well the institutions serve the purpose of generating genuine common knowledge. A sovereign might become corrupt and disseminate false public reports of who is to be regarded as an enemy of the public. A system of credit exchange could break down if too many of the reports submitted by credit grantors are inaccurate, or if the online credit reporting programs are compromised. But this only underscores the more general point that according to the folk theorem interpretation I attribute to Hobbes, the Foole has good reason to keep Hobbes' law of nature requiring promise keeping, given a proper context. Such a proper context includes common knowledge that allows individuals to reliably distinguish between the innocent and the guilty, and this common knowledge must typically be generated by reliable institutions.

Hobbes can also grant the Foole that in a community of agents capable of following a convention characterized by a Hobbesian-Humean strategy there are many equilibria available to them, but he might contend that the Hobbesian-Humean strategy he assumes in his argument against the Foole is the strategy that ideally rational agents adopt. As I have argued above, the Foole can counter that there is no uniquely "correct" strategy for an agent in a system of repeated Covenant games. True, if all in the community follow the h^* strategy with the unforgiving innocence and guilt conditions Hobbes assumes, they follow the profile of an optimal equilibrium of their supergame. But there are many other optimal equilibria, including equilibria where some of the parties exploit other parties some of the time and hence fare even better than they would fare at the all-h^*

49. Credit bureaus play a role analogous to the law merchants who would adjudicate disputes between traders at interregional trading fairs in twelfth- and thirteenth-century Europe. In a now classic essay, Paul Milgrom, Douglass North, and Barry Weingast argued that the law merchant institution sustained successful impersonal exchange at these fairs, and proved a folk theorem establishing the existence of an equilibrium of no cheating in trades where traders can lodge complaints with a law merchant. See Paul R. Milgrom, Douglass C. North, and Barry R. Weingast, "The Role of Institutions in the Revival of Trade: The Law Merchant, Private Judges and the Champagne Fairs," *Economics and Politics* 2 (1990), pp. 1–23. Avner Greif analyzes a variety of related past institutions in *Institutions and the Path to the Modern Economy: Lessons from Medieval Trade* (Cambridge: Cambridge University Press, 2006).

equilibrium.[50] So even if one assumes that ideally rational agents would follow the strategy of an optimal equilibrium, it does not follow that they would adopt Hobbes' assumed strategy.

Still, perhaps one can at least partially rescue Hobbes' response to the Foole if one allows for another possibility Hobbes does not consider, namely, that strategies like a Hobbesian-Humean strategy that require performance in covenants with innocent partners might evolve in societies. In 1984 Robert Axelrod published *The Evolution of Cooperation*, where he presented a variety of historical case studies, analytical results, and computer simulation findings to defend his claim that in many situations having a repeated Prisoner's Dilemma structure, the engaging agents will tend to settle into an optimal equilibrium characterized by a strategy that is initially cooperative but will punish uncooperative conduct.[51] Axelrod's work had great impact both in academia and far beyond, and it helped launch a research program on the evolution of history-dependent strategies. It is now known that there is a whole family of history-dependent strategies that characterize optimal equilibria of an indefinitely repeated Prisoner's Dilemma where agents cooperate with partners who obey certain norms of cooperation and punish disobedient partners. And for many of these strategies the innocence and guilt conditions are *forgiving*, so an agent who disobeys becomes eligible to receive the benefits of mutual cooperation once more after n periods of punishment. There are also models where the equilibria characterized by such forgiving punitive strategies tend to evolve.[52] These results for repeated Prisoner's Dilemma are easily adaptable to supergames of covenant interactions, such as an indefinitely repeated Figure 7.4 Covenant game. So one can argue that Hobbesian-Humean strategies tend to evolve in human communities where the evolved strategies

50. David Kreps gives an accessible demonstration that an indefinitely repeated Prisoner's Dilemma can have an optimal and asymmetric equilibrium where one of the agents periodically exploits the other; see *Game Theory and Economic Modeling* (Oxford: Oxford University Press, 1990), pp. 97–99. In Vanderschraaf (2007) I give an analogous proof that in a system of indefinitely repeated Covenant games, optimal equilibria where some parties sometimes exploit others can exist.

51. Axelrod (2006). The specific strategy Axelrod argued would tend to evolve is *tit-for-tat*. In a repeated Prisoner's Dilemma between a pair of fixed agents where at each period each Agent i can either perform (P_i) or defect (D_i), as in the Figure 1.6 game, tit-for-tat requires Agent i to follow P_i at period $t = 1$ and at each period $t > 1$ to imitate the choice of his partner at period $t-1$.

52. Here I will cite three of the most important works in this now large research area. Sugden (2004), §6.3–4, and Boyd (1989) proved some of the central results regarding the properties of standing strategy equilibria and the evolution of standing strategies in repeated Prisoner's Dilemma. Martin Nowak and Karl Sigmund developed related *image scoring* models of repeated Prisoner's Dilemma in "Evolution of Indirect Reciprocity by Image Scoring," *Nature* 393 (1998), pp. 573–577.

have forgiving guilt and innocence conditions such that a guilty agent regains innocence after a punishment cycle of *n* periods of being shunned. Such an argument puts an evolutionary "patch" on a gap in Hobbes' rational choice folk theorem argument. Moreover, if such evolved Hobbesian-Humean strategies are somewhat forgiving, this does no real violence to Hobbes' own view and might in fact might be advantageous to him. In real human societies, everyone makes mistakes. If it were literally true that people generally follow a completely unforgiving Hobbesian-Humean strategy, then in time in a community of fallible individuals everyone would become guilty because of some past violation committed either deliberately or by mistake, and ultimately no covenants would form at all. A Hobbesian-Humean strategy that forgives after a finite punishment cycle of some length *n* is still punitive but eventually forgives transgressions, which is likely to reflect the way real people react to offensive violations of most covenants. Indeed, Hobbes' own sixth law of nature in *Leviathan* requires one to forgive the past offense of a person who repents and promises future good conduct, though he does not specify how quickly one must forgive.[53] Nevertheless, the most such an evolutionary argument shows is that conventions characterized by Hobbesian-Humean strategies might tend to emerge in certain communities. There is no guarantee that the Foole's community is regulated by such a convention. Once again, the Foole can conclude that Hobbes' response to his challenge is persuasive only given the right background conditions.

§7.4. An Invisible Foole

Suppose the ring that once belonged to the Lydian Shepherd falls into the hands of the Foole. Now he can turn invisible whenever he wishes, so I will rename him the *Invisible Foole*. And suppose further that after some experimentation the Invisible Foole learns that the ring has another power the Shepherd did not notice: Using the ring, the Invisible Foole can appear to others as some person other than himself. With the ring, the Invisible Foole can enter into covenants appearing to be someone else and then turn invisible and abscond when it is his turn to perform. He can commit injustices at will against others, all while concealing his identity perfectly. After he completes his direct reply to the Foole, Hobbes states: "As for the Instance of gaining the secure and perpetuall felicity of heaven, by any way; it is frivolous: there being but one way imaginable, and this is not breaking, but

When $n = 1$, the corresponding standing strategy in Sugden's and Boyd's works is a self-correcting version of tit-for-tat, since if either of a pair who follow this standing strategy defects against her innocent partner "by mistake," they can return to a pattern of repeated mutual co-operation after the offender is punished for one period.

53. *Leviathan* 15:17.

keeping of Covenant."[54] But the Invisible Foole still does not believe in God, so he would scoff at Hobbes' statement, just as he would scoff at a Thomist who warns him that his unjust conduct could cause him to suffer hell in the next life.

Indeed, the Invisible Foole appears to have no use for any talk of goods allegedly inseparable from justice. Before he had the ring, the Foole seemed interested in only external goods such as money and labor, which he would willingly seek by being just if he had to but would seek by other means that would spare him the costs of being just if he could. If we suppose that the Invisible Foole cares for only these sorts of external goods, then of course no justice-Platonist argument will make any impression on him. Hobbes' Foole claimed that injustice is the better course of action if he receives the benefits of the others' justice no matter what he does. The Invisible Foole appears to have the power to ensure that he is indeed guaranteed to receive the benefits of others' justice whatever he may do. Given the power of the Shepherd's ring, the Invisible Foole can ask quite simply, "Why should I *ever* do as justice requires?"

At first blush, the challenge of the Invisible Foole might leave defenders of justice dumbfounded. As already noted, inseparable-goods arguments will be wasted on the Invisible Foole. And as he possesses the ring of Gyges, the Invisible Foole seems to have no good social-sanctions reasons to refrain from injustice. Nevertheless, justice-reciprocalists like Hobbes and Hume can present two types of social-sanctions arguments to the Invisible Foole in an attempt to persuade him that he still can have good prudential reasons to be just. These arguments are analogous to the folk theorem argument I have attributed to Hobbes in his response to the ordinary Foole. The leading idea in these arguments is that the members of a community might follow somewhat more complex and sometimes more punitive strategies than the forgiving Hobbesian-Humean strategies discussed above if they are confronted with offensive violators who possess the power the ring of Gyges confers. In particular, an Invisible Foole who offensively violates using the ring might spark a punishment cycle either more severe or more indiscriminate than the punishment cycles of ordinary Hobbesian-Humean strategies, and one that will cost the Invisible Foole in the long run. If this is the case, then the Invisible Foole can have good reason to refrain from offensive violations in order to minimize the risk of launching such a punishment cycle.

The first such social-sanctions response to the Invisible Foole is motivated by another objection Socrates might have raised against Glaucon and Adeimantus' challenge, namely, that the concealment power of the invisibility ring could be transitory. After all, the Shepherd might one day discover to his surprise that his ring no longer works, for it turns out the ring was powered by

---

54. *Leviathan* 15:6.

a nuclear battery that has expired. Or the Shepherd might one day realize his ring is no longer on his finger moments after flushing the toilet. Additionally, if one has in the past taken advantage of absolute or near absolute power to exploit others and then loses this power, one is liable to suffer a particularly severe reprisal for these past exploitations. According to Thucydides' account, the Melians issued the Athenians just such a warning in their negotiations, and events ultimately proved the Melians right. One could present the Invisible Foole with these and other examples, and advise the Invisible Foole against offensive violation on the grounds that should the he lose the concealment power of the invisibility ring, he will be liable to suffer a similarly severe punishment.

To show how this response to the Invisible Foole can have bite, suppose the members of a community are engaged in the indefinitely repeated game described in §7.3 where at each period one is matched in a Covenant game with a counterpart in the community and the counterparts can vary over time. Suppose further that the relevant institutions exist to facilitate the generation of the common knowledge that enables community members to follow Hobbesian-Humean strategies correctly under ordinary circumstances, where no one can effectively conceal her identity. And suppose that in fact under these ordinary circumstances a forgiving Hobbesian-Humean strategy h^* characterizes the incumbent community convention. The Invisible Foole will then be tempted to use his ring to enter into a given covenant while appearing to be someone else, and then become invisible when it is his time to perform. If the community follows an all-h^* equilibrium, they will identify the individual the Invisible Foole impersonated as guilty and punish her instead of punishing the Invisible Foole. Each of the Invisible Foole's hapless victims will have to suffer the punishment of being shunned for the duration of the punishment cycle defined by h^*. But suppose the community members all follow a variant of the h^* strategy:

T^*: Follow S_i with a counterpart Agent $i(t)$ identified as having used an invisibility ring in an offensive violation, and otherwise follow h^* with Agent $i(t)$.

In other words, community members willingly forgive an offensive violator who is not discovered concealing her identity and who serves out her punishment according to h^*, but they never forgive one identified as an invisibility ring user in offensive violations. A community might employ such a draconian rule for dealing with a known ring user partly because ring users are so dangerous to deal with in individual covenants and partly because ring users lead others to mistakenly punish innocent partners. Community members can follow T^* in a nontrivial manner if there is a non-negligible chance that the power of an invisibility ring fails in a given use, so the community discovers the identity of the ring user.

If there is such a non-negligible chance, then one can prove a folk theorem showing that if the community members are all sufficiently patient, then they follow an optimal equilibrium if they all follow T^*. If everyone in the community does follow this T^*-equilibrium, then the Invisible Foole can expect to do worse if he deviates from T^* and offensively violates using the ring than if he performs in his covenants with the innocent as T^* requires.[55] So if one relaxes the assumption that the invisibility ring is certain to conceal a user's identity perfectly for all time, then the Invisible Foole can have good justice-conventionalist reasons to be just after all.

The assumption that the Invisible Foole could lose the ring's concealment power might be plausible, but of course one might object that this assumption produces a desired conclusion on the cheap. What if the Invisible Foole presses his case and claims he is confident he will never lose the power of perfect concealment the ring gives him? Then by hypothesis the community will never be able to identify the Invisible Foole as the guilty agent when he offensively violates. So it would seem that the community members cannot punish the Invisible Foole, in which case he has apparently won his case. But there is another social-sanctions response to the Invisible Foole's challenge. The Invisible Foole needs to consider the possibility of suffering *untargeted* punishment. If the Invisible Foole offensively violates covenants while concealing his identity, then his conduct might tend to undermine the willingness of others to enter into covenants with counterparts who are not known offensive violators, and perhaps with anyone at all. And if the community members generally stop following the norm requiring them to perform in covenants with the innocent, then no one will be able to enjoy the benefits of others' performance in covenants, including the Invisible Foole.

One can again use game theory to show how this response to the Invisible Foole can have persuasive force. Suppose the members of a community are once more engaged in the indefinitely repeated Covenant game described above, but this time they follow a *roundabout punishment* strategy defined partly in terms of a Hobbesian-Humean strategy h^* that does not always distinguish between the guilty and the innocent:

R^*: Follow h^* when conditions are *normal* and follow S_i when conditions are *abnormal*,

where conditions are abnormal in case there has been a public report at a past time of an *abnormal defection*, that is, a defection involving the use of an invisibility ring, and otherwise conditions are normal. For an R^* strategy the time of

55. See Proposition A3.4 of Appendix 3.

a public report of an abnormal defection that establishes abnormal conditions may but need not be within a fixed recent past time. I call R^* a roundabout punishment strategy because punishment is targeted against the guilty only under normal conditions. A defector who renders conditions abnormal by using an invisibility ring does not suffer targeted punishment but still suffers punishment, since everyone in the community is effectively treated as if she was guilty and worthy of punishment according to h^*. How is an abnormal defection known to have occurred? Community members will have some ability to detect an abnormal defection even if a ring user can successfully impersonate some other agent when entering into a covenant, as suggested above. For if a ring user defects at a time t and the agent the ring user has impersonated performs at time t in another covenant with other partners, then community members other than the ring user may conclude that the defector is not whom she has impersonated and that this defector is a ring user.

As indicated in the definition, either the untargeted punishment cycle of R^* can be completely unforgiving or it can end at some specified length, in which case the system can be self-correcting. The shunning cycle that R^* requires in case of an announced abnormal defection is similar to a *contagion strategy* for engaging in a repeated Prisoner's Dilemma with partners who change over time.[56] In a community whose members follow such a contagion strategy, an agent who violates the required pattern of mutual cooperation "infects" the community, so its members start defecting indiscriminately in all their Prisoner's Dilemmas, with the result that the original violator eventually suffers along with everyone else.[57] One might also think of the shunning cycle that R^* launches under abnormal conditions as a "class detention" strategy, since this part of R^* resembles the situation where a teacher has every pupil in a class serve detention for some offense in case no pupil admits to being the offender. R^* is in a sense a restrained contagion strategy, since community members start a punishment cycle of shunning everyone only under abnormal conditions and otherwise mete out only targeted punishment against members who become guilty the "ordinary" way. If there is positive probability that abnormal defection is detected and reported publicly, then one can prove yet another folk theorem establishing that community members can be at optimal equilibrium if they all follow R^* for a given punishment cycle length.

56. Kandori (1992) and Ellison (1993) propose and analyze such contagion strategies.

57. In the contagion strategy he develops, Ellison enables the system to be self-correcting by having a punishment cycle end when a public announcement is issued at some random time following the start of punishment. This public announcement in effect resets the whole system of Prisoner's Dilemmas back to the state where each community member cooperates with her current partner. The contagion strategies Kandori discusses do not have self-correcting mechanisms.

The all-R^* equilibrium is closely related to the "blinking" equilibrium of a repeated Three-in-a-Boat game, discussed in §3.4, where if any agent deviates from the path where all contribute, then all respond by withholding their contributions for the duration of a punishment cycle. The Invisible Foole can expect to fare strictly worse if he deviates from this all- R^* equilibrium and offensively violates.[58] In this case, the Invisible Foole should perform in his covenants as justice requires even if he is sure he can conceal his identity in covenants, because he prefers to avoid the untargeted punishment that he will suffer should he trigger a contagion of shunning by offensively violating while using his ring.

Plainly, the two social-sanctions responses to the Invisible Foole proposed here are inconclusive, much as Hobbes' response to the Foole of *Leviathan* interpreted as a proto-folk-theorem response is inconclusive. In particular, the Invisible Foole can note that he has no a priori reason to assume that those he encounters really will launch into punishment cycles that are either so relentless or so indiscriminate as those that are the backbone of the targeted and untargeted punishment strategies described here. He might also add that historical examples of the terrible punishments that follow after some mighty individual or state falls from power are at best thin anecdotal evidence for the claim that these punitive strategies would tend to evolve in societies in which some members had the concealment power of the invisibility ring. The most the analysis here shows is that the Invisible Foole can have good social-sanctions reasons to refrain from injustice. If conditions are such that the members of society can and do follow sufficiently punitive strategies of targeted or untargeted punishment, then the Invisible Foole should obey Hobbes' law of nature requiring promise keeping even if he has the ring of Gyges. Under different conditions, where the members of society cannot or will not be so punitive, then to commit injustices using the ring might be the Invisible Foole's prudentially rational choice.

Hume acknowledges both the importance of untargeted punishment and its limits in his response to the Knave's challenge. The Knave thinks that in some exceptional cases he can profit from a breach of justice that will not appreciably undermine the system of justice regulating his society.[59] When such golden opportunities arise, the Knave expects to suffer no untargeted punishment, since he can expect the others in his society to continue obeying their system of justice, including the requirements he offensively violates on these occasions. The Knave does not mention targeted punishment, but if the Knave expects to suffer no untargeted punishment, then presumably he expects to suffer no targeted

58. See Proposition A.3.5 of Appendix 3.

59. *Enquiry* 9.2:22.

punishment, either. For targeted punishment should tend to be less costly and hence easier for members of society to carry out so long as they know whom to punish. Why then, asks the Knave, should he not offensively violate when such golden opportunities come his way? In the end, the challenge of the Knave is much like that of the Invisible Foole. Indeed, I regard the Invisible Foole as an individual like Hume's Knave who possesses identity concealment technology but perhaps lacks some of the Knave's acumen. Having the power of the ring, the Invisible Foole might see no reason to restrain himself at all, so in the end he may spark a cycle of untargeted punishment because he has provoked too many too often. The Knave believes he can commit injustices much more judiciously, avoiding all social sanctions as he profits from his offenses. Can the Knave's skeptical challenge against justice be refuted?

§7.5. Combining the Social-Sanctions and the Inseparable-Goods Approaches

So far I have distinguished between two approaches to completing the Reconciliation Project, one that appeals to goods inseparable from justice and the other that appeals to the social sanctions of justice and injustice. Justice-Platonism and justice-reciprocalism have distinguished histories in philosophy. But in my opinion, philosophers have been disposed to consider the inseparable-goods and the social-sanctions approaches separately. In fact, one can regard justice-Platonism and justice-reciprocalism as complementary approaches to completing the Reconciliation Project. One could be interested in securing for oneself the goods of both these approaches. If one believes in and values relevant goods inseparable from justice as well as the benefits of others' good conduct toward oneself, then one has two sets of reasons to be just. Hume's response to the Knave's challenge makes this very point. Hume is seldom so passionate as he is in this response. In one representative pair of sentences from his response, Hume extols the advantages an honest person has over people who are like the Knave:

> Such a one has, besides, the frequent satisfaction of seeing knaves, with all their pretended cunning and abilities, betrayed by their own maxims; and while they purpose to cheat with moderation and secrecy, a tempting incident occurs, nature is frail, and they give into the snare; whence they can never extricate themselves, without a total loss of reputation, and the forfeiture of all future trust and confidence with mankind.
>
> But were they ever so secret and successful, the honest man, if he has any tincture of philosophy, or even common observation and reflection, will discover that they themselves are, in the end, the greatest dupes, and

> have sacrificed the invaluable enjoyment of a character, with themselves at least, for the acquisition of worthless toys and gewgaws.[60]

In *Treatise*, Hume presents conventionalist arguments to establish the prudential rationality of obeying the requirements of justice. In his *Enquiry* response to the Knave's challenge, Hume retains the proto-folk-theorem reasoning of *Treatise*, noting that individuals who follow the Knave's advice are likely to be identified and to suffer the social consequences of a damaged reputation. But he also appeals to the goods of a clear conscience and satisfaction in one's own integrity, and stresses just how valuable these goods are to honest, reflective persons.[61] Hume clearly thinks one can take both justice-reciprocalist and justice-Platonist considerations seriously.[62]

Is either justice-Platonism or justice-reciprocalism satisfactory on its own? This is, does either justice-Platonism or justice-reciprocalism work as a stand-alone platform upon which philosophers can complete the Reconciliation Project? I believe this is at bottom an empirical question. In a world whose inhabitants have common knowledge that everyone is a justice-Platonist, this common knowledge would be sufficient to give everyone sufficient prudential reason to be just. In another world whose inhabitants have common knowledge that everyone accepts justice-reciprocalist arguments like the arguments Hobbes and Hume give, this common knowledge would also be sufficient to give everyone sufficient prudential reason to be just. Matters are more complicated in our own world, given the heterogeneous beliefs its inhabitants have regarding justice and accounts of the good. The justice-reciprocalist might not be able to convince the justice-Platonist that expectations of reciprocity are the primary reason it can be prudentially rational to be just. But the justice-reciprocalist can rightly observe that many in the actual world accept the Foole's account of the good as socioeconomic benefit and nothing else. This has important implications for the justice-Platonist. For the justice-Platonist will be loath to ever offensively violate a requirement of justice, but she might also be loath to enter into covenants with partners like the Foole or the Knave who are willing to

60. *Enquiry* 9.2:24–25.

61. In the concluding section of *Treatise*, Hume asserts that having inner peace and being satisfied with one's own character as well as having the high regard of others depends upon one strictly observing the social virtues, and that these goods are more valuable than any increase in fortune one gains by breaching these virtues (*Treatise* 3.3.6:6). But in *Treatise* Hume does not connect this point to his conventionalist analysis of justice.

62. In different ways Hobbes and Plato make this same point. As noted in §7.4, following his direct reply to the Foole Hobbes adds that keeping covenants is a necessary condition for gaining the felicity of Heaven (*Leviathan* 15:6). Near the end of *Republic*, Socrates declares that the just person can typically expect to enjoy the social rewards of a good reputation as well as the intrinsic goods of justice (*Republic* 613b–614a).

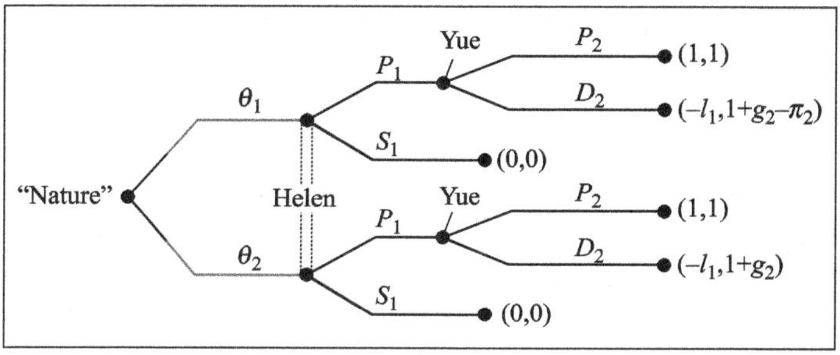

$g_i > 0, l_i > 0, \pi_i > 1 + g_i, i \in \{1, 2\}$

θ_1 = Yue has justice-Platonist preferences, θ_2 = Yue has Foole's preferences

FIGURE 7.8 A Justice-Platonist Considers Entering into a Covenant

exploit others when they think this will bring them socioeconomic gain. And what if parties cannot easily distinguish between the types of counterpart parties they might encounter in Covenant situations?

Suppose Helen, a justice-Platonist, is approached by Yue, who wishes to form a covenant. If Yue is also a justice-Platonist, then she will be sure to perform if Helen agrees to covenant. But if Yue has a conception of the good like the Foole's, then it appears that Helen can expect to be exploited if she enters into the covenant. Figure 7.8 summarizes this situation as a one-sided game of incomplete information. In this game, a justice-Platonist Agent i absorbs a cost π_i for offensively violating reflecting the inseparable good lost by the unjust. Helen does not know in advance whether Yue is a θ_1-type who has justice-Platonist preferences or a θ_1-type who has Foole's preferences. Yue's unique best strategy is P_2-if-θ_1;D_2-if-θ_2. For Helen, agreeing to covenant and then performing (P_1) is a best response only if the probability x she assigns to Yue being a θ_1-type satisfies $x \geq \frac{l_1}{1+l_1}$.[63] Otherwise, shunning (S_1) is Helen's best response.[64] Plainly, given this summary of a covenant interaction, a justice-Platonist like Helen would be reluctant to enter covenants if the likelihood that she encounters partners who are not justice-Platonists like herself is sufficiently great. But this summary of course does not take into account the possibility

---

63. For Helen, given Yue's strategy $s_2 = P_2$ - if - θ_1; D_2 - if - θ_2,

$$E_1\left(u_1\left(P_1, s_2\right)\right) = 1 \cdot x - l_1 \cdot (1-x) = x - l_1 - l_1 x \geq 0 = E_1\left(u_1\left(S_1, s_2\right)\right)$$

exactly when $x > \frac{l_1}{1+l_1}$.

64. Defecting is not also an option for Helen since Helen is a justice-Platonist.

of repeated interactions and history-dependent strategies. A justice-Platonist might be willing to enter into a covenant even if she believes it likely that her partner has Foole's preferences if she also believes this partner accepts a justice-reciprocalist rationale for why he should perform in covenants. Even if a justice-Platonist does not herself find the justice-reciprocalist defense of the rationality of being just necessary or even compelling, she has good reason to hope that others who reject justice-Platonism find the justice-reciprocalist defense convincing. Otherwise, given that we live in a world in which many have Foole's preferences, it might not make sense to covenant with others after all. In other words, the justice-Platonist can rely on justice-reciprocalist arguments in an indirect way, since others' direct reliance on these arguments gives the justice-Platonist a good reason to enter into covenants with others.

What about the justice-reciprocalist? A carefully developed set of folk theorem arguments may persuade many individuals like the Foole, and perhaps also individuals like the Invisible Foole, that they have good prudential reasons to abstain from offensively violating covenants. But as discussed above in §7.3, the Foole can raise a number of serious objections against such justice-as-following-an-equilibrium arguments. I will briefly recapitulate these objections here. Even if some social states that require universal compliance with justice can be social equilibria, the Foole has no a priori reason to suppose that the members of his community will be following any of these equilibria. Beyond this, the epistemic background conditions needed to support an equilibrium characterized by a Hobbesian-Humean strategy are quite demanding, and they presuppose reliable institutions for information transmission. If a community lacks the means for generating common knowledge, or if these means are sufficiently corruptible, then its members will be incapable of following a Hobbesian-Humean strategy correctly because they will be incapable of knowing who really is innocent and who really is guilty. Beyond this, the folk theorem arguments presuppose that the members of the community all are sufficiently patient to make the state where all follow the relevant Hobbesian-Humean strategy h^* an equilibrium of the repeated game. If some in the community do not assign probabilities of continued interaction sufficiently high to make the all-h^* state an equilibrium, then offensive violation when the opportunity arises might be the best course of action after all. The Foole might conclude that in the end the idealizing assumptions of folk theorems are simply too strong to enable a justice-reciprocalist to refute him decisively using folk theorem arguments alone. The Foole can add that some contemporary social scientists, including some who have made important contributions of their own to game-theoretic analyses of social cooperation, have expressed similar concerns regarding the idealizing assumptions of folk theorems and similar reservations regarding how well folk theorems by themselves can explain such cooperation.[65] As Herbert Gintis puts it, perhaps we should all raise only "one cheer for the folk theorem."[66]

Finally, the Foole has Kavka's backward induction argument. This argument amounts to denying that there can be any folk theorem equilibrium of cooperation in a community having common knowledge of a least upper bound to the number of interactions involving covenants. As noted in §7.3, it is plausible to suppose that community members lack this specific piece of common knowledge, in which case Kavka's argument is blocked. But the Foole might respond that this is an odd move for a proponent of folk theorem arguments to make given how much the folk theorem arguments rely upon common knowledge of other facts about the community. Moreover, the Foole can point out that if all or even only some in his community are indeed relatively impatient or lack reliable knowledge of much of the past histories of their partners, then he can apply backward induction in another way. The Foole might be able to ascertain that in some of his encounters his partner has limited if any knowledge of his past conduct and limited if any ability to inform others of the details of his current conduct. And when the Foole meets such a partner, he might expect to interact with her only a few times over his own lifetime. The Foole knows that if he offensively violates a covenant he enters into with such a partner, this partner will never covenant with him again. But if the Foole knows a least upper bound on the number of possible interactions with this partner, the Foole can apply backward induction reasoning similar to that of Kavka's argument to conclude that performing in any covenant they might form is never rational. So if Foole happens to find himself matched with such a partner and they have formed a covenant, perhaps because this partner is a "sucker," then he should defect and enjoy the fruits of offensive violation if this partner performs, which shows that he was right to endorse offensively violating covenants all along.

People do not consistently follow the Foole's advice, either in their ordinary interactions or in the laboratory. Many empirical studies confirm that individuals who engage in interactions where it "pays" to take advantage of others when possible settle into patterns of mutually beneficial conduct where each side far more frequently refrains from exploiting interaction partners than they apparently "should." The empirical findings on Ultimatum game and public good experiments discussed in Chapter 5 illustrate how individuals often tend to "play fair" when apparently they could do better by exploiting their partners. And

65. See, for example, Elinor Ostrom, Roy Gardner, and James Walker, *Rules, Games and Common-Pool Resources* (Ann Arbor: University of Michigan Press, 1994), ch. 1; Gintis (2009), §10.6; Bowles and Gintis (2011), §5.6.

66. Gintis (2009), p. 195.

there are many other such illustrations. As I argued in Chapter 5, one can explain such apparently anomalous conduct by postulating different types of agents, not all of whom have payoffs defined solely in terms of the personal gains in external goods such as money or labor from the interaction. In the games that summarize the interactions where it pays to take advantage, the agents can achieve outcomes corresponding to reciprocal compliance with norms of fairness or justice due to the influence of some who have a preference for following such norms that is at least somewhat independent of the personal gains in such external goods from the game.

This idea is not new. Much of the now vast body of analytical and empirical results on single and repeated Prisoner's Dilemmas, Stag Hunts, bargaining problems, public goods, and other related games confirms the following general hypothesis: Even small uncertainties regarding all the agents basing their payoffs solely on their personal gains or losses in external goods can radically transform their situation so that cooperation becomes a rational course of action. In particular, a rational agent with Foole's preferences might evaluate covenant situations very differently if she knows that there is some chance that some of her partners' payoffs are such that they will not necessarily follow the course of action the Foole would recommend. The Foole himself might be rational to perform in all his covenants if he believes that some of his future partners are willing to shun offensive violators whether or not they are sufficiently patient to make the corresponding Hobbesian-Humean strategy their part of a folk theorem equilibrium of the sort discussed above. Or the Foole might be rational to perform in a given covenant with a partner he expects to interact with only a limited number of times even in cases where his reputation is not at stake if he believes this partner may have some preference for performing in her covenants independent of what she might gain from the Foole in external goods. For then the Foole cannot assume this partner would surely fail to perform at the last possible covenant interaction, and so the Foole would not be able to anchor a backward induction argument that would justify offensively violating against this partner at the outset. The Foole might do best to perform in at least many of the interactions with this partner in order to maintain her willingness to covenant with him, so that he can enjoy the benefits of continued mutual performance in covenants with this partner in the relatively few covenant interactions he expects with her.[67] More generally, if it is known that some in the community have a tendency to "play

67. The Foole could contend that if he accepts this argument, he still should defect in the last possible interaction because performance can then no longer sustain an ongoing pattern of mutual performance in covenants with this partner. The Foole would be right on this point if he could be sure that he knows the least upper bound of interactions with this partner. And if the Foole were to reach what he believed at the outset had to be the last possible such interaction, this might throw him into doubt as to whether or not this initial belief was correct.

fair" (discussed in Chapter 5 in the context of covenant interactions), then this might tend to make conditionally cooperative strategies such as the Hobbesian-Humean strategies more salient for all in this community, thereby enhancing the prospects for Hobbesian-Humean strategies to evolve and endure. The upshot is that one may be able to strengthen the justice-reciprocalist responses to the Foole considerably if one allows for some heterogeneity in the preferences of the community members.

Are agents who have preferences to perform their parts of the covenants they enter into independent of the relevant external goods simply suckers? Likewise, are agents ready to shun offensive violators whether or not their discount factors make it "profitable" for them to mete out such punishment just dupes? These questions amount to asking whether or not individuals who have at least some of the characteristics of strong reciprocators are simply irrational. In Chapter 5 I discussed the explanatory power of strong reciprocity and how the presence of some strong reciprocators can help to sustain norms of fairness in a community. But while analytical and computer models and the evidence of field studies and laboratory experiments may tell us much regarding how strong reciprocity might support cooperation and the mechanics of the evolution of minorities of strong reciprocators in human communities, the question remains: Why do those who exhibit the characteristics of strong reciprocity act as they do? One way to answer this question—a way that allows these individuals to claim they are in fact acting rationally—is to suppose these individuals are justice-Platonists. And, in fact, some people in the actual world do accept justice-Platonist arguments. So the justice-reciprocalist can mount her strengthened response to the Foole by starting with a claim he would certainly accept, namely, that it is common knowledge that some people are justice-Platonists. In this manner, the justice-reciprocalist can rely indirectly on justice-Platonism.

Conclusion

Can the Reconciliation Project be completed once and for all? In this long look at the challenges of the Foole, the Lydian Shepherd, and the Sensible Knave I hope at least to have identified some of the reasons this ancient project is so challenging and to show that conventions, properly understood, are a valuable tool for philosophers who address this project. Working through and trying to respond to each of these challenges yields valuable philosophical morals. Even a surface reading of Hobbes' response to the Foole's challenge highlights how one might try to reconcile duty and self-interest by appealing to social sanctions. And even a surface reading of Glaucon and Adeimantus' challenge points one to *the* great alternative route to showing that duty and self-interest coincide, namely, appealing to special goods that are allegedly inseparable from justice. As Hume's own response suggests, the Knave's challenge shows both that there are limits to how far philosophers can go toward completing the Reconciliation Project and that the most persuasive responses to skeptical challenges against justice will incorporate both social-sanctions reasons and inseparable-goods reasons for being just.

Another general moral to draw from confronting the three challenges is that folk theorem arguments can go far, and perhaps farther than one would first expect, in reconciling justice with rational prudence. This might seem a surprising claim for me to make at this stage, since I have taken care to state along the way the various objections the Foole and the Invisible Foole can raise against the folk theorem arguments I have proposed. It is true that folk theorem arguments rest upon demanding assumptions. If the members of the Foole's community cannot generate certain common knowledge or if some are insufficiently patient, then they cannot follow a folk theorem convention that would make obeying the requirements of justice the Foole's rational response. And if conditions are such that they can follow this type of convention, then these same conditions also make a huge number of other folk theorem conventions possible. So doing what justice requires is the Foole's best choice only given the right incumbent convention. Again, the folk theorem arguments have persuasive force against individuals like the Foole only when the background conditions are "just right." But these conditions may be "just right" in a great many if not most of the communities in which the Foole and others with the Foole's preferences are liable to find themselves. Social scientists have documented in a wealth of field research and laboratory experiments that human communities can and very often do settle into and sustain norms of reciprocal cooperation that they enforce via *indirect reciprocity*. Examples range from food-sharing norms of hunter-gather societies that are enforced by members suspending their exchanges with violators to norms enshrined in law in industrialized societies that are enforced partly by a police and court system and partly by social stigma. In an indirect reciprocity community, members follow Hobbesian-Humean strategies that reward the innocent and punish the guilty.[68] The Foole has much to learn from this research. Perhaps Hobbes and Hume were cavalier to simply assume in their arguments against offensive violation that one's interaction partners follow Hobbesian-Humean strategies. But

68. The literature on indirect reciprocity is now very large and diverse, and in my opinion no one source gives a complete current overview of the field. Three of the works that laid the initial foundations of research on indirect reciprocity are Sugden (2004), §6.3–4; Richard D. Alexander, *The Biology of Moral Systems* (Hawthorne, NY: Aldine de Gruyter, 1987); and Boyd (1989). Henrich and Henrich (2007) is perhaps the most systematic empirical study of indirect reciprocity among the members of a community living in an industrialized society published so far.

given the widespread phenomenon of indirect reciprocity, Hobbes' and Hume's assumption may be on the mark with respect to many if not most actual human communities. If the Foole is likely to interact with partners in an indirect reciprocity community, then the folk theorem arguments of targeted punishment should give him pause when he is tempted to commit offensive violations.

The discussion of the Invisible Foole shows that folk theorem arguments of a different stripe can be mounted in response to the challenge of the Shepherd. The challenge of the Shepherd is designed to elicit an inseparable-goods response. And in fact Socrates willingly accepts Adeimantus' admonition to abstain from appealing to any considerations of reputation or social sanctions and to use inseparable goods reasons only in developing his own response, at least until he has established his main conclusion that justice is valuable for the sake of preserving the integrity of one's soul.[69] But Socrates could have accepted Glaucon and Adeimantus' assumption that the ring's cloaking power always shields the Shepherd's identity perfectly and still not have limited himself to inseparable-goods arguments in the main part of his response. The ring prevents anyone from punishing the Shepherd directly, but if the Shepherd takes seriously the possibility of untargeted punishment, then he might be wary of using his ring to commit injustices and starting a cycle of indiscriminate punishment that will reach him in the end. Like the Invisible Foole, the Shepherd can have good social-sanctions reasons for being just if his community can follow a convention where an abnormal offensive violation triggers a cycle of untargeted punishment. The challenge of the Shepherd is sometimes thought to be unanswerable because any inseparable-goods argument will simply be too weak to persuade someone who has the power of a god. To this initial version of the challenge, the right response is to grant Glaucon that if the powers of the ring are strengthened so as to make its user invulnerable as well as invisible, then indeed one can appeal only to inseparable-goods reasons to be just, and some will not find any such appeal persuasive. In this initial version of the challenge, the Shepherd is simply outside the circumstances of justice.[70] In the second and more plausible version of the challenge, Glaucon and Adeimantus claim "merely" that so long as one can surely prevent any damage to her own reputation, one has no social-sanctions reason to be just. I have argued in this chapter that Glaucon and Adeimantus' claim is mistaken.

---

69. See note 62.

70. In "Three Against Justice," Gauthier (1990) considers only this first version of the challenge as proposed by Glaucon, and he takes the conclusion I have just stated here to be a central moral of the challenge of the Shepherd.

It is the Knave's challenge, for all its simplicity, that is the most intractable of the three. Hume presents the Knave's challenge so succinctly that one can easily miss its force. The Knave claims he can choose between two alternatives: (1) obey the requirements of justice without exception, and (2) obey the requirements of justice except in golden opportunity cases, where offensive violation will add substantially to one's personal fortune and will result in no negative social sanctions.[71] The Knave admits that alternative (1) may serve him well as a general policy, but he claims that (2) will serve him better. The Knave effectively argues that alternative (2) weakly dominates alternative (1). And the Knave can argue further that if there is any positive probability that he will encounter at least one golden opportunity situation, then rationality requires him to adopt alternative (2). In his response to this challenge, Hume effectively admits that to complete the Reconciliation Project perfectly may be beyond any philosopher's reach. Indeed, in his response Hume gives the impression that he is willing to try anything to finish off this project short of appealing to divine sanctions, which Sidgwick later portrays as something of a desperation move. Yet Hume acknowledges that his Knave might not find any social-sanctions or inseparable-goods arguments persuasive.[72] Hume portrays the Knave as a mild-mannered individual who merely has an unsettling thought regarding his duty to be just. But beneath the surface, if the Knave believes his own words and is right about his ability to detect golden opportunities, then he might well be an individual of the sort most hope never to encounter: a perfect psychopath capable of committing perfect crimes. Perhaps, as Hume suggests, such a Knave is to be pitied for being incapable of appreciating the goods inseparable from justice. But from the perspective of such a Knave, the "ordinary" people who value the so-called inseparable goods are simply deceived, perhaps mainly by themselves. If such a Knave cannot in the end be persuaded that he really cannot know when golden opportunities for offensive violations arise, and if he cannot be persuaded to take intrinsic-goods arguments seriously, then there really is no way to show this Knave he has good prudential reasons to be just.

But is this really so bad? One might worry that if there are sufficiently many such Knaves in a given society, then all in this society would eventually be unwilling to enter into covenants at all once the aggregate injustices of these Knaves exceed

71. In a 1990 graduate seminar he led at the University of California at Irvine, Gregory Kavka would use the phrase "golden opportunities" to refer to situations that looked particularly favorable for offensive violation from the Foole's perspective. Partly to honor Kavka, I have used his terminology in this chapter, although in that seminar Kavka did not connect the idea of a golden opportunity with Hume's Sensible Knave.

72. *Enquiry* 9.2:23.

a certain threshold. A cycle of untargeted punishment resembling Hobbes' State of Nature would then ensue, so following the Knave's advice would produce self-defeating results. Happily, such Knaves are relatively few and far between. Were they not, then Hume's Knave would see little point in raising his challenge in the first place. Moreover, to ask philosophers to finish the Reconciliation Project in a manner that satisfies *everyone* may simply be asking for too much. Kavka, for one, thought that no proposed resolution of the Reconciliation Project would satisfy a determined immoralist like Thrasymachus, but he also thought that some resolutions might prove acceptable to a "puzzled ordinary person" like Glaucon.[73] And as Hume would point out, the fact that some aspire to follow the Knave's advice is no proof that the rest of us would be wrong to conclude that justice does coincide with rational prudence, perhaps for both social-sanctions reasons and inseparable-goods reasons.

A final lesson of the Knave's challenge is that the most successful attempts to complete the Reconciliation Project will integrate elements of justice-reciprocalism and justice-Platonism. In §7.5 I argued that a justice-reciprocalist can present a much stronger case if she incorporates even small uncertainties parties might have regarding whether or not all calculate their payoffs solely in terms of personal material gain. Such uncertainties could reflect the presence in the community of strong reciprocators, whose motivations can be consistent with Bayesian rationality if they are justice-Platonists. In §7.5 I also argued that, conversely, a justice-Platonist can rely upon justice-reciprocalism indirectly since social-sanctions arguments may persuade those who reject inseparable-goods arguments and consequently make it rational for the justice-Platonist to enter into covenants with parties who are not justice-Platonists like herself. My argument above that justice-reciprocalism and justice-Platonism can be mutually supportive raises many further questions. What mixtures of justice-Platonists and justice-reciprocalists in a population can produce an environment where making and keeping covenants is rational for them all? Exactly what facts must be known mutually or commonly in such mixed societies in order for equilibria of reciprocal cooperation to be viable? How much offensive violation by Fooles and Knaves can a mixed society of justice-reciprocalists and justice-Platonists tolerate and yet maintain an equilibrium of general compliance with norms of justice? I have left such questions unanswered here.

Still, the admittedly incomplete arguments given in this chapter yield a practical conclusion: Empirical beliefs regarding one's own society always matter in one's interactions involving covenants. At the extreme condition where it is common knowledge that all members of society accept inseparable-goods

73. Kavka (1984), p. 297.

arguments or that all accept social-sanctions arguments, everyone has good prudential reasons to enter into and perform in covenants. At the opposite extreme, where all know that no one in society accepts either inseparable-goods arguments or social-sanctions arguments, no one has good prudential reasons to enter into covenants. Actual societies tend to be more heterogeneous, with some of their members accepting inseparable-goods arguments, some accepting social-sanctions arguments, some accepting both, and even some, like Hume's Knave, accepting neither. And the fact that a population may be mixed in such a manner may well be common knowledge among its members. In these mixed cases, it may or may not serve one's own expected interests to enter into and perform in covenants, depending upon how likely one thinks it is that one's partners accept certain proposals for completing the Reconciliation Project. In general, the prudential rationality of entering into and performing in covenants varies according to one's beliefs about others' commitments to either justice-Platonism or justice-reciprocalism as well as one's own commitments.

8 JUSTICE AS MUTUAL ADVANTAGE?

> [I]f by convention be meant a sense of common interest, which sense each man feels in his own breast, which he remarks in his fellows, and which carries him, in concurrence with others, into a general plan or system of actions, which tends to public utility; it must be owned, that, in this sense, justice arises from human conventions. For if it be allowed (what is, indeed, evident) that the particular consequences of a particular act of justice may be hurtful to the public as well as to individuals; it follows that every man, in embracing that virtue, must have an eye to the whole plan or system, and must expect the concurrence of his fellows in the same conduct and behavior. Did all his views terminate in the consequences of each act of his own, his benevolence and humanity, as well as his self-love, might often prescribe to him measures of conduct very different from those which are agreeable to the strict rules of right and justice. . . .
>
> Whatever is advantageous to two or more persons, if all perform their part; but what loses all advantage if only one perform, can arise from no other principle. There would otherwise be no motive for any one of them to enter into that scheme of conduct.
>
> —DAVID HUME, *An Enquiry Concerning the Principles of Morals*

Introduction

Justice as mutual advantage, the idea of defining and analyzing justice as a system of rules that people follow because these rules benefit them all, has a distinguished history in political philosophy. Philosophers in ancient Athens proposed early accounts of justice as mutual advantage,[1] and Plato certainly regarded justice as mutual advantage sufficiently important to merit a presentation and refutation in the *Republic* exchanges among Socrates, Glaucon, and Adeimantus. Justice as mutual advantage theories appear in the works of Epicurus, Thomas Hobbes, Hugo Grotius, and David Hume. David Gauthier, Robert Sugden, Brian Skyrms, and Ken Binmore have added to the justice as

---

1. Nicholas Denyer gives an overview of proposed theories of justice as systems of mutually beneficial rules current in the Athens of Plato's and Aristotle's time in "The Origins of Justice," in *Suzetesis: studi sull' epicureismo greco e romano offerti a Marcello Gigante* (Naples: Macchiaroli, 1983), pp. 133–152.

mutual advantage tradition in their contemporary works.[2] Despite this distinguished history, I think that historically justice as mutual advantage has held a minority position among philosophers. Starting with Plato, most philosophers who engage seriously in discussions of morals and politics seem to have believed that justice, whatever it might be, has to be based upon ideas more exalted than mutual benefit. At the same time, justice as mutual advantage seems an idea that simply will not disappear, no matter how wrongheaded some regard the theories of figures such as Hobbes, Hume, and Gauthier.

Interestingly, philosophers have spent far less effort trying to identify the conditions that characterize justice as mutual advantage than they have spent defending or criticizing specific accounts of justice as mutual advantage. Much of the contemporary discussion proceeds as if one should have no trouble understanding what justice as mutual advantage is and why this general theory of justice is obviously correct or obviously defective. Perhaps this situation has arisen because the notion of a general theory or a conception of justice is somewhat vague and indeed relatively new in philosophy. Identifying and analyzing general conceptions or general theories or "schools" of justice is a project that began mainly in the twentieth century, and many of the basic issues in this young project remain unsettled. Indeed, the very names "general theory" and "conception" indicate how challenging it can be to distinguish the type from some of its tokens. Are the theories of justice of Plato, Aristotle, Hobbes, Hume, Kant, and Rawls specific examples of more general theories of justice, or do at least some of these theories qualify as general theories of justice in their own right?

I believe that that justice as mutual advantage is indeed a distinct general theory or conception of justice. But characterizing justice as mutual advantage precisely turns out to be quite an interesting challenge. In §8.1 I specify four necessary conditions of justice as mutual advantage. These conditions imply that the requirements of a justice as mutual advantage system are conventions as defined in Chapter 2. In §8.2–§8.4 I discuss a common view regarding justice as mutual advantage, namely, that according to this theory the vulnerable members of society would be excluded from the benefits of justice. In §8.2 I lay out this *Vulnerability Objection* and discuss why critics have thought this objection fatal for justice as mutual advantage. In §8.3 I discuss several possible responses to this objection that I conclude in the end are inadequate. In §8.4 I present my own response to the Vulnerability Objection by introducing

2. See especially Gauthier (1986), Sugden (2004), Skyrms (2014), and Binmore (1994, 1998). In §8.6 I argue that Gauthier's and Binmore's theories are actually hybrid theories rather than purely justice as mutual advantage theories.

a game, the indefinitely repeated *Provider-Recipient game*, that has equilibria where benefits of mutual aid are extended to all the agents engaged in the game, including those who are effectively vulnerable. This shows by example that a justice as mutual advantage system can extend benefits to the vulnerable in society after all. In §8.5 I address the issue of specifying which beings are to be included in the community of those who are eligible for benefits in a justice as mutual advantage system. In this section I argue that on salience grounds this community is very likely to consist of all of the resident humans, either following birth or including the prenatal humans. I complete my description of justice as mutual advantage in the concluding section, §8.6. Here I argue that justice as mutual advantage needs criteria for reducing the set of conventions that satisfy the necessary conditions spelled out in §8.1 so that the remaining conventions are those defining distributions of benefits that at least roughly match widely held beliefs regarding what sorts of regimes are genuinely just. To achieve the necessary reduction, I introduce a fifth *Baseline Consistency* requirement for justice as mutual advantage. The leading idea of Baseline Consistency is that the rules of a justice as mutual advantage system remain stable with respect to possible renegotiation in case the community experiences certain changes in their circumstances, including becoming able to provide less or more in the way of mutual benefits than before.

§8.1. Necessary Conditions for Justice as Mutual Advantage

Brian Barry's work provides a useful starting point for the purpose of identifying certain necessary features of any account of justice as mutual advantage. While Barry fervently rejects justice as mutual advantage, in my opinion no contemporary philosopher has done more to establish the importance of justice as mutual advantage as a general conception of justice. In *Theories of Justice*, Barry takes justice as mutual advantage to be the one serious competitor to his own preferred general theory of justice, a theory Barry calls *justice as impartiality*.[3] Early in this work Barry describes justice as mutual advantage thus:

> Justice is simply rational prudence pursued in contexts where the cooperation (or at least forbearance) of other people is a condition for our being able to get what we want. Justice is the name we give to the constraints on themselves that rational self-interested people would agree to as the minimum price that has to be paid in order to obtain the cooperation of others.[4]

---

3. Barry (1989), p. 7.

4. Barry (1989), pp. 6–7.

In his later *Justice as Impartiality*, Barry says that justice as mutual advantage consists of an attempt to complete the following project:

> we are to imagine people with different conceptions of the good seeking a set of ground rules that holds out to each person the prospect of doing better (on each person's conception of what 'doing better' consists of) than any of them could expect from pursuing the good individually without constraints.[5]

Each of these descriptions highlights what I think is an important condition that must be part of any account of justice as mutual advantage. The second description addresses the structure of interaction. As will be the case with any specific system of justice based upon any general theory of justice, a justice as mutual advantage system will consist of rules or requirements binding upon the members of a society. Such a system requires individuals to restrain their pursuit of their personal interests to some extent. The members of society are in the Generic Circumstances of Justice as outlined in Chapter 3, and the restraining requirements are the remedy for their predicament. Hobbes' account of civil society is a prototype example of such a system. Hobbes argues that if individuals all submit to the requirements of a sovereign, they have a commonwealth where general compliance with the laws of nature is possible and they all do better than they would do in an utterly unconstrained State of Nature. Barry's first description addresses motivation. In justice as mutual advantage, each individual conforms for exactly one reason: each wants the cooperation of the others in society. Hobbes and Hume each summarize this rationale for compliance particularly well regarding specific requirements. Here I repeat two key passages quoted in earlier chapters. Hobbes' second *Leviathan* law of nature addresses the requirement to abstain from trying to seize the goods others possess without permission:

> *That a man be willing, when others are so too, as farre-forth, as for Peace, and defence of himself he shall think it necessary, to lay down this right to all things; and be contented with so much liberty against other men, as he would allow other men against himselfe.* For as long as every man holdeth this Right, of doing any thing he liketh; so long are all men in the condition of Warre. But if other men will not lay down their Right, as well as he; then there is no Reason for any one, to divest himself of his. For that were to expose himselfe to Prey, (which no man is bound to) rather than to dispose himself to Peace.[6]

5. Barry (1995), p. 32.

6. *Leviathan* 14:5, quoted above in §1.1.

In *Treatise* Hume explains why a party to a covenant keeps her promise in situations structurally similar to the Farmer's Dilemma:

> I learn to do a service to another, without bearing him any real kindness; because I foresee, that he will return my service, in expectation of another of the same kind, and in order to maintain the same correspondence of good offices with me or with others. And accordingly, after I have serv'd him, and he is in possession of the advantage arising from my action, he is induc'd to perform his part, as foreseeing the consequences of his refusal.[7]

Put very roughly, justice as mutual advantage holds out the promise that all who follow its requirements can fare better than they would fare at a baseline where no one follows the requirements. As this description suggests, justice as mutual advantage lends itself quite naturally to game-theoretic analysis. Conflictual coordination games, indefinitely repeated games such as the indefinitely repeated Covenant game, and especially Nash bargaining games are invaluable tools for developing and evaluating contemporary accounts of justice as mutual advantage. In the first part of *Theories of Justice*, Barry uses Richard Braithwaite's Matthew-Luke problem, discussed earlier in Chapters 1, 4, and 5, to illustrate how he thinks a justice as mutual advantage theorist might try to resolve a problem of fair division.[8] And some of the most important contemporary justice as mutual advantage theorists, including Gauthier, Sugden, Skyrms, and Binmore, have employed Nash's bargaining problem extensively in their works.

In light of the above discussion I now propose the following three conditions as necessary conditions for a system S_N of rules to be a system of justice as mutual advantage for the members of a society N. My pronoun usage in stating these conditions reflects the idea that typical members or parties in the society N will be individual persons, but these conditions can in principle apply to societies where the parties are groups. These conditions are obviously related to the Generic Circumstances of Justice discussed in Chapter 3. They are compatible with Barry's two sketches of justice as mutual advantage quoted above, but they do not clearly address one important element in his account, which I will address at the end of this section.

(M1) *Conflicting interests.* S_N requires each Party i capable of pursuing interests to restrain pursuit of her own interests to some extent in order to advance the interests of other parties to some extent.

---

7. *Treatise* 3.2.5:8, quoted above in §7.1.

8. Barry (1989), chs. 1–3.

(M2) *Pareto improvement for contributors.* If no party violates the requirements of S_N, then for each Party i capable of pursuing interests who follows the requirements of S_N, Party i's own interests are better satisfied than they are at the state σ_0^* where no party restrains her pursuit of her own interests.
(M3) *Negative mutual expectations.* Any given Party i capable of pursuing interests obeys the requirements of S_N only because violating these requirements is a sufficient condition for losing at least some of the benefits of other parties' restrained conduct toward herself. That is, if Party i obeys the requirements of S_N, she does so because she expects that if she were to violate these requirements, then other parties would consequently reduce their restraint of their conduct with respect to her and her interests would consequently be less well satisfied. Moreover, if Party i violates the requirements of S_N, then the parties' subsequent reduction of their restraint with respect to Party i is compatible with the requirements of S_N (because Party i is a violator).

I will call σ_0^* the *free-for-all* or *baseline state.* As I did in Chapter 3, here I will use Gauthier's helpful terminology and call the additional benefits that members of society generate by following any system of rules that satisfies conditions (M1), (M2), and (M3) the *cooperative surplus.* I will assume that one contributes positively to the cooperative surplus exactly when one restrains pursuit of one's own interests somewhat in order to allow others to pursue their interests more effectively. I will also assume that if one violates the requirements of S_N by pursuing one's own interests without restraint when the others keep the requirements of S_N, then one subtracts from the cooperative surplus. It is important to note that any motivation parties might have for complying with the system's requirements is built into justice as mutual advantage. The Pareto improvement condition (M2) guarantees that if all who can comply with the requirements of S_N do comply, then those who have added to the cooperative surplus by their compliance receive benefits of the cooperative surplus and that they do better than they would do at the baseline of no restraint. But the negative mutual expectations requirement (M3) ensures that those who pursue their own interests without restraint are liable to be denied some of the benefits of the cooperative surplus. It is also important to note that conditions (M1)–(M3) do not presuppose that the members of society have only egoistic preferences. In addition to their own selfish concerns, members might wish to advance the conflicting agendas of various communities represented in society, such as political movements or religions. Even a society whose members' interests are purely altruistic can satisfy (M1)–(M3), same as such a society of perfect altruists can satisfy the conditions of the Generic Circumstances of Justice. Justice as mutual advantage requires only that the interests of the members of society both coincide and conflict to some

		Party 2	
		M	G
Party 1	M	$(2, 2)$	$(0, 3)$
	G	$(3, 0)$	$(1, 1)$

M = perform, G = defect

FIGURE 8.1 Prisoner's Dilemma

extent, again same as in the Generic Circumstances of Justice.[9] Contributors to the system improve their prospects over what they can expect in the free-for-all state σ_0^*, and the system requires the contributors to give in to the interests of others to some extent.

I have presented (M1)–(M3) as necessary conditions of justice as mutual advantage. I believe these conditions do not by themselves describe a full account of justice as mutual advantage. Figure 8.1 summarizes a Prisoner's Dilemma.[10] In this setting, N is a society of two. Suppose that these two parties are Bayesian rational and know the payoff structure of their Prisoner's Dilemma and that they have a system S_N consisting of a single rule: Follow M. Then conditions (M1)–(M3) are satisfied, but they will not follow the (M,M) outcome, even though both can infer that (M,M) is a Pareto improvement over (G,G).[11] By dominance reasoning they settle into the suboptimal (G,G) equilibrium, which characterizes their baseline state. In fact, Barry maintains that justice as mutual advantage has the structure of a Prisoner's Dilemma and consequently is unstable.[12] Here Barry blurs the distinction between the structure of interaction and the rules that are to regulate conduct in this interaction. But if he were correct in thinking that the relevant interaction structure is a Prisoner's Dilemma, then indeed justice as mutual advantage would be unstable. I think Barry is not correct. The interactions that any system of justice regulates in an actual society are too complex to be even roughly summarized by a single game. But one can use specific games to illustrate specific rules of justice. Figure 8.2 presents a Hawk-Dove game.[13] In Chapter 2 I used the Hawk-Dove game to analyze the problem of property acquisition. If the parties are Bayesian rational and know the structure of their Hawk-Dove game, then they

9. See the parallel discussion in §3.5.

10. This is the Figure 1.6 game with a relabeling of strategies and agents.

11. Condition (M3) is satisfied vacuously because the rule requiring one to perform specifies no specific conduct in case one's counterpart fails to perform.

12. Barry (1995), p. 51.

13. This is the Figure 2.5 game with a relabeling of agents.

		Party 2 M	Party 2 G
Party 1	M	$(6,6)$	$(2,7)$
	G	$(7,2)$	$(0,0)$

M = "dove," G = "hawk"

FIGURE 8.2 Hawk-Dove

can infer that both would fare better if both were to follow a requirement to follow the pure strategy M and try to share the good with the other than they would be were each to follow G in an attempt to claim ownership of the good. As is the case in the Prisoner's Dilemma, in Hawk-Dove (M,M) is a Pareto improvement over (G,G) but is not a stable outcome. In Hawk-Dove, neither (M,M) nor (G,G) is an equilibrium. But there are a variety of correlated equilibrium conventions available to the two parties in this Hawk-Dove game that are Pareto improvements upon the free-for-all (G,G) outcome.[14] One of these is the first finder convention described in Chapter 2 where the parties follow the outcomes (M,M), (G,M), and (M,G) with equal probability. This partially correlated equilibrium convention is characterized by the rule: Follow G when I ascertain I am first finder and follow M otherwise.[15] When both follow their parts of the first finder convention, each party restrains her conduct some of the time to allow the other to benefit more. So this rule satisfies the conditions (M1)–(M3), so far identified as necessary parts of justice as mutual advantage.

Of course, for actual human communities a single rule that settles questions of original ownership is but one part of a complete system of justice. But the first finder convention illustrates a more general point: If all of the rules of the system characterize equilibria of the relevant interactions, then the system of justice as mutual advantage is stable. So I propose an additional condition:

(M4) *Positive mutual expectations.* Any Party i capable of pursuing interests expects that if she follows the requirements of S_N, then the other parties will restrain their conduct with respect to her, as S_N requires.

---

14. Some argue that in a conflictual coordination game such as Hawk-Dove the baseline state should be the mixed Nash equilibrium rather than the fully unrestrained (G,G), on the grounds that the mixed Nash equilibrium is the best outcome the agents can expect to achieve if they fail to correlate their strategies. For Hawk-Dove, the Pareto optimal conventions such as the first finder conventions are Pareto improvements upon both (G,G) and the mixed Nash equilibrium.

15. See §2.3.

Given (M3) and (M4), a given member of the population does better to follow the requirements of S_N than to violate these requirements. So these conditions together guarantee that each requirement of the system defines an equilibrium of the relevant interaction. Not surprisingly according to the conditions (M1)–(M4) I identify as necessary conditions of justice, the rules of justice characterize special conventions according to the Chapter 2 analysis of convention. However, before continuing, I wish to note that the analysis that follows immediately below in this section and in §8.2–§8.5 does not require, as I require, that justice as mutual advantage be a stable social state. The arguments below prior to §8.6 will still apply if one supposes that justice as mutual advantage requires (M1), (M2), and (M3) only.

I must address one final and crucial point here. Condition (M4) implies that following the requirements of the system S_N is a sufficient condition for receiving the benefits of the compliance of others with the system. Is following the requirements also a necessary condition for receiving the benefits of the system? The answer to this question might seem obvious, as condition (M3) explicitly states that if one violates the requirements of the system, then one expects to lose out on some of its benefits. Much of the best recent literature on justice as mutual advantage does suppose that complying with the system is indeed a necessary condition for receiving the benefits of others' compliance. While Barry does not say so explicitly, some of his criticisms of justice as mutual advantage plainly imply that he thinks compliance is a necessary condition. In their discussions of justice as mutual advantage, Allen Buchanan and David Gauthier are explicit. Gauthier makes compliance a prerequisite for receiving benefits in his theory,[16] and Buchanan maintains that justice as mutual advantage in general is committed to this prerequisite.[17] I will state this prerequisite formally as the following:

(C*) *Contribution requirement.* S_N requires that parties will restrain their conduct with respect to a given Party i only if Party i increases the cooperative surplus by following the requirements of S_N herself.

In the discussion below I will attribute (C*) to Barry, Buchanan, and Gauthier. In the following section it will become apparent that all three recognize that

16. Gauthier (1986), p. 17. Gauthier repeats his view that noncontributors would have no rights on p. 268 of Gauthier (1986) and on p. 125 of his later essay "Mutual Advantage and Impartiality," in *Impartiality, Neutrality and Justice: Re-Reading Brian Barry's* Justice as Impartiality, ed. Paul Kelly (Edinburgh: Edinburgh University Press, 1998), pp. 120–136.

17. Buchanan (1990), pp. 230–231, and Allen Buchanan, *Justice, Legitimacy, and Self-Determination: Moral Foundations for International Law* (Oxford: Oxford University Press, 2004), p. 97.

the contribution requirement has implications for actual human societies that are unsettling, to put it mildly. Condition (C*) might look redundant in light of (M3). Indeed, (M3) would be redundant if each member necessarily either follows the requirements of the system or violates them. But to assume this is to overlook an important third possibility. Perhaps some members of society are simply unable to pursue interests at all. Such members might have interests, but they are in no position either to pursue these interests or to limit the pursuit of their interests through their own efforts. Once one admits this possibility, one must at once face the Vulnerability Objection.

§8.2. The Vulnerability Objection

I will define the *vulnerable* members of a society as those humans living in this society who are unable through their own efforts to contribute to the cooperative surplus. The vulnerable in a society might include very young children, some of the very elderly, the seriously ill, and the seriously injured. Individuals who live with severe and permanent disabilities turn out to be a particularly troublesome class of vulnerable members of society both for some critics of justice as mutual advantage and for some defenders of the theory. For the present, I will limit membership in society to humans, recognizing that some might wish to extend the analysis here to members of other species. I also recognize that this definition of vulnerability is not perfectly adequate. The ability to contribute to the cooperative surplus varies across several dimensions. A healthy adult is likely to be able to contribute more to her society's cooperative surplus than can a healthy ten-year-old child, who in turn is likely to be able to contribute more to the surplus than can a healthy three-year-old child. An adult battling a treatable form of cancer might be able to contribute less to the surplus than adults who are physically healthier, but more than someone who is so ill as to be continually bedridden. Additionally, Buchanan rightly argues that one's ability to contribute to the cooperative surplus can also vary according to the way one's society structures its frameworks for cooperation. For example, Buchanan argues that individuals who suffer from mild retardation and dyslexia might be vulnerable in a highly literate society where contributing to the cooperative surplus requires one to be able to follow complicated rules and practices often communicated in writing. Yet these same individuals might be able to contribute to the cooperative surplus as well as anyone in a hunter-gatherer society.[18] Perhaps out of politeness to the academic profession, Buchanan did not add that in all likelihood some university professors who could contribute in the literate society would be vulnerable in the hunter-gatherer society.

---

18. Buchanan (1990), p. 237.

In short, vulnerability is really best thought of as an attribute that any individual may have to a certain degree that can vary both according to one's particular society and according to one's individual circumstances. However, I will assume that if one holds the structures for cooperation of a given society fixed, then one can identify some members of this society as vulnerable in the sense given here, that is, these members of society cannot contribute to the cooperative surplus at all. This assumption is plausible for any sizable human society that endures for at least more than a single generation, and it is all that is needed to develop the Vulnerability Objection. One can state the objection quite simply: Justice as mutual advantage denies the vulnerable any of its advantages, which shows that justice as mutual advantage is in fact no proper account of justice at all. For those who are not instantly persuaded by this statement that justice as mutual advantage is a nonstarter, I supply a more developed argument.

P1. If a system of rules is merely a system of rules members of a society follow only for mutual advantage (that satisfy (M1), (M2) and (M3)), then the vulnerable members of society have no claim to any of the benefits of the cooperative surplus.
P2. By definition, a member of society is owed benefits of justice if, and only if, this member has some claim to some benefits of the cooperative surplus.
P3. So if justice is merely a system of rules that members of a society follow only for mutual advantage (that satisfy (M1), (M2) and (M3)), then the vulnerable members of society are not owed any benefits of justice.
P4. The vulnerable members of society are owed some benefits of justice.
C. So justice is not merely a system of rules that members of a society follow only for mutual advantage (that satisfy (M1), (M2) and (M3)).

The key moves in this argument are, of course, P3, P4, and the *modus tollens* conclusion. The preliminary P1 and P2 serve two purposes. P1 and P2 together clarify what it means to say that one is, or is not, owed the benefits of justice. More importantly, stating P1 explicitly makes it all the more clear that the Vulnerability Objection relies upon the contribution requirement. If ability to contribute to the cooperative surplus really is a prerequisite for receiving any of the benefits of others' contributions, then the vulnerable by definition are ineligible to receive any benefits.

Since I will later argue against the contribution requirement, I do not include it as a premise in the argument above. However, as noted already, some of the best critics and defenders of justice as mutual advantage maintain that this theory of justice must include the contribution requirement. And they take the Vulnerability Objection to be an especially serious, even fatal, problem for justice as mutual advantage.

§8.3. Three Unsatisfactory Responses

The task for a defender of justice as mutual advantage is clear. The defender must respond to the Vulnerability Objection without turning justice as mutual advantage into something else. A first response to the Vulnerability Objection is to simply accept that the vulnerable fall outside the scope of justice. Gauthier eventually bites the bullet and declares openly that the vulnerable in society indeed have no claim on any of the benefits of justice as mutual advantage.[19] One might claim that the Vulnerability Objection has no real force, because the objection assumes that the vulnerable are owed justice with no regard to mutual advantage. In other words, the Vulnerability Objection assumes what it allegedly proves, namely, that justice is not merely mutual advantage. Referring back to the §8.2 argument, defenders of justice as mutual advantage can complain that their critics assume the truth of P4 far too casually, and assert that P4 is simply false. And however vehemently some might attack justice as mutual advantage, those who reject P4 can point out that at least they are not hypocrites. With characteristic frankness, Ken Binmore, who in fact argues that justice as mutual advantage need not necessarily exclude the helpless, describes the conduct of many who claim to oppose justice as mutual advantage:

> The unwelcome truth is that practical morality—the morality by which we actually live—does in fact endorse the exploitation of those powerless to resist. We dismiss the homeless and the destitute as being an unfortunate consequence of the necessity that a productive society provide adequate incentives for its workers. Is this not to accept that an underclass must suffer in order that the rest of us can enjoy a higher standard of living? We do not, of course, say this openly. Instead, we square things with our consciences by dehumanizing those excluded from the feast.[20]

To be sure, not all critics of justice as mutual advantage accept this dismissal of the Vulnerability Objection.[21] But whether one accepts this first rebuttal or not, one can view the Vulnerability Objection in a different way. Even if one concedes that the objection has no a priori force, the objection raises a serious explanatory problem. A time-honored method for evaluating any account of justice is to

---

19. Gauthier (1986), pp. 268, 282–288. Here Gauthier calls justice as mutual advantage "a morality tied to mutuality" (1986, p. 268).

20. Binmore (1998), pp. 258–259.

21. Buchanan, for one, mounts a vigorous rebuttal to the claim that P4 has no basis in theory (1991, §III).

consider how well this account coheres with and explains certain commonly held beliefs regarding justice that for Sidgwick are parts of "the Morality of Common Sense" and for Rawls are *considered judgments*.[22] Rawls declares:

> These are questions we feel sure must be answered in a certain way. For example, we are confident that religious intolerance and racial discrimination are unjust. We think that we have examined these things with care and have reached what we believe is an impartial judgment not likely to be distorted by an excessive attention to our own interests. These convictions are the provisional fixed points which we presume any conception of justice must fit.[23]

Taken as an explanatory criticism, the Vulnerability Objection has bite, and on a standard otherwise favorable to justice as mutual advantage. Both defenders and critics of justice as mutual advantage argue that one of the chief advantages of this theory of justice is its explanatory power. Barry thinks that the main reason one should seriously examine justice as mutual advantage is its substantial overlap with our ordinary beliefs regarding justice.[24] But the overlap presumably does not extend to our beliefs regarding the vulnerable. Even Gauthier expresses some squeamishness regarding the way his theory treats, or rather fails to treat, the severely disabled. I suspect that, like the hostile critics of justice as mutual advantage, Gauthier believes that one considered judgment regarding justice is that the vulnerable are not to be denied the benefits of justice merely because they are vulnerable. One can counter the Vulnerability Objection by denying P4. But to deny P4 is to deny a considered judgment regarding justice. So if one tries this move, one should provide a convincing case that all who hold and have held this considered judgment are and always were mistaken. And this case had better include reasons other than the consequences of assuming that justice as mutual advantage is the right theory of justice. Here I side with Barry and the other critics of justice as mutual advantage who press the Vulnerability Objection. I think there are no such independent reasons for thinking that so many have been wrong and that the vulnerable really are owed no justice because of their vulnerability. So I find the first response to the Vulnerability Objection unacceptable.

Two other unsatisfactory responses to the Vulnerability Objection can be dealt with more quickly. One could deny that the vulnerable make no important

---

22. *Methods of Ethics*, pp. 214–215; Rawls (1971), pp. 20–21.

23. Rawls (1971), pp. 20–21.

24. Barry (1989), p. 163, (1995), p. 45 n. c.

contributions to the welfare of society. For instance, one could argue that since the vulnerable are incapable of violating the requirements of justice, they support the system of justice as mutual advantage in a passive manner.[25] I reject this proposal because I think such passive "contributions" would give those who can contribute positively to the cooperative surplus little reason to restrain their conduct with respect to the vulnerable. Indeed, these contributors might be tempted to regard the care and other resources the vulnerable need simply to continue living as a drain on the cooperative surplus, and consequently be tempted to withhold such care and resources from the vulnerable. One might claim that if contributors to the system for mutual advantage do not confer benefits to the vulnerable, then the contributors will be more tempted not to contribute to the system at all. But I see no reason to believe that this claim is true. Moreover, this claim assumes that one's willingness to comply with the requirements of the system for mutual advantage depends directly to a certain extent on how much of the benefits of the system the vulnerable receive, and this plainly goes against the negative mutual expectations requirement.

A variant of this response appeals to contributions that people value even though they do not add to the cooperative surplus. Mother Teresa once said, "The poor are wonderful. The poor are very kind. They have great dignity. The poor give us more than what we give them."[26] One might argue that even if the vulnerable cannot increase the material wealth of society or other parts of this society's cooperative surplus, they contribute invaluable intangibles such as love, and consequently should not be stigmatized as noncontributors. Love and similar goods are without doubt terribly important. Still, this variant is an unsatisfactory response to the Vulnerability Objection. Many of the vulnerable, such as those who are comatose, are just as incapable of expressing love or contributing other intangibles as they are of contributing to the cooperative surplus. So the scope of this variant appears to be too narrow. Is a system of justice satisfactory if this system extends some benefits to very young loving children but none to more mature persons whose conditions leave them unable to give goods such as love to others? Yet even if one sets this problem aside, the variant is still unsatisfactory. By definition, the intangible goods referred to here are not contributions to the cooperative surplus. If one appeals to such goods as reasons for extending benefits of justice, then one adopts an account of justice that is not a justice as mutual advantage account according to conditions (M1)–(M4).

---

25. My thanks to Ned McClennen and Susanne Sreedhar for suggesting this proposal and the underlying idea of the response given here.

26. Mother Teresa, *In My Own Words*, comp. Jose Luis Gonzalez-Balado (Ligouri, MO: Ligouri Publications, 1996), p. 83.

A third inadequate response is to argue that justice as mutual advantage will provide the benefits of justice to the vulnerable without requiring that their interests be taken into account directly. According to this line of reasoning, justice will protect the vulnerable because they have active advocates, such as their friends and families, who want the vulnerable protected and cared for. Gregory Kavka, for example, suggests that Hobbesian contractors would build provisions on behalf of the disabled into their system of justice. According to Kavka, these contractors would want their own disabled friends and family members covered in the system of justice. Moreover, as they are both a needy and a nonthreatening minority, the disabled would be likely targets of whatever sympathy or altruism the contractors might have.[27]

Christopher Morris presents a sophisticated account of *moral standing* to address the general problem of providing benefits for the vulnerable in a contractarian system of justice.[28] Kavka and Morris are not trying to rescue justice as mutual advantage as I characterize it here, but their work provides a basis for developing this response to the Vulnerability Objection. According to Morris' analysis, one has moral standing exactly when one is owed moral consideration by others.[29] Put another way, one has moral standing when others are obligated to treat one with some restraint, so that one receives some of the benefits of justice. Party i has *primary moral standing* with respect to Party j if Party i and Party j can restrain their conduct toward each other so that the other benefits and in fact Party i and Party j do restrain their conduct in this manner. Party i has *secondary moral standing* with respect to Party j if for some Party k, Party j has primary moral standing with respect to Party k and Party k would be unwilling to restrain her conduct toward Party j if Party j were to fail to restrain his conduct toward Party i so that Party i benefits. In this case Party i is an object of Party k's preferences, that is, Party k cares for Party i enough that Party k would be willing to punish someone who does not treat Party i with restraint.[30] So a contributor to the cooperative surplus could be required to treat a vulnerable individual with some restraint if the vulnerable individual has secondary moral standing. For example, one is required to treat an infant with some restraint if one has primary

---

27. Kavka (1986), p. 242.

28. Christopher Morris, "Moral Standing and Rational-Choice Contractarianism," in Vallentyne, ed. (1991), pp. 76–95; "Justice, Reasons, and Moral Standing," in Coleman and Morris, eds. (1998), pp. 186–207; and "The Idea of Moral Standing," in *The Oxford Handbook of Animal Ethics*, ed. Tom L. Beauchamp and R. G. Frey (Oxford: Oxford University Press, 2011), pp. 257–275.

29. Morris (1991), p. 81, (1998), p. 191.

30. Morris (1991), pp. 89–90.

moral standing with respect to the infant's parents and the parents love their child to a degree that makes their child an object of their preferences. As Morris notes, on this account moral standing is a relational concept. One could have moral standing with respect to some of the people with whom one interacts, but perhaps not with others, including those with whom one never interacts or who are unwilling to treat one with restraint.

Moral standing is an ingenious framework for analyzing the obligations in contractarian systems of morality. However, I think moral standing does not provide an adequate basis for responding to the Vulnerability Objection. One can appeal to secondary moral standing to explain why contributors to the cooperative surplus could have good reason to treat the vulnerable with restraint. The vulnerable cannot punish nasty individuals who treat them with no restraint, but others who are not vulnerable can punish these nasty individuals. Indeed, I will employ this idea of indirect punishment to enforce compliance with requirements of a justice as mutual advantage system in the following section. But secondary moral standing relies upon motivating forces such as altruism and affection that lie outside of the scope of justice as mutual advantage as this theory of justice is characterized by both its defenders and its critics. Vulnerable members of society have secondary moral standing when they have advocates who care for them to the degree that they are objects of their advocates' preferences. But if one "sweetens" the pool of motivating forces among the members of society to include enough altruism and affection to generate secondary moral standing, then it is no longer so clear that one can proceed within the framework of justice as mutual advantage given the explicit assumption of this general theory that parties obey the requirements of justice solely as a means to receiving benefits of the cooperative surplus. One cannot rescue justice as mutual advantage from the Vulnerability Objection by turning it into something quite different. Moreover, moral standing would introduce an element of partiality into the system of justice that jars with another considered judgment, namely, that justice should be impartial. If one employs the moral standing approach, then in the human societies we know of, many of the vulnerable would receive no benefits of justice simply because these vulnerable people have no family or friends. A final problem with moral standing, a problem Morris clearly acknowledges, is that this idea produces certain strikingly counterintuitive results. While secondary moral standing could explain why individuals who care nothing for the welfare of certain vulnerable people still have moral obligations to these vulnerable people, secondary standing cannot always account for the relevant moral obligations of the advocates of these vulnerable people. For example, if parents care for their infant child to a sufficient degree, then relative strangers who interact with the parents might have moral obligations to this infant due to secondary moral standing. But if no one other than the parents happens to care for this infant, then this infant has no moral standing with respect to her own parents. She is not capable of having primary moral standing with respect to her parents, and she also has no other advocates whose care for her would generate secondary moral standing with respect to her parents.[31] Because of its dependence upon the motivations, or lack thereof, of relevant third parties, moral standing can fail to ground the obligations of justice in sufficient generality. In particular, moral standing can fail to ground the duties family members have toward each other.

§8.4. The Indefinitely Repeated Provider-Recipient Game

I favor a different response to the Vulnerability Objection: Leave the contribution requirement out of the account of justice as mutual advantage. This move allows one to deny P1 in the §8.2 argument, so that this argument does not go through after all. But without the contribution requirement, can any system of rules still be a system of justice as mutual advantage? In this section I will show why one can give an affirmative answer to this question.

I begin by considering a community whose members interact repeatedly over discrete time periods. Community members are sometimes *active* and sometimes *inactive*. Members play the role of *provider* for a fraction $\alpha \in \left(2^{-1}, 2^{-\frac{1}{2}}\right)$ of the time periods when they are active, and of *recipient* the rest of the time. In particular, members are always recipients when inactive. At each period, every recipient is matched with a provider. The requirement that $\alpha > \frac{1}{2}$ ensures that every recipient has an available provider at every period. When she is a provider, an active member Party i produces a quantity V of a perishable good that can benefit herself as well as others in the community. An active recipient can destroy the good her current provider produces. An inactive recipient can do nothing. The benefit a member Party i receives from consuming a fraction λ of a provider's good is summarized by the payoff function $u_i(\lambda) = (\lambda V)^{\frac{1}{2}}$, reflecting Party i's diminishing marginal utility for additional increments of the good.[32] For the total number of periods Party i interacts in the community, ε_{i1} is the expected proportion of periods during which she is inactive, and ε_{i2} is the expected proportion of

31. Morris (1991), p. 95.

32. In Appendix 4 I show that the argument to follow can be extended to any increasing von Neumann–Morgenstern utility function $u_i(\lambda)$ with diminishing marginal utility such that $u_i\left(\frac{1}{2}\right) > \alpha u_i(1)$.

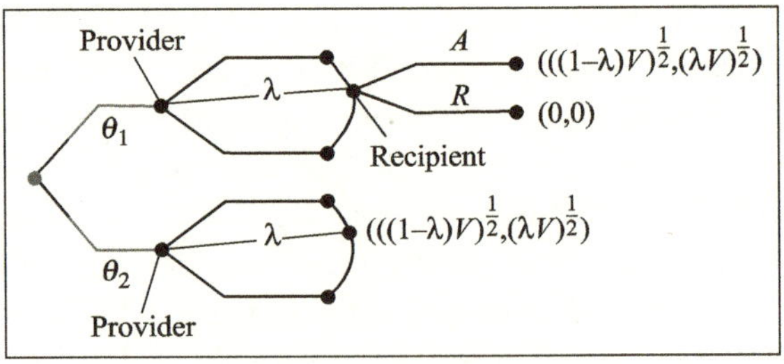

$\lambda \in [0,1]$, $A =$ accept, $R =$ reject

$\theta_1 =$ recipient is active, $\theta_2 =$ recipient is inactive

FIGURE 8.3 Provider-Recipient Game

periods that she is matched with an inactive recipient. Figure 8.3 summarizes the *Provider-Recipient* game that characterizes one of these pairwise encounters. In this game, "Nature" selects the type of recipient the provider meets. The Figure 8.3 game is similar to a game of incomplete information in that the parties fall into distinct subgames according to the party type selected by "Nature," but in this game the parties have no uncertainty regarding each other's payoffs at the possible outcomes. If the recipient is of θ_1-type, then this recipient is active. The provider can then offer any share $\lambda \in [0,1]$ and the recipient can then either *accept* the provider's offer (A), leaving the provider with $1-\lambda$, or *reject* the offer (R) and destroy the good. If the recipient is of θ_2-type, then this recipient is inactive and the provider simply takes whatever share $1-\lambda \in [0,1]$ of the good she likes, leaving whatever λ is left for the recipient. When the recipient is of θ_1-type, the proper subgame starting with the provider's move is an Ultimatum game. When the recipient is of θ_2-type, the degenerate proper subgame where the provider takes what she will is known among game theorists as a *Dictator* game because the provider's choice alone completely determines the outcome.

Next I compare the results in the indefinitely repeated Provider-Recipient game when all providers are *fully greedy*, each consuming all of the good she produces, and when all are *equitable*, so that each provider shares half of the good she produces with her current recipient. That is, a fully greedy provider offers $\lambda = 0$ and an equitable provider offers $\lambda = \frac{1}{2}$. The average payoff for a given Party i when all are fully greedy is $\alpha(1-\varepsilon_{i1})V^{\frac{1}{2}}$, since Party i receives a positive payoff only when she is a provider. On the other hand, if every provider is equitable, then every member of the community receives a one-half share of the good at every period, so the average payoff to each community member is $\left(\frac{1}{2}V\right)^{\frac{1}{2}} = 2^{-\frac{1}{2}} \cdot V^{\frac{1}{2}}$.

Since $2^{-\frac{1}{2}} > \alpha$, it follows immediately that $2^{-\frac{1}{2}} \cdot V^{\frac{1}{2}} > \alpha(1-\varepsilon_{i1})V^{\frac{1}{2}}$, so a community whose providers are all equitable achieves a Pareto improvement over a community whose providers are all fully greedy. What if the providers share only with their active recipients, who are able to punish their providers by rejecting offers they find unsatisfactory? If the members of the community follow this harsher pattern where inactive members receive nothing, then the average payoff for a given Party *i* is

$$\gamma_i = (1-\varepsilon_{i1})(1-\varepsilon_{i2}) \cdot 2^{-\frac{1}{2}} \cdot V^{\frac{1}{2}} + (1-\varepsilon_{i1})\varepsilon_{i2} \cdot V^{\frac{1}{2}}.$$

If $\varepsilon_{i1} = \varepsilon_{i2}$, that is, all members are inactive for the same portion of time periods, then $2^{-\frac{1}{2}} \cdot V^{\frac{1}{2}} > \gamma_i$ and so a community whose providers always share half the good with recipients Pareto dominates a community whose providers share half only with active recipients.[33] However, for reasons that will become apparent below, it is important to consider cases where ε_{i1} and ε_{i2} vary across members. In particular, if $\varepsilon_{i2} = 1$, so that Party *i* when active is always matched with an inactive partner, then if Party *i* follows the harsher pattern, her average payoff is $(1-\varepsilon_{i1})V^{\frac{1}{2}}$.[34] Note that even in this extreme case, $2^{-\frac{1}{2}} \cdot V^{\frac{1}{2}} > (1-\varepsilon_{i1})V^{\frac{1}{2}}$ when $\varepsilon_{i1} > 1-2^{-\frac{1}{2}} \approx 0.2929$.

Naturally, if any community member expects the other members to be equitable, this raises the possibility of free-riding. Why should Party *i* not take advantage of the others' generosity by being fully greedy when she is a provider? The community may be able to forestall free-riding if members follow this history-dependent strategy:

---

33. If $\varepsilon_{i1} = \varepsilon_{i2} = \varepsilon$, then

$$\begin{aligned}
(1-\varepsilon_{i1})(1-\varepsilon_{i1}) \cdot 2^{-\frac{1}{2}} V^{\frac{1}{2}} + (1-\varepsilon_{i1})\varepsilon_{i2} V^{\frac{1}{2}} &= (1-\varepsilon)^2 \cdot 2^{-\frac{1}{2}} V^{\frac{1}{2}} + (1-\varepsilon)\varepsilon V^{\frac{1}{2}} \\
&= 2^{-\frac{1}{2}} \cdot V^{\frac{1}{2}} + V^{\frac{1}{2}}\varepsilon\left(1-2^{\frac{3}{2}}+2^{-\frac{1}{2}}\varepsilon-\varepsilon\right) \\
&< 2^{-\frac{1}{2}} V^{\frac{1}{2}}
\end{aligned}$$

because $1-2^{\frac{3}{2}}+2^{-\frac{1}{2}}\varepsilon-\varepsilon<1$.

34. In this case, Party *i* never meets any active counterparts, so γ_i reduces to

$$\gamma_i = (1-\varepsilon_{i1})(1-1) \cdot 2^{-\frac{1}{2}} \cdot V^{\frac{1}{2}} + (1-\varepsilon_{i1}) \cdot 1 \cdot V^{\frac{1}{2}} = (1-\varepsilon_{i1}) \cdot V^{\frac{1}{2}}.$$

g^*: When a provider, always offer $\lambda = \frac{1}{2}$ to an *innocent* recipient and $\lambda = 0$ to a *guilty* recipient, and when an active recipient, follow A given the offer from an innocent provider and follow R given the offer of a guilty provider,

where a given Party i is innocent until she offers some value $\lambda < \frac{1}{2}$ when matched with an innocent recipient, at which point she becomes guilty. This strategy g^* requires active recipients to accept any offer, no matter how stingy, from an innocent provider and to reject any offer, no matter how generous, from a guilty provider and then to destroy all of the good the guilty provider has produced. The strategy g^* is obviously much like the Hobbesian-Humean strategies of repeated Covenant-type games, discussed in Chapter 7, that require one to perform in covenants with innocent partners and to shun guilty partners. I will refer to g^* as a Hobbesian-Humean strategy below. If Party i remains innocent, she receives an average payoff of $2^{-\frac{1}{2}} \cdot V^{\frac{1}{2}}$ over time. If, when a provider, Party i fails to offer at least half the good to an innocent recipient, then afterward the best this now guilty Party i can achieve is an average payoff of $(1-\varepsilon_{i1})V^{\frac{1}{2}}$, assuming she has the good luck to be matched always with inactive recipients after her offense. As shown in the last paragraph, this payoff can be worse than the average payoff of conforming to the Hobbesian-Humean strategy g^* when one's own proportion of inactive periods is sufficiently high. So each member of the community can have decisive reason to conform with this Hobbesian-Humean strategy. This informal argument is developed in more detail in Appendix 4. There it is shown that under fairly general conditions, the Hobbesian-Humean strategy g^* characterizes a folk theorem equilibrium of this system of repeated Provider-Recipient games.

What does this toy example show? This is a simple case of a community whose members can enjoy mutual benefits when they provide for the welfare of others at some personal cost. The state where all providers are always fully greedy corresponds to the free-for-all state where no one restrains conduct so that anyone else may benefit. This always fully greedy state is an equilibrium of the system, since the best average payoff any Party i can achieve if all her counterparts are always fully greedy providers is the payoff she achieves by being an always fully greedy provider herself. The state where all active members follow the Hobbesian-Humean strategy g^* can also be an equilibrium of this system, and this all-g^* state yields every member a higher average payoff than that of the always fully greedy state. The all-g^* folk theorem equilibrium of the Provider-Recipient game illustrates a very simple example of justice as mutual advantage, where the population is obligated to follow the single restraining requirement g^* so that each Party i must offer half the good she produces to her recipient when this recipient is innocent.

The Provider-Recipient game differs from many other game-theoretic examples of justice as mutual advantage in that members are not always able to affect the prospects of their counterparts. The key idea behind the Hobbesian-Humean all-g^* equilibrium is that a norm of sharing with all is enforced indirectly. A Party i who offensively violates this norm by being fully greedy in an encounter might not expect to be punished by the victim, who might be indefinitely or even permanently inactive. But such an offensive violator can expect other active community members to punish her. This underlying idea is of course analogous to the community enforcement of covenants that Hobbes and Hume discussed in their discussions of the obligations of promises and which is the object of so much research in contemporary social science. However, in this system of indefinitely repeated Provider-Recipient games, not every innocent community member is required to participate in the indirect punishment all of the time, and indeed at any particular time it is likely that some in the community are currently incapable of carrying out punishment. The indefinitely repeated Provider-Recipient game is also similar to some of the *overlapping generations games* studied by Peter Hammond, Ken Binmore, and V. Bhaskar.[35] In these earlier overlapping generations games, each agent enters into an indefinitely repeated base game, is active for a fixed number of periods and inactive for a fixed number of periods, and exits after completing all her active and inactive periods. These overlapping generations games have equilibria where agents share some of a good at stake when they are active and receive shares of the good when they are inactive. The indefinitely repeated Provider-Recipient game is more flexible than these earlier overlapping generations games, in part because this game allows the proportion of inactive periods across members to vary and even to occur at random. Hence, in the indefinitely repeated Provider-Recipient game, agents can follow an equilibrium at which all providers share with recipients even if some of the recipients can never be providers themselves. The presence of inactive members in the system mimics the facts that all humans are vulnerable at certain points in life and that some are vulnerable all their lives. In this system of repeated games, interacting parties might be inactive both early and late in their interaction histories, and might even be inactive intermittently throughout their interaction histories. This, of course, reflects the actual life histories of most humans who live into adulthood, and who are occasionally seriously ill or injured. The indefinitely repeated Provider-Recipient game even allows for the possibility that some members are

35. Peter Hammond, "Charity: Altruism or Cooperative Egoism?," in *Altruism, Morality and Economic Theory*, ed. Edmund S. Phelps (New York: Russell Sage, 1975), pp. 115–131; Binmore (1994), pp. 73–74, (1998), pp. 329–330; and V. Bhaskar, "Noisy Communication and the Evolution of Cooperation," *Journal of Economic Theory* 82 (1998), pp. 110–131.

never active. Permanently inactive members correspond to the severely disabled members of real human societies. The repeated game system shows that a society whose members work together only for mutual advantage can require that all its members receive the benefits of cooperation, even those members who can never contribute to the supply of these benefits. This system satisfies all of the conditions I have claimed are necessary conditions of justice as mutual advantage: (M1), (M2), (M3), and even (M4). Moreover, the all-g^* equilibrium is such that all parties, including the vulnerable, receive *equal* benefits. While I have not yet proposed any official conditions for which conventions qualify as parts of a justice as mutual advantage system, I will propose this simple system where N are all of the parties who can be in the role of either provider or recipient and S_N consists of the single requirement that active parties must follow the Hobbesian-Humean g^* strategy as part of such a system. Of course, I do not claim that the indefinitely repeated Provider-Recipient game even roughly approximates the cooperative structures of any actual human society. But the all-g^* Hobbesian-Humean equilibrium of this repeated game establishes the main point of this section: Justice as mutual advantage need not exclude the vulnerable from its benefits after all.

§8.5. Setting the Boundaries

I have argued that a system of justice as mutual advantage can require that all of the vulnerable in society receive some of the benefits of justice. The Hobbesian-Humean strategy equilibrium of the indefinitely repeated Provider-Recipient game of §8.4 shows that it is even possible that a justice as mutual advantage system provides the vulnerable with the same benefits of the cooperative surplus all the contributors receive. If I am right, then the Vulnerability Objection is not the "silver bullet" that liquidates justice as mutual advantage after all. To be sure, one must not slide into the conclusion that justice as mutual advantage will guarantee that the vulnerable are to receive adequate benefits of justice. That would be a mistake much like the mistake discussed in Chapter 7 of concluding that folk theorem arguments show that justice is necessarily prudentially rational. Human societies adopt many alternative systems of cooperative equilibria that settle the competing interests of their members in different ways. Such a system might provide benefits to only some of the vulnerable, or even to none. Or whatever benefits the vulnerable do receive might be inadequate, possibly even to the point that they are granted so little that their expected life spans are far shorter than the expected life spans of their contributing fellow community members.[36] This is

36. I will not attempt to give precise conditions for an adequate share of the cooperative surplus here. This is not necessary for the discussion in this section.

of course the sad lot of many of the vulnerable in many of the actual societies in human history. Perhaps no actual human society has yet adopted a system of social requirements that provides adequate benefits to all its vulnerable. All I maintain here is that nothing in the analysis of justice as mutual advantage offered here blocks this possibility. Justice as mutual advantage can ensure that the vulnerable receive adequate shares of the system of justice.

If society does follow a system of mutual advantage that benefits all of the vulnerable, then an important extension of the Vulnerability Objection is also avoided, or at least significantly mitigated. Suppose the system grants all some minimal immunity rights, including rights not to be killed or abused physically, and also grants all at least some of the means to sustain their lives. These are plausible requirements if one maintains that all are to benefit from the cooperative surplus. Then if the relatively powerful do tamper with the cooperative structures of society so that more of a targeted segment of the population become vulnerable, there are consequently more vulnerable mouths to feed. So according to the necessary conditions of justice as mutual advantage laid out in §8.1, no one would be tempted to create conditions that render any particular members vulnerable unless doing so somehow increases one's share of the cooperative surplus. This is conceivable if, for example, according to the system the costs of maintaining the vulnerable are so much lower than the costs of paying the least productive contributors their shares that one actually nets savings by turning the least productive into vulnerable members. I see no reason to think a society regulated by mutual advantage would have such a peculiar incentive structure. In any event, there will be no temptation to make targeted members of society vulnerable in a system that makes one responsible for the care of those one renders vulnerable and requires that the vulnerable receive at least as much from the cooperative surplus as the contributors who receive the smallest rewards in the system. A system of justice as mutual advantage that requires that the vulnerable receive benefits might even encourage the relatively powerful to alter the cooperative frameworks to make otherwise vulnerable members contributors.

At this point, one might object that I have "rescued" justice as mutual advantage from the Vulnerability Objection by illegitimately tinkering with the account of this general theory of justice that proponents such as Gauthier and critics such as Buchanan and Barry adopt. My preferred account of justice as mutual advantage replaces the contribution requirement with a weaker requirement, one that in effect requires only those who can contribute to the cooperative surplus to actually contribute. Does this not just allow me to get a desired result on the cheap? In fact, I think clinging to the contribution requirement leads to a surprise that gives an additional reason for relaxing this requirement. Before I discuss this surprise, I will first consider a different but related issue.

Philosophers who think the vulnerable are owed justice frequently reject justice as mutual advantage on the grounds that this theory of justice is too exclusive.

If one accepts conditions (M1)–(M4) outlined in §8.1 as necessary conditions of justice as mutual advantage, then one might have the reverse worry: Justice as mutual advantage might turn out to be too *inclusive*, at least for some. For if a system of justice as mutual advantage extends benefits to all of the vulnerable, then apparently every human in the community regulated by this system is to benefit, including those humans in the earliest stages of life and those in a persistent vegetative state. Indeed, one might also argue that if justice as mutual advantage has no contribution requirement, then a system of justice could require that all of the nonhuman creatures that can benefit from the cooperative surplus are to receive benefits.[37] However, a great many would object that this is casting too wide a net, including some philosophers who defend unusually inclusive accounts of which beings are to be treated with some restraint. Animal liberationists such as Peter Singer would approve of requirements in a system of justice as mutual advantage that forbid humans from factory-farming and then slaughtering chickens, pigs, and other animals belonging to many species now commonly factory-farmed and then killed for human consumption. New natural law theorists such as John Finnis would approve of requirements in such a system that forbid induced abortion of human fetuses and the destruction of so-called excess human embryos conceived in fertility clinics.[38] But neither Finnis, Singer, nor many of their intellectual allies would approve of justice as mutual advantage if this theory of justice sets no limits at all on the class of beings that are to receive the benefits of justice.

I do not think the potential inclusiveness of justice as mutual advantage is a problem for the theory in principle. But I admit that there may be no determinate way to set limits on the scope of justice as mutual advantage that many will want to set if one uses only the resources of this theory of justice. One might try to exclude nonhuman animals by arguing that only humans can benefit from the system in a particular way. For example, one might claim that only humans can benefit from certain basic liberties, such as freedom of thought, freedom of one's own person, and the right to own property, that the system can protect on behalf of its members and which John Rawls argues support the especially important good of self-respect.[39] But I believe such a move steps outside of justice as mutual advantage. Even if certain benefits of the system such as goods that purportedly underwrite

37. Such a system might resemble the system Martha Nussbaum develops in *Frontiers of Justice* (2006), where some nonhuman creatures are extended benefits of the cooperative surplus. Of course, I do not claim that Nussbaum endorses justice as mutual advantage.

38. I should perhaps add that the new natural law theorists generally condemn the in vitro conception of human embryos in fertility clinics and research laboratories, although they maintain that these embryos should not be deliberately killed after they are conceived.

39. Rawls (1971), §11, §29, §67.

self-respect are characteristically human benefits, this alone is not a good reason to discriminate against nonhuman creatures from a purely justice as mutual advantage perspective. Why not conclude that any of the creatures that can benefit from any of the goods of the cooperative surplus are eligible for shares of those goods that can benefit them? For that matter, why not conclude instead that the system should be redesigned so as to produce only benefits that all sentient creatures can enjoy? Perhaps humans do have some special status implying that only they can be owed justice. But what would confer such status uniquely upon humans? To argue, as some do, that only humans have immortal souls, or that only humans have genuinely free will, or that God values humans above all other creatures might be to argue that humans indeed are distinct in some important way from other living creatures. But using metaphysical claims of this sort as the basis for making the beneficiaries of justice a "humans-only club" transforms the theory of justice under consideration into something radically different from justice as mutual advantage, unless these claims imply that humans are all equals according to the relevant metaphysical criteria. Otherwise the resulting system ends up resembling Plato's Kallipolis more than a justice as mutual advantage system. On exactly what metaphysical grounds would humans be both equal with respect to each other and so superior to all nonhuman creatures that only the humans are worthy of the benefits of justice? Suppose, for example, one were to first claim that in God's sight, all humans are equal and all nonhuman animals are inferior to humans, and then to conclude that consequently the community of those eligible to receive the benefits of justice is bounded so that humans are "in" and nonhumans "out." Then the corresponding system of justice could possibly be a justice as mutual advantage system. But such a rationale for setting this membership boundary could only work for a community if all its constituent humans capable of understanding it were willing to accept that their membership rests upon claims, like this claim about God's regard for humans and other species, that are contentious, to understate the matter. One fundamental reason for taking justice as mutual advantage so seriously as a conception of justice is that this is one of the conceptions that can avoid importing this sort of controversial metaphysical baggage.

In fact, I think the view that nonhuman creatures cannot be owed justice is another considered judgment regarding justice, although this judgment is challenged in our time more frequently than in times past. This considered judgment has a long history in philosophy, which one can trace backward in time in the writings of figures such as Rawls, Kant, Hume, Hobbes, Aquinas, Epicurus, and Aristotle.[40]

40. Rawls, *A Theory of Justice*, §77; Kant, *Anthropology from a Pragmatic Point of View*, Academy Edition, Volume 7, p. 127; Hume, *Enquiry* 3.1:19; Hobbes, *Leviathan* 14:22; Aquinas, *Summa Contra Gentiles*, Book III, Part II, Chapter 112; Epicurus, *Principal Doctrines* XXXII; Aristotle, *Nicomachean Ethics* 1137a26–30.

The various arguments philosophers such as these have offered for excluding nonhuman creatures from justice share a core idea. In *Politics* Aristotle asserts that "it is peculiar to human beings, in comparison to the other animals, that they alone have perception of what is good or bad, just or unjust, and the rest."[41] Most philosophers over the centuries have accepted Aristotle's empirical claim or a more refined version of it: Only humans have the capacity for a sense of justice. Some, such as Rawls, then conclude directly that nonhuman animals fall outside the scope of justice. Others including Epicurus, Hobbes, and Hume incorporate this idea when they argue that nonhuman animals are excluded from justice because they cannot participate in creating the requirements of justice or deliberately obey or disobey these requirements. What matters for the many who accept some version of Aristotle's claim is that humans are presumably naturally superior to nonhuman animals in a way that renders nonhuman animals nonbeneficiaries of justice. To be sure, one can also argue that even if justice does not protect nonhuman creatures, these creatures still should be treated with some restraint, and Aquinas, Hume, and Rawls do just this. But they also make it clear that any such requirements with respect to nonhuman creatures are rooted in compassion, in humanity, or even in an indirect concern for other humans, not in justice. Those who in our time propose extending the boundary of justice to include at least some nonhuman species question the inclusionary standard of having some capacity for a sense of justice or the empirical claim that only humans can meet this standard. Whether one agrees with this traditional rationale for excluding nonhuman creatures or not, the relevant point here is that this standard is not built into the necessary conditions of justice as mutual advantage as I have characterized these conditions. Moreover, granting, as Rawls does, that a sense of justice is an attribute a being might possess to a certain degree,[42] like an ability to converse in a language, then this standard raises questions of vagueness that are also not answered by appealing to these necessary conditions. What is the minimum degree of a sense of justice beings must have the capacity to reach in order to be included as beneficiaries of the system of justice? What precisely can count as satisfactory evidence that a being has some capacity for a sense of justice to at least this minimal degree? Questions such as these have no easy answers, particularly when one has not yet settled upon a clear answer to the question "What is justice?" And if such questions are answered in a certain way, then members of some nonhuman species could fall within the boundary of inclusion and be afforded benefits of justice.

All this underscores how hard it may be to justify setting a boundary that excludes nonhuman creatures from the benefits of the cooperative surplus,

---

41. Aristotle, *Politics* 1253a15.

42. Rawls (1971), p. 505.

assuming that is what one wants. Of course, some may object to extending the boundary of inclusion to encompass all of the humans. One might propose, for example, that human embryos and at least some of the more developed human fetuses lie outside the system of justice on the grounds that these humans are not persons. According to this now familiar line of argumentation, human embryos, human fetuses, and even newly born human infants cannot be persons because they cannot function in certain ways thought to be characteristic of personhood, such as having awareness of one's own existence as a continuing individual and forming and having plans for one's own life.[43] To be sure, such a *functionalist* standard, sometimes also called a *performance* or *achievement* standard, can be applied to exclude from the class of persons certain humans who have ceased functioning "well enough" after having qualified as persons in earlier periods of their lives. As is now very old news in bioethics, humans identified as having fallen into a persistently vegetative state could fall outside the class of persons, according to such a standard. I happen to doubt that inability to function in special ways such as these is proof that a being is not a person.[44] But even if one could establish on either functionalist grounds or some other grounds that some humans are not persons, to claim that personhood is a prerequisite for inclusion in the system of justice is to again appeal to a criterion that is not intrinsic to justice as mutual advantage.

An account of how to set the inclusion boundary is no more intrinsic to justice as mutual advantage than is an account of equilibrium selection to the Nash and correlated equilibrium concepts of game theory. But this observation points to how a justice as mutual advantage theorist might go about setting this boundary, namely, in terms of certain salient characteristics of beings that determine which of these beings are "in" and which are "out." In earlier chapters I discussed one form of salience that agents engaged in a game can use to single out an equilibrium to follow. There is another form of salience that in effect picks out those who are counted as agents in the games that characterize the social situations that call for regulation by norms of justice. The requirements of a justice as mutual advantage system characterize equilibria that community members maintain with their compliance.

---

43. Michael Tooley launched this literature with his classic 1972 article "Abortion and Infanticide," *Philosophy and Public Affairs* 2 (1972), pp. 37–65. A fine gateway to some of the most important parts of this now large literature is Section 4 of Agnieszka Jaworska and Yue Tennenbaum, "The Grounds of Moral Status," *The Stanford Encyclopedia of Philosophy*, summer 2013 ed., ed. Edward N. Zalta, http://plato.stanford.edu/archives/sum2013/entries/grounds-moral-status.

44. For a fine recent discussion of the pitfalls of such functionalist analyses of personhood, see Christopher Kaczor, *The Ethics of Abortion: Women's Rights, Human Life, and the Question of Justice*, 2nd ed. (New York: Routledge, 2015).

Hobbes would say that obeying these requirements reflects the principle "You shall love your neighbor as yourself."[45] If any community member who wishes to know how to obey correctly asks, "And who is my neighbor?," one can answer, "Any being like yourself," or, to be more clear, "Any being like yourself in certain psychologically prominent respects." For example, the community falling within the inclusion boundary could consist of all of the resident humans, including possibly the resident fetal humans, since these humans are so similar to this curious member and to each other, being of the same species and being capable of enjoying benefits and of suffering harms in such similar ways. To be sure, one could propose a different criterion for drawing the boundary, say, by including exactly those creatures that currently have the capacity for feeling physical pain and pleasure. That boundaries much or even exactly like the boundary that includes all resident humans, or at least all resident born humans, in fact are in place in many actual systems of justice while boundaries such as the one suggested in some of Peter Singer's works have not gained wide acceptance is not hard to explain in salience terms. One can argue that boundaries like the all-resident-humans boundary tend to prevail over other sorts of boundaries like a capacity-for-physical-pain boundary because membership in the very species that creates and maintains the requirements of justice is both psychologically prominent and unambiguous in ways that the criteria of these other boundaries are not. I acknowledge that this sort of salience explanation of how inclusion boundaries are set perhaps takes aboard ideas similar to the contribution requirement, since contributors to the cooperative surplus are presumably also those having the power to enforce these boundaries. But if this is a problem at all, it is not a problem unique to justice as mutual advantage, since salience explanations could be used to define the inclusion boundary in other theories of justice. Moreover, justice as mutual advantage is not committed to such salience explanations, although in fact I think these sorts of explanations of the inclusion boundary dovetail well with this theory of justice. In any event, as shown in the §8.4 analysis of the indefinitely repeated Provider-Recipient game, justice as mutual advantage is by no means committed to an inclusion boundary that extends benefits exactly to those who meet the contribution requirement. In fact, one might plausibly argue that the criterion of being a resident human is more salient than that of being a resident contributor, since, as noted in §8.2, ability to contribute to the cooperative surplus is a matter of degree and consequently might be harder for community members to use as the basis for setting the inclusion boundary than the unambiguous human species membership criterion.

This last claim might shock many who have engaged in the long debates over the moral permissibility of abortion and various forms of euthanasia and the

45. See *De Cive* 17:8. Versions of this biblical commandment are stated in Leviticus 19:18, Matthew 22:39, and Luke 10:27.

more recent debate over the in vitro creation and subsequent treatment of human embryos in laboratories and fertility clinics. Many contributors to these debates have argued with great vigor that mere membership in the human species cannot confer any rights, including of course the immunity right against being killed. As already discussed above, some propose functionalist criteria for distinguishing human persons who can have rights from other humans who cannot. But the various proposed functionalist criteria, such as self-awareness, problem-solving ability, or having life plans, raise serious puzzles. Like the sense of justice that Aristotle claims is characteristic of humans and like the ability to contribute to the cooperative surplus, these functionalist criteria can all be satisfied to a certain degree and are consequently somewhat ambiguous. Moreover, there is the well-known problem of functional intermittence. Even mature humans ordinarily capable of exercising the proposed functions maximally do not in fact exercise these functions all of the time, and they might not even have the capacity for exercising these functions all of the time. Someone unconscious following a concussion, under general anesthesia, in a reversible coma, or merely in a deep dreamless sleep might temporarily lack the capacity for performing various proposed functions, but no one claims that such an individual temporarily loses her status as a rights-bearing individual until she regains full consciousness. But then just why would someone who loses these capacities permanently also lose her status as a rights-bearing individual? And for that matter, why would a developing human who is yet too immature to have acquired these capacities not be a rights-bearing individual merely for lack of a history of having these capacities and exercising these functions? Yet another problem for the functionalist approach to attempt to distinguish between humans who are persons and those who are not is that no one set of functionalist criteria appears to be *the* set of functionalist criteria that establishes personhood. Indeed, some of those who adopt this approach frankly admit to having difficulty giving sufficient conditions for personhood according to functionalist criteria. They argue that for practical purposes, functionalist criteria serve for specifying necessary conditions for personhood, so a being who fails to fulfill any of the items on a certain list of such criteria is disqualified from the class of persons.[46] But even if one could without difficulty use one or more of these functionalist criteria to identify some humans as falling out of the class of persons, who would fall *in* according to criteria of this sort? Proponents of functionalist accounts of human person have their answers to all of these questions.[47]

46. Probably the best-known work representing this position is Mary Anne Warren's essay "On the Moral and Legal Status of Abortion," *Monist* 57 (1973), pp. 43–61.

47. Following her landmark *Monist* essay, Warren herself developed a complex account of moral status that incorporates a variety of criteria, not all of which are functionalist, and which

I certainly do not claim it would be impossible to set the boundary of inclusion using functionalist criteria. But I do think that using the best-known proposed functionalist criteria for this purpose is liable to produce a boundary many would continually challenge as at least somewhat vague and therefore hard to apply.

So if, as I believe is quite plausible, a community is likely to settle upon an inclusion boundary on the basis of salience, then in the end functionalist criteria might fail to serve as the basis for setting this boundary. As I have just indicated, functionalist criteria are somewhat ambiguous and also of dubious psychological prominence. I think this is borne out by our difficulties answering the question "Who *are* persons?" in terms of functionalist criteria. What other kinds of criteria could serve for setting the inclusion boundary? Some of the other traditionally proposed criteria for granting at least the immunity right against being killed, such as viability, sentience, or the ability to move, are also ambiguous, hard to detect in certain circumstances, not characteristic of humans, or all of the above. I think a more recently proposed criterion, some form of brain activity, is gaining a certain salience. Some already seriously consider brain activity a criterion marking the onset and cessation of rights-bearing for humans.[48] Brain activity is closely connected with how persons characteristically function and in particular how persons *think*. But unlike thinking and other forms of activity commonly found on functionalists' criteria lists, brain activity is not discontinuous. And with proper equipment brain activity is unambiguously detectable. On the other hand, brain activity simpliciter is not characteristically human and the forms of brain activity involved in functioning as only persons allegedly function are not fully understood and develop only gradually. So for the time being, I think brain activity has insufficient salience for serving as the criterion for drawing the inclusion boundary, although I think this could change as understanding develops of various forms of brain activity and the ability to detect these activities easily and cheaply improves.

---

can be applied to analyze the possible moral status of nonhuman creatures as well as humans of varying functional capacities. See Mary Anne Warren, *Moral Status: Obligations to Persons and Other Living Things* (Oxford: Clarendon Press, 1997).

48. Baruch Brody gave an early defense of the view that brain activity is the criterion that establishes certain crucial rights in various works, especially *Abortion and the Sanctity of Human Life: A Philosophical View* (Cambridge, MA: MIT Press, 1975). Following Brody's foundational work, a number of authors have argued that organized cortical brain activity is a necessary condition for a human to have an immunity right against being killed. For two fine recent defenses of this latter position, see David Boonin, *A Defense of Abortion* (Cambridge: Cambridge University Press, 2003), §3.6, and Jeff McMahan, *The Ethics of Killing: Problems at the Margins of Life* (Oxford: Oxford University Press, 2002), especially §1.5 and §4.1–2.

In the meantime, in my opinion the two currently most salient criteria for determining the inclusion boundary are (i) membership in the class of living born humans and (ii) membership in the class of all living humans, both born and unborn. These criteria are unambiguous, easy to verify, and I think without doubt psychologically prominent. The criterion of birth is obviously salient, if for no other reason than the fact that humans immediately following birth began to interact with other humans in profoundly new ways for the rest of their lives. But conception, which marks the beginning of membership in the human species, is also psychologically prominent. Evidence for the psychological salience of conception is the fact that all who are engaged seriously in the abortion and in vitro fertilized embryos debates, including those who conclude that the immature humans in question do not in fact have rights, regard the questions of fetal and embryonic rights as worthy of careful consideration. If anything, I believe the salience of conception is greater than in times past, given the modern understanding of conception as the union of the effectively equal biological contributions of a woman and a man resulting in a genetically original human. True, conception has certainly not won as a defining criterion of inclusion in modern cultures. But unless some more salient set of inclusion criteria emerges, I believe conception together with birth will remain the most serious contenders.

Some may in the end think it rather odd that membership in the community of beings who are owed benefits of justice could depend upon salience, rather than some other, grander standards. But if one sticks with a commitment to limiting the theories of justice under serious consideration to those that do not rest upon robust and controversial metaphysical premises, then frankly no grander criteria of inclusion are likely to be available. And from the specific perspective of justice as mutual advantage, setting the inclusion boundary via salience seems quite natural. Hume would remind us that many of the specific rules of justice that regulate actual societies might seem much like superstitions, and that in a conventionalist account of justice such as his, communities settle into many of these rules according to the guidance of seemingly mundane precedents, analogies, and relationships that in fact express general principles of salience.[49] Again, if salience can serve to pick out some of the equilibria of norms of justice in the relevant games, why should salience not also serve to pick out who can be the agents in these games?

Now I am ready to return to the charge that I should not have dropped the contribution requirement. I think that authors such as Barry, Buchanan, and Gauthier quite naturally conclude that justice as mutual advantage includes the contribution requirement because so many of the most important accounts of

---

49. *Enquiry* 3.2:35–38, *Treatise* 3.2.3.

justice as mutual advantage, from Glaucon's account in *Republic* to Gauthier's account in *Morals by Agreement*, are expressly contractarian. And one might think that if a member of society can be a contractor, then she can be a contributor. Suppose these and like-minded authors reject my claim that justice as mutual advantage can extend benefits to the vulnerable, and insist I include the contribution requirement. If I restore this requirement, so that justice as mutual advantage must satisfy at least (M1), (M2), (M3), and (C*), then I agree that the Vulnerability Objection is unanswerable. However, I now draw upon a distinction seldom made in discussions of justice with respect to the vulnerable, namely, the distinction between the permanently vulnerable and the intermittently vulnerable. Gauthier hints at this distinction when he says that his version of justice as mutual advantage might extend benefits to the aged but not to the severely disabled.[50] Gauthier gives only the beginnings of an argument for this claim, but his insights are crucial. The aged in his system can receive benefits because they have already contributed to the cooperative surplus. Gauthier assumes that the severely disabled are never able to contribute to the surplus, and consequently are ineligible to receive benefits. According to Gauthier, the contribution requirement necessarily excludes only the permanently vulnerable. Indeed, justice as mutual advantage cannot exclude all of the intermittently vulnerable. Many of us are vulnerable late in life, many are vulnerable for limited amounts of time long before the end of life, and we are all vulnerable very early in life. So at least some of the intermittently vulnerable must receive benefits if anyone receives benefits. Again Gauthier has the key insight. An intermittently vulnerable member of society can be eligible for benefits from the cooperative surplus, even when this member is vulnerable, because this member fulfills the contribution requirement when she is not vulnerable. The Melians have a similar insight in their exchange with the invading Athenians.[51] The Melians warn these Athenians not to treat them unjustly even though they are currently helpless, because if these Athenians yield to the temptation to breach justice and wreak destruction upon the Melians, then they and the rest of the Athenians cannot expect just treatment should they ever find themselves helpless in the future. The Melians rely upon the idea that vulnerable parties can be eligible to receive the benefits of justice, and that currently nonvulnerable parties can forfeit this eligibility by violating the requirements of justice.

I suggest that Gauthier's insight leads to a conclusion some will find unsettling: In a society that rigorously enforces the contribution requirement, the

---

50. Gauthier (1986), p. 18 n. 30.

51. The exchange between the Athenians and the Melians that Thucydides reports in *The History of the Peloponnesian War* is discussed above in §1.1 and §1.3.

severely disabled are owed no benefits, but most if not all the unborn are owed some benefits. Again, I think it plausible that these benefits include at the very least immunity rights against being killed or otherwise physically abused and rights to sufficient resources to sustain life.[52] Gauthier in fact declares that the unborn fall outside the scope of a morality based upon mutual advantage.[53] But this conclusion need not follow from the contribution requirement. Gauthier allows that the aged might receive benefits in payment for past contributions to the cooperative surplus.[54] Binmore shows with an overlapping generations game example that a requirement to reward community members who can no longer produce for their past contributions can be part of a social equilibrium.[55] The indefinitely repeated Provider-Recipient game of §8.4 also shows this, but it shows more. As shown in §8.4, the individuals in the Provider-Recipient game can follow an equilibrium where providers share with all recipients, including the permanently inactive. But they can follow another equilibrium in which providers are required to share only with the intermittently inactive. In this equilibrium, the rule is once more "Share with the innocent and punish the guilty," but the conditions for guilt and innocence are now different. Permanently inactive members are now guilty by definition. An intermittently inactive member remains innocent so long as she shares half of the good she produces when she is a provider and when matched with an innocent recipient, who by definition also must be intermittently inactive. This equilibrium incorporates the contribution requirement. And this equilibrium does not reward past contributions only. The equilibrium also rewards expected future contributions. If community members are inactive in the early periods of their lifetimes, then providers share with them in these early periods because they expect these currently inactive members to reciprocate when they become active. Similarly, if aged persons in a contribution-requirement-based society can receive benefits in payment for past contributions, then gestating fetuses can receive benefits in down payment for expected future contributions.[56] But the permanently severely disabled would still receive no benefits at all.

---

52. A corollary that many would also find unsettling is that in such a society, abortion rights might be limited or even nonexistent, since the fetus a pregnant woman carries is expected to be a contributor later in life. However, in such a society a pregnant woman might have the right to insist that the fetus she carries be removed from her body if the fetus could be placed in a different life-sustaining environment such as an artificial womb.

53. Gauthier (1986), p. 268.

54. See note 50.

55. Binmore (1994), pp. 73–74, (1998), pp. 329–330.

56. There would most likely be exceptions. Any fetuses known, perhaps by genetic screening, to have conditions that render them permanently vulnerable would have no rights in this system.

This possibility is another considered-judgment reason for rejecting the contribution requirement. Opponents of abortion rights press what they regard as a consistency criterion of minimal immunity rights, namely, that if all of the born children have a serious right not to be killed, then the unborn must have this right as well. Indeed, antiabortion activists frequently use terms such as "unborn children" or "unborn babies" to refer to unborn humans in order to emphasize their view that the unborn have the very same immunity right against being killed that all infants and older children presumably have after they are born. As legions of students who enroll in applied ethics courses are informed, many proponents of abortion rights deny this alleged consistency claim, including many who are careful to acknowledge that human embryos and fetuses are members of the same species to which human infants, older children, and adults also all belong. I think it is far less well appreciated that both opponents and proponents of abortion rights generally accept another claim: No born children are to be granted *less* from a system of justice than are any of the unborn. I take this claim to be a considered judgment regarding justice. And without taking a poll of those who have seriously considered the issues of abortion and infanticide and more generally the minimal rights, if any, of children and the unborn, I am confident that even many of those who deny that both the unborn and newly born infants have a serious right to life will not challenge this claim. And given how I have stated it, the contribution requirement, when rigorously enforced, will lead to flagrant violations of the claim. Unless one is prepared to argue that this is a claim that should be demoted from considered judgment status, one should be willing to drop the contribution requirement.

§8.6. Too Many Equilibria?

So far I have argued that the contribution requirement is not a necessary part of justice as mutual advantage. So a justice as mutual advantage theorist need not plead guilty to the charge that according to her preferred theory of justice the vulnerable are sure to be owed nothing. But opponents of justice as mutual advantage can raise a related and in my opinion more serious charge. Brian Barry presents the basics of this charge, although not quite in the way I will state it myself. In his discussions of justice as mutual advantage, Barry insists this theory necessarily allows the terms of agreement to depend upon differences in bargaining power.[57] As a consequence, argues Barry, many social regimes that anyone should regard as plainly unjust are in fact justice as mutual advantage systems. For those who fall low on the relative bargaining power scale can expect to receive correspondingly

57. See Barry (1989), §1, (1995), §7, and §III of "Something in the Disputation not Unpleasant," in Kelly, ed. (1998), pp. 186–257.

small shares of the cooperative surplus. One can view the Vulnerability Objection as a special case where some parties have no bargaining power at all and therefore are purportedly entitled to no shares of the cooperative surplus. The upshot of the §8.4 discussion is that community enforcement conventions can extend benefits from the cooperative surplus to community members who are powerless. However, the most I or any other defender of justice as mutual advantage can assert on the basis of this discussion is that all members of a given society, including the completely powerless, may be extended *some* benefits of justice. The necessary conditions of justice as mutual advantage summarized in §8.1 do not themselves rule out distributions of benefits that are so asymmetric across the members of society, both vulnerable and nonvulnerable, that only a Thrasymachus would with a straight face declare them examples of justice.

Ancient Sparta is but a single example of the many long-lived social regimes in human history that satisfy the §8.1 conditions of justice as mutual advantage and where many of its members receive benefits that only barely improve their condition with respect to the baseline. The helots of ancient Sparta undoubtedly contributed greatly to the cooperative surplus of their regime and did receive some of its benefits, as their Spartiate masters did treat them with some minimal restraint. And one could argue that all who obeyed the requirements of this regime were better off than they would have been in the free-for-all state of no reciprocal restraint at all. But who would laud the Spartiate regime as just? Evidently not the helots themselves, since they rebelled against their masters several times, even after they had suffered savage reprisals following unsuccessful rebellions. And yet the Spartiate regime appears to qualify as a justice as mutual advantage system. If the Spartiate regime so qualifies, then the rebellious helots were simply mistaken in thinking their subordinate status was unjust. If one extends this conclusion to the rest of the social regimes of human history, then a great many of the have-nots of these regimes apparently were or have been flat-out wrong to complain, protest, and even rebel against their regimes on the grounds of injustice. Should not the long laundry list of serfdoms, slaveries, and other institutionalized deep inequalities of the "mutually beneficial" regimes of human history embarrass the justice as mutual advantage theorist?

A perhaps simpler example of grossly asymmetric power where the interaction is of limited duration is the encounter recounted by Thucydides between the Athenians and the Melians. The Figure 1.15 extensive form game summarizes in a rough manner the structure of the interaction problem facing the Athenians and the Melians following the arrival of the invading Athenian force. As discussed in §1.3, had both sides accepted that they were in effect engaged in the Figure 1.15 game and had they followed ordinary backward induction reasoning, then they would have followed the unique equilibrium outcome where the Athenians attack and the Melians surrender without a fight. The fact that the Melians did have

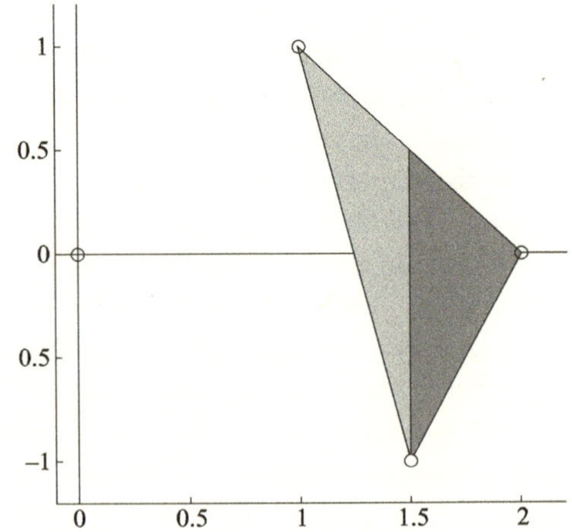

FIGURE 8.4 Feasible Set of the Melian Invasion Game I

some minimal power to resist explains why the Athenians bothered to negotiate before they attacked, and this minimal power can be reflected in a corresponding bargaining problem. Figure 8.4 depicts the feasible payoff set that is defined by the Figure 1.15 game. Given the nonagreement point $\left(\frac{3}{2},-1\right)$, corresponding to the $(A,R\text{-if-}A)$ outcome of the Figure 1.15 game where the Athenians attack and the Melians resist, the Melians do have some minimal bargaining power in this bargaining problem. By resisting when attacked, the Melians lower the Athenians' payoff relative to the outcome $(2,0)$, corresponding to the $(A,S\text{-if-}A)$ outcome in the Figure 1.15 game where the Athenians attack and the Melians surrender. But this minimal bargaining power is evidently too weak to do the Melians much good. The dark shaded region of the Figure 8.4 feasible set where both sides fare at least as well or better than they fare at the nonagreement point $\left(\frac{3}{2},-1\right)$ excludes the $(1,1)$ point corresponding to where both sides remain at peace. The only outcome corresponding to the best-known solution concepts of axiomatic bargaining theory is the point $(2,0)$.[58] Technically, rules that require the Melians and

58. Given the nonagreement point $\left(\frac{3}{2},-1\right)$, the Nash and the Kalai-Smorodinsky solutions coincide at $(2,0)$. If this feasible set is extended to be comprehensive, so that each side is effectively permitted to discard any of the gains it receives, then $(2,0)$ is also the *leximin solution*, an extension of the egalitarian solution. See Thomson and Lensberg (1989), Chapter 9, for a definition and analysis of the leximin solution concept.

Athenians to follow their parts of the corresponding $(A, S\text{-if-}A)$ outcome satisfy the conditions of a justice as mutual advantage theory laid out in §8.1. But many, including myself, would agree with the Melians that justice requires the Athenians to follow P so that both sides remain at peace.

Now, a natural way to try to rescue justice as mutual advantage from such presumably unacceptable consequences parallels the folk theorem response to Hobbes' Foole. One can argue that parties like the Athenians in their encounter with the Melians or the Spartiates in their interactions with the helots are tempted to commit injustices because they misunderstand their situations. Or, to use game-theoretic terminology: Like the Foole, such parties may need some instruction or reminder of which games they are actually engaged in and what strategies their counterparts follow. The Melians in effect suggest that the Athenians should understand their interaction as part of a larger repeated game when they warn the Athenian representatives that should the Athenians unjustly destroy them, others will punish Athens severely in the future. To illustrate this idea, I will use the Combined Melian Invasion game of incomplete information of Figure 1.17, discussed in §1.3. Figure 8.5 depicts a feasible payoff set based upon the Figure 1.17 game payoffs where with probability $\frac{2}{3}$ the Athenians are against inferior Melians they can defeat easily and with probability $\frac{1}{3}$ they are against superior Melians capable of defeating them. For this game, the payoff vector $(1,1)$ of peace is now a Nash equilibrium payoff vector. The outcome of peace can be sustained as an equilibrium both of the corresponding Figure 1.17 game with agents who engage only once and of this game repeated indefinitely often. But in

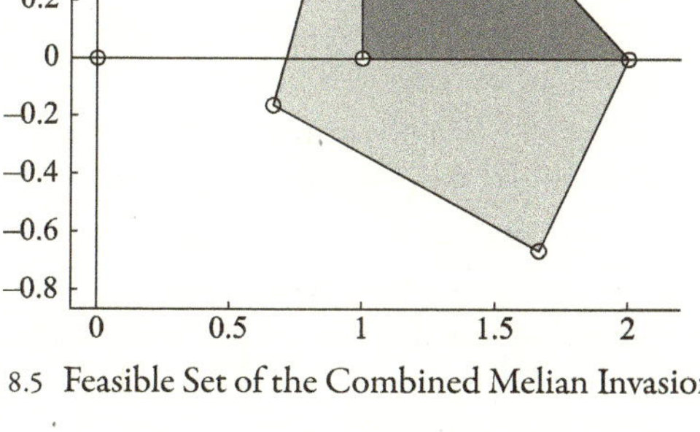

FIGURE 8.5 Feasible Set of the Combined Melian Invasion Game

the indefinitely repeated game, all of the points in the dark shaded region of the feasible set can be sustained by various history-dependent strategy equilibria, including the point (2,0) corresponding to the Athenians attacking and the Melians surrendering whether they are weak or strong. All of these equilibria are Pareto improvements over the payoff vector $\left(\frac{2}{3}, -\frac{1}{6}\right)$ of the free-for-all outcome. This simple example illustrates a more general phenomenon. By adopting the "right" games, one can very often ensure that the "just" outcomes are included among a set of equilibria where all receive better payoffs than they receive at the baseline state. But in general for these games, the set of distinct equilibria that share the property of being Pareto improvements upon the baseline state is huge and will typically include many highly asymmetric equilibria that look like the equilibria of unjust regimes.

The real problem for justice as mutual advantage as some of its most perceptive critics conceive of it is that it threatens to collapse into an alternative description of the Circumstances of Justice with the caveat that the parties follow *some* equilibrium. A theory of justice should be good for evaluating alternative social regimes and in particular for identifying some of these regimes as acceptable and others as needing reform or even replacement. If justice as mutual advantage were fully characterized by the §8.1 conditions, then according to this theory all stable social regimes that Pareto improve upon the free-for-all would be acceptable. Anyone who claimed that any such regime is unjust would simply be mistaken, no matter how great the social asymmetries of the status quo. I grant that as I have characterized this theory thus far, justice as mutual advantage has a "too many equilibria" problem. The justice as mutual advantage theorist can deal with this problem by adopting some criteria for narrowing down the set of equilibria that Pareto improve upon the baseline so that only the genuinely just equilibria remain. This move might then complete the general description of justice as mutual advantage.

But which such criteria should the justice as mutual advantage theorist adopt? Salience and learning can go far in explaining the origins of many equilibria. The salience-learning approach has certainly sparked an important body of research into the origins of norms of cooperation and fairness. I have applied elements of this approach myself to 2-agent bargaining problems and Augmented Stag Hunt games in Chapter 5. However, I think that by itself the salience-learning approach will not suffice for the present purpose of completing the description of justice as mutual advantage. Taken alone, the criteria of this approach may still admit too many equilibria. As many of the Chapter 5 examples have illustrated, in populations that engage in a conflictual coordination game an equilibrium corresponding to a norm of fair division or mutual cooperation might indeed be the equilibrium that evolves most often when there is a learning process, but other equilibria of unfair division or where no one cooperates still can evolve also. David Lewis pointed out that agents might regard an equilibrium as salient because it is a "uniquely bad" equilibrium.[59] I think learning and salience are invaluable at the micro level for explaining and analyzing the emergence of certain specific norms of justice. But at the macro level, I believe, it is simply not enough to say that justice as mutual advantage is a system of equilibria that are salient in a certain way or that are certain endpoints of learning. Even Hume, who gave both one of the greatest justice as mutual advantage theories and perhaps the greatest account of equilibrium selection by salience, did not give clear criteria for distinguishing unjust from just equilibria in terms of learning and salience.

What if one adopts a rational choice approach? This would be much more in line with some of the most prominent contemporary theories of justice. One could, for example, adapt the idea proposed by John Harsanyi and John Rawls of identifying the principles of justice as the principles that rational agents would choose from behind a veil of ignorance that prevents these agents from choosing principles biased in favor of anyone in particular.[60] Or one could adapt T. M. Scanlon's idea of identifying principles of justice as the product of a different choice situation where rational agents are not constrained by a veil of ignorance but are equipped with an additional motive besides that of advancing their own individual interests, specifically, "the desire to find and agree on principles which no one who had this desire could reasonably reject."[61] The general idea here is that rational agents in special and possibly hypothetical circumstances select the equilibria that define the system of justice. In fact, Ken Binmore has developed just such an equilibrium selection account of justice. According to Binmore's account, the equilibrium that defines a just distribution is that which would be chosen by any party constrained by a veil of ignorance who knows her choice is subject to revision by any other party under the same constraint.[62] Binmore's theory yields results that look good in the sense that it selects equilibria that resemble commonly accepted norms of fairness. Nevertheless, I think Binmore's theory illustrates how the rational choice approach can produce a theory of justice that is really more of a hybrid theory than a bona fide justice as mutual advantage

59. Lewis (1969), p. 35.

60. Harsanyi (1953, 1955); Rawls, "Justice as Fairness," in Rawls (1999), pp. 47–72, and (1971).

61. Thomas M. Scanlon, "Contractualism and Utilitarianism," in *Utilitarianism and Beyond*, ed. Amartya Sen and Bernard Williams (Cambridge: Cambridge University Press, 1982), pp. 103–128. The quoted passage appears on p. 111.

62. Binmore (1994), (1998), and Ken Binmore, *Natural Justice* (Oxford, New York: Oxford University Press, 2005).

theory.[63] In Binmore's theory, as in Harsanyi's, Rawls', and Scanlon's theories, the hypothetical choices in special circumstances do a great deal of the heavy lifting. In Harsanyi's, Rawls', and Scanlon's theories, mutual advantage plays at most a background role. In fact, it is by no means a foregone conclusion in Harsanyi's, Rawls', and Scanlon's theories that the choice of principles of justice will constitute a social equilibrium.[64] Binmore's theory is an equilibrium selection theory, so the outcome of his hypothetical choice procedure is guaranteed to be mutually advantageous. But for purposes of identifying the content of justice, the real general theory of justice at work here is something more like what Brian Barry calls justice as impartiality, that is, a theory where "justice should be the content of an agreement that would be reached by rational people under conditions that do not allow for bargaining power to be translated into advantage."[65]

In *Morals by Agreement*, David Gauthier proposes an alternative rational choice approach.[66] Like Harsanyi, Rawls, Scanlon, and Binmore, Gauthier develops his account of justice as the product of a hypothetical choice of ideally rational parties. But unlike Harsanyi, Rawls, and Binmore, Gauthier does not deprive choosing parties of the knowledge of their individual social positions. And unlike Scanlon, Gauthier does not give his parties preferences for reaching any particular kind of agreement. Gauthier makes the hypothetical choice circumstances themselves game-theoretic by placing his parties in a Nash bargaining problem.[67] Remarkably, Gauthier recognized the "too many equilibria" problem some time before critics started using this problem to attack justice as mutual advantage. To block severely asymmetric distributions, Gauthier requires the parties to start from a nonagreement point reflecting what he calls the *Lockean proviso*.[68] As the name suggests, the baseline characterized by this proviso is much like Locke's

63. To be sure, Binmore is not trying to defend his as a purely justice as mutual advantage theory.

64. Certainly Rawls appreciates this, since he devotes so much of the later parts of *A Theory of Justice* to arguing that his version of justice as fairness does characterize a social equilibrium, and presents a new set of arguments for this claim in *Political Liberalism* (New York: Columbia University Press, 1993). Paul Weithman presents a fine analysis of both sets of Rawls' arguments and the evolution of Rawls' thought on this question in *Why Political Liberalism? On John Rawls's Political Turn* (Oxford: Oxford University Press, 2011).

65. Barry (1989), p. 7.

66. Gauthier (1986), especially Chapters V and VII.

67. As discussed in §5.1, especially n. 26 and n. 27, in *Morals by Agreement* Gauthier defended a minimax relative concession solution of the bargaining problem as the product of hypothetical bargaining, and in his more recent (2012) essay defended the related maximin proportionate gain solution.

68. Gauthier (1986), p. 192.

State of Nature, where all have free and equal access to resources and a minimal property rights structure is in place. As Gauthier argues, the proviso ensures that the final distribution of the cooperative surplus is the product of a noncoerced agreement. That is, the proviso blocks distributions based upon initial positional advantages that could lead weaker parties to effectively surrender to stronger parties. Like Binmore's theory, Gauthier's theory produces nice-looking results. But I also think that, like Binmore, Gauthier imports elements of a different theory of justice into his own theory.[69] Despite Gauthier's dogged efforts to show otherwise, his baseline contains at the outset too much of the moral structure he aspires to develop as the output of the final agreement. If Gauthier sticks to assuming that parties will follow the agreement only on account of mutual advantage, then he should not be entitled to suppose that these parties would be willing to begin from a baseline where their actions are already significantly constrained by property rights. Such property rights really should be regarded as part, and a very important part at that, of the cooperative surplus. Recognizing that Gauthier would resist my opinion, I believe that Gauthier has effectively incorporated into his theory fundamental natural rights the way Locke conceives of such rights, so that his is no longer a purely justice as mutual advantage theory.

Plainly, the justice as mutual advantage theorist needs criteria that on the one hand do real work in identifying acceptable sets of equilibria and on the other hand do not smuggle in elements from some fundamentally different theory of justice. In the remainder of this section I will consider a criterion I believe does the job. This criterion is defined in terms that lean neither toward explicit rational choice nor toward explicit salience-learning. But one could analyze the set of conventions this criterion selects from either a salience-learning perspective or a rational choice perspective.

First I will state this *Baseline Consistency* criterion more precisely. The baseline I have used in defining the necessary conditions of justice as mutual advantage in §8.1 is much like the Hobbesian State of Nature, and in fact in many cases *is* the Hobbesian State of Nature, in that at this baseline the parties act without any restraint toward each other. According to these conditions, for a given population N the requirements S_N of an incumbent justice as mutual advantage system define a body of conventions that together define a complex social equilibrium that is also a Pareto improvement over the free-for-all σ_0^*. If the background conditions of society change so that the cooperative surplus diminishes or increases, then the distribution of the benefits and burdens of justice can be modified according to the requirements of S_N. But should this new distribution be based upon the

69. And Gauthier would take issue with my complaint, since he is self-consciously trying to develop a justice as mutual advantage theory. This comes out most clearly in Gauthier's essay "Mutual Advantage and Impartiality," in Kelly, ed. (1998), pp. 120–136.

original baseline? Or should this new distribution be based upon the distribution of the status quo? The following condition stipulates that for justice as mutual advantage, either answer is acceptable.

(M5) *Baseline Consistency*. Let $s^*_{C_0}$ denote the social state defined by S_N applied with respect to a given cooperative surplus C_0 with baseline σ^*_0 where the parties act without any restraint toward each other. Given an increase in cooperative surplus, then at the larger cooperative surplus C' each Party i fares as well when S_N is applied with respect to C' with baseline defined by $s^*_{C_0}$ as Party i fares when S_N is applied with respect to with baseline σ^*_0.

Baseline Consistency says that the requirements of S_N should be effectively renegotiation-proof with respect to changes in the baseline. Given Baseline Consistency, if the parties anticipate some change in their situation that will result in their generating a different cooperative surplus, then they should all be willing to continue using the requirements of S_N starting exactly from where they are. With a Baseline Consistent set of requirements S_N, the parties of N can make a transition from one given cooperative surplus to another that is "smooth" or "seamless" in the sense that applying S_N starting from their current status quo yields a result as good for all as would effectively beginning from scratch and applying S_N starting from the free-for-all σ^*_0. One can apply Baseline Consistency to define what the parties will do given a decrease in their cooperative surplus, which could result from some calamity such a long drought or a war, as well as what they will do given an increase that might stem from the discovery of new natural resources or successful use of new technologies. Indeed, the Baseline Consistency criterion can be applied inductively, so that the distribution of benefits resulting from a system S_N of Baseline Consistent requirements can in principle be derived either directly, using the free-for-all state as the baseline, or as the limit of a sequence of systems, each of which is reached using as the new baseline the status quo defined by its predecessor system applied to the predecessor cooperative surplus.

The basic idea of Baseline Consistency is easy to illustrate using Nash bargaining problems. Here I will use the Braithwaite game once more together with a variation on this game.[70] Suppose that $N = \{\text{Luke, Matthew}\}$ and that Luke and Matthew can generate some cooperative surplus of time for playing an instrument undisturbed by correlating the times when each plays while the other remains silent. Figure 5.9 illustrates the feasible payoff set of Braithwaite's bargaining problem based upon the Figure 5.7 basis game together with its Nash,

70. See §1.3 for a summary description of the Braithwaite game and §5.2 for a discussion of alternative solutions to the associated bargaining game.

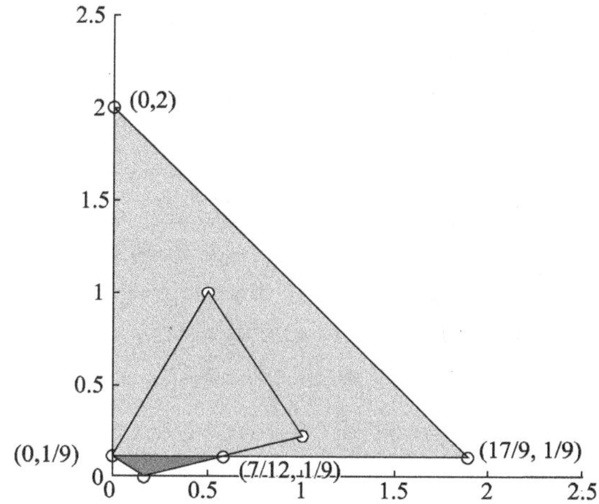

FIGURE 8.6 Expanded Braithwaite Game

Kalai-Smorodinsky, and egalitarian solutions. If we interpret this bargaining problem as a simple setting where parties are in the Circumstances of Justice, the free-for-all σ_0^* is characterized by the nonagreement point with payoff vector $\left(0,\frac{1}{9}\right)$ where Luke and Matthew both try to claim all of the available playing time. At the Nash solution, the payoff vector is $\left(\frac{15}{28},\frac{17}{18}\right) \approx (0.536, 0.944)$, while at the egalitarian solution, the payoff vector is $\left(\frac{15}{23},\frac{158}{207}\right) \approx (0.652, 0.763)$. Now suppose that $S_N^{(1)}$ consists of the single rule that requires Luke and Matthew to each follow his part of the Nash solution, and that $S_N^{(2)}$ consists of the rule that requires Luke and Matthew to each follow his part of the egalitarian solution. Then $S_N^{(2)}$ is a Baseline Consistent system, but $S_N^{(1)}$ is not. Figure 8.6 depicts an expansion of Luke and Matthew's original feasible payoff set. In Figure 8.6 the lightly shaded region depicts the part of the expanded set where Matthew and Luke both receive payoffs at least as good as their payoffs at the original nonagreement point. This region is isomorphic to the feasible set of the Chocolate Cake game of Figure 5.8 in the sense that one of these sets is equivalent to a linear rescaling of the other.[71] Here I assume that the change in the feasible set and consequently in the cooperative surplus is the result of an increase in the amount of available good at stake.

71. If Λ is the feasible set of the Figure 5.8 game and Υ is the region of the Figure 8.6 feasible set where both agents' payoffs are greater than or equal to their payoffs at $\left(0,\frac{1}{9}\right)$, then $\Lambda = \frac{17}{9}\cdot\Upsilon$.

Harking back to Braithwaite's original interpretation, one can think of Matthew and Luke's landlord arranging for them to have the use of a single studio room for playing on condition that they cease playing in their apartments, which bothers the landlord and their other neighbors. Given the studio room's convenient location, each can revise his schedule so that they now have same two hours for playing each day, where in their original problem they had only one. Luke's and Matthew's respective payoffs reflecting their relative aversions to the outcome where they play simultaneously remain as they were in their original problem. But since there are no walls in this studio room, neither finds the other's playing at all pleasant in their new situation. If Matthew and Luke follow $S_N^{(1)}$, then by applying $S_N^{(1)}$ to their new situation starting from $\left(\frac{15}{28},\frac{17}{18}\right)$ as their baseline, at the new Nash solution they will achieve the new payoff vector $\left(\frac{401}{504},\frac{607}{504}\right) \approx (0.796,1.204)$, as illustrated in Figure 8.7.

However, Luke may at this point protest. They first achieved the Nash solution where Luke's expected payoff was $\frac{15}{28}$ and Matthew's expected payoff was $\frac{17}{18}$ by deriving this solution from the $\left(0,\frac{1}{9}\right)$ nonagreement point, and then from the

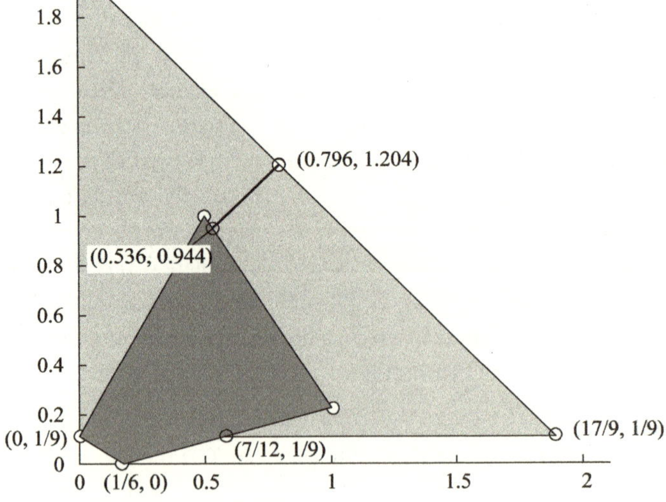

FIGURE 8.7 Expanded Braithwaite Game with Nash Solution Derived from the Nash Solution of the Original Braithwaite Game

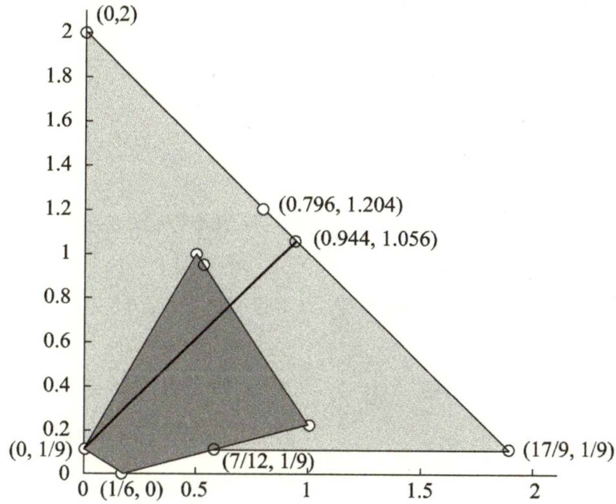

FIGURE 8.8 Expanded Braithwaite Game with Nash Solution Derived from Original Nonagreement Point

point $\left(\frac{15}{28},\frac{17}{18}\right)$ they reached the second Nash solution with associated payoff vector $\left(\frac{401}{504},\frac{607}{504}\right)$. But had Luke and Matthew based their new Nash solution on one application of $S_P^{(1)}$ only, using their original $\left(0,\frac{1}{9}\right)$ nonagreement point to define their baseline, then they would have arrived at the Nash solution with payoff vector $\left(\frac{17}{18},\frac{19}{18}\right) \approx (0.944, 1.056)$, a solution much more favorable to Luke than the two-stage solution. Figure 8.8 depicts this new single-stage solution.

This difference in Nash solutions presents a real problem for Luke and Matthew. Luke will likely complain that the new Nash solution should not depend upon a status quo that that was so lopsided in favor of Matthew to begin with. Why should they not start anew from their original nonagreement point? But Matthew might well retort that they should not have to start all over as if they had not been sharing their cooperative surplus successfully in their original problem. If the status quo was good enough for them both to follow in their original problem, then why should it not serve as the basis for distributing their new cooperative surplus? In the end, Matthew and Luke are likely to have trouble applying $S_N^{(1)}$ to their revised situation because $S_N^{(1)}$ is not Baseline Consistent.

If, on the other hand, Luke and Matthew follow $S_N^{(2)}$, then the windfall that changes their cooperative surplus and its corresponding feasible set poses no

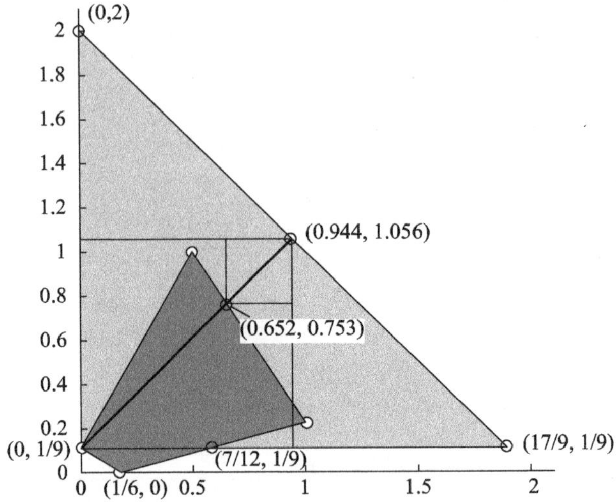

FIGURE 8.9 Expanded Braithwaite Game with Egalitarian Solutions

problem. If they use payoff vector $\left(\frac{15}{23}, \frac{158}{207}\right)$ of the egalitarian solution in their original problem to define their baseline, then in the expanded feasible set at the new egalitarian solution $\left(\frac{17}{18}, \frac{19}{18}\right)$ is the payoff vector they achieve. But if they disregard their earlier problem and its egalitarian solution, then from the original $\left(0, \frac{1}{9}\right)$ nonagreement point they achieve the very same egalitarian solution that they achieved in their two-stage solution. This result is depicted in Figure 8.9.

It is no coincidence that the payoff $\left(\frac{17}{18}, \frac{19}{18}\right)$ vector of the egalitarian solution of the expanded bargaining problem from the original nonagreement point is also that of the Nash solution for this very same bargaining problem. Given the almost entirely symmetric structure of the expanded problem, the Nash and egalitarian solutions here coincide, even though these two solutions are distinct in the smaller original bargaining problem. But if one applies the rule of $S_N^{(1)}$ in stages, then, as shown above, one cannot be assured of reaching the same solution as one would reach by applying the axioms of the Nash solution directly to the expanded problem with the original nonagreement point, forgetting the solutions that may have been reached in the past. The egalitarian solution does not have this defect. In fact, one might say that for the egalitarian solution, history always matches up with starting fresh. The Figure 8.9 diagram depicts this property of the egalitarian solution geometrically. In fact, the line segment joining $\left(0, \frac{1}{9}\right)$

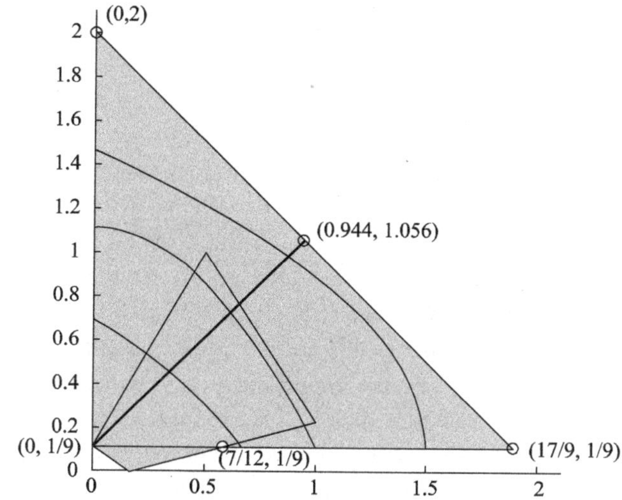

FIGURE 8.10 Bargaining Problems Bounded by the Expanded Braithwaite Game with Their Egalitarian Solutions

and $\left(\frac{17}{18},\frac{19}{18}\right)$ traces an entire family of egalitarian solutions of various bargaining problems that characterize subsets of the expanded feasible set, all based upon on the original $\left(0,\frac{1}{9}\right)$ nonagreement point of the original bargaining problem. Figure 8.10 depicts several of these bargaining problems together with their egalitarian solutions. For each of these bargaining problems, the egalitarian solution is the point of intersection of the feasible set Pareto frontier with the line segment joining $\left(0,\frac{1}{9}\right)$ and $\left(\frac{17}{18},\frac{19}{18}\right)$.[72] Along this path, any of the corresponding egalitarian solutions is in effect reachable from any of the others by successive applications of the egalitarian solution axioms. In an important essay, Ehud Kalai proved that the egalitarian solution had this property of *decomposability*, that is, the final solution is the same whether one computes it in stages or computes it directly from the original nonagreement point.[73] For this simple 2-agent

72. This is a consequence of the fact that the egalitarian solution is *strongly monotone*, in the sense that if the feasible set is expanded, then the resulting new solution must be weakly Pareto superior to the solution of the unexpanded problem. Informally, with a strongly monotone solution concept no one loses and at least some gain if the pie to be divided increases in size. Thomson and Lensberg (1989) give a splendid discussion of strong monotonicity and related concepts that include a proof of the strong monotonicity of the egalitarian solution.

73. Ehud Kalai, "Proportional Solutions to Bargaining Situations: Interpersonal Utility Comparisons," *Econometrica* 44 (1977), pp. 1623–1630.

population N, the system $S_N^{(2)}$ characterized by the one rule requiring the parties to follow their parts of the egalitarian solution is Baseline Consistent.

With Baseline Consistency I finish my own definition of justice as mutual advantage. According to this definition, a body S_N of requirements is a justice as mutual advantage system for its population N exactly when S_N satisfies conditions (M1)–(M5). Since I have used a baseline σ_0^* where there are no preexisting restraints and the equilibrium conditions (M1)–(M4) together with the refining condition (M5) do not make reference to or depend upon any restraining conditions other than the set S_N itself, this definition does not rely upon parts of any different theory of justice. I think Baseline Consistency also coheres well with some of the most important specific past accounts of justice as mutual advantage, at least in principle if not in all the actual details. For example, in Hobbes' theory, the regime of one's current sovereign is supposed to be more or less isomorphic to the regime one would have by returning to the State of Nature and recreating the regime from scratch. And in Hume's theory, one's incumbent regime is subject to the review of an impartial examiner, presumably with an eye toward possible reform in case from this examiner's perspective the status quo is sufficiently unsatisfactory.[74]

But do the criteria (M1)–(M5) characterize an honest theory of justice? Do these criteria separate the acceptable regimes from the plainly unjust regimes like those of the grossly lopsided helot-Spartiate equilibria? As I indicated in the introduction, the answer to such questions will depend to a significant extent upon the intuitions that defenders and especially critics of justice as mutual advantage have and expect others to share regarding which social systems are definitely just or unjust. At least at the micro level, where the underlying interaction structure is sufficiently simple to be summarized by a single game or a set of related games, then (M1)–(M5) do quite well in this regard. In particular, when (M1)–(M5) are applied to a set of problems having an underlying bargaining problem structure with a common baseline, the resulting set of equilibria always includes the set of egalitarian solutions and in fact reduces to the set of egalitarian solutions if the parties are assumed to have equal natural bargaining ability.[75] And as discussed in Chapter 5, one can interpret the egalitarian solution as an application of

74. See §6.2–4 for related discussion.

75. In axiomatic bargaining theory this assumption is made precise by the symmetry axiom, according to which if the feasible set remains geometrically the same if one interchanges the positions of the agents, then the solution remains the same. In my account of justice as mutual advantage I want to allow for the possibility that parties might have some differences in their natural bargaining ability, and so I do not assume an additional condition that would imply the symmetry axiom in related bargaining problems.

the principle of proportionate distribution that Aristotle claims all agree is the standard we all endorse.[76]

Conclusion

Above I have argued that justice as mutual advantage, properly understood, is justice where the rules define conventions that are proof against renegotiation in the face of certain changes in the social background. These conventions share out among the members of a society benefits from the cooperative surplus generated by the compliance of its contributing members. And when the available cooperative surplus contracts or expands, the members of this society are just as willing to apply their conventions for dividing their old cooperative surplus to the new cooperative surplus using the old status quo distribution as their baseline as they would be were they to start all over with a baseline of no restraint and no cooperative surplus. Put in less precise but also less clumsy terms, justice as mutual advantage defines rules for dividing the social pie that all are willing to continue using in case their pie changes size given either the choice of redividing the entire changed pie or starting with their original shares of the original pie and only dividing the difference between the old and the new pies.[77] The pie division rules of justice as mutual advantage characterize certain distinguished conventions that define only a subset of many possible divisions. Like all conventions, a convention of a justice as mutual advantage system is discretionary-sense arbitrary with respect to the family of alternative conventions of its specific coordination problem. But such a justice as mutual advantage convention is of course not indifference-sense arbitrary with respect to all these other conventions.

Justice as mutual advantage is a theory with staying power. Even some of its harshest critics take justice as mutual advantage quite seriously, treating this theory as an especially dangerous threat to their own preferred theories of justice. Just why does justice as mutual advantage have enduring appeal? And just why have so many been so confident this theory is false? One great advantage of justice as mutual advantage is that it employs weak and therefore widely appealing assumptions regarding what the members of society believe and what motivates them, and it includes an account of rational choice that is simple and widely accepted, at least in the social sciences. Justice as mutual advantage attributes no specific religious or metaphysical doctrines or even any specific desires to the various parties who are to be subject to what their system of justice will require

76. See the conclusion to Chapter 5.

77. As discussed in §8.6, this difference can be negative in case the pie shrinks.

of them.[78] The parties are assumed to be *homo economicus* parties, in the proper and simple sense that for any one of them to choose rationally is to seek maximum satisfaction of her own particular interests.[79] If the parties can generate the appropriate reciprocal expectations of their expected conduct, then they are able to obey the requirements that characterize the conventions of their justice as mutual advantage system, and Bayesian rationality explains quite simply *why* they should obey. Other theories of justice rely on much more controversial presuppositions. Philosophers in modern times are reluctant to embrace a theory like Plato's or Aristotle's because in such theories important social inequalities are justified with claims of deep natural or metaphysical disparities across classes of humans. Theories with a more egalitarian base, like the theories discussed in §8.6 that incorporate hypothetical choice, by design eschew these sorts of contentious natural or metaphysical claims regarding humans. But such theories also rely upon what look suspiciously like ad hoc special motivations, choice situations or accounts of rational decision that are rigged to get a desired result or perhaps even beg the question. The veil of ignorance theories of Harsanyi, Rawls, and Binmore illustrate this, as the parties in their alternative theories produce different results according to how they are allowed to make their choices.[80] Scanlon's theory illustrates this too, since his parties are specifically motivated by a desire to adopt principles no one having this desire would reasonably reject. And Gauthier's theory illustrates this, since his rational bargainers begin from a baseline that respects certain natural rights. Justice as mutual advantage does not require any such special devices. Justice as mutual advantage aspires to build justice completely from scratch.

The other great strength of justice as mutual advantage is its explanatory power. To the fundamental question "Why should I obey the requirements of justice?" the justice as mutual advantage theorist will respond with a simple

78. Hobbes may be a partial exception, since he attributes certain near-universal desires to people, such as a desire to preserve one's own life. However, as Kavka (1986, p. 82) observes, Hobbes' texts indicate that he thinks the reason people desire continued life is because this is a prerequisite to acquiring other goods they may desire, not because they regard life itself as intrinsically valuable.

79. David Gauthier argues that his *Morals by Agreement* theory rests upon a similar basis (1986, Chapter 1), although, as I argue in §8.6, Gauthier in fact bases this theory in part on natural rights.

80. As is well known, Harsanyi's and Rawls' theories differ in content because Harsanyi's parties choose according to the principle of Bayesian rationality while Rawls' parties choose in a manner consistent with maximin reasoning. Binmore's equilibrium selection theory produces results consistent with maximin choice because any party's choice constrained by the veil of ignorance is always subject to revision.

equilibrium answer: "Obedience serves your own interests on condition that you expect others to obey as well." To the other fundamental question, "What are these requirements?," the justice as mutual advantage theorist will answer, "Conventions that share out the benefits and the burdens of life in society." When the social contract is understood in its most generic sense, as the body of rules that regulate a community, then justice as mutual advantage is the theory that can best account for the most important part of the social contract, namely, its rules of justice. I think all theorists of justice can agree that justice consists of rules that regulate conduct in conflictual coordination problems. In actual societies, rules of this sort are numerous, complicated, sometimes idiosyncratic, and above all inflexible. No one appreciated these points better than David Hume, who argued that the best and indeed only satisfactory explanation for all these systems of rules with all their peculiarities has to be a conventionalist explanation. A justice as mutual advantage theorist such as Hume or Hobbes can tell a cogent general story of where all these systems come from and how they are maintained. Justice as mutual advantage theorists do not all give the same story. Hobbes, for example, derives the rules of justice partly as the product of rational choice and partly as the results of the actions of particular sovereigns, who act as arbiters for their own particular subjects. Hume explains the rules of justice as primarily the product of salience and learning from experience. I think one can give a larger story of where the rules of justice come from and why they persist that includes elements of both Hobbesian and Humean stories. I give parts of such a larger story in the earlier chapters of this book. A complete justice as mutual advantage explanatory story would fill many volumes. But details aside, the key idea underlying the idea remains that justice is at bottom a system of special conventions. This idea makes justice as mutual advantage the theory best suited for explaining the complexity, diversity, and inflexibility of the actual systems that determine social inequalities.

Of course, this great strength of justice as mutual advantage is also its great apparent weakness. The critics of justice as mutual advantage insist that this theory explains too much. Or, to state the matter another way, these critics argue that justice as mutual advantage does not properly explain what really matters. To briefly recapitulate the most serious general criticism of justice as mutual advantage discussed in this chapter: Justice as mutual advantage is too indeterminate to serve as a stand-alone theory of justice. Critics ask pointedly, "Are just *any* such conventions that share out the benefits and the burdens of life in society really just?" Historically, people have always tried to use justice as the Melians tried to do—as a standard for justifying or challenging the power relationships that exist and their fallouts. Perhaps every social regime that has ever existed has also been criticized, either openly or in private, by some under its rule for being unjust to some extent. Hobbes observes that in any commonwealth subjects are prone to grumble about their sovereign,[81] but should everyone follow Hobbes in dismissing out of hand such grumblings as the product of shortsightedness? To state the banal, people routinely engage in vigorous and even shrill debates over questions of the justice of their institutions. Foes of justice as mutual advantage do not take this phenomenon lightly. They can argue that if justice as mutual advantage, as many have conceived it, is the true theory of justice, then all of these debates are really quite without point.

I for one am sensitive to this general criticism of justice as mutual advantage, though, as I have discussed above, I am certainly not the first contemporary theorist with a strong justice as mutual advantage orientation who tries to address the underlying "too many equilibria" problem. I accept Rawls' view that a satisfactory theory of justice should make a good fit with a body of considered judgments regarding social arrangements as being definitely unjust or acceptable. One running theme of this book is that a more satisfactory justice as mutual advantage theory is possible given a better analysis of convention. Using game theory, the contemporary formal theory of interactive decisions, I have tried to present an analysis of convention that serves for analyzing problems of justice. This analysis serves to embed the requirements of justice into the larger system of conventions that regulate a society. But to distinguish the bona fide conventions of justice, one must address the "too many equilibria" problem. Gauthier tried to deal with this problem by eliminating at the outset any baseline equilibria where coercion might occur that therefore would be prone to lead to excessively lopsided final distributions.[82] Binmore used a variation of Harsanyi's and Rawls' original position where parties choose from behind a veil of ignorance to select the set of equilibria that define a just distribution. As discussed above, Gauthier's and Binmore's responses to the "too many equilibria" problem produce final results that cohere well with widely accepted beliefs regarding just social arrangements, but at the price of incorporating parts of general theories of justice lying outside the true scope of justice as mutual advantage. My own approach is to require the set of conventions eligible to serve as conventions of justice to satisfy Baseline Consistency. This criterion narrows down the set of conventions that can be parts of a justice as mutual advantage system to those that define relatively egalitarian distributions. In fact, the resulting set of conventions of justice, according to my account of justice as mutual advantage, is quite similar to that of

81. *Leviathan* 18:20.

82. However, Gauthier is not trying to show that his own theory matches up with considered judgments of morals and justice. In *Morals by Agreement* Gauthier states clearly that his is a normative theory and that the consequences of this theory might differ significantly from commonly held beliefs regarding specific questions of morals and justice (1986, p. 6).

Binmore's theory, which in turn produces results that are quite similar to those of Rawls' justice as fairness and that conform with Aristotle's proportionality of distributive justice. So for practical purposes, the end result of the conventionalist account of justice as mutual advantage proposed here is not all that different from those of other prominent theories of justice. But the end result comes from a genuinely just theory based on justice as mutual advantage. And such a genuinely just theory does not need the powerful and contentious assumptions or the suspect machinery of other theories of justice.

APPENDIX 1

FORMAL DEFINITION OF CONVENTION

In this appendix I restate the §2.4 definition of convention so as to make more explicit some of the analytical details this definition incorporates. As I define the notion in §2.4 and here, a convention is a practice the members of a group follow that characterizes an equilibrium that is discretionary-sense arbitrary. In game-theoretic vocabulary, the members of a group who follow a convention follow a correlated equilibrium of a certain game, which might be a larger game constructed from several constituent games. But how are the games that can be these constituent games related to each other? I believe that the games of a family that can be the family of a given convention must be such that (i) each Agent i has the same available moves across these games and (ii) if in any one of these games Agent i achieves her kth most preferred outcome by following the move a_j when the other agents follow a_l, then Agent i achieves her kth most preferred outcome by following the move a_j when the other agents follow a_l in all of these games. I will call a set of games such that properties (i) and (ii) are satisfied an *act equivalent set*, since it is at least possible that a given agent can achieve an outcome equally good from her perspective in each of these games by following the same move in all of them. For example, the Prisoner's and the Farmer's Dilemma games of Figures 1.3 and 1.5 form another act equivalent set, since in both of these games one agent achieves her most preferred outcome when she follows D and the other follows P, her third most preferred outcome when both follow D, her second most preferred outcome when both follow P, and her least preferred outcome when she follows P while the other follows D. Note that I refer to an agent's *move* rather than a pure strategy, since I wish to allow for the possibility that agents can follow a convention over a set of games where the strategic and the extensive form games of the set all have the same moves but possibly not the same pure strategies across all players, as in the case when the games of the act equivalent set are Prisoner's and Farmer's Dilemma games. Figure A.1.1 summarizes the larger extensive form game where the constituent games are an act equivalent set where two agents can engage in either a Prisoner's Dilemma or a Farmer's Dilemma.

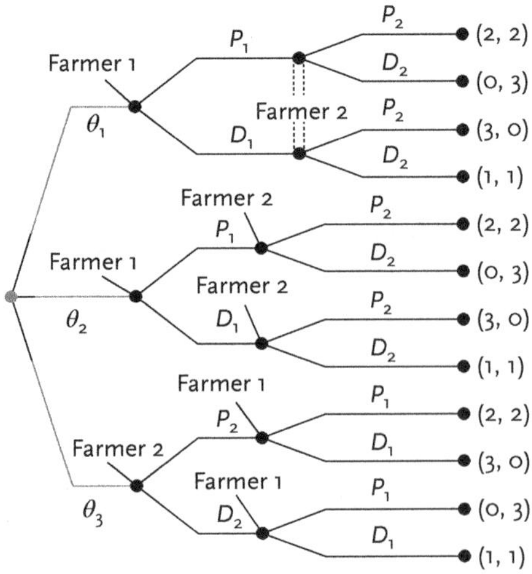

θ_1 = Subgame is Prisoner's Dilemma
θ_2 = Subgame is Farmer's Dilemma with Farmer 1 moving first
θ_3 = Subgame is Farmer's Dilemma with Farmer 2 moving first

FIGURE A1.1 Extensive Form Game with Act-Equivalent Prisoner's Dilemma and Farmer's Dilemma Constituent Games

In this larger game, "Nature" moves first by selecting the constituent game in which the two agents engage.

$N = \{1, 2, \ldots\}$ is a set or community of parties or agents that may have either finitely or infinitely many members. At each successive time period $t \in \{1, 2, \ldots\}$, a finite and nonempty subset $N_t \subseteq N$ is sampled with replacement. At period t, each *matched* Agent i in N_t engages in a *base game* Γ_t that has constituent act equivalent subgames in the position of one of the agents in this base game and is matched with other *partner agents* in their respective positions in Γ_t. The sequence (Γ_t) is a *supergame*.[1]

Since the constituent subgames of Γ_t are act equivalent, there is for each Agent i a fixed set of pure strategies $A_i = \{a_{i1} \ldots, a_{im_i}\}$ of the base game Γ_t that are available to Agent i at period t if Agent i is matched at this period.[2] For a given period t, if Agent i is

1. Michael Taylor was perhaps the first to use the term "supergame" to refer to any sequence of individual noncooperative games in Taylor (1976), p. 28, and Taylor (1987), p. 60. In the early history of game theory, this term was used to refer to a sequence consisting of a single noncooperative game with a single fixed set of agents repeated over time—a special case of supergames, as Taylor and I use the term. In more contemporary literature, a sequence of this sort is typically referred to as an *indefinitely repeated game* or more simply as a *repeated game*. Another special case, where the number of agents and agents' pure strategies are fixed and the payoffs can vary across time periods, is sometimes referred to in the literature as a *dynamic game* or a *stochastic game*.

2. This set might be dependent upon which roles in the supergame Γ_t that Agent i might possibly engage in.

not matched, then Agent i does not engage in a base game at this period and is assigned an "empty" move denoted by $\underline{a}$. So at a given period $t \geq 1$ each Agent i follows some act $s_{it} \in \{\underline{a}, a_{i1}, \ldots, a_{im_1}\}$, and so at period t the parties follow the *act profile* $s_t = (s_{1t}, s_{2t}, \ldots)$. At each act profile s_t, Agent i receives a payoff $u_i(s_t)$ with $u_i(s_t) = 0$ if $s_{it} = \underline{a}$. At each period $t \geq 1$, $m_t = (s_1, \ldots, s_{t-1})$ is the *ex ante history* of interactions. With the supergame (Γ_t) is an associated set Ω of *possible worlds*. At each period t, one world $\omega(t) \in \Omega$ is *actual*. The actual world can depend on the *ex ante* history of interactions. Each Agent i has a private *information partition* $\mathcal{H}_i$ of Ω and a *conjecture* $\mu_i(\cdot)$ over $\mathcal{H}_i$ and the strategies of her counterparts. A full description of $\omega(t)$ includes all of the information relevant to the agents' decisions at period t, including a description of the base game, the assignments of the agents in N_t to base games, the private information partitions and the conjectures each matched Agent i has regarding the partners.[3]

A function $f_i : \Omega \to A_i$ defined over the possible worlds that is constant on each cell of $\mathcal{H}_i$ is an *individual strategy* for Agent i's and $f = (f_1, f_2, \ldots)$ is a *strategy profile* over all the agents of N.[4] Each Agent i has a *discount factor* $\delta_i \in (0,1)$ that can be interpreted as the probability Agent i assigns to engaging in the supergame for one additional period or how much Agent i discounts the expected payoff at the following period compared to the current period. Given the strategy profile $f = (f_1, f_2, \ldots)$, Agent i's *expected payoff* is

$$E_i\left(u_i(f)\right) = \sum_{t=1,\omega\in\Omega}^{\infty} u_i\left(f(\omega)\right)\mu_i\left[\omega(t) = \omega\right]\delta_i^t.$$

f is a *correlated equilibrium* of the supergame (Γ_t) if for each $i \in N$,

$$E_i\left(u_i(f)\right) \geq E_i\left(u_i(h_i, f_{-i})\right)$$

for any strategy $h_i \neq f_i$, that is, if each Agent i maximizes her overall expected payoff by following her end f_i of f given that the others follow their ends of f.[5] Such an equilibrium f is *path-observance strict* if for any strategy $g_i \neq f_i$ that requires an Agent i to deviate unilaterally from the strategy profile defined by $f_i(\omega(t))$ at any period,

$$E_i\left(u_i(f)\right) > E_i\left(u_i(g_i, f_{-i})\right)$$

that is, (g_i, f_{-i}) yields Agent i a strictly lower expected payoff than f.

---

3. For more discussion on this way of understanding the possible worlds, see Aumann (1987) and Eddie Dekel and Faruk Gul, "Rationality and Knowledge in Game Theory," in *Advances in Economics and Econometrics: Theory and Applications, Seventh World Congress Volume I*, ed. D. M. Kreps and K. F. Wallis (Cambridge: Cambridge University Press, 1997), pp. 87–172.

4. The property that f_i be constant on each cell of Agent i 's information partition $\mathcal{H}_i$ is also known as $\mathcal{H}_i$*-measurability*.

5. The subscript $-i$ is the "jackknife" notation that indicates the result of removing the i th component of an ordered n-tuple or n-fold Cartesian product. Here,

$$\left(f_i', f_{-i}\right) = \left(f_1, \ldots, f_{i-1}, f_i', f_{i+1}, \ldots, f_n\right).$$

This notation is used throughout these appendices.

With these preliminaries all made explicit, the definition of convention can be restated in a manner almost identical to the §2.4 definition:

Definition. Given a community N of agents who can be matched in each period t in the supergame (Γ_t), the strategy profile f is a *convention* if, and only if,

(C1) f is a path-observance strict equilibrium of (Γ_t).
(C2) There is some strategy profile $f' \neq f$ such that f' is also a path-observance strict equilibrium of (Γ_t).
(C3) (C1) and (C2) are common knowledge among the members of N.

If, in addition,

(C4) Each Agent i's conjecture is such that following her end of f is her unique best response to her expectations regarding the other agents in N.
(C5) (C4) is common knowledge among the members of N.
then f is the *incumbent convention* for the members of N.

Some of the refinements of the §2.4 definition can also be restated with somewhat greater technical detail. Certain refinements of this definition characterize previous and less general accounts of convention. A strategy profile f is *history independent* if the probability that $\omega(t) = \omega'$ for a given $\omega' \in \Omega$ is independent of the *ex ante* history m_t. A convention f is *simple* if f is history independent. A convention f is *basic* if f is simple and at each period t the matched agents always engage in the same r-agent base game Γ, that is, the base game Γ has no constituent subgames. The equilibrium f of a simple convention is a strict correlated equilibrium of the base game Γ_{θ_t} at each period t as well as a strict correlated equilibrium of the supergame (Γ_{θ_t}), and the alternative f' is also a strict correlated equilibrium of Γ_{θ_t} at each period t. A simple convention f is a *Lewis-convention* if for each Agent i,

$$E_j\big(u_j(f)\big) \geq E_j\big(u_j(g_i, f_{-i})\big)$$

for every Agent j, that is, f is a coordination equilibrium.

The definition of convention incorporates common knowledge. As discussed in Chapter 2, David Lewis gave an early analysis of common knowledge in *Convention*.[6] Common knowledge has since become an important area of research in its own right, and a number of different analyses of common knowledge have been proposed and analyzed.[7] In the remainder of this appendix I summarize in more detail this account of common knowledge, which is based upon the reconstructions of Lewis' account

6. Lewis (1969), pp. 52–60.

7. Vanderschraaf and Sillari (2014) discuss some of the history of common knowledge and its alternative formulations.

given in earlier work by myself, by Robin Cubitt and Robert Sugden, and by Giacomo Sillari.[8] In his own presentation of common knowledge in *Convention*, Lewis makes it clear that the infinite hierarchy of epistemic claims that characterizes common knowledge forms a chain of implications, not actual steps in anyone's reasoning.[9] In his analysis of common knowledge Lewis does not adopt an explicit analysis of knowledge itself such as the justified-true-belief account common among philosophers. Most formal analyses of common knowledge incorporate a knowledge operator that satisfies several standard properties of logic with such an intensional operator. Cubitt and Sugden reconstruct Lewis–common knowledge in terms of *reasons to believe*, following Lewis' use of "reason to believe" in his own definitions of indication and common knowledge.[10] As Cubitt and Sugden clearly acknowledge, according to their own reconstruction the members of a group could have Lewis–common knowledge without any group members necessarily having any actual beliefs that A obtains or that any group member actually believes any nested epistemic claims regarding what she or the others actually believe regarding A. I give a reconstruction of Lewis–common knowledge in terms of the more usual knowledge operator approach that makes no distinction between reasons to believe and actual belief, although it is usual to interpret this operator as implying actual belief. I also adopt a possible-worlds approach to analyzing Lewis–common knowledge, although, as Cubitt and Sugden note, Lewis does not adopt this approach himself.[11] The possible-worlds approach dovetails naturally with the definitions of correlated equilibrium and convention where each agent predicates her own choices upon her information regarding the possible worlds.

The possible worlds are a set Ω where some $\omega_\alpha \in \Omega$ is the actual world. A proposition $A \subseteq \Omega$ obtains at world $\omega \in \Omega$ if $\omega \in A$. The operator R_i, when applied to some proposition A, produces the new proposition $R_i(A)$, which can be read "Agent i has reason to believe that A obtains." If one assumes actual belief, then $R_i(A)$ can be read as "Agent i knows that A obtains." but I here will follow Cubitt and Sugden, and Lewis before them, and remain noncommittal regarding the agents' specific actual beliefs. The R_i operator functions in much the same manner as the knowledge operator used in

8. Vanderschraaf (1998b); Cubitt and Sugden (2003); Giacomo Sillari, "A Logical Framework for Convention," *Synthese* 147 (2005), pp. 379–400; Vanderschraaf and Sillari (2014).

9. Lewis (1969), p. 53.

10. Cubitt and Sugden (2003); Lewis (1969), pp. 53, 56.

11. Cubitt and Sugden abandon the possible-worlds approach in favor of an alternative formalism that enables them to give a deeper formal analysis of the notion of *indication* in Lewis' definition of common knowledge. Sillari (2005) proposes a reconciliation between Cubitt and Sugden's approach and the possible-worlds approach where Lewis-common knowledge is formalized in a richer possible-worlds semantic framework that can represent the distinction between reasons to believe and actual beliefs.

much of the literature on epistemic logic and formal common knowledge. The operator R_i satisfies the following axioms:

(R1) $R_i(A) \subseteq A$
(R2) $\Omega \subseteq R_i(\Omega)$
(R3) $R_i(\cap_k A_k) = \cap_k R_i(A_k)$
(R4) $R_i(A) \subseteq R_i R_i(A)$

(R1) says that if Agent i has reason to believe A, then A must be the case. (R2) says that Agent i has reason to believe that that some possible world in Ω occurs no matter which possible world $\omega \in \Omega$ is actual. (R3) says that Agent i has reason to believe a conjunction if, and only if, Agent i has reason to believe each conjunct. (R4) is a *positive reflection property*, which says that if Agent i has reason to believe A, then Agent i has reason to believe that she has reason to believe A.[12]

A crucial assumption in Lewis' analysis of common knowledge is that agents know they share the same "rationality, inductive standards and background information" with respect to a state of affairs A',[13] that is, if an agent can draw any conclusion from A', then she knows that all can do likewise. This idea is made precise in the following definitions.

Definition. Given a set of agents N and a proposition $A' \subseteq \Omega$, the agents of N are *A'-symmetric reasoners* if, and only if, for each $i, j \in N$ and for any proposition $A \subseteq \Omega$, if $R_i(A') \subseteq R_i(A)$ and $R_i(A') \subseteq R_i R_j(A')$ then $R_i(A') \subseteq R_i R_j(A)$.

The definiens says that for each Agent i, if Agent i can infer from A' that A is the case and that everyone has reason to believe that A' is the case, then Agent i can also infer that everyone has reason to believe that A is the case.

Definition. A proposition A is *Lewis–common knowledge at* $\omega \in \Omega$ among the agents of a set $N = \{1, \ldots, n\}$ if, and only if, there is a proposition A^* such that $\omega \in A^*$, the agents of N are A^*- symmetric reasoners, and for every $i \in N$,

(L1) $\omega \in R_i(A^*)$
(L2) $R_i(A^*) \subseteq R_i(\cap_{j \in N} R_j(A^*))$
(L3) $R_i(A^*) \subseteq R_i(A)$

12. The axioms (R1)–(R4) correspond to (S4) systems of modal logic. If one adopts an additional *negative reflection* axiom

$$(R5): \neg R_i(A) \subseteq R_i \neg R_i(A)$$

then the axioms (R1)–(R5) together correspond to (S4) systems of modal logic.

13. Lewis (1969), p. 53.

A^* is a *basis* for the agents' common knowledge. $L_N^*(A)$ denotes the proposition defined by (L1)–(L3) for a set N of A^*-symmetric reasoners, so we can say that A is Lewis–common knowledge for the agents of N if, and only if, $\omega \in L_N^*(A)$.

(L1) says that Agent i has reason to believe A^* at ω. (L2) says that if Agent i has reason to believe that A^* obtains, then Agent i has reason to believe that everyone has reason to believe that A^* obtains. (L3) says that Agent i has reason to believe A if Agent i has reason to believe A^*.

If one does assume actual belief, then Lewis' analysis inspires a simple way to characterize common knowledge informally: A proposition A is common knowledge among a group of agents if each agent in the group knows that all know A and knows that all can infer the consequences of this mutual knowledge. This implies a hierarchy of nested knowledge claims, so that a proposition A is common knowledge for a set of agents if the agents have all orders of mutual knowledge of A, that is, each agent knows A, each agent knows that each agent knows A, and so on. The following result shows that Lewis–common knowledge implies a hierarchy of nested claims of the form "Each agent has reason to believe A, each agent has reason to believe that each agent has reason to believe A, and so on."

Proposition. For each $m \geq 1$, $L_N^*(A) \subseteq R_{i_1} R_{i_3} \cdots R_{i_m}(A)$ for all agents $i_1, i_2, \ldots, i_m \in N$.[14]
PROOF. Suppose that $\omega \in L_N^*(A)$. By definition, there is a basis proposition A^* such that $\omega \in A^*$. By (L3), $R_{i_1}(A^*) \subseteq R_{i_1}(A)$ for each $i_1 \in N$. Since (L2) is the case and the agents of N are A^*-symmetric reasoners, $R_{i_1}(A^*) \subseteq R_{i_1} R_{i_2}(A)$ for each $i_1, i_2 \in N$. Applying (L2) and the definition of A^*-symmetric reasoning again, $R_{i_1}(A^*) \subseteq R_{i_1} R_{i_3} R_{i_2}(A)$ for each $i_1, i_2, i_3 \in N$. Continuing to apply (L2) and the definition of A^*-symmetric reasoning successively, we have for each $m \geq 1$ and for all agents $i_1, i_2, \ldots, i_m \in N$,

(1) $\omega \in R_{i_1} R_{i_3} \cdots R_{i_m}(A)$

and (1) implies that $L_N^*(A) \subseteq R_{i_1} R_{i_3} \cdots R_{i_m}(A)$.□

One might have actual beliefs regarding only a small proper subset of the propositions one has reason to believe. Such a small proper subset of the epistemic claims one has reason to believe according to Lewis' and my own analysis of convention might be all that each member of a community need actually believe in order to maintain a convention. One way to model the distinction between an actual belief and having reasons to believe is to introduce *awareness structures* over possible worlds. Giacomo Sillari was one of the first to introduce formal analyses of awareness into an analysis of common knowledge by using awareness structures.[15] Awareness structures play a

14. This was first proved in Vanderschraaf (1998b), Appendix Proposition A.1.
15. Sillari, (2005); "Common Knowledge and Convention," *Topoi* 27 (2008), pp. 29–39.

role analogous to knowledge partitions in the more standard actual-beliefs common knowledge literature. An agent's awareness structure specifies for each possible world a set of propositions of which the agent is said to be aware. An agent actually believes that a proposition *A* obtains if and only if she has reason to believe that *A* obtains *and* *A* is in her *awareness set* at the actual world. How much actual belief must the agents involved in a convention have? Answers to this question vary. As noted above, Cubitt and Sugden's analysis leaves open the possibility that no specific actual beliefs are necessary for the agents who follow a Lewis-convention. Giacomo Sillari argues that the agents involved need have only actual beliefs regarding specific instances of a convention involving specific counterparts, and points out that Lewis devotes much attention to discussing agents' knowledge of specific instances only.[16] I myself think it would suffice to require that each individual each actually believes only in a small body of propositions that imply the full entire hierarchy, even though each individual does not of course actually reason through all the steps of this hierarchy. In any event, the recent work on formal models of awareness and unawareness provides a basis for developing an analysis of common knowledge that actual individuals can attain and that underwrites their compliance with conventions.

16. Sillari (2008). Lewis gives his corresponding discussion on pp. 64–68 of *Convention*.

APPENDIX 2

COMPUTER SIMULATIONS OF INDUCTIVE LEARNING IN GAMES*

INDUCTIVE LEARNING DYNAMICS

As discussed in Chapter 4, the *weighted fictitious play* process is an extension of Rudolf Carnap's final system of inductive logic.[1] This process is defined for a set $N = \{1, \ldots, n\}$ agents who engage in an n-agent game repeatedly over time periods as follows: At each period $t \geq 0$, each Agent i follows a pure strategy $s_i(t)$ that is a best response given her current *conjecture* over the other agents' strategy choices, which is a subjective probability distribution $\mu_i^t(\cdot)$ over the pure strategy profiles the agents of $N_{-i} = \{1, \ldots, i-1, i+1, \ldots, n\}$ can follow.[2] At each period $t > 0$, Agent i updates her conjecture according to the recursive rule

$$\text{(A.2.1)} \qquad \mu_i^{t+1}(s_{-i}) = \frac{1-\theta_i}{1-\theta_i^{t+1}} \cdot 1_{s_{-i}}(t) + \theta_i \cdot \frac{1-\theta_i^t}{1-\theta_i^{t+1}} \cdot \mu_i^t(s_{-i})$$

where (i) $\mu_i^0(s_{-i}) = 1_{s_{-i}}(0)$ is Agent i's prior probability that the agents of N_{-i} follow strategy profile s_{-i}, (ii) for $t > 0, 1_{s_{-i}}(t)$ is the indicator function for s_{-i} at t,[3] that is,

* All of the computer simulations discussed in these appendices and in the main text were constructed and run in MatLab. The MatLab programs used to run these simulations are available upon request

1. Carnap (1980) (cited in Chapter 4, note 54).

2. I use the "jackknife" notation summarized in Appendix 1, note 5.

3. In general, an indicator function for some defining proposition A has the form

$$1_A = \begin{cases} 1 \text{ if } A \text{ obtains} \\ 0 \text{ otherwise} \end{cases}.$$

$$1_{s_{-i}}(t) = \begin{cases} 1 \text{ if the agents of } N_{-i} \text{ followed } s_{-i} \text{ at period } t \\ 0 \text{ otherwise} \end{cases},$$

and (iii) $\theta_i \in (0,1)$ is Agent i's *decay* or *weighting factor* by which Agent i discounts the past.[4] One can interpret weighted fictitious play either as a *fixed agent process*, where the same set of agents engage in the game repeatedly with each other, or as a *population process*, where members of a large population at a given time enter into and engage in a game with partner agents, form their conjectures according the history they have observed, and then at future times might engage with different partners or even drop out of the sequence of engagements. As discussed in §4.3, data from experiments where subjects are matched in 2-agent games show that weighted fictitious play is a learning model that fits these subjects' learning patterns fairly well. Experimental investigators have imputed median values for θ_i across subjects between 0.25 and 0.50.[5] The simulation results presented below all incorporate discount factors or distributions of the discount factors that are compatible with these experimental results.

For a given noncooperative game, the set Δ of all possible conjectures the agents in the game can have over their counterparts' strategy profiles is the *belief simplex* of this game. The initial conjectures, that is, the prior probabilities that each agent has over her counterparts' pure strategy profiles is a point in Δ. Beginning from the initial conjectures point, the weighted fictitious play process traces an *orbit* of updated conjectures points. Any rest point of weighted fictitious play is a Nash equilibrium, and if a weighted fictitious play orbit converges, the limit is a Nash equilibrium in conjectures. Any strict Nash equilibrium is an absorbing state of weighted fictitious play in the sense that if agents updating according to this process best respond by following their ends of a strict equilibrium at any stage, they continue to follow this equilibrium for all subsequent stages.[6] Strict Nash equilibria are attracting points of this dynamic, and the *basin of attraction* $\Delta_{s^*} \subseteq \Delta$ for weighted fictitious play of a strict Nash equilibrium s^* is the set such that if $x_0 \in \Delta_{s^*}$ is the initial conjectures point, the orbit starting from x_0 generated

4. A related process is *straight fictitious play*, where

$$\mu_i^{t+1}(s_{-i}) = \frac{1}{t+1} \cdot 1_{s_{-i}}(t) + \cdot \frac{t}{t+1} \cdot \mu_i^t(s_{-i})$$

so that there is no discounting of the past. The convergence properties of weighted and straight fictitious play are similar, but precisely because there is discounting of the past in weighted fictitious play, this process tends to converge far more rapidly than straight fictitious play.

5. Cheung and Friedman (1997), Camerer (2003), p. 284, cited in Chapter 4, note 55.

6. For proofs of these results for straight fictitious play see Propositions 2.1 and 2.2 of Drew Fudenberg and David K. Levine, *The Theory of Learning in Games* (Cambridge, MA: MIT Press, 1998), pp. 33–34, and Propositions 3.2.3, 3.2.6, and 3.2.7 of Vanderschraaf (2001b), pp. 125, 130–131. The corresponding results for weighted fictitious play follow from essentially the same proofs for straight fictitious play.

by the weighted fictitious play process converges to the s^* equilibrium in conjectures. The *size* $m(\Delta_{s^*})$ of the basin Δ_{s^*} is the fraction of the simplex of all possible conjectures defined by the conjectures of this basin.

For any deterministic fictitious play process it is possible for an orbit to settle into a limiting sequence where the agents' actual payoffs at each period are strictly less than their expected payoffs given their conjectures. A variation on the deterministic weighted fictitious play process defined by (A.2.1) has agents *experiment* in case they fall into a cycle where their achieved payoffs are less than their expected payoffs. According to this perturbed fictitious play process, at each $t+1$st stage of updating, Agent i follows a best response given her current conjecture $\mu_i^{t+1}(s_{-i})$ unless at the tth period the realized payoff was less than her maximin payoff, in which case Agent i is *dissatisfied* at period $t+1$ and follows a best response with probability $1-\zeta_i(t)$ and experiments by choosing a pure strategy at random with probability $\zeta_i(t)$. The probabilities $\zeta_i(t)$ of mixing in case of dissatisfaction can be, but need not be, constant across the representatives over time. Allowing the agents to experiment when their achieved payoffs are inconsistent with their expected payoffs dramatically improves their ability to reach strict equilibria in coordination games.[7]

By introducing into the weighted fictitious process external *signals* that agents can observe when they engage in the game, the limits of this process can be correlated equilibrium conventions.[8] The weighted fictitious play process can also be perturbed by *mutation*, where with some probability $\varepsilon_i > 0$ an Agent i chooses a pure strategy at random instead of following her best response given her current conjecture. One can interpret a mutation as a mistake or an experiment. Mutations are assumed to be independent and identically distributed across agents. One can use the perturbed fictitious play to test the stability of equilibria. When experimentation or a positive mutation rate is introduced into the weighted fictitious play process, the sequence of updated conjectures becomes a stochastic process that can fail to have permanent rest points. Nevertheless, the orbits of a perturbed fictitious play process can still converge. When the orbit of a perturbed weighted fictitious play process converges to a limit, this limit is a Nash equilibrium in conjectures.[9]

An alternative *representative weighted fictitious play* process is especially well suited for a population interpretation.[10] The updating rule for this process is defined as

---

7. I introduce this *maximin-regarding weighted fictitious play* process in "Security Regarding Weighted Fictitious Play" (unpublished manuscript, 2012).

8. This is demonstrated in Vanderschraaf (2001b), Chapter 4.

9. Fudenberg and Levine (1998), Chapters 2, 4, and 5, give proofs that the limits of versions of perturbed straight fictitious play are always Nash equilibria. The companion results for weighted fictitious play have similar proofs.

10. I introduce this process in Vanderschraaf (2012).

(A.2.2) $$\mu_i^{t+1}(s_{-i}) = \frac{\sum_{k=0}^{\tau_i(t)+1} \bar{\theta}^k \cdot 1_{s_{-i}}(\tau_i(t)+1-k)}{\sum_{k=0}^{\tau_i(t)+1} \bar{\theta}^k}$$

where (i) $\bar{\theta}$ is a random variable defined by

$$\bar{\theta} = 1_{[\theta+a_1\chi_1<0]} \max(\theta + a_1\chi_1, 0) + 1_{[\theta+a_1\chi_1\geq 0]} \min(\theta + a_1\chi_1, 1)$$

where $\theta \in (0,1)$ and $a_1 > 0$ are constants and $\chi_1 \sim N(0,1)$, that is, χ_1 is normally distributed with mean zero and variance 1, and (*ii*) for each representative in the role of Agent *i* at period *t*, $\tau_i(t)$ is a Poisson distributed random variable with mean λ that is independent of the $\tau_j(T)$s for other representatives where $j \neq i$ or $T \neq t$. $\bar{\theta}$ is defined in this manner to ensure that $0 \leq \bar{\theta} \leq 1$. Agents are also allowed to experiment in case of inconsistency between achieved and expected payoffs. The underlying idea here is that each representative enters into the game with her own personal weight that discounts the past and observes only the most recent $\tau_i(t)+1$ plays, which she uses together with her discounting weight to form her conjecture. The random distribution of the $\tau_i(t)$s allows for the amount of observed information from the past to vary across representatives, so this weighted fictitious play process also incorporates two sources of randomness into each updating, namely, the variations on the weights and on the number of most recent observations. This dynamic does not incorporate common prior conjectures across representatives and does not require each representative to recall the entire history of past plays, only the history of some of the most recent past plays.

Weighted fictitious play is a discrete time updating process. The continuous time analog of weighted fictitious play is the *weighted best response* dynamic, which is defined by the differential equation

(A2.3) $$\frac{d\mu_i^t}{dt} = r_i\left(B_i^t - \mu_i^t\right)$$

where B_i^t is a strategy that is a current best response for Agent *i* and $r_i > 0$ is a discount rate defined by $\theta_i = e^{r_i(t_k - t_{k-1})}$ where $t_k - t_{k-1} \to 0$.[11] Weighted best response is best interpreted as a population process where at any given point in continuous time, a fraction of the population update their conjectures. The equilibrium and convergence properties of the weighted best response dynamic are similar to those of the companion weighted fictitious play discrete time process. One can perturb the weighted best response dynamic

11. If the current best response is not a unique pure strategy, then the value of B_i^t can be defined as a selection of one of Agent *i*'s pure strategies that is a current best response or as a mixture of Agent *i*'s pure strategies that is a current best response. The weighted fictitious play process is discussed in Vijay Krishna and Tomas Sjöström, "On the Convergence of Fictitious Play," *Mathematics of Operations Research* 23 (1998), pp. 479–511.

with mutation so that at any given point in continuous time, $\delta > 0$ of the population follow a strategy chosen at random while the remaining $1-\delta$ update according to their best responses. As with the discrete time weighted fictitious play process, an orbit of a perturbed best response dynamic is a stochastic process that can approach a limit. For any $\delta > 0$, if an orbit of the perturbed weighted best response dynamic approaches a limit, this limit is a Nash equilibrium.

Computer Simulations of Learning in Threshold Public Good Games Discussed in Chapter 5: Introduction

The extensive form representation of the variation on the Three-in-a-Boat game discussed in §5.1 where reciprocators are present in the population is given in Figure A.2.1. In this game there are eight possible states of the world denoted by $\theta_{i_1 i_2 i_3}$ where $i_j = 0$ if Agent j is an "ordinary" egoist and $i_j = 1$ if Agent j is a reciprocator, and the probability that any given agent is a reciprocator is $\frac{1}{10}$, with the event that an Agent i is a reciprocator being probabilistically independent of the others being reciprocators. If Agent i is an egoist, then her pure strategies are either to perform (P_i) or defect (D_i). But if Agent i is a reciprocator, then she effectively has the one choice of first performing and then punishing in case one or both of the others defect (R_i). In this game "Nature" chooses the true state of the world $\theta_{i_1 i_2 i_3}$ and agents engage without knowing in advance the types of their counterparts. When this game is converted to strategic form it is the Figure 5.4 threshold public good game.

To the threshold public good games of Figure 1.12 and Figure 5.4, I applied the weighted fictitious play process defined by (A.2.1) with discount factor $\theta = 0.375$, which is the midpoint of the range $[0.25, 0.50]$ of median discount factors imputed to subjects in experimental studies. For both of these games I simulated 100,000 orbits of 100 time periods each where each orbit was set to begin at a prior conjectures point chosen at random in the belief simplex Δ. This process can be interpreted as a fixed agent process where the same three agents engage in the same threshold public good game 100 times and each updates her conjectures over the others' pure strategy profiles according to the (A.2.1) updating process. For both the Figure 1.12 and the Figure 5.4 games, all 100,000 orbits of weighted fictitious play converged to a strict Nash equilibrium over the 100 cycles, illustrating that weighted fictitious play updaters can learn to follow an equilibrium fairly rapidly. For each of these threshold public goods games, the sizes of the basins of attraction were estimated by taking relative frequencies of the convergent orbits. For example, in the Figure 1.12 game simulations, 12,601 orbits converged to the conjectures of the (D, P, P) equilibrium, 12,570 orbits converged to the conjectures of the (P, D, P) equilibrium, 12,498 orbits converged to the conjectures of the (P, P, D) equilibrium, and the remaining 12,570 orbits converged to the conjectures of the suboptimal (D, D, D) equilibrium, so that $m\left(\Delta_{(D,P,P)}\right) \approx 0.1260$, $m\left(\Delta_{(P,D,P)}\right) \approx 0.1257$,

μ[Agent j is a reciprocator] $= \frac{1}{10}$, $r = 1$, $p = 3$

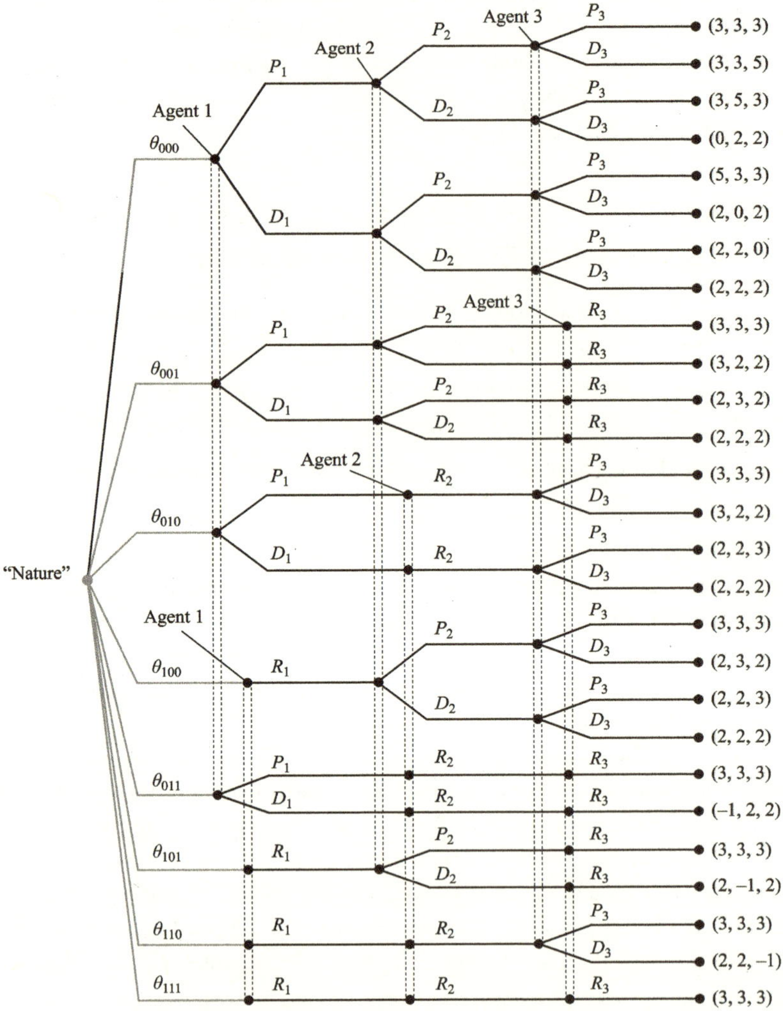

$\theta_{i_1 i_2 i_3} \in \{\theta_{000}, \theta_{001}, ..., \theta_{111}\}$, $i_j = 0$ if Agent j is an "ordinary" egoist,
$i_j = 1$ if Agent j is a reciprocator,
$P_j =$ perform if $i_j = 0$, $D_j =$ defect if $i_j = 0$,
$R_j =$ perform, then punish if a counterpart defects if $i_j = 1$, $j \in \{1, 2, 3\}$

FIGURE A.2.1 Extensive Form of Threshold Public Good Game with Reciprocators

$m\left(\Delta_{(P,P,D)}\right) \approx 0.1250$ and $m\left(\Delta_{(D,D,D)}\right) \approx 0.6233$. Hence, as stated in the text, for the Figure 1.12 game approximately 62.33% of the weighted fictitious play orbits converged to the suboptimal equilibrium (D, D, D), while only approximately 37.67% of the orbits converged to an optimal equilibrium.

The phase diagrams of Figures 5.3 and 5.5 were generated by simulating and then plotting 1000 orbits of one of the three agents' updated conjectures according to the weighted fictitious play process (A.2.1) with $\theta = 0.375$ the initial conjectures point chosen at random. As discussed in the text,[12] for each of these $3\times2\times2$ games, the conjecture for an agent is characterized by a point (x_1, x_2, x_3, x_4) in a tetrahedron where each vertex corresponds to one of the counterparts' four available pure strategy profiles, and for these games each vertex of this tetrahedron characterizes one of the four pure strategy Nash equilibria.

Computer Simulations of Division Problems Discussed in §5.1

To explore the properties of weighted fictitious play applied to the 2-agent bargaining problems discussed above, for each of the demand games discussed in §5.1 I simulated 100,000 orbits of 100 time periods each for the weighted fictitious play processes, where each orbit was set to begin at a prior probability distribution that was a point chosen randomly in the belief simplex. Agents updated their conjectures according to a perturbed version of the (A.2.1) rule, where they were allowed to experiment in case of inconsistency between achieved and expected payoffs. In this context the weighted fictitious play process is interpreted as a fixed agent process where each of the 100,000 orbits constituted a sequence of updated conjectures for a fixed pair of agents who engaged in the same demand game with each other over 100 periods. For every game examined, the majority of the orbits converged to an equilibrium over 100 or fewer periods, confirming that weighted fictitious play learners tend to reach a limit point of learning relatively quickly. For each orbit, each Agent i's weighing factor was set at $\theta_i = \overline{\theta} + \sigma$ where $\overline{\theta} = 0.375$ and σ was sampled from a normal distribution with mean 0 and standard deviation 0.125. These weighting factors were selected so as to vary across orbits in a manner consistent with known experimental results. For each demand game, the claim precision was $\delta = \frac{1}{100}$, that is, the agents in the roles of Claudia and Laura each could follow one of 101 pure strategies $s_0, s_1, \ldots, s_{100}$ where Agent i follows s_m by claiming $m\cdot\delta$ of the good, $m \in \{0,1,\ldots,100\}$. The resulting strategic form game had $101^2 = 10{,}201$ pure strategy profiles, and approximated the completely continuous bargaining problem quite well in that each agent could claim any whole-number percentage of the good. This game had 101 Nash equilibria in pure strategies of the form (s_m, s_n) where $m \in \{0,1,\ldots,100\}$ and $n = 100 - m$, so that Agent 1 in Claudia's role claims $m\cdot\delta$ and Agent 2 in Laura's role claims $(100-m)\cdot\delta$. The ninety-nine of these equilibria where $m \in \{1,\ldots,99\}$ are strict and correspond to efficient divisions where Claudia and Laura each receive a positive share of the good. The remaining two equilibria (s_{100}, s_0) and (s_0, s_{100}) respectively characterize the Nash equilibria of the basis game (G, M)

12. See Chapter 5, note 14.

where Claudia is greedy and Laura is modest and (M,G) where Claudia is modest and Laura is greedy. For each of the demand games discussed in §5.1, the distribution of sizes of the basins of attraction was estimated by taking relative frequencies of the convergent orbits. These distributions are summarized in Figures 5.10, 5.12, 5.14, and 5.15.

Computer Simulations of Learning in Stag Hunt and Augmented Stag Hunt Discussed in §5.2

To estimate the sizes of the basins of attraction of representative weighted fictitious play for the specific Stag Hunt and Augmented Stag Hunt games discussed in §5.2, for each of these games I simulated 100,000 orbits of 100 time periods each where each orbit was set to begin at an initial conjectures point chosen at random in the belief simplex. Agents updated their conjectures according to the (A.2.2) rule with parameters $\bar{\theta}=0.375$ and $a_1=0.05$ and where the number $\tau_i(t)$ of most recent interactions that Agent i observes at period t is Poisson distributed with mean $\lambda=3$. Again these parameters were chosen so that the discounting factors would vary across the representatives who update their conjectures in a manner consistent with experimental results. In this context the weighted fictitious play process is interpreted as a population process where at each of the 100 stages of each of the 100,000 orbits, the two agents who meet in the Stag Hunt or Augmented Stag Hunt game are fresh representative agents of a larger population who update their conjectures according to the partial history of interactions each observes prior to their engagement in the game. In all of these simulations virtually every one of the 100,000 orbits reached an equilibrium in the 100 cycles, indicating that learning was very rapid for representative weighted fictitious play updaters who engage in Stag Hunt or Augmented Stag Hunt. The sizes of the basins of attraction were estimated by taking relative frequencies of the convergent orbits.

The phase diagrams of Figures 5.21 and 5.22 were generated by simulating and then plotting in the triangle that characterizes the belief simplex 300 orbits with initial conjectures point chosen at random of a perturbed weighted best response dynamic where the deterministic dynamic is defined by (A.2.3) and the mutation rate is defined by $\delta=0.01$.

Computer Simulations of Learning in State of Nature Interaction Discussed in §4.3

The strategies the parties in the Variable Anticipation Threshold model of §4.3 follow depend crucially upon how they form their probabilities over their partners' strategies. Intuitively, one would expect a Party i's probability $\lambda_i(t)$ that a current partner will Anticipate to increase monotonically with the number of his past partners who Anticipated. The Variable Anticipation Threshold model reflects this intuition by incorporating a generalization of the weighted fictitious play process discussed above.

At each period t, if Party i has at least one partner, then she updates her probability $\lambda_i(t)$ according to the rule

$$\begin{aligned}\lambda_i(t+1) &= \frac{1-\theta_i}{1-\theta_i^{t+1}} \cdot \sum_{k=0}^{t} \theta_i^k A_i(t-k) \\ &= \frac{1-\theta_i}{1-\theta_i^{t+1}} \left(A_i(t) + \theta_i \cdot \frac{1-\theta_i^t}{1-\theta_i} \cdot \lambda_i(t) \right)\end{aligned} \tag{A2.4}$$

where $A_i(0) = \lambda_i(0)$ is Party i's prior probability that a partner Anticipates, $A_i(m)$ is the fraction of Party i's partners who Anticipate at period $m \in \{1,\ldots,t\}$, and $\theta_i \in (0,1)$ is Party i's weighting factor. If Party i has no partners at period t, then $\lambda_i(t+1) = \lambda_i(t)$. This updating rule generalizes standard weighted fictitious play processes for 2×2 games, which assume that each inductive learner is matched in the game with exactly one other partner at each period.

The simulations explore how behavior evolves in particular instances of the Variable Anticipation Threshold model discussed in Chapter 4, where parties who neighbor each other in a two-dimensional lattice play games with payoff functions that conform with the Figure 4.6 matrix. The updating according to (A2.4) is to be interpreted as a population process, since parties can migrate and change partners over time. The lattice has m^2 sites, where the user defines m, each of which has an index (j,k), $j,k \in \{1,\ldots,m\}$. In all simulations summarized here, $m = 50$, which defines a lattice with 2,500 sites.[13] Topologically the lattice is equivalent to a torus, and can be mapped onto a square whose edges "wrap around." The program simulates a sequence of M generations of play, or *run* of length M, between neighboring agents in the lattice who update their beliefs according to the weighted fictitious play formula (A2.4). At the start of a run, a set of agents are randomly distributed in the lattice as follows: For each (j,k), $j,k \in \{1,\ldots,m\}$, a value $U_1(j,k)$ is sampled from the uniform distribution over $[0,1]$ and site (j,k) is initially occupied if $U_1(j,k) < \rho$, where the user chooses the density $\rho \in [0,1]$. Hence there are $n \le m^2$ agents in the system, and $n = m^2$ if $\rho = 1$. X_1, X_2 and X_3 denote independent normally distributed random variables with mean 0 and variance 1, and v_α, v_β, and v_θ are constants chosen by the user. For each Party i, α_i was sampled from the random variable $Y = v_\beta \cdot \text{abs}(X_1)$, $x_i = 2 + \beta_i$ where β_i was sampled from the random variable $Z = v_\beta \cdot X_2$ and θ_i was sampled from the random variable $W = v_\theta \cdot X_2 + \mu_\theta$. The user can also set the prior $\lambda_i(0)$ and the initial strategy $s_i(0)$ for each party according to the formula

$$s_i(0) = \begin{cases} C \text{ if } U_2(j_i,k_i) \le \sigma \\ A \text{ if } U_2(j_i,k_i) > \sigma \end{cases}$$

13. I have explored several simulations with larger lattices, such as the 10,000 -site lattice defined when $m = 100$. However, these simulations require far more computer resources and are harder to interpret visually than the simulations summarized here where $m = 50$. In the larger simulations I attempted, I obtained results similar to those where $m = 50$.

where $U_2(j_i, k_i)$ is sampled from the uniform distribution over $[0,1]$, (j_i, k_i) is Party i's site at $t = 0$, and $\sigma \in [0,1]$ is chosen by the user.

If Party i occupies site (j_i, k_i) at a given period t, then the set

$$\mathcal{M}^t(j_i, k_i) = \{\{j, k\} : |j_i - j| = 1 \text{ mod } m \text{ and/or } |k_i - k| = 1 \text{ mod } m\}$$

is Party i's *Moore-8 neighborhood*, and the set

$$\mathcal{V}^t(j_i, k_i) = \{\{j, k\} : |j_i - j| = 1 \text{ mod } m \text{ or } |k_i - k| = 1 \text{ mod } m\}$$

is Party i's *von Neumann neighborhood*. The user can choose to have each Party i play all of the other parties that lie in either Party i's Moore-8 neighborhood or Party i's von Neumann neighborhood.

In each run, parties in the lattice can migrate according to either of two rules chosen by the user. According to the first rule, at the end of each period t, if a party in $\mathcal{M}^t(j_i, k_i)$ (or $\mathcal{V}^t(j_i, k_i)$, depending upon the user's choice) followed A and at least one cell $\mathcal{M}^t(j_i, k_i)$ in (or $\mathcal{V}^t(j_i, k_i)$) is unoccupied, then at period Party i migrates into of these unoccupied cells. Otherwise, if a cell in $\mathcal{M}^t(j_i, k_i)\left(\text{or } \mathcal{V}^t(j_i, k_i)\right)$ is unoccupied, then Party i migrates into this cell with probability $\frac{\eta}{8}\left(\text{or } \frac{\eta}{4}\right)$ where η is chosen by the user. The second migration rule is simply the second part of the first rule. Parties that migrate according to the second rule simply move about in the lattice at random. Parties that migrate according to the first rule deliberately move away from Anticipators and otherwise move at random. In the special case where $\rho = 1$, every cell in the lattice is occupied and the network of interactions is uniform and fixed.

In the simulations summarized here, the fictitious play weights were distributed normally with a median value $\mu_\theta = 0.375$ and a standard deviation $v_\theta = 0.125$. These parameters ensured that the fictitious play weights of the parties were concentrated along the interval of fictitious play weights compatible with the experimental studies of coordination games played by human subjects. A variant of the model uses perturbed weighted fictitious play, where with some probability $\varepsilon > 0$, a party *mutates* or chooses a strategy at random instead of best responding given current beliefs.

Tables A.1–A.4 summarize the results of a variety of simulations of interaction in the Hobbesian State of Nature. Run 1.1 is the first simulation of a population of all moderates discussed in §5.3. A population $N = \{1, \ldots, 1256\}$ of 1256 moderates interacted in the 50^2 sites of the lattice. In this simulation, $v_\alpha = 0.20$ and $v_\beta = 0.10$. Consequently, in this system the parties' payoff function parameters were distributed so that $x_i > 1 + \alpha_i$ for all $i \in N$. The initial strategies were distributed so that initially 47.93% of the parties cooperated and 52.07% Anticipated. Parties migrated according to the rule where each party moved if possible when any of its Moore-8 neighbors Anticipated and otherwise migrated at random if possible with $\eta = 0.25$. By the end of the run of $M = 1000$ generations, 0.0% of the parties Anticipated. Run 1.3 is the first simulation of a mixed population discussed in §5.3. A mixed population $N = \{1, \ldots, 1256\}$ of 1256 interacted in the 50^2 sites of the lattice. This time the priors were all set at $\lambda_i(0) = 0$. Once again, at each successive time period parties actively moved away from Anticipators if possible and otherwise moved at random with $\eta = 0.25$. However, here $v_\alpha = 0.35$ and $v_\beta = 0.10$, so in this population the payoff functions were distributed so that $1 + \alpha_i > x_i$ for approximately 0.88% if the $i \in N$. That is, approximately 0.88% of the parties were strict dominators. At the start of the run of $M = 1000$ generations, only 0.88% of the population Anticipated, namely, the strict dominators. By the end of this run, 100.0% of the parties in this system Anticipated.

Tables A2.1 and A2.2 summarize simulations where parties moved according to the rule where parties deliberately fled Anticipators when possible. Tables A2.3 and A2.4 summarize simulations where parties moved at random only. Tables A2.1 and A2.3 (Tables A2.2 and A2.4) summarize simulations where parties interact with counterparts who lie in their Moore-8 neighborhoods (von Neumann neighborhoods). With only a single exception (the mutation rates in $r = 5$), in each run $1.r$, $2.r$, $3.r$, and $4.r$, $r \in \{1,\ldots,15\}$, the other parameters of the simulation are the same for each r in order to compare the properties of the dynamics across movement rules and interaction rules. In general, in these simulations the presence of dominators was always a sufficient condition to produce a contagion of Anticipation, and dominators were needed in order to produce this contagion in all but the 4.5 simulation, discussed in the following paragraph.

The runs where $r = 5$ test the stability of the all-C equilibrium when no dominators are present in the population. In these runs all are moderates and all start by following C except for mutants. In both runs where parties interact with partners in their Moore-8 neighborhoods, the system remains near the all-C equilibrium over 10,000 generations even at a mutation rate of $\varepsilon = 0.05$. In run 2.5, where parties interacted with partners in their von Neumann neighborhoods and tried to move away from Anticipators, they remained near the all-C equilibrium over 10,000 generations at the relatively high mutation rate of $\varepsilon = 0.02$. But in run 4.5, where parties interacted with partners in their von Neumann neighborhoods and moved at random only, with $\varepsilon = 0.02$ the system approached the all-A equilibrium after than fewer than 1000 generations. In this case, the all-C equilibrium could not withstand the high "bombardment" of mutants for long. These runs show that the stability of the all-C equilibrium is somewhat sensitive to rules governing partnership and movement. When all are moderates, the all-C equilibrium is quite stable when parties have the relatively many partners who lie in their Moore-8 neighborhoods or actively flee Anticipators. But when they have the relatively few partners who lie in their von Neumann neighborhoods and they move at random only, the all- C equilibrium is less stable in the face of random mutation.

In runs where $r = 6, 7$, or 8 and where population density ρ was varied across values less than or greater than $\rho = 0.5$, the system always converged to the all-A equilibrium where the percentage of Anticipators was $A(M) = 100.0$ even though in general the percentage of dominators was $D < 1.0$. So the attracting power of the all-A equilibrium is fairly robust to changes in population density, so long as some movement is possible. In the runs where $r = 9$, $\rho = 1.0$ and the system would remain near the all-C

Table A2.1 Simulations Where Parties Interact with Neighbors in $M^t(j_i, k_i)$ (Parties Deliberately Move Away from Anticipators if Possible)

Run	M	ρ	n	ν_α	ν_β	σ	$\in$	η	D	$A(1)$	$A(M)$
1.1	1000	0.50	1256	0.20	0.1	0.5	0.0	0.25	0.0	52.07	0.0
1.2	10,000	0.50	1257	0.20	0.1	0.5	0.02	0.25	0.0	49.09	0.072
1.3	1000	0.50	1256	0.35	0.1	1.0	0.0	0.25	0.88	0.88	100.0
1.4	10,000	0.50	1268	0.35	0.1	1.0	0.02	0.25	0.71	1.03	98.97
1.5	10,000	0.50	1198	0.20	0.1	1.0	0.05	0.25	0.0	2.25	3.01
1.6	1000	0.25	608	0.35	0.1	1.0	0.0	0.25	0.49	0.49	100.0
1.7	1000	0.75	1859	0.35	0.1	1.0	0.0	0.25	0.75	0.75	100.0
1.8	1000	0.90	2231	0.35	0.1	1.0	0.0	0.25	0.77	0.77	100.0
1.9	1000	1.00	2500	0.35	0.1	1.0	0.0	0.25	0.56	0.56	0.60
1.10	1000	1.00	2500	0.45	0.1	1.0	0.0	0.25	3.44	3.44	100.0
1.11	1000	0.5	1255	0.35	0.1	1.0	0.01	0.0	0.72	1.04	99.36
1.12	1000	0.5	1225	0.35	0.1	1.0	0.01	0.5	0.65	0.90	99.27
1.13	1000	0.5	1258	0.35	0.1	1.0	0.01	1.0	0.87	1.51	99.60
1.14	1000	0.5	1261	0.30	0.2	1.0	0.01	0.25	0.71	1.59	99.44
1.15	1000	0.5	1268	0.25	0.3	1.0	0.01	0.25	0.79	1.50	99.53

$A(1)$ = percentage of parties that follow A in period 1

$A(M)$ = percentage of parties that follow A in period M

D = percentage of dominators in the population

Table A2.2 Simulations Where Parties Interact with Neighbors in $V^{\tau}(j_i, k_i)$ (Parties Deliberately Move Away from Anticipators if Possible)

Run	M	ρ	n	ν_α	ν_β	σ	$\in$	η	D	$A(1)$	$A(M)$
2.1	1000	0.5	1221	0.20	0.1	0.5	0.0	0.25	0.0	50.78	0.0
2.2	10,000	0.5	1233	0.20	0.1	0.5	0.02	0.25	0.0	50.28	2.27
2.3	1000	0.5	1271	0.35	0.1	1.0	0.0	0.25	0.55	0.55	100.0
2.4	10,000	0.5	1230	0.20	0.1	1.0	0.02	0.25	0.89	1.06	99.11
2.5	10,000	0.5	1267	0.20	0.1	1.0	0.02	0.25	0.0	1.18	1.34
2.6	1000	0.25	610	0.35	0.1	1.0	0.0	0.25	0.49	0.49	100.0
2.7	1000	0.75	1862	0.35	0.1	1.0	0.0	0.25	0.70	0.70	100.0
2.8	1000	0.90	2235	0.35	0.1	1.0	0.0	0.25	0.67	0.67	100.0
2.9	1000	1.0	2500	0.35	0.1	1.0	0.0	0.25	0.56	0.68	0.68
2.10	1000	1.0	2500	0.45	0.1	1.0	0.0	0.25	3.64	3.64	100.0
2.11	1000	0.5	1221	0.35	0.1	1.0	0.01	0.0	0.82	1.31	99.67
2.12	1000	0.5	1226	0.35	0.1	1.0	0.01	0.5	0.49	0.82	99.51
2.13	1000	0.5	1244	0.35	0.1	1.0	0.01	1.0	0.88	1.37	99.44
2.14	1000	0.5	1260	0.30	0.2	1.0	0.01	0.25	0.71	0.95	99.37
2.15	1000	0.5	1255	0.25	0.3	1.0	0.01	0.25	1.59	1.91	99.52

$A(1)$ = percentage of parties that follow A in period 1

$A(M)$ = percentage of parties that follow A in period M

D = percentage of dominators in the population

Table A2.3 Simulations Where Parties Interact with Neighbors in $M^t(j_i, ki)$ (Parties Move at Random)

Run	M	ρ	n	ν_α	ν_β	σ	$\in$	η	D	$A(1)$	$A(M)$
3.1	1000	0.50	1184	0.20	0.1	0.5	0.0	0.25	0.0	49.07	0.0
3.2	10,000	0.50	1283	0.20	0.1	0.5	0.02	0.25	0.0	48.56	1.40
3.3	1000	0.50	1244	0.35	0.1	1.0	0.0	0.25	0.40	0.40	100.0
3.4	10,000	0.50	1264	0.35	0.1	1.0	0.02	0.25	1.03	1.66	98.66
3.5	10,000	0.50	1267	0.20	0.1	1.0	0.05	0.25	0.0	1.82	2.76
3.6	1000	0.25	614	0.35	0.1	1.0	0.0	0.25	0.65	0.65	100.0
3.7	1000	0.75	1891	0.35	0.1	1.0	0.0	0.25	0.53	0.53	100.0
3.8	1000	0.90	2238	0.35	0.1	1.0	0.0	0.25	0.54	0.54	100.0
3.9	1000	1.00	2500	0.35	0.1	1.0	0.0	0.25	0.68	0.68	0.68
3.10	1000	1.00	2500	0.45	0.1	1.0	0.0	0.25	3.00	3.00	100.0
3.11	1000	0.5	1280	0.35	0.1	1.0	0.01	0.0	0.86	1.09	14.14
3.12	1000	0.5	1229	0.35	0.1	1.0	0.01	0.5	0.49	0.90	99.84
3.13	1000	0.5	1292	0.35	0.1	1.0	0.01	1.0	0.54	1.01	99.61
3.14	1000	0.5	1240	0.30	0.2	1.0	0.01	0.25	0.73	1.37	99.27
3.15	1000	0.5	1271	0.25	0.3	1.0	0.01	0.25	1.18	1.81	99.37

$A(1)$ = percentage of parties that follow A in period 1

$A(\mathrm{M})$ = percentage of parties that follow A in period M

D = percentage of dominators in the population

Table A2.4 Simulations Where Parties Interact with Neighbors in $V^t(j_i, k_i)$ (Parties Move at Random)

Run	M	ρ	n	ν_α	ν_β	σ	$\in$	η	D	$A(1)$	$A(M)$
4.1	1000	0.50	1253	0.20	0.1	0.5	0.0	0.25	0.0	49.40	0.0
4.2	10,000	0.50	1310	0.20	0.1	0.5	0.02	0.25	0.0	50.23	98.63
4.3	1000	0.50	1259	0.35	0.1	1.0	0.0	0.25	0.64	0.64	100.0
4.4	10,000	0.50	1252	0.35	0.1	1.0	0.02	0.25	0.32	0.96	99.20
4.5	1000	0.50	1226	0.20	0.1	1.0	0.02	0.25	0.0	0.65	79.45
4.6	1000	0.25	626	0.35	0.1	1.0	0.0	0.25	1.28	1.28	100.0
4.7	1000	0.75	1894	0.35	0.1	1.0	0.0	0.25	0.53	0.53	100.0
4.8	1000	0.90	2272	0.35	0.1	1.0	0.0	0.25	0.44	0.44	100.0
4.9	1000	1.00	2500	0.35	0.1	1.0	0.0	0.25	0.60	0.60	0.64
4.10	1000	1.00	2500	0.45	0.1	1.0	0.0	0.25	3.40	3.40	11.64
4.11	1000	0.5	1218	0.35	0.1	1.0	0.01	0.0	0.82	1.15	42.86
4.12	1000	0.5	1282	0.35	0.1	1.0	0.01	0.5	0.16	0.39	99.45
4.13	1000	0.5	1241	0.35	0.1	1.0	0.01	1.0	0.81	1.13	99.92
4.14	1000	0.5	1275	0.30	0.2	1.0	0.01	0.25	0.55	0.94	99.29
4.15	1000	0.5	1207	0.25	0.3	1.0	0.01	0.25	1.16	1.66	99.50

$A(1)$ = percentage of parties that follow A in period 1

$A(M)$ = percentage of parties that follow A in period M

D = percentage of dominators in the population

equilibrium even though some dominators were present. This is not surprising when one takes into account the fact that in these systems parties could not migrate, so that the few dominators are "trapped" in the lattice and cannot spread their aggressive behavior. On the other hand, in several of the runs where $r = 10$, the all-A equilibrium took over the system because $v_\alpha = 0.45$ even though $\rho = 1.0$ once more. So it is possible in a fixed network of parties with no migration for the all-A equilibrium to take over even when all moderates initially cooperate, so long as there are sufficiently many strict dominators. The runs where $r = 11, 12$, and 13 suggest that if dominators are present, the attracting power of the all-A equilibrium is robust with respect to changes in the probability of random movement. In the runs where $t = 14$ and 15, the values of v_α and v_β are varied. In these runs strict dominators are again present and the systems all quickly move to near the all-A equilibrium. Again, what drives the system near all-A is the fact that dominators are in the system, not the specific parameter values that introduce the dominators. (In the runs where $r = 11, \ldots, 15$ the systems do not converge exactly to all-A because the mutation rate is set at $\varepsilon = 0.01$.)

APPENDIX 3

FOLK THEOREMS FOR THE INDEFINITELY REPEATED COVENANT GAME

Several of the concepts summarized in this appendix reflect those used in the formal definition of convention given in Appendix 1. The folk theorems proved in this appendix are community enforcement theorems, where each Party i is a member of a community who can be matched in a base Covenant game with other counterpart parties that can vary over periods in a supergame consisting of an indefinitely repeated sequence of Covenant games. First I will give a formal summary of how individual parties interact in pairwise Covenant games. $N = \{1,\ldots,n\}$ is a set or community of *parties* where $n \geq 2m$, $m \in \mathbb{N}^{+} = \{1,2,\ldots\}$ and $m \geq 2$. $\Omega = \{0,1\}^{n}$ denotes the set of possible worlds for this indefinitely repeated game. Ω consists of the 2^{n} vectors

$$\omega_{00\cdots0} = (0,0,\ldots,0), \omega_{10\cdots0} = (1,0,\ldots,0),\ldots, \omega_{11\cdots1} = (1,1,\ldots,1)$$

and each Party i's information partition of Ω is defined by $\mathcal{H}_i = \{\{\omega_{00\cdots0}\},\{\omega_{10\cdots0}\},\ldots,\{\omega_{11\cdots1}\}\}$, so that all parties know which possible world $\omega \in \Omega$ is the actual world. At each time period or *stage* $t \in \mathbb{N}^{+}$, one world $\omega(t) \in \Omega$ obtains as the actual world at stage t. A full description of each possible world at stage t includes all of the information relevant to the parties' decisions at stage t, including a description of the stage Covenant game and a description of the history of past plays that defines the current $\omega(t) \in \Omega$. Each Party $i \in N$ has a subjective probability distribution $\mu_i(\cdot)$ over the propositions in Ω and an expectation operator $E_i(\cdot)$ based upon $\mu_i(\cdot)$. I write $\mu(A) = \mu_1(A)$ for the special case where $\mu_1(A) = \cdots = \mu_n(A)$ for a given $A \subseteq \Omega$. For the base game, $u_i(\cdot)$ denotes Party i's payoff function. At each stage t, a nonempty subset $N_t \subseteq N$ with m_t members of N where m_t is divisible by 2 is sampled from N with replacement. Each sampled Party $i \in N_t$ is matched with exactly one counterpart $i(t) \in N_t$. In the special case where $N_t = N$ at every stage, so that every party is sampled and matched at every stage, then the parties are in an *ordinary repeated matching game*. If Party i is unmatched at some stage t, then at this stage Party i

Party i \ Party $i(t)$	P	D	S
P	1	l_i	0
D	$1+g_i$	$-c_i$	0
S	0	0	0

$g_i > 0, l_i > 0, c_i > 0, g_i - l_i < 1$

FIGURE A3.1 Party i 's Covenant Game Payoffs

receives a constant *noninteraction* payoff $\underline{u}=0$. If Party i is matched at stage t, then Party i and counterpart Party $i(t)$ engage in a Covenant game and her payoffs are defined by the Figure A3.1 matrix.

Now I define formally the strategies that the parties in N can follow in the indefinitely repeated Covenant game. A generic *strategy* for Party i is a sequence of functions $f_i=(f_i^t)$ where $f_i^t:\Omega\to\{P,D,S\}$ and is $\mathcal{H}_i$-measurable, that is, f_i^t is constant on each cell of $\mathcal{H}_i$. $f=(f_1,\ldots,f_n)$ is a generic *strategy profile*. S_i denotes the set of all strategies Party i can follow. At a given stage t, $f_i^t(\omega(t))\in\{P,D,S\}$ defines the pure strategy $a_i(t)$ that Party i follows in the base Covenant game at stage t. I stipulate that $f_i^t(\omega(t))=S$ if $i\notin N_t$ at stage t in order to avoid trivial complications. At stage t,

$$f^t(\omega(t))=\left(f_1^t(\omega(t)),\ldots,f_n^t(\omega(t))\right)\in\{P,D,S\}^n$$

is the set of pure strategies $(a_1(t),\ldots,a_n(t))$ the parties follow in the base Covenant game. Party i's expected payoff at stage t given $\omega(t)\in\Omega$ is

$$E_i\left(u_i\left(f^t(\omega(t))\right)\right)=\sum_{j\neq i}E_i\left(u_i\left(f_i^t(\omega(t)),f_j^t(\omega(t))\right)\right)\mu_i\left[i(t)=j\right].$$

Let $\delta_i\in(0,1)$ be Party i's discount factor. Party i's overall expected payoff is

$$E_i(u_i\circ f)=\sum_{t=1}^{\infty}E_i\left(u_i\left(f^t(\omega(t))\right)\right)\delta_i^t.$$

A strategy profile f is a correlated equilibrium of the indefinitely repeated Covenant game if, and only if, for each $i\in N$,

$$E_i(u_i\circ f)\geq E_i\left(u_i\circ(f_i',f_{-i})\right)\text{ for all } f_i'\in S_i.$$ [1]

1. I use the "jackknife" notation summarized in Appendix 1, note 5.

Basic Community Enforcement Folk Theorems

The following results are similar in spirit to the folk theorems Michihiro Kandori and Glenn Ellison have proved for indefinitely repeated Prisoner's Dilemma played in random matching models.[2] However, the matching model of this appendix does not assume that every party is matched with a counterpart in every period. The strategies considered below also allow for the possibility that an offensive violation starts no punishment cycle. Kandori and Ellison assume that every party is matched at every period and that an offensive violation is certain to start a punishment cycle. Note that in the results discussed here, the only restriction placed on matching is that the probability a Party i is matched remains constant over the stages of play.

Each Party i has a *marker function* $z_i(t): \mathbb{N}^+ \to \{0,1\}$ that indicates at each stage t whether Party i is currently *innocent*, in which case $z_i(t)=1$, or *guilty*, in which case $z_i(t)=0$. Let $\omega(t)=(z_1(t),...,z_n(t))$. Then Party i's *Humean strategy* is defined by $h^* = \left(h^*\left(\omega(t)\right)\right)$ where

$$h^*\left(\omega(t)\right) = \begin{cases} P \text{ if } i(t) \in N_t \text{ and } z_{i(t)}(t)=1 \\ S \text{ if } i(t) \in N_t \text{ and } z_{i(t)}(t)=0 \end{cases}.$$

That is, according to h^*, Party i performs in the base Covenant game if matched with an innocent counterpart and shuns if matched with a guilty counterpart.

To complete the description of a given Humean strategy one needs to specify the conditions for guilt and innocence. Here I define two special types of innocence-guilt conditions. The first of these is the basis for a punishment cycle of indefinite length. Party i's *grim marker* is defined recursively as

$$\text{(M.1)} \qquad z_i(t) = \begin{cases} 1 \text{ if } t=1 \\ 1 \text{ if } t>1,\ z_i(t-1)=1 \text{ and } a_i(t-1)=h^*\left(\omega(t-1)\right) \\ 1-\overline{X}_i \text{ if } t>1,\ z_i(t-1)=1 \text{ and } a_i(t-1)\neq h^*\left(\omega(t-1)\right) \\ 0 \text{ if } t>1 \text{ and } z_i(t-1)=0 \end{cases}$$

where $\overline{X}_i$ is a random variable with range $\{0,1\}$ where $\overline{q}_i = \mu\left[\overline{X}_i = 1\right]$. According to the grim marker function, a given Party i is innocent at stage 1 and retains innocence at stage t if she was innocent at stage $t-1$ and followed the Humean strategy h^* at $t-1$. But if Party i is innocent at stage $t-1$ and deviates from h^* at this stage, then Party i with probability $\overline{q}_i$ becomes guilty at stage t. And once Party i becomes guilty, she remains guilty at every subsequent stage. The grim marker function gets its name from its obvious similarities to the grim strategy for playing a repeated Prisoner's Dilemma with a fixed partner. If Party i becomes guilty at stage t, then starting at this stage the community begins a punishment cycle of indefinite length by shunning Party i at every

2. Kandori (1992); Ellison (1993).

stage $T \geq t$ where $i \in N_t$. One can think of $\overline{q}_i$ as the probability that an offensive violation on Party i's part is detected and announced to the community, in which case Party i becomes permanently guilty. When $\overline{q}_i = 1$, one becomes guilty exactly when one offensively violates. The $\overline{q}_i = 1$ case describes a punishment regime that is working "perfectly," in that offensive violators are certain to be detected and punished. The opposite extreme where $\overline{q}_i = 0$ describes a situation where a Party i is certain to escape detection if she offensively violates, as if Party i had a foolproof ring of Gyges technology. Note that in the definition of the grim marker function, any unilateral deviation from h^* at a given stage constitutes an offensive violation, so a Party i can become guilty for failing to shun a guilty partner as well as for defecting against an innocent partner. Hence the grim marker defines a Humean strategy that incorporates second-order punishment for failing to punish the guilty. It is of course possible to define a more lenient innocence-guilt condition leading only to first-order punishment where the only offensive violation is defecting against an innocent partner.

Proposition A3.1. If each Party i's marker is the grim marker defined by (M.1), and if

(A3.1.1)
$$\delta_i \geq \frac{g_i}{g_i + \overline{q}_i}$$

for $i \in N$, then $\boldsymbol{h}^* = (h^*, \ldots, h^*)$ is a correlated equilibrium of the indefinitely repeated Covenant game with matching over N.

Note that for any value of $\overline{q}_i > 0$, there will be values of that satisfy (A3.1.1).

PROOF. Let $\overline{p}_i = 1 - \overline{q}_i$, that is, $\overline{p}_i$ is the probability that no punishment cycle begins at stage t if Party i offensively violates at $t-1$ and becomes guilty at stage t. Let $x_i = \sum_{j \neq i} \mu_i[i(t) = j]$ and $1 - x_i = \mu_i[i \notin N_t]$, that is, x_i is Party i's probability of being matched at a given stage. Note that at stage t, Party i's undiscounted expected payoff for following her end of $\boldsymbol{h}^*(\omega(t)) = (h^*(\omega(t)), \ldots, h^*(\omega(t)))$ is

$$\begin{aligned} E_i\left(u_i\left(\boldsymbol{h}^*(\omega(t))\right)\right) &= 0 \cdot \mu[i \notin N_t] + \sum_{j \neq i} u_i(P,P) \cdot \mu[i(t) = j] \\ &= 0 \cdot (1 - x_i) + u_i(P,P) \cdot x_i \\ &= x_i \end{aligned}$$

because by hypothesis all the parties in N follow their respective ends of $\boldsymbol{h}^*$. So we have

$$E_i(u_i \circ \boldsymbol{h}^*) = \sum_{t=1}^{\infty} x_i \delta_i^t = x_i \cdot \frac{\delta_i}{1 - \delta_i}.$$

Note that if $x_i = 0$, that is, Party i is never matched, then $E_i(u_i \circ \boldsymbol{h}^*) = 0$ and Party i can never gain by deviating from $\boldsymbol{h}^*$ because she never interacts. The interesting case is where $x_i > 0$. Now consider any strategy $f_1^* \neq h^*$ where Party i deviates from the sequence $\left(h^*(\omega(t))\right)_{t=1}^{\infty}$ for the first time at stage $t = 1$. Here we note that

$$E_i\left(u_i\left(f_1^*, \boldsymbol{h}_{-i}^*\right)\right) \leq \sum_{t=1}^{\infty}\left(x_i \cdot \left[(1+g_i)(\bar{p}_i)^{t-1}\delta_i^t\right]\right)$$

because if Party i follows f_1^* when the others follow $\boldsymbol{h}_{-i}^*$, then starting at $t=1$ the best expected continuing payoff Party i can possibly achieve is the discounted payoff $(1+g_i)\delta_i^t$ of exploiting Party $i(t)$ if Party i is matched at t, assuming that no punishment cycle has already started at $t \geq 1$, an event that occurs with probability $(\bar{p}_i)^{t-1}$. So we have

$$\begin{aligned}\bar{p}_i \cdot E_i\left(u_i\left(f_1^*, \boldsymbol{h}_{-i}^*\right)\right) &\leq \bar{p}_i \cdot \sum_{t=1}^{\infty}\left(x_i \cdot \left[(1+g_i)(\bar{p}_i)^{t-1}\delta_i^t\right]\right) \\ &= \sum_{t=1}^{\infty}\left(x_i \cdot \left[(1+g_i)(\bar{p}_i)^{t}\delta_i^t\right]\right) \\ &= x_i \cdot (1+g_i) \cdot \frac{\bar{p}_i\delta_i}{1-\bar{p}_i\delta_i}\end{aligned}$$

and so

$$E_i\left(u_i\left(f_1^*, \boldsymbol{h}_{-i}^*\right)\right) \leq x_i \cdot (1+g_i) \cdot \frac{\delta_i}{1-\bar{p}_i\delta_i}.$$

Hence we have

$$E_i\left(u_i \circ \boldsymbol{h}^*\right) \geq E_i\left(u_i\left(f_1^*, \boldsymbol{h}_{-i}^*\right)\right)$$

when

$$x_i \cdot \frac{\delta_i}{1-\delta_i} \geq x_i \cdot (1+g_i) \cdot \frac{\delta_i}{1-\bar{p}_i\delta_i}$$

or

(A3.1.2)
$$\frac{\delta_i}{1-\delta_i} \geq (1+g_i) \cdot \frac{\delta_i}{1-\bar{p}_i\delta_i}$$

and (A3.1.2) is satisfied when

$$\delta_i \geq \frac{g_i}{1+g_i-\bar{p}_i} = \frac{g_i}{1+\bar{q}_i},$$

which establishes that if (A3.1.1) is satisfied, then a given Party i cannot improve her expected payoff by deviating unilaterally from $\boldsymbol{h}^*$ for the first time at $t=1$.

Now note that if Party i follows a strategy f_T^* where $f_1^*(\omega(T)) \neq h^*(\omega(T))$ for the first time at some $T>1$, then at stage T she faces the same sequence of strategy profiles defined by $\boldsymbol{h}_{-i}^*$ that she faced at stage $t=1$, and if Party i continues to follow h^* from stage T onward, then she also faces the same sequence of strategy profiles defined by $\boldsymbol{h}_{-i}^*$. The respective expected payoffs starting at stage T of following h^* and f_T^* satisfy

$$\sum_{t=T}^{\infty} x_i \delta_i^t = \delta_i^{T-1} \cdot \sum_{t=1}^{\infty} x_i \delta_i^t = \delta_i^{T-1} \cdot E_i\left(u_i \circ \boldsymbol{h}^*\right)$$

and

$$\delta_i^{T-1} \cdot \sum_{t=1}^{\infty}\left(x_i \cdot \left[(1+g_i)(\overline{p}_i)^{t-1} \delta_i^T\right]\right) = \sum_{t=T}^{\infty}\left(x_i \cdot \left[(1+g_i)(\overline{p}_i)^{t-1} \delta_i^T\right]\right)$$
$$\geq \delta_i^{T-1} E_i\left(u_i\left(f_1^*, \boldsymbol{h}_{-i}^*\right)\right).$$

Hence the same argument just given for the $t=1$ case applies to the case where Party i deviates unilaterally from $\boldsymbol{h}^*$ for the first time at $T>1$, and so in general $E_i(u_i \circ \boldsymbol{h}^*) \geq E_i\left(u_i(f_t^*, \boldsymbol{h}_{-i}^*)\right)$ for $t \geq 1$ when (A3.1.1) is satisfied for $i \in N$. □

Corollary A3.2. For $N=\{1,2\}$ and $\overline{q}_1 = \overline{q}_2 = 1$, if each Party i's marker is the grim marker and $\delta_1 \geq \frac{1}{1+g_1}$ and $\delta_2 \geq \frac{1}{1+g_2}$, then (h^*, h^*) is a correlated equilibrium of the indefinitely repeated Covenant game played between fixed partners.

PROOF. Since $N_t \neq \varnothing$, $N_t = \{1,2\}$ for each stage, that is, Party 1 and Party 2 are matched with each other at each stage. Since $\delta_1 \geq \frac{1}{1+g_1}$ and $\delta_2 \geq \frac{1}{1+g_2}$, (A3.2.1.1) is satisfied, so by Proposition A3.1, (h^*, h^*) is an equilibrium. □

Note that the assumption that $\overline{q}_1 = \overline{q}_2 = 1$ in this corollary is actually not very demanding, since given that each party in a fixed pair is matched at every stage with the same partner, either of these parties is certain to know if the other offensively violates at a given stage. Given these hypotheses, (h^*, h^*) is like the grim equilibrium (Tr, Tr) for playing indefinitely repeated Prisoner's Dilemma except that offensive violation is punished with shunning rather than with defection. Note also that in this case where $N=\{1,2\}$, only first-order punishment ever takes place.

A second main type of innocence-guilt marker is the basis for a limited punishment cycle where an offensive violation is punished for K stages of shunning, after which Party i regains innocence. Party i's *K-stage guilt marker* is defined recursively as

$$\text{(M.2)} \quad z_i(t) = \begin{cases} 1 \text{ if } t=1 \text{ or if } t>1,\ z_i(t-1)=1 \text{ and } a_i(t-1)=h^*\left(\omega(t-1)\right) \\ 1-\hat{X}_i \text{ if } t>1,\ z_i(t-1)=1 \text{ and } a_i(t-1)\neq h^*\left(\omega(t-1)\right) \\ 0 \text{ if } t>1 \text{ and for some } T<t,\ z_i(T-1)=1,\ z_i(t)=0 \text{ and } t-T<K \\ 1 \text{ otherwise} \end{cases}$$

where $\hat{X}_i$ is a random variable with range $\{0,1\}$ where $\hat{q}_i = \mu[\hat{X}_i = 1]$. The K-stage guilt marker function is similar to the grim marker function except that if a Party i offensively violates and then becomes guilty as a result, she remains guilty for only K stages.[3]

3. Note there is some redundancy in the innocence-guilt conditions as I have defined them here.

As is the case with the grim marker, the K-stage guilt marker establishes conditions for second-order punishment for failing to punish the guilty. But in this case, after K stages of shunning, the community effectively forgives an offensive violation.

Proposition A3.3. If each Party i's marker is the K-stage guilt marker defined by (M.2), and if

$$\text{(A3.3.1)}\quad \left(1-\delta_i\left(1-\hat{q}_i\right)\right)\left(\delta_i^{K+1}-1\right)-\left(\left(\delta_i\left(1-\hat{q}_i\right)\right)^{K+1}-1\right)\left(1-\delta_i\right)\left(1+g_i\right)\leq 0$$

for each $i \in N$, then $\boldsymbol{h}^*$ is a correlated equilibrium of the indefinitely repeated Covenant game with matching over N.

Note that if $\hat{q}_i = 1$, so that a unilateral deviation by Party i from is certain to render Party i guilty, then (A3.3.1) reduces to

$$\text{(A3.3.2)}\qquad \delta_i^{K+1}-\left(1+g_i\right)\delta_i+g_i\leq 0.$$

In this special case, the corresponding Humean strategies are nearly identical to the *standing strategies* that Sugden and Boyd propose for playing a repeated Prisoner's Dilemma,[4] except that offensive violation is punished with shunning instead of defection. Note also that as $K \to \infty$, so that the punishment cycle approaches indefinite length, (A3.3.1) converges to

$$-\left(1-\delta_i\left(1-\hat{q}_i\right)\right)+\left(1-\delta_i\right)\left(1+g_i\right)\leq 0$$

and this inequality is equivalent to inequality (A3.1.1) when $\hat{q}_i = \overline{q}_i$. So for any values of $\hat{q}_i > 0$ and $g_i > 0$, there will be a value $K_{\hat{q}_i, g_i} > 0$ such that for $k \geq K_{\hat{q}_i, g_i}$ there are values of $\delta_i \in (0,1)$ that satisfy (A3.3.1). Note that a larger value of g_i may require a larger value of K in order to make $\boldsymbol{h}^*$ an equilibrium, which makes intuitive sense since a larger and more tempting value of g_i may make it necessary for a community to apply a longer punishment cycle in order to make conforming with the corresponding Humean strategy each Party i's best response.

PROOF. As in Proposition A3., if x_i denotes the probability that $i \in N_t$ at any stage t, then Party i's expected payoff for following her end of $\boldsymbol{h}^*$ when the others do likewise is

$$E_i\left(u_i \circ \boldsymbol{h}^*\right)=\sum_{t=1}^{\infty} x_i \delta_i^t = x_i \cdot \frac{\delta_i}{1-\delta_i}.$$

Consider any strategy $f_1' \neq h^*$ where Party i deviates unilaterally from the sequence $\left(h^*\left(\omega(t)\right)\right)_{t=1}^{\infty}$ at stage $t=1$. If a punishment cycle starts at stage $t=2$, then Party i's counterparts follow S at each stage t where $i \in N_t$ and where $2 \leq t \leq K+1$, and then revert back to P at stage $t = K+2$ if $i \in N_t$, so that Party i now faces the sequence

$$\left(h^*\left(\omega(t)\right)\right)_{t=K+2}^{\infty}=\left(h^*\left(\omega(t)\right)\right)_{t=1}^{\infty},$$

4. Sugden (2004), §6.3–4; Boyd (1989).

that is, at stage $t = K+2$, Party i faces the same situation she faced at the beginning stage $t=1$, except that her overall expected payoff is multiplied by the discount factor δ_i^{K+1}. Let $\hat{p}_i = 1-\hat{q}_i$ denote the probability that no punishment cycle begins at stage $t \in \{2,\ldots,K+1\}$. Now note that over the $K+1$ stages from $t=1$ to $t=K+1$ Party i's expected payoff if she follows f_1' is no greater than

$$\begin{aligned} x_i \cdot (1+g_i) \cdot \sum_{t=1}^{\infty} (\hat{p}_i)^{t-1} \delta_i^t &= x_i \cdot (1+g_i) \cdot (\hat{p}_i)^{-1} \cdot \sum_{t=1}^{\infty} (\hat{p}_i)^t \delta_i^t \\ &= x_i \cdot (1+g_i) \cdot (\hat{p}_i)^{-1} \cdot \frac{\hat{p}_i \delta_i - \left(\hat{p}_i \delta_i\right)^{K+2}}{1-\hat{p}_i \delta_i}, \\ &= x_i \cdot (1+g_i) \cdot \frac{\delta_i - (\hat{p}_i)^{K+1} \delta_i^{K+2}}{1-\hat{p}_i \delta_i} \end{aligned}$$

which Party i achieves only when she gains the discounted exploitation payoff each time she is matched over these K stages and no punishment cycle starts at any of these K stages. If, on the other hand, Party i follows h^* from $t=1$ to $t=K+1$, then over these stages Party i's expected payoff equals

$$\sum_{t=1}^{K+1} x_i \delta_i^t = x_i \cdot \frac{\delta_i - \delta_i^{K+2}}{1-\delta_i}.$$

So in order for f_1' to be Party i's best response to $\boldsymbol{h}_{-i}^*$, we must have

$$x_i \cdot (1+g_i) \cdot \frac{\delta_i - (\hat{p}_i)^{K+1} \delta_i^{K+2}}{1-\hat{p}_i \delta_i} > x_i \cdot \frac{\delta_i - \delta_i^{K+2}}{1-\delta_i}$$

or

$$(1+g_i) \cdot \frac{1-(\hat{p}_i)^{K+1} \delta_i^{K+2}}{1-\hat{p}_i \delta_i} > \frac{1-\delta_i^{K+1}}{1-\delta_i}.$$

Hence $E_i(u_i \circ \boldsymbol{h}^*) \geq E_i\left(u_i(f_1', \boldsymbol{h}_{-i}^*)\right)$ when

$$\left(\frac{1-\delta_i^{K+1}}{1-\delta_i}\right)\left(\frac{1-\hat{p}_i \delta_i}{1-(\hat{p}_i \delta_i)^{K+1}}\right) \geq 1+g_i$$

or

$$(1-\delta_i \hat{p}_i)\left(\delta_i^{K+1}-1\right) - \left((\delta_i \hat{p}_i)^{K+1}-1\right)(1-\delta_i)(1+g_i) \leq 0,$$

that is,

$$\left(1-\delta_i(1-\hat{q}_i)\right)\left(\delta_i^{K+1}-1\right) - \left(\left(\delta_i(1-\hat{q}_i)\right)^{K+1}-1\right)(1-\delta_i)(1+g_i) \leq 0.$$

Now, if Party i follows any strategy $f_T' \neq h^*$ where $f_T'\left(\omega(T)\right) \neq h^*\left(\omega(T)\right)$ for the first time at stage $T>1$ when the others follow $\boldsymbol{h}_{-i}^*$ at every stage, then starting at stage T, Party i can gain no higher an expected payoff than the highest expected payoff discounted by a factor of δ_i^{T-1} that she could have gained by following f_1', and starting at T her expected payoff of continuing to follow $\boldsymbol{h}^*$ is the same as that of following $\boldsymbol{h}^*$ from stage 1 onward discounted by a factor of δ_i^{T-1}. So we can apply to f_T' the argument just applied to f_1' for $t=1$ to conclude that h^* is a best response to $\boldsymbol{h}_{-i}^*$ in general when (A3.3.1) is satisfied for each $i \in N$. □

Folk Theorems for Covenant Game with Matching and Identity Concealment Technology

I will first define a strategy T^* that forgives an "ordinary" offensive violation after a finite punishment stage but never forgives an offensive violation involving the use of identity concealment technology if the user is detected. Let iQt denote the proposition that at stage t, Party i commits an offensive violation using identify concealment or ring of Gyges technology and is discovered. Let $z_i'(t)$ be the K-stage guilt marker as defined above, and define the function $w_i : \mathbb{N}^+ \rightarrow \{-1,0,1\}$ by

$$w_i(t) = \begin{cases} 1 \text{ if } t=1 \\ z_i'(t) \text{ if } t>1 \text{ and } \neg iQ(t-1) \\ 1-X^* \text{ if } T>1 \text{ and } iQ(t-1) \\ -1 \text{ if } t>1 \text{ and } w_i(t-1)=-1 \end{cases}$$

where X_i^* is a random variable with range $\{0,2\}$ and where $q_i^* = \mu[X_i^*=1]$. Then the T^*-marker is defined as follows:

(M.3)[5]
$$z_i(t) = \begin{cases} 1 \text{ if } w_i(t)=1 \\ 0 \text{ if } w_i(t) \in \{-1,0\} \end{cases}.$$

Then T^* is defined as

$$T^*(\omega(t)) = \begin{cases} P \text{ if } i(t) \in N_t \text{ and } z_{i(t)}=1 \\ S \text{ if } i(t) \in N_t \text{ and } z_{i(t)}=0 \end{cases},$$

that is, T^* is a Humean strategy like h^* as defined above except that T^* uses a marker defined in a somewhat more complex manner that makes it possible for community members to mete out targeted punishment against a Party i who offensively violates in the "ordinary" way or who offensively violates using ring of Gyges technology that fails, so Party i is caught red-handed using such technology.

---

5. Defining the T^* in this indirect manner, rather than using $w_i(\cdot)$ itself as the T^*-marker, makes it possible to use the same possible world space Ω used to define the Humean strategies above.

The following elementary result assumes that an "ordinary" offensive violation is certain to be detected and announced but that an offensive violation where the violator uses ring of Gyges technology is discovered only with probability q_i^*. More general folk theorems where both types of offensive violation might escape detection are possible, but of course the conditions under which the discount factors make T^* an equilibrium are liable to be more restricted.

Proposition A3.4. For $i \in N$, let Party i's marker be the T^*-marker defined by (M.3) and let $\hat{q}_i = 1$. If for $i \in N$, there is a $\delta_i^* \in (0,1)$ satisfying (A3.3.2) and

$$\delta_i \geq \max\left\{ \delta_i^*, \frac{g_i}{g_i + q_i^*} \right\},$$

then $\boldsymbol{T}^* = (T^*, \ldots, T^*)$ is a correlated equilibrium of the indefinitely repeated Covenant game with matching.

PROOF. For each $i \in N$, δ_i satisfies the hypotheses of both Proposition A3.1 and Proposition A3.3. By Proposition A3.3, Party i cannot improve her expected payoff by deviating unilaterally from T^* in the "ordinary" way, and by Proposition A3.1, Party i cannot improve her expected payoff offensively violating using ring of Gyges technology. □

Finally I will consider an example of a roundabout punishment strategy R^*. A variety of such roundabout punishment strategies are possible, but in the following example, if indirect punishment occurs, it occurs only for some finite cycle. Let N_tQt denote the proposition that at stage t, some Party i in N_t commits an offensive violation using ring of Gyges technology and that this event is publicly announced, and let $\mu^* = \mu[N_tQt]$. If N_tQt obtains at stage t, then over a cycle of stages starting at stage $t+1$ conditions are *abnormal*, denoted by $\neg Bt$, and otherwise conditions are normal, denoted by Bt. More specifically, $\neg Bt$ exactly when $B(t-1)$ and N_tQt or if for some $T < t$ and some K_2, $B(T-1)$, $\neg BT$ and $t - T < K_2$. Let $z_i''(t)$ be the K_1-stage guilt marker for as defined above. Then Party i's R^**-marker* is defined by

$$z_i(t) = \begin{cases} 1 \text{ if } t = 1 \\ z_i''(t) \text{ if } t > 1 \text{ and } Bt \text{ obtains.} \\ 0 \text{ if } t > 1 \text{ and } \neg Bt \text{ obtains} \end{cases}$$

That is, when conditions are normal, Party i's innocence or guilt is defined according to the K_1-stage guilt marker, and when conditions are abnormal, then Party i is guilty. The R^*-marker clearly creates the conditions for untargeted punishment. If a given party offensively violates using ring of Gyges technology when conditions are normal and this event is publicly announced, then for the next stages every party is guilty. Then, given the R^*-marker, R^* is defined as

$$R^*(\omega(t)) = \begin{cases} P \text{ if } i(t) \in N_t \text{ and } z_{i(t)} = 1 \\ S \text{ if } i(t) \in N_t \text{ and } z_{i(t)} = 0 \end{cases},$$

so R^* is a Humean strategy, although with innocence-guilt conditions that permit untargeted punishment.

Proposition A3.5. For $i \in N$, let Party i's marker be the R^*-marker defined by (M.3). If for each $i \in N$, δ_{i1}^* satisfies (A3.3.2) for $K = K_1$ and δ_{i2}^* satisfies (A3.3.1) for $K = K_2$ and $\mu^* = \hat{q}_i$, and

$$\delta_i \geq \max\{\delta_{i1}^*, \delta_{i2}^*\},$$

then $\boldsymbol{R}^* = (R^*, \ldots, R^*)$ is a correlated equilibrium of the indefinitely repeated Covenant game with matching.

PROOF. For each $i \in N$, since $\delta_i \geq \delta_{i1}^*$ and δ_{i1}^* satisfies (A3.3.2) for $K = K_1$, by Proposition A3.3 Party i cannot improve her expected payoff by deviating unilaterally from $\boldsymbol{R}^*$ in the "ordinary" way. And since $\delta_i \geq \delta_{i2}^*$ and δ_{i2}^* satisfies (A3.3.1) for $K = K_2$ and $\mu^* = \hat{q}_i$, again by Proposition A3.3 Party i cannot improve her expected payoff offensively violating using ring of Gyges technology. □

Note that in the special case where $\mu^* = 1$, so that any use of ring of Gyges technology is certain to start an indirect punishment cycle of shunning by all against all, then the resulting $\boldsymbol{R}^*$ equilibrium resembles the "blinking" equilibrium of a repeated public goods game where an offensive violation triggers a cycle where all withhold contributions for a certain number of stages. Note also that any combination of punishment cycle lengths K_1 and K_2 is possible, including $K_1 > K_2$ and $K_1 = K_2$, but it may be most plausible to assume that $K_2 > K_1$, since this reflects the intuition that a community may make a cycle of indirect punishment more severe than a targeted punishment cycle in order to better deter the use of ring of Gyges technology.

APPENDIX 4

HUMEAN CONVENTIONS OF THE HUMEAN SOVEREIGNTY GAME AND THE REPEATED PROVIDER-RECIPIENT GAME

HUMEAN SOVEREIGNTY GAME

Figure 6.5 summarizes the stage game of the Humean Sovereignty game that the Subjects and the Sovereign engage in over successive time periods. As discussed in Chapter 6, at the start of each period $t \geq 1$, the Subjects and Sovereign are at a state $\theta \in \{\theta_0, \theta_1\}$ where θ_0 denotes being in the State of Nature and θ_1 denotes being in an established commonwealth, with $\theta = \theta_0$ at the initial period $t = 1$. For a given period t, when $\theta = \theta_1$, the Subjects move first and can *obey* (P) or *disobey* (D), and if they follow P, then the Sovereign moves next and chooses $x_t \in [0, c]$ and $\theta = \theta_1$ at period $t+1$, and if the Subjects follow D, then $\theta = \theta_0$ at period $t+1$. If the Sovereign moves, then $x_t = x$ is *performing to the degree* x. For period t, when $\theta = \theta_0$, the Sovereign moves first and chooses the signal $\pi_t \geq 0$, placing Subjects and Sovereign in a subgame that proceeds as if the initial game were at $\theta = \theta_1$. The Subjects' and Sovereign's respective payoff functions are defined by

$$u_1(s_1, s_2) = \begin{cases} V(x_t) - c \text{ if } s_1 = P \text{ and } s_2 = x_t \\ 0 \text{ if } s_2 = D \end{cases}$$

and

$$u_2(s_1, s_2, \theta) = \begin{cases} W(c - x_t) \text{ if } s_1 = P \text{ and } s_2 = x_t \text{ and } \theta = \theta_1 \\ W(c - x_t) - \pi_t \text{ if } s_1 = P \text{ and } s_2 = \pi_t, x_t \text{ and } \theta = \theta_1 \\ -\pi_t \text{ if } s_1 = D \text{ and } \theta = \theta_0 \\ 0 \text{ if } s_1 = D \text{ and } \theta = \theta_1 \end{cases}$$

where $V(\cdot)$ and $W(\cdot)$ are strictly increasing functions, so that $V(x)$ strictly increases and $W(c-x)$ strictly decreases in x, and $W(0)>0$ and $V(c)>c>V(0)$. Note that the Subjects' payoff function is the same at either state.

Following the discussion of Appendix 1, when the Subjects and the Sovereign engage in this stage game repeatedly, at each period $t\geq 1$ they follow the act profile $s_t=(s_{1t},s_{2t})$, and $m_t=(s_1,\ldots,s_{t-1})$ is the *ex ante history* of interactions. The Subjects' and the Sovereign's respective discount factors are δ_1 and δ_2, so their overall respective expected payoffs are

$$E_1\left(u_1\left(h_1,h_2\right)\right)=\sum_{t=1}^{\infty}u_1\left(h_1(t),h_2(t)\right)\cdot\delta_1^t$$

and

$$E_2\left(u_2\left(h_1,h_2\right)\right)=\sum_{t=k_{0t}+1}^{\infty}u_2\left(h_1(t),h_2(t)\right)\cdot\delta_2^{t-k_{0t}}$$

for a given profile (h_1,h_2) of history-dependent strategies h_1 and h_2 and where k_{0t} is the most recent period where $\theta=\theta_0$.[1] The $t=k_{0t}+1$ indexing on the Sovereign's payoff reflects the idea that at the start of each period where $\theta=\theta_0$, the agent in the Sovereign's position is replaced with a fresh candidate.

As discussed in §6.3, if the agents engage in the Figure 6.5 state game only once, the Subjects' best choice is D at either state and the Sovereign's best choices are $\pi_t=0$ at state θ_0 and $x_t=0$ if the Subjects obey at either state, so the unique subgame perfect equilibrium is (s_1^*,s_2^*) where $s_1^*=D$ and $s_2=(\pi_t=0 \text{ and } x_t=0 \text{ if } \theta=\theta_0; x_t=0 \text{ if } \theta=\theta_1)$, which yields the payoff vector (0,0) of the State of Nature. But as also discussed in §6.3, under certain conditions the Subjects and the Sovereign can follow an equilibrium better for both sides if they follow the contingency strategy profile (f_1,f_2) where

$$f_1(m_t)=\begin{cases} P \text{ if } \pi\geq\pi^* \text{ and } \theta=\theta_0 \\ P \text{ if } x_{t-1}\geq x^* \text{ and } \theta=\theta_1 \\ D \text{ otherwise}\end{cases}$$

and

$$f_2(m_t)\begin{cases} \pi_t=\pi^*; x_t=\bar{x}\geq x^*\text{-if-}P \text{ if } \theta=\theta_0 \text{ and } \pi_t'\geq\pi^* \\ \pi_t=0; x_t=0\text{-if-}P \text{ if } \theta=\theta_0 \text{ and } \pi_t'<\pi^* \\ x_t=\bar{x}\geq x^*\text{-if-}P \text{ if } \theta=\theta_1 \text{ and } \pi_{k_{0t}}\geq\pi^* \\ x_t=0\text{-if-}P \text{ if } \theta=\theta_1 \text{ and } \pi_{k_{0t}}<\pi^*\end{cases}$$

1. Note that the state θ is determined by the *ex ante* history and consequently does not need to be made an explicit argument of each overall payoff function.

where $\pi^* > 0$ is the Subjects' *signaling threshold*, $x^* > 0$ is the Subjects' *performance threshold*, $\pi_t' > 0$ reflects the Sovereign's signaling ability at period t, and k_{0t} is the most recent period where $\theta = \theta_0$, with the added assumption that if $\pi_t' \geq \pi^*$, then the Sovereign is capable of performing at any level $x_t \in [0, c]$.[2] The possible worlds of these contingency strategies are characterized by the *ex ante* histories over time periods and the state θ, all of which are known by the Subjects and the Sovereign.

If the Subjects follow the strategy f_1, then if $\theta = \theta_1$ or if $\theta = \theta_0$ and the Subjects have followed P, the Sovereign has been authorized and is effectively engaged in an indefinitely repeated game where its counterpart adopts a policy similar to the Tr-strategy of repeated Prisoner's Dilemma. In this case, for any $x^* > 0$, if the Sovereign deviates unilaterally from the path that (f_1, f_2) requires at $t = k_{0t} + 1$, the best payoff it can achieve is $W(c)$, where the Sovereign follows $x_1 = 0$ and is then deposed at period $t = k_{0t} + 2$. If the Sovereign conforms with (f_1, f_2) then its expected payoff is

$$E_2\left(u_2\left(f_1, f_2\right)\right) = \sum_{t=k_{0t}+1}^{\infty} W\left(c - \bar{x}\right) \cdot \delta_1^{t-k_{0t}} = W\left(c - \bar{x}\right) \cdot \frac{\delta_2}{1 - \delta_2},$$

so the Sovereign does best to follow f_2 when $W\left(c - \bar{x}\right) \cdot \dfrac{\delta_2}{1 - \delta_2} \geq W(c)$ or

$$\delta_2 \geq \frac{W(c)}{W(c) + W\left(c - \bar{x}\right)}. \tag{A.4.1}$$

By a similar argument, the same condition obtains if the installed Sovereign deviates unilaterally from (f_1, f_2) at any period $t > k_{0t} + 1$. Under all other circumstances, where the Sovereign is not authorized, f_1 requires the subjects to follow D and the Sovereign's best response is $\pi_t = 0$ or $x_t = 0$ in case the subjects unexpectedly followed P, which is what f_2 requires. So f_2 is a best response to f_1 when (A.4.1) is satisfied, and there are always values of δ_2 satisfying (A.4.1) because $W\left(c - \bar{x}\right) > 0$.

The conditions under which f_1 is the Subjects' best response to f_2 are very strong but fairly general. The discussion that follows is based upon Stokey and Lucas' analysis of the employee search model.[3] As already stated, $V(x)$ is strictly increasing in x, and here I now assume the stronger condition that $V(x)$ is continuously differentiable with $V'(x) > 0$ everywhere. I further assume that $V(x)$ is strictly concave and that $V'(x) < \infty$. Also, as already stated, the signal of a Sovereign candidate is assumed to be closely correlated with ability to perform and that in particular $\pi_t \geq \pi^*$ implies that the Sovereign candidate is capable of performing at any level $x_t \in [0, c]$, including x^*. So if at period $t = 1$ when the state is $\theta = \theta_0$ and if $\pi_t \geq \pi^*$, the Subjects can achieve at least their

2. As is the case with the overall payoff functions, since the state θ is determined by the *ex ante* history, θ does not need to be made an explicit argument of the contingency strategies.

3. Stokey and Lucas (1989), §10.7.

desired threshold payoff $V(x^*)-c$ at the current period and at each subsequent period by following f_1 if the Sovereign follows f_2, since then the Subjects achieve the overall expected payoff

$$E_1\left(u_1\left(f_1,f_2\right)\right)=\sum_{t=1}^{\infty}\left(V\left(\bar{x}\right)-c\right)\cdot\delta_1^t=\left(V\left(\bar{x}\right)-c\right)\cdot\frac{\delta_1}{1-\delta_1}$$
$$\geq\left(V\left(x^*\right)-c\right)\cdot\frac{\delta_1}{1-\delta_1}>0$$

the expected payoff of remaining in the State of Nature. Similarly, the Subjects achieve $V(\bar{x})-c\geq V(x^*)-c$ at any future period where $\theta=\theta_0$ and $\pi_t\geq\pi^*$ at subsequent periods by following f_1 if the Sovereign follows f_2. The key question for the Subjects is setting the value of x^* so that deposing an incumbent Sovereign that fails to perform adequately is the Subjects' best response. To identify this value, let $K=c-V(0)$ and define $U(x)=V(x)-c+K$. Since $V(0)-c<0$, $K>0$ and $U(0)=0$. Because they differ only by the constant K, $U(x)$ also inherits the assumed properties of $V(x)$ of being continuously differentiable with $U'(x)>0$ everywhere, strictly concave, and satisfying $U'(x)<\infty$. Now suppose at current period t the Subjects infer that the Sovereign will serve at the level $x_t=x$, either because $\theta=\theta_1$ and the Sovereign is an incumbent who served at level $x_{t-1}=x$ or because $\theta=\theta_0$ and the Subjects infer this value from the Sovereign's signal π_t as a candidate aspiring to be authorized by the Subjects. The Subjects want to choose so as to maximize a *value function* v that is defined recursively. The Subjects' discounted value of obeying is

$$U(x)+\delta_1\left[(1-\alpha)v(x)+\alpha v(0)\right]$$

and the discounted value of disobeying is

$$\delta_1\int_0^c v(w)p(w)dw$$

where the values of w are distributed on the interval $[0,c]$ according to the probability density $p(\cdot)$. So the Subjects' decision problem is defined by the *Bellman equation*

$$v(x)=\max\left\{U(x)+\delta_1\left[(1-\alpha)v(x)+\alpha v(0)\right],\delta_1\int_0^c v(w)p(w)dw\right\}.$$

As discussed in §6.3, this problem corresponds to that of an employee who must choose between working at an accepted wage x_t with the probability α of losing this job at each period and rejecting the offered wage x_t in favor of searching for a more satisfactory wage with some other employer, and x^* corresponds to the employee's reservation wage. In the employment interpretation, the employee should accept the current offer x_t precisely when $x_t\geq x^*$ and otherwise should search. In the governing convention interpretation I propose in §6.3, the Subjects should obey and authorize or maintain an incumbent Sovereign when $x_t\geq x^*$ and otherwise should go to or remain in the State of Nature, in which case new Sovereign candidates are drawn for the Subjects' consideration with a distribution that has density p. There are several ways to characterize x^*, including the following equation:

$$v(x^*) = \delta_1 \cdot \int_0^c v(w)p(w)dw. \tag{A.4.2}$$

Equation (A.4.2) has a unique solution in x^*, which implies that for a function $U(\cdot)$, and equivalently a function $V(\cdot)$, satisfying the stated assumptions, the threshold value x^* is well defined. This establishes that for a sufficiently high factor δ_1, f_1 is the Subjects' best response if the Sovereign follows f_2. Since the Subjects and the Sovereign can also follow the suboptimal equilibrium where they remain in the State of Nature at all periods, for sufficiently high discount factors the (f_1, f_2) equilibrium of the indefinitely repeated Humean Sovereignty game characterizes a convention as defined in Chapter 2. This governing convention can involve some uncertainty regarding the payoffs of one's counterpart. One way to account for why the Sovereign would perform at a level $\bar{x} > x^*$ that is strictly better than the Subjects acceptability threshold is to suppose that agents in the Sovereign role might be uncertain as to the exact value of x^*.

Repeated Provider-Recipient Game

As was the case in Appendix 3, several of the concepts summarized here are based upon the formal definition of convention given in §2.4. I first summarize how community members interact in pairwise Provider-Recipient meetings. This summary is quite similar to that given for the matching model of the indefinitely repeated Covenant game in Appendix 3, except that here the community can have infinitely many members, each of which will enter and exit the indefinitely repeated Provider-Recipient game at certain stages. $N = \mathbb{N}^+ = \{1,2,...\}$ is a set of parties that form the community who will engage in the supergame consisting of Provider-Recipient games. At each stage $t \in \mathbb{N}^+$, $2m$ parties are sampled with replacement from N where $m \in \mathbb{N}^+$ and $m \geq 2$. The set $N_t \subset N$ of parties selected at stage t are the parties that will engage in the Provider-Recipient game at this stage. There are eight ordered pairs of the form $(x_i, y_i) \in \{-1,0,1,2\} \times \{0,1\}$. The set Ω of possible worlds consists of all vectors of the form $(x_1, y_1, x_2, y_2, ...)$ where $x_i \in \{-1,0,1,2\}$ and $y_i \in \{0,1\}$. If $\omega_\tau \in \Omega$ is any such vector, then $\{\omega_\tau\}$ is a cell of each Party i's information partition $\mathcal{H}_i$ of Ω, so that all parties know which world $\omega \in \Omega$ is the actual world. At each time period or stage $t \in \mathbb{N}^+$, one world $\omega(t) \in \Omega$ obtains and is the actual world at t. The possible worlds of Ω will be characterized below. As in Appendix 3, here a description of each possible world at t includes all of the information relevant to the parties' decisions and acts at stage t, including a description of the stage games, the status of each party at stage t, and the beliefs each party has regarding the counterparts. Each Party $i \in N$ has a subjective probability distribution $\mu_i(\cdot)$ over the propositions in Ω, a private information partition $\mathcal{H}_i$ of Ω, and an expectation operator $E_i(\cdot)$ based upon $\mu_i(\cdot)$. At each stage t, each Party $i \in N_t$ is matched with exactly one *counterpart* Party $i(t) \in N_t$, so that there are m matched pairs at each stage.

At each stage t, one party in each matched pair is a *provider*, and the other party in this pair is a *recipient*. Each Party i plays the role of provider for $\alpha > \frac{1}{2}$ of the time periods when she is *active*. If Party i is a provider at stage t and her counterpart Party $i(t)$ is also active, then they play an Ultimatum game where Party i offers Party $i(t)$ a share $\lambda \in [0,1]$ and then Party $i(t)$ may either accept (A) or reject (R) the offer. If active recipient Party $i(t)$ chooses A, then Party i receives a payoff of $u_i(1-\lambda)$ and Party $i(t)$ receives a payoff of $u_{i(t)}(\lambda)$. If active recipient Party $i(t)$ chooses R, then both Party i and Party $i(t)$ receive a payoff of 0. If Party i is a provider at stage t and her counterpart Party $i(t)$ is *inactive*, then they play a Dictator game where Party i offers Party $i(t)$ a share λ and then Party i receives a payoff of $u_i(1-\lambda)$ and Party $i(t)$ receives a payoff of $u_{i(t)}(\lambda)$. For each Party i, the payoff function $u_i(\lambda)$ where $u_i(0)=0$ is an increasing von Neumann–Morgenstern utility function with diminishing marginal utility such that in particular $u_i\left(\frac{1}{2}\right) > \alpha u_i(1)$. One can ensure that $u_i(\lambda)$ satisfies these conditions by requiring that in addition to $u_i(0)=0$ and $u_i\left(\frac{1}{2}\right) > \alpha u_i(1)$ the function $u_i(\cdot)$ is twice differentiable in $\lambda \in [0,1]$ where the first derivative is always strictly positive, $u_i'(\lambda) > 0$, and the second derivative is always strictly negative, $u_i''(\lambda) < 0$, for all $\lambda \in [0,1]$.[4]

Next I define formally the strategies that the parties in N can follow in the indefinitely repeated Provider-Recipient Game. A generic *strategy* for Party i is a sequence of functions $f_i = (f_i^t)$ where $f_i^t : \Omega \to [0,1] \times \{A,R\}$ and f_i^t is $\mathcal{H}_i$-measurable. $f = (f_1, f_2, \ldots)$ is a generic *strategy profile*. S_i denotes the set of all strategies Party i can follow, and $S = S_1 \times \cdots \times S_n$ denotes all of the strategy profiles that parties in N can follow. At a given stage t, $f_i^t(\omega(t)) \in [0,1] \times \{A,R\}$ defines the pure strategy $a_i(t)$ that Party i follows in the Provider-Recipient Game at stage t. The vector

$$f^t(\omega(t)) = \left(f_1^t(\omega(t)), f_2^t(\omega(t)), \ldots\right) \in [0,1]^\infty \times \{A,R\}^\infty$$

defines the set of pure strategies $(a_1(t), a_2(t), \ldots)$ the parties follow at t. Note that when Party i is a provider at stage t, then $a_i(t)$ is $\lambda_i \in [0,1]$, that is, Party i offers some share λ_i to her recipient. When Party i is an active recipient at stage t, then $a_i(t)$ is either A or R, that is, Party i either accepts or rejects the offer her provider makes her. When Party i is an inactive recipient at stage t, then $a_i(t) = R$, that is, Party i makes no choice and simply receives the share offered her. To avoid trivialities I stipulate that when Party i is

---

4. A specific function that satisfies all these conditions for any value of $\alpha \leq \left(\frac{1}{2}\right)^{\frac{1}{2}} \approx 0.7071$ is $u_i(\lambda) = \lambda^{\frac{1}{2}}$, which is the function used to illustrate Proposition A.4.1 in Chapter 8.

unmatched at stage t, then $a_i(t) = R$ and in this case Party i receives the noninteraction payoff $\underline{u} = 0$. Party i's expected payoff at stage t given $\omega(t) \in \Omega$ is

$$E_i\left(u_i\left(f^t\left(\omega(t)\right)\right)\right) = \sum_{j \neq i} E_i\left(u_i\left(f_i^t\left(\omega(t)\right), f_j^t\left(\omega(t)\right)\right)\right)\mu_i\left[i(t) = j\right].$$

Let $\delta_i \in (0,1)$ be Party i's discount factor. Party i's overall expected payoff is

$$E_i\left(u_i \circ f\right) = \sum_{t=1}^{\infty} E_i\left(u_i\left(f^t\left(\omega(t)\right)\right)\right) \cdot \delta_i^t.$$

A strategy profile f is a *correlated equilibrium* of the indefinitely repeated Provider-Recipient Game if, and only if, for each $i \in N$,

$$E_i\left(u_i \circ f\right) \geq E_i\left(u_i \circ \left(f_i', f_{-i}\right)\right)$$

for all $f_i' \in S_i$.[5]

I now need to define a Humean strategy for playing this repeated game that in effect rewards innocent parties and punishes guilty parties and to show that the parties of N can follow an equilibrium characterized by this Humean strategy. First, I identify two particular strategies for playing the base one-shot Provider-Recipient Game at a given stage t. To facilitate the definitions of these strategies I define a *role marker* function for each Party i at each state at each state t as

$$r_i(t) = \begin{cases} 1 \text{ if Party } i \text{ is a provider} \\ 2 \text{ if Party } i \text{ is an active recipient} \\ 0 \text{ if Party } i \text{ is an inactive recipient} \\ -1 \text{ if if Party } i \text{ is not selected} \end{cases}.$$

For the one-shot Provider-Recipient Game, strategy $\sigma_{i,\lambda}(t)$ is defined as follows:

$$\sigma_{i,\lambda}(t) = \begin{cases} a_i(t) = \lambda \text{ if } r_i(t) = 1 \\ a_i(t) = A \text{ if } r_i(t) = 2 \end{cases}$$

Strategy $\pi_i(t)$ is defined as follows:

$$\pi_i(t) = \begin{cases} a_i(t) = 0 \text{ if } r_i(t) = 1 \\ a_i(t) = R \text{ if } r_i(t) = 2 \end{cases}$$

Strategy $\sigma_{i,\lambda}(t)$ requires a given Party i at stage t to share λ of the good if at this stage she is a provider and to accept any offer if at this stage she is an active recipient. Strategy $\pi_i(t)$ requires Party i at stage t to offer nothing if at this stage she is a provider and reject any offer if at this stage she is an active recipient. Next I define an indicator function for

5. I use the "jackknife" notation summarized in Appendix 1, note 5.

use in defining the desired Humean strategy. For $i \in N$, define $z_i : t \to \{0,1\}$ by $z_i(0)=1$ and for $t>0$,

$$z_i(t)=\begin{cases} 0 \text{ if for some } T<t, z_{i(T)}=1, r_i(T)=1 \text{ and } a_i(T)=\lambda<\frac{1}{2} \\ 0 \text{ if for some } T<t, z_{i(T)}=1\ r_i(T)=2 \text{ and } a_i(T)\neq A \\ 0 \text{ if for some } T<t, z_{i(T)}=0 \text{ and } a_i(T)\neq \pi_i(T) \\ 1 \text{ otherwise} \end{cases}.$$

In words, a Party i is *innocent* at stage t if she has always followed the sharing strategy $\sigma_{i,\frac{1}{2}}(t)$ over the first $t-1$ stages with other innocent counterparts and has always followed the punitive strategy $\pi_i(t)$ with any counterpart who is not innocent or *guilty*. Party i becomes guilty if she ever deviates from strategy $\sigma_{i,\frac{1}{2}}(t)$ when paired with an innocent counterpart by offering less than $\lambda=\frac{1}{2}$ if she is the provider or by rejecting if she is the active recipient, or if she fails to follow $\pi_i(t)$ when paired with a guilty counterpart. $z_i(t)$ is Party i's *innocence-guilt marker*, and $z_i(t)=1$ if Party i is innocent and $z_i(t)=0$ if Party i is guilty.

The role markers and standing markers of the parties in N characterize the possible worlds in Ω. Let $\omega(t)=(r_1(t),z_1(t),r_2(t),z_2(t),\ldots)$. Then the *Humean strategy* for the indefinitely repeated Provider-Recipient Game is defined by $g^*=(g^*(\omega(t)))$ where

$$g^*(\omega(t))=\begin{cases} \sigma_{i,\frac{1}{2}}(t) \text{ if } z_{i(t)}(t)=1 \\ \pi_i(t) \text{ if } z_{i(t)}(t)=0 \end{cases}.$$

That is, the Humean strategy requires a selected Party i to follow the sharing strategy $\sigma_{i,\frac{1}{2}}(t)$ with an innocent counterpart and to follow the punishing strategy $\pi_i(t)$ with a guilty counterpart.

The following result gives conditions under which a strategy profile where all follow this Humean strategy forms an equilibrium of the indefinitely repeated Provider-Recipient Game.

Proposition A.4.1. Let ε_{i1} denote the expected proportion of stages that Party i is inactive, and let ε_{i2} denote the expected proportion of stages that Party i is matched with an inactive counterpart. Then if for each $i \in N$,

$$\text{(1)} \qquad \delta_i \geq \frac{u_i(1)-u_i\left(\frac{1}{2}\right)}{u_i(1)(1-\varepsilon_{i1}+\varepsilon_{i1}\varepsilon_{i2})}$$

then $\mathbf{g}^*=(g^*,g^*,\ldots)$ is a correlated equilibrium of the indefinitely repeated Provider-Recipient Game.

PROOF. Given $i \in N$, we have

$$E_i\left(u_i \circ g^*\right) = \sum_{t=1}^{\infty} E_i\left(u_i\left(\sigma_{1,\frac{1}{2}},\ldots,\sigma_{n,\frac{1}{2}}\right)\right)\cdot \delta_i^t. \tag{2}$$
$$= \sum_{t=1}^{\infty} u_i\left(\frac{1}{2}\right)\cdot \delta_i^t$$

Now consider any strategy f_i' where Party i deviates from the sequence $(g^*(\omega(t)))$. Let T_0 be the first stage such that $f_i'(\omega(T_0)) \neq h(\omega(T_0))$. Then

$$E_i\left(u_i\left(f_i', g_{-i}^*\right)\right) \leq \left(\sum_{t=1}^{T_0-1} u_i\left(\frac{1}{2}\right)\delta_i^t\right) + u_i(1)\delta_i^{T_0} + \left(1-\varepsilon_{i1}\right)\varepsilon_{i2}\cdot \sum_{t=T_0+1}^{\infty} u_i(1)\delta_i^t \tag{3}$$

because (i) if Party i deviates from g^* for the first time at $t = T_0$, then at stage T_0 he will net at most the discounted gain $u_i(1)\delta_i^{T_0}$ of exploiting Party $i(T_0)$, and (ii) at each subsequent stage $t > T_0$, Party i receives 0 when matched with an active counterpart, and so after T_0 Party i can receive a positive payoff only when matched with an inactive counterpart. So by (2) and (3), g^* is a best reply to g_{-i}^* if

$$\frac{u_i\left(\frac{1}{2}\right)\delta_i^{T_0}}{1-\delta_i} = \sum_{t-T_0}^{\infty} u_i\left(\frac{1}{2}\right)\cdot \delta_i^t \geq u_i(1)\delta_i^{T_0} + \left(1-\varepsilon_{i1}\right)\varepsilon_{i2}u_i(1)\cdot \frac{\delta_i^{T_0+1}}{1-\delta_i} \tag{4}$$

and simplifying inequality (4) we have

$$\frac{u_i\left(\frac{1}{2}\right)}{1-\delta_i} \geq u_i(1) + \left(1-\varepsilon_{i1}\right)\varepsilon_{i2}u_i(1)\cdot \frac{\delta_i}{1-\delta_i}$$

or

$$\delta_i \geq \frac{u_i(1) - u_i\left(\frac{1}{2}\right)}{u_i(1) - \varepsilon_{i1}u_i(1) + \varepsilon_{i1}\varepsilon_{i2}u_i(1)}. \quad \square$$

For example, if $u_i(1) = 3$, $u_i\left(\frac{1}{2}\right) = 2$ and $\varepsilon_{i1} = \varepsilon_{i2} = \frac{1}{10}$ for each $i \in N$, then g^* characterizes an equilibrium of the indefinitely repeated Provider-Recipient Game when

$$\delta_i \geq \frac{3-2}{3 - \frac{3}{10} + \frac{3}{100}} \approx .3663.$$

REFERENCES

Ademollo, Francesco. 2011. *The* Cratylus *of Plato: A Commentary*. Cambridge: Cambridge University Press.

Alexander, Richard D. 1987. *The Biology of Moral Systems*. Hawthorne, NY: Aldine de Gruyter.

Alston, William. 1964. *Philosophy of Language*. Englewood Cliffs, NJ: Prentice Hall.

Aquinas, Thomas. 1948 (ca. 1274). *Summa Theologiae*. Trans. Fathers of the English Dominican Province. New York: Benzinger Brothers.

Aquinas, Thomas. 1975 (ca. 1263). *Summa Contra Gentiles*. Trans. Vernon J. Bourke. Notre Dame, IN: University of Notre Dame Press.

Aristotle. 1998. *Politics*. Trans. C. D. C. Reeve. Indianapolis: Hackett.

Aristotle. 2000. *Nicomachean Ethics*. Trans. and ed. Roger Crisp. Cambridge: Cambridge University Press.

Aumann, Robert. 1974. "Subjectivity and Correlation in Randomized Strategies." *Journal of Mathematical Economics* 1: 67–96.

Aumann, Robert. 1987. "Correlated Equilibrium as an Expression of Bayesian Rationality." *Econometrica* 55: 1–18.

Aumann, Robert. 1995. "Backward Induction and Common Knowledge of Rationality." *Games and Economic Behavior* 8: 16–19.

Axelrod, Robert. 2006 (1984). *The Evolution of Cooperation*, revised ed. New York: Basic Books.

Baldwin, Jason. 2004. "Hume's Knave and the Interests of Justice." *Journal of the History of Philosophy* 42: 277–296.

Barry, Brian. 1989. *Theories of Justice*. Berkeley: University of California Press.

Barry, Brian. 1990 (1965). *Political Argument: A Reissue with a New Introduction*. Berkeley: University of California Press.

Barry, Brian. 1995. *Justice as Impartiality*. Oxford: Oxford University Press.

Bernheim, B. Douglas. 1984. "Rationalizable Strategic Behavior." *Econometrica* 52: 1007–1028.

Bhaskar, V. 1998. "Noisy Communication and the Evolution of Cooperation." *Journal of Economic Theory* 82: 110–131.

Bicchieri, Cristina. 1993. *Rationality and Coordination*. Cambridge: Cambridge University Press.

Bicchieri, Cristina. 2006. *The Grammar of Society: The Nature and Dynamics of Social Norms*. Cambridge: Cambridge University Press.

Binmore, Ken. 1994. *Game Theory and the Social Contract,* Volume I, *Playing Fair*. Cambridge, MA: MIT Press.

Binmore, Ken. 1998. *Game Theory and the Social Contract,* Volume II, *Just Playing*. Cambridge, MA: MIT Press.

Binmore, Ken. 2005. *Natural Justice*. Oxford: Oxford University Press.

Binmore, Ken, and Adam Brandenburger. 1990. "Common Knowledge and Game Theory." In *Essays on the Foundations of Game Theory*, ed. Ken Binmore, pp. 105–150. Oxford: Basil Blackwell.

Boonin, David. 2003. *A Defense of Abortion*. Cambridge: Cambridge University Press.

Bowles, Samuel, and Herbert Gintis. 2011. *A Cooperative Species: Human Reciprocity and Its Evolution*. Princeton: Princeton University Press.

Boyd, Robert. 1989. "Mistakes Allow Evolutionary Stability in the Repeated Prisoner's Dilemma." *Journal of Theoretical Biology* 136: 47–56.

Boyd, Robert, and Peter J. Richerson. 1985. *Culture and the Evolutionary Process*. Chicago: University of Chicago Press.

Braithwaite, Richard. 1994 (1955). *Theory of Games as a Tool for the Moral Philosopher*. Bristol: Thoemmes Press.

Brams, Steven. 1975. *Game Theory and Politics*. New York: Free Press.

Brandenburger, Adam, and Eddie Dekel. 1987. "Rationalizability and Correlated Equilibrium." *Econometrica* 55: 1391–1402.

Brandenburger, Adam, and Eddie Dekel. 1988. "The Role of Common Knowledge Assumptions in Game Theory." In *The Economics of Missing Markets, Information and Games*, ed. Frank Hahn, pp. 46–61. Oxford: Clarendon Press.

Broad, Charlie D. 1930. *Five Types of Ethical Theory*. Oxford: Clarendon Press.

Brody, Baruch. 1975. *Abortion and the Sanctity of Human Life: A Philosophical View*. Cambridge, MA: MIT Press.

Buchanan, Allen. 1990. "Justice as Reciprocity Versus Subject-Centered Justice." *Philosophy and Public Affairs* 19: 227–253.

Buchanan, Allen. 2004. *Justice, Legitimacy, and Self-Determination: Moral Foundations for International Law*. Oxford: Oxford University Press.

Camerer, Colin. 2003. *Behavioral Game Theory: Experiments in Strategic Interaction*. Princeton: Princeton University Press.

Carnap, Rudolf. 1980. "A Basic System of Inductive Logic, Part 2." In *Studies in Inductive Logic and Probability*, vol. II, ed. Richard Jeffrey, pp. 7–155. Berkeley: University of California Press.

Cheung, Yin-Wong, and Daniel Friedman. 1997. "Individual Learning in Normal Form Games: Some Laboratory Results." *Games and Economic Behavior* 19: 46–76.

Coleman, Jules, and Morris, Christopher Morris, eds. 1998. *Rational Commitment and Social Justice: Essays for Gregory Kavka*. Cambridge: Cambridge University Press.

Copp, David. 1997. "The Ring of Gyges: Overridingness and the Unity of Reason." *Social Philosophy and Policy* 14: 86–106.

Cubitt, Robin, and Robert Sugden. 2003. "Common Knowledge, Salience and Convention: A Reconstruction of David Lewis' Game Theory." *Economics and Philosophy* 19: 175–210.

Curley, Edwin. 1994. "Introduction to Hobbes' *Leviathan*." In Thomas Hobbes, *Leviathan*, ed. Edwin Curley, pp. viii–xlvii. Indianapolis: Hackett.

Dagger, Richard. 2010. "Political Obligation." In *The Stanford Encyclopedia of Philosophy*, summer 2010 ed., ed. Edward N. Zalta. http://plato.stanford.edu/archives/sum2010/entries/political-obligation.

Davis, Michael. 2009. "Fourteen Kinds of Social Contract." *Journal of Applied Ethics and Philosophy* 1: 8–19.

Dekel, Eddie, and Faruk Gul. 1997. "Rationality and Knowledge in Game Theory." In *Advances in Economics and Econometrics: Theory and Applications, Seventh World Congress,* Volume I, ed. D. M. Kreps and K. F. Wallis, pp. 87–172. Cambridge: Cambridge University Press.

Denyer, Nicholas. 1983. "The Origins of Justice." In *Suzetesis: studi sull' epicureismo greco e romano offerti a Marcello Gigante*, pp. 133–152. Naples: Macchiaroli.

Ellison, Glenn. 1993. "Learning, Local Interaction and Cooperation." *Econometrica* 61: 1047–1071.

Ensminger, Jean, and Joseph Henrich, eds. 2014. *Experimenting with Social Norms: Fairness and Punishment in Cross-Cultural Perspective*. New York: Russell Sage Foundation.

Epicurus. 1994. Principal Doctrines. In *The Epicurus Reader: Selected Writings and Testimonia*, pp. 32–36. Trans. and ed. Brad Inwood and Lloyd P. Gerson. Indianapolis: Hackett.

Fehr, Ernst, Urs Fischbacher, and Simon Gächter. 2002. "Strong Reciprocity, Human Cooperation and the Enforcement of Social Norms." *Human Nature* 13: 1–25.

Fehr, Ernst, and Simon Gächter. 2000. "Cooperation and Punishment in Public Goods Experiments." *American Economic Review* 90: 980–994.

Flood, Merrill M. 1958. "Some Experimental Games." *Management Science* 5: 5–26.

Fudenberg, Drew, and David K. Levine. 2008. *The Theory of Learning in Games*. Cambridge, MA: MIT Press.

Gaus, Gerald. 2008. *On Philosophy, Politics, and Economics*. Belmont, CA: Thomson Wadsworth.

Gaus, Gerald. 2011. *The Order of Public Reason: A Theory of Freedom and Morality in a Diverse and Bounded World*. Cambridge: Cambridge University Press.

Gauthier, David. 1969. *The Logic of Leviathan: The Moral and Political Theory of Thomas Hobbes*. Oxford: Clarendon Press.

Gauthier, David. 1974. "Rational Cooperation." *Nous* 8: 53–65.

Gauthier, David. 1986. *Morals by Agreement*. Oxford: Clarendon Press.

Gauthier, David. 1990. *Moral Dealing: Contract, Ethics and Reason*. Ithaca, NY: Cornell University Press.

Gauthier, David. 1992. "Artificial Virtues and the Sensible Knave." *Hume Studies* 28: 401–428.

Gauthier, David. 2012. "Twenty-Five On." *Ethics* 124: 601–624.

Gaylord, Richard J., and Louis J. D'Andria. 1998. *Simulating Society: A* Mathematica *Toolkit for Modeling Socioeconomic Behavior*. New York: Springer.

Gert, Bernard. 1967. "Hobbes and Psychological Egoism." *Journal of the History of Ideas* 27: 503–520.

Gibbard, Allan. 1973. "Manipulation of Voting Schemes: A General Result." *Econometrica* 41: 587–601.

Gintis, Herbert. 2009. *The Bounds of Reason: Game Theory and the Unification of the Behavioral Sciences*. Princeton: Princeton University Press.

Gintis, Herbert, Samuel Bowles, Robert Boyd, and Ernst Fehr, eds. 2005. *Moral Sentiments and Material Interests: The Foundations of Cooperation in Everyday Life*. Cambridge, MA: MIT Press.

Gilbert, Margaret. 1989. *On Social Facts*. Princeton: Princeton University Press.

Gilbert, Margaret. 2008. "Social Convention Revisited." *Topoi* 27: 5–16.

Granovetter, Mark. 1978. "Threshold Models of Collective Behavior." *American Journal of Sociology* 83: 1420–1443.

Greif, Avner. 2006. *Institutions and the Path to the Modern Economy: Lessons from Medieval Trade*. Cambridge: Cambridge University Press.

Grotius, Hugo. 2005 (1625). *The Rights of War and Peace*. Ed. Richard Tuck. Indianapolis: Liberty Fund.

Güth, Werner, Rolf Schmittberger, and Bernd Schwarze. 1982. "An Experimental Study of Ultimatum Bargaining." *Journal of Economic Behavior and Organization* 3: 367–388.

Hammond, Peter. 1975. "Charity: Altruism or Cooperative Egoism?" In *Altruism, Morality and Economic Theory*, ed. Edmund S. Phelps, pp. 115–131. New York: Russell Sage.

Hampton, Jean. 1986. *Hobbes and the Social Contract Tradition*. Cambridge: Cambridge University Press.

Hampton, Jean. 1990. "The Contractarian Explanation of the State." *Midwest Studies in Philosophy* 15: 344–371.

Hampton, Jean. 1991. "Two Faces of Contractarian Thought." In *Contractarianism and Rational Choice: Essays on David Gauthier's* Morals by Agreement, ed. Peter Vallentyne, pp. 31–55. New York: Cambridge University Press.

Hampton, Jean. 1994. "Democracy and the Rule of Law." In *The Rule of Law*, ed. Ian Shapiro, pp. 13–44. New York: New York University Press.

Hampton, Jean. 1997. *Political Philosophy*. Boulder, CO: Westview Press.

Hardin, Garrett. 1968. "The Tragedy of the Commons." *Science* 162: 1243–1248.

Hardin, Russell. 1982. "Exchange Theory on Strategic Bases." *Social Science Information* 2: 251–272.

Hardin, Russell. 1988. *Morality Within the Limits of Reason*. Chicago: University of Chicago Press.

Hardin, Russell. 1999. *Liberalism, Constitutionalism and Democracy*. Oxford: Oxford University Press.

Hardin, Russell. 2003. *Indeterminacy and Society*. Princeton: Princeton University Press.

Harper, William. 1988. "Causal Decision Theory and Game Theory: A Classic Argument for Equilibrium Solutions, a Defense of Weak Equilibria, and a New Problem for the Normal Form Representation." In *Causation in Decision, Belief Change, and Statistics II*, ed. W. Harper and B. Skyrms, pp. 25–48. Dordrecht: Kluwer.

Harper, William. 1991. "Ratifiability and Refinements (in Two-Person Noncooperative Games)." In *Foundations of Decision Theory*, ed. M. Bacharach and S. Hurley, pp. 263–293. Oxford: Blackwell.

Harrison, Jonathan. 1981. *Hume's Theory of Justice*. Oxford: Oxford University Press.

Harsanyi, John. 1953. "Cardinal Utility in Welfare Economics and the Theory of Risk Taking." *Journal of Political Economy* 61: 343–345.

Harsanyi, John. 1955. "Cardinal Welfare, Individualistic Ethics, and Interpersonal Comparisons of Utility." *Journal of Political Economy* 63: 309–321.

Harsanyi, John. 1967. "Games with Incomplete Information Played by 'Bayesian' Players, I–III: Part I. The Basic Model." *Management Science* 14: 159–182.

Harsanyi, John. 1968a. "Games with Incomplete Information Played by 'Bayesian' Players, I–III: Part II, Bayesian Equilibrium Points." *Management Science* 14: 320–334.

Harsanyi, John. 1968b. "Games with Incomplete Information Played by 'Bayesian' players, I–III: Part III. The Basic Probability Distribution of the Game." *Management Science* 14: 486–502.

Harsanyi, John. 1977. *Rational Behavior and Bargaining Equilibrium in Games and Social Situations*. Cambridge: Cambridge University Press.

Hart, Herbert L. A. 2012 (1961). *The Concept of Law*, 3rd ed. Oxford: Clarendon Press.

Henrich, Natalie, and Joseph Henrich. 2007. *Why Humans Cooperate: A Cultural and Evolutionary Explanation*. Oxford: Oxford University Press.

Herodotus. 2007. *The Landmark Herodotus: The Histories*. Trans. Andrea L. Purvis. Ed. Robert B. Strassler. New York: Anchor Books.

Hobbes, Thomas. 1962 (1655). "Elements of Philosophy." In *The English Works of Thomas Hobbes of Malmesbury*, vol. I. Ed. Sir William Molesworth. London: John Bohn.

Hobbes, Thomas. 1991 (1651). *Leviathan*. Ed. Richard Tuck. Cambridge: Cambridge University Press.

Hobbes, Thomas. 1994 (1640). *The Elements of Law: Human Nature and De Corpore Politico*. Ed. L. C. A. Gaskin. Oxford: Oxford University Press.

Hobbes, Thomas. 1998 (1640). *De Cive (On the Citizen)*. Trans. and ed. Richard Tuck and Michael Silverthorne. Cambridge: Cambridge University Press.

Hoekstra, Kinch. 1997. "Hobbes and the Foole." *Political Theory* 25: 620–654.

Hubin, D. Clayton. 1979. "The Scope of Justice." *Philosophy and Public Affairs* 9: 3–24.

Hume, David. 1994. *Political Essays*. Ed. Knud Haakonssen. Cambridge: Cambridge University Press.

Hume, David. 1998 (1751). *An Enquiry Concerning the Principles of Morals: A Critical Edition*. Ed. Tom Beauchamp. Oxford: Clarendon Press.

Hume, David. 2000a (1740). *A Treatise of Human Nature*. Ed. David Fate Norton and Mary J. Norton. Oxford: Oxford University Press.

Hume, David. 2000b (1748). *An Enquiry Concerning Human Understanding*. Ed. Tom Beauchamp. Oxford: Oxford University Press.

Jaworska, Agnieszka, and Julie Tennenbaum. 2013. "The Grounds of Moral Status." In *The Stanford Encyclopedia of Philosophy*, summer 2013 ed., ed. Edward N. Zalta. http://plato.stanford.edu/archives/sum2013/entries/grounds-moral-status.

Jenkins, John J. 1967. "Locke and Natural Rights." *Philosophy* 42: 149–154.

Kaczor, Christopher. 2015. *The Ethics of Abortion: Women's Rights, Human Life, and the Question of Justice*, 2nd ed. New York: Routledge.

Kagel, John H., and Alvin E. Roth, eds. 1995. *Handbook of Experimental Economics*. Princeton: Princeton University Press.

Kalai, Ehud. 1977. "Proportional Solutions to Bargaining Situations: Interpersonal Utility Comparisons." *Econometrica* 44: 1623–1630.

Kalai, Ehud, and Meir Smorodinsky. 1975. "Other Solutions to Nash's Bargaining Problem." *Econometrica* 16: 29–56.

Kandori, Michihiro. 1992. "Social Norms and Community Enforcement." *Review of Economic Studies* 59: 63–80.

Kant, Immanuel. 1996 (1793). "On the Common Saying: That May Be Correct in Theory, but It Is of No Use in Practice." In *Practical Philosophy*, pp. 279–309. Trans. and ed. Mary J. Gregor. Cambridge: Cambridge University Press.

Kant, Immanuel. 2006 (1798). *Anthropology from a Pragmatic Point of View*. Trans. and ed. Robert B. Louden. Cambridge: Cambridge University Press.

Kavka, Gregory. 1983. "Hobbes's War of All Against All." *Ethics* 93: 291–301.

Kavka, Gregory. 1984. "The Reconciliation Project." In *Morality, Reason and Truth*, ed. David Copp and David Zimmerman, pp. 297–319. Totowa, NJ: Rowan and Allanheld.

Kavka, Gregory. 1986. *Hobbesian Moral and Political Theory*. Princeton: Princeton University Press.

Kavka, Gregory. 1989. "Political Contractarianism." Unpublished manuscript.

Kavka, Gregory. 1995. "The Rationality of Rule-Following: Hobbes's Dispute with the Foole." *Law and Philosophy* 14: 5–34.

Kelly, Paul, ed. 1998. *Impartiality, Neutrality and Justice: Re-Reading Brian Barry's* Justice as Impartiality. Edinburgh: Edinburgh University Press.

Keyt, David. 1991. "Aristotle's Theory of Distributive Justice." In *A Companion to Aristotle's* Politics, ed. David Keyt and Fred D. Miller Jr., pp. 238–278. Oxford: Basil Blackwell.

Kreps, David. 1990. *Game Theory and Economic Modeling*. Oxford: Oxford University Press.

Krishna, Vijay, and Tomas Sjöström. 1998. "On the Convergence of Fictitious Play." *Mathematics of Operations Research* 23: 479–511.

Lewis, David. 1969. *Convention: A Philosophical Study*. Cambridge, MA: Harvard University Press.

Lloyd, Sharon. 1992. *Ideals as Interests in Hobbes's* Leviathan: *The Power of Mind over Matter*. Cambridge: Cambridge University Press.

Lloyd, Sharon. 2005. "Hobbes's Reply to the Foole: A Deflationary Definitional Interpretation." *Hobbes Studies* 18: 50–73.

Lloyd, Sharon. 2009. *Morality in the Philosophy of Thomas Hobbes: Cases in the Law of Nature*. Cambridge: Cambridge University Press.

Locke, John. 1988 (1690). *Two Treatises of Government*. Ed. Peter Laslett. Cambridge: Cambridge University Press.

Luce, R. Duncan, and Howard Raiffa. 1957. *Games and Decisions: Introduction and Critical Survey*. New York: John Wiley and Sons.

Macpherson, Crawford B. 1962. *The Political Theory of Possessive Individualism: Hobbes to Locke*. Oxford: Oxford University Press.

Marmor, Andrei. 1996. "On Convention." *Synthese* 107: 349–371.

Marmor, Andrei. 2009. *Social Conventions: From Language to Law*. Princeton: Princeton University Press.

Maynard Smith, John. 1982. *Evolution and the Theory of Games*. Cambridge: Cambridge University Press.

McCall, John J. 1970. "Economics of Information and Job Search." *Quarterly Journal of Economics* 84: 113–126.

McMahan, Jeff. 2002. *The Ethics of Killing: Problems at the Margins of Life*. Oxford: Oxford University Press.

McNeilly, Francis S. 1968. *Anatomy of* Leviathan. London: Macmillan.

Milgrom, Paul R., Douglass C. North, and Barry R. Weingast. 1990. "The Role of Institutions in the Revival of Trade: The Law Merchant, Private Judges and the Champagne Fairs." *Economics and Politics* 2: 1–23.

Mill, John Stuart. 1948 (1836). "On the Definition of Political Economy; And on the Method of Investigation Proper to It." In *Essays on Some Unsettled Questions of Political Economy*, pp. 120–164. London: London School of Economics and Political Science.

Morris, Christopher W. 1991. "Moral standing and rational-choice contractarianism." In *Contractarianism and Rational Choice: Essays on David Gauthier's* Morals by Agreement, ed. Peter Vallentyne, pp. 76–95. New York: Cambridge University Press.

Morris, Christopher W. 1998a. *An Essay on the Modern State*. Cambridge: Cambridge University Press.

Morris, Christopher W. 1998b. "Justice, Reasons, and Moral Standing." In *Rational Commitment and Social Justice: Essays for Gregory Kavka*, ed. Jules Coleman and Christopher Morris, pp. 186–207. Cambridge: Cambridge University Press.

Morris, Christopher W. 2011. "The Idea of Moral Standing." In *The Oxford Handbook of Animal Ethics*, ed. Tom L. Beauchamp and R. G. Frey, pp. 257–275. Oxford: Oxford University Press.

Mother Teresa. 1996. *In My Own Words*. Comp. Jose Luis Gonzalez-Balado. Ligouri, MO: Ligouri Publications.

Nash, John. 1996. *Essays on Game Theory*. Cheltenham, UK: Edward Elgar.

Nowak, Martin A., and Karl Sigmund. 1998. "Evolution of Indirect Reciprocity by Image Scoring." *Nature* 393: 573–577.

Nussbaum, Martha. 2007. *Frontiers of Justice*. Cambridge, MA: Harvard University Press.

Olson, Mancur. 1965. *The Logic of Collective Action*. Cambridge, MA: Harvard University Press.

Osborne, Martin J., and Ariel Rubinstein. 1990. *Bargaining and Markets*. Bingley, UK: Emerald Publishing Group.

Ostrom, Elinor. 1990. *Governing the Commons: The Evolution of Institutions for Collective Action*. Cambridge: Cambridge University Press.

Ostrom, Elinor, Roy Gardner, and James Walker. 1994. *Rules, Games and Common-Pool Resources*. Ann Arbor: University of Michigan Press.

Ostrom, Elinor, James Walker, and Roy Gardner. 1992. "Covenants with and Without a Sword: Self-Governance Is Possible." *American Political Science Review* 86: 404–417.

Pareto, Vilfredo. 1971 (1927). *Manual of Political Economy*. Trans. Ann S. Schwier. Ed. Ann S. Schwier and Alfred N. Page. New York: Augustus M. Kelley.

Parfit, Derek. 1979. "Is Common-Sense Morality Self-Defeating?" *Journal of Philosophy* 76: 533–545.

Pearce, David. 1984. "Rationalizable Strategic Behavior and the Problem of Perfection." *Econometrica* 52: 1029–1050.

Plato. 1997. *Complete Works*. Ed. John M. Cooper and D. S. Hutchinson. Indianapolis: Hackett Publishing Company.

Plato. 2004. *Republic*. Trans. C. D. C. Reeve. Indianapolis: Hackett Publishing Company.

Postema, Gerald J. 1988. "Hume's Reply to the Sensible Knave." *History of Philosophy Quarterly* 5: 23–40.

Pufendorf, Samuel. 1994 (1672). "On the Law of Nature and of Nations." In *The Political Writings of Samuel Pufendorf*, pp. 93–268. Ed. Craig L. Carr. Trans. Michael Seidler. New York: Oxford University Press.

Quine, Willard. 1983 (1936). "Truth by Convention." In *Philosophy of Mathematics: Selected Readings*, 2nd ed., ed. Paul Benacerraf and Hilary Putnam, pp. 329–354. Cambridge: Cambridge University Press.

Raiffa, Howard. 1953. "Arbitration Schemes for Generalized Two-Person Games." In *Contributions to the Theory of Games*, vol. 2, ed. H. Kuhn and A. W. Tucker, pp. 361–387. Annals of Mathematics Studies, no. 28. Princeton: Princeton University Press.

Ramsey, Frank. 1990 (1926). "Truth and Probability." In *Philosophical Papers*, ed. D. H. Mellor, pp. 52–94. Cambridge: Cambridge University Press.

Rawls, John. 1971. *A Theory of Justice*. Cambridge, MA: Harvard University Press.

Rawls, John. 1993. *Political Liberalism*. New York: Columbia University Press.

Rawls, John. 1999. *Collected Papers*. Ed. Samuel Freeman. Cambridge, MA: Harvard University Press.

Rawls, John. 2001. *Justice as Fairness: A Restatement*, 2nd ed. Ed. Erin Kelly. Cambridge, MA: Harvard University Press.

Rawls, John. 2007. *Lectures on the History of Political Philosophy*. Ed. Samuel Freeman. Cambridge, MA: Harvard University Press.

Reny, Philip. 1992. "Rationality in Extensive Form Games." *Journal of Economic Perspectives* 6: 103–118.

Roth, Alvin. 1979. *Axiomatic Models of Bargaining*, Berlin: Springer.

Rousseau, Jean-Jacques. 1997 (1755). "Discourse on the Origin or Foundations of Inequality Among Men." In *The Discourses and Other Early Political Writings*, ed. Victor Gourevitch, pp. 111–231. Cambridge: Cambridge University Press.

Rubinstein, Ariel. 1982. "Perfect Equilibrium in a Bargaining Model." *Econometrica* 50: 97–109.

Russell, Bertrand. 1921. *The Analysis of Mind*. London: George Allen and Unwin.

Satterwaithe, Mark. 1975. "Strategy-Proofness and Arrow's Conditions: Existence and Correspondence Theorems for Voting Procedures and Social Welfare Functions." *Journal of Economic Theory* 10: 187–217.

Scanlon, Thomas M. 1982. "Contractualism and Utilitarianism." In *Utilitarianism and Beyond*, ed. Amartya Sen and Bernard Williams, pp. 103–128. Cambridge: Cambridge University Press.

Schelling, Thomas. 1960. *The Strategy of Conflict*. Cambridge, MA: Harvard University Press.

Schelling, Thomas. 1978. *Micromotives and Macrobehavior*. New York: W. W. Norton.

Selten, Reinhard. 1965. "Spieltheoretische Behandlung eines Oligipolmodells mit Nachfragtragheit." *Zeitschrift für die gesamte Staatswissenschaft* 121: 301–334, 667–689.

Sen, Amartya. 1967. "Isolation, Assurance and the Social Rate of Discount." *Quarterly Journal of Economics* 81: 112–124.

Sidgwick, Henry. 1981 (1907). *The Methods of Ethics*, 7th ed. Indianapolis: Hackett.

Sillari, Giacomo. 2005. "A Logical Framework for Convention." *Synthese* 147: 379–400.

Sillari, Giacomo. 2008. "Common Knowledge and Convention." *Topoi* 27: 29–39.

Simmons, A. John. 1989. "Locke's State of Nature." *Political Theory* 3: 449–470.

Simmons, A. John. 1993. *On the Edge of Anarchy: Locke, Consent and the Limits of Society*. Princeton: Princeton University Press.

Skyrms, Brian. 1990. *The Dynamics of Rational Deliberation*. Cambridge, MA: Harvard University Press.

Skyrms, Brian. 1998. "The Shadow of the Future." In *Rational Commitment and Social Justice: Essays for Gregory Kavka*, ed. Jules Coleman and Christopher Morris, pp. 12–22. Cambridge: Cambridge University Press.

Skyrms, Brian. 2014 (1996). *Evolution of the Social Contract*, 2nd ed. Cambridge: Cambridge University Press.

Skyrms, Brian. 2004. *The Stag Hunt and the Evolution of Social Structure*. Cambridge: Cambridge University Press.

Smith, Adam. 1982 (1759). *The Theory of Moral Sentiments*. Ed. D. D. Raphael and A. L. MacFie. Indianapolis: Liberty Fund.

Sobel, Jordan Howard. 1994. *Taking Chances: Essays on Rational Choice*. Cambridge: Cambridge University Press.

Sobel, Jordan Howard. 2009. *Walls and Vaults: A Natural Science of Morals (Virtue Ethics According to David Hume)*. Hoboken, NJ: John Wiley & Sons.

Sreedhar, Susanne. 2010. *Hobbes on Resistance: Defying the Leviathan*. Cambridge: Cambridge University Press.

Stähl, Ingolf. 1972. *Bargaining Theory*. Stockholm: Economic Research Institute.

Stokey, Nancy L. and Robert E. Lucas Jr. 1989. *Recursive Methods in Economic Dynamics*. Cambridge, MA: Harvard University Press.

Sugden, Robert. 2004 (1986). *The Economics of Rights, Co-operation and Welfare*, 2nd ed. Houndmills, UK: Palgrave Macmillan.

Taylor, Michael. 1976. *Anarchy and Cooperation*. London: John Wiley & Sons.

Taylor, Michael. 1987. *The Possibility of Cooperation*. Cambridge: Cambridge University Press.

Taylor, Michael, and Hugh Ward. 1982. "Chickens, Whales and Lumpy Goods: Alternative Models of Public-Goods Provision." *Political Studies* 30: 350–370.

Thomson, William, and Terje Lensberg. 1989. *Axiomatic Theory of Bargaining with a Variable Number of Agents*. Cambridge: Cambridge University Press.

Thrasher, John. 2014. "Uniqueness and Symmetry in Bargaining Theories of Justice." *Philosophical Studies* 167: 683–699.

Thucydides. 1993. *On Justice, Power and Human Nature: Selections from* The History of the Peloponnesian War. Trans. and ed. Paul Woodruff. Indianapolis: Hackett.

Tooley, Michael. 1972. "Abortion and Infanticide." *Philosophy and Public Affairs* 2: 37–65.

Ullmann-Margalit, Edna. 1977. *The Emergence of Norms*. Oxford: Oxford University Press.

Vallentyne, Peter, ed. 1991. *Contractarianism and Rational Choice: Essays on David Gauthier's* Morals by Agreement. Cambridge: Cambridge University Press.

Van Damme, Eric. 2002. *Stability and Perfection of Nash Equilibria*, 2nd ed. Berlin, Springer-Verlag.

Van Damme, Eric, Reinhard Selten, and Eyal Winter. 1990. "Alternating Bid Bargaining with a Smallest Money Unit." *Games and Economic Behavior* 2: 188–201.

Vanderschraaf, Peter. 1998a. "The Informal Game Theory in Hume's Account of Convention." *Economics and Philosophy* 14: 215–247.

Vanderschraaf, Peter. 1998b. "Knowledge, Equilibrium and Convention." *Erkenntnis* 49: 337–369.

Vanderschraaf, Peter. 2001a. "Instituting the Hobbesian Commonwealth." *Pacific Philosophical Quarterly* 82: 383–405.

Vanderschraaf, Peter. 2001b. *Learning and Coordination*. New York: Routledge.

Vanderschraaf, Peter. 2003. "Justice-Conventionalism, Justice-Platonism and the Social Contract." In *The Social Institutions of Capitalism: Evolution and Design of Social Contracts*, ed. Pursey Heugens, Hans van Oosterhout, and Jack Vromen, pp. 141–163. Cheltenham, UK: Edward Elgar.

Vanderschraaf, Peter. 2006a. "The Circumstances of Justice." *Politics, Philosophy and Economics* 5: 321–351.

Vanderschraaf, Peter. 2006b. "War or Peace? A Dynamical Analysis of Anarchy." *Economics and Philosophy* 22: 243–279.

Vanderschraaf, Peter. 2007. "Covenants and Reputations." *Synthese* 157: 167–195.

Vanderschraaf, Peter. 2008. "Game Theory Meets Threshold Analysis: Reappraising the Paradoxes of Anarchy and Revolution." *British Journal for the Philosophy of Science* 59: 579–617.

Vanderschraaf, Peter. 2010. "The Invisible Foole." *Philosophical Studies* 147: 37–58.

Vanderschraaf, Peter. 2011. "Justice as Mutual Advantage and the Vulnerable." *Politics, Philosophy and Economics* 10: 119–147.

Vanderschraaf, Peter. 2012. "Security-Regarding Weighted Fictitious Play." Unpublished manuscript.

Vanderschraaf, Peter. 2013a. "A Governing Convention?" *Rationality, Markets and Morals* 4: 131–156.

Vanderschraaf, Peter. 2013b. "Game Theoretic Interpretations of Hobbes." In *The Bloomsbury Companion to Hobbes*, ed. Sharon A. Lloyd, pp. 39–49. London: Bloomsbury Academic.

Vanderschraaf, Peter. 2016. "In a Weakly Dominated Strategy Is Strength: Evolution of Optimality in Stag Hunt Augmented with a Punishment Option." *Philosophy of Science* 83: 29–59.

Vanderschraaf, Peter. Forthcoming. "Learning Bargaining Conventions." *Social Philosophy and Policy*.

Vanderschraaf, Peter, and Andrea Christelle. 2012. "Convention and Natural Law." Unpublished manuscript.

Vanderschraaf, Peter, and Diana Richards. 1997. "Joint Beliefs in Conflictual Coordination Games." *Theory and Decision* 42: 287–310.

Vanderschraaf, Peter, and Giacomo Sillari. 2014. "Common Knowledge." In *The Stanford Encyclopedia of Philosophy*, spring 2014 ed., ed. Edward N. Zalta. http://plato.stanford.edu/archives/spr2014/entries/common-knowledge.

Venezia, Luciano. 2015. *Hobbes on Legal Authority and Political Obligation*. Houndmills, UK: Palgrave Macmillan.

Von Neumann, John. 1928. "Zur Theorie der Gesellshaftsspiele." *Mathematische Annalen* 100: 295–320.

Von Neumann, John, and Oskar Morgenstern. 2004 (1944). *Theory of Games and Economic Behavior*. Princeton: Princeton University Press.

Warren, Mary Anne. 1973. "On the Moral and Legal Status of Abortion." *Monist* 57: 43–61.

Warren, Mary Anne. 1997. *Moral Status: Obligations to Persons and Other Living Things*. Oxford: Clarendon Press.

Warrender, Howard. 1957. *The Political Philosophy of Hobbes: His Theory of Obligation*. Oxford: Oxford University Press.

Watkins, John W. N. 1965. *Hobbes's System of Ideas: A Study in the Political Significance of Philosophical Theories*. London: Hutchinson.

Weithman, Paul. 2011. *Why Political Liberalism? On John Rawls's Political Turn*. Oxford: Oxford University Press.

INDEX

Printed in the USA/Agawam, MA
October 7, 2020

762376.014